An Introduction to American Government

Kenneth Prewitt University of Chicago
Sidney Verba Harvard University

An Introduction to American Government

Second Edition

Harper & Row, Publishers
New York, Hagerstown, San Francisco, London

Sponsoring Editor: Dale Tharp
Project Editor: Elizabeth Dilernia
Designer: Howard S. Leiderman
Production Supervisor: Will C. Jomarrón
Photo Researcher: Myra Schachne
Compositor: Ruttle, Shaw & Wetherill, Inc.
Printer: The Murray Printing Company
Binder: Halliday Lithograph Corporation
Art Studio: Eric G. Heiber Associates Inc.

Photograph Credits

All photographs are from Wide World Photos except the following: pp. 8 *(top)*, 30, 36–37, 51, 67 *(bottom)*, 82–83, 126–127, 215, 420–421, 494: Beckwith Studios; pp. 60–61, 67 *(top)*, 160–161, 172 *(center right)*, 462, 466: Joel Gordon; p. 41: New York Public Library Picture Collection; p. 66: Library of Congress; p. 77: Wendy Watriss, Woodfin Camp; p. 111: Mimi Forsyth, Monkmeyer; p. 194 *(top)*: Tim Egan, Woodfin Camp; p. 194 *(bottom)*: Irene Bayer, Monkmeyer; p. 205 *(bottom)*: U.S. Public Health Service; p. 219: Exxon; pp. 335, 340: Bettmann Archives; p. 373: Richard Collins, DPI; p. 427 *(top right)*: Henry Monroe, DPI; p. 427 *(bottom left)*: Grete Mannheim, DPI; p. 427 *(bottom right)*: Sybil Shelton, DPI.

An Introduction to American Government, Second Edition

Library of Congress Cataloging in Publication Data

Prewitt, Kenneth.
    An introduction to American Government.

    Includes bibliographies and index.
    1. United States—Politics and government—
Handbooks, manuals, etc.   I. Verba, Sidney, joint
author.   II. Title.
JK274.P76 1976   320.4'73   75-28282
ISBN 0-06-045286-2

Contents

CONTENTS

vii

CONTENTS

ix

Preface

The main problem one faces in writing a textbook on American government is how to create order out of chaos and complexity. American politics is not orderly. Much political activity bypasses formal channels, and the institutional patterns themselves are not clear. Furthermore, so much goes on in so many places! Issues, personalities, and crises appear, disappear, and reappear at a breathless pace.

We have tried to give some order to the complexity of day-to-day politics by focusing on recurring patterns. This is not a book on current events. We do use some of the important issues of recent times as illustrations of the underlying patterns of politics. But we hope our analyses transcend the specific issues of the day. Those issues are unlikely to be the ones the citizen will face in future years. We want the student to think about the patterns, structures, and processes that give meaning to the helter-skelter of daily politics.

Our book presents no single political thesis. It is not organized around structural functional theory, elite theory, pluralist theory, or any other all-encompassing theory. We wish we had such a theory around which to organize our book—it would make things simpler. We believe theory is important in helping us understand politics. But we do not know of any overall theory into which one can fit the reality of American politics without distorting that reality. However, we do draw on many of the theoretical interpretations of American politics and have tried in each section of the book to use those that seem most appropriate.

Just as we have no all-encompassing theory, we have no particular political axe to grind. This is not a "point of view" book. It is our purpose neither to praise nor to condemn the American political system. Our stance toward American politics is critical, but in the strict sense of the word: We try to be objective so as to locate both strengths and weaknesses. The result is that we cannot present *the* interpretation of American politics based on this year's intellectual (or political) trend. We stress *alternative* interpretations. In fact the theme of controversy is central to the book. At the end of most chapters we raise a controversial issue in which we explore alternative interpretations of American politics. If at times the student is uncertain as to which interpretation is correct, he or she will have gotten our message. Uncertainty is not a comfortable feeling with which to leave an introductory text, but it is healthier than a false certainty.

Consistent with the theme that we do not yet have all the answers about American politics is our concern with the ways in which we can improve our understanding. We do not intend to train students in methodology. But in several places we provide special sections on the ways political scientists go about trying to understand politics. One of these is on studying public opinion and participation, another on the use of documentary evidence to study public policies and political leaders.

We have tried to base this book on the latest and most sophisticated research in political science. But it is not a compilation of research findings. We use the research to make the political process more understandable to the student who is not technically trained. Nor do we limit ourselves to recent research. It is important for the student to know about the arguments in *The Federalist Papers* as well as current research on elections.

In each section of the book we attempt to make an argument, using facts about American politics to clarify the political process. We appreciate that the attempt to develop an intellectual argument may make it somewhat difficult for the student to learn the basic structural facts of American politics. Therefore we have provided separate "nuts and bolts" sections, in question-and-answer format, describing how some key institutions work—for instance, how cases come before the Supreme Court, the procedures for replacing the President, and how a bill becomes a law.

The story is told of a British actor who, when applying for a visa to visit the United States, was asked if he intended to engage in activities aimed at overthrowing the government. His reply was, "I wouldn't know where to begin." This problem is faced not only by someone trying to overthrow the government but also by someone trying to understand it.

The government of the United States is a complex system: complex because it has many parts, a system because the many parts interrelate. One has to understand the federal government with its internal complexity as well as its relationship to the states and to the many local governments. A government is interconnected with the rest of society. It has an impact on all parts of society: the economy, the family, the educational system, the media. And it is affected by what goes on in economic institutions, in families, in schools, and in cultural institutions. A proper understanding of American government requires an understanding of the connections among the parts of the government and the links between the government and the rest of society.

We begin with a pair of chapters dealing with the fundamental basis of American politics: a particular economic system and a particular constitutional structure. The first chapter deals with the nature of the American economy and how it interrelates with the political process. We do not believe economics explains all. But given the overlap between politics and economics, we feel that one cannot begin without an understanding of how they interrelate. The second chapter traces the historical evolution of the constitutional structure, followed by a chapter tying the separate themes of the first two together—a chapter on the nature of citizenship in America, focusing on how economic and political inequalities relate to each other.

The next two chapters deal with the way in which citizens are linked to the political process. Chapter 4 discusses the ways citizens participate in and attempt to influence politics; Chapter 5 deals with the process by which political leaders are recruited. Chapter 6 outlines the basic political beliefs of Americans and shows how these beliefs affect the political process. In Chapter 7 we focus on a fundamental question, What is political conflict all about? Here we present and analyze the various kinds of divisions in American society that form the basis for political conflict.

The first seven chapters provide the basis for considering the major institutions of American political life. The two chapters that follow discuss the institutions linking the citizen to the political process. Chapter 8 deals with the role of interest groups and Chapter 9 with that of political parties.

In Chapters 10–13 we consider the major institutions of the federal government: Chapter 10, Congress, Chapter 11, the Presidency, and Chapter 12, the judiciary. Chapter 13 deals with the complex interaction among these three branches of the government and the general principles of the separation of powers.

Having provided a thorough grounding in the workings of the federal government, we turn in Chapter 14 to an analysis of the relationship between the government and the individual and in Chapter 15 between the federal government and the state and local governments.

Chapters 16 and 17 attempt to tie together the previous chapters by looking at the way public policy is actually made. Chapter 16 considers the policy process in general, while Chapter 17 shows how that process works by looking at some of the key policies that have evolved in recent years. Chapter 18 concludes the text with alternative explanations of American politics.

We finished the first edition of this book under the shadow of Watergate. Watergate produced both anguish and joy (or at least relief) in the American public: anguish that such events could happen, joy or relief that the system could correct itself (though how much correction there has been is one of those uncertainties about American politics that we leave unresolved.)

Watergate also produced anguish and joy in a pair of political scientists trying to write an introductory text in American politics. The anguish was what to write about one of the most important crises in American political history in the midst of events that were moving so rapidly. Yesterday's newspaper was already dated. How dated our book would be when it was read, some months after we finished writing it! The joy came from the way the Watergate events underlined the features of American government: the role of the President, Congress, the courts, the media. The student of government could hardly hope to find a "better" crisis. Watergate is in one sense behind us, but it has left its mark. This new edition of our book allows us to deal with its meaning for the political process.

We have many debts to acknowledge for help in the preparation of this book. The major debt is to the scholars upon whose work we have drawn. Political scientists often complain that little is known about fundamental political matters; we have been impressed with how much *is* known. Many colleagues wrote to give us their reactions to our book. Many liked it, and many sent in suggestions for additions and improvements. We bless the former and thank the latter. In most cases we agreed with the comments and have incorporated them.

We owe a special debt to Robert Gamage for tireless and imaginative assistance. Professor Kay Schlozman of Boston College has been a close collaborator and constructive critic. Finally, we wish to thank the following people for their valuable comments on various stages of the manuscript: Jean Douglas Andrew, Edinboro State College; Richard L. Cole, George Washington University; Stephen L. Daigle, University of Texas, Arlington; Elmer Anthony DeShazo, Southwest Texas State University; Steve J. Mazurana, University of Northern Colorado; and Gordon T. Randall, Chabot College.

K. P.
S. V.

An Introduction to American Government

Government and Politics: Some Fundamentals

Why Government?

We are so used to government that we rarely question why we have it. However, the answer to the question, Why government at all? is not obvious. Even though we may take government for granted, there is a good argument against it: Government makes us do things—pay taxes, drive at certain speeds, respect other people's property, serve on juries, pay our bills, and so on. What's more, we are not free to decide whether or not to obey. We must obey; if we don't, we are likely to be punished. Thus by forcing citizens to do things governments diminish individual choice and freedom. If we agree that choice and freedom are valuable and good, then the case against government is a strong one. If governments coerce, restrict, regulate, tax, and sometimes even imprison citizens, why do people put up with them?

Maintaining Social Order

One answer stresses the role of government in maintaining social order. Without government civilized life would be impossible. If everybody were allowed to live just as he pleased, society would be chaotic and full of conflict. We support government because it, in turn, provides law and order. It provides the social stability within which a citizen can raise a family, work at a job, get an education, enjoy leisure, and plan for the future.

In just about every area of life, government helps provide the orderly conditions necessary for even the most mundane activities. Take, for instance, economic activities. To work for a salary, to invest savings, to buy or produce a product depends on contracts— between worker and manager, lender and borrower, or seller and buyer. Some guarantee is needed to make sure people don't back out on contracts—to make sure the car buyer doesn't drive off and quit making his payments; the employer doesn't decide at the end of the month not to pay his workers; the bank doesn't close its doors and keep the savings deposits. One reason such contracts, which are necessary for economic exchange, are usually honored is that they are backed up by the authority of the government; that is, people fulfill their contracts because the government makes sure they do and may punish those who don't. Thus people comply with their obligations both out of fear for the consequences if they don't and out of respect for the government. In the area of social life and leisure activities, we depend on government to provide security for our lives and property. A man will be reluctant to buy an expensive hi-fi set if he thinks it will be stolen; a parent will not want his 5-year-old to start school if there are no traffic laws to make street crossings safe; a woman will refuse an invitation to a party if to go across town at night is to risk assault. Even more important, we

One task of government is providing protection for private property.

expect government to provide for our security as a nation, to protect our borders from foreign invasions and international outlaws.

This, then, is the classic justification for government. The legal processes, the police powers, and the national-security policies establish the social order essential to civilized life. However, the government engages in many activities that cannot reasonably be considered as providing basic law and order: for example, repaving an interstate highway in Nevada; supporting a graduate student writing a dissertation on the tools used by prehistoric man in Central Africa; raising the tax on gasoline to conserve energy; publishing a booklet naming the trees and plants along a trail in the Smoky Mountains; sending a monthly check to a blind pensioner in New York.

Obviously we must look beyond the maintenance of social order to answer the question, Why government?

Providing Collective Goods

Governments often make binding decisions when individuals have goals that cannot be achieved without government intervention. For example, all automobile drivers are interested in seeing that all cars drive on one side of the road or the other. It matters little which side is chosen as long as all drivers choose the same side. In such a case all benefit if they can turn over to the government the power to make a rule that each driver must drive on a particular side.

To understand why social goals may require binding decisions by government, we must understand the concept of collective goods. Governments often provide collective goods—benefits available to every individual whether or not he has worked toward the attainment of that benefit. If the government opens a new park, it be-

comes available for my use whether or not I actively worked to create it. This helps explain why *binding* decisions are needed to create public facilities. If I benefit in any case, why should I voluntarily help create the park? I will benefit from it if *others* work to create it, so I will be wise to sit back and take advantage of their effort. On the other hand, even if I were to try to help create a public park, it would probably do no good, because my effort—the money or labor I could contribute—would be relatively small unless I were a millionaire.

A park is quite different from a noncollective good such as a camper. I can get access to a camper only if I use my private resources. Therefore my efforts to buy a camper can be quite effective. If I put my resources into it and if I have enough resources, I can have the camper.

In short, for any *single* individual it makes a lot of sense to wait until others have created the collective good and then to take advantage of it. In that case, however, collective goods would never be created. Only a binding governmental decision that *makes* all people contribute to the park through tax revenues can lead to a beneficial collective gain for all citizens. No government has ever been supported through voluntary payments by citizens.

Here's another example. Air pollution caused by automobiles is a serious problem facing many communities. Reduction of air pollution would be a collective good in that all would benefit whether or not they did anything to help reduce it. Suppose a highly efficient pollution-control device for cars is invented that costs $300. All Americans would benefit from the reduction of pollution that would come from installing such a device on all cars. But can the installation and the beneficial social goal of pure air come from the voluntary activities of the citizens? It is unlikely.

The situation from the point of view of the individual citizen deciding whether to spend his $300 is as follows: No citizen acting alone can have much impact on the overall pollution in his community. If Citizen A buys an antipollution device, the quality of the air in the city will not change very much if others do not. If Citizen A does not buy a pollution device but all the other citizens in the community do, he will benefit from the cleaner air and save himself $300.

Thus it is rational for the individual citizen not to purchase such a device. He does not get clean air if he buys one and others do not, and he gets fairly pure air even if he does not buy one, if others do so. If every individual acts in the way that is most rational, a situation is created in which all lose. This is why all citizens gain if there is some way of *coercing one another* to buy the device. And the most likely way to do this is a law requiring all cars to be equipped with the pollution-control device. Only when individual choice is taken away can the overall social goal be achieved.

Summary
We have discussed two different answers to the question, Why government? First, government provides the domestic order and the security that make it possible for citizens to go about such normal activities as raising a family, going to school, earning a living, or enjoying leisure. Second, binding government decisions make it possible to convert individual goals into collective goods, thus satisfying the desires of the members of society.

Why Politics?

Government would be simple indeed if all government decisions were like the decision that all cars must drive on the right side of the road. For one thing, most drivers don't care whether they drive on the right or the left side, as long as everyone drives on the same side. Besides, this type of policy is costless. No one loses money because traffic laws require that one drive on the right. If government were simply a matter of using state authority to obtain goals that all citizens favor and from which all benefit equally, it would not be the complicated business it is.

Different Citizen Preferences
Government, however, is not always a matter of achieving goals that all citizens favor and that benefit all citizens equally. In fact government decisions are nearly always sources of conflict. The reasons are clear. It is not easy to agree on what collective goods government should provide or who should pay how much for them. Not every group benefits equally from any collective good, and not every group pays equally or even pays in proportion to its use of that good. Thus government involves a competitive struggle in which individuals and groups seek to maximize the benefits they receive from government while minimizing their costs.

Consider, for example, public highways. Certainly they are a col-

Government action to stop strip mining would protect the environment but might harm the mining industry.

lective good in the sense that no single individual could afford to build one. They are also a collective good in the sense that they are not reserved for particular groups but are open to any adult willing to obey the traffic laws. Yet the politics of highway construction and location can become very intense indeed. Downtown merchants may want an expressway to come directly into the central city; apartment dwellers about to lose their homes to the bulldozers will fiercely oppose such a plan. Truckers and automobile manufacturers will be on the side of more and faster expressways; conservationists insist that cities would be more livable if resources went to mass transit and public parks instead. Another group, favoring lower taxes, doesn't want the expressway no matter where it is located and opposes public transit and parks as well. And still another group, perhaps the largest one, is indifferent to the whole issue.

Thus the first important point about politics and government is this: Individuals and groups have different preferences. A large, diverse nation like ours must include groups with different goals: labor and management, doctors and patients, whites and blacks, Catholics and Protestants, producers and consumers, landlords and tenants, and so on.

Doctors may want less government involvement in medical care; elderly citizens may want more complete care programs. Blacks may want the government to encourage integrated housing in suburbs; white suburbanites may want the government to stay out of it. Catholics may seek government aid for parochial schools; Protestants may oppose it.

The number of alternative preferences to be found in America is vast indeed. There are many issues, and on any issue we are likely to find some citizens on one side, some on the other side, and others indifferent. Different preferences by different groups lead of course to arguments over what collective goods the government should provide and who should pay the costs of these goods. It is these arguments that set in motion the struggle to control and influence government.

Differential Impact Leads to Different Levels of Involvement

If the political struggle begins with differential preferences, it is spurred by a second fundamental point about government and society: Government decisions have differential impact. Any given policy is likely to benefit one group a lot, benefit another a little, and leave another unaffected. It may even hurt some people. The decision to build a highway next to my house benefits the highway builders a lot, benefits commuters a little, leaves most citizens unaffected, but may hurt me and a few of my neighbors substantially. That government decisions have differential impacts implies that on any particular issue we will find not only citizens with different preferences but citizens who hold those preferences with *different levels of intensity.*

Those few citizens who have intense preferences—those most severely affected—will be concerned and active. Differential intensity leads to different levels of political involvement. With regard to any particular policy, some individuals and groups will be more active and will try harder to affect the outcome.

Unequal Political Resources

In terms of one of the means citizens use to influence the outcome of political struggles, we are all roughly equal: Each citizen has one vote. Beyond this equality, however, are great inequalities. Citizens differ in the resources they use to influence the government. They differ in their economic resources, and this makes some more politically powerful than others. Each citizen may have one vote, but heavy campaign contributors can influence a lot more votes than those who have no money to contribute. And citizens are unequal in more than economic resources—they are unequal in the skills they bring to political matters, in how well they are organized, in the connections they have, and in the time they can devote to political affairs.

Government and Politics: The Democratic Struggle

Our introductory comments have brought us to an interesting conclusion. We started by asking why governments are tolerated, given their many distasteful activities and their limitations on individual freedom. We answered that they are tolerated because they

Politics occurs when people have different preferences and feel strongly about them: The coal miners want the government to allow strip mining, while the environmentalists want the government to ban strip mining.

provide collective goods such as national security, law and order, and state services, but then we learned that such collective goods can have differential impact, benefiting some groups in society while leaving others unaffected and hurting still others. Even such collective goods as mass transit systems, schools, defense policies, and social-security programs are not provided at equal cost to all citizens and are not equally beneficial to all citizens. Thus there is in society a continuous, often intense struggle to influence what

GOVERNMENT AND
POLITICS: SOME
FUNDAMENTALS

collective goods will be provided, who will bear the greatest cost, and who will receive the greatest benefit.

Who wins? You have probably learned that in a democracy the majority *should* win. But the issue is really much more complicated. Certainly the majority does not in fact always win, and it may even be that the majority should not always rule.

For one thing, there may not be a majority on one side or the other. On any given issue there may be several major groups all wanting something very different. For example, we have already discussed the various preferences of the groups that might want to influence whether a road gets built, and if so, where. Downtown merchants want one thing, commuters another, conservationists still another, and so on. Rather than a majority and a minority, there are many minorities.

Differences in Intensity of Preferences

Besides, as we have seen, not all groups feel equally intensely about the issues. Should the voice of someone whose home will be bulldozed and whose neighborhood will be destroyed by the expressway count equally with that of another citizen who simply wants to reduce by five minutes the time it takes to get from his suburban home to a movie in the city? Simple democracy would ignore differences in intensity of preferences. As we shall see when we study political participation and pressure-group activity, the actual political process is influenced by such differences.

Even if we were to say that the majority should always win, we would have to admit at once that it doesn't. Groups bring different resources, economic and otherwise, to the political struggle; hence very often the resources of a small group outweigh those of a majority. Many collective goods are provided for an intense and well-organized minority, for example, subsidies for farmers, tax allowances for oil interests, research grants for university professors, training programs for blacks, and loans for home builders.

Government in the United States

Politics is a struggle over government policies. It is a struggle among individuals and groups that have different preferences, different levels of concern, and different amounts of resources. These statements could be applied to most governments. But they apply particularly well to American politics because of some important characteristics of the American government and people.

The American People

The United States Has a Large Population The 1970 census counted 203 million Americans. A population of this size creates big problems: Do we have enough natural resources? Enough space? Schools? Jobs? The solution to these problems involves governmental action. A big population implies big government.

The United States Has a Changing Population   There were 213 million Americans in 1975. A generation earlier there were 70 million fewer: In 1940, 72 million Americans lived in metropolitan areas; by 1970, the number had almost doubled, reaching 130 million. In 1940, there were about 3½ million Americans with college degrees. By 1972, the number had grown to 13½ million.

And more population growth is expected in the future. Demographers estimate that in the year 2000 there will be between 264 million and 300 million Americans.

One could go on listing changes, not only in population but in the economy, technology, education, and almost everything else. The conclusion for American government is this: If a big population creates pressures for governmental action, a changing population creates even greater pressures because the government must constantly deal with new problems.

The United States Is a Varied Nation   The American public is remarkably varied in terms of race, ethnic background, language, occupation, place of residence, and so forth. Twenty-three million Americans are black. Twelve million or more are Spanish speaking. In 1971 almost 3 million families earned over $25,000 a year; 7 million families earned under $4,000 a year.

An Iowa corn farmer has little in common with a ghetto black on the south side of Chicago. A Scarsdale stockbroker has little in common with a Houston truck driver. This variety also has important implications for American government. It means the American public is divided into many subgroups with different interests and preferences. The size of the public and the fact that it is changing rapidly means there are pressures on government policy. Its variety means there are often contradictory pressures on public policy.

The American Government

The American Government Is Democratic   *Democracy* has many meanings. But most definitions of democracy are based on the idea that the decisions of governing officials are supposed to be influenced by the public. This is what makes the variety of interests found among the American public so important. Because the political system is "open," these interests can be expressed, and the government is supposed to pay attention to them. (How "open" is the political system and how responsive? This is a complex question, and much of this book will be devoted to an attempt to answer it.)

The American Government Is Representative   This means the public is supposed to control the actions of government officials mainly through the election of officials—the President, governors, mayors, members of Congress, state legislatures, the local governing bodies. The elected officials make public policy. This means that to understand the way policy is made in America one must study the election process.

The American Government Has a Federal Structure This means power is divided between the federal government in Washington and the state governments. And it is further divided among many, many local governments. The varied interests of the American public can be expressed in many places. Citizens who want to affect governmental policy can pressure the federal, state, or local government.

The American Government (or Governments) Is Large and Complex The budget of the federal government for 1973 was about $250 billion; if one adds together the budgets of the federal, state, and local governments, the figure for all government spending is closer to $650 billion. In 1974 the federal government employed more than 2.5 million civilians; if we look at all governments together, they employed nearly 14 million people. This governmental system is organized into countless bureaus, agencies, departments, and the like. This means there are many different governmental bodies making policy and, in turn, many different places where members of the public can apply pressure.

The result is the American political system in all its complexity: many people with many preferences; a government divided into many different levels and, on each level, many different agencies and organizations. Yet out of that complexity come policies that affect our daily lives. We will try to show in some detail how that happens.

How We Find Out About Politics: I

Few would argue with the statement that politics is important. The outcome of the struggle to control government affects us in many specific ways—the cleanness of the air we breathe and the water we drink, the standards (and costs) of the health care and education we receive, the security of the contracts we sign, the safety of the planes and trains we travel in, the honesty of advertisements we hear, and the quality of merchandise we purchase. The ongoing and seemingly mundane activities of government add up to public policies that go far toward determining whether our own lives are healthy and happy, or perhaps mediocre and disappointing.

Yes, politics counts. And it does so whether we like it or not, whether we pay attention or are indifferent, whether we understand or are puzzled. Politics counts because some of the largest issues of life are at stake: security and safety, justice and liberty, equality and happiness. The unending, often intense struggle to control the activities of government matters—very much indeed.

For this reason, if for no other, some effort to understand politics is worthwhile.

But understanding is not easy. Politics is puzzling. Issues are complicated and changeable and often seem to be affected by past history. The language of political debate is obscure at best, as if an effort were being made to disguise the "real" facts. Besides, political personalities come and go. The effort to "keep up with politics" can be very great. A busy undergraduate hardly has time to read a daily newspaper, let alone listen to and digest the amount of information necessary to even begin to understand current events. And even when you know what is going on, you may continue to be puzzled as to why it is happening.

In this book we wish to help the student understand why things happen as they do in American political life. We will concentrate on the struggle over governmental policies. Although we take for granted that the government provides collective goods, we know also that these goods are not equally beneficial or equally costly to all citizens. We focus on who reaps the benefits and who pays the costs.

We will first look at several aspects of American society that affect the way political struggle takes place. For one thing, the beliefs of citizens about politics affect how policies are chosen and carried out. Also important are the many conflicts and divisions among political groups. We will study the economic system as well, because economics and politics are very closely intertwined in our society.

Our attention will then turn to the actors in the political struggle. Chief among these are the pressure groups, the political parties, the voting public, and the political leaders. These actors play out the political game within a definite framework—a framework provided by the basic features of American government: constitutionalism, federalism, separation of powers, due process of law, majoritarian democracy. We will discuss these principles and the institutions that give them substance: the Supreme Court, Congress, the Presidency. We will constantly ask the question, How do these principles and institutions affect the democratic struggle over government policies? In the final chapters the policy-making process itself will interest us.

This is a lot to cover, considering that there are millions of facts about the politics, principles, institutions, and policies of American government. We will be very selective in the facts we give, and you as a student deserve an account of why we choose this set of facts and not another.

An understanding of politics rests on two kinds of knowledge: knowledge of facts and explanations of facts. We cannot study politics without some knowledge of the two parties, the role of pressure groups, the meaning of judicial review, the importance of federalism. It is useful also to have some detailed information about public policies and the way they have come to be.

But all facts are not equally important to an understanding of politics. The child who has memorized every state capital knows some political facts but does not understand much about politics. Even the adult who can name his congressman and all the members of the President's Cabinet does not have very useful knowledge.

Such facts are of relatively little use for a variety of reasons. For one thing, they are temporary: Congress and the Cabinet change with each election. Moreover, names by themselves do not answer the more important questions one might have about the operation of the government. Why do the President and his Cabinet often favor one kind of legislation, while Congress favors another? Why does Congress more often than the Cabinet consider the particular needs of local areas? Why can there be wide shifts in the portion of the vote going to the Democratic and Republican candidates for President (Johnson, a Democrat, won in a landslide in 1964; Nixon, a Republican, barely won in 1968, but then won by a landslide in 1972) with the Congress remaining steadily in the hands of the Democrats? And why do the Democratic Congresses sometimes give as much support to Republican Presidents as to Democratic ones?

To answer questions like these we need more relevant facts than the names of the members of Congress. We need to know about the social backgrounds and careers of Cabinet members and congressmen, for these facts help explain different views about policy. We need to know about party loyalties among voters and how these sometimes lead them to support a candidate from one party for President and from the other for Congress, for this will help explain why a Republican can win the White House but then face a Congress controlled by the Democrats. And we need to know about the organization of Congress and the party ties of congressmen, because this will help explain why a Democratic Congress may support a Republican President and vice versa.

Why are facts about the backgrounds and careers of congressmen useful? Some facts can be linked to other facts to help us understand how members of Congress act in office. Most important, the information is useful in understanding congressional action on such topics as why Congress takes the stand it does on tax bills, or why it usually leaves foreign policy to the President.

This gives some clues to the principles of selection we use in this book. We cannot describe all the facts of American politics and draw connections among all of them. Nor can we keep up with the latest events as reported in the daily press. Rather, we must choose what to discuss. Our principle is to choose our material in terms of what will give us the most generalizable knowledge.

Politics and Controversy

"Let's not talk about politics. It will ruin the evening." Why does political discussion often lead to argument, sometimes very bitter argument? Because people have different political values, and they often hold those values with passionate conviction. Neutrality about politics is difficult.

Those who write about politics—in the press, in magazines, in books—also usually are commited to one political position or another. They are tempted to describe and explain politics from that viewpoint. Thus for any political issue we can usually find many interpretations, often completely opposed to one another. Nor is the study of politics an exact science in which the objective observer can always find one side clearly right and the other clearly wrong.

In this book we try to pay attention to the varying interpretations of American politics. We do not present one interpretation as gospel truth. Rather we try to focus on some of the leading controversies in the interpretation of American politics. Understanding political controversies may well be the first step toward understanding politics.

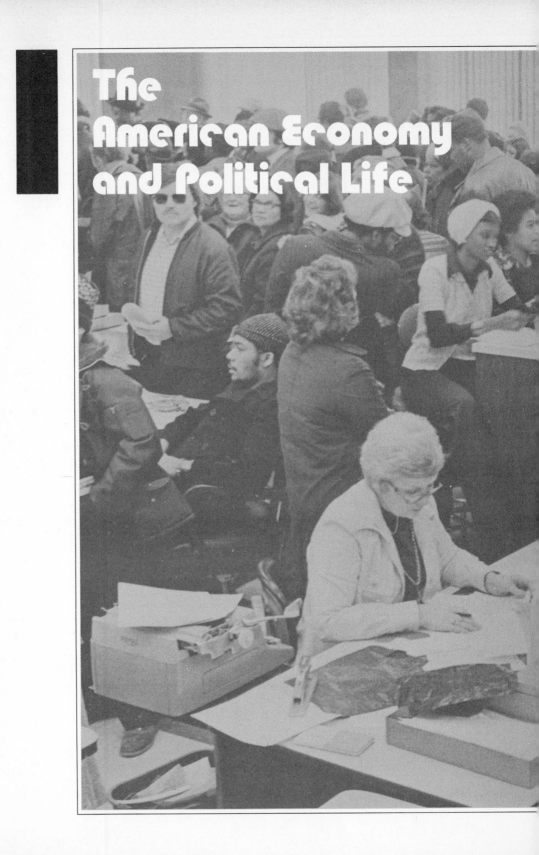

The American Economy and Political Life

Recent news headlines:

Federal Reserve Board Eases Interest Rates
Labor Department Acts to Head Off Coal Strike
White House Acknowledges Recession, Promises to Act
Federal Program for Unemployment Provides City Jobs
Government Investigates Soaring Sugar Prices

What do these headlines have in common? They all refer to an *economic* issue or problem: interest rates, strikes, recession, unemployment, inflation. They all refer as well to a *government* action or program.

Here are some more headlines; note what they have in common:

Consumer Group Demands Price Controls on Foods
Taxpayer Revolt Predicted If Surcharge Becomes Law
Bank Depositors Threaten Withdrawal Unless Government Increases Protection
Auto Workers Support Congressmen Who Promise Higher Tariffs on Foreign Cars
Defense Plant Employees Out of Work, Claim Unemployment

Again we see the connection between economics and politics. In these headlines a citizen's economic role leads to a political act.

We cannot explain American politics without understanding how the government affects the economy and the economy affects the government. We cannot explain individual political beliefs and actions without understanding the connection between government and the citizen as consumer, taxpayer, investor, and worker.

What Is Economics?

Economics is the study of how society chooses to use *scarce* resources —labor, minerals, land, water, capital, knowledge—to produce various goods and to distribute those goods, now and in the years ahead, among different groups and people in society.

This definition of economics poses interesting questions. For what purposes should scarce resources be used? Difficult decisions have to be made, such as whether limited oil supplies should be used to heat homes or to keep gasoline prices down or to maintain the military at full strength. How much should go to satisfying current needs and how much to investing in long-range goals? Again there are difficult decisions, such as whether to close down a factory in Gary, Indiana, and throw some breadwinners out of work, or to keep the factory operating even though it is contributing to the pollution of Lake Michigan. How should the goods in society be distributed among many competing groups? More difficult decisions; for example, providing free medical care for the elderly may mean reducing research on children's diseases.

Underlying all of these difficult questions is the most difficult question of all: Who in society will make the decisions about the use of scarce resources, the balance between present needs and long-term goals, and the distribution of goods among many groups? Should these decisions be made by the government?

There was a time in American history when it was out of the question to consider the government an agency for making economic decisions. The American economy was based on the principles of free enterprise, which, roughly translated, meant government should keep its blankety-blank hands out of economic affairs. An unregulated and unplanned free interplay among workers and owners, sellers and buyers, producers and consumers would be just the thing for a healthy, growing economy.

Things never quite worked out in practice the way they were supposed to in principle. As we shall see, right from the start of American history the government was called upon to perform certain economic functions. The government's involvement in economic affairs has increased steadily since then. That involvement will be reviewed under three headings in this chapter: "A Supported Economy," "A Regulated Economy," and "A Managed Economy."

What has resulted from the government's economic activities is not, however, the destruction of the free-enterprise system. Many important features of the capitalistic economy have been kept, though they have been changed by the role of the government. This we review in the section called "A Capitalistic Economy."

What is difficult for the student to understand is the very complex relationship between a capitalistic economy and a government involved in economic activities. For while the government exercises economic controls, it does not in fact control the economy. This we try to make clear in the final section of the chapter, where we bring in the term *state capitalism*.

A Supported Economy

Economic activities benefit from government supports in dozens of ways. First, the government provides the legal framework needed in a free-enterprise economy. Second, it provides direct subsidies to many economic activities. Third, it is a major, sometimes *the* major, customer for producers in the economy.

The Legal Framework for a Free-Enterprise Economy

When James Madison, chief draftsman of the U.S. Constitution, wrote in 1787 that the first goal of government is to protect the different and unequal ability of men to acquire property, he was echoing themes from Europe and England. In Europe democracy began as a reform movement led by a commercial middle class against the oppression of absolute rulers and hereditary nobilities. The privileges and special status enjoyed by the king and his noblemen blocked the commercial activities of a small but growing group of merchants, traders, and craftsmen.

These early "capitalists" knew that a free-enterprise economy depends on the right of individuals to enter into valid contracts and to have those contracts upheld by law; it depends on the right to sell one's products and labor in the free marketplace; and it depends on the right to use one's abilities to gain material goods. Free enterprise cannot survive when legal restrictions block the exchange of goods and labor and when social position is fixed at birth.

In the beginning the assault on class privilege was a reform movement that freed commerce and trade. In doing so it introduced democratic principles such as due process of law, equal status as citizens, protection from arbitrary arrests and unfair seizure of property, and at least limited voting. Stated differently, the U.S. Constitution reflects the victory of individual rights and limited government over class privileges and royal absolutism. Just as the European middle-class reformers expected, such a constitution would also make possible a free-enterprise economy.

Although capitalism as we know it did not take hold until after the Civil War, the legal framework and constitutional system necessary to a free-enterprise economy was fairly well established as early as 1800. Even then a police force protected private property, a court system dealt with violations of contracts, a monetary system provided the bills and coins used in economic transactions, and a system of common weights and measures, patents, and copyrights provided the necessary uniformity and protection for exchanges of goods and titles. These have been accepted government functions since 1789, and they continue today—on a larger scale—to provide the legal framework that allows a capitalistic system of production and exchange to operate.

Subsidies to Private Enterprise

Direct support of private enterprise through state powers and with public moneys is as old as the nation itself. Alexander Hamilton, first Secretary of the Treasury, insisted that the new government set up a national bank. Credit would be increased this way, and according to Hamilton, this would help "the operations of commerce among individuals. Industry is increased, commodities are multiplied, agriculture and manufacturers flourish; and herein consists the true wealth and prosperity of a state." As the most decisive member of President Washington's Cabinet, Hamilton got his way, and the government has been supporting private business ever since.

Support for Transportation The first large-scale support began after the Civil War. Between the 1860s and the end of the century, great economic growth took place. Although a strong and innovative private sector was largely responsible for this transformation, government support played an important role. For example, the

Private industry is constructing the Alaskan oil pipeline, but only after permission was granted by the federal government.

canals, harbors, and roads necessary for commercial expansion were built and maintained at public expense. The most notable subsidy, however, was for railroads. By 1870, some 131 million acres — an area larger than Texas — had been granted to private railroad builders; in return the railroads agreed to carry the U.S. mail at a very low cost.

Direct public support for private business has continued to the present day. For example, a modern version of the nineteenth-century railroad subsidy is the federal highway program, which benefits the trucking, automobile, and petroleum industries and of course motorists. In addition, when the government builds airports with public money the airlines are essentially getting a subsidy.

The reason given for the earliest forms of direct support to private business is the same one used today: that these subsidies make possible collective goods that benefit all the members of society and that no single individual or corporation has enough resources to provide.

Protection of Industry — the Protective Tariff When President Nixon imposed a surtax on foreign cars — thereby trying to make them less competitive with American cars — he was acting in a tradition dating back to the nineteenth century. In order to protect American industry from foreign competition, the government has from time to time imposed protective tariffs in the form of high import taxes on foreign products.

Federal Loans The government not only subsidizes and protects businesses but also lends them money. For example, the Small Business Administration makes loans to small businessmen, and a variety of agencies make loans to encourage homeownership and housing construction. Such loans are not made only to average citizens and small businessmen; from time to time the government bails a huge corporation out of financial trouble with a federal guaranteed loan.

Agricultural Subsidy Programs One of the largest government subsidy programs is in agriculture. Farm prices fluctuate widely. If it were not for major government supports that ensure a fair price for his products, the individual farmer would suffer from considerable income instability, often due to causes he cannot control.

The Government as Customer

The gross national product (GNP) is the dollar figure obtained by adding together all the consumption goods, services, and investments produced by the land, labor, and capital resources of society. GNP is the yardstick that tells a society how well it is doing. When more goods are being produced (apples, tanks, medicines), more services are available (health care, police protection), and more investments are being made (new factories, skill training), the GNP of

Figure 1.1
Federal Outlays as a
Percent of GNP

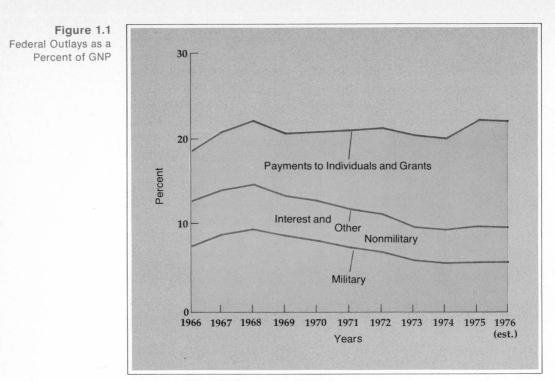

Source: U.S. Office of Management and Budget.

a society is increasing. When there is a slowdown in the production of goods, services, and investments, the GNP drops.

The importance of government to the private economy can be seen in the percent of GNP accounted for by government expenditures. Figure 1.1 shows for the last decade how large this has been. The federal government alone accounts for more than one-fifth of the GNP. A large part of the government's contribution to the GNP figures is in the government payroll: salaries for the military, for teachers, for judges, for clerks in the State Department, for the FBI, for medical researchers. But government is also a consumer of goods produced by private industry: It buys food for school lunches; type-writers to type order forms to buy more typewriters; cars to drive people around on "government business"; paper to publish the an-nual budget; military hardware to keep the armed forces equipped.

Since World War II the U.S. government has become the largest single customer for American industrial products and services. Were government purchases to stop, huge gaps would be left in the econ-omy. This is especially true of the industries that supply the military. As shown in Table 1.1, many of the nation's largest and most power-ful corporations hold direct contracts with the various defense-related agencies of the federal government, especially the Pentagon. Not only do these contracts involve huge amounts of money, but some of the largest defense contractors—notably General Dynamics and Lockheed Aircraft—depend on government contracts for almost

Table 1.1
The Military-Industrial
Alliance: Contracts

Selected Contractors	Prime Military Contracts, 1968 (in Billions)	Military Contracts as Percent of 1968 Sales
General Dynamics	$2.24	84%
Lockheed Aircraft	1.87	84
General Electric	1.49	18
United Aircraft	1.32	55
McDonnell-Douglas	1.10	34
Boeing	0.76	23
North American Rockwell	0.67	26
Grumman Aircraft Engineering	0.63	55
Martin Marietta	0.39	57
Northrop	0.31	64

Source: Based on data from *Congressional Record,* March 24, 1959, p. S3074; "500 Biggest Industrial List," *Fortune,* May 15, 1969; and "Where the Military Contracts Go," *Fortune,* August 1, 1969.

all their business. Defense contractors include many of the nation's largest corporations; 65 of the 100 leading firms are heavily involved in the military market. Besides, direct defense contracts are only the tip of the iceberg. The companies that provide the raw materials like aluminum and plastics and the manufactured parts like airplane tires and gaskets are equally dependent on the government's involvement in vast defense spending.

A Regulated Economy

Government economic regulation dates back to the latter part of the nineteenth century, when a nation of farmers and traders was slowly being transformed into one of factory workers and industrialists. It was in the post-Civil War era that the nation was crisscrossed with railroads. Canals and harbors were opened up for shipping. Natural resources—especially coal, lumber, and oil—were being put to industrial use. Factories were beginning to mass-produce everything from shoes to stoves. The telegraph and then telephones were spreading. Electricity was being introduced into the home, at least into city homes. American exports were being shipped around the world.

The growth and transformation of the economy had some harmful effects. But the government took little notice of them. A free-enterprise system should benefit from government supports and protection but not be hampered by government regulations. Thus the government provided little help to those hurt by an unregulated capitalist economy—small businessmen forced out of the market by the ruthless practices of monopolies like Standard Oil, farmers gouged by the high prices charged by the railroads that shipped their crops, workers who toiled long hours in unsafe and unsanitary conditions for very little pay. As a matter of fact, not only were judges and politicians unsympathetic to the cause of industrial regulation; they often owed their jobs to industrial interests. "Capitalists, seeking land grants, tariffs, bounties, favorable currency policies, freedom from regulatory legislation, and economic reform, supplied campaign funds, fees, and bribes and plied politicians with investment opportunities.[1] Few politicians resisted the temptations: "One might search the whole list of Congress, Judiciary, and Executive during the twenty-five years 1870 to 1895," concluded Henry Adams, "and find little but damaged reputation."

Correcting the Flaws

It was not until the 1890s that discontented farmers, middle-class reform groups working with small-business interests, protesting consumers, and labor agitators began to call for government regulation of the economy. Although they had only limited success, they did establish a political climate in which the flaws of a capitalist system— child labor, economic insecurity, deceptive advertising, price fixing, shoddy merchandise, unsafe working conditions—could be seen and corrected through government regulation.

A second, and perhaps more significant, stimulus toward regulatory legislation came from the business community itself. An unregulated economy was difficult to manage. Some corporation chiefs recognized that the federal government could be very helpful in bringing order to the sometimes chaotic economic situation if the business community could define the limits of government intervention in the economy. Business was largely successful in doing this. Thus the early regulatory legislation meant not the "triumph of small business over the trusts," as has often been suggested, but "the victory of big business in achieving the rationalization of the economy that only the federal government could provide."[2]

Today government activities to regulate the economy are many and varied. There are regulations on the training necessary to become a licensed barber; the number of exits from an airplane or a movie theater or a day nursery; the wording of wills and contracts; the advertising claims made by a medicine or food or automobile manufacturer; the price of electricity and gas. Government regulations affect how a corporation sells stocks, whether it will be allowed to expand its operations, the way it advertises its products, and how often and in what way it must make a public accounting of its transactions.

"Trust-Busting"

The romanticized version of early American capitalism stated that the force behind economic expansion was the small businessman. This was not the case. Starting in the nineteenth century and con-

---

[1] Richard Hofstadter, *The American Political Tradition* (New York: Vintage, 1954), p. 170. The quotation from Henry Adams appears in this work as well, p. 107.
[2] Gabriel Kolko, *The Triumph of Conservatism* (New York: Quadrangle, 1967), p. 284.

Offshore oil drilling is tightly regulated by the government.

tinuing today, industrial corporations, not small businessmen, have put together the necessary capital and know-how for opening canals and harbors, cutting timber, mining oil and coal, building railroads, inventing new production techniques, and experimenting with new products. The early "captains of industry" are remembered for the industrial empires they established: Rockefeller (oil), Carnegie (steel), Armour and Swift (meat-packing), Pillsbury (milling), Vanderbilt and Stanford (railroads), and Morgan (banking).

The new way of doing business sometimes gave rise to monopolies, as when a single firm (say, Standard Oil of New Jersey) could so monopolize an industrial sector (mining, refining, and distribution of oil) that it could set prices at will. No other firm would be big enough to provide serious competition.

These conditions were considered the very root of the economic evils so distressing to the late-nineteenth-century reformers. The reformers wanted to break up the enormous concentrations of economic power. "Trust-busting" became a popular political slogan; Supreme Court Justice Louis D. Brandeis, speaking of "industrial absolutism," warned of the danger to democracy when "there develops within the State a state so powerful that the ordinary social and industrial forces existing are insufficient to cope with it." Regulatory legislation was passed, such as the Sherman Antitrust Act of 1890, which prohibits monopolistic activities in restraint of trade, and the Federal Trade Commission Act of 1914, which prohibits unfair competition. Laws were also passed regulating working conditions and hours of work, especially for children and women.

From Monopoly to Oligopoly

Antitrust legislation has enabled the government to limit monopolistic power. Whenever a single corporation takes over a large share of the market for its products, the antitrust division of the Attorney General's Office begins to investigate. In recent years two giant corporations, IBM in the field of computers and electronics and ITT in the field of communication, have been the subjects of antitrust court action.

Government regulation of monopolies, however, has not eliminated concentration of economic power and resources. Much of the economy is under the control of what economists call *oligopolies*, in which only a few corporations control a particular part of the economy. A good example is in automobile manufacturing, where three giant corporations—Ford Motor, General Motors, and Chrysler— jointly dominate the manufacture and sale of automobiles.

Economic concentration can occur even when there are many firms producing the same service or goods, as in the following examples:

- There are 67,000 separate corporations actively involved in the utilities and communication industry. Of these corporations, only 33 control half of all assets in electricity, natural gas, transportation, and communication.
- There are 13,511 commercial banks in the United States. The 50 largest banks, 0.1 percent, control about half of all banking assets.
- In 1970 the Securities and Exchange Commission listed 202,710 manufacturing corporations. But only 100 of them (0.05 percent) controlled more than half of all manufacturing assets in the nation. This concentration has been steadily increasing for the last two decades. Here is the portion of all manufacturing assets controlled by only 100 corporations:

1950	1955	1960	1965	1970
39.8%	44.3%	46.4%	46.5%	52.3%

Not all industrial sectors show equal amounts of oligopolistic control. For example, in retail clothing and food distribution the assets are more evenly divided. It is in the key sectors of the economy—transportation, iron and steel, oil, banking and finance, communication, industrial chemicals—that concentration is greatest. Note that this concentration has not been reduced by government regulation. Regulation has made it difficult for a firm to gain monopolistic control but not for huge industrial corporations to pile up large amounts of economic resources.

A Managed Economy

Regulation should not be confused with management of the economy. Regulatory activities are piecemeal—they attempt to correct particular flaws in the economic system. The flaw might be decep-

Unemployment has been a persistent problem for the American economy: In 1975 nearly one out of ten workers was seeking unemployment benefits.

tive advertising: The government steps in to protect the consumer from being misinformed about what he or she is buying. Or the flaw might be something as substantial as monopoly control: Here the government steps in to break up the monopoly. But regulation has never intended to manage the economy. It was not until the Great Depression of the 1930s that the government turned its attention to management questions.

Establishing Economic Policy

During the period of industrial growth between the Civil War and the Great Depression of the 1930s, it was believed that a capitalist economy was self-adjusting. Full employment and price stability could occur if workers freely traded their labor for pay, if supply and demand regulated production and prices, and if profits guided the rate of growth and investment.

Until the depression of the 1930s, this view was challenged only by a few "radical" economists and business leaders who said that a "boom-bust" cycle, in which periods of economic growth are followed by periods of recession and unemployment, is built into an unmanaged capitalist system and, thus, that capitalism is by nature unstable.

Economic Policy in the 1930s

As unemployment climbed, banks failed, and factories closed, the argument that the economy would straighten itself out began to be less persuasive. Government leaders began to pay attention to a new argument put forward by John Maynard Keynes. He stated that government intervention in the economy—adjusting taxes, increasing or decreasing government spending on public projects, controlling the supply of money and credit—could stop the boom-bust cycle.

A MANAGED ECONOMY

25

These economic tools began to be used in the 1930s, during what is generally called the New Deal of Franklin D. Roosevelt. Today government economic policy is a major force in the free-enterprise system. In accepting such policies the business and political leaders were in effect admitting that no citizen—whether worker, pensioner, investor, or owner—was secure during depression. Government assumed responsibility for monitoring the business cycles and trying to maintain a relatively low level of unemployment while at the same time keeping prices from creeping up to destroy the value of the dollar.

The responsibility of the government for the health of the privately owned economic sector was firmly established by the Employment Act of 1946, which declared that "it is the continuing policy and responsibility of the federal government . . . to promote maximum employment, production, and purchasing power." The economy remains privately owned but it is increasingly subject to public management.

Government policy has not been entirely successful in managing the economy. Americans still suffer through business cycles, though to date none as severe as that of the 1930s. The 1970s have seen particularly difficult times. Unemployment has been on the increase; by 1975 it had reached levels well above what is considered "safe" by government economists. At the same time, inflation has been a major problem for many Americans. The prices of food, services, and goods have been increasing as much as 12–15 percent a year. This is a much greater increase than normal wage increases can match. The dollar is buying less and less.

There have been, then, louder demands for the government to "do something." The government has tried various things, even wage and price controls, but so far nothing has worked. The failure

The government called an Economic Conference on Inflation in late 1974 to seek new ways to manage the economy.

of the government to manage the economy is one thing. The very fact that the government is trying to manage the economy is another.

A story about the stock market crash in 1929 shows just how much has changed in recent decades. The economic crisis in 1929 was severe, the worst in American history. The stock market closed and banks failed. J. P. Morgan, the nation's leading banker, called a meeting of major bankers and financial figures. This group, meeting in New York, issued a statement saying *they* would act to correct the economy. Newspapers reported the statements of the bankers as if the crisis was a problem for Wall Street to solve. Few thought of an *economic* crisis as something *government* should deal with.

Much has changed since 1929. Today when there are economic problems we naturally look to the White House and government leaders for action, not to Wall Street and the bankers. The responsibility for managing the economy has shifted to government.

The federal government has tried to manage the economy with the tools introduced by President Roosevelt and his advisers in the 1930s: fiscal policy, primarily the powers of taxation and government spending; and monetary policy, primarily the powers to set interest rates for money loaned by the government and to affect the money supply. To aid the government in using these tools, a small group of economists serve as the President's Council of Economic Advisers.

The federal government has not attempted to *plan* the economy, at least not yet. But as the problems of the 1970s persisted, people started talking about a major economic planning agency. Such an agency would coordinate the many activities of government that affect the present and future state of the economy. Included along with taxation, the government budget, interest rates, and the money supply would be energy policy, a cost-of-living policy, and international trade policy. If such an agency is formed—and it would be much larger and more powerful than the present Council of Economic Advisors—then the partnership between government and economy would require even closer cooperation. More than ever would it be true that every major economic issue is also a political one and every major political issue also an economic one.

Thus far we have learned that the government is actively supporting, regulating, and to an extent managing the economy. Later in the text we will see that the government provides economic welfare for individual citizens through such programs as social security, unemployment compensation, medicare, education, and aid to disabled people—adding up to increasingly growing government involvement in the economy. Is America, then, still a capitalistic society?

A Capitalist Economy

What defines a society as capitalistic involves a number of complex things. We can touch briefly on only three matters: private ownership, individual economic choices, and material incentives.

The Privately Owned Economy

The United States was founded on the idea that the job of government is to protect life, liberty, and property. Individual citizens own property, and the government must ensure that a citizen can acquire, use, and dispose of his or her property according to personal choice. This idea is as central to our political life now as it was two centuries ago.

But if the principle of private property has remained firm, the kind of property that is privately owned has dramatically changed character. To the nation of farmers and small tradesmen in 1880, land itself was the most valuable form of property. And though land remains valuable, many other forms of property have become increasingly important to an industrial nation. Especially valued are the natural resources and the productive processes that convert natural resources into consumer goods. Iron, the natural resource, becomes steel, which becomes automobiles, the consumer goods.

Natural resources, productive processes, chemical patents, means of transporting goods, and related components of an industrial economy are privately owned in the United States. And the economy is run so as to return a profit for the owners. In this sense the economy is still very much a capitalistic one. Private individuals and institutions, not the public or the state, own and reap the profits of the economy.

In this way the United States is unusual among industrial nations. Of course we expect that in socialist nations such as the Soviet Union or East Germany much of the economy is state owned. But it is easy to overlook that there is much public ownership of economic enterprises even in Western democracies such as France or Great Britain. The United States is an exception, for there is very little government ownership and operation of natural resources, factories, transportation and communication systems, and basic social services.

Table 1.2 makes this very clear. Public ownership of major industries and services is compared for five Western nations: France, Britain, West Germany, Canada, and the United States. The amount

Table 1.2
Public Ownership of Various
Industries and Services

	Roads	Postal Services	Electricity	Railways	Telephones	Airlines	Radio, Television	Gas	Coal	Oil	Steel	Banks
France	S	S	S	S	S	S/p	S	S	S	S	—	S/p
Great Britain	S	S	S	S	S	S/p	S/p	S	S	s	S	—
West Germany	S	S	S	S	S	S	S	S	s	—	—	—
Canada	S	S	S/p	S/p	s	S/p	S/p	—	—	—	—	—
United States	S	S	s	—	—	—	—	—	—	—	—	—

S = predominantly state ownership.
s = element of state ownership in predominantly private system.
S/p = state and private sectors both substantial.
Source: Anthony King, ''Ideas, Institutions and the Policies of Governments: A Comparative Analysis: Parts I and II,'' *British Journal of Political Science*, 3 (July 1973), 296.

of private ownership in the United States is striking. Note that this table presents data on *ownership,* not on government regulation or support. The airline industry is as closely regulated in the United States as it is in the other four nations. But each of the other nations has a major government-owned airline: Lufthansa in Germany, Air France in France, British Airways in Britain, and Air Canada in Canada. There is no publicly owned airline in the United States. Gas and electricity are wholly state owned in the three European democracies, and 80 percent state owned in Canada. In the United States, the manufacture and distribution of gas are overwhelmingly in private hands. The ownership of electricity is mixed; some firms are privately owned (Pacific Gas and Electric) and some publicly owned (Tennessee Valley Authority).

The resistance in America to public ownership of major businesses can be seen in the recent history of the railroads. Railroads, especially in the northeastern part of the nation, have been operating at a loss. Under a free-enterprise system a business that could not make a profit would simply close up shop. Yet if the product of that business is a collective good—defined earlier as a socially valued product that is too expensive for private enterprise to maintain—closing down the business would be socially harmful. Certainly a transportation network that carries thousands of passengers and millions of tons of freight each day is an important asset to society.

In most countries a bankrupt but important transportation system would be taken over by the government. Or such a valuable national asset would have been state owned in the first place. People who have used the efficient rail services in Holland or Switzerland, indeed throughout Europe, have used state-owned and state-managed railroads.

The response in the United States has been different. A government agency was formed, the U.S. Railway Association, to restructure rail service in 17 northeastern and midwestern states. In early 1975 this agency announced a vast long-term plan, eventually to cost $7 billion. No public ownership is involved. Instead, there will be a private corporation, aided with large amounts of federal money, to take charge of the restructuring and to manage the new rail system.

Individual Economic Choice

The economy is regulated and managed by government. And many resources and powers are concentrated in large corporations. Yet we live in a society where many economic activities are the result of thousands and even millions of uncoordinated and unregulated individual choices. Consider New York City, residence of eight million people and working place for thousands more who pour into the city each day. How are these millions of people to be fed? Certainly they do not grow their own crops or fatten their own livestock. Rather, they depend on a daily supply of food coming into the city—a supply that comes from 50 states and dozens of nations:

Despite government intervention in the economy, many economic transactions are based on individual choices.

Wisconsin milk, Iowa beef, French cheeses, Brazilian coffee. Some of the food has been traveling for months. Were the supply to be cut off, the residents and workers of New York would come close to starving within a few days.

What can be said about the process that puts food on the tables of New Yorkers? There is an immense network of food production and processing, packaging and transportation, marketing and sales. This network functions without direction or coordination by any central agency. It rests on millions of individual economic activities: growing, producing, exchanging, selling, transporting.

This example reminds us that much economic life occurs without the involvement of either government planning bureaus or corporate oligopolies. The example of feeding New York is only one of many that could be cited. Consider the thousands of American families that move each week. These moves reflect economic decisions as breadwinners seek new jobs, new neighborhoods, or new housing. No agency regulates or coordinates the population shifts that take place in America.

If an economy is capitalistic when it allows citizens to choose what to buy, where to live, what jobs to seek, how much of their earnings to save and how much to spend, then the American economy is capitalistic. We often take note of how much government does to control economic activities. And we often see that the powers of corporations restrict the choices open to the individual citizen. We will discuss the controls and restraints in the next section, where we describe state capitalism. But it would not do to leave out the many ways economic activities are based on individual choices.

A Material Incentive System

Democratic ideology rejects inequalities based on "natural" superiority or inferiority. In the words of the Declaration of the Rights of Man and Citizens proclaimed in France in 1789, "Men are born and remain free and equal in rights." But democratic ideology does not reject inequality itself, as that radical declaration makes clear: "Social differences can only be based on general utility."

"Social differences based on general utility" can be translated into three propositions:[3]

1. Certain jobs are more important to society than others; some are so important that if they are poorly performed society itself suffers.
2. Certain jobs, often the socially important ones, require long and difficult training periods and are not easy to carry out.
3. People will work only if given suitable rewards.

It is the third proposition that is of interest: People work when rewarded. If they are not rewarded, they do not work, or at least work less. The question arises: What are the rewards to be? A capitalist society stresses money as the reward, though of course

---

[3] What is often called "the functional theory of social stratification" is an elaboration on these propositions. The argument is developed in Kingsley Davis and Wilbert E. Moore, "Some Principles of Stratification," *American Sociological Review*, 10 (April 1945), 242–249.

Table 1.3
Salaries and Bonuses of
Leading Executives, 1973

Company	Name and Title	Remuneration
CBS	William S. Paley, Chairman	$385,481
Chrysler	Lynn A. Townsend, Chairman	672,200
Ford	Henry Ford 2d, Chairman	865,000
General Motors	R. C. Geustenberg, Chairman	923,000
Goodyear	Russell DeYoung, Chairman	395,070
IBM	Frank T. Cary, Chairman	446,900
ITT	Harold S. Geneen, Chairman	814,299
RCA	Robert W. Sarnoff, Chairman	375,000

payment of different wages for different jobs is not true only of capitalism. It occurs in communist countries such as China or socialist countries such as Tanzania.

But capitalism declares differential wages for different jobs to be a basic principle. A person's worth is measured by the income he can attract when he places his talents and skills on the market. If the shop foreman earns twice what the assembly-line worker does, this is because the foreman's job requires more experience, skill, and responsibilities. If the owner of the factory, in turn, earns several times what the foreman does, this is because the owner, after all, took the risk and established the business that now provides employment and income in the community. If a line worker is good at production, his reward is in his paycheck, perhaps even in a promotion. If the foreman fails to manage his workers, his punishment is the suggestion that he seek a job elsewhere. If the owner makes an error in judgment, perhaps bankruptcy follows. If he is innovative, perhaps a fortune follows.

Table 1.3 gives some idea of the higher salaries paid in the United States. The chairman of Ford Motor, for instance, was paid $865,000 in 1973. His salary plus those of another half-dozen or so Ford executives totaled more than $4 million, or an amount about equal to what 500 people on the assembly line would earn.

The deliberate use of unequal wages to attract talent to important positions and to motivate effort is found throughout the economy. As the Ford example shows, the gap between the highest and lowest wages can become very large. American society accepts this. Here, then, is further evidence of the strength of a capitalist system in spite of the growing involvement of the government in economic affairs. The progressive income tax, discussed in Chapter 3, only modestly changes the pattern of income inequality associated with the widespread use of material rewards.

State Capitalism

Two facts are now clear. First, the government is heavily into economic affairs. This is shown in the importance of the annual government budget, possibly the single most critical document produced by the government. (See Chapter 13.) It is shown in the structure of government. The Presidential Cabinet includes secretaries of Commerce, Agriculture, Labor, Treasury, Transportation; important executive agencies include the Federal Trade Commission, the Interstate Commerce Commission, the Securities and Exchange Commission; the most powerful committees in Congress are those dealing with taxation, budget review, and appropriations. (See Chapters 10 and 11.) Through its involvement in the economy, the government supports private enterprise, regulates economic activities, and attempts to manage general economic conditions.

The second fact, however, balances this picture of government involvement. Major features of capitalism remain. Private individuals own the mines, the trucks, the chemicals, the factories, the grocery stores, and the land of America. These private individuals are very often organized as corporations, and the amount of resources and wealth controlled by the larger corporations is great indeed. Because the economy is privately owned, it is run in order to make profits for the owners.

We now reach an important point in our discussion. We have on the one hand an interventionist government. We have on the other hand huge privately owned corporations that can be influenced, for better or worse, by the activities of the government. What is the outcome of this situation?

Most observers agree that the United States has evolved into a form of *state capitalism*. Large economic units, including not only corporations such as General Motors or Sears Roebuck but also organized labor, have joined in a partnership with the government. This partnership is not without strains and differences of opinion, but it is held together by some important shared goals.

Economist John Kenneth Galbraith, in *The New Industrial State*, spells out the chief goals of the state: "The state is strongly concerned with the stability of the economy. And with its expansion or growth. And with education. And with technical and scientific advance. And, most notably, with the national defense."[4] These national goals have their counterparts in the corporate sector: Stability is necessary to long-term planning; economic growth brings profits, promotions, and prestige; trained manpower, scientific research, and technical development are necessary to a modern industrial system; defense spending directly supports, through government contracts, a large part of the economy. There are, then, shared goals between the public and the private sectors, between government and corporation leaders.

Critics of State Capitalism

Although most observers agree on the facts of the partnership between economy and government, not all feel comfortable with these facts. The critics note that the growth of concentrated economic

[4] John Kenneth Galbraith, *The New Industrial State* (Boston: Houghton Mifflin, 1967), p. 304.

Demanding government action on inflation leads to new government bureaucracies, such as the Council on Wage and Price Stability.

and political power, and especially the joint operation of these powers, makes it more and more difficult for a citizen to control his own life.

Milton Friedman, a professor at the University of Chicago, is one such critic. Freedom, he writes, "is a rare and delicate plant." Great care is necessary to protect it. "Our minds tell us, and history confirms, that the great threat to freedom is the concentration of power." Friedman is especially concerned about concentration of power in the government. Although government is necessary to preserve freedom, it can also threaten freedom. The true free man will ask: "How can we keep the government from becoming a Frankenstein that will destroy the very freedom we establish it to protect?"[5]

In this analysis it is the concentration of power in the government that is to be avoided. The government has grown huge because it is so involved in the economy. If it allowed the economy to take care of itself, the need for large government bureaucracies and budgets would be less. And there would be less danger that the government would restrict individual freedoms.

Other critics give more attention to the dangers of concentrated economic power. This criticism takes note of the ease with which great wealth in the hands of a small group can be converted to political control. If there are great inequalities of control over economic resources, the argument goes, it is hard to see how there can be the equal political influence promised by a democracy.

Paul Baran and Paul Sweezy, noted Marxist economists, claim that "the incessant repetition that the political regime in the United States today is a democracy" is a falsehood "devoid of all descriptive or explanatory validity." In the United States, they continue, "the

STATE CAPITALISM

33

[5] Milton Friedman, *Capitalism and Freedom* (Chicago: University of Chicago Press, 1962), p. 2.

propertyless masses have never been in a position to determine the conditions of their lives or the policies of the nation's government." A tiny group "resting on vast economic power and in full control of society's political and cultural apparatus makes all the important political decisions. Clearly to claim that such a society is democratic serves to conceal, not to reveal, the truth."[6]

Whether they express fear of government power or of corporate power, the critics share a concern that the political-economic partnership in the United States is a threat to individual liberty and democratic values.

Supporters of State Capitalism

Balanced against the critics of state capitalism are the voices of other observers who believe the partnership between government and economy is healthy. In this view a powerful government and a powerful corporate economy have joined forces to secure beneficial goals: a steady growth in production based primarily on improved technology and efficiency; a steady increase of consumer goods, which means higher standards of living; international stability and larger world markets for American products; constant improvement of public education to supply trained men and women. Those who speak in favor of the U.S. political economy take into account the problems of poverty, unemployment, and inflation but believe the best way to solve such problems is to strengthen rather than weaken the partnership between a public government and a private economy.

State Capitalism: Context for Analysis

The critics as well as the supporters of state capitalism raise important points; these points will be considered from a variety of viewpoints in later chapters. Indeed the picture of the American economy and government that emerges from this chapter is in large part the context within which many aspects of politics must be examined. In Chapter 3, for example, we look more closely at the tension between citizenship equalities, on the one hand, and economic inequalities, on the other. In later chapters we review how citizens' political participation and the choice of leaders are affected by the distribution of wealth. State capitalism also sets the context within which many political conflicts take place. For example, interest groups compete to attract federal moneys to the causes they represent, as when a truckers' association wants more money spent on the federal highway program and a citizen action group wants that money spent on mass transportation. Because so many of the issues of American politics derive from state capitalism, the formulation of public policies in the legislative, executive, and judicial branches of government is closely linked with the political economy.

[6] Paul A. Baran and Paul M. Sweezy, *Monopoly Capital: An Essay on the American Economic and Social Order* (London: Pelican, 1968), p. 327.

As briefly noted earlier, the organization of government reflects concern with the economy. There are huge government programs that fund research and train personnel; there are huge government bureaucracies that regulate economic activities; there is the taxing and spending power of government, which is used to influence prices, employment, and private investment.

As we turn to the actual working of the national, state, and local governments in the United States, we will be constantly reminded that there are political-economic conditions—summarized under the term *state capitalism*—that loom large in the who, what, how, and why of American politics.

2 The Constitutional Framework

The economy is not the only major factor in American politics. Also important is the constitutional framework. The Constitution is the "basic rule" from which all other rules derive. If something is "unconstitutional," it is not done, or at least it is not supposed to be done. If it is done, we expect that whoever does it will be punished. The criminal code and the civil code that govern the people living in the United States, as well as U.S. citizens living abroad, are made with an eye to what is constitutional and what is not.

Understanding the Constitution

A farmer in the 1790s was free to grow whatever crops he wished; to pay his help any wages they agreed to; to prepare, transport, and market his products however he chose; and to set his own prices. Today, however, dozens of regulations affect how foodstuffs are grown, processed, and marketed. Which crops are planted, and in what amounts, are subject to government regulation; so also is the use of fertilizers and insecticides; so are farm wages and crop prices.

If the farmer in 1790 was wealthy, he sent his children to private schools or perhaps hired a tutor to educate them at home. If he became ill, he depended on his family or neighbors to care for the farm until he could go back to work. As he grew old and could no longer run the farm, he lived off his savings and the good will of his children. Today the average farmer sends his children to public schools, and he can rely on public health services and a state social-security system as protection against sickness and old age.

The growth of government regulation and services has greatly changed the relationship between citizen and state over the past two centuries. But no sooner do we recognize this than we come face to face with an interesting point: The same basic rule, meaning the Constitution, that governed American society in 1790 governs it today. In other words, the growth of the "service" and "regulated" state has taken place within a legal framework and set of political principles hammered out one hot summer in Philadelphia nearly 200 years ago. What is this Constitution that could so long endure and accommodate itself to a society that has changed so much?

To understand the constitutional foundation of our government, we need to review a bit of American history. As we go back to the 1780s to study the politics that led to the Constitutional Convention and influenced the Constitution itself, we will see that our Constitution grew out of a period of turmoil. We will point out that although a constitution is supposed to "live for the ages," those who wrote it and those who argued for and against passing it were living in their own age. They had an eye on the immediate advantages and disadvantages of the new document as well as its future implications.

Then we will discuss the way our Constitution handles the

fundamentals. To survive, a political community needs procedures for defending itself from external and internal enemies, a means for settling conflicts between its own members, methods of making and carrying out rules, and a basis for agreement on how to select the rule makers. It is also wise for it to have some way of limiting the uses to which authority can be put. It is often said that the way the U.S. Constitution handled these fundamentals accounts for its enduring so long.

Finally, we will examine how the Constitution has managed to adapt itself to the great political, economic, and social changes that have taken place since 1787.

The Founding

Between the early 1770s and the early 1790s, political events changed the eastern seaboard from 13 separate colonies under British rule into a nation of 13 states. Especially critical in this process were the events of the decade between the signing of the Declaration of Independence in 1776 and the writing of the Constitution in 1787. Following is a list of the major events of this period.

AMERICAN POLITICAL HISTORY:

1774   The First Continental Congress, formed extralegally. Fifty-six delegates from 12 colonies meet in Philadelphia to discuss problems common to all of the colonies.

1775   Military action between Britain and the colonies becomes stronger. The famous ride of Paul Revere; the British expedition against the Concord Minutemen; the Battle of Bunker Hill.

1776   Thomas Paine publishes "Common Sense," a radical call to break all ties with Great Britain. Signing of the Declaration of Independence.

1777   The Articles of Confederation are drafted. They link the 13 states in a loose "League of Friendship" and are finally adopted in 1781.

1782   The War for Independence comes to an end. Peace talks begin in Paris, and the treaty is ratified the following year.

1786   Shays' Rebellion in Massachusetts, an attack by debtors on their creditors.

1787   An assembly to draft a constitution meets in Philadelphia.

1788   Enough states ratify the new Constitution so it can be put into effect.

1789   George Washington is elected first President of the United States.

1791   Bill of Rights added to the Constitution.

Establishing a Nation: A Two-Stage Process

The process of creating a new nation during the 1770s and 1780s involved two stages. During the first stage, the Declaration of Independence and the War for Independence, the existing ties with Great Britain were broken. A new government, a league of free and independent states, was set up under the Articles of Confederation. The Articles had a number of weaknesses, however, so there followed a second phase during which divisive forces threatened to disrupt the fragile confederation. In order to cope with these forces, a new government framework was drafted and adopted. The U.S. Constitution shifted the center of political power from a loose league of states to a strong federal union, thus checking the divisive forces.

Those who have studied the process of nation building in other parts of the world will recognize this as an eighteenth-century version of a pattern common today. During the first stage colonial rulers are overthrown: Just as the American colonies gained their independence from Great Britain, so Kenya gained its independence from Great Britain, Indonesia from Holland, the Congo from Belgium, and Algeria from France. Simply gaining independence does not guarantee the establishment of a new nation. A second phase, in which centers of power struggle to maintain their authority against the forces that threaten to fragment and divide the new society, often follows. The civil wars in many new nations indicate how powerful such divisive forces can be.

The War for Independence

During the War for Independence the inhabitants of the thirteen colonies were divided on the wisdom and justice of the war. To justify their positions the Tories and the Patriots appealed to different political principles. Tories, opposed to the war, stressed that it was in the best interests of the colonies to remain loyal to the authority of Parliament and the legal system of the British Empire. The Patriots, on the other hand, asserted that both economic self-interest and natural right dictated that a continent should not be governed by an island. In Jefferson's elegant phrases in the Declaration of Independence,

> We hold these truths to be self-evident, that all men are created equal, that they are endowed by their Creator with certain unalienable Rights, that among these are Life, Liberty, and the pursuit of Happiness. That to secure these rights, Governments are instituted among Men, deriving their just powers from the consent of the governed. That whenever any Form of Government becomes destructive of these ends, it is the Right of the People to alter or to abolish it, and to institute new Government, laying its foundations on such principles and organizing its powers in such form, as to them shall seem most likely to effect their Safety and Happiness. Prudence, indeed, will dictate that Governments long established should not be changed for light and transient causes; and accordingly all experience hath shown, that mankind are more disposed to suffer, while evils are sufferable, than to right themselves by abolishing the forms to which they are accustomed. But when a long train of abuses and usurpations, pursuing invariably the same Object evinces a design to reduce them under absolute Despotism, it is their right, it is their duty, to throw off such Government, and to produce new Guards for their future security. Such has been the patient sufferance of these Colonies and such is now the necessity which constrains them to alter their former Systems of Government. . . .

Jefferson's concerns included economic interests as well as human rights. The immediate "abuses and usurpations" he referred to were the arbitrary taxes and trade restrictions imposed by Great Britain without the consent of the colonies.

Major Consequences of the War

To see the War for Independence simply as a struggle over economic interests is to miss some of its important aspects. Mobilized by propaganda stressing the principles stated in the Declaration, many citizens became committed to a view of individual freedom that emphasized the right to rebel against central authority; authority was illegitimate unless it was based on the consent of the people.

In addition, the small group of leaders who had served in the initial Continental Congress, written the Declaration of Independence, and financed and fought in the war began to think of themselves as a national political elite. Of course there was no real "nation"—only thirteen independent states, formerly separate colonies, loosely linked together by the Articles of Confederation. Nevertheless the men who led the colonies during the war years were aware of their role in establishing a nation.

These national leaders recognized that in spite of the revolutionary emphasis on individual liberties, stable, effective government demands obedience. Newly formed governments often have difficulty reasserting authority after a period of rebellion. During the 1780s the founding fathers took it as their job to make sure authority would be reasserted.

The Articles of Confederation: Their Weaknesses

The Articles of Confederation, framed in the spirit of the War for Independence, were ratified in 1781; they lasted less than a decade. The Articles were a compromise between complete state sovereignty and a strong central government. For the most part they reflected the belief that local self-rule could best preserve the liberties gained in the successful war. Even to establish a confederation, however, was to recognize that some centralized coordination among the thirteen states might benefit all. The inability of the Articles to provide such coordination quickly discredited them.

What kind of government was provided for in the Articles of Confederation? First of all, there was no executive power—no king, no president, and thus no one to administer the laws. Congress consisted of delegates from the thirteen states, who, like ambassadors, served entirely at the pleasure of their home states. Deadlock was almost inevitable in Congress. Regardless of size or resources, each state had only one vote; nine votes—more than a two-thirds majority—were required to pass legislation; the vote of only one state could veto an amendment to the Articles.

Furthermore, Congress had many limitations on its powers. First of all, it exercised no direct power over individuals. Men held citizenship only in their respective states. Any congressional law—say, a law drafting men into the military—would not be binding on an individual unless his state chose to enforce it. Many regulations were never enforced by state authority. A comparison can be made with the United Nations. If the UN Assembly passes a resolution calling for trade sanctions against Rhodesia, no manufacturer or shipper can be punished for trading there unless his own nation passes similar legislation.

In addition, Congress could not tax. The confederation was supposed to be supported by state contributions. However, just as the UN cannot collect dues from any nation that refuses to pay, Congress could not enforce such contributions. Thus the confederation verged on bankruptcy. Finally, Congress could neither regulate commerce nor impose tariffs. This not only closed off an important source of potential revenue but also led to economic warfare among the states.

Economic Groups Hurt by the Government's Lack of Powers

The interests of several economic groups were hurt by the weakness of the Articles. First of all, those who had lent money for the war effort would lose everything if the government went bankrupt. Men like Hamilton were aware that if the government defaulted on its debts, it would be hard to raise money in the future. Land speculators who wished to open the vast areas west of the Appalachians to settlement and trade felt that their interests were hurt by the weakness of the Articles. The inability of the central government to protect settlers from Indians and to dislodge the British from their trading posts severely hurt land speculators. In addition to creditors, land speculators, and settlers moving west, the merchant and commercial interests, small though they may have been, were suffering under the Articles of Confederation. State-imposed tariffs often crippled small industries in a neighboring state. General restrictions on interstate trade and the lack of common regulations on shipping slowed the growth of the kind of national economy necessary for commercial interests to prosper.

In short, economic interests were severely hampered by the inability of the central government to maintain a standing army, to tax citizens in order to pay its debts, to regulate commerce among the states, to impose tariffs on foreign goods, and to protect economic investments.

The Conflict Between Debtors and Creditors

It should be obvious that some groups—particularly debtors—were not hurt by the weakness of the central government under the Articles. Many farmers who were in debt benefited from the cheap paper money being issued by state governments. Using their influence in state legislatures, they were able to pass laws delaying the collection of debts.

Debtors benefited not only from some of the economic conditions but also from the central government's lack of effective police power. Incidents of open rebellion against creditors, the most famous of which was led by Daniel Shays, were fairly common. Although the rebellion was put down by a mercenary army, the lesson of Shays' Rebellion was not lost on citizens concerned about protecting property. Many citizens felt that the central government was too weak.

The Constitutional Convention

By the mid-1780s political leaders felt that something had to be done. What they did was to write the Constitution that established the United States of America. This time, however, national leadership stressed authority over liberty.

Congress had requested the 13 states to send representatives to Philadelphia "for the sole purpose of revising the Articles of Confederation." Without question the 55 men who gathered in May 1787 did more than revise the Articles. As soon as they arrived they agreed to two principles. First, the meetings were to be held in strict secrecy, and second, the Articles were so inadequate that nothing would do but to create an entirely new Constitution. Knowing that not all states would adopt the Constitution, they decided that it would go into effect when only nine states had ratified. It is clear that they violated the authority under which they were gathered, but the country was ready for something new, and these were the men who provided the leadership.

Writing a constitution is a difficult business. Political leaders are often strong willed, and if they differ in their views of the social order, in personal interests, and in the people they represent, they are unlikely to write a document agreeable to all.

Yet during a single summer these 55 men succeeded in writing a constitution that is still perhaps the most effective such document

ever written. The statesmanship of Washington, the tactical brilliance of Hamilton, the profound insights of Madison, and the practical wisdom of Franklin have become political folklore passed on from generation to generation of American citizens.

The men gathered in Philadelphia were in fact a remarkable group. The document they wrote reflected their political experience as well as close study of political philosophy. As many as 20 of the delegates had had previous experience writing state constitutions, and in many respects the federal Constitution was an extension of basic rules that had proved their worth in the different states. Thirty of the delegates were serving in state legislatures at the time of the convention. Thus they knew well the weaknesses of some of the existing charters and were able to avoid certain mistakes. More than three-fourths had been members of the national Congress established by the Articles of Confederation. Their disappointment with this institution played a large part in the Philadelphia convention.

If the founders could draw on personal experience, they could also draw on political theory. John Locke's *Two Treatises on Government*, James Harrington's *Commonwealth of Oceana*, both seventeenth-century writings, and Montesquieu's *Spirit of the Laws*, written forty years before the Philadelphia convention, were familiar to all men of education. In these writings were many of the basic ideas that found their way into the Constitution. More than half of the delegates were trained in law and had read some of the great commentaries on English common law, a system that remains the basis of our own legal system.

It was nevertheless a difficult document to draft. Any constitution must balance freedom and authority—the freedom of citizens from arbitrary or unjust government, yet the authority of government to settle disputes and manage the society. It is important to recognize that the politics in the convention hall (and outside it) were as instrumental in the balance between freedom and authority as the personal traits of the founders. Three political factors are relevant to understanding the considerable success of the Constitutional Convention: The founders agreed on certain basic issues, the convention skipped the hardest issue, and the delegates were willing to compromise when feelings ran high.

Agree on Basic Issues   Missing from the convention were conservatives who might have opposed the more liberal provisions of the Constitution. Also missing were several forceful democrats who might have refused to give so much authority to a central government. Patrick Henry, for instance, refused to attend and commented, "I smelt a rat." He was to be a vigorous opponent of adoption of the Constitution.

The men who dominated the convention reflected solid, conservative financial interests. Thus they had no difficulty in agreeing that the Articles of Confederation be dropped and an entirely new document written. They shared a philosophy that included mistrust of human nature, belief in the sanctity of property, anxiety about the excesses of democracy, and confidence in their right to fashion a new government. But if they were conservative in these respects, they were also committed in varying degrees to the experiment of self-government.

Through a process of self-selection and self-elimination, the writing of the Constitution was left largely to men of influence with a basically similar political philosophy. Others either chose to ignore the convention or were not sent as delegates. Perhaps for this reason the most difficult battles over the Constitution occurred not in Philadelphia but in the various state legislatures. For instance, the founders completely ignored the question of a bill of rights and were able to win ratification in several states only when the first ten amendments were promised.

Skip the Hardest Issue The strongest political feelings of the time centered on the question, Should there be state sovereignty such as existed under the Articles, or should there be a unitary government in which sovereignty rests with the central power? *Federalism*, in which sovereignty is shared between the states and the central government, was a brilliant compromise and was probably the major reason the Constitution was finally adopted. Yet the Constitution simply avoided the hardest issue of all, whether member states had the right to secede. If the right to secede had been written into the Constitution, it is doubtful that the Union would have lasted more than a few decades. If the right to secede had been expressly prohibited, it is doubtful that there ever would have been a "united states." The founders simply passed this question along to a later generation, and it finally took a bitter civil war to settle it.

Compromise When There Is Strong Political Opposition The Constitution was a compromise document on many counts. For instance, there is evidence that among the men gathered in Philadelphia were many who recognized that slavery was basically inconsistent with a government proclaiming the inalienable rights of men. A Virginia delegate, George Mason, attacked the slave trade as "infernal traffic" and warned that slavery "would bring the judgment of heaven on a country." Other delegates, however, said their states would not join the union if the Constitution made slavery illegal. The compromise, found in Article I, prevented Congress from banning the slave trade until 1808. Congress did outlaw the slave trade, though not slavery itself, in that year. But southern states continued to import slaves until the beginning of the Civil War.

The most famous compromise was in the makeup of Congress. The question was whether the individual states would be represented in Congress in proportion to their population, giving an advantage to larger states, or on an equal basis, giving an advantage to smaller states. The latter arrangement prevailed under the Articles of Confederation and was considered unworkable by representatives from the populous states. But delegates from small states like Maryland and New Jersey were strongly opposed to giving seats in Congress on the basis of population. A few large states could easily outvote all the smaller states.

In what is known as the Connecticut Compromise, the Constitution established a Congress in a form familiar today. There would be a House of Representatives in which seats would be granted depending on the size of the state. And there would be a Senate, or upper house, in which each state, no matter how small, would have two seats. Because most important legislation must be passed by both the House and the Senate, this compromise allowed the smaller states to check the larger ones.

Summary

We have reviewed the events that led to the creation of the United States of America and to the writing of the U.S. Constitution. We have discussed the way many of the concerns that arose during the War for Independence shaped later political events and the kind of government that was created. We saw that the Articles of Confederation proved unworkable, having created a government that was too weak and decentralized to govern effectively. Then we saw that the men who gathered at the Constitutional Convention were anxious to create a strong and effective government without repeating the mistakes of the Articles.

How were they able to handle the difficult task of writing such a constitution? In part, because they all combined a conservative philosophy and financial preferences with a belief in democracy, they agreed on the basic issues. Furthermore, they were willing to compromise on certain issues, such as the representation of large and small states. Finally, they simply skipped the hardest issue, that of sovereignty, by creating a federal system and not answering the question of whether the states had the right to secede.

Constitutional Principles

The constitution of a society will reflect the philosophical ideas acceptable to that society. And our Constitution does have a philosophical basis, one acceptable to many citizens in the 1790s and, we suspect, to many citizens today. Here is what John Adams had to say to his cousin Samuel Adams:

> Human appetites, passions, prejudices and self-love will never be conquered by benevolence and knowledge alone. . . . 'The love of liberty,' you say, 'is interwoven in the soul of man.' So it is (also) in that of a wolf; and I doubt whether it be much more rational, generous, or social in one than in the other. . . . We must not, then, depend alone upon the love of liberty in the soul of man for its preservation. Some political institutions must be prepared, to assist this love against its enemies.

In other words, Adams was saying that without institutional restraints men are not to be trusted. They would break their contracts. Their passions and ambitions would dominate their reason and self-restraint. Minorities, if they were in control, would tyrannize majorities and plunder in order to expand their own privileges. Majorities, if unrestrained, would destroy the rights of minorities, forcing them to conform to majority wishes.

What was behind the writing of the Constitution, and imbedded in it, was a pessimistic view of human nature but an optimistic view of social and civil institutions. A good political constitution, backed by the government, could protect liberties and guard the social order.

But if there must be authority, it too must be curbed. No single group—be it a minority within government, the government itself, or the majority outside the government—must be allowed final control. It is a tribute to the founders that they were consistent in applying these principles. They feared the unchecked ambitions of leaders just as they feared the excesses of the public. They were as careful to impose constraints on those in authority as they were to guarantee the authority needed to govern the community.

The checks on authority were expressed through three constitutional fundamentals: popular control over elected representatives, fragmentation and separation of governmental powers, and the idea of limited government.

A Representative Form of Government

Distrustful as the founders were of the excesses of democracy, they were also strongly opposed to arbitrary rule. They were sympathetic to republican government, and in this they followed the seventeenth-century English political idealists who favored political representation and popular rule. Did not the Declaration of Independence speak of the "consent of the governed"? And did not Madison report that "a dependence on the people is, no doubt, the primary control on the government"?

Titles of Nobility Abolished   One of the first acts of the founders was to abolish hereditary titles of nobility and hereditary positions of power. This trend had started in the state legislatures, but to put it into the Constitution was to break sharply from a practice common in Europe and England. Time and again the founders stressed their belief in the principle that no arbitrary standard, especially birth, should give to some men the right to rule and deny it to other men. *The Federalist* (No. 57) asserts:

> Who are to be the objects of popular choice? Every citizen whose merit may recommend him to the esteem and confidence of his country. No qualification of wealth, of birth, of religious faith, or of civil profession is permitted to fetter the judgment or disappoint the inclination of the people.

Open Access to Office   The founders did feel that the "right" people should rule. And they did retain a belief in the natural aristocracy of wealth, talent, and education. They themselves were far from a random sample of the total population. But the principle they asserted was that no man had a right to rule *just* because he was born of parents already in positions of authority. Office was open to the talented and ambitious, whatever their social origins.

Periodic Elections   "Consent of the governed" found its most concrete expression in periodic elections. *The Federalist* explained the House of Representatives as follows:

> As it is essential to liberty that the government in general should have a common interest with the people, so it is particularly essential that the branch of it under consideration should have an immediate dependence on, and an intimate sympathy with, the people. Frequent elections are unquestionably the only policy by which this dependence and sympathy can be effectually secured.

The right of suffrage extended only so far, of course. Individual states were allowed to legislate their own voting regulations. Moreover, only members of the House of Representatives were directly elected by citizens. Senators, expected to be members of a more "aristocratic" house, were indirectly elected, being nominated and chosen by the state legislatures. (Indirect election of senators was changed to popular election in 1913, with final ratification of the Seventeenth Amendment.) The President and Vice-President were even further removed from popular election; they were chosen by an electoral college, which, in turn, was appointed by the state legislature. And judicial posts of course were filled by appointment.

Though limited, the right to vote was firmly stated in the Constitution. And elections were to become a major prop supporting the evolution of representative government. Periodic elections mean office holding is probationary. Leaders serve limited terms, at the end of which they face the electorate (or other agencies) that granted them power in the first place. The purpose was to create in political leadership a "habitual recollection of their dependence on the peo-

Periodic elections give meaning to the concept of representative government: Here ballots are being sorted by the Chicago Board of Elections Commissioners.

Figure 2.1
Conception of Representative
Government Today

A belief in

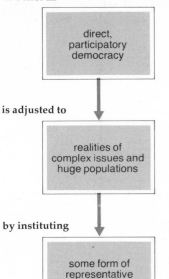

direct,
participatory
democracy

is adjusted to

realities of
complex issues and
huge populations

by instituting

some form of
representative
government.

Founders feared

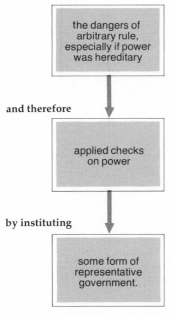

the dangers of
arbitrary rule,
especially if power
was hereditary

and therefore

applied checks
on power

by instituting

some form of
representative
government.

ple," as stated in *The Federalist* (No. 57). In a manner recalling the founders' shared belief with Lord Acton that "power tends to corrupt," this passage continues:

> Before the sentiments impressed on their minds by the mode of their elevation can be effaced by the exercise of power, they will be compelled to anticipate the moment when their power is to cease, when their exercise of it is to be reviewed, and when they must descend to the level from which they were raised; there forever to remain unless a faithful discharge of their trust shall have established their title to a renewal of it.

This passage contains much that is relevant to an understanding of representative government. Being elected to political office is to be "elevated," and being evicted from that office is to be "punished." Officeholders therefore use power in a manner "faithful" to the trust placed in them by the electorate.

Representative Government The Constitution established a government based on the consent of the governed. In reading back into history present-day conceptions of democracy, we very often misinterpret what happened in 1787 and either see the founders as more radical than they actually were or blame them for being too cautious. Neither of these views fits the facts.

Today we think of representative government as a compromise between the principles of "perfect" democracy, direct popular participation in making the laws that govern the people, and the realities of complex and huge nations. Because there is no way for the people to assemble, debate, and decide, we compromise our commitment to these principles and institute representative government, in which a select group of people meet and decide on the issues of the day but are always aware of the wishes of those who sent them. We can diagram the logic of this position as shown in Figure 2.1.

What the founders had in mind was something far different. Because they feared arbitrary rule, they believed men with political power must somehow be checked in their use of power. And because they felt some sympathy toward republican government, they saw a system of political representation as an appropriate check. Representative government was not a compromise with a deep commitment to democracy; it was a cautious move away from prevailing practices of hereditary rule. Compare Figure 2.2 with Figure 2.1, and you will see that the initial conception of political representation was very different from how it is often thought of today.

The same point can be stressed from another angle. Whereas today we view representational processes as means by which the larger population can express itself on political issues, the founders saw the possibility of limiting the impact of the public. The representatives would be wiser and more cautious of the social order than the masses. As Madison put it, representative government would "refine and enlarge the public views by passing them through the medium of a chosen body of citizens.''

In addition to external checks, whereby citizens could restrain the use of authority, the founders considered internal checks, whereby those in authority checked one another.

Fragmentation of Powers

The Constitution is a search for the means by which governments can rule and yet not rule unfairly. It is a search for the delicate balance between authority, or ability to rule, and liberty, or protection against unfair rule. We have seen that the writers of the Constitution wanted a strong national government, one strong enough to create a single nation out of thirteen separate states. Yet the founders worried that in setting up a national government they would be establishing the tool with too much power. One check on this power, periodic elections and limited tenure of office, has just been reviewed.

The founders were not satisfied. As it was put in *The Federalist* (No. 51), ''a dependence on the people is, no doubt, the primary control on the government; but experience has taught mankind the necessity of auxiliary precautions.'' These extra precautions were to be found in the fragmentation of powers *within* government.

Federalism Some powers went to the national government. Some were reserved to the individual states. This is fragmentation of powers across the layers of government. It was a great act of political engineering, for it served two seemingly contradictory ends. The first goal was to establish a strong, effective central government. Nothing short of this would guarantee social order, pay the public debt, provide a monetary system, and make it possible to develop the country's resources. Yet it was also necessary to preserve the independence of the state governments, for this would check the concentration of powers in the federal government. Out of the tension between these two goals grew the federal system. In Chapter 15 federalism is reviewed in detail.

Separation of Powers The writers of the Constitution were not content with federalism. They also divided powers across three different branches of government, giving different powers and resources to the legislative, executive, and judicial branches. Here was the protection against political tyranny, defined in *The Federalist* (No. 47) as ''the accumulation of all powers, legislative, executive, and judiciary, in the same hands.'' It was not enough to have popular control over government. It was not enough to have two layers of government. Beyond these controls was the need to further fragment the powers of government. Again *The Federalist* (No. 51) makes the case clear:

In the compound Republic of America, the power surrendered by the people is first divided between two distinct governments (Federal government and the States), and then the portion alloted to each is subdivided among distinct and separate departments. Hence, a double security rises to the rights of the people. The different governments will control each other, at the same time that each will be controlled by itself.

Separation of powers, like federalism, is such a central principle of our political system that we will devote an entire chapter (Chapter 14) to seeing how it has worked out in practice.

Limited Government

A third basic principle of the Constitution is limited government. Here there are two things to keep in mind.

The Bill of Rights   First, there are certain things government cannot and should not do. It cannot restrict the protections for the individual citizen stated in the first ten amendments, the Bill of Rights. The government was explicitly prevented from denying citizens the right to practice the religion of their choice, the right to say and write what they pleased, the right to assemble for political purposes, and the right to bear arms. Moreover, the government could not take life, liberty, or property without due process of law, which included the right to a speedy, public, and fair trial and to a trial by a jury of peers in certain cases.

The complications of applying such principles in concrete cases are discussed in Chapter 13, and throughout the book are examples showing that the protections promised by the Bill of Rights have had a checkered political history. At this point, however, we are interested in constitutional *principles* rather than political realities. The principle of limited government holds that the rights of man are derived from a higher law than government (natural law) and should be protected by placing limits on government, as in the Bill of Rights.

"Government of Laws, Not of Men" The second idea behind the principle of limited government is constitutionalism itself. By this is meant simply the familiar phrase "government of laws, not of men." There is a basic law against which all lesser laws should be measured. This law, the written Constitution in our case, is based on the consent of the governed. Any lesser laws passed in accordance with the Constitution, then, should have the same basis. Moreover, the basic law as well as the lesser laws regulate the operation of government and, thus, the governors. No one is "a law unto himself" or should "stand above the law," not even the President of the United States — as was so dramatically demonstrated by Richard Nixon's fall from power.

The Court System The court system in the United States provides the means for testing the constitutional character of the government. A citizen hurt by an act of the government can challenge that action in the courts. If the courts accept jurisdiction, the government must show that its action was based on an authorizing law. A policeman cannot simply arrest any citizen; the citizen must be charged with violating a specified statute, and the policeman must be able to show the legal basis for the arrest. Welfare officials cannot simply issue checks to friends or refuse to pay those whose hair styles they dislike; in each instance they must be prepared to show in court that their decision was controlled by whether or not the applicant for welfare was in one of the welfare categories authorized by law. In principle, if not always in practice, courts offer the citizen the means to check arbitrary governmental power.

But the courts play an even more important role in American politics. Even if a government official can show that his act was in accordance with a local, state, or national law, his act can still be reversed if it can be shown in court that the *law itself* is contrary to the Constitution. The American system of government thus allows courts to limit what the popularly elected branches of government may authorize the government to do. Only a constitutional amendment — a cumbersome, time-consuming, politically awkward expedient — can reverse the United States Supreme Court's interpretation of the Constitution.

Like the Bill of Rights, the idea of a "government of laws" has had a checkered history. Secrecy, duplicity, and lawlessness are not unknown in the highest government circles. The law can be, and often is, bent for those with power and money. Some examples appear in the chapter on the Supreme Court (Chapter 12) and throughout the text. But however misshapen by political pressures, the principle of constitutionalism remains a constant check on arbitrary government.

Summary

We have covered two major topics: how the Constitution came to be written and the fundamental principles on which it rests. The material provides a partial answer to the question at the beginning of the chapter, What is this Constitution that could so long endure and accommodate itself to a society that has changed so much over the past two centuries? One part of the answer is that the Constitution was and is a political document. And at least some of the political conflicts of the 1780s are still with us today, though in different forms. An example is the conflict between central power and local control. Thus a document sensitive to political realities remains workable because those realities remain important.

Another partial answer lies in the constitutional fundamentals. Popular control over elected representatives, fragmentation and separation of governmental powers, and limited government were attractive enough ideals in 1787 so that the Constitution could be adopted. We can only guess that they remain attractive enough, despite major changes in society, so that the Constitution continues to be supported. Political history reveals only one major challenge to the U.S. Constitution in 200 years—the attempted secession of the Confederacy. The Civil War was fought to "defend and maintain the supremacy of the Constitution and to preserve the union," in the words of a congressional resolution of July 1861. Except for the Civil War, no significant political movement has tried to call into question the Constitution.

But these are partial answers. A further explanation rests on the adaptability of the Constitution and its constant reinterpretation to deal with new political realities and social conditions.

A Flexible Constitution

"The Constitution belongs to the living and not to the dead," Jefferson wrote. No document of a few thousand words written in 1789 could possibly anticipate and resolve the political-legal issues that would emerge as the nation developed and changed. Jefferson, speaking of the Constitution, said that "as new discoveries are made, new truths disclosed, and manners and opinions changed . . . institutions must advance also, and keep pace with the times."

The Constitution has kept pace with the times, or else it would long ago have been discarded. Three factors have contributed to its flexibility: constitutional generalities, constitutional silences, and a formal amendment process.

Constitutional Generalities

The Constitution seems in places to have been purposely ambiguous. Maybe this was the best way the founding fathers had of winning approval of the various factions. In any case this ambiguity has allowed later generations to interpret the Constitution as giving broad grants of authority to key institutions. We will see in Chapter 12 that the power of the Supreme Court to declare acts of Congress unconstitutional is not explicitly stated in the Constitution, nor is it denied. But the Supreme Court ruled that it did have the power of judicial review, a decision that greatly enlarges its political significance. The executive power of the President is not clearly spelled out in the Constitution either. The change from George Washington's staff of a half-dozen clerks to the huge federal bureaucracy of the 1970s has been justified by the simple constitutional phrase, the President "shall take care that the laws be faithfully executed."

New Meanings Given to Old Words   Using a general language allows new meanings to be given to old words. Consider the example of "unreasonable searches." The founders disliked the way colonial officers searched private homes at will, so in the Fourth Amendment they declared that "the right of the people to be secure in their persons, houses, papers, and effects, against unreasonable searches and seizures, shall not be violated. . . ." This expresses a clear principle in such general language that it can still be applied today, despite an entirely different technology of search and seizure. Today the right of government agents to use electronic surveillance techniques—telescopic cameras, wiretaps, and hidden microphones—is challenged according to the principle and with the language of the Fourth

The Fourth Amendment of the Constitution prohibits unreasonable searches: This amendment protects citizens from government use of such bugging devices as the one shown here.

Figure 2.3
Standard Practice of Amending
the Constitution

**Amendments are
proposed**

by a two-thirds vote
in both the Senate and
the House of
Representatives.

**Amendments are
ratified**

when legislatures in
three-fourths of the
states (38 states) vote
in favor.

Amendment as adopted in 1791. A new technology, yes, but an old argument that places individual rights above the government's right to know.

Constitutional Silences

One of the best examples of a constitutional silence permitting political flexibility is the matter of political parties. The political party system is entirely extraconstitutional, yet who could imagine twentieth-century politics in the United States without some form of political parties? We will see that every major elected official, and most appointed ones, take office under the banner of a political party (Chapter 9). And political parties largely organize and manage the elections, including primaries and nominating conventions. All of this takes place outside the framework of the Constitution, and indeed largely outside of any type of federal law at all.

Thus it is that political institutions and the formal government adapt themselves to the requirements of twentieth-century politics, very often because the Constitution has nothing to say on the matter.

The Amendment Process

The writers of the Constitution knew that very specific changes would become necessary as the conditions in society changed. So they provided for a formal amendment process. It is a two-step process: proposing an amendment and then ratifying it. It is complicated because there are two separate ways amendments may be proposed, and there are two separate ways they may be ratified. The standard practice, however, has not been as complicated; the procedure is shown in Figure 2.3.[1]

The formal amendment process has been used infrequently (leaving out the Bill of Rights, only sixteen times), sometimes for minor changes in the mechanics of government. Most of the amendments, however, have been significant in adapting government to new social conditions. The famous "Civil War amendments" (Thirteenth, Fourteenth, and Fifteenth) outlawed slavery; defined the privileges and immunities of national citizenship and set limits on state interference with equal protection and due process; and gave the right to vote without regard to race, color, or prior servitude. Other amendments have broadened the democratic meaning of the Constitution, providing for direct election of senators, women's suffrage, repeal of the poll tax, and a voting age lowered to 18. One of the most important amendments, the Sixteenth, ratified in 1913, authorized the income tax.

The proposed Twenty-Seventh Amendment, the Equal Rights Act,

[1] Amendments also may be proposed by a special national convention called by Congress at the request of two-thirds of the state legislatures. This has never happened. And amendments may be ratified by special conventions in three-fourths of the states. This procedure has been used once, when the Twenty-First Amendment, which repealed prohibition, was ratified by state conventions rather than state legislatures.

is currently being debated in state legislatures. This amendment will require equal treatment of males and females (see the discussion in Chapter 3).

The Dynamics of Constitutional Change

To say that the Constitution is flexible is another way of saying that it does not provide ready-made answers for new political questions and social issues. We have identified aspects of the Constitution that give it flexibility, but we have not yet accounted for specific examples of major constitutional change.

No general formula can account for each major change and reshaping of the Constitution, but it would help to hold in mind the following: The genius of the Constitution is also its weakness. A document that gives powers to different political institutions is sooner or later going to be caught in a squeeze when the interests of those institutions are in conflict. The clashes leading to constitutional crises have been of four general sorts: (1) clashes between the federal and state governments, (2) clashes over the authority of a particular branch of government, (3) clashes over the separation-of-powers doctrine, and (4) clashes over the extension of citizenship rights.

Federalism   In Chapter 15 we will learn how easy it is for conflicts to occur over which level of government is responsible and authorized to do what. The genius of the Constitution in splitting government powers between the national government and the independent states is also its weakness when different levels are in conflict. The Civil War was fought to establish the supremacy of the national government, a supremacy ratified by the adoption of the Thirteenth, Fourteenth, and Fifteenth Amendments. The war did not end disputes among the branches of government, and the principle of federalism is constantly being tested.

Scope of Authority   Many of the new social conditions government has had to deal with over the past two centuries have been handled within the guidelines set by the Constitution. But some conditions have presented such new and complicated problems that traditional definitions of government authority have been of little use. The interpretation of the Constitution has shifted in response to these problems. As we shall see in Chapter 12, sometimes the courts have resisted the process of constitutional adaptation. For example, the great economic depression of the 1930s seemed to require broad new government authority and programs. But the Supreme Court declared important new legislation unconstitutional, claiming that the Presidency was increasing its authority illegally. Heavy political pressure from the Roosevelt administration led the Court to reverse itself. In other times it was the Court itself that stimulated constitutional adaptation. Thus citizenship rights and liberties were greatly enlarged in a series of decisions by the Warren Court (so called because the Chief Justice was Earl Warren) in the 1950s and 1960s.

Separation of Powers We have noted that the writers of the Constitution feared a government in which all powers were centered in only one institution, and that they therefore devised one in which each branch would have the means and the incentive to keep the others in their proper place. The constitutional situation has led to many disputes and conflicts between the Presidency and Congress, between Congress and the courts, or between the courts and the Presidency. Most of these disputes have been settled without major constitutional revision, but at present we are in the midst of a separation-of-powers conflict that has broad constitutional implications.

It remains uncertain even today how important Watergate will prove in bringing about any constitutional change in the relationship between the branches of government. As will be discussed in Chapter 14, there are some signs that one effect of Watergate may be to spur Congress in particular to become more vigorous both in its own right and as a more active check on the executive branch. If we can take some comfort and even pride in the resiliency of the Constitution as shown in the Watergate crisis, we must at the same time take heed that—as Watergate makes clear for better and for worse—the integrity of the Constitution is inseparable from that of those who govern by its authority.

The Meaning of Citizenship American political history has given many severe tests to the Constitution, but perhaps none as severe as the problem of defining the goals of equal citizenship. This issue is the topic of the next chapter.

How Institutions Work: I
The Structure of the
U. S. Government

On what basis is the U.S. government structured?

The general structure of American government is based on the Constitution and on two principles in particular: federalism and separation of powers. Organized as a federal system, the powers and functions of government are divided between the national government and the states. Then, in accordance with the separation-of-powers principle, the authority given the national government is divided among three separate branches: the legislative, the executive, and the judicial.

What are the institutions and agencies of government that make up each of the three branches?

Legislative

All power to make laws lies in a Congress composed of two houses, the Senate and the House of Representatives. Their authority and limitations are set forth in the Constitution. The Senate consists of 100 members (2 from each state) and the House of 435 members (the number from each state determined by population). The Constitu-

Figure 2.4   The Government of the United States

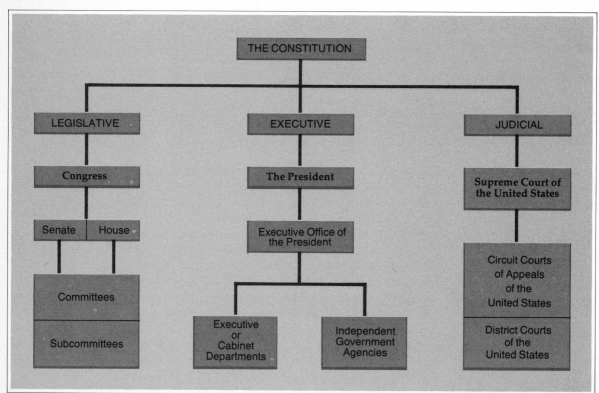

tion does not say how Congress is to be organized internally, but both bodies have chosen a committee structure.

Executive

The executive power is in the President alone; no other executive body is called for in the Constitution. However, an enormous establishment has grown up around the President. Directly serving the President is the Executive Office, which consists of several operating units established either by the President or by law. The executive Office serves the President's managerial needs and includes the White House Office, the Office of Management and Budget, and the National Security Council.

The executive branch also includes the eleven Executive Departments that together make up the Cabinet. As with the Executive Office, the Constitution makes no provision for a Cabinet. All of the Executive Departments have been created by acts of Congress, the most recent addition being the Department of Transportation in 1966.

In addition to the major departments, there is a group of independent government agencies of two general types: independent executive agencies and independent regulatory commissions. The former perform specialized tasks; the CIA, NASA, and the Veterans Administration are in this category. Also grouped with the executive agencies are the government corporations such as the U.S. Postal Service and the Tennessee Valley Authority. The independent regulatory commissions include such bodies as the Interstate Commerce Commission and the Federal Power Commission. Although formally part of the executive branch, they have been designed to be independent of the President.

Judicial

The Constitution locates the judicial power in one Supreme Court and in lower courts established by Congress. Even the size of the Supreme Court is a matter left open to congressional decision. Over the years Congress has created a structure of lower federal courts made up of the U.S. circuit courts of appeals and the U.S. district courts.

3 Political Equality, Social Inequality

As a result of a new federal law passed in 1974, Little League baseball teams are made up of "young people" rather than "boys." Karen no longer cheers for the Redbirds; she now pitches for them. For the first time women in the executive branch of government can use the White House gym. Equal rights for women, equal rights for blacks, equal rights for Indians, equal rights for Chicanos, equal rights for the poor—these demands go back to promises in the Declaration of Independence.

Democracy and Equality

"We hold these truths to be self-evident," says the Declaration of Independence, "that all men are created equal." The men who signed this document knew, of course, that all men were not created equal; differences in ability, intelligence, ambition, and talent could hardly be denied. Yet they were not just spouting empty political slogans. The signers wanted to go on record against a political order in which members of society were *legally* unequal.

In medieval times citizenship was classified, and privileges and rights were allowed to one class of citizens but denied to others. The nobility, for instance, was given public authority, but commoners or serfs were subordinate by law. The aristocratic justification of first- and second-class citizenship is well summarized in the following passage:

> The lot of the poor, in all things which affect them collectively, should be regulated for them, not by them. They should not be required or encouraged to think for themselves, or give to their own reflection or forecast an influential voice in the determination of the destiny. It is the duty of the higher classes to think for them, and to take responsibility for their lot. . . . The rich should be [like parents] to the poor, guiding and restraining them like children.[1]

Democratic thought contrasts sharply with this aristocratic point of view. It rejects the idea that people who are richer, more accomplished, more intelligent, or of nobler birth than others are somehow "better." The principle of citizenship elbows aside those ancient beliefs that formed the basis of monarchies, aristocracies, hereditary privileges, a class system, and racial prejudice. It is no accident that the principle of equal worth developed at the same time as radical religious movements. The idea that all men are equal in the eyes of God gave rise to the idea that all men are equal in the eyes of the state.

It is of course true that the principle of equal worth is not completely accepted, and probably never will be. Nevertheless it is

POLITICAL EQUALITY,
SOCIAL INEQUALITY

[1] John Stuart Mill, *Principles of Political Economy*, II (Boston: Little, Brown, 1848), pp. 319–320. Here Mill is summarizing the aristocratic viewpoint, not endorsing it.

deeply rooted in Western political systems. Justifications for special status or hereditary rights have been undermined, and this in itself is a major achievement. This does not mean privileges and special rights no longer exist, but it does mean that they no longer have the open protection of the state.

The constitutional guarantees of citizenship are supposed to bring about the equality promised by the Declaration of Independence. The two major forms of citizenship protected by the Constitution are *legal citizenship* and *political citizenship*.

Legal Citizenship

Early American political history was dominated by legal-constitutional issues. The problems to be solved included the definition of citizenship rights and the extension of these rights to the entire population. Legal citizenship, or what we today call civil rights, includes the basic freedoms of speech, worship, and assembly. It also includes economic rights, especially the right to acquire and dispose of property, the right to choose one's place and type of work, and the right to enter into valid contracts knowing they will be upheld in courts of law.

The institutions central to legal citizenship are the courts. And here the basic citizenship principle is called *due process of law*. This refers to many things: A citizen is presumed innocent until proved guilty. A citizen has the right to be tried by a jury of fellow citizens. No one can be kept in jail unless there is reasonable evidence that he or she is guilty of a crime. Due process of law also includes the right to legal counsel, the protection against self-incrimination (no one can be forced to testify against himself), the right to face and to question witnesses, and protection from unreasonable searches such as telephone taps.

In later chapters, where we review the role of the courts and discuss basic freedoms in detail, we will see that the translation of citizenship principles into specific laws is an ongoing process.

Political Citizenship

The second major form of citizenship is political participation. Democratic theory states that government should be based on the consent of the people. Because all members of society are governed, they should all have equal right to choose the governors. The principle of equal political citizenship is clearly stated in *The Federalist* (No. 57):

> *Who are to be the electors of the federal representatives?*
> Not the rich, more than the poor; not the learned, more than the ignorant; not the haughty heirs of distinguished names, more than the humble sons of obscurity and unpropitious fortune. The electors are to be the great body of the people of the United States.

Perhaps the authors of *The Federalist Papers* believed the Constitution they had helped write guaranteed these equalities. However, they forgot two things: Many barriers were placed between the voter and the government, and the Constitution did not actually guarantee universal suffrage. Until the Seventeenth Amendment was passed in 1913, senators were chosen by state legislatures rather than by the voters. Of course, as prescribed by the Constitution, the President is not directly elected but is chosen by the electoral college. Furthermore, Supreme Court justices are appointed rather than elected.

The Growth of Voting Rights

The Constitution did not really answer the question of who may vote and under what conditions. This has required no fewer than four amendments.

Initially the Constitution left voting laws to the states; if a person could not vote in a state election, he could not vote in a federal election. Generally states restricted the vote to white male property owners. And in some states as few as 10 percent of the white males could vote. During the Presidency of Andrew Jackson (1829–1837), most property standards were dropped, and universal (white) manhood suffrage became the rule. America was hailed as a model for the democratic world. It was fifty years before Britain reached the same level of voting rights.

Still, as Figure 3.1 shows, fewer than 40 percent of the adult population could vote at the time of the Civil War. Blacks of course were forbidden to vote in the South, and with few exceptions they were also unable to vote in the North. After the Civil War the Fifteenth Amendment established that "the right of citizens of the United States to vote shall not be denied or abridged by the United States

Figure 3.1
Proportion of the Adult Population Eligible to Register to Vote, 1860–1970

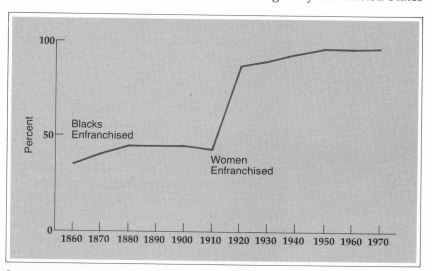

Source: Robert Lane, *Political Life* (New York: Free Press, 1959), p. 21; U.S. Department of Commerce, Bureau of the Census, *Statistical Abstract of the United States: 1969* (Washington, D.C., 1969), p. 369.

POLITICAL EQUALITY,
SOCIAL INEQUALITY

or by any State on account of race, color, or previous condition of servitude." But in the South the reality of blacks' voting faded with the end of Reconstruction. When white southerners got back in control of their state governments, they moved quickly to undermine the Fifteenth Amendment through such means as the poll tax (one had to pay to vote), phony literacy tests, and the all-white primary, as well as intimidation and violence.

Throughout the late 1800s the electorate continued to grow as new states were added and large numbers of immigrants arrived. However, although some blacks could vote in some areas, and although women were gaining the right to vote a little at a time, most of the electorate in the early twentieth century was white and male.

The next major expansion of the electorate was the addition of women. In 1869 Wyoming became the first state to grant voting rights to women; it was followed by several other states, chiefly in the West. The drive for women's rights — the Suffragette Movement — was led by, among others, Susan B. Anthony and Elizabeth Cady Stanton. Beginning in 1917 the suffragettes began marching in front of the White House only to be arrested and jailed. Their cause triumphed in 1920 with adoption of the Nineteenth Amendment, which states that the right to vote cannot be denied on account of sex.

Over the past decade federal action has been taken to remove barriers set up by certain states and localities. In 1964 the Twenty-Fourth Amendment banned the use of the poll tax in federal elections, and the Voting Rights Act of 1965 extended the ban to cover state elections. But the real significance of the Voting Act was to put federal authority behind the drive to enable southern blacks to vote; federal examiners were given the power to register voters. The effect of this legislation was dramatic: Between 1964 and 1968 black registration in the 11 southern states increased by over 50 percent. (See Table 3.1.) In 1970 Congress extended and broadened the Voting Rights Act to suspend the use of literacy and character tests in all states and to establish uniform residency requirements (30 days) for voting in federal elections.

Table 3.1
Estimated Percent of
Blacks Registered to Vote in
Southern States, 1940–1970

Year	Percent Registered
1940	5%
1952	21
1960	28
1964	45
1968	62
1970	66

Source: Based on data reported in *The American Negro Reference Book* (Englewood Cliffs, N. J.: Prentice Hall, 1966); Harry A. Polshi and Ernest Kaiser, eds., *The Negro Almanac* (New York: Bellweather, 1971).

POLITICAL CITIZENSHIP

The suffrage was extended again in 1971 with the Twenty-Sixth Amendment, which lowered the voting age to 18. About 10.5 million people were thus added to the electorate.

The history of citizenship rights starts with the principle that all citizens are to be treated equally. There is to be no such thing as first- and second-class citizens, with one group having rights and privileges denied to the other. We have already begun to see that actual practice has often failed to live up to this principle. In particular, black Americans and other minorities as well as women of all races have found their legal and political rights to be less than those of white males.

Second-Class Citizenship: Slavery

The essence of slavery is the denial of citizenship. Slavery was protected by law in the United States until after the Civil War, and of course in the eighteenth century most American blacks were slaves. Slaves could not say what they wanted to, be with people they wanted to be with, do with their labor as they pleased, or enter into binding contracts. American citizenship gave a man the right to the product of his labor; slavery forbade this right. Despite the promises of the Declaration of Independence, the Constitution allowed a double standard. One class of people had rights and privileges denied to another class.

At first this double standard was not a racist doctrine. It separated free men and slaves, but it did not separate whites and blacks. And there were free blacks. Nearly 100,000 had escaped slavery; they had bought their freedom or been given it by their owners and lived in the North and West much as other citizens. They paid taxes, voted, and in a few cases held political office. But in 1857 this was changed by the infamous Dred Scott case, which held that blacks, free or slave, "had no rights which the white man was bound to respect."

Dual citizenship based on race continued long after the Civil War had officially ended slavery. The clear language of the Fourteenth Amendment, "all persons born or naturalized in the United States, and subject to the jurisdiction thereof, are citizens of the United States. . . . No state shall make or enforce any law which shall abridge the privileges or immunities of citizens," was modified by later court decisions and blocked by the "Jim Crow" society.

Jim Crow laws allowed nearly total segregation of the blacks into separate and inferior institutions. As described by the Commission on Civil Rights (1963), Jim Crow was applied to "waiting rooms, theaters, boardinghouses, water fountains, ticket windows, streetcars, penitentiaries, county jails, convict camps, institutions for the blind and deaf, and hospitals for the insane." This is just a partial list. Jim Crow laws affected schools, businesses, clubs, churches, and the U.S. Armed Services. Facilities reserved for blacks were always inferior, though equal prices had to be paid for the unequal services.

Negroes for Sale.

A Cargo of very fine stout Men and Women, in good order and fit for immediate service, just imported from the Windward Coast of Africa, in the Ship Two Brothers.—
Conditions are one half Cash or Produce, the other half payable the first of January next, giving Bond and Security if required.
The Sale to be opened at 10 o'Clock each Day, in Mr. Bourdeaux's Yard, at No, 48, on the Bay.
May 19, 1784.   JOHN MITCHELL.

Thirty Seasoned Negroes

To be Sold for Credit, at Private Sale.

AMONGST which is a Carpenter, none of whom are known to be dishonest.

Also, to be sold for Cash, a regular bred young Negroe Man-Cook, born in this Country, who served several Years under an exceeding good French Cook abroad, and his Wife a middle aged Washer-Woman, (both very honest) and their two Children. Likewise, a young Man a Carpenter.
For Terms apply to the Printer.

POLITICAL EQUALITY,
SOCIAL INEQUALITY

66

Racist ideologies received the backing of the Supreme Court. As Justice Brown remarked in *Plessy* v. *Ferguson* (1896), the case that established the "separate but equal doctrine," remaining in force until 1954: "If one race be inferior to another socially, the Constitution of the United States cannot put them upon the same plane. . . ." So much for the Fourteenth Amendment, and so much for the idea that citizenship placed everyone on an equal footing before the law.

In Chapter 12 and elsewhere we will review the court cases and political programs that have slowly been reversing the racist doctrines that established slavery in the first place and led to the Jim Crow society after the Civil War. Here it is important to understand that the principle of equal citizenship has been the chief weapon in the struggle against second-class citizenship for black Americans.

Second-Class Citizenship: Women

"Equality of rights under the law shall not be denied or abridged by the United States or by any state on account of sex." These are the terms of the Equal Rights Amendment, which has been passed by Congress and by 34 of the 38 states that must ratify it before it becomes the Twenty-Seventh Amendment to the Constitution. Women, 200 years after the Declaration of Independence, are trying to gain the same rights in society as men.

Women have long been second-class citizens. Except in some state and local elections, women were not allowed to vote until 1920. Certain government jobs, especially in the military, have until recently been reserved for males. Many states have laws that discriminate against women in property ownership, in employment and salaries, and in the terms of marriage and divorce. Women find it hard to get loans because credit agencies see them as "bad risks."

In addition to legal and political discrimination, there are many informal barriers to full women's rights. Women are paid less than men, even for doing the same work. (See Figure 3.2.) And women have had a difficult time reaching high positions. A survey by *Fortune* magazine found only 11 women among the directors and officers of the 1300 largest corporations in America. There are 300,000 doctors in the United States; fewer than 8 percent are women. The number of women in political office is small: There are at present no women in the Senate, only 18 (out of 435) women in the House of Representatives, and one woman governor.

The Equal Rights Amendment attempts to eliminate the legal barriers that have prevented women from enjoying equal rights with men. It states that women are to be absolutely equal to men. For this reason some women's groups have opposed it on the ground that it provides "too much" equality. For instance, it makes women equally liable for child support when a couple gets a divorce, equally subject to the military draft (should it ever be reinstated), and no longer exempt from dangerous jobs such as mining.

POLITICAL CITIZENSHIP

Figure 3.2
Women Doing the Same Work
as Men Receive Less Pay

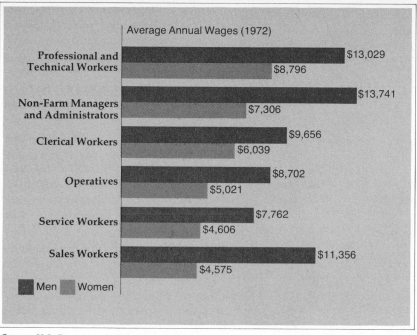

Average Annual Wages (1972)

	Men	Women
Professional and Technical Workers	$13,029	$8,796
Non-Farm Managers and Administrators	$13,741	$7,306
Clerical Workers	$9,656	$6,039
Operatives	$8,702	$5,021
Service Workers	$7,762	$4,606
Sales Workers	$11,356	$4,575

Source: U.S. Department of Commerce, Bureau of the Census, *Current Population Reports,* Series P-60, no. 90 (Washington, D.C., December 1973).

Second-Class Citizenship: Minors

In 1971 nine students were suspended from Columbus, Ohio, high schools after a period of student unrest and racial demonstrations. The suspensions were for less than 10 days, but they went onto the students' records. The action took place without any formal hearings. The suspended students challenged the procedures, claiming that they were deprived of liberty (though no proof of involvement in the demonstrations was provided) and of property (their legal right to an education) without due process of law. Thus, the students argued, the action by the school authorities violated the Fourteenth Amendment.

In 1975 the case of the students came before the Supreme Court. In a split decision (five to four) the Court ruled in favor of the students.[2] Public school authorities cannot suspend students without following certain basic procedures: giving formal notice of the charges, explaining the evidence against the student, and allowing students to present their side of the story.

In other words, students had rights. And these rights could be supported in federal courts. The case has important implications for school systems around the country. It is estimated that as many as 10 percent of all students in urban schools are suspended at least once a year; in New York City alone there are 20,000 suspensions a year. Because these suspensions become part of a student's record,

[2] *Goss* v. *Lopez* 73–898 U.S. (1975).

no doubt having a negative effect on job and college applications, the majority of the Supreme Court felt that students should be allowed at least to present their case.

Note, however, that the Court did not grant full rights of due process. A suspended student cannot hire a lawyer, cross-examine witnesses, call his own witnesses, or have a jury trial. A suspension is not the same as a crime, and it is understandable that the full range of rights given an accused criminal are not given a suspended student. The Court did leave open the possibility that more formal proceedings would be required when students were suspended for a long time or were expelled from school.

The Supreme Court ruling has opened wider than ever the complex issue of rights of minors. It is true that minors have always been "second-class" citizens in the sense that they do not vote, cannot run for office, cannot enter binding contracts without parental permission, and are politically and legally limited in lots of other ways. It is also true that minors receive special protection from the state. A minor convicted of a crime, even murder, is treated much less harshly than an adult convicted of the same crime.

Citizenship rights for minors is a new area into which constitutional lawyers and judges are moving. It is too early to know the end result of what is sure to be a long and sometimes painful process. But it is clear that the momentum that has forced major changes in the citizenship rights of minority groups and women will change the way minors are treated in the legal and political processes of the nation.

Affirmative Action

The early 1970s saw a new aspect of the definition of citizenship rights. American society is being asked whether it will tolerate discrimination to compensate for past acts of discrimination. In 1971 Marco DeFunis, a white male college graduate, was denied admission to the University of Washington Law School. His college grades and his application test scores were higher than those of some of the 36 blacks, Chicanos, and Indians who were admitted to the law school. DeFunis claims he was the victim of reverse discrimination — that he was denied equal protection of the law just because he is white. The University of Washington responded that discrimination to aid minorities that have long been held back by racial barriers is within the law. DeFunis took his case to court, and a local judge ruled that he should be admitted. The University admitted DeFunis, but it appealed the decision. The case was argued before the United States Supreme Court in the spring of 1974.[3] Because by that time DeFunis was about to graduate, the Court let the earlier ruling stand and did not decide on the merits of the case.

[3] *DeFunis* v. *Odegaard* 416 U.S. 312 (1974).

Nevertheless the DeFunis case raised one of the most complicated questions in the history of citizenship rights: Is affirmative action that benefits one group over another constitutional? Should law schools or medical schools reserve places for blacks, Chicanos, or women so that eventually the society will have lawyers and doctors from all social groups other than white males? Should the government award building contracts only to construction firms that hire workers from all racial and ethnic groups?

Affirmative action programs apply racial or sex standards in the short run to cut down on discrimination in the long run. But of course if university admissions or government contracts or hiring practices deliberately favor minorities and women, then whites and males are being discriminated against. And where does this leave the principle of equal citizenship rights?

Arguments Against Affirmative Action

Those who oppose affirmative action point out that the Constitution does not allow for "special treatment" based on race or sex. A brief written for DeFunis by two well-known professors of constitutional law makes a strong argument:

> If the Constitution prohibits exclusion of blacks and other minorities on racial grounds, it cannot permit exclusion of whites on racial grounds. For it must be the exclusion on racial grounds which offends the Constitution, and not the particular skin color of the person excluded.[4]

These professors argue that DeFunis was denied admission to law school *because* he was white. This was racial discrimination; it was therefore unconstitutional. "Discrimination on the basis of race is illegal, immoral, unconstitutional, inherently wrong and destructive of democratic society."

Arguments for Affirmative Action

Those who support affirmative action take seriously the idea of equal protection of the law. But they argue that equal protection is not enough to overcome years and years of unequal treatment. It is as if there were a race between two people, one of whom had been in training for ten years while the other had been in chains for ten years. If the chains were removed, both runners started at the same point on the track, and the rules of the race were applied to the runners equally, would we say each runner had an equal chance to win? Affirmative action, supporters argue, is to help the chained runner get in condition so the race will be fair.

Affirmative Action and Citizenship

The questions raised by the DeFunis case will be with us for a long time. Affirmative action is a new and troublesome chapter in

[4] Philip Kurland and Alexander M. Bickel, quoted in Nina Totenberg, "Discrimination to End Discrimination," *The New York Times Magazine,* April 14, 1974.

the history of citizenship. It moves beyond equal protection of the law and even beyond equal opportunity to a new concept of citizen rights: the right to be treated unequally, though favorably, in order to undo previous unequal and unfavorable treatment.

Such treatment cannot avoid being called reverse discrimination. Groups that have struggled to succeed under the old rules—white union leaders, for example—will resent the change in the rules that would seem to penalize them just because they are white and male. (The controversy at the end of this chapter provides an opportunity to discuss the complexities of affirmative action.)

We have reviewed two general themes in citizenship—equal legal rights and equal political rights. These were the rights the Constitution was primarily concerned with. And normally it is thought that if these rights can truly be equally available to all members of society, then the promise of democracy will have been kept. But there is a third form of citizenship that occupies more political attention today than either of the others.

Social-Rights Citizenship: A New View of Equality

President Roosevelt's twelfth State of the Union Address, delivered in 1944, contained a surprising departure from earlier definitions of citizenship. His speech began on a familiar note: "The Republic," he said, "had its beginning and grew to its present strength, under the protection of certain unalienable political rights—among them the right of free speech, free press, free worship, trial by jury, freedom from unreasonable searches and seizures. They were our rights of life and liberty." As he continued, however, he spoke of America's failure to provide for its citizens and stated the principle behind a whole new area of citizens' rights:

> As our Nation has grown strong in size and stature, however—as our industrial economy has expanded—these political rights proved inadequate to assure us equality in the pursuit of happiness. . . . We have come to a clear realization of the fact that true individual freedom cannot exist without economic security and independence.

He was saying that the legal and political rights set forth in the Constitution were not enough and that citizenship must include social well-being and security against economic injustices. Roosevelt also mentioned areas in which the rights of social citizenship should apply:

> We have accepted, so to speak, a second Bill of Rights under which a new basis of security and prosperity can be established for all—regardless of station, race, or creed.

Among these rights are:

- The right to a useful and remunerative job in the industries or shops or farms or mines of the Nation.

- The right of every farmer to raise and sell his products at a return which will give him and his family a decent living.
- The right to earn enough to provide adequate food and clothing and recreation.
- The right of every businessman, large and small, to trade in an atmosphere of freedom from unfair competition and domination by monopolies at home or abroad.
- The right of every family to a decent home.
- The right to adequate medical care and the opportunity to achieve and enjoy good health.
- The right to adequate protection from the economic fears of old age, sickness, accident, and unemployment.
- The right to a good education.

When Roosevelt used the word *right,* he was describing a new concept of citizenship, a citizenship enlarged far beyond what was included under the original concept of due process of law.

This concept has produced much social legislation by both Republican and Democratic administrations over the past three decades. A large number of programs—social security, urban renewal and housing, job training and manpower development, medicare—have been undertaken. During this period, in addition, the earliest "welfare program," public education, has grown. These programs have given rise to great controversy, and even today many of the most hotly debated issues are in the area of social-rights citizenship: federal support for education, the negative income tax, the minimum wage, a national health-insurance program, public housing, and increasingly, consumer protection. What is interesting about these debates, however, is that even conservatives accept some form of welfare state. This is a major change from earlier conservative thought.

Social-rights citizenship breaks with tradition in two important ways. First, it changes what used to be done by private charity into a duty of the state. To say a decent standard of living is a citizenship right is to deny that it depends on the charity of the wealthier classes. Critics claim that replacing the Christmas basket from the local church with a welfare check destroys one of the most important traditions in American society. But they overlook the implicit snobbishness in giving charity and the explicit self-abasement in receiving it. They may also forget that hunger does not come only when the wealthy feel charitable; social welfare is regular and consistent.

The second break with tradition is even greater. Social-rights citizenship separates social services from the price system. People who are strongly committed to the free-enterprise system don't like this. Medical care, housing, food, insurance, and even education have traditionally been priced in terms of what the market will bear. Who gets what quantity of these various social benefits depends on purchasing power. Those who can pay get better medical treatment, better housing, more nourishing food, more security against illness

POLITICAL EQUALITY,
SOCIAL INEQUALITY

and old age, and better education. Those who are "worth less" get fewer of these benefits of society, or the quality of the benefits they receive is lower.

Social-rights citizenship separates social services from the price system by shifting them from the private to the public domain in the name of citizenship. A decent standard of living is said to be a right rather than a privilege to be paid for or a gift.

Citizenship Equality vs. Economic Inequality

We have reviewed three forms of citizenship equality: (1) Legal citizenship promises equal application of the law and equal access to the courts; (2) political citizenship promises the vote and other political rights, including the right to campaign and run for public office, equally to all citizens; (3) social citizenship promises equal protection from economic disasters beyond individual control, including protection for the old against major health problems.

The equality promised by citizenship has definite limits. There is no promise of equal condition, especially economic condition. For example, the catch phrase "one man, one vote," which describes an important part of political equality, is not matched with the phrase "one man, one dollar," which would suggest equal distribution of the wealth in society.

We have already noted (Chapter 1) that society is based on economic inequality, accepting as both a principle of fairness and a practical arrangement the idea of differential material rewards. People who work harder or are more talented or do important jobs should be rewarded more than the lazy, the untalented, and those who do less important jobs. Anything else would be unfair to the hard workers and the achievers. It would also be socially harmful, for the growth of the economy is said to depend on such talent and ambition.

Citizenship and Equal Opportunity

Citizenship is, however, related to economic inequality in a way that cuts down on some of the inequalities in society. For citizenship has been used to increase the opportunities to compete for the unequal rewards. Economic inequality means people have different standards of living: Some have big, comfortable houses, have jobs they enjoy doing, can take vacations, can send their children to college, and can save enough to protect them against illness or unemployment. At the other end of the economic scale are people who live in crowded and poor-quality housing, do the dirty, dull jobs, worry more about feeding their children than what college to send them to, are usually in debt and always worry about sickness or unemployment.

Citizenship equalities have not caused a major redistribution of wealth. Legal, political, and even social citizenship exist along with

great inequalities in standard of living. What citizenship amounts to is equal opportunity to compete for the unequal rewards of society. Americans are much less likely to call unequal rewards unfair than to complain of blocked opportunities. What they think is appropriate is to give everyone a chance to go after the best jobs and the highest incomes. This was made explicit in the War on Poverty.

The War on Poverty The usual approaches to social services and public welfare were greatly extended in the mid-1960s. The antipoverty programs, with an annual budget of around $2 billion, introduced Head Start, Job Corps, VISTA, and various other such programs. We will not review the failures and successes of President Johnson's War on Poverty (greatly modified by President Nixon), but will simply ask how antipoverty programs affect inequality.

The purpose of antipoverty policy is to raise the floor level of society. The poor are those living below some socially acceptable standard. An affluent society should not have poor people in its midst. No one should be so poor that he cannot enjoy his political and economic rights. A successful antipoverty program moves every citizen above the tolerable level, which, in the words of the War on Poverty, eliminates poverty "by opening to everyone the opportunity for education and training, the opportunity to work, and the opportunity to live in decency and dignity."

The goal is to increase the portion of the population who compete in an economic system based on wage differentials and wealth earned from private property. This is no small accomplishment, but it should not be confused with egalitarianism. The only way the elimination of poverty can affect inequality is by reducing slightly the distance between the rich and the poor, not by making the rich less wealthy but by making the poor better off. The War on Poverty did not close the gap between rich and poor by very much.

The War on Poverty is only one of the federal programs lumped under the heading of welfare policies. The relationship of other welfare policies—what we call social-service programs—to economic inequality is complex and deserves our attention.

Social-Service Programs Social security, unemployment compensation, public education, and medicare are the major social-service programs in America. A strong case can be made that these programs have made citizens more equal. But the relationship is a complicated one. First we must describe two different types of inequality: inequality of distance and inequality of scope.

Inequality of distance refers to the size of the gap between the richest and poorest, or between any two points along the income distribution. In a society where the richest group earns 20 times as much as the poorest group, the inequality of distance is great. In a society where the richest group earns only 5 times as much as the poorest group, inequality of distance has been reduced. The kinds of social-

The purpose of the antipoverty program is to help all citizens lead a tolerable life: This American family lives in a tent and cooks meals on an open wood fire.

74

service programs that provide a cushion for the sick, the old, and the unemployed do not greatly reduce the distance between rich and poor. The major social-service programs are simply government-managed insurance plans to which the worker contributes during his working years. For instance, nine out of ten working people in America are now contributing to social security. Other social-service programs, such as medicare, help out a citizen in time of financial need, in this case older citizens who cannot afford high medical costs. But these programs do not "level" society in the sense of cutting heavily into the wealth of the rich and increasing that of the poor.

Does this mean social-service programs are unrelated to equality in America? Not at all. But now we must speak of *inequality of scope.* This term refers to the number of ways the rich are better off than the poor.

Assume the following extreme case: *Every* social benefit is available only through the private sector and is priced so that its owners make the highest profit possible. Education, medical care, insurance, recreation, transportation, communication services, and even security against personal attack are available in unequal amounts and unequal quality. The wealthy person, therefore, has greater access to these services than the poor. He even hires his own security force to protect his possessions. The less wealth you have, the less of any of these services you can get, until we get to the bottom of the scale, where none are available—there is no public education, no free medical care, no public parks, no social security, no transportation or communication systems except those used by the wealthy, not even a police force. Under such conditions inequalities of scope would be enormous. Every social value would be more available, and in a better form, to the wealthy than to the poor.

Now assume the opposite case: *No* social benefit is priced; all are equally available to every citizen. Public schools are excellent, and educational attainment is based on intelligence; health and insurance programs protect all citizens equally against illness, accident, and disability; there are many public parks and entertainment is widely available; transportation is efficient, as are telephone and mail services; and the standing army and police force protect everyone's possessions. Under such conditions inequalities of scope are greatly narrowed. There are still rich and poor, and the rich can afford luxuries denied the poor. But the rich cannot buy superior social services. The advantage of wealth is limited to certain areas of consumption.

Inequalities of distance refer to *how much* better off the rich are; inequalities of scope refer to *how many ways* they are better off. *Welfare policies are egalitarian in the sense that they increase the number of services for which wealth is unnecessary.* The point is well made by Julius Nyerere, President of socialist Tanzania, when he urges that inequalities be reduced through "the provision of social services which are available to all, regardless of income; for a man who suddenly has new medical services available to him and his family, or a new house, or a new school or community center, has had an improvement in his standard of living, just as much as if he had more money in his pocket."

If citizenship reduces inequalities of scope, it has made a major contribution to equality. This has happened, though less than either supporters or critics of the service state admit. For one thing, the benefits of social programs are not always directed toward the poorer groups in society. Free higher education, for instance, has serviced the middle class and to a lesser extent the working class, and has not done much for really poor families. Even the benefits of programs directed specifically to the poor end up only partially in their pocketbooks or bank accounts. A large portion of the antipoverty money goes to the middle-class professionals who administer the programs and provide the services. Research grants to university professors to evaluate antipoverty programs are subtracted from the money used to reduce poverty. The impact of welfare programs has also been lessened by the method of paying for them. For the most part the relevant taxes are spread across the population, meaning that the poorer groups pay for services designed to equalize their income in exact proportion to what they pay in taxes anyway. Their payments would have to be subtracted from any exact calculation of benefits.

The results of social citizenship have been less egalitarian than some hoped and others feared; nevertheless if decent social services are provided by the government, either free or at minimal cost, then inequalities of scope are reduced. The rich can still support private universities and send their children to them, but excellent public universities reduce this advantage. Government programs therefore equalize somewhat the opportunities to compete for the benefits of quality education.

Citizenship and the Progressive Income Tax

When equal political rights were first proposed, many opposed the idea. They feared that those without money would use their voting power to tax away the profits and savings of the talented and hardworking citizens. More correctly, they feared that the rights of property would be threatened by, as they put it, "too much democracy." In 1821 political leaders in New York were debating the merits of extending the vote to all white males. An active opponent was Chancellor James Kent, the highest official in the state. He felt:

That extreme democratic principle, universal suffrage, has been productive of corruption, injustice, violence, and tyranny. . . . The apprehended danger from the experiment of universal suffrage applied to the whole legislative department, is no dream of the imagination. It is too mighty an excitement for the moral constitution of men to endure. The tendency of universal suffrage is to jeopardize the rights

The progressive income tax has not redistributed wealth to the extent that the middle class of America cannot continue to enjoy itself.

of property and the principles of liberty. There is a constant tendency in human society, and the history of every age proves it; there is a tendency in the poor to covet and to share the plunder of the rich—in the debtor to relax or avoid the obligation of contracts—in the indolent and the profligate to cast the whole burthens of society upon the industrious and the virtuous. . . .[5]

Echoes of this statement could be heard nearly 100 years later, when the progressive income tax became the federal government's chief method of raising revenue. The principle behind the progressive income tax is simple enough: The more money you earn, the higher the portion you pay in taxes. One might imagine that the progressive income tax would lead to redistribution of wealth. The poorer citizens would vote for sharply graduated taxes, taking a very low percent from people like themselves but a very high percent from the richer classes. This would be the method by which political equality ("one man, one vote") would lead to economic equality ("one man, one dollar").

In practice nothing like this has happened. Table 3.2 presents relevant figures. The first column gives different income levels; the next shows what portion of income should be paid. The poorest family, for instance, would pay only 1.9 percent of its income in taxes, while the richest families, those making $1 million or more, would pay 60 percent. The table shows the average amount actually paid by different income levels and the average amount saved because of tax loopholes. It is clear that the progressive income tax is not as progressive as it is supposed to be. Why is this so?

The Sixteenth Amendment, which authorized the progressive income tax, allows Congress to tax income "from whatever sources derived," but tax legislation has played havoc with this principle. Dollars earned from some sources, though they are worth just as much in consumer goods, leisure, or the like, are not taxed at the same rate as dollars earned from other sources. The dollars most

[5] Quoted in Alpheus T. Mason, ed., *Free Government in the Making,* 2d ed. (New York: Oxford University Press, 1956), p. 399.

Table 3.2
Portion of Family Income Paid in Income Taxes

Family Income	Payment Required by Tax Law	Average Paid After Deductions	Average Amount Saved via Loopholes
$ 2,500	1.9%	0.5%	$ 35
5,000	7.5	2.8	235
10,000	12.4	7.6	480
20,000	20.8	12.1	1,740
75,000	46.0	26.8	14,400
250,000	58.0	29.6	71,000
1,000,000	60.5	30.4	301,000

Source: Based on data from Philip M. Stern, *The Rape of the Taxpayer* (New York: Random House, 1974), p. 11.

CITIZENSHIP EQUALITY VS. ECONOMIC INEQUALITY

heavily taxed are earned in wages and salaries; those least heavily taxed are earned on various types of investments: long-term capital gains, real estate, stock options, oil, and state and local bonds. For example, a family of four earning an income of $10,000 would, under existing laws, pay the following federal income taxes:

- $905 if the income is all in the form of wages and salaries
- $98 if the income is all in the form of profits from selling stocks or land
- $0 if the income is all in the form of interest on state and local bonds

Thus the person who gains his income by working pays a greater share of it in taxes than the one who gains it without lifting a finger. Furthermore, since the income of the wealthy is derived primarily from nonwage sources, it is the wealthy, not the low- and middle-income wage earners, who benefit from these different rates of taxation.

Every year a lot of money is lost to the government through tax deductions and loopholes. Such uncollected taxes are a gift to those who are able to take advantage of such deductions, generally the wealthy. If this money could be collected, the official tax rates could be cut nearly in half, or perhaps needed social services such as mass transit or clean air and water could be provided. It is ironic that the annual budget of the antipoverty program is less than 3 percent of the loss from the "tax welfare" program, but what is even more ironic is the distribution of these tax handouts: The 6 million poorest families receive about $92 million; the wealthiest 3000 families receive $2.2 billion, or about 24 times as much.

The progressive income tax does flatten out the income distribution at the lower end of the scale. For example, the income tax brings the family with an income of $16,000 closer to the family with an income of $8,000. But its impact on the top of the income scale is much less. Before taxes the average income of the richest 20 percent in the country is about 10 times that of the poorest 20 percent; the effect of the income tax is to reduce this only to 9 times as much. In general, under present laws the progressive income tax is not nearly as progressive as is often thought; it does not greatly reduce the distance between the wealthy and the poor. Other types of taxes are even less progressive. The sales tax, for instance, takes a much larger share of the income of the poor than of the rich. Say, for example, a family earns $5,000 and pays a 5 percent sales tax on the

Table 3.3
Portion of Total Income in U. S. Received by Highest 20 Percent of Population, After Taxes

1929	1941	1950	1954	1956	1959	1962	1969
54%	47%	44%	43%	43%	43%	44%	41%

Source: "Inequality in Income and Taxes," by Edward C. Budd. Reprinted in Maurice Zeitlin, ed., *American Society, Inc.* (Chicago: Markham, 1970), p. 148. Originally published by W. W. Norton & Company, Inc., © 1967. Reprinted by permission. Figure for 1969 taken from a report of the Joint Economic Committee, March 1972.

$4,000 it spends on consumer goods and basic necessities. This family would pay $200, or 4 percent of its total income, in sales taxes. A family that earns $25,000 and spends $8,000 on items bearing the 5 percent sales tax would spend $400, or 1.6 percent of its total income, in sales taxes. Thus the poorer family is being taxed at a higher rate.

The Political Challenge to Economic Inequality: An Assessment

The War on Poverty, the growth of social-service programs, and the progressive income tax have helped equalize economic conditions. But they have not caused a major redistribution of wealth. Table 3.3 shows the percent of total income received by the wealthiest one-fifth of the population for the 40 years from 1929 to 1969. This period covers the decades in which various egalitarian programs have been introduced. There has been some reduction in the amount of income received by the wealthier groups, but most of this reduction took place more than 20 years ago.

Other evidence, reported by a congressional committee, shows that the income gap between America's poorest and richest families has nearly doubled in the past two decades. In 1949 the gap between the average income of the poorest one-fifth and that of the wealthiest one-fifth was about $10,000; by 1969 this gap had increased to nearly $20,000. Thus great inequalities remain after nearly a half-century of progressive income taxes and various social-welfare programs.

Figure 3.3 shows the basic income distribution in the United States as we approach the 200th anniversary of the Declaration of Independence. It is clear that equal legal and political rights have not led to a leveling of society. American society tolerates economic in-

Figure 3.3
Income Distribution, 1972

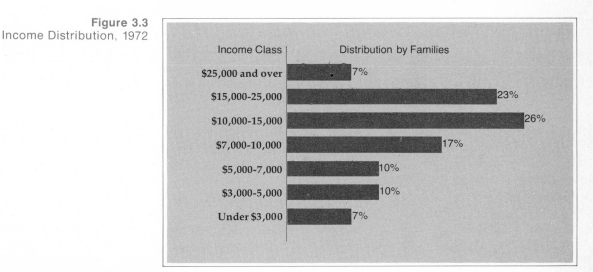

Source: U.S. Department of Commerce, Bureau of the Census, *Statistical Abstract of the United States: 1974* (Washington, D.C., 1974), p. 382.

equality while extending citizenship equalities. Charles A. Beard, in his famous book *The Economic Basis of Politics,* saw this as a major paradox:

> Modern equalitarian democracy, which reckons all heads as equal and alike, cuts sharply athwart the philosophy and practice of the past centuries. Nevertheless, the democratic device of universal suffrage does not destroy economic classes or economic inequalities. It ignores them. Herein lies the paradox, the most astounding political contradiction that the world has ever witnessed.[6]

This "astounding political contradiction" influences many aspects of American politics, as we will see in the next chapter, where we look more closely at the practice rather than the theory of equal political participation.

Controversy

Systematic discrimination over a long period leads to a social situation nearly impossible to reverse by ordinary means. If, for example, the black minority has been discriminated against by the white majority in schooling, housing, health care, and employment, then turning to "equal status before the law" will not greatly improve the status of blacks relative to that of whites. The 1970 census was taken at the end of a decade that gave a lot of attention to racial justice—more books were written, more meetings held, more marches organized, more legislation passed, more programs started, more commissions formed, more money spent on solving "the American dilemma" than in any other period of our history. At the end of that decade, the median income of white families was $9,961 whereas for black families it was $6,067. And this was not due simply to the fact that whites have better jobs. Blacks are paid less than whites for similar jobs. The median income of white male "professional, managerial and kindred workers" in 1970 was $11,108. The median for the *same category* of blacks was $7,659. The situation is similar in all job categories.

If these are the facts, what should be done?

One Side

It is the government's duty to put its enormous powers behind compensatory programs. An excellent place to begin would be educational and employment quotas. Universities and colleges

[6] Charles A. Beard, *The Economic Basis of Politics* (New York: Vintage, 1960), p. 69.

should be required to hold approximately 10 percent of their places for black applicants. Entering classes in medical schools should admit 10 percent blacks. If someday there is to be a fair share of black ownership of investment capital, all training programs and junior employees in banks, investment houses, insurance companies, and so forth, should include 10 percent blacks. Similar quotas should be applied to construction unions, army officers, college professors, publishing firms, and so on.

There is a moral case to be made for reverse discrimination. After more than 200 years of slavery and another 100 years of Jim Crow laws, white prejudice, and institutional racism, American society does after all owe something to its black citizens. But in addition to the moral case, and perhaps more important, is the very practical argument that equality will result only if we go through a period of reverse discrimination and affirmative action.

The Other Side

The government should treat men and women simply as citizens, "regardless of race, creed, color, or sex." If public and private life discriminates on the basis of race (or any other arbitrary standards), then government should banish the practice.

But to replace one form of discrimination with another is to violate the principle of neutrality. No matter what moral or practical case can be made, it goes too far to say that government should favor one group. This would be once again to make laws on the basis of race, which is what the principle of equality before the law forbids.

Quota programs, for instance, can be fair only if applied to every group equally. If there is a "black quota" there should be an "Irish quota" or a "southern quota" or a "woman quota." If there is a black studies program, there should be an Italian-American studies program and a Jewish studies program and a women's studies program. Violating the principles of equality does not rid society of discrimination. It only changes its form.

4

Political Participation in America

How does the American citizen participate in the political life of his country? How active is he? In what way does he participate? And which citizens participate?

How American democracy works depends largely on who participates and how. Through participation citizens tell the government what they want: what goals they want it to set up and how they want it to allocate resources. If citizens do not participate, government officials are not likely to be aware of their needs and desires. If some citizens participate while others are passive, government officials are much more likely to pay attention to the needs and desires of the active citizens and ignore the inactive ones. Thus to understand the role of participation in American politics we have to consider *which* citizens are active.

Participation is important for another reason. Not only does it tell the government what citizens want; it has more direct benefits. The ability to participate in decisions that affect one's life is an important source of human dignity. Participation is thus an end in itself. In a democracy it is probably the best evidence of full membership in the society.

How Do Citizens Participate?

Participation refers to the ways in which citizens influence what the government does, and this can be accomplished in many ways.

Voting

Through his vote the citizen helps choose his political leaders. The vote of any single individual is not a very powerful political tool. But elected officials are sensitive to the needs and desires of groups of voters.

Campaign Activity

Each citizen is limited to one vote in an election. That vote is only one of thousands or millions and can play only a small role in the results. But a citizen can increase his voting influence in one perfectly legal way—he can try to influence the vote of others. One of the most common forms of political activity takes place at the time of an election. Citizens ring doorbells, work at the polls, and talk to their friends and neighbors to try to affect their votes. Or they give money to a candidate or party. And if political leaders pay attention to voters, they may pay even more attention to those citizens who supply the work and money needed to conduct a campaign.

Communal Activity

Elections are an important way citizens influence government officials. But elections have a big drawback—they are very blunt instruments of citizen control. Elections take place only at fixed intervals: every two, or four, or six years, depending on the office. And the choice is between only two or maybe three or four candidates.

Citizens, on the other hand, have many and varied interests. In fact one can imagine each group as having a "list of priorities" it would like to see the government act on. Sometimes these interests have to do with broad national policies—American Jews are concerned with Middle East policy, conservationists with nuclear testing, blacks with federal laws on segregation. Sometimes these are local interests—a group of neighbors want to prevent the building of a road in their section of town, a group of parents want to improve school facilities, a group of high school students want the community to provide a recreation center.

These interests are indeed varied. An election could not possibly offer a choice in all of these areas. Citizens often find that the issues that concern them the most are not election issues, for both candidates take the same position or none. Furthermore, the problems and interests citizens want the government to deal with do not arise only at election time. Thus participation in election campaigns is not enough to tell government officials what citizens want.

Other means of participation are needed to fill in the gaps left by elections—some way specific sets of citizens can tell their more precise concerns to the government as they arise. We call this communal activity, meaning groups of citizens working together to try to influence the government. They may work through informal groups, as when neighbors join to protest to city hall about some issue. Or they may work through more formal organizations such as unions, PTAs, or civic associations. This kind of activity—which, as we will show, is very common in the United States—has two important features. First, citizens work together. This is important because the government is influenced more by a group than by a single individual. Second, the citizens are active on the problems that concern them most—parents will work in the PTA, welfare recipients in a welfare mothers' group, and so forth.

Citizen-Initiated Contacts

So far we have mentioned ways citizens participate along with others—as part of the voting population, in campaigns, or in cooperation with their fellow citizens. But some citizen activity is carried on alone, as when someone writes to his congressman or to a newspaper, or visits a government office to make a complaint. We do not often think of this as political participation, for citizens may be dealing with very narrow and specific problems that concern only them. They may ask their congressman to help a relative get a discharge from the army, or they may complain about the condition of the sidewalk in front of their house. But this is another way citizens influence what the government does—and often in areas important to them.

Direct political protest often replaces "politics as usual," especially when feelings are strong, as they are for this group of parents who resent the textbooks used in their West Virginia school district.

Protests, Marches, Demonstrations

Citizens sometimes use more dramatic and direct means of showing their points of view. They may march to protest American foreign policy, busing for integration, or the lack of school busing. Such protests, called by some "demonstration democracy," have become more common in recent years. Some of these activities are ways of showing political preferences in a more dramatic way. Some are ways of directly affecting the workings of the government—blocking the entrance to a military induction center, preventing school buses from running. Such means of participation are used by citizens who feel that the "ordinary" means won't work or who think the problem is so urgent that it cannot wait for the ordinary political processes.

How Active Are Americans?

One can hear quite contradictory things about political participation in America. Some say it is very active. Others say there is very little. This contraction may come in part from what people expect. If one expects all citizens to be fully active in politics, the finding that only 10–20 percent of the population is active will be disappointing. If one expects citizens to be private, home-centered individuals, he might be surprised to find that *as many as* two out of ten Americans bother to take part in election campaigns.

The reader will have to judge for himself whether participation in America is high or low. But we will give some standards for comparison. Table 4.1 reports the percentages of citizens who are active in various ways—voting, campaign activity, communal activity, and contacting the government.

A number of facts are shown by data on participation rates. Only in Presidential elections do we find a majority of the people active. The turnout in Presidential elections is usually 60–65 percent of the voting-age population, though it fell to a low of 55 percent in 1972. In local elections a little less than half vote regularly. Note that voting is the easiest political act. It takes little time and, more important, little initiative. Thus it is not surprising to find the highest activity rates in voting. (Another important question about voting, to be considered in Chapter 6, is: How rationally do citizens vote?)

Campaign activity takes more time, initiative, and commitment to a particular candidate or party. And it is clear that this is not an activity for everyone. Less than a third of all citizens say they try to persuade others how to vote; only about a quarter have done work for a political party, and other campaign activities are performed by even smaller portions of the population. Only 13 percent have given money to a campaign.

About a third of the citizens participate in communal activity— work with some local group on a community problem. And a similar number has worked through formal organizations.

Table 4.1
Activities Performed
by Citizens

Mode of Activity	Percent Active
A. Voting	
Voted in 1972 Presidential election	55%
Voted in 1968 Presidential election	62%
Votes regularly in local elections	47%
B. Taking Part in Campaign Activities	
Persuade others how to vote	28%
Ever worked for a party	26%
Attended political rallies	19%
Contributed money in a political campaign	13%
Member of a political club or organization	8%
C. Cooperative Activities	
Worked through local group	30%
Helped form local group	14%
Active member of organization engaged in community activities	32%
D. Contacting Officials	
Contacted local officials on some problem	20%
Contacted extralocal officials on some problem	18%
Wrote a letter to a public official	17%
Wrote a letter to an editor	3%

Source: All but the first two and last two items based on data from Sidney Verba and Norman H. Nie, *Participation in America: Political Democracy and Social Equality* (New York: Harper & Row, 1972); the last two items in D: based on data from 1964 Presidential election study, Survey Research Center of the Institute for Social Research, University of Michigan.

A Presidential campaign often generates political activity.

Finally, citizens often say "I'm going to write to my congressman!" about all sorts of problems. But only about one American in six has ever written to any public official. And only about one in five has ever contacted a local official or an official outside of the community on a problem.

What about more dramatic political activities—protest marches, demonstrations, and the like? It is hard to get accurate figures, but it is likely that few citizens have taken part in such activities. During the height of the Vietnam war protests in the late 1960s, one study found only eight citizens (out of 1500 interviewed) who had ever taken part in a demonstration about Vietnam—about 0.1 percent. Another study of a city in upstate New York found that only about 2–3 percent of the white citizens had ever been in a street demonstration, and only 4 percent said that they had gone to a protest meeting.

But one point should be made about such activity. Only a small percentage of all citizens may take part in demonstrations, but larger portions of particular groups may do so. Thus the same study that found that only 2–3 percent of whites had taken part in a street demonstration found that 11 percent of blacks had. And over half of the students in college during the Vietnam war reported taking part in anti-war demonstrations.

Is There Much or Little Participation?

The reader can look at the figures and judge. But we can give some guidelines for judgment. In the first place, we should be careful how we read the data. Remember that, aside from voting, no more than a third of the population is politically active—that's the portion that participates in local organizations—and the most usual campaign activity (convincing others how to vote) is reported by only 28 percent. But this does not mean that only a third of the American public is involved in any activity besides voting. The citizens involved in activity in their community are not always the same ones who work in campaigns. Thus the 28 percent who have tried to convince others how to vote and the 30 percent who have worked in an informal group on some community matter only partially overlap.

Types of Participants

We can divide the American public into six "types of participants" based on how active they are in politics and the kind of activity in which they participate.[1]

1. INACTIVES   These citizens, 22 percent of the population, never take part in campaigns, are involved in no communal activity, and never contact an official. They are not regular voters, though they may vote from time to time. In other words, about one-fourth of all Americans are not politically active.

2. VOTING SPECIALISTS   Some citizens are very regular about voting in elections; they almost always vote. But that is all they do. This group is similar in size to the inactives—about 21 percent.

3. PAROCHIAL PARTICIPANTS   These citizens contact government officials. In this sense they are active. But the reason they do this is some problem affecting them or their family. And that is all their political activity. They avoid all activity likely to affect more public issues. These "parochial" participants form 4 percent of the population.[2]

4. COMMUNAL ACTIVISTS   A fairly large part of the population is active in the life of its community, but only in nonpartisan activities—voluntary groups, school issues, and the like. These citizens join civic groups, work in charitable campaigns, and keep all kinds of community activities going. They form about 20 percent of the population.

5. CAMPAIGN ACTIVISTS   A group of similar size takes part fairly regularly in political campaigns but is not involved as much in the less partisan community activities. They form 15 percent of the population.

6. COMPLETE ACTIVISTS   This is a small but important part of the population—11 percent. They are active in every way. They rarely miss an election, are active in nonpartisan community affairs, and ring doorbells and participate in other partisan activities at election time.[3]

[1] Sidney Verba and Norman H. Nie, *Participation in America: Political Democracy and Social Equality* (New York: Harper & Row, 1972), chap. 4.

[2] Note that this figure is lower than the number who write to government officials, just as the figure for "voting specialists" is lower than the number of voters. We are talking about people who *only* vote or *only* write to their congressman.

[3] Seven percent of the sample studied was unclassifiable because of mixed patterns or missing information.

Participation in the United States and Other Nations

To see whether American participation is high or low it may be useful to compare it with participation in other nations. One point should be made first: Americans are more "participation oriented" than citizens elsewhere. They are more likely to believe they can influence the government if they want to than citizens in other countries, and this makes them more likely to act. And perhaps more important, they are more likely to feel that the citizen has a *responsibility* to be active in the life of his community. In a study conducted in five democratic nations, people were asked what responsibility a citizen had to his community. In the United States, as Table 4.2 indicates, over half of those who answered said a citizen should take an active part in the life of his community—many more than in any of the other countries. By an "active role" they meant participation in local government (willingness to run for office, to serve on boards, and to attend meetings) as well as activity of a nongovernmental nature (working for the local Red Cross or the PTA).

When it comes to actual participation, the pattern is mixed. Voting turnout is usually lower in the United States than in many of the European democracies. Turnout in U.S. Presidential elections tends to be between 60 and 65 percent. In many European countries turnout is 80 or 90 percent. This does not necessarily reflect a lower level of political interest and involvement in the United States than elsewhere. The best explanation of such low voting rates is that election laws sometimes make voting difficult. Many areas have residency rules that prevent new residents from voting until some time has passed.

Table 4.2
How Active Should the Ordinary Person Be in His Local Community?

Percent Who Say the Ordinary Man Should:	United States	Great Britain	Germany	Italy	Mexico
Be active in his community	51%	39%	22%	10%	26%
Only participate in more passive ways (be interested, etc.)	27	31	38	22	33
Only participate in church affairs	5	2	1	—	—
Total who mention some outgoing activity	83%	72%	61%	32%	59%
Only be upright in personal life	1%	1%	11%	15%	2%
Do nothing in local community	3	6	7	11	2
Don't know	11			35	30
Other	2	—	—	7	7
Total percent	100%	100%	100%	100%	100%
Total number of cases	970	963	955	995	1007

Source: Gabriel Almond and Sidney Verba, *The Civic Culture: Political Attitudes and Democracy in Five Nations*. Copyright © 1963 by Princeton University Press. Reprinted by permission of Princeton University Press.

IS THERE MUCH OR LITTLE PARTICIPATION?

	United States	Great Britain	Germany	Italy	Mexico
Attempted to influence a decision of the local government	28%	15%	14%	8%	6%
Attempted to influence a decision of the federal government	16%	6%	3%	2%	3%

Source: Based on data from Gabriel Almond and Sidney Verba, *The Civic Culture: Political Attitudes and Democracy in Five Nations* (Princeton, N. J.: Princeton University Press, 1963).

Participation in political activities that take more time and effort may be more important. Data on this subject are harder to find, since they are not recorded officially the way voting turnout is, but some are available. Only a small minority of Americans have ever tried to influence a decision of their local government (28 percent say they have) and an even smaller portion say they have tried to influence a decision of the national government (16 percent). But in both cases the portions are substantially larger than those found in other nations, as Table 4.3 shows: Political participation is more likely to be an important activity in the United States than in other democracies.

In one way participation in the United States seems particularly well developed compared with other nations. This is in communal activity, when citizens come together to work on some community problem or join in some group to pressure the government. Citizens in several countries were asked how they would go about influencing the government. In the United States, over half of those who thought they could have some influence felt that they could best do so by joining with others. In the other countries studied, citizens would more likely work alone or through some more formal organization like a political party. And the willingness to work with others— friends, neighbors, and others at work—is found in all social groups in the United States.

Data on the actual behavior of citizens show that in the United States there is much more community-oriented activity involving the cooperation of citizens: more groups of citizens formed to deal with some local problem and more active associations connected with the schools, recreational problems, and the like. In fact this type of behavior is not new in America. It was noted over 100 years ago by the Frenchman Alexis de Tocqueville, who commented on the zest for cooperative activity he found in America compared with Europe.

And, as noted, such activity is important because it can deal with the most immediate problems of citizens. In this way the individual citizen increases his own influence on the government—because many voices generally carry more weight with government officials than a few.

Equality of Political Access

Compared with other nations, citizens in the United States feel a fairly high level of responsibility to be active and are relatively active. But there is another standard by which we can measure political participation in the United States: How *equally* do citizens participate in America? Are all types of citizens equally active, or is participation mostly in the hands of a few? The answer is very important in understanding how participation works in America. Citizens *communicate* their needs and desires to government leaders through participation. They also use participation to pressure leaders to act on these needs and desires. Thus the citizen who does not participate may be ignored. The government will respond to the participant.

But the issue is not whether all citizens participate but whether the citizens who do are *representative* of the rest. As we have seen, not everyone is active in politics; nor is it realistic to expect them to be. But if the activists have the same problems, needs, and preferences as the nonactivists, they may speak for those who do not take part. On the other hand, if they are different from the rest of the population—come from selected social groups, have particular problems, want the government to do special things—then the fact that only a subgroup of the population participates means that the government will act on only some of the needs and desires of the population.

Who Are the Participants?

Citizens from all walks of life participate in American politics—no group is totally barred. But certain kinds of citizens participate much more than others.

Close studies come to the following conclusions about which citizens are likely to be active in politics:

1. EDUCATION   If you have a college education, you are much more likely to be politically active than if you have less education.
2. INCOME   People with higher incomes are likely to be active; the poor much less likely.
3. RACE   Black Americans are, on average, somewhat less active than whites. But the difference is not very great for most types of activity.
4. SEX   Men are somewhat more active than women, but the difference between the sexes is less in America than in most other nations.
5. AGE   Both young and old citizens tend to be somewhat less active than those in the middle years.

In sum, if you are highly educated and wealthy, you are much more likely to be a political activist than if you are less well educated and poor. Being white, male, and middle-aged helps as well. But race, sex, and age are less important than education and income. The important point is that the difference in participation rates

Figure 4.1
Problems Facing Inactive and
Active Citizens

Proportion Saying They Have
Recently Been Faced with a Serious
Problem of Employment, Paying of
Medical Care, or Adequate Housing

Inactive Citizens	Most Active Citizens
38%	22%

Inactive Citizens   **Most Active Citizens**

Source: Based on data from Sidney
Verba and Norman H. Nie, *Participation in America: Political Democracy
and Social Inequality* (New York: Harper & Row, 1972), chap. 15.

Figure 4.2
Differing Opinions of Inactive
and Active Citizens on Problem
Solving Among the Poor

Proportion Saying the Poor Have
the Prime Responsibility for
Solving Their Economic Problems

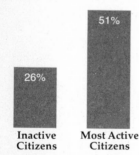

Inactive Citizens   **Most Active Citizens**

26%   51%

Source: Based on data from Sidney
Verba and Norman H. Nie, *Participation in America: Political Democracy
and Social Inequality* (New York: Harper & Row, 1972), chap. 15.

among these various groups does make a difference in what the government is told. Those who are inactive—the poor, the less educated—have different problems than those who are more active. And inactive citizens have different ideas about what the government should do. Suppose we compare the problems of the most active citizens with those faced by the least active. (See Figure 4.1.) We find that the inactive citizens are nearly twice as likely as active ones to say they have recently faced serious problems in paying for medical care, getting a job, or finding adequate housing.

In other words, if participation is how government officials find out about the problems of citizens, these leaders will not be aware of some of the more serious economic problems citizens face. The ones who have these problems are inactive. Nor do the inactives let the government know how they think it should deal with social and economic problems. If they did, the government would see a different picture of citizen desires than it gets from the activists. Consider the data in Figure 4.2. Active citizens believe the poor must solve their problems through their own effort. Those who are inactive are less likely to think this. They think the government should deal with such problems. But their views are not communicated. The government official who learns what the public wants by considering the preferences of the active citizens will find a majority who feel that the economic problems of the poor are their own responsibility and not an area for government action.

Campaign Contributions and the "Fat Cats"

Educated and wealthy citizens are more active in many ways. They are more likely to ring doorbells in campaigns, write to their congressman, and take part in community organizations. But the difference in participation between wealthy citizens and others is greatest in the area of campaign contributions. Election campaigns have become terribly expensive. The 1972 Presidential campaign cost at least $100 million. And congressional campaigns are expensive as well. The average cost of a senatorial campaign in 1972 was about $500,000; many candidates spent a lot more. One Republican senator, John Tower of Texas, spent $2,301,870 on his reelection campaign. House races are less expensive, but candidates in close races spent an average of over $100,000.

Where does this money come from? Most of it comes from a small number of wealthy contributors. One estimate is that about 90 percent of the campaign funds come from 1 percent of the population. The list of campaign donors who gave $40,000 or more to the Nixon campaign in 1972 fills three columns of small print in a *Congressional Quarterly* report and reads like a Who's Who of American business. Nor are such large donors missing from the Democratic support lists (though there were fewer of them).[4]

[4] "Dollar Politics: The Issue of Campaign Spending," *Congressional Quarterly*, 2 (October 1974), 66–67.

Senators Jackson and Kennedy look at stacks of petitions protesting gasoline price increases. But even millions of signatures are only a small portion of the citizenry.

The importance of large contributions in political campaigns illustrates a major generalization about politics in America: The struggle among citizens for a voice in governmental policy is an unequal one.

Participation and Equality   The data show up a major problem of American politics: Those who need governmental intervention the most—the poor, the less educated, the victims of racial discrimination—are the ones who are least active. Those who need governmental help the least—because they are already wealthier, better educated, less discriminated against—are the most active. Because of the inactivity of the poor and the greater activity of the rich, the government may underestimate citizens' need and desire for governmental intervention.

What causes this situation? Why do those who need help least participate the most? The answer is that what makes them better off in social and economic terms makes them better able to participate.

Education and wealth provide the resources needed for participation. Wealth is the most obvious resource. Few citizens can give tens of thousands of dollars to political candidates. Those who can are likely to have greater political influence. Skills are another resource, and these come from education. The educated are more likely to "know the ropes" of politics: whom to see and what to say.

The wealthy and the better educated are more active in politics for another reason. Many studies have shown that the more educated citizens are more motivated to take part in politics. Political motivation is important: It is not enough to have the necessary resources; one must be willing to use them. Education creates a set of attitudes—a belief that one can be effective in politics, that one has a responsibility to be active—that leads citizens to participate. We pointed out earlier that half the citizens in America think the ordinary person should be active in the affairs of his community—a much larger figure than in other countries. But in Table 4.4 notice the way educational groups differ in that sense of responsibility. Among those with no high school education, only a third think the ordinary person should be active in his community; among those with some college training, two-thirds think the ordinary person should be politically active.

Table 4.4
Which Citizens Think the Ordinary Man Should Be Active in His Community?

	Among Those Without High School Education	Among Those with Some High School	Among Those with Some College
Percent saying the ordinary man should be active	35%	56%	66%

Source: Based on data from Gabriel Almond and Sidney Verba, *The Civic Culture: Political Attitudes and Democracy in Five Nations* (Princeton, N. J.: Princeton University Press, 1963).

EQUALITY OF POLITICAL ACCESS

	Among Those Without High School Education	Among Those with Some High School	Among Those with Some College
Percent saying they could influence a decision of the local government	60%	82%	99%

Source: Based on data from Gabriel Almond and Sidney Verba, *The Civic Culture: Political Attitudes and Democracy in Five Nations* (Princeton, N. J.: Princeton University Press, 1963).

Similarly, educated citizens are more likely than less educated ones to have a sense of *political efficacy,* to think they can influence the government. Table 4.5 shows this. These two beliefs—that one *has a responsibility to be active* and that one *can influence the government*—lead to political activity. Those who hold such views are likely to be active.

Equalizing Political Participation

Can political participation be made more equal so citizens who are less well off in income or education are not the least effective participants? There are several ways to achieve greater political equality.

Put a Ceiling on Political Activity One way is to limit individual political activity. The most obvious place to do this is at the polls. Each citizen, no matter how rich or well educated, is limited to one vote for each political office.

If voting were the only way citizens took part in politics, the rule of "one man, one vote" would make all citizens equal politically—at least they could easily be equal if they all voted. But as we have seen, there are many other forms of participation, and these are often more powerful than voting. A millionaire, like a factory worker, has one vote, but his contributions to candidates give him a lot more voice than the factory worker. Can one put a ceiling on campaign contributions?

In the wake of the Watergate episode, Congress passed the Public Finance Bill of 1974. Under this law individuals can give no more than $1000 to a candidate in any federal election. (A person can give $1000 to a Presidential candidate, $1000 to a Senate candidate, and so forth. The limit is $1000 in any single race.) This hardly makes campaign contributions as equal as the vote; very few citizens can give $1000. But it should reduce somewhat the great influence of those who traditionally gave campaign contributions well above $1000.

The 1974 law limiting campaign contributions also introduces public financing of campaigns. We look at some of the ways this may affect political campaigns in a later chapter.

But limits on campaign contributions would not completely equalize political participation. There are many kinds of political activity that cannot easily be limited without severely limiting free speech. Nor would anyone want to limit such activities, since the essence of democracy is that citizens be free to express their preferences to the government. But since such activities depend on motivation, and the better educated are more likely to be motivated toward political activity, it is the better educated and the wealthy who are most likely to participate.

Mobilizing the Disadvantaged

Another way to equalize participation is to mobilize the disadvantaged. Rather than putting a ceiling on the activity of the wealthy, one *raises* the level of activity of the poor. Two things are necessary to mobilize citizens so their activity level will rise to that of the wealthy and better educated: (1) awareness of their disadvantaged position and (2) organization.

Awareness   Observers of American politics—particularly those who compare it with politics in Europe—often comment on the absence in the United States of any strong sense of economic class. This is very noticeable among American workers. It is particularly striking because a sense of class can be found in many other industrialized democracies. The American worker sometimes thinks of himself as a worker and makes political decisions from that point of view. But sometimes he thinks in terms of other groups. He may think politically as a Catholic, a suburbanite, a white or a black, and so forth. This separates him from other workers, from Protestants if he is Catholic, from blacks if he is white. A sense of membership in a *working class* is absent.

Organization   What about organization? Two kinds of organization might help disadvantaged citizens participate more in politics: political parties and voluntary groups. They might help by providing channels for activity and by increasing a sense of group identity. In many countries political parties are organized along class lines— they are parties of the working class, parties of the farmers, parties of the middle class. Parties that are limited to a particular class tend to do a better job of recruiting the members of that class. Thus socialist or workers' parties tend to mobilize working-class citizens. But the parties in the United States have no such clear class basis. Democrats are more likely to receive support from workers and Republicans from business. But both parties get support from all levels of society. The result is that citizens of lower social status have no party organizations trying to bring them into politics.

The same can be said for voluntary groups. These organizations can help citizens become more active. We discuss how this happens in Chapter 8. But here we can note that members of these associa-

Table 4.6
Which Citizens Belong
to Organizations?

	Among Those Without High School Education	Among Those with Some High School	Among Those with Some College
Percent who are members of an organization	49%	67%	78%
Percent who are active in an organization	27%	43%	59%

Source: Based on data from Sidney Verba and Norman H. Nie, *Participation in America: Political Democracy and Social Equality* (New York: Harper & Row, 1972).

tions tend to be of higher social status. As Table 4.6 shows, citizens with higher education are more active in organizations: Only about one-half of the citizens who have not finished high school belong to a voluntary organization; over three-quarters of those with some college training do. And only about one-fourth of those without a high school degree are active in an organization, whereas over half of the college group is.

If organization is a way to make groups of citizens politically meaningful, then it is clear that this resource is also more available to upper-status citizens.

Black vs. White: Political Mobilization of a Disadvantaged Group

Among black Americans—at least in recent decades—one can observe the beginnings of a break in the participation cycle that leaves the disadvantaged even more disadvantaged. And the break comes, we believe, through organization and self-awareness. American blacks have a history of relatively effective organization—at least more effective than that of white Americans of similar social and economic status. There are many reasons for this, perhaps the most important one being the fact of segregation and social separation. Forced to live apart from whites, they are better able to organize as a separate group. In addition, numerous black organizations—from the NAACP to more militant groups—have played an important role. Nor should one forget the role of the black churches. It is clear that blacks have developed an organizational base.

In addition, they have developed—as whites have not—a clear sense of identity. The slogans "Black Power" and "Black is Beautiful" are examples of this awareness. And their separation from the mainstream of white society makes this possible. The point is that the segregation of American society—which finds blacks living apart, going to school apart, holding certain kinds of jobs—produces more unity and less of the multiple identification that hampers self-awareness and organization among disadvantaged white citizens.

Studies show that through black self-awareness citizens who might not otherwise participate can be active in politics. Black

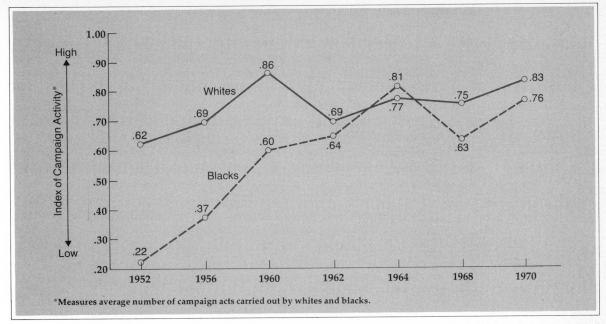

*Measures average number of campaign acts carried out by whites and blacks.

Figure 4.3
Level of Campaign Activity
Among Blacks and Whites

Source: Based on data from Sidney Verba and Norman H. Nie, *Participation in America: Political Democracy and Social Inequality* (New York: Harper & Row, 1972), chap. 14.

Americans, on the average, participate in politics somewhat less than white Americans. This is what one would expect, given the fact that blacks are generally of lower income and education. But if we consider blacks who have a sense of group identity (who, for instance, mention problems of race when asked what are the most important problems for themselves or the nation), we find that they are as active in politics as whites. In other words, the sense of black identity is a way to overcome the disadvantage in political activity that blacks have because of their lower educational and income levels.[5]

The situation can be seen more clearly if we look at the situation over time. A series of studies of American voting behavior has been made by the University of Michigan since 1952. This lets us trace the difference in black and white participation rates in political campaigns over a long period. These data are presented in Figure 4.3.

In 1952 — two years before the Supreme Court's historic school desegregation decision and three years before the first bus boycott led by Martin Luther King in Montgomery, Alabama — black Americans were much less active in political campaigns than the average white. In the 1960s the difference between black Americans and white Americans declined. The average level of black activity has remained a touch below that of whites, but the difference is much less than at the beginning of the awakening of black self-awareness.

The data on black-white differences do not mean political prob-

[5] Verba and Nie, chap. 10.

lems for black citizens are over. Their participation rate still remains below that of whites. And of course we have information only on how much activity they attempt, not on the all-important question of how effective that activity is. Blacks may have increased their political activity, but they remain a minority group and their political activity is not always—perhaps not often—effective.

Most participation still comes from the white population, and, among that population, from those who are richer and better educated. But because blacks have developed a group identity and are relatively well organized, their disadvantage in political activity compared to whites has been reduced. Compare 1952 with the years since 1962 in Figure 4.3.

Two more conclusions can be drawn from these data. Both have to do with the relationship between the more ordinary ways of participating—elections, community work, letters to one's congressman—and the more dramatic, more direct, and sometimes illegal kinds of political activity—protest demonstrations, marches, and the like.

One conclusion is clear from the last figure on black-white differences in campaign participation over the past two decades. Although direct political activity among blacks, and the origin of that activity in an increased sense of black identity, has attracted much attention, it is quite clear that along with this has come more ordinary political activity.

The second conclusion is that the increase in "demonstration democracy" may in part be explained by some of the differences in participation rates found among social groups in America. If indeed the ordinary ways of participating are so heavily in favor of the "haves" rather than the "have-nots," citizens unhappy with the results might seek other, more direct means of political pressure.

Political Activity of Women

Women have generally been less active in politics than men. Traditionally they were less likely to vote, to be active during election campaigns, or to run for office. Some of the same reasons why poorer and less educated citizens are less politically active probably apply to women as well. We have seen that those with lower levels of education were more likely to feel that they had no responsibility to take part in politics and that they had a weaker sense of their ability to influence politics. Studies of schoolchildren have shown that girls are raised to believe that politics is not for them. The result is that women—at least until recently—felt less politically able and were therefore less active.

But there is evidence that in recent years this gap between women and men has been narrowing. Women are more active in political campaigns than they once were, and more are running for office. In 1974 a greater number of women were elected than ever before. As in the case of blacks, the source of the increase in participation by women appears to be their growing sense of self-awareness. One

Growing self-awareness among women has increased their levels of political participation.

study found that the growth in political activity was particularly strong among women who could be considered feminists.[6]

The Politics of Protest:
A Closer Look

So far we have given most of our attention to the "ordinary" means of participation: political campaigns and community group activity. But a full account of political activities in America has to pay close attention to direct political activity: political demonstrations, marches, and violence. These activities have become more important in recent years. Protests have focused on racial matters and the war in Vietnam, but they have spread to other issues as well. Although there are no clear data on the subject, it seems likely that groups are more willing to disrupt (to seize a building, to march on an office) than in the past. Is this something new in America—a new political style that grew out of the tensions of the 1960s?

Violence, Protests, and the Record

To begin with, we must make clear that protest and violence are not the same thing. A study done for the National Commission on the Causes and Prevention of Violence found that only about one-third of the protests recorded in the press involved violence; most were nonviolent. In fact the figure of one-third may be somewhat large, since the newspapers pay more attention to violent incidents.

Furthermore, violence is hard to define. "Violent language"—rude and insulting—is often used in political confrontations, but is that violence? Also, as studies of clashes between police and demonstrators have shown, it is hard to tell "who started it" when confrontations turn violent. As the report to the commission put it, "it is often difficult to determine who was 'responsible' for the violence. The reports of our study teams, however, clearly suggest that au-

[6] Kristie Andersen, "Working Women and Political Participation," *American Journal of Political Science,* forthcoming. Ms. Andersen also found that political activity was highest among working women.

thorities bear a major responsibility. . . . Of the violent incidents [analyzed], in only half did the violence seem to be initiated by the demonstrators."[7]

Although the recent growth of political protest (and the violence that sometimes goes with it) is often thought of as a new development, this is not the case. U.S. history is filled with the uses of political violence and conflict. Not only was the nation born in violent protest against the British; less well known is the history of violent protests against the government by poor Appalachian farmers throughout the second half of the seventeenth century. Violence was used by the southern states in trying to secede from the Union and by the North in preventing it. It was used by WASPs (White Anglo-Saxon Protestants) against various immigrant groups in American cities in the nineteenth century. It was used by worker groups to protest economic conditions, and it was used by the authorities to put down those protests. None of the demonstrations against the war in Vietnam matched the violence of the antidraft riots in New York during the Civil War, when draft offices were burned and many people were killed.

Above all, there was violence in the South after the Civil War— violence against blacks (with the approval of the authorities) that successfully maintained the power of white over black in that area.

What Are Protests About?

In recent years protest activity has focused on two issues: the war in Vietnam and racial matters. The busing of schoolchildren to achieve integration is another major issue. But, as the historical record makes clear, there have been protests on many issues. Such activities are often thought of as irrational, with no political goal. But this does not seem to be the case. Usually there is some political goal. It may not be clear in the mind of the demonstrator, but then neither is the goal of voting always clear in the mind of the voter.

There is also the so-called riff-raff theory: The demonstrators are those who are the least well integrated into society. Among blacks these would be the jobless, the young, and the most poverty stricken. But studies show that protests do not have such a narrow base. They find that most urban rioters are young and unemployed, but they are drawn from all parts of the community and have at least the passive support of the majority. Thus the makeup of the protest groups also shows that these are political activities.

The Motivation for Direct Action Most protests have one thing in common: a belief that the ordinary political channels are unresponsive or (perhaps the same thing) too slow. As the Chicago Riot Study Committee put it, "there is a conviction on the part of a clear ma-

[7] Jerome H. Skolnick, *The Politics of Protest,* Staff Report to the National Commission on the Causes and Prevention of Violence (New York: Ballantine, 1969), pp. 3–4.

Direct action is used by
Boston parents opposed
to school busing.

jority of our Black citizens that political representation is entirely
unsatisfactory and must be improved."[8]

Direct action, furthermore, is likely to take place under certain
conditions: when a group lives apart from the rest of the society, has
its own lifestyle, and has little (or believes it has little) in common
with others. There are no ties to the rest of the society; the group
feels that other channels are not open to it. If the ordinary political
channels are closed, the buildup of tensions and frustrations may
result in the use of more direct means.

Is Direct Action Appropriate?   Here of course is a big problem for
those who try direct action. Some argue that such activities are never
appropriate in a democracy, where there are other, more peaceful
channels. Certainly the ordinary channels must be tried first. And
even then the switch to direct action is inappropriate. If everyone
who could not get his way used violence, society would become a
war of all against all.

Others answer that in many cases all channels have been tried.
Furthermore, the democratic channels are not available equally
to all: Some groups are excluded and have no choice but direct activity. Finally, those favoring direct activity argue that some issues
are so important—stopping a war or providing civil rights or preventing the busing of children away from a neighborhood school—
that one must act firmly and directly.

It is not our job to decide who is right. Part of the debate is a factual one: Are channels open to all and were all channels tried before
direct action? But these questions have no easy answer. And the

[8] *Chicago Riot Study Committee Report* (Chicago, 1969), p. 112.

legitimacy of stepping outside of the ordinary political channels, as well as the tougher question of the legitimacy of violence, are not factual questions but moral ones.

Is Protest Effective?

Protests are political acts by citizens who want some response from the government. In this sense we can judge them by asking how effective they are.

This again is an area where it is hard to find clear answers. It is difficult to tell how much more effective protest is than the slower processes of ordinary participation. Many people—particularly government leaders who would like to discourage such activity—claim that they pay no attention to them. President Nixon once made quite a point of watching a football game on TV while the White House was surrounded by and much of Washington filled with Vietnam war protesters. Others—particularly the leaders of demonstrations—claim that they are the only effective political activity.

Probably the truth lies in between. The most effective political activity often is the slowest and hardest—the doorbell ringing and the patient talk that goes with campaigning. Protest activities sometimes flash quickly and then fade, leaving no results. But the opposite often happens. An urban demonstration ending in violence, a big march on Washington by angry war protesters, attempts by citizens to block school integration—all such activities may cause government leaders to change their course sharply.

We can find examples showing clearly that direct action caused changes. The Riot Commission Report says:

> Northern violence ended Southern slavery, and Southern terrorism ended radical Reconstruction. The transformation of labor-management relations was achieved during a wave of bloody strikes, in the midst of a depression and widespread fear of revolution. And black people made their greatest political gains, both in Congress and in the cities, during the racial strife of the 1960's.[9]

Protests are particularly important as "signals." The dramatic nature of protests and their coverage by the media make them a powerful tool for signaling discontent to political leaders. And they may often attract participants as well. It is not accidental that the growth of black participation in the electoral process came when direct protests were becoming more common.

Yet there is another side to the coin. Direct action is generally disapproved of by the majority of Americans—even when they approve of its goals. A great majority (75–85 percent) of the American people disapproved of student protests on the war in Vietnam. Indeed one study showed that this view was held even by citizens who thought the war in Vietnam was a mistake.[10]

[9] Skolnick, p. 16.
[10] Milton J. Rosenberg, Sidney Verba, and Philip E. Converse, *Vietnam and the Silent Majority* (New York: Harper & Row, 1970), pp. 44–45.

Public opinion polls on racial matters make clear that there is a "white backlash" to black militant activities. The 1960s was an era of increasing acceptance by whites of the goals of blacks—better housing, integration, and the like—coupled with greater disapproval of militant activities.

Does militant activity do more harm than good? It is hard to tell, partly because the results are mixed and hard to measure and partly because one's judgment on these issues depends on his values. Some may believe violence (or the risk of violence) is wrong in almost any case. Others may feel that it is necessary if social change is to happen. Out of such differences come "ordinary" politics as well as violent politics.

5

Recruitment of Political Leaders

In the early weeks of 1975, President Ford announced a major economic program, one that involved tax cuts, energy conservation programs, federal government actions, and goals for the business community. Immediately there were news stories reporting what the Democratic party leaders felt about the program, what business leaders said, whether the labor leaders thought the program was fair to working men and women, what congressional leaders had to say, and how the leading economists felt.

Who were all these "leaders"? How did they get to be leaders? For whom did they speak when they announced that the President's proposals were good or bad? Are they the same leaders who led the nation into its economic trouble in the first place? These are the kinds of issues we raise in this chapter.

Leadership: A Tiny Group

The most striking fact about national leadership is how few people are directly involved in it.

> In all assemblies and groups and organized bodies of men, from a nation down to a committee of a club, direction and decisions rest in the hands of a small percentage, less and less in proportion to the larger size of the body, till in a great population it becomes an infinitesimally small proportion of the whole number. This is and always has been true of all forms of government.[1]

This is easy to prove. There are 136 million adult citizens in the United States, yet how many of them are directly involved in planning and directing government programs? About 1500 congressmen, higher officials in the executive branch, governors, top federal and state judges, big city mayors, national party committee members, and various other key state and local officials. From 136 million possible candidates, then, comes the tiny, tiny group of important political leaders.

Definition of National Leadership

Defining leadership is not easy. A person who has leadership at one level of society, say, a local businessman, may be unimportant in national affairs. Or a person who plays an important role on some issues, say, the role of a general in planning military strategy, may count for nothing when economic policy is being planned.

The definition we use in this text describes *national* leaders, that is, people whose positions provide national visibility and influence that can be felt on a national scale. And the definition is *institutional*.

[1] J. Bryce, *Modern Democracies* (New York: Macmillan, 1942), p. 542.

Leaders in America are people who hold high positions in specific institutions: banks, public bureaucracies, corporations, newspapers, universities, law firms, Congress, labor unions, hospitals, churches, civic organizations, and so forth.

Institutions differ in importance; some are much more significant to the society than others. They can be classified as dominant and nondominant. Here are examples of dominant and nondominant institutions in different social sectors:

Social Sector	Dominant, Nationally Important Institutions	Nondominant, Less Important Institutions
Business	IBM	Brown Shoe Company
Government	Department of Agriculture	Oshkosh County Mosquito Control Agency
Newspapers	New York *Times*	Oak Creek *Herald*
Banks	Chase Manhattan Bank of New York	City National Bank of Kansas City
Professional Associations	National Academy of Sciences	Southern Political Science Association
Military	The Pentagon	Utah National Guard
Civic Organizations	Kennedy Center	Linda Hall Library

A close look at various parts of American society shows that a fairly small number of institutions control a very large share of the total resources of society. Chapter 1 told how economic resources are

DEFINITION OF NATIONAL
LEADERSHIP

concentrated in a few corporations, banks, and insurance firms. For instance, 0.1 percent of all manufacturing corporations control more than half of all manufacturing assets in the country. Although there are over six thousand foundations in the United States, the dozen largest ones control approximately 40 percent of all foundation assets. Although there are more than 2500 colleges and universities, about 20 of them receive well over half of all government contracts and control a very large share of college endowment money.

National leaders have important positions in the dominant institutions of American society. They are the officers and directors of IBM, the secretary, assistant secretaries, and program directors in the Department of Agriculture, the publisher and editors of the New York *Times*, the officers and trustees of the Chase Manhattan Bank of New York, and so forth.

How Many National Leaders Are There?

It is hard to give an exact number of national leaders. Should we count all congressmen, or just those with enough seniority to influence legislation? Should we count the presidents of the 20 largest and richest universities or of the 50 largest and richest universities? One study has attempted such a count and reports that fewer than 4000 people

> control half of the nation's industrial assets, half of all assets in communications, transportation and utilities, half of all banking assets, and two-thirds of all insurance assets; they control nearly 40 percent of all the assets of private foundations, half of all private university endowments; they control the most prestigious civic and cultural organizations; they occupy key federal government positions in the executive, legislative, and judicial branches; they occupy all of the top command positions in the Army, Navy, Air Force, and Marines.[2]

This estimate may be low because it leaves out leaders of important social movements such as civil rights groups or consumer protest organizations; it also overlooks institutions with few financial resources but great prestige, such as scientific organizations. But even adding another 1000 or 2000 people does not change the fact that American society is led by a very small number of people.

Starting from this fact, we ask three questions about the leaders, the "C questions" of leadership in a democratic society:

CHOICE: Who is chosen to be a national leader?
COHESION: How cohesive is the leadership group?
CHANGE: In what ways and how fast can the leadership group be changed?

Most of the discussion and examples will focus on political leaders, that is, on top elected and appointed officials in the government. Space does not permit full attention to corporate executives, univer-

[2] Thomas R. Dye and John W. Pickering, "Governmental and Corporate Elites: Convergence and Differentiation," *Journal of Politics*, November 1974, 905.

Figure 5.1
Which Few Citizens Will
Achieve Leadership Roles?

sity presidents, leading scientists, newspaper publishers, or military generals, but much of what we say here applies equally well to these other leaders.

Choosing National Leaders

How do people move into and out of the top circles? Are particular groups given special advantages? What political viewpoints dominate within the governing group? What actions or mistakes typically result in the downfall of individual leaders or even in the fall of entire ruling groups? If, for instance, in Figure 5.1 the box on the left represents the entire adult population of the United States, and the speck on the right stands for the political leaders, which few citizens will succeed in reaching leadership positions?

For much of human history there was no question who would rule. People either were or were not born into the ruling class. Birth determined leadership, just as it determined who owned property and who did not. Of course hereditary rule did not prevent quarrels within the ruling group and palace revolutions. But it did prevent recruitment from the lower social orders. Political office and its privileges were matters of birthright.

The democratic revolution changed this. It separated birthright from officeholding. Authority could no longer be claimed because of family name. The powerful positions had somehow to be earned.

Sometimes it is thought that the democratic revolution was a challenge to leadership itself. Although this might have been intended by a few radicals, it was not a major part of the democratic revolution. The challenge was to inherited leadership. Our own Constitution recognized that a few would govern many, while insisting that power and position were to be won through merit, performance, and talent.

Standards for Choosing Leaders

We can understand leadership choice in American politics by looking again at Figure 5.1. Think of the ancient Chinese box puzzle. In this puzzle different-sized boxes are designed so that the smallest box fits into the next largest one, which, in turn, fits into the next-largest one, and so forth. The largest box contains all the others. To find the very smallest box you have to open all the boxes between it and the largest one.

Now imagine that the largest box represents the entire population and the smallest box represents the leadership group. The other boxes would represent smaller and smaller "recruitment pools" that supply people from the larger to the smaller groups. Recruitment is the gradual but continuous process of selection and elimination that narrows the large population to the few who hold the highest positions. Figure 5.2 is a diagram of that process, showing four stages between the many and the few.

Figure 5.2
Recruitment Criteria for
Political Leadership

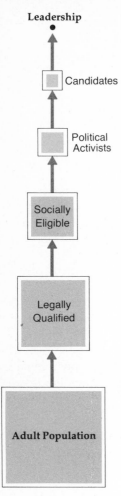

Leadership

Candidates

Political
Activists

Socially
Eligible

Legally
Qualified

Adult Population

Legally Qualified   Within the adult population there is a group of people who meet the legal qualifications for political officeholding. For instance, the Constitution sets minimum ages for some positions. Other legal qualifications include residency requirements (you must live in the state from which you would like to be a senator, for instance) and, for certain positions, professional credentials (especially for judicial offices, which are often limited to persons with legal training). Legal qualifications, however, do not play a very significant part in political recruitment. Almost any adult citizen is legally qualified to hold public office. This has not always been the case. In the seventeenth century only property owners could stand for office; blacks were barred from office as well as from voting until after the Civil War, and women could not hold certain positions until fairly recent times. One way to trace the growth of democratic principles in any society is through the progressive elimination of laws that bar particular groups from office.

Socially Eligible   The next standard for choosing political leaders is that they be "socially eligible." A large percentage of leaders consistently come from particular social groups in the population. Leaders are not typical in their social origins, in their educational levels, and in their occupations before holding office.

Imagine that we were to study the way a tiny portion of your own generation will eventually come to hold the highest political offices. We might make up a list of people between the ages of 18 and 25, and then follow them through their careers until, say, 30 years from now, when a few of them will have risen to important positions. Suppose this list of younger citizens included the following:

- The son of a corporation lawyer who heads a law firm in Washington, D.C. He has just graduated from Princeton, where he was active in student politics and was editor of the campus newspaper. Next year he will enter Harvard Business School.
- A black longshoreman in San Francisco who is keenly interested in trade union affairs. He has already been elected secretary of his multiracial local. His formal education is limited to community college, but he is a good organizer and popular with fellow workers. He has campaigned actively for local Democratic candidates.
- A student body president of a large state university in the Midwest. She is the daughter of a small-town mayor and has served her father as an unofficial consultant on ending sex discrimination in the town's schools and hospitals. Although she is known to be very sharp politically, her academic record is mediocre. Still, she has been admitted to the university's graduate school of education.
- A farmer's son who graduated with honors from Jerseyville High School but decided against further education. He was a football hero in the community and has recently joined the Elks, partly because some local businessmen have hinted that they would like him to serve on the town planning commission.

Although practically every citizen is legally qualified for high office, a much smaller number are "socially eligible."

Now ask: What are the chances that 30 years from now any one of these four will have reached top government positions? We would rank their chances in the order in which they are listed, even though each has leadership skills. For every 100 people like the Princeton graduate, perhaps one will end up in a top position; while for every 10,000 budding labor leaders, only one is likely to get that far. However, this particular labor leader is black, which may be an advantage during a period when great attention is given to racial equality. The next person on the list is disadvantaged by her sex and by the fact that she is taking advanced work in education rather than law or business. Finally we come to our high school hero, whose chances of reaching a high position are practically nil.

Trying to predict which of these four 20-year-olds will become a national leader helps us see that leaders are chosen from a small portion of the general population. To come from a wealthy family, to be white and male, and to attend a good university or college greatly increases the chances of moving into the circles from which leaders are selected. Consider two people on the list. The Princeton graduate has begun a career that often puts people of his background and ability in line for the highest positions in society. His family, his father's business associates, his Princeton classmates or Harvard professors would not consider it odd if he announced that his ambition is the U.S. Senate or a well-known New York law firm.

The social setting of the farm boy is far different. How unusual it would be for him to consider himself a future member of the highest political circles. There are few models for him to look up to, no contacts to help him on his way, and little reason for him to think of himself as on a level with the very wealthy and powerful. His idea of success is to own his own farm and maybe become village mayor. Such a self-image is realistic, like the self-image of the Princeton graduate. The point is clear: People eliminate themselves from as well as select themselves for the race for the few top positions. Patterns of self-elimination and self-selection cannot be separated from social position. Some are born with a foot on the ladder to power, but most are not. Those who are not have trouble finding the ladder, let alone getting a foot on it.

Moreover, movement into leadership positions is always influenced by the judgments of people already holding high office. This is true even if great stress is placed on "objective standards," for those standards can never be separated from the prejudices of the people responsible for them. No matter how talent is defined, it must be discovered by those who have already proved themselves to have it. Those in leadership positions will encourage people of similar status and background. This selectivity from the top down contributes to a process in which certain social groups continue to supply recruits for the top political positions.

Social background, however, is only one among several factors

Candidates for top political office come from those who assert themselves.

that account for who reaches the top. All four of the people listed earlier have a chance if for no other reason than that they have shown some leadership skill. In this way their chances are higher than those of schoolmates who have shown no such skill. Another Princetonian might come from the same social level, but he might have concentrated on chemistry for the past six years. He is now in graduate school and avoids activities that distract him from his academic work. This chemist is not a realistic candidate for a top political position.

Political Activists Approximately one in twenty adult citizens is a political activist, and it is from this group that leadership eventually comes. As Chapter 4 made clear, the activists pay close attention to political matters, serve on committees and work in campaigns, know and are known by the people actually in office, and are in positions that traditionally supply the recruits for public office. This group is largely, though not entirely, made up of middle- and upper-middle-class citizens.

The boundaries that separate the politically active from the less active are neither firmly established nor easily recognized. People move back and forth across these boundaries as their interests change, as their careers take them closer to or further away from politics, and as their own ambitions respond to the chance to have a political career. In some important ways the active citizens are self-selected. There are no universal standards for entry into the loose network that supplies candidates for the highest positions. Political activists do, though, often come from families with a tradition of political involvement; they are exposed to politics early in life and simply carry these habits into their adult careers. Approximately one-third of the officeholders in the United States trace their earliest political involvement to the influence of the family. This may be seen in such families as the Roosevelts, Tafts, and Kennedys.

Candidates Within the politically active group is an even smaller number of people who become candidates for top leadership positions. This includes those who are actually nominated for elective positions as well as those whose names appear on lists when appointments are being made to the Cabinet, the Supreme Court, executive agencies, and so forth. How some activists become serious contenders for the leadership positions and others do not is not well understood. One factor, however, is self-assertiveness. This is illustrated in President Johnson's view of the world as "a vacuum of non-wills in which the strong man with a 'will to power' automatically takes charge. Most people drop off the political ladder at the bottom and middle rungs; private values intrude; conflicts arise. The restless few who remain become the political leaders of the day." It was no accident that Johnson himself belonged to the restless few: "As long as I can remember I've always been the kind of person who takes over in any group, who takes responsibility for calling the gathering together, getting the agenda for the meeting and carrying out the assignments."

Another factor is the attitude of those already in powerful positions. They can sponsor careers in the way they make opportunities available and fill key apprenticeship positions. For instance, Lyndon Johnson, when he was majority leader in the Senate, greatly aided John F. Kennedy's career by helping the freshman senator gain appointment to the Senate Foreign Relations Committee. This gave Kennedy a platform from which he could launch his drive for the Presidential nomination of the Democratic party.

The Test of Achievement in Leadership Selection

The Chinese box puzzle shows how a very large population is gradually narrowed until a small number of candidates are competing for the even smaller number of top political positions. But this leaves unanswered the question of ability. Because so many leaders come from well-to-do families and are white males, some observers of American politics say *who you are* is more important than *what you can do*. This is a hasty and incorrect conclusion. It is clear that social background provides advantages, but it can neither guarantee a place among the political leaders nor completely block entry.

The people who govern American society are achievers. They have shown they can manage large enterprises or direct the efforts of others or attract the loyalty of large numbers of people. Thus at any given time the President's Cabinet will probably include former chief officers of giant corporations, perhaps someone who has been head of a foundation or a university president, a member of a leading law firm, an ex-labor union leader.

We appear to be inconsistent. First, leaders are largely white males from relatively high-status families. Second, they are able and talented people. It looks as if we have to conclude that ability and talent are concentrated among sons of wealthy, white families. But this conclusion is untrue. Some have a greater opportunity to develop and display their abilities than others.

Display of Talent on a Grand Scale To be in line for national political leadership, it is necessary to show your ability on a grand scale. It is better to succeed at running Ford Motor than at selling worn-out Fords on the used-car lot, though the latter may involve greater skill than the former. It is better to be an innovative president of a well-known university than an innovative grade school teacher where the president sends his children, though teaching a roomful of 8-year-olds may take more innovation than overseeing a university. It is better to be the popular vote-getting mayor of New York than of Brisbane, though it may take more popularity to turn out the vote in Brisbane than in New York.

It is therefore not just achievement but very specific achievements that move one into leadership positions. This suggests why the wealthy provide so many of the top leaders. They have the education and contacts necessary to reach positions through which ability can be shown on a grand scale. The used-car salesman may be as skilled, personable, and hardworking as the president of the company whose worn-out products he sells. But the salesman was born into the working class, not the upper class; he attended a local junior college, not Harvard Business School; his friends also sell used cars, they don't direct the corporations that make them; he is sometimes active in precinct politics, but he does not give thousands of dollars to Presidential campaigns. When the list is made of possible appointees to the Cabinet or possible nominees for the governorship or possible candidates for an ambassadorship, it never includes the skilled, personable, hardworking used-car salesman, but often includes the head of the company whose cars he sells.

Top leaders are people who have achieved a lot. But the achievements that count are easier to display if you start life as a white male from a fairly well-off Protestant family. This is how you get the education and job opportunities that, in turn, launch the careers that take some people, but not many, to the top.

Ability to Win Elections It is true that American politics often rewards with power those who have proved that they can direct the large institutions of commerce and business, of banking, and of law, education, and philanthropy. But also rewarded are those with a very different kind of skill—the ability to win elections.

The electorate in a democracy necessarily controls entry into certain key leadership posts. Thus what matters is the simple achievement of winning elections. Nixon built on a series of election victories, starting with his campaign for the House of Representatives in 1946 and ending in his landslide reelection to the Presidency in 1972. Johnson also went from the House to the Senate to the Vice Presidency to the Presidency. Of course not all major electoral victories build on a series of lesser victories. Eisenhower transfered his great popularity as wartime general into voter popularity and won the Presidency without ever having been active in politics. The past governor of California, Ronald Reagan, moved into that position directly from his career as a movie actor. Charles Percy was a corporation executive before being elected Illinois senator.

Voter appeal can be used to advantage by people from any background. Indeed in American politics it makes up for the lack of family wealth or a high-status education. Only one President out of the last six (Kennedy, in contrast to Truman, Eisenhower, Johnson, Nixon, and Ford) started with the advantage of wealth.

We see, thus, that achievement is weighed in two different though sometimes related ways. There is the achievement shown by becoming a corporation executive or a senior partner in a leading law firm or the president of a foundation or university. Such people are candidates for the highest political positions, as when Robert McNamara moved from head of Ford Motor to Secretary of Defense or Edward Levi moved from president of the University of Chicago to Attorney General. There is also the achievement of election victories.

Although the first group of achievers come almost entirely from the wealthier social classes, for the second group this is not necessarily so. This gives political recruitment in America one of its distinctive characteristics. Members of the lower classes are almost never chosen for high *appointive* office, but they sometimes make it to *elective* office. Most political leaders will come from higher-status groups—but not all.

How Cohesive Are the National Leaders?

There is, on the one hand, the argument that national leaders generally think the same way about public policy. Only small differences are allowed. Leaders are a cohesive group, and it is nearly impossible to introduce new ideas unless the "establishment" agrees to them. There is, on the other hand, the argument that leaders are very much divided into different and competing groups. Leaders have varying ambitions. They represent different economic groups, regions, or political movements. The important fact about leadership is not agreement but conflict. Which view is correct?

Political Leadership in Disagreement

Leaders hold a great variety of viewpoints. Sharply different views are held on such issues as tax reform, inflation controls, defense expenditures, and so forth. It could not be otherwise. *The political recruitment process carries into leadership circles some of the basic conflicts and divisions of society.* This happens in many ways. For instance, we see in Chapter 9 that Republicans and Democrats do differ. In addition, leaders become spokesmen for the many political and social divisions in society: North vs. South, Protestant vs. Catholic, workers vs. management. Then of course there are conflicts between state leaders and the federal bureaucracy, between Congress and the Presidency.

One of the more important types of disagreement between institutions could be seen in the Watergate affair. This is the conflict between the news media and the government. At one level this was simply reporters trying to expose criminal activities in the White House. But the conflict between press and government is deeper than Watergate and will have lasting effects.

Political leaders often complain that they are being unfairly treated by the news media; and editors, reporters, and announcers often complain that political leaders do not really respect the free press.

In the 1960s these complaints took on new force. The press began to see its job as more than reporting the news. The phrase "advocatory journalism" was heard, showing that the press was beginning to argue strongly for or against particular public policies. "The national media," as Theodore H. White observed, "have put themselves into the role of permanent critical opposition to any government which does not instantly clean up the unfinished business of our time."[3] Of course this means no government can ever satisfy the press.

The media and the government have different institutional interests. "The media have an interest in exposure, criticism, highlighting and encouraging disagreement and disaffection within the executive branch." The media want to spur political debate. In contrast, national leaders, especially those in the executive branch, "have an interest in secrecy, hierarchy, discipline, and the suppression of criticism."[4] The federal bureaucracy wants to limit political debate.

Before he left the government in disgrace, Spiro Agnew, Vice President under Nixon, spoke forcefully against the role the national press had taken upon itself.

> This little group . . . of network commentators and self-appointed analysts . . . not only enjoy a right of instant rebuttal to every presidential address but, more importantly, wield a free hand in selecting, presenting, and interpreting the great issues in our nation . . . a tiny, enclosed fraternity of privileged men elected by no one.[5]

TV commentator David Brinkley responded to the Nixon administration's criticism of the press by pointing out that

> if, over the last generation, the politicians and the bureaucrats in Washington have made such a mess of things with the press keeping some kind of watch over them, what would they have done with nobody watching?[6]

The disagreement between media and government is but one of several examples we could use to show that national leaders are far from a cohesive group. Other examples appear throughout the text, where we discuss conflict between interest-group leaders, between party leaders, between bureaucrats and congressmen, between those outside and those inside government.

It is, then, incorrect to assert that the leaders are a cohesive group. From this, two things follow. First, conflicts within leadership circles put a great strain on government. It is not easy to settle on a policy when the policy makers cannot agree. The result is often compromise and negotiation. Second, disagreements within the leadership group allow the public to play off one set of leaders against another. The

---

[3] Quoted in Samuel P. Huntington, "Postindustrial Politics: How Benign Will It Be?," *Comparative Politics*, January 1974, 184.
[4] Ibid.
[5] Television address, November 13, 1969.
[6] *Parade*, January 14, 1973.

Democrats can be replaced by the Republicans, or leaders who favor an expanded military budget can be replaced by those who support military cuts. Thus competing viewpoints within the leadership help maintain popular control over public policy.

Conflict and competition among leaders are, however, only part of the story. The political recruitment process also makes for agreement in many areas.

Political Leadership in Agreement

Leaders share many experiences. They often come from similar backgrounds. They know how hard it is to get and use power. They worry about how to keep the economy working effectively and how to keep the government intact. Out of these shared experiences, backgrounds, challenges, and worries comes a form of leadership consensus. This is because leaders are recruited from the political *mainstream,* a term with both a substantive and a procedural meaning.

Substantive Consensus The political mainstream includes those broad policies that most Americans actively support, or at least willingly tolerate. Take military policy as an example. Most Americans agree that the nation should maintain military preparedness and that the United States should, if necessary, defend its national interests with military force. Most, but not all, citizens take this view. There are some who oppose the whole idea of military preparedness and believe the United States should disarm. Such a view is considered "outside the mainstream of American thinking." Equally outside the mainstream is the view that the United States should make nuclear strikes against its supposed enemies.

The recruitment process tends over and over again to select leaders from the political mainstream. One reason is that the electorate is not likely to support candidates whose viewpoints conflict with its own. This does not mean every political leader is equally acceptable to every voter. A congressman elected by white rural Mississippians probably has views on race relations that are obnoxious to northern black voters. But if individual leaders are generally disliked by particular electorates, the leadership group as a whole has policy views that go along with majoritarian, mainstream thinking.

There is, then, a certain consensus among the leaders on the policies the American public is willing to tolerate. Within the political mainstream, and thus within the leadership, are many divergent viewpoints. Take again the example of military policy. To say there is broad agreement that the United States should be prepared to defend its interests is not to agree about the size of the budget for "preparedness" or about "national interests." Despite these differences, the recruitment process bars from the top leadership circles those views that strike most Americans as "extreme" or "going too far."

Senator Edward Kennedy, liberal Democrat, and ex-Governor Ronald Reagan, conservative Republican, manage to find common political ground with George Wallace, a southern populist.

Procedural Consensus There is a second sense in which leaders are recruited from and reflect the political mainstream. Much that is important about American politics, or any politics, may be found in the oft-repeated phrase of the 1960s, "working within the system." Here the emphasis is on procedural consensus. There is an acceptable way of doing things and an unacceptable way. Political hostility toward peaceniks, eco-freaks, black militants, and hippies stemmed from the belief that without "the system" there is no hope for the goals sought by such groups—no hope for lasting peace, clean air, racial justice, cultural tolerance. Political dissidents can vote the rascals out, but they will not be allowed to destroy the system that permits a later group of rascals to be voted out; they can petition and demonstrate, but they cannot abolish the system that allows petitions and demonstrations; they can condemn acquisitiveness, but they cannot ruin the system that gives to others the right to acquire.

Leaders agree on the importance of "working within the system," and in this way they reflect the political mainstream. Consensus on *how* to bring about change cuts across sharp policy disagreements on *what* changes, if any, are necessary. The recruitment process maintains this procedural consensus. The long climb to high office generally breeds commitment to the rules of the game, and the result is a common approach to governing despite different points of view.

Sometimes, however, political leaders fail to "play by the rules of the game." This sends shock waves through the political system, as in the Watergate affair. People in powerful positions were caught in such activities as illegal raising of campaign funds, political spying, and attempts to undermine the election process during the months before the 1972 election.

RECRUITMENT OF POLITICAL LEADERS

Perhaps most disturbed by Watergate were certain elite groups that fully understood the implications of these activities. These groups—an independent judiciary, important media figures, and congressmen—quickly saw the importance of ridding Washington of people whose ideas and methods conflicted with the "procedural consensus" on which successful political leadership depends.

National Leadership in Changing Circumstances

Membership in the national leadership group is not permanent, particularly for individuals, who leave in a variety of ways: defeat, old age, withdrawal. Nor is it permanent for particular groups. New social forces—women's liberation, black power, consumer protest, labor unions—enter the scene, and very often they push aside some established groups. This is called *elite circulation,* a process through which new viewpoints, new groups, and new skills find a place in leadership circles.

The Continuing Skill Revolution

The main job of leadership can be simply stated: Be prepared for and solve the problems of society. This task is unevenly performed. Consider today's social problems: pollution of air and water; congested cities; inflationary costs of social services; and racial, ethnic, and social class tensions. Would these problems be less severe today if previous leaders had been more aware of the drift toward pollution, urban decay, and other current problems? To put the question another way: Today are there signs of future problems that are not noticed by the current leaders but that will crowd the political agenda when today's college students are trying to raise their families?

Such questions are very hard to answer, but they point out an important issue for political recruitment. Leadership skills change as the problems facing society change. We ask, then, whether leadership skills have caught up to social problems. The struggle to keep up is what causes the continuing skill revolution.

The Political Agenda and Leadership Changes In the Depression of the 1930s, none of the traditional economic solutions seemed to work. Then in 1932 the Roosevelt administration took over. Dozens of new social reforms and programs were tried. The people in leadership positions had very different economic and social philosophies from preceding administrations. They had a new range of skills. Out of this "skill revolution" came the New Deal, a collection of government programs and social services and an attitude toward fiscal management unheard of a decade earlier.

This shows the link between a skill revolution and the political agenda. Pressing problems form the agenda. When the right skills are lacking, the problems get worse. When the right skills are pro-

Governor Ella T. Grasso of Connecticut symbolizes the changing status of women in politics.

vided, appropriate programs are begun. What are often called "national crises" occur during the lag time between the emergence of serious problems and the recruitment of people with skills and outlooks to deal with them.

It is helpful to compare the past three decades with the present decade. In the thirty years from 1940 to 1970, the political agenda of the United States was dominated by issues of national security and international politics: World War II, the cold war, the Korean War, the North Atlantic Treaty Organization (NATO) and other mutual security alliances, the Berlin crisis, the arms race and nuclear stockpiling, the missile gap between the United States and the USSR, the Cuban blockade, and, of course, the long-drawn-out war in Vietnam.

This agenda of issues had a great effect on the skills and outlooks recruited into top leadership positions. Thus, for instance, the man elected to the Presidency in 1952, Dwight D. Eisenhower, had no record and few known positions on domestic policy questions. Indeed *both* of the major parties had approached him about running for the Presidency. With national security and international politics dominating public attention, leadership fell into the hands of those skilled at diplomacy and military matters, people like John Foster Dulles, Secretary of State to Eisenhower, or, more recently, Henry Kissinger. The 1950s and 1960s produced the "military-industrial complex," but we should not be surprised that a nation with war, weapons, and security on its mind would turn to the Pentagon, the CIA, and the weapons manufacturers.

Now, however, the military-industrial complex is in disfavor. Americans are dissatisfied with the cold war policies of the past decade, and they were disillusioned by the Vietnam war. Domestic political questions are demanding attention—pollution, drugs, crime, social services, taxes, inflation. This shift in the social-political agenda is, according to some, causing a transfer of political power from the military-industrial complex to the social services-industrial complex, with a demand for leaders able to solve problems in health and education, transportation, consumer protection, urban life, conservation, and environmental quality.

Thus, to sum up, we choose as our political leaders people from particular social groups and people who have proved their ability, but we also choose them from particular skill groups. The challenge of any society is to recruit the skills appropriate to the problems it faces. The drift into one crisis or another is due partly to the failure to recruit leaders able to prepare for and solve social problems. Otherwise the problems grow until they become crises, as when the "problems" of city life become the "crisis" of urbanized America. Some feel that it is past time for a major skill revolution, arguing that those who have managed America over the past decades have been concerned too much with national security and too little with the quality of life for American citizens.

RECRUITMENT OF POLITICAL LEADERS

Table 5.1
Number of Black Members
and Women Members
in Congress, 1947–1974

| Congress[a] | Black Members in the | | Women Members in the | |
	SENATE	HOUSE	SENATE	HOUSE
80th		2	1	7
81st		2	1	9
82nd		2	1	10
83rd		2	3	12
84th		3	1	16
85th		4	1	15
86th		4	1	16
87th		4	2	17
88th		5	2	11
89th		6	2	10
90th	1	5	1	11
91st	1	9	1	10
92nd	1	12	2	13
93rd	1	15	0	14
94th[b]	2	16	0	18

[a] Each congressional session lasts two years. There are a total of 435 members of the House and a total of 100 members of the Senate.

[b] As of November 1974 election.

Source: Based on data from *Current American Government* (Washington, D.C.: *Congressional Quarterly,* Spring 1973), pp. 25–26; and *Current American Government,* Spring 1975, p. 17.

Emergence of New Social Groups

Earlier we pointed out that some social groups provide most of our political leaders. National leadership has long been a white male club. But within this club some important changes have taken place over the years. Its social makeup is not completely fixed. The ministers, lawyers, and wealthy landowners who founded the nation did not expect that a century later the United States would be governed by men who made their millions by building up giant industries. And the industrialists and bankers of the late nineteenth and early twentieth century did not expect that a few decades later they would be sharing power with leaders of powerful labor unions. During this transition white males continued to dominate leadership positions, but the groups they represented changed dramatically.

Now, in the last quarter of the twentieth century, new social groups are getting into the club. Each year more blacks and women are counted among the national leaders. Table 5.1, for example, shows the number who have entered Congress over the past quarter-century. Connecticut has a woman governor, and several large cities have black mayors. Changes are taking place in business, universities, newspapers, hospitals, and law firms as well. It is a slow process but, once started, continues to put pressure on the leadership group.

Summary

A small group of people govern the nation. These are the people who have important positions in the dominant institutions of society. Through these institutions—the banks, universities, govern-

Top leaders in recent years have been those involved in security and diplomatic affairs.

ment agencies, businesses, legislatures—the leaders decide how the resources of the society are used. The level of government spending on the military is such a decision; so is the interest rate on money borrowed by a homeowner, the tuition at colleges and universities, the type of scientific research that is funded.

We have said that leaders are recruited in a way that gives advantages to particular social groups. They share common experiences and background, though they do not agree about the kinds of policies the nation should be following. We have also said that the leadership group is under continual pressure to change, pressure to allow new social groups to have a voice in the governing of the society, and pressure to recruit new skills as the agenda of society changes.

We have not discussed the democratic controls on the leaders. In some ways this whole book is about these controls. Thus we have already discussed the Constitution, with its provision that the nation is to have a government of law, not of men. This certainly is intended to restrict what the leaders can do. And we have reviewed public participation. Later we discuss political parties and elections, which also try to place democratic controls on the leaders. Then also we want to deal with separation of powers, and especially the way the various branches of government must cooperate for public policy to be made.

For democracy to work the leaders must be responsive to the non-leaders. In this chapter we learned that the leaders are a very small group. Throughout the text we will ask how well the democratic promise of government by, for, and of the people is protected.

RECRUITMENT OF POLITICAL
LEADERS

Controversy

Citizens have varying amounts of political influence and involvement. At the bottom are the inactive citizens who care little about political matters and probably do not even bother to vote. Then comes the mass of Americans who vote and are involved in some political activity now and then. Then come the real activists, who are very involved in the political life of their community or of the nation. Then come those who try for public office: the candidates. Then come those who succeed: the officeholders. And these range from minor local jobs up through the ranks to the top national offices.

At each of these levels one would find a population that was more and more "elite" in social and economic terms. At each step upward the portion from high-status families would increase. At each step upward the portion with higher levels of education would increase. Some say this reflects the proper working of American democracy. Others think of it as a major flaw.

One Side

That wealthier and better-educated citizens find their way to the top of American politics implies nothing bad about American democracy. They do so mostly because they choose to do so. Lower-status citizens are less interested. And if because of that they have less influence over the government than their wealthier fellow citizens, it is they who are to blame, not the system. As long as citizens are *free to participate* and *free to run for office,* democracy is working. If some do not take advantage of these opportunities, it does not mean democracy is not working well.

Furthermore, the situation has good results in terms of the kinds of people in positions of leadership. The higher you go, the more qualified the group you find. Recruiting skilled people is difficult under the best of circumstances. Turning to the successful businessmen, lawyers, and civil leaders as candidates for high office means fewer mistakes. These people have shown that they can succeed where the competition is toughest. They have graduated from the hardest schools. They have achieved in highly competitive situations. They have proved that they can run the largest institutions in American society, and governing requires the skill to run such superinstitutions as the Pentagon or the Department of Health, Education and Welfare. We should recruit as top leaders those who have shown such skill.

Earlier we described four young citizens: the Princetonian headed for a career as a corporation executive, the black longshoreman active in local politics, the politically skilled feminist preparing for a career in education, the popular small-town boy who will soon have experience in community planning. The chances of the corporation executive's reaching high political office are much, much greater than those of any of the other three. And he is likely to be the one with the background to grasp the complex problems of American society. The black trade-union activist will know how to develop race-relations programs that make sense for the docks of San Francisco. It is not clear, however, that he will have the experience necessary for a broadly based program on the same issue. A creative program will have to take into account the race relations on Alabama farms, on army bases in Europe, in the sales forces of Boston insurance agencies. Moreover, it will have to coordinate with a program for police colleges in the Department of Justice or a student-exchange program with Africa planned by the Department of State. Perhaps the Princeton graduate—now an IBM executive who spent two years as a consultant in Nairobi, served on the Civil Rights Commission, is a member of the board of trustees of several colleges, and recently advised the Ford Foundation on its program for grants to inner-city schools—is the best person to direct a federal agency on race relations.

We should choose our leaders from the small group of citizens who have proved their ability. It is of course unfortunate that this small group is mostly white, mostly male, and mostly from wealthy and Protestant families. These facts should be changed, but they should be changed by ending race, sex, and class discrimination.

The color or sex or social background of leaders is not at issue. But the skills and outlook are. American society will suffer if it chooses as leaders people of low achievement.

The Other Side

Democracy works only when all citizens have equal voice; the more it fails in this respect, the less effective it is. That the rich and better educated are more active in politics and more successful in climbing the political ladder is therefore a major flaw in American democracy. It is not fair to say poorer citizens do not go far politically because they choose not to. The opportunities to participate are not equal across social groups. If lower-status citizens participate less than others, it is not because they don't care but because they lack resources. If election campaigns cost millions, those who cannot give large sums are not "equally free" to participate effectively. And they are even less likely to be able to run for office themselves.

Nor does this mean that only the "best" make it to the top leadership positions. Maybe they have more education, but there are important skills and outlooks they may not have. The skills that might establish racial harmony, provide decent education and health care, and plan communities as places to enjoy life are not necessarily found in white upper-class males. Leaders should be drawn from the groups who have direct experiences with the problems of American life.

The white corporate executive may have more organizational ability and more advanced education than the black union leader. But whose career is likely to develop the skills necessary to ease racial tension within the American working class? Might not the feminist be able to bring fresh approaches to the Department of Health, Education and Welfare? And might not the Jerseyville town planner be sensitive to protecting community well-being against urban sprawl?

American society may be short-changing itself by always choosing leaders from the successful business and professional classes.

6

Political Beliefs in America

To understand American politics we must understand the American people—their beliefs and feelings about politics and government, and how they act in politics. The point seems clear, but it is often ignored. Some observers think politics can be understood by studying the formal structures of government. If we asked them what the important features of the American political system are, they would reply: In the United States we have a presidential rather than a parliamentary system; we have a federal system with power divided between the national and the state governments; we have a Constitution with formal guarantees of liberty. These features of the formal structure of government are of course important. But in this chapter we deal with something more basic—the beliefs and feelings of the American people about the American political system.

There is a simple reason why knowing the formal structure of government is not enough unless one understands the beliefs of those who live under that structure: Those beliefs affect how the political structure works. This lesson has been learned the hard way by those who have tried to transfer political forms from one society to another. A classic example is the Weimar Republic in Germany, founded after World War I. This new republic replaced the empire of the Kaisers and had one of the most carefully worked-out democratic constitutions ever written. But the constitution never took root among the people—it was not respected; the democratic institutions it set up were challenged from the left and the right. And after a short, stormy existence the new democracy fell to the totalitarian rule of the Nazis.

Similar results have been seen in many of the new nations in Africa and Asia. Constitutions have been borrowed from countries with long histories of functioning democracy—Britain or the United States. These constitutions provide for the basic institutions of democracy: periodic elections, the right of political opposition, basic freedoms, and so forth. But in many cases the democratic governments have been replaced by military regimes or one-party states. The explanation given is that the institutions were "motivationally hollow"; the democratic forms were there but the democratic beliefs were not. This experience of other nations has reinforced a widely held belief about American democracy: that it has its roots in the "hearts and minds" of the American people.

Political Beliefs and Democracy

What is the set of citizen beliefs that are most basic to democracy? Many agree that the following are particularly important:

1. If democracy is to *survive*, citizens must believe the government is *legitimate*, that is, that it deserves the support of the citizens.

2. If democracy is to *survive*, citizens must support the *democratic rules of the game;* they must be in favor of key democratic procedures such as free speech and free elections. If citizens do not believe the government is legitimate and do not support the rules of the democratic game, democracy will not long survive, for it will have little public support. But democracy depends on more than support for its rules. In a democracy the government is supposed to respond to the preferences of the public. And it is kept responsive when citizens elect candidates whose policies they approve of. Thus political scientists think citizens have to have another characteristic.

3. If democracy is to *work,* citizens must make *rational choices* as voters. They must decide what policies they prefer and vote for candidates who support those policies. In this way the government becomes responsive to the preferences of the public.

Political scientists have argued that belief in the legitimacy of the government, support for the rules of the game, and rational voting are basic to democracy. But it was hard to know whether the American public actually held this set of beliefs. Fortunately in recent years social scientists have developed such methods as the in-depth sample survey of public attitudes. We can look at actual data about the beliefs of the American public. As we shall see, the public does hold the beliefs just listed, but only in part.

Legitimacy of the Government

If democracy is to work, citizens must be committed to it. And that support must be continuous, not given one day and taken away the next. The term *legitimacy* is used to refer to the belief that those in authority deserve support and that the laws they pass must be obeyed. It is easy to see why legitimacy is basic to democracy. Democracy depends on *voluntary consent* of citizens. If most citizens do not give such consent, the government is likely to rely more and more on force. Citizens, in turn, are likely to be attracted to political movements opposed to democratic government.

Do Americans give their trust and loyalty to the political process? One way such trust and loyalty is shown is through commitment to the *symbols* of American democracy. Over the years studies have found that Americans have, in general, a deep commitment to the symbols of the American political community. Reverence for the flag and the Constitution is taught in the schools and maintained throughout the life of the average American.

A major study of democratic attitudes in 1959 compared the political beliefs of Americans with those of citizens in four other countries. (See Table 6.1.) The researchers asked what citizens were proud of about their countries. Two results are important. For one thing, few Americans—only 4 percent—replied that there was nothing they were proud of, a response showing general hostility to the political community. (In the other four countries, the portions who were proud of "nothing" ranged from 10 percent to 27 percent.) More in-

Respect for the flag and other symbols of government authority is taught to American children at a young age.

	United States	Great Britain	Germany	Italy	Mexico
Percent who are proud of "nothing"	4%	10%	15%	27%	16%
Percent who are proud of the political institutions	85%	46%	7%	3%	30%

Source: Based on data from Gabriel Almond and Sidney Verba, *The Civic Culture: Political Attitudes and Democracy in Five Nations* (Princeton, N. J.: Princeton University Press, 1963).

teresting is what they were proud of. Compared with the citizens in other nations, Americans showed pride in political aspects of society—the Constitution, political freedom, democracy. Eighty-five percent of those interviewed in the United States—twice the percentage in the next-highest country—mentioned such political aspects.

American politics has changed a lot since 1959. But the basic attitude toward the political system does not seem to have changed as much as one might expect. In 1972 a sample of the American public was asked to choose between two statements: "I am proud of many things about our form of government" and "I can't find much about our form of government to be proud of." Eighty-six percent chose the first alternative. And in response to the question of whether there is a need for major change in our form of government, only 15 percent said that a "big change is needed."[1]

The public may still respect the American form of government, but it has become much more dissatisfied with the way the government has been run. Over the years researchers have asked citizens questions about their trust and confidence in the government: Do they think the government is run for all the people, or for a few special interests; do they trust the government to do what is right? In the past decade there has been a large increase in the portion of the public that responds in ways that show dissatisfaction. (See Figure 6.1.) In 1958, 18 percent of the public thought the government was for the benefit of a few; by 1973, this percentage had risen to 67 percent.[2]

Along with the decline in trust in the government has come a general decline in optimism about the future. One group of scholars has been studying the hopes and fears of Americans for a number of years. In 1959 and 1964 they found that Americans had a clear view of steady progress: The present was better than the past; the future would be better yet. But in 1971 they found a striking change. The citizens viewed the last half of the 1960s as a time of decay, not progress. Things had gotten worse. They still believed America

[1] Jack Citrin, "The Political Relevance of Trust in Government," *American Political Science Review*, 68 (September 1974), 975.

[2] Data for 1958 from University of Michigan Survey Research Center election study of that year. Data for 1973 from National Opinion Research Center study.

Figure 6.1
The Growth of Distrust in the
Government

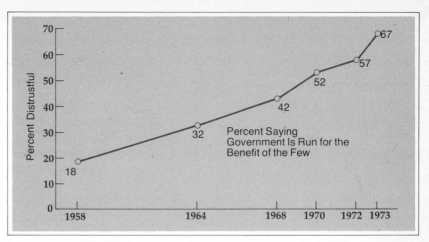

Source: Data for 1958–1972: Survey Research Center studies, Institute for Social Research, University of Michigan; data for 1973: National Opinion Research Center study, University of Chicago.

Declining confidence in
government policies eventually
leads to alienation from the
system of government.

would recover lost ground and hoped for future progress, but the view of continuous progress had been shattered.[3]

The decline in optimism and trust in political leaders had begun well before the Watergate scandal. Watergate increased public dissatisfaction, but the decline in confidence seems to have its roots in a belief that the government could not cope with the many serious problems it faced during the late 1960s and in the 1970s—racial tension, Vietnam, law and order, pollution, and so on.

The long-term implications of this decline in trust in government are unclear. Some believe the decline is a temporary reaction to specific policies and personalities. Others argue that there is a deeper *alienation* in the land that could threaten democracy. Thus far the evidence shows that the public is dissatisfied with political leadership, not yet with the "form of government." They seem to be saying that "the system is all right; it is just working badly." But a long period of dissatisfaction with "the way the system works" might lead to a more general loss of legitimacy for the political process as a whole. As yet there is little evidence that this is happening. But the firm support for the government once found among the American people is no longer there.

Citizens' Belief in Their Political Efficacy   Another citizen attitude is closely related to belief in the legitimacy of the government is *political efficacy*. This is the belief of citizens that they have a voice in the government. Democratic government is supposed to be responsive to the people. If citizens do not believe they can influence the government, they are less likely to feel that it deserves support.

Do Americans have a sense of political efficacy? In general, yes; but as with trust in government, the number who feel that way has

[3] Albert H. Cantril and Charles W. Roll, Jr., *The Hopes and Fears of the American People* (New York: Universe Books, 1971).

Table 6.2
Can You Do Something
About a Regulation
You Consider Unfair?

	United States	Great Britain	Germany	Italy	Mexico
Percent saying yes in relation to local government	77%	78%	62%	51%	52%
Percent saying yes in relation to national government	75%	62%	38%	28%	38%

Source: Based on data from Gabriel Almond and Sidney Verba, *The Civic Culture: Political Attitudes and Democracy in Five Nations* (Princeton, N. J.: Princeton University Press, 1963).

declined recently. Most Americans believe the vote is effective for controlling government officials, and they believe government officials are basically responsive to the people. In short, they feel that they have some political influence. If we compare Americans to citizens of other nations, we find that they are more likely than most others to think they can have some effect on a local government regulation or a law of Congress they consider unfair or unjust. (See Table 6.2.) About three out of four Americans say they could do something about such a regulation. The percentages are generally smaller elsewhere.

American citizens, this suggests, do not feel helpless before the government. And, to some extent at least, believing they are not helpless makes them less helpless. The same study shows that those who feel able to influence the government are likely to try.

In addition, Americans believe one has an obligation as a citizen to try to influence the government. When asked what role the individual should play in his local community, a majority of Americans replied that they should take some *active* part — a portion higher than in the other countries studied.

The data reported here come from a 1959 study. How have things changed since then? We have no information from other nations to see if the relative position of the United States has changed. But we do have periodic measures of "citizen efficacy" during the 1950s and 1960s. And the best evidence shows that feelings of efficacy rose in the 1950s and fell in the 1960s and early 1970s. In 1952, 69 percent of a sample agreed that "people have some say about what the government does"; by 1960 the figure had risen to 72 percent. But by 1973 the portion agreeing with that statement had fallen to 49 percent. The figure is still high — higher probably than in other nations — but the decline is significant.[4]

Support for the Democratic Rules of the Game

Agreement on the "rules of the game" means agreement on the basic procedures of democracy such as periodic elections and free speech. Again it is easy to see why some have argued for the need

[4] Data from University of Michigan Survey Research Center studies.

to agree on the rules of the game. The argument goes as follows. Certain political elements are necessary if a democracy is to work: Opposing groups must be able to organize and to express their views; there must be public control over officials through periodic elections; government leaders must be willing to step down when the voters choose other leaders. These elements are written into the Constitution and formal laws. However, they survive only because the people of the United States are committed to them. The Constitution states that the winning Presidential candidate replaces the former President. The change takes place, however, not only because it is in the Constitution but also because there is agreement that this is the way things should be. Supporters of both parties—even that of the loser—agree that it is right for the winner of a Presidential election to take office.

Those who argue that the survival of democracy depends on the commitment of the citizens to democratic procedures stress the importance of citizen support for free speech. The Bill of Rights may provide formal guarantees of free speech, but unless the public supports the right of free speech the Bill of Rights will be meaningless. Democracy depends, they claim, on the willingness of the majority to tolerate unpopular political views.

If Americans agree on these basic rules, so the argument goes, they will be able to disagree on other issues. Should there be federal control of the railroads? Should there be laws against abortion? Americans disagree on such matters, sometimes quite sharply. But as long as all tolerate the right of opponents to express themselves and as long as they accept the outcome of the dispute when it is settled according to the rules of the game, democracy survives.

Do Americans in fact agree with the rules of the democratic game? In part the answer is implied in the fact that the symbols they are committed to include the Constitution and the Bill of Rights. When they talk about the political institutions they are proud of, they mention the symbols of democracy. Furthermore, several studies have shown that the American people generally agree with the principles of democratic government. (By "generally" we mean that usually more than nine out of ten agree.) They agree that the rights of minorities to free speech should be protected, that all people should have the right to vote, that political leaders should be responsive to the people, and that democracy works best when there is strong competition between political parties.[5] For example, in the early 1970s the Harris poll found that 91 percent agreed that "every citizen has the right to express any opinion he wants to" and only 5 percent disagreed.[6] In short, most Americans support basic rules of the democratic game.

[5] James W. Prothro and Charles M. Grigg, "Fundamental Principles of Democracy: Bases of Agreement and Disagreement," *Journal of Politics*, 22 (Spring 1960), 276–294; Herbert McClosky, "Consensus and Ideology in American Politics," *American Political Science Review*, 58 (June 1964), 361–382.
[6] Louis Harris, *The Anguish of Change* (New York: Norton, 1973), p. 278.

A greater number of citizens support free speech for a group of neighbors than for black militants.

Commitment to Democratic Procedure—How Consistent Is It?

But there is other research on the political beliefs of Americans showing that commitment to the rules of democratic procedure seems to be greatest in the abstract; it seems less firm in particular cases. The same American population agreeing that free speech in general is a good thing is less sure certain groups should have that freedom. When one asks if groups with unpopular views (communists, socialists) should be allowed to make speeches, the American people are not sure speech should be that free. Indeed a large portion of Americans are opposed to letting groups of this sort make speeches in their community, and large numbers would remove their books from the local library. For communists or atheists, about two-thirds would oppose such freedom.[7] The same Harris poll that found in the early 1970s over nine out of ten Americans in favor of free speech in general, found that two out of three favored outlawing "organizations that preach the violent overthrow of the government." One study in Tallahassee, Florida, found that there was broad agreement that minority groups should have full right to participate in politics. But among the same people 42 percent thought that a black should not be allowed to run for mayor of their city.[8]

In theory one should favor free speech no matter how one feels about the speaker or the content of his speech — at least if the speaker does not directly preach violence or breaking the law. In 1971 the National Opinion Research Center studied this subject. It is clear from this study that citizens would allow free speech for things they favor but not for things they oppose. "Should a group of people be allowed to circulate an anti-pollution petition?" Ninety-three percent of the people said yes. "Should a group be allowed to circulate a petition calling for the legalization of marijuana?" Only a bare majority, 52 percent, said yes.

[7] Samuel Stouffer, *Communism, Conformity and Civil Liberties.*
[8] Prothro and Grigg, 294.

Table 6.3
Citizens Approve Free
Speech When They
Like the Group

	Percent Saying Yes
Should a *group of your neighbors* be allowed to circulate a petition?	95%
Should a *group of black militants* be allowed to circulate a petition?	69%
Should a *group of radical students* be allowed to circulate a petition?	71%

Source: National Opinion Research Center study, University of Chicago, 1971.

Table 6.4
Citizens Favor Free Speech
More When They Approve
of the Views of the Speakers

	Percent Saying Yes
Should a group be allowed to petition *to stop a factory from polluting the air?*	93%
Should a group be allowed to circulate a petition expressing *concern with crime* in their community?	95%
Should a group be allowed to circulate a petition calling for the *legalization of marijuana?*	52%
Should a group be allowed to circulate a petition calling on the government to make sure that *blacks can buy and rent homes in white neighborhoods?* (asked of whites only)	70%
Should a group be allowed to circulate a petition calling on the government to *prevent blacks from buying or renting in white neighborhoods?* (asked of blacks only)	51%

Source: National Opinion Research Center study, University of Chicago, 1971.

Similarly people would allow freedom of speech for those they like but not for those they dislike. Ninety-five percent of the population said yes when asked if "a group of your neighbors" should be allowed to circulate petitions to ask the government to act on some issue—a clear commitment to democratic procedures. But only about 70 percent thought that "black militants" or "radical students" should be allowed to circulate a petition. (See Table 6.3 and 6.4.)

That citizens like free speech in general does not mean they support it where it really counts—when the speakers come from unpopular groups with unpopular views. The commitment to democratic rules is hardly meaningful if they are applied narrowly.

So the data present a puzzle. If democracy depends on commitment to the values of democracy, democracy would be weak indeed if the values are supported only in general terms but are not supported when it comes to specific application. But fortunately we can go one step further. We have seen that citizens take a strong position in favor of democratic freedom when asked general questions and a more limited one when asked more concrete questions. But how in fact do they act? They act differently from what one might expect from some of their answers. In Tallahassee, Florida—where 42 percent of a sample said a black should not be allowed to run for mayor —a black *had* campaigned for mayor a few months earlier. No one had tried to stop him. And in the communities where citizens said various unpopular speakers should not be allowed to speak and their books should be removed from the library, these opinions were not acted upon.

Thus the position of the American people on the rules of the democratic game is by no means clear. Americans support the rules in general. When you ask about specific cases, they are less supportive of democracy, but when you get even closer to reality and ask about what they do, you find that they do not act on these political views. One thing this tells us is that people are not consistent; their general values may not be consistent with the specific ways they apply their values, and their values and attitudes may not be consistent with their actions.

One possible explanation of why the citizens of Tallahassee would report in large numbers that they thought a black should not be allowed to run for mayor and yet do nothing to stop him is that they were expressing negative feelings toward blacks when the question about a black running for mayor was asked, but their actions were guided by the more general value of equal opportunity to run for office. And this may in part be true. But there is another explanation. Individuals express political views to researchers, but often these views are lightly held and are not acted upon. Studies suggest that much of what individuals say about public issues during an interview represents positions in which they believe, but not very strongly, or at least not strongly enough to act upon.

This is not true of all Americans. For some, politics is a very important activity. The people that are politically concerned and active form, as we have seen, a minority of the population. They are more likely to have advanced education, and they are particularly committed to democratic rules. Like the rest of the public, political activists agree with the general principles of democracy, but they also support these principles when they are applied to specific cases.

Thus the study that found Americans—up to two-thirds—opposing free speech for various unpopular groups also found that most *leaders* of local organizations or local government officials were in favor of allowing unpopular speech. (See Table 6.5.) Two-thirds of a cross-section of the American people would bar a communist from speaking in their community, but a majority of the leaders (though a bare majority) would allow it. Or, as another study found, almost one-third of Americans thought that the majority has the right to deny freedom to minorities; a much smaller percentage—7 percent— of the political leaders (in this case, delegates to the national conventions) took this undemocratic position.[9]

These data suggest that democratic values may be less firmly held

9 McClosky, 365.

Table 6.5
Community Leaders Are More
Tolerant Than Ordinary
Citizens of Unpopular Views

	Among a Cross-Section of Citizens	Among Community Leaders
Percent saying they would allow an admitted communist to speak in public	27%	51%
Percent saying they would allow a socialist to speak in public	58%	84%
Percent categorized as "more tolerant" of minorities	31%	66%

Source: Based on data from Samuel Stouffer, *Communism, Conformity and Civil Liberties.* Copyright © 1955 by Samuel A. Stouffer. Reprinted by permission of John Wiley & Sons, Inc.

among most of the American people than is generally believed, but stronger among those who are likely to have a greater voice in how things in fact are run — those who are active in politics and in organizations. Democracy may be based on democratic political commitments, but it may be a narrow base.

Several additional points can be made — some discouraging, some encouraging for democracy. A discouraging point is that a large group in the population is not in favor of political freedom for unpopular groups and may therefore tolerate antidemocratic politics. This discouraging thought must be measured against two others. For one thing, the general commitment to the values of democracy — vague though it may be — counteracts the less democratic views. At least it provides a set of values one can appeal to. And further, all evidence shows that commitment to democratic values — in both the general and the concrete sense — is strongest among people with higher education. As the population becomes more and more educated — as will happen over time, since the college population is growing — one can expect a large portion of the population to have political views that are consistently democratic.

Summary

We have looked at some data on the beliefs of Americans and compared them to what we would expect of a democratic public. The data and the expectations were similar in some ways, different in others.

We expected that citizens would believe the government is legitimate and give it trust and support. In general, citizens do so, but they have recently expressed strikingly high levels of distrust for those in the government. We expected that citizens would be committed to the democratic rules of the game. In general, they are; the commitment is vaguer in specific cases. However, this lack of clear commitment to democratic values is offset by the fact that those who are least consistently committed are the least active.

In short, the system works, but not exactly as democratic theory might have us believe. There is commitment to democratic values and to the political system, but it may not be as strong as is generally thought.

The Citizen as Rational Voter

We have been discussing the amount of agreement in the American public on the basic rules of democracy. But democracy involves a clash of specific interests as well. Politics is about the allocation of benefits to members of the society and the clash among citizens for a larger share of those benefits.

How can citizens take part in this conflict so that the government is as responsive as possible to their interests? Again democratic theory has an answer: The citizen acts as a *rational voter*. What is a rational voter? It is someone who knows his or her own interests, who looks around to see which party or candidate is most likely to favor those interests and who votes accordingly.

Do citizens behave as rational voters? Studies of the American public give us an answer. And again we will find that citizens behave somewhat like the theory would have us believe, but not exactly.

The Party-Oriented Voter

Detailed survey studies of the American electorate began in the 1950s. The classic study was conducted by a group of University of Michigan scholars and reported in their book, *The American Voter*. They found that the American voter was quite different from the rational voter of democratic theory.

For one thing, the public was relatively ill informed about political matters. It often lacked the information on the positions of candidates that would be needed in deciding which candidate to support. Even more striking was the fact that citizens did not appear to have well-formed opinions on a large number of public issues. They might give researchers answers to questions on all sorts of issues, but the answers were usually not carefully formed opinions. (In one study a researcher asked a sample of Americans their opinion on the "Metallic Metals Act." The act did not exist, but 70 percent had an opinion for or against it.)[10]

Furthermore, these studies showed that most Americans did not think about politics in ways that were familiar to better-informed citizens. Journalists, scholars, and politicians themselves are likely to have consistent positions on many issues. One can call them "liberal" or "conservative" or "radical" because they will take a consistent stand on a variety of political matters. Thus a liberal is

[10] Stanley J. Payne, *The Art of Asking Questions* (Princeton, N.J.: Princeton University Press, 1951), p. 18.

someone who takes the following positions: He favors faster school desegregation and supports programs to reduce segregation in housing; on matters of social welfare he favors increased federal spending; on foreign affairs he favors a more conciliatory attitude toward the communist world. And the conservative would hold the opposite position: He would want to go slowly on integration, reduce welfare spending, and take a hard line in foreign affairs. In each case the positions on specific issues would be the parts of a more general outlook.

The studies of the American public in the 1950s and early 1960s found that the average American rarely held such clear political views. People rarely thought in liberal or conservative terms when they evaluated candidates. Most striking was the fact that there was almost no relationship between a citizen's position on one issue and his position on other issues. If he was conservative on matters of race, the average citizen was as likely to be liberal as conservative on matters of welfare policy or foreign policy. Any one position could not be predicted from other positions.

This had important implications for American politics. It meant the results of elections did not depend on the issues, since the public was uninformed about where the candidates stood on the issues and, in any case, did not hold consistent positions on those issues. The lack of clear positions on issues also meant there was less chance of a sharp division of the American people into conservative and liberal camps. The citizen who was conservative on one matter was likely to be liberal on another—and therefore would not easily fit into one camp or another.

Thus it is no wonder citizens were not rational voters. They could not vote for the candidate whose position they favored because they did not have information about the positions of the candidates and, worse, did not have clear and consistent opinions that could guide their vote. Why did they vote the way they did? Researchers found that one of the major forces determining a citizen's vote was his or her *partisan identification*. Seventy-seven percent of the public identified with one or the other of the major parties. This identification appeared to be a long-term and stable one. Most citizens inherited such identification from their parents (just as one might inherit religion), and most people kept it throughout their lives.

Furthermore, party identification was a key to the vote. Most citizens voted for the candidate of the party they identified with. This was especially true in races for such offices as congressman. In 1956, 91 percent of the voters stuck to their party in the congressional race. Voters might leave their party to vote for a popular Presidential candidate—millions of Democrats voted for Eisenhower in 1952 and 1956. But they did so because of his personal popularity, not because they agreed with his issue positions. And though they crossed the line to vote for the candidate of another party, they continued to consider themselves Democrats.

Figure 6.2
Frequency of Evaluation of
Candidates in Terms of Party
Ties, Personal Attributes, and
Issue Positions

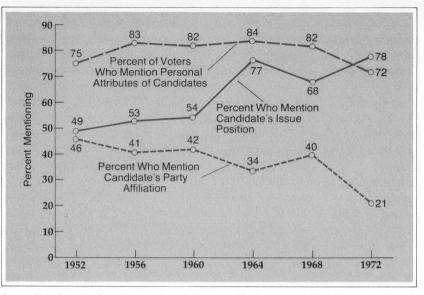

Source: Based on data from Survey Research Center studies, Institute for Social Research, University of Michigan.

Studies done during the 1950s found the American voter quite different from the model of the rational voter. The voter identified with a political party and voted along party lines. If he left his party, it was not because he disagreed with the candidate of his own party.

But the 1950s were an unusual period in American history: A popular World War II hero, Dwight Eisenhower, was in the White House; there were no serious domestic or foreign problems; and political conflict was relatively calm. In periodic studies since then we can trace some important changes in the public.

Over the years since the 1950s, citizens seem to have become more issue oriented. More and more citizens have relatively consistent political attitudes. If they are conservative on one issue, they are conservative on other issues; if they are liberal on one, they are liberal on others. Political opinions are less random than in earlier years. Furthermore, citizens more often judge candidates on the basis of their issue positions. In each Presidential election since 1952, the University of Michigan Survey Research Center has asked citizens what they liked and disliked about the candidates. Some people mention the personality of the candidate; some mention the party of the candidate ("I like X because he is a good Democrat"); others talk about the issues the candidate stands for. Figure 6.2 shows the percentages of the public in each of the elections since 1952 that mention the personality of the candidate, his party, and his issue positions. Note that citizens still give a lot of attention to the personality of the candidate. About 80 percent mention this in each election year. But the striking change is the fall in the percentage of citizens who like or dislike a candidate on the basis of their party

Figure 6.3

As the Correlation of Party Identification and the Vote Has Gone Down, the Correlation of Issue Position and the Vote Has Gone Up

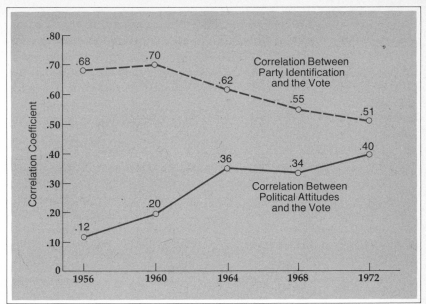

Source: Based on data from Survey Research Center studies, Institute for Social Research, University of Michigan.

affiliation coupled with the rise in the portion of citizens who judge candidates by their issue positions.

There are many indications that political parties are no longer as important as they used to be. In 1956, almost all Americans—77 percent—had a long-term commitment to one or the other party; by 1974, the percentage had fallen to about 60 percent. A majority still identified with one or the other party, but the portion had fallen quite a bit. More important, perhaps, young voters coming into the electorate at the end of the 1960s and early 1970s were as likely to call themselves independents as to identify with one of the major parties—a big change from earlier times. And even among those who continued to identify with a party, more and more were voting for the other party's candidate or splitting their tickets.

And as the importance of party as a guide to the vote has gone down, the importance of issues has gone up. Figure 6.3 shows the correlations between the issue positions of citizens and their vote and between their party identification and the vote. The higher the correlation between issue position and the vote, the more it means citizens vote in ways consistent with their issue positions (that is, vote for a liberal candidate if they are liberal themselves, for a conservative if they are conservative). The higher the correlation between party identification and the vote, the more it means citizens vote in ways consistent with their party affiliation (vote for a Democrat if they are Democrats, for a Republican if they are Republicans). Note how as the correlation of party identification with the vote declines, the correlation of issue position with the vote goes up.

This does not mean the average voter carefully weighs the issue positions of candidates before deciding how to vote. Studies continue to show that the public often lacks basic political information. In 1972 a study found that only about half of the citizens (53 percent) know the name and party affiliation of *one* of their senators; only 36 percent could name both senators and identify their parties.[11] And even when issues become more important, as Figure 6.3 shows us it does in recent elections, the correlation of issue position with the vote is still weaker than that of party identification and the vote. In short, citizens are voting on the issues and are less closely tied to their parties. But this does not mean citizens have become fully rational voters.

Where Do Political Attitudes Come From?

When individuals are acting—either by giving an opinion or by voting—they are likely to seek guidance. How do they know their opinions or choices are right? Citizens usually have no direct information about an issue: "What really is going on in China?" "Who is to blame for inflation?" When a citizen cannot test his opinions against reality, he tests them against the opinions of others. Or, if he has an opinion on a subject but others have a different opinion, he is likely to change his opinion. This is especially true if those "others" are individuals or groups whose views he respects or from whom he wants acceptance.

Who are these "others"? They include peers, political authorities such as the President or Supreme Court, and one's political party.

Peers

Studies have shown that groups of individuals in contact with one another are likely to have similar opinions. This is particularly true of what are called primary groups—friends, families, neighbors, and others who come into face-to-face contact. In part the opinions of members of such groups are similar because they are in similar real circumstances—members of primary groups tend to come from the same occupations, to live near one another, and so forth. Thus they may face similar political and social problems.

In addition, individuals will change their opinions to fit those that are dominant in the groups they belong to. This becomes a way of increasing one's acceptance by such groups, reduces tensions with friends and relatives, and gives the individual some sense that his view is right—others agree with him when he gives his opinion.

Is this irrational behavior? Yes and no. It may be irrational in the sense that an individual's positions—how to vote, what to do about inflation—are not based on the "real" political situation. In other

[11] U.S. Senate Subcommittee on Intergovernmental Relations of the Committee on Government Operations, *Confidence and Concern: Citizens View Their Government*, December 3, 1973.

words, they are not based on consideration of the issues or on the merits of a candidate. Rather, they are derived from social forces within the group—the desire to be socially accepted, for instance. On the other hand, under certain circumstances this may be a reasonable way to come to a political position (given that one cannot afford the time and full effort to find out all the information on an issue). The opinions of one's associates are perhaps as good a guide as any to political beliefs.

Political Authorities

Another place one can turn for guidance in political uncertainty are leading political authorities. The Supreme Court holds such authority for many Americans. If it has taken a position, many Americans feel it must be the right one. Another such figure is the President. In one sense he may be less useful than the Supreme Court as a guide for public opinion, since he represents only one opinion and one political party, while the Supreme Court is a non-partisan institution representing nine opinions. But the President is well covered by the news media, so his views are widely known and usually respected. This is particularly true on issues that are "distant" from the average American, such as foreign policy.

During the war in Vietnam, for instance, observers noticed an interesting fact. Over time, popular support for the war declined. Polls showed a steady drop in the portion of the people who thought the President was doing a good job with Vietnam. But whenever the President did something dramatic—increasing bombing or stopping bombing, taking a new hard line or a softer line—the portion approving his activities went up, only to fall again shortly. The increase in Presidential support when he made a dramatic announcement was due largely to his importance in the public mind and the willingness of the people to be guided by him in matters they do not understand.

The Watergate scandal and the resignation of President Nixon probably made citizens less likely to think of the President as an authority figure. But the President will probably continue to hold a dominant role as a source of political beliefs. No other figure gets as much attention from the public.

One's Political Party

For a long time party identification was a major source of political opinions. And though its importance has faded somewhat, it remains an important guide on many issues. Issues themselves are complicated, and they change all the time. Furthermore, a candidate's position on an issue may be unclear. It is therefore understandable that many citizens use their party as a guide to political positions. It represents a handy anchor-point for political beliefs in a rapidly changing world.

Currents and Crosscurrents

In this chapter we have been looking at the American public in rather broad terms, and one may get the impression that all Americans are the same. But that is not the message of this chapter. Indeed when we look more closely at American opinion, what seems at first glance like consensus — say, on democratic values — appears on closer study to represent much greater variety of opinion. All (or at least most) Americans agree with the general principles of democracy, but when it comes to specific cases the portion supporting these principles falls to one-third, one-half, or two-thirds, depending on the groups we are talking about. And figures such as one-third or one-half taking a particular position indicate just the opposite of consensus. They indicate quite a bit of disagreement.

Social Bases of Political Conflicts

So far we have not asked which groups disagree with which in American society. This is, of course, one of the main questions about politics in any society: What groups of the population are opposed to one another, or, in other words, what are the social bases of political conflicts? In the United States there are many such bases — people in different regions, people with different occupations, people of different races, ages, religions, or ethnic origins may well have different political views. This theme is so important that we shall devote the next chapter to it. The struggle among opposing groups — and the problem of which groups are important — goes to the heart of American politics. Here we want to glance at some of the different viewpoints of such groups in terms of the underlying set of American political values.

There are, as just suggested, many ways to divide up the American population: into northerners and southerners, men and women, young and old, rich and poor, black and white — that is, by region or sex or age or income or race — and many other ways as well. Each such division of the population would reveal some interesting differences in political viewpoint. But when it comes to some of the basic political beliefs we have been discussing in this chapter — basic commitment to political freedoms, sense of ability to influence the government, basic trust in the government, and basic sense of obligation to participate in politics — many of these divisions of the population would reveal little difference in overall attitudes. Although there are some differences, inhabitants of different regions, the young and the old, men and women do not differ very much on these basic political principles.

The division of the population that makes the most difference in attitude on these basic matters is that between the better educated, on the one hand, and the less well educated, on the other. We have already seen that commitment to democratic values is strongest among political activists and leaders of organizations. This is probably because such commitment is most often found among people of higher education, and such people are also likely to be the political activists and the organization leaders.

The model of the democratic citizen — a person committed to the values of democracy, with a strong sense of obligation to participate, and with well-thought-out and consistent political views — does not fit the American population very well, but it fits the educated part best. Americans, as we have seen, are much more likely than citizens in other countries to believe a citizen should be active in his local community — an important part of the democratic model. But the portion who feel this obligation is different at different levels of education. Only a third of those citizens who have a primary education feel such an obligation, in contrast with two-thirds among the college educated. Or consider the sense of ability to influence the government. In 1972 citizens were asked whether they could do anything about an unjust or corrupt public official. Fifty-eight percent said yes. But among those with only a grade school education 35 percent said yes, while among the college educated 71 percent said yes.[12]

Black Americans and White Americans

Suppose we turn from the average white middle-class American to those who have generally been deprived of the full benefits of citizenship and of the full opportunity to participate in its political life — the blacks, the Chicanos, the Appalachian poor. What are their political attitudes? One might expect less general belief in the "system," more demand for rapid change. Detailed data are hard to get

[12] Ibid.

for all deprived minority groups, but we know quite a bit about the political attitudes of blacks. And what we know confirms that they only partly share the outlooks of the average white American.

In some ways black and white Americans have similar political attitudes. When it comes to some general views about the American political system, we do not find as much difference as we might expect. Yet when asked about the workings of the government as it affects them, blacks respond much more negatively than whites.

Consider the kind of treatment citizens expect from officials of the government. A study of political attitudes found that Americans were much more likely to expect equal treatment in a governmental office than citizens in most other nations. Table 6.6 shows how different the attitude of the average American is from that of the citizen in, say, Italy or Mexico. The American has much more trust in governmental agencies. Indeed the percentages expecting equal treatment are so different that the authors of that study suggest that citizens in the United States and in Mexico live in "different political worlds." The majority of Americans expect fair treatment; Mexicans are much less likely to.

But it can also be said that the average black American lives in a different world from the average white American. Consider the difference between the races on expectations of equal treatment, as shown in Table 6.7. Almost 90 percent of white Americans expect equal treatment from the government; a little less than half of the blacks have such expectations.

These differences between blacks and whites, first noted in 1959, have appeared again and again in more recent studies. Most dramatic have been differences between the races in attitudes toward

Table 6.6
Attitudes Regarding Equal Treatment in Government Offices in Five Nations

	United States	Great Britain	Germany	Italy	Mexico
Percent saying they expect equal treatment in a government office	83%	83%	65%	53%	42%

Source: Based on data from Gabriel Almond and Sidney Verba, *The Civic Culture: Political Attitudes and Democracy in Five Nations* (Princeton, N.J.: Princeton University Press, 1963).

Table 6.7
Attitudes Regarding Equal Treatment in Government Offices Among Black and White Americans

	White Americans	Black Americans
Percent saying they expect equal treatment in a governmental office	87%	49%

Source: Based on data from Gabriel Almond and Sidney Verba, *The Civic Culture: Political Attitudes and Democracy in Five Nations* (Princeton, N.J.: Princeton University Press, 1963).

the police. Urban blacks have less confidence in the honesty of the police, less favorable expectations of fair treatment by them, and less favorable experiences in dealing with them. Furthermore, blacks are less satisfied with public services in their neighborhoods; they complain more about high prices and the quality of the goods in neighborhood stores.

In sum, when it comes down to their actual lives and their relations with the government, blacks differ sharply from whites in attitude.

Do the different outlooks of black and white Americans mean the consensus one sees in the "average" American covers up basic differences when one looks more closely at a minority group like the blacks? Since the issue of race relations is a major one in American politics today, it is useful to look fairly closely at some evidence before answering the question.

Racial Hostility

Have blacks and whites become more hostile to each other over the years? Certainly someone comparing the newspapers in the early 1950s with those in the early 1970s would have to conclude that hostility had grown. Twenty years ago one read little about racial issues in the papers; today hardly a day goes by without some news of racial conflict. But this is merely to say that racial differences have come into the open. It does not mean bitter race hatred has developed.

In 1971 the National Opinion Research Center asked people how they felt about various groups in America. Those interviewed were given a scale on which they could rate various groups in terms of how much they liked them. Figure 6.4 shows how white and black Americans differ in the ratings they give each other. Note that whites have a more favorable view of whites than they have of blacks; blacks favor blacks more than whites. That is not unexpected. More important, both racial groups place the opposite group on the favorable side of the neutral point. On the average, blacks do not say they dislike whites; whites do not say they dislike blacks.

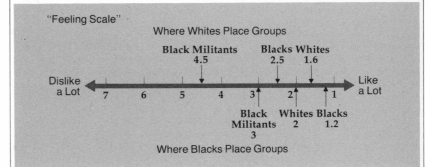

Figure 6.4
How Whites and Blacks Feel About Each Other and About Black Militants

Source: National Opinion Research Center study, University of Chicago, 1971.

The racial groups differ in their views toward black militants. Whites, on the average, say they dislike such militants and place them far down the scale. Blacks are not hostile to black militants. But even if blacks are more favorable toward black militants than are whites, they still rate them only neutrally. Indeed the average black reports more favorable views of whites than of black militants. The data suggest a major difference in viewpoint, but not racial hatred.

In the years since the racial issue "exploded" in America, white attitudes toward blacks have undergone striking, but somewhat ambivalent, changes. In general, whites have become more favorable to blacks, more responsive to their demands. In 1949, the National Opinion Research Center asked if "Negroes were as intelligent as whites." At that time only 42 percent of whites thought so. By 1956, the percentage had risen to 78 (where it has stabilized). In 1942, only 30 percent of white Americans said white and black children should go to the same schools. By 1956 (shortly after the Supreme Court decision), the percentage had risen to 48, and by 1968, to 60 percent. In 1972, the Harris poll found that 71 percent of white Americans favored desegregated schools. And the same has been true for attitudes toward integration of housing. From 1942 to 1972 the percentage of whites who would not object to integration of housing had risen from 35 percent to over 70 percent. The era of more open racial conflict was also one in which white attitudes toward blacks improved a lot.

But there are several qualifications to that generalization. For one thing, as the data indicate, many whites still oppose integration. Furthermore, white support for the goals of blacks has been accompanied by a general and growing rejection of black tactics—at least of militant tactics. We have seen the negative attitudes of whites toward black militants. And whites have generally rejected direct action by black groups, even when it is peaceful and fully within the law. Thus the Harris poll found in 1968 that 80 percent of black Americans favored Martin Luther King's Poor People's March on Washington—a massive, peaceful rally at the Lincoln Memorial— whereas only 29 percent of whites did. Or consider the data in Table 6.8 on the proper speed of integration: Whites seem to think things are beginning to go too fast. Thus as whites are starting to accept some of the goals of blacks, they are beginning to feel that things are moving too quickly, that blacks are pushing too hard with inappropriate tactics.

The picture is quite mixed: more favorable attitudes of whites toward blacks coupled with less favorable attitudes. One explanation of the ambivalence of whites may lie in the "rugged individualist" beliefs of the Americans. Whites have come less and less to believe blacks are racially inferior, but they remain firm in the belief that people should get ahead on their own steam and that in America anyone who wants to get ahead can, if only he will try. Thus they see lower levels of black education or income as a result of lack of effort.

February 1964	30%
April 1965	34%
July 1966	46%
September 1966	52%
August 1967	44%
April 1968	39%
October 1968	54%
July 1969	44%
March 1970	48%
November 1972	52%

Source: Gallup poll data, cited in Jerome H. Skolnick, *The Politics of Protest,* Staff Report to the National Commission on the Causes and Prevention of Violence (New York: Ballantine, 1969). 1970 data from Gallup poll; 1972 data from Harris poll.

If blacks do not succeed, it is because they do not try hard enough. Such an attitude leads to reluctance to favor social programs aimed at improving the conditions of blacks.

The ambivalent nature of white attitudes toward blacks can be seen in Figure 6.5, which compares the attitudes of whites and blacks on racial issues. People were asked to choose between opposing positions on what to do about urban unrest and on the speed of progress for blacks. On the question about what do do about urban unrest, people could choose between using all necessary force to put down riots, and solving the underlying problems of poverty. Blacks clearly favor the latter course. The position of whites falls between the two alternatives. A similar pattern is seen in relation to the proper speed for further progress for blacks. Blacks, as one might

Figure 6.5
Differing Positions of Whites
and Blacks

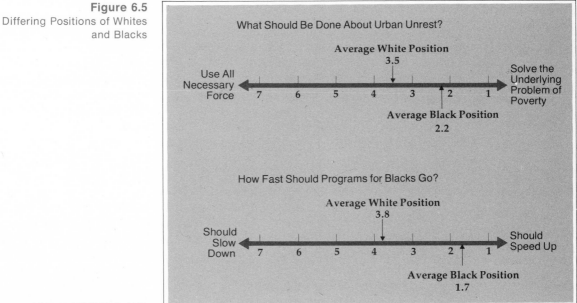

Source: National Opinion Research Center study, University of Chicago, 1971.

Figure 6.6

Differing Positions of Whites
and Blacks on the Govern-
ment's Role Regarding
Residential Segregation

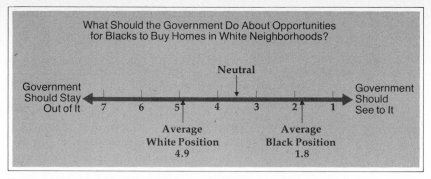

Source: National Opinion Research Center study, University of Chicago, 1971.

expect, want faster rather than slower progress. Some whites would prefer a slower pace. On these two issues one finds blacks firmly in favor of faster change; whites are not completely opposed, but they are certainly holding back compared with the blacks.

Some issues, however, lead to greater division between whites and blacks. Consider Figure 6.6, which shows how whites and blacks differ on what the government should do about segregated housing. Here is an issue that more sharply divides the population: Whites want the government to stay out of it; blacks want the government to see to it.

The data on black and white political differences suggest both the basis for continuing conflict and some hope for cooperative progress. The progress could be based on the commitment of the two groups to the democratic system, at least in a general sense. It also could be based on the absence of racial antagonism between blacks and whites, and on greater acceptance by whites of black goals.

But the danger of continuing conflict lies in the greater differences between the races when one gets down to specifics. Blacks may trust the system in general, but they have less confidence in actual government officials. Whites may accept black goals but are more hesitant about specific aspects of those goals, are opposed to pressure from blacks to achieve those goals, and have begun to feel that things are moving too fast.

Radical Politics in America

Traditionally the United States has been described as the wrong place for radical politics. This, so the argument went, was not because radicals were suppressed. Rather, there were tendencies in American politics that took away many of the issues around which radical politics might be organized. And the two major political parties were good at "stealing the thunder" of such groups by taking up some of their positions.

The 1960s and early 1970s called into question the assumption that radicalism was out of place in America. We cannot discuss basic

political values in America without asking why some black and Chicano and student radical groups have challenged the workings of the political system in recent years.

We are not interested here in groups that are radical on some issue, who want basic changes in our foreign policy or in the economic structure of our country. Rather, we are interested in those who have radical attitudes toward the democratic process itself, who think decisions should be made by some other rules. Such radicalism can come from either end of the political spectrum. Democratic procedures may be rejected by those who see them as blocking rapid social change—"Problems such as war, pollution, the cities, poverty, racism are too great to be dealt with through the 'system,'" they might argue. Or the rules of democracy might be rejected by those who see such rules as the cause of violence and decay in our society—"We have too much free speech. We cannot tolerate the political views of those who would destroy the 'system.'"

In fact few groups take such a position. As we have seen, the commitment to the rules of democratic procedures (at least on the general level) is widespread—even among those who would be expected to be very dissatisfied with the operation of that system. The young are much more critical of political institutions in America than the population as a whole. A poll in 1972 asked young adults about American democracy. About six out of ten thought the country was democratic in name only and was run by special interests. But only 18 percent thought the system was inflexible and needed radical change. Sixty-two percent thought political parties needed major change; only 12 percent thought the Constitution did.[13]

Many of the more radical criticisms of American politics come not from those who would prefer other rules but from those who see the rules working poorly and would prefer to see more effective democracy in the United States. These would include those who want more real participation in the political process or who want greater local government power.

Where one sees direct radical criticism of the rules—rejection of elections or free speech—it seems to come less from the belief that such rules are bad *per se* than from the belief that these rules have made for a poor performance on some issue.

Summary

It may be useful to summarize what we have learned about the basic beliefs of Americans and how they affect politics.

It has long been believed that democracy is based on consensus on certain democratic values such as free speech. In the United States we find consensus on general principles, along with a tendency to limit these values in practice. This tendency is, however,

RADICAL POLITICS IN AMERICA

[13] Daniel Yankelovich, *The New Morality: A Profile of American Youth in the 1970's* (New York: McGraw-Hill, 1973), p. 116.

partly offset by the fact that the citizens who are likely to be most politically involved and active—the better educated, the leaders of organizations—have a greater commitment to democratic values.

Perhaps the most striking thing about the basic political beliefs of Americans is the fact that there have been important changes in the past decade. For one thing, Americans are no longer as optimistic about their nation as they once were. And this has happened at a time when politics has become more visible to the average citizen and when citizens seem to be developing more consistent sets of political attitudes.

These changes in political attitudes, coupled with powerful and divisive issues—race, the urban crisis, Vietnam—can lead to a situation in which hostile groups of citizens are in conflict on a wide range of issues. The data on the political beliefs of blacks and whites suggest that this may be happening, but not as much as would be the case if one considered only the views of the most militant members of each group.

This theme is so important in America today that we will devote a good deal of the next chapter to it.

Does Public Opinion Make a Difference?

We have looked at American attitudes toward government in general and some specific issues such as race. But a major question has not yet been answered: What difference, if any, does public opinion make? Does it shape government programs? Or do officials pay it lip service and largely ignore it?

When the public opinion poll was started in the 1930s, some thought it would be a great thing for democracy. Now the officials in Washington could get an accurate idea of the feelings of the American people on the important issues of the day. Policy could really follow the views of citizens. An accurate poll could tell what the American people thought of unemployment insurance, defense spending, farm supports. At the same time, other observers expressed concern. Polls would cause trouble: The public was too ill informed, too fickle, too "irrational" to guide public policy. Good policy requires careful study and thought, something possible only if officials are protected from the day-to-day opinions of the majority.

Actually the public opinion poll was never used to set government policy as the optimists hoped and the pessimists feared.

Two somewhat contradictory points can be made about the impact of public opinion on governmental leaders. One is that most officials—especially elected ones—pay great attention to the public opinion polls, to the mail, to all sorts of indicators of public opinion. Not only do politicians follow the Gallup and Harris polls, they also have special polls taken for them to find out public opinion on a particular issue. Furthermore (and this is important), political leaders believe public opinion is important and should be followed—at least up to a point. On the other hand, policy is rarely made directly on the basis of public opinion.

Why is this the case?

Public Opinion Does Not Always Become Public Policy

One might imagine that if the polls showed that the majority favored a particular position, that position would sooner or later become law. But this is clearly not the case. In 1972 the Harris poll asked a sample of Americans whether there should be a strict federal law requiring that hand guns be registered. Seventy percent said yes. Yet no such federal law has been passed. One might answer that such things take time; if the public continues to feel that way, a law is likely to be passed. But in one of the earliest public opinion polls, in 1940, the Gallup poll asked an almost identical question. At that time 79 percent favored the gun control law.

How can the public overwhelmingly favor a particular piece of legislation for 35 years and yet have no response from Congress? The answer is simply that the large majority favoring gun control does not feel very strongly about it; some members of the minority that oppose gun control do feel strongly on the matter and are active in support of their position.

The example of gun control teaches two important lessons. One has to do with the making of policy in America. It is that a small, intense minority is usually more effective than a large majority that is not as concerned with the problem. This fact is so central to American politics that it will form the theme of the next two chapters. The second lesson is that public opinion polls can sometimes give misleading information on the preferences of the public. We gave the reason for this when we discussed polls as a means of understanding the public: Most public opinion polls give equal weight to the opinions of all who answer. "Do you favor gun control?" Four out of five say yes, one out of five says no. But if those who say yes do not care much while those who say no are committed to their position, it would be misleading to see the results as showing great support for the position of the majority.

Public Opinion Tends to React to, Not Guide, Current Policy

The public official trying to choose a policy does worry about the public and usually tries to keep informed about its attitudes. But on most issues the public is ill informed and its policy preferences unclear. We have seen evidence of this statement.

But the official also knows the public may react negatively if he does badly. Thus much of his concern is worry about public reaction. He does not learn from the public opinion polls what policy to pursue. But he often learns what troubles he is likely to face at the next election if he does not deal with certain problems. The public will not tell the political leader how to deal with inflation, but it will let him know if it is concerned about high prices.

The history of public attitudes on the war in Vietnam illustrates this point. No war has ever aroused as much public concern and disapproval. From the time the war first became a leading public issue—around 1964 or 1965—the portion of the American people satisfied with governmental policy went down and down. The low point was reached around the time of President Johnson's 1968 decision not to run for office again. And public unhappiness with the war probably had something to do with that decision.

Yet public opinion was a far-from-adequate guide for specific policy. When pollsters asked citizens for their preferences on the war—Should we escalate to win, deescalate and get out, or keep up our present policy—they typically found the public divided across all three positions. How can a President follow that lead? Furthermore, the public seemed to be pleased whenever the President did anything—increased our military commitment or decreased it—as long as something was done. The pleasure lasted only briefly when it became clear that the new move was not going to end the war. But the conclusion was obvious: The public was unhappy and wanted results. And political leaders had to pay attention to that unhappiness or they would lose in the next election, as the Democratic party learned in 1968. But what the public wanted done was less clear. The administrations involved—the Johnson and Nixon administrations—were under public pressure to do something, but not under pressure to do something specific.

Limits to Public Tolerance

There is another way to look at the role of public opinion in the policy process. This is that public opinion sets certain limits to what is acceptable policy: Some things the public will not stand for. There is probably some truth to this. Public tolerance sets some outer boundaries to acceptable policies. But even here the role of public opinion is by no means clear. One reason is that one can never tell what those boundaries are from the answers to questions in public opinion polls. We do not know the limits to public tolerance in advance; we may have to test the public to find out.

An example will help make the point and teach us some important lessons about public opinion. For many years observers claimed that the American public set definite limits to foreign policy. The public, we were told, would not stand for recognition of China or allowing it to join the United Nations. Students of foreign policy often complained that this kept American political leaders from forming better relations with China. And indeed public opinion polls over the years showed that a large majority of the American public was against recognition of China.

But when President Nixon made his historic trip to China in 1972, the Harris poll found that 73 percent of the people approved. The notion that public opinion stood in the way of better relations with China was probably a myth. This shows the importance of leadership in setting public opinion. Policy on China did not reflect public attitudes; rather, public attitudes reflected government policy. Change the policy and the attitudes change.

The case of China may exaggerate the changeability of public opinion and the real flexibility this leaves to leaders. Such flexibility is probably greater in foreign affairs, about which citizens do not have firmly fixed opinions. On issues closer to home the limits set by public opinion may be more rigid. Attitudes on racial matters are less easily manipulated, and the threat of electoral punishment by an unhappy public on such an issue may be more real to an elected official than the supposed threat of public disapproval for a new China policy. On such matters public attitudes may have a strong effect on leadership. Yet even in these areas, where public opinion seems firmer, one can never be sure how much it can be manipulated. As we have seen, public support for integrated schools showed a large increase after the Supreme Court declared segregated schools unconstitutional.

A Nation of Many Publics

We can end our discussion of the impact of the public on government policy by making one major point. In most cases one cannot think of *the public* as a single entity. There are many *publics:* There are the citizens who are inactive in politics; there are those who are active. There are those who are uninterested in political matters, and a smaller number who are interested. There are, above all, differences in what it is that interests citizens. Different citizens become interested in and active on different sets of problems. This is important in understanding how the attitudes of the public affect governmental policy. Political leaders are likely to be responsive to certain parts of the public, especially those that are active on a particular issue. Rather than asking about the impact of public opinion as a whole, we have to ask about the impact of the special publics. We turn to this topic in the next chapter.

How We Find Out About Politics: II
Public Opinion and Voting

Because politics is so complicated and political realities are sometimes hidden, political scientists worry a lot about their methods of study. Their concerns are realistic, for it is easy to get distorted information about politics. When you are given "information" about politics, you should always ask: Where did that information come from? How was it gathered? What are its possible biases?

Public Opinion: How Do We Find Out About It?

Throughout this book we present information about attitudes and behavior of the American public. We look at their political beliefs, the ways they act politically, how they vote, and how they decide to vote the way they do. How do we find out about the American public?

Everybody thinks he knows how the American public feels about things. In a sense we have a right to think so. For one thing, each of us is a member of the American public, and thus our own views are part of public opinion. For another, we talk to many other people who are also members of the public; we read newspapers, where we see reports of public attitudes or letters to the editor; and we watch television. But for several reasons such information—based on observation of the world around us—can often be wrong, sometimes seriously wrong.

1. First of all, we often look at our own views and assume that other people share them. This is not a safe assumption. People have widely differing views on political issues and react to political events in varied ways.

2. Sometimes we feel that we learn more about public opinion by talking to our friends, neighbors, or fellow workers. Such conversations are likely to give distorted views of public opinion. Most of us meet only certain kinds of people.

An example is the college campus. During the late 1960s students on some campuses, noticing that there was a great deal of activity against the war in Vietnam, began to think everybody under 30 was against the war and to talk of a "generation gap" between their generation, which seemed to be solidly anti-war, and the older generation, which was pro-war. However, if one looked at the entire younger generation—students on all campuses and those who did not go to college—one found a much wider range of opinions and a great deal of support for the war in Vietnam. Thus by talking only to people like themselves some students got a distorted view of public opinion.

3. Even reading newspapers or watching television can give us a distorted view of public opinion. For example, it is difficult to know whether people who write letters to the editor—people who obviously have time, interest, and the ability to express themselves—are representative of the general public. Furthermore, the mass media have a well-known tendency to look for the dramatic. The expressions of public opinion likely to wind up on the evening news are a demonstration by a small minority or a speech by a well-known celebrity. This, too, is information about one part of the public. It is difficult to know if this small part is representative of the larger public.

The Sample Survey: Its Strengths and Weaknesses

The sample survey, or public-opinion poll, was developed to get around the weaknesses of the commonsense approach to public opinion. Such surveys—the Gallup or Harris polls, surveys by scholarly organizations, and surveys done for political candidates—can be very accurate in estimating public opinion. Sample surveys must be used with care, however, if one is to arrive at an undistorted picture of Americans' views on a given subject.

To understand how sample surveys can give us more accurate information than our commonsense observations of public opinion, we must consider

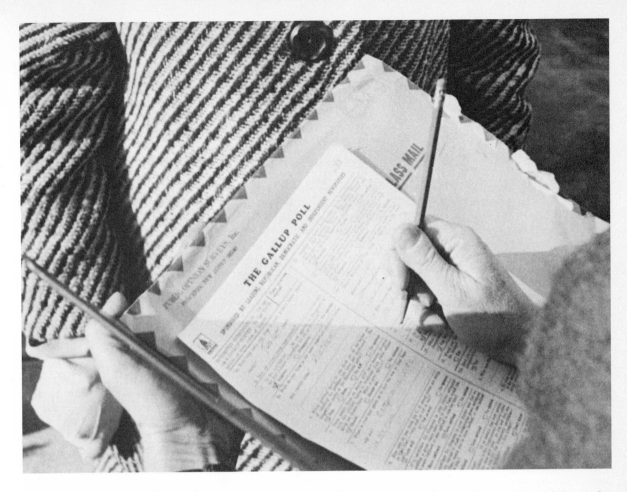

the sample used and the instrument, or questionnaire, applied to the sample, that is, who the pollster talks to and what questions he asks.

Sampling

The notion of sampling is basic to the survey. To know about public opinion it would be ideal to talk to all Americans. But obviously that is not feasible; it would be too costly and time-consuming. One can talk to only some Americans. The important point is that one should try to choose people who are representative of the public as a whole. That is, one takes a sample of the American population and tries to generalize to the population as a whole.

But what is a good sample? Imagine a government inspector who wants to find out whether the jam produced by a certain company meets government standards of purity. To find out if the jam is pure, he must open a jar and test it. But he cannot open all the thousands of jars produced by this company; that

would be too costly for him and would leave the company with no unopened jars to sell.

Thus the inspector decides to take a sample of the jars and check them—just as a public-opinion pollster takes a sample of citizens. What kind of sample does he look for?

1. An adequate number: The government inspector will probably not be satisfied by looking at one or two jars of jam. Any particular jar may be unlike all the others. He will want enough so that he is likely to find contamination if it exists.

2. A wide geographic spread: If the company produces jam at a large number of factories, the inspector should not be satisfied by going to the factory nearest his own office, even though that would save him time and effort. Since the various plants may differ in cleanliness, a careful inspector would select jars from all the jam factories owned by the company.

3. A wide range of types: If the company makes all kinds of jam, the inspector would do well to sample the various kinds and not limit his inspection to strawberry jam. Again, the reason is simple: What he finds out about the strawberry jam will not tell him about the raspberry jam.

4. A random selection: The inspector selects at random; he does not let anyone else select for him. The clever inspector will be careful to avoid any kind of bias in the particular jars he looks at. He will not sit in his office and allow company officials to bring him a few jars of each kind of jam, for they might select jars from the cleanest part of the factory or from the newest, most sanitary equipment. Rather, he will go out into the factory and *randomly* choose which jars to test.

How does the public-opinion pollster deal with this kind of issue?

1. An adequate number: A good survey researcher will not be satisfied to talk to one, two, or a few dozen citizens. Even if they are chosen at random, they will be too few to tell us much about the general population. There is too much chance that one will accidentally find people who are very different from the rest of the public. Most good public-opinion polls interview about 1500 people.

2. A wide geographic spread: It is important that those interviewed come from a wide range of places, not just the pollster's home town. Survey organizations conduct interviews all over the country to get a good geographic spread.

3. A wide range of types: The most important thing about a sample is that it allow all types of citizens an equal chance to be interviewed. If the selection process is biased so that one type of person is eliminated, the resulting sample will not represent the population as a whole. In former years many surveys were taken of people who happened to pass by in public places such as railroad stations. It is not difficult to see why such surveys were often inaccurate. They omitted those who do not commute by railroad—housewives, college students, elderly pensioners, automobile riders, and so on. Certain groups, such as working men, were overrepresented, and other groups were not represented at all.

4. A random selection: The pollster selects; he does not let the respondent self-select. An important aspect of a good sample is that a pollster chooses—on the basis of statistics—who it is that he wants to interview. He does not wait for people to volunteer to be interviewed. This point is important, and it is this that makes the sample survey different from the ways of finding out public opinion used in everyday politics.

The congressman who judges public opinion on the basis of letters written to him is acting very differently from a professional pollster. The congressman is assuming that the opinions of those who *voluntarily* write to him are representative of the opinions of his constituents as a whole or of the public as a whole. As we have discussed, this is probably an incorrect assumption, for letter writers may differ in important ways from those who don't write.

That the pollster talks to all kinds of people—those who do not volunteer their opinions as well as those who do—is the greatest strength as well as the greatest weakness of the public-opinion poll. The great strength of the poll is that it gets at the opinions of all citizens, whether or not they have chosen to volunteer their views. In this sense a good survey represents all citizens—the articulate few who volunteer their views as well as the "silent majority."

But this can be a source of weakness as well, because the pollster records the opinions of many citizens who basically have no opinion. Often a person has not thought about a particular problem until a public-opinion pollster appears to ask about it. Rather than saying he or she has no opinion or doesn't know anything about the issue, the uninterested or uninformed person will usually give an offhand answer. Such a response is highly changeable; if the pollster returned the following day, a different answer might be given. Every sample survey contains such answers by respondents who don't really know or care about the issue; this must be borne in mind when interpreting sample-survey data.

The Questions Used

Sometimes two different polls will come up with what seem to be different or contradictory results. When this happens it is usually because the two polls have asked different questions. This, then, is another general principle of survey technique: The answers you get depend on the questions you ask.

Those who have worked professionally with sample surveys know how even small changes in question wording can change the results. People respond to the symbols contained in questions. If you ask a question about "Russia," people will respond one way. If you ask a question about "Communist

Russia," people will respond more negatively, simply because you have added the negative symbol of communism. Similarly if you asked about "aid to families with dependent children," you would get a different set of answers than if you had asked about "welfare" or "government giveaway programs."

Thus polls are quite accurate in telling you how Americans responded to a particular question. But the wording of the question always has an effect on the response. Public-opinion polls provide very useful information about the American public, but the information is valuable only if used carefully.

7

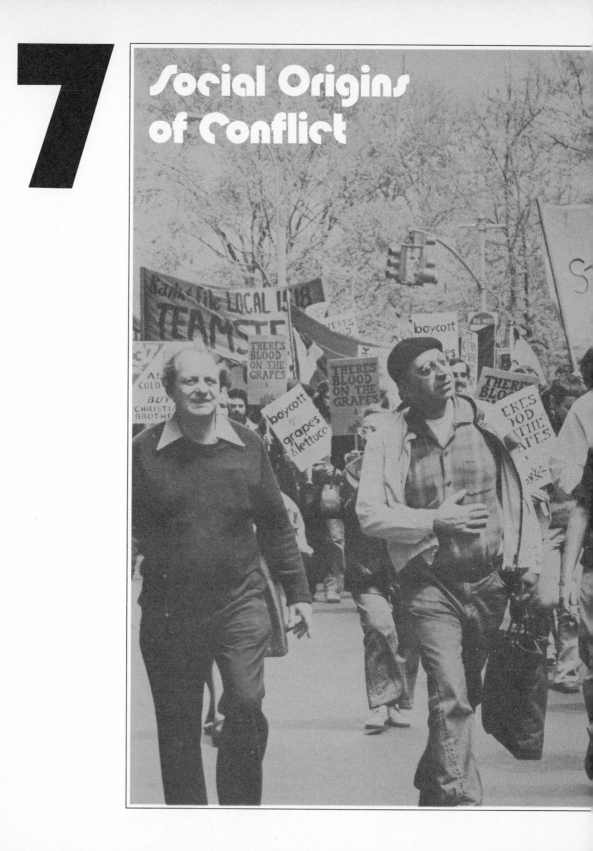

Social Origins
of Conflict

Politics in America—as everywhere—is about conflict and competition. The reason is obvious. The government allocates benefits to the citizens in the society. And the major decisions of the government involve the questions of who gets the benefits and who pays the costs. There would be conflict in America even if there were no differences of opinion on what kinds of policy the government should pursue, simply because the pie the government is dividing is not infinite. Suppose everyone thought the most important thing for the government to do was to spend more on roads. Conflict over government policies would still arise, since choices have to be made as to what kind of road to build and where. Citizens in one part of the country would try to pressure the government to favor their area. Citizens in one town would prefer to have the new superhighway close enough to be convenient, but not so close as to disrupt their community. They would prefer that it run through the neighboring town.

But of course not everyone wants roads. Some citizens think more should be spent on mass transportation and less on roads. Some think spending on transportation is not as important as spending on education or housing. And some think what is most important is cutting spending to cut taxes.

Thus conflict arises not only about who should benefit from a particular policy but also about which policy to pursue. And, to take it one step further, conflict also arises because a policy to benefit one group is seen by others as a policy that hurts them; a decision to place public housing projects in suburban communities may be favored by blacks and others who want integrated housing, but opposed by some suburban residents. Higher tariffs on imports of textiles from Japan may be favored by American textile manufacturers, but opposed by some clothing manufacturers who like to use the cheaper Japanese textiles or by consumer groups who prefer the lower-priced imports.

This chapter is about the groups who compete for benefits. Note that we talk about "groups" that compete, not about individuals. Political competition is usually among groups. Consider the following newspaper headlines:

Auto Workers Question Wage Guidelines
Legislature Seat for Chicanos Demanded
Republicans Ask Court to Nullify Convention Seats
Pilots Call for Hijack Protection
Women's Group Challenges All-Male Court Nominations
Parents' Group Calls for Busing Boycott
Fishermen Protest Shortened Season
Conservationists Sue to Block Superhighway

In each case we see a group of citizens demanding something, challenging something, expressing some position. They become politically relevant because they are groups of citizens, not separate individuals. Groups like these are sometimes called *interest groups*, sometimes *pressure groups*. The members of these groups have interests in common. This forms the basis for their working together in politics. And they *pressure* the government to further those interests. Both terms are important—for not all groups of individuals have interests in common, and not all of those that have such interests put pressure on the government. Which brings us to the question, Which groups in America are politically relevent and why?

What Makes a Group Politically Relevant?

Anything a set of individuals have in common can be the basis of a group. In the headlines we see groups based on sex (women), occupation (auto workers), leisure preference (fishermen), political belief (Republicans), and ethnic background (Chicanos). But almost anything might form the basis of a group. What about citizens of Japanese descent, tea drinkers, red-haired citizens, hot-rod racers, people who live in odd-numbered houses, people opposed to vivisection, sausage makers? Not all the groups are politically relevant. Chicanos and blacks are relevant political groups. A few years ago women were not; now they are. Suburbanites may or may not be, depending on the particular suburb. Hot rodders usually are not but might be if they want a local town to set up a drag strip. But residents in odd-numbered houses are unlikely ever to be a politically relevant group.

Since politics is about competition among groups making claims on the government, it is important to ask why some social groups are politically relevant while others are not. Why are Chicanos politically relevant but tea drinkers not? Why women now, but not fifteen years ago? Three things make a group of people politically relevant: a common interest, awareness of that interest, and organization. In addition, groups are likely to be successful in achieving their political goals if they can get their members to give time, effort, and resources to the group.

Common Interests

A group is likely to be politically relevant if the thing that defines the group—sex or race or occupation or type of house—is something that creates a common interest, particularly a common interest for which governmental policy is relevant, that is, an interest that can best be served by some action by the government. Blacks clearly have such common interests in housing policy, desegregation policy, voting rights, and so forth. Tea drinkers have a common interest in government tariff policy on tea. But residents of odd-numbered houses do not, and it is hard to believe they ever would.

However, not all common interests lead to the formation of politically relevant groups. Some interests are more important than

A common interest sent these Hopi Indians to Senate hearings on land disputes between Hopis and Navajos.

others. Tea drinkers may have interests in common, but they are not important enough to get them to act. The change in the price of tea that might come from a change in tariff has too little impact on them to make any difference. It is hard, on the other hand, for an American black to be unaware of policies that affect blacks.

But, though tea drinkers may not consider the price of tea important, tea importers do. The price of tea, as affected by tariff policy, has a large impact on the lives of those who earn their living from the import and sale of tea; it has a small impact on those for whom it is just one item in a shopping bag.

This illustrates a most important principle of American political life. Different groups of citizens are interested in different areas of governmental policy. Tea importers and tea drinkers may be interested in tea tariffs. Coffee drinkers could probably not care less. Chicanos—citizens of Mexican-American descent—will be interested in Spanish-language teaching in the schools. Citizens in states with no Spanish-speaking minority will be uninterested. Furthermore, even when several sets of citizens are interested in a particular area of governmental policy, the interests may be very strong for some but relatively mild for others. Chicanos will be interested in Spanish-language teaching in the public schools, and so will the non-Spanish-speaking residents of their communities. But for the former it is an important issue relevant to their culture, to the latter perhaps a less important issue having to do with the costs of schools. What this means is that on any policy some citizens may be very concerned, others will be only mildly involved, and many others will not care. This fact structures much of the political conflict in America. A vast range of possible interests can form the basis of politically relevant groups.

SOCIAL ORIGINS OF CONFLICT

Economic Interests These are the ones that come to mind most easily when one thinks of the interests citizens pursue in political

activity. Workers seek higher wages. If the government tries to hold wages down by direct or indirect controls, this interest in wages is likely to form the basis of political activity on the part of workers and unions. Businessmen are concerned about price controls, tariffs, and government policies that affect the "economic climate"—all because such policies affect their incomes. And of course all citizens have interests in that inevitable governmental policy—taxes.

Power Interests   We can also talk of power interests—citizens want, demand, and work for political control over their own lives and over the government of their community. Thus there are conflicts over what kind of person gets elected or appointed to office, who may vote, how districts are zoned for elections. Such political control can, to be sure, be used to further economic interests. And it is often used for that purpose. But political power is also desired as an end in itself. Many of the most bitter conflicts in America are over the question, Who controls the government?

Way-of-Life Interests   It is hard to give a more precise term to this broad set of interests. They are not clearly economic or political but represent the desire to lead a particular kind of life. Citizens may want to keep a community the way it is—residential and not industrial; white and nonintegrated; small and not large. Or they may want to change a community—integrate it, improve its cultural life. These interests, too, can form the basis of political groups.

Self-Awareness

It is not enough that a group of citizens have interests in common; they have to be aware of those interests. Interests become politically important when they are not merely objective but subjective as well. American blacks have such objective interests, and, further, they are aware of them. In many cases groups may have objective interests in common for a long time, but these interests become politically relevant only with group self-awareness. In recent years women's groups have been active in trying to equalize the pay received by men and women. The objective problem—lower pay for women when they do work equal to that of men—is not a recent one. Such unequal treatment was traditional. But it is only when people become *concerned* about such unequal treatment that they become politically relevant.

Organization and Leadership

Groups that are organized can pressure the government more effectively; groups that have leadership have spokesmen who can represent them to the government. And such leadership can get greater efforts and commitment from group members.

Self-awareness and leadership reinforce each other. One of the main tasks of a leader is to arouse the self-awareness of followers.

WHAT MAKES A GROUP
POLITICALLY RELEVANT?

When that happens social movements are born. If not, one has leadership but no one to lead.

Common interests, self-awareness, organization—these make for relevant political groups. Blacks in America have all three. Many economic and professional groups such as unionized workers, farmers, and doctors have all three. In some cases one finds the first two but not the last. Until recently groups such as migratory farm workers have had common interests and some self-awareness, but little organization. Groups with interests in common but little shared sense of group membership and little organization have been called *potential groups*. For a long time such a description might have fit consumers or city dwellers who suffered from polluted air. Potential groups become more active groups as they become aware of their common interest and form organizations dedicated to furthering these interests.

Motivating Group Members

Why do citizens join in political activity with others who have similar interests? Why do they give time and effort to work with others to further such interests? At first the answer seems obvious. Citizens work together because they want to pressure the government to respond to their needs. Women work with other women to influence government policy in relation to sex discrimination; blacks join with other blacks to get the local government to improve neighborhood facilities; businessmen join with other businessmen to lobby for favorable economic laws.

Goals like these are the "policy goals" of political groups; they are what the group wants the government to do. Some have argued that it would not be "rational" for a citizen to become involved actively in a group in order to achieve such policy goals. To see why they make this argument, we can return to a point we made at the beginning of this book about government in general. In the introductory chapter we talked about "collective goods" and why citizens might not voluntarily contribute to their achievement. A collective good is something available to each individual whether or not he has contributed to the creation of the good. If I can use the park my city opens even if I do not contribute to its creation, why not sit back and let others work and pay for it? But if everyone felt that way, no park would be created and all would lose.

In the introductory chapter we argued that "binding decisions" are often needed to achieve such collective goods; all benefit if citizens can be made to contribute such benefits. Thus tax funds (which citizens must pay whether they want to or not) are used to build parks.

This is related to the question of why citizens join with others in political activity to achieve some group interest. Why should a woman work with other women to achieve equal-pay legislation? The effort of one more person would not have much effect on the outcome. So it should make little difference if she does nothing.

Furthermore, she benefits from the regulation if it is passed, even if she did not work for it.

Why should a black join a community group working for better facilities in the neighborhood? His effort does not add that much. And he can use the facilities when they are provided even if he did not help get them.

As with collective goods that the government provides, the "logic" of the situation would result in no activity by women or blacks (or any other group that wanted something done). For each individual woman or black it would be "rational" to wait for the others to act and get a "free ride." The result: No one would act and all would be worse off.

Furthermore, groups of citizens with common interests cannot make "binding decisions" and force their members to contribute to the policy goals of the group. The government can make citizens pay taxes to support the park just as it can make them obey laws in other respects. But the women's movement cannot force other women to join, nor can a black community group force blacks to take part. People have to volunteer.

Why do people contribute time and effort to group causes despite the "logic" that says it would be irrational to do so? One answer is that people don't think in terms of logic. People work for the group cause even if it might not be logical. But the groups that are successful in getting people to work for them usually offer something more than a chance to work for the group's policy goal. Successful groups offer their members other rewards. One such reward is the feeling of solidarity that comes from participating with others to achieve some goal. The feeling of solidarity—of belonging to a group—is, at least in part, the "payoff" for participation. Social movements like the women's movement or the black movement give participants a sense of belonging, and this plays a big role in keeping members committed and active.

There are other rewards for members of groups as well. Some political groups can provide economic benefits—one makes job contacts through the group. Or the group provides recreational opportunities. For some, activity in a political group is a way of meeting people.

We are not saying that members of political groups say they are committed to the group's policy goals but really take part to make friends or get a sense of solidarity. Participants may be strongly committed to the policy goals of the group. But the other rewards the group offers reinforce their activity. Those political groups are likely to be successful that can offer these additional rewards.

Groups in America: Many and Varied

This ability to form groups of like-minded citizens is typical of American political life. In one study that compared Americans with citizens elsewhere, people were asked how they would go about

Table 7.1

The Use of Informal
Groups to Influence
the Government

	United States	Great Britain	Germany	Italy	Mexico
Percent saying they would form an informal group to protest an unjust law	56%	34%	13%	7%	26%

Source: Based on data from Gabriel A. Almond and Sidney Verba, *The Civic Culture: Political Attitudes and Democracy in Five Nations* (Princeton, N.J.: Princeton University Press, 1963).

trying to influence their local government. In the United States, over half said they would try to get their friends and neighbors to join in with them. This way they could approach the government as a group. In other nations, fewer citizens gave such a response. (See Table 7.1.)

In recent years there has been a growing tendency for groups of citizens who were previously politically irrelevant (because they were not aware of their common interests, nor were they organized) to become politically relevant. We have mentioned women as an example. Many other types of groups have recently become more politically involved. One reads of groups of consumers, commuters, homosexuals, welfare recipients, tenants, and so on. These groups have had interests in common for a long time, but they have recently added to those common interests the self-awareness and organization that make them important politically. In this they are following the footsteps of groups that have been organized for many years, such as factory workers, businessmen, and farmers.

Let us consider some of the different types of political groups in America.

Ethnicity and Race

If we wish to describe the various groups on the American political scene, it is best to start with something basic like ethnic identity. When we talk of ethnics or ethnic politics, we tend to think of Irish Americans, Polish Americans, Jewish Americans, or perhaps black Americans. There is no generally agreed-upon definition of ethnicity, but what we're talking about is fairly clear. Ethnicity refers to that fundamental sense of identity that is based on national origin. This sense of identity is transmitted through the family. It is associated with where one lives or comes from. It forms the core of the answer an individual might give if asked: "What are you?"

One's ethnic identity is often associated with more specific things such as language. If people speak the same language, they have a fundamental bond—the ability to communicate. True, they may not communicate or they may communicate hostile messages. But the identification based on one's language—especially when the people around one speak another language—is important. In addition, people who have lived together for a long time often develop an ethnic identity. Or—and this is particularly true in the United States—common place of origin may be the basis of an ethnic group. Other ties such as race or customs hold such ethnic groups together.

The power of these ties is apparent around the world. They divide nation from nation, and they divide within nations as well. And the divisions can create open conflict. Nigeria, Belgium, Canada, Ireland, India, Yugoslavia—we could make a long list of nations where ethnic differences lead to divisions, conflict, and violence.

But, we are told, not in the United States, "one nation indivisible." America, so the saying goes, is a melting pot. It is inhabited by people from Europe, Asia, and Africa who melted together, mixed, and formed the American people. This is essentially true. For one thing, these immigrants have by and large become American citizens. (In some countries immigrants may live for generations without obtaining local citizenship—either because they prefer not to or because they are not allowed to. So this fact is not as obvious as it may sound.)

Furthermore, the stamp of "Americanization" was placed on all these immigrants in terms of language. The people who poured into the United States in the late nineteenth and early twentieth centuries wound up a generation later speaking a single language. The earlier language sometimes (but rarely) survived. But English became the dominant language. Again, this was not inevitable. In many lands two or more languages continue to be spoken and sooner or later form the basis of conflict. The dominance of English America is in part the result of policy. Teachers and government officials believed that to be an American meant to speak English, and the schools enforced this in the training of immigrant children. Former Justice Felix Frankfurter of the United States Supreme Court, who came from Austria, reports that he said something in German on one of his first days in school. The teacher slapped him and told the rest of the class not to speak to him unless he spoke English. It is important to note that the immigrants themselves largely accepted the argument that to be an American meant to speak English.

Thus, say the history books, out of the immigrants from Europe and Asia and Africa the melting pot made one nation. Not quite. Some groups did not melt easily. Those of other races did not fit the melting-pot model. Blacks of course were denied citizenship and freedom until the Civil War. Even then they did not get the real benefits of citizenship. Similarly—though not as openly—immigrants from Asia were denied full citizenship. The only Americans who were not immigrants—the American Indians—were also denied full citizenship. The melting pot never fully applied to non-Caucasians.

But neither did it apply fully to white immigrants. Long after the melting pot was supposed to have done its work, ethnic identity remains, ethnic organizations flourish, and ethnic interests come into conflict. And language is still an issue. We consider ourselves an

English-speaking nation, but 12 million Americans are Spanish speaking. And in recent years they have been pressing to have their language accepted.

Ethnic patterns are found throughout American politics. Groups like Irish Catholics or Polish Catholics traditionally support the Democratic party, usually voting over 70 percent Democratic. Or they support candidates of the same ethnic group. Sometimes ethnic politics takes the form of concern about the "old country"—Americans from Eastern Europe are concerned with political problems in that area of the world, Jewish Americans with developments in Israel.

There are two reasons for ethnic politics, both having to do with the interests, direct and indirect, of the various ethnic groups. The direct interests involve the desire—despite the melting pot—to preserve ethnic identity. In earlier times this meant the desire to live near, depend on, or marry others with a similar background and language—for only in that way could one find security in a strange land. Nor have things changed very much. Americans who should have been assimilated long ago have been rediscovering the language, culture, history, and customs of the old country. The richness of American life that was almost lost through pressure for Americanization may still be preserved by the self-awareness of ethnic groups.

More important politically may be the indirect interests associated with ethnicity. The fact that many ethnic groups were immigrants is important here. The groups who today form the various ethnic communities tended to come as immigrants. And each group in turn found itself the most deprived. When the Irish came in the mid- and late nineteenth century, they found themselves in the poorest neighborhoods, with the worst jobs, and in communities controlled by established residents. Their struggle was with the older Yankee residents for better jobs and housing and political power. A generation later, when the Italian immigrants came, history repeated itself—with the Irish likely to be in a somewhat more stable economic position and in control of the local government.

The history of black immigration from the South to northern cities repeated this story, at least in part. Like the older immigrants, the blacks find themselves in the lowest positions in relation to housing, jobs, and income. And they often face a city government controlled by other ethnic groups. The struggle takes the same form—for better living conditions and for political control of the local government. But the analogy between blacks and other ethnic groups is far from perfect.

Let us consider some of these ethnic groups more closely.

The "White Ethnics" American politics—particularly in the large cities—was for many years an ethnic politics. The waves of immigrants who came to America in the late nineteenth and early twentieth centuries often settled in the cities. And because such immigrants came in groups, joining family members or seeking places where they would find familiar faces or a familiar language, large numbers from the same place of origin would concentrate in particular cities. These groups—the Irish, the Poles and Slavs, the East European Jews, the Italians—usually occupied the lowest economic levels. But their numbers, and the ease with which they could become citizens, gave them one basis of power: the vote.

The large urban political machines in New York, Boston, and Chicago were based on the ethnic vote. In return for the vote, the machine offered the new immigrant help in getting a job, aid if there was trouble with the police, perhaps a Christmas basket— important comforts in a hostile new country.

These white ethnic groups have usually been mostly Democratic, particularly the Catholics and Jews. There are many reasons for this. The established groups—the white Protestant Yankees—tended to be Republican and to control the local government, and the Democratic party became a political channel for their opponents. The Democratic party, furthermore, being somewhat less a party of the business elite, was more willing to provide the social services needed by these new groups—though such services more often took the form of informal benefits than legislation to help those in need.

These immigrant groups of course cannot be thought of as a single group. The important point about them may be the order in which they came. Thus the Italian groups in many American cities started out supporting the Republican party because the Democratic party was dominated by the Irish who had come a generation earlier. This was the case in New York. But the Italians switched to the Democratic party over time, often replacing the Irish in leadership positions.

The white ethnics show the three factors that make a set of citizens into a politically relevant group. They had common interests because they were newcomers in an unfamiliar country; they were aware of these common interests because they lived in ethnic neighborhoods; and they were organized by the political parties who wanted their votes. These groups also could get members to work on political matters by providing a sense of solidarity. The social services promised by the machine also encouraged political activity.

All this happened early in this century. For several decades, observers have, for a number of reasons, been predicting the end of ethnic politics. As the generations pass, the common set of interests that hold the ethnic groups together fade. They are no longer new residents holding the low-level jobs; their children move into the mainstream of the American economy. Many move out of the ethnic neighborhoods to the newer suburbs, into areas that are ethnically mixed. This reduces the level of common interest and the possibility of developing strong self-awareness. Finally, the urban machine has lost much of its power; the welfare services it provided have been

Politically active groups and political demands in American society continue to reflect the ethnic and racial diversity of the population.

SOCIAL ORIGINS OF CONFLICT

taken over by federal social-security and other welfare programs. In short, the basis for ethnic politics seems to be fading.

But though ethnicity is not as powerful a political factor as it once was, it has remained strong. After a generation of attempts to bury the customs and identities of the Old World, many third-generation immigrant children are returning to a sense of ethnic self-awareness. Ethnic voting continues in many cities—the candidate with the right ethnic name can count on support from many of similar background. And studies show ethnicity plays a role in Presidential elections. Ethnic associations and, in some cities like Chicago, ethnic neighborhoods remain.

Likewise, ethnic groups have continued to support the Democratic party. Many observers expected this support to weaken as the white ethnics moved to the suburbs and improved their social and economic status. For a time in the 1950s it looked as if this was happening when the Republicans came close to winning the Catholic vote in the Presidential elections of 1952 and 1956. (Even in those elections the Jewish vote remained solidly Democratic.) But the switch of Catholic ethnics to the Republican party may have been due to the appeal of Dwight Eisenhower and not a permanent shift. Today, young, upwardly mobile Catholic college graduates, several generations removed from immigrant status, are still more likely than young Protestants to vote for Democratic candidates. Indeed this situation illustrates a point made in the last chapter. Party identification tends to be a stable and long-term aspect of an individual's political makeup. Once it is formed, it is likely to be passed on from generation to generation. Thus the party identification of ethnic groups persists even after the circumstances that led to that identification fade. (See Table 7.2.)

In part this renewal of ethnic politics is a reaction to a challenge from other groups—in particular from black Americans. Many of the American ethnic groups have "made it"—skilled work, a reasonably good income, a house and car, children in a good school. Challenged by what they see as a threat from expanding black neighborhoods, and by a group with what seems to be a firmer sense of

Table 7.2
Ethnic support for the
Democratic Party

Percent Identifying Themselves as Democrats	
White Protestants (Anglo-Saxon, Scandinavian, or German origin)	47%
Catholics, Irish origin	70%
Catholics, Italian origin	67%
Catholics, Polish origin	77%
Jews	62%
Blacks	89%
Among all citizens	60%

GROUPS IN AMERICA: MANY
AND VARIED

Source: Based on data from Sidney Verba and Norman H. Nie, *Participation in America: Political Democracy and Social Equality* (New York: Harper & Row, 1972).

identity—the black militants—white ethnics have begun to renew their ethnic ties.

Blacks   The melting pot, as we have pointed out, never applied to blacks. Other groups might participate fully in America, but the racial barrier was harder to cross. Black Americans have been, from the beginning, important in American politics—but as the subjects of government policy, not as participants in politics. The history of America from the early nineteenth century through the Civil War was largely one of conflict about blacks. And since the Civil War politics has often centered on the issue of race.

Before the Civil War, blacks were barred from political life. Even in states where there was no slavery, free blacks were usually denied the vote. As suggested earlier, there is some similarity between the current position of black Americans as the newest immigrants to northern cities and the position of the earlier white immigrants. Such an analogy is useful, for it helps us see some general patterns underlying the experiences of various groups. But in relation to the position of blacks in America it would be unrealistic not to notice the vast differences between the position of the blacks and that of the Irish, Italian, or Eastern European immigrants to America. The major differences can be summed up in two words: slavery and race.

Consider the position of the white immigrants to the United States in the nineteenth century. They were poor and often uneducated. They were looked down on and discriminated against. They were crowded into urban ghettos. But their situation was sharply different from that of blacks. The white immigrants entered a nation where the dominant principle was one of equality; where the aristocratic tradition of Europe in which one's position in life was determined at birth had been rejected. And they entered a society where the laws supported this principle. By the 1840s almost all men could vote. But the principle of equality and the ability to vote were clearly limited to whites—in the North as well as in the South.

The Civil War and the constitutional changes that followed it—the Thirteenth, Fourteenth, and Fifteenth Amendments—tried to change this situation. The American black could not be denied citizenship, the vote, or the protection of the laws.

At least so the Constitution said. It had still to be fully applied in practice. As part of the process of reconciliation of the North and South (of northern whites and southern whites, that is), the meaning of these amendments was watered down. Votes were effectively taken away from blacks in the South. Segregated facilities were legally accepted. And in many ways the gains of blacks at the end of the Civil War were seriously reduced.

Political conflict, as we have pointed out, arises when groups have conflicting goals but are interdependent. If they have no conflicting goals, there is no conflict. If they are not interdependent, they can each go their own way and there is no need for conflict over what policy the government should pursue. The conflict between American blacks and American whites arises because of a combination of interdependence and conflicting goals. Where the conflict between goals is severe and there appears to be little chance of agreement, one solution is to reduce the interdependence—to separate. And throughout the history of the blacks in America this has been done. In the early days of the Republic, many white leaders thought the solution to the issue of slavery would be to return blacks to Africa. And black leaders have often supported that position—as in the movement under Marcus Garvey in the 1920s for a return of blacks to Africa. This movement—though it was supported by part of the black population—never received support among the bulk of American blacks and has never been a realistic alternative. Its more recent forms—the various versions of black nationalism and separatism—call for separation within the United States: separate communities, separate schools and institutions, sometimes separate states or sections of the country.

The failure and unreality of these movements point up the fact that political conflict will continue. The black nationalist movements are significant not for their goal but for the increased sense of black identity they foster. As we have pointed out, one of the factors that makes a group of citizens politically important and effective is the sense of identity that binds them together. And this has been fostered to a large extent by the sense of deprivation of blacks in America.

American blacks have become a strong political force in recent years because they have developed self-awareness and organization. The third factor—common interests—is something they have had from the beginning. But common interests are not enough if the group is not aware of these interests. This self-awareness grew in the 1950s and 1960s.

The growth of black self-awareness has many sources. The role of the civil rights movement of the 1950s and 1960s is important. So is the role of the mass media—especially television—in communicating the new movement to the black community. In earlier times a civil rights demonstration in one part of the country might have little impact on others. But when a nation is linked together by the media, it is easier to create a community among people living in different regions, in cities and in rural areas.

The increased importance of blacks in American political life depends also on organization. The history of the recent black movement has been a history of organization as well: the NAACP, the Southern Christian Leadership Council, CORE, the Black Muslims, the Black Panthers, Operation Breadbasket. The list—and it could be much longer—shows how many and varied the bases of black political organization are. Blacks are by no means organized in one common group, nor are they all organized. But organizations of all sorts are making blacks a political force.

Other Minority Groups   Blacks are not the only racial or ethnic minority. We have seen how white ethnic politics has responded to what is seen as a black challenge. Other minority groups—Chicanos, American Indians—have also moved into active politics. In each case their activity shows how interests or needs in common, self-awareness, and organization make a group politically relevant.

Chicanos, for instance, have long had common interests and needs. Speaking a language that was foreign in the United States, often given only the lowest-paying agricultural jobs, discriminated against in housing and schools, the Chicanos were not politically active until recent times. However—again perhaps in response to similar activities among black Americans, but also in response to such leaders as Cesar Chavez—they have moved into the center of political conflict.

They form an interesting contrast to another group—Americans of Japanese origin—many of whom, like the Chicanos, live on the West Coast. Japanese-Americans also have a long history of common problems and discrimination. They were long barred from American citizenship and from owning land. And in World War II most Japanese-Americans were put in concentration camps—called relocation centers—as dangerous aliens. In addition, Japanese-Americans have a fairly strong sense of group identification.

But unlike Chicanos and blacks, Japanese-Americans are not an active political force. One of the three factors is missing. There is a sense of identification and even some organization, but little common political interest. Japanese-Americans face almost no housing or schooling discrimination and have moved into high-status jobs in most places. With little common political interest—that is, no set of policies they want the government to pursue—they do not become a potent political force.

Other Types of Groups

There are so many ways citizens group together that we could go on describing them endlessly. As we began to run out of relevant groups at one point in time, new ones would be forming and old ones fading from political involvement. Let us, then, look at some of the other *types* of groups one finds in America. We can then turn to the more interesting question of how they relate to one another.

Occupational Groups   Occupation is an important concern to most Americans; people are interested in how well teachers, farmers, doctors, or plumbers are doing. But occupational groups vary in political relevance in terms of common interests, self-awareness, and organization.

Not all occupational groups have common interests to the same extent. Small shopkeepers represent an important occupational group, but the members of the group do not have a "common fate": One shopkeeper may do well while another goes bankrupt. Of

Occupational groups, whether doctors or truckers, share common concerns and may act politically.

course sometimes they will have common problems. All shopkeepers may be hurt by inflation or a business downturn, but in these cases it will have an impact on them as members of the general economy, not as shopkeepers. Or the shopkeepers in a particular town may be hurt by the development of a shopping center outside the town. But in this case they will probably form a politically relevant group on a local basis.

Compared with shopkeepers or lawyers, such groups as teachers or automobile workers are much more likely to have a common fate

GROUPS IN AMERICA: MANY AND VARIED

177

and a set of common interests. Teachers have common interests because their salaries and working conditions are all set by the governments for which they work; automobile workers, because they depend on a single industry.

In addition, there is the question of how much these interests are affected by governmental policy. The more the government is active in relation to a particular occupation, the more the occupational group is likely to be politically involved. Doctors and lawyers show a contrast here. Governmental policies that affect the practice of medicine—from community and state hospitals to medicare to drug regulations—are much more extensive than those that affect the practice of law. And doctors as an organized occupational group have, through the American Medical Association (AMA), been most active in politics. This illustrates a point made earlier about the different degrees of citizen concern about particular interests. All citizens have an interest in health care. But the medical profession—because it earns its living through health care, because it is organized and has leadership—has had a greater voice in such matters than the much larger number of ordinary citizens.

Note that we are dealing here with the extent to which various occupational groups become politically active *in relation to the interests of that occupation*. Lawyers are generally more active in politics than doctors; indeed they are more active than members of most other professions. They are more likely than members of other professions to run for office or to take government appointments. But they do so not as representatives of the interests of the legal profession.

This difference among occupational groups is related to a simple but important generalization about politics: Where the government is active, citizens are likely to be active as well. When new government programs touch the lives of particular groups, they are likely to become more politically involved.

Occupational groups also differ in self-awareness and organization. These two characteristics are of course linked. The better a group is organized, the more likely it is that its members will be aware of their common problems and the relevance of the government to them. Farmers have been an important political force because they have participated in a variety of farm organizations. Or, rather, those farmers who have been organized have been a strong force; those who have not organized (poorer farmers, tenant farmers, and so on) have been weak politically. A most important distinction is between organized and unorganized labor. Workers who are not unionized are politically weak—both because they have no organization to speak for them and because they have no self-awareness. This was the case for many decades for such groups as teachers and migratory workers. Teachers remained unorganized because they believed unionization was not appropriate for such a professional group; migratory workers remained unorganized because the conditions of their work made it hard to form groups. In recent years, as both groups have begun to develop organization, they have become more politically active and effective.

We have not mentioned one way the American population might divide up occupationally. Rather than being divided into specific groups—auto workers or high school teachers or small shopkeepers or doctors—politics could be based on broad divisions between "workers" and "management." In other countries workers have organized into a socialist or communist party while another party or parties represents management. For a variety of reasons, some of which we shall discuss later when we consider the American parties, this has not happened in America. One can argue about whether this is due to a lack of objective interests in common among workers or a lack of self-awareness or a failure of leadership and organization. Or perhaps, as some argue, the needs of workers are satisfied by a strong union movement. Whether this is good (because it lowers the intensity of conflict in America) or bad (because it prevents the adequate representation of the needs of workers) is also debatable.

Income Groups   Income is of course closely related to occupation, and the two go together to create what is often called social class. Many have wondered why the poor do not form a more clear-cut political movement. Why don't farmers and laborers join to form a political party that would redistribute the resources in America?

Attempts have been made to form such parties. And in recent years there have been poor people's groups cutting across occupation and race. Such movements could be an important force in America, and one cannot predict their future success or failure. But the fact that they are often described as coalitions indicates one of the problems with the formation of political groups based on income. It is true that the poor have interests in common, but they also have much that keeps them from coming together to work on those interests. For one thing, as we have seen, political action depends on resources such as time and money. The poor have less money by definition, and time is often something they cannot afford. And the poor are themselves divided by occupation—farmers and laborers have some interests in common but many differences—and by race and ethnicity. As a political group the poor could become important, but income is not yet a strong basis for cohesive political action.

Regional Groups   The place where people live and work also forms the basis for common interests. Different regions, different states and cities, suburbs vs. central cities—all these differences may have political importance. Regional politics has of course been important in U.S. history. The South is the most distinctive region in terms of culture, history, and political behavior. Its voters tended to vote in a distinctive way—traditionally for the Democratic party long after the basis for that identification had faded. And its representatives in

Congress formed a bloc—often voting with northern Republicans to form a strong conservative force. The solid South has become less solid since Republicans began to make inroads in the Eisenhower years. Industrialization and population migration, as well as the political awakening of the southern black, have changed the social and political life of the region.

With the South one sees another example of the importance of common interests and common experiences with government policy. Southerners had the shared experience of the Civil War and Reconstruction. Even when long past, these experiences could be seen in the South's heightened self-awareness as a region.

Regional politics in the United States is important because it is always well organized. By that we simply mean elections in America have a regional structure. We elect representatives to Congress from particular districts or states. The point is so obvious that we may miss its importance. Why not elect representatives from occupational groups—all plumbers elect a certain number, all lawyers, all farmers? Or by race—the blacks elect theirs, the whites theirs, the Chicanos theirs? Why not indeed? Other countries have experimented with such alternatives, and one can make an argument for them. The argument for geographic representation is that citizens living in the same area have similar interests, but this is only partially true. In some ways we have interests in common with those who live in the same congressional district, but in some ways we may have more interests in common with citizens of similar occupation or religion or race living in other parts of the state or nation.

But whatever the basis of representation (and probably none is perfect), the fact is that the American system is organized on the basis of place of residence, and this is unlikely to change. This automatically makes geography important as a basis of citizen interests. As we shall see in Chapter 10, where we discuss the representativeness of Congress, this basis of representation has a major impart on how the government operates.

Recently conflict has arisen between citizens who have moved to suburbs to avoid the noise, crowding, and social tensions of the cities and those who remain in the central cities, for whom the noise, crowding, and social tensions are an unavoidable part of life. The latter claim that the problems of the central city could be solved if those in the suburbs would help—if their schools were open to central-city children, if their communities would construct low-cost housing. The suburban citizens often reply that these are the problems of the cities, and they are pleased to have left them behind. That the central city resident is often black and the suburban citizen white does not make the problem easier to solve.

Religious Groups In many nations religious conflict is severe. In America religious divisions have been politically relevant but not the source of severe conflict. Catholics have had a traditional identi-

Creating self-awareness has been a goal of such feminist organizations as the National Organization of Women.

fication with the Democratic party; Jewish groups have been active on American policy in the Middle East; fundamentalist Protestant groups have lobbied for Blue Laws and the like. When the first Catholic candidate (Al Smith) ran for the Presidency in 1928, he was bitterly opposed by many Protestant groups who thought his election would represent a takeover by the Catholic Church. When the second Catholic candidate (John F. Kennedy) ran and won in 1960, he was also opposed for similar reasons. But his behavior in office could in no way be considered distinctively Catholic. It may be that the Kennedy experience will lead to a decline in the religious basis for political groups.

Perhaps the major reason for the lack of severe religious conflict in American politics is the constitutional ban on laws affecting religious belief. If our generalization is correct, groups become politically active when governmental policy is directed at them. The constitutional ban on legislation affecting religion may explain why religion has not been the explosive issue it might have been. On the other hand, the Constitution does not eliminate all religious-based issues. The exact meaning of the constitutional provision for the separation of church and state has given rise to conflict in the past and continues to do so. Is it a violation of the Constitution if a city pays for school buses for children going to Catholic schools? Is it a violation if there is prayer in the schools? On such issues one finds religious groups active and concerned. Similarly religion can affect a group's attitude on foreign policy—as is shown by the strong views of American Jews on relations with Israel.

Sex and Age Groups   Is either sex or age the basis for politically relevant grouping? Ten years ago one might have said "maybe" for age (there have been politically relevant movements among old and retired people from time to time in American history) but "no" for sex. Men and women, at least since the women's suffrage movement, did not seem to have different political interests. In recent times of course, because of the "generation gap," the increasingly large numbers of elderly citizens, the vote for 18-year-olds, youth movements and the youth culture, age may have become politically relevant. Evidence suggests that organized youth was a small portion of that group during the 1960s and a rather distinct portion at that—those on college campuses.

Women are not a minority group. They form 51 percent of the population. But the history of the women's movement parallels in many ways that of other groups in American politics. The case of women shows the importance of self-awareness as well as common interest in creating a politically relevant group. The leaders of women's groups complain of various forms of discrimination. But they do not speak of problems invented in the few years since that movement has burst on the scene. Rather, the things they complain of—job discrimination, stereotyping, and so forth—are old ones. But the awareness of such practices, encouraged by a few active leaders and the mass media, is what creates the group.

Critics of social movements such as women's liberation or black militant movements often accuse these groups of inventing the problems they complain of. "Women never knew they were discriminated against until the women's lib types told them." But that is exactly what political leadership must do if it is to succeed in creating a movement. It must create awareness of problems within a group in order to make that group politically active.

Special-Concern Groups We have been describing groups of American citizens in terms of ethnic background, occupation, sex, age, place of residence. These things are likely to be at the base of lasting political groups, but they become politically relevant, we have argued, only if accompanied by an awareness of some common interest — a black political interest, a women's political interest.

But there are times when groups are based more directly on shared interests and less on basic social characteristics. As with social characteristics, the variety of specific interests is also vast. Groups form around common recreational interests (skiing, hunting, bird watching); around social concerns (mental health, pollution, governmental corruption); around intellectual or cultural interests (book clubs, literary groups, art groups).

As with the other groups, these special-concern groups become politically relevant when there is some way their interests are affected by government action or inaction. For instance, recreational groups may begin as organizations with no particular interest in government policy; they may be simply groups of citizens with common interests in skiing or hiking or bird watching. But as the pursuit of these nonpolitical interests becomes dependent on governmental programs — on the preservation of a wilderness area, for instance — these groups can become politically active.

Multiple Memberships

As we have seen, Americans have many different group identifications. To understand how these affect political life, we must look at the relationships among these identifications. There are two points to note:

1. There is a great variety of groups and potential groups in America. There is no set of dominant groups.
2. More important is the fact that the groups can overlap. Each citizen belongs to many groups at once. Citizens have at the same time ethnic identity, occupational status, regional location, religion, and so forth.

Which of these group affiliations will be important politically? The answer is that it varies. At some times and on some issues, one group affiliation will be important, at other times others will matter. The Catholic steelworker living in a suburb of Cleveland will sometimes act politically as a steelworker. He will support policies or candidates based on his view of the interests of steelworkers or on the advice of his union. At other times he may act as a Catholic, perhaps voting for a candidate who is of the same faith or considering an issue such as abortion law or aid for parochial schools from that point of view. Another time he may act as a suburbanite, perhaps opposing plans to tax suburban dwellers who work in the cities. In short, citizens have many potential political interests. At times they act in terms of one such interest, at other times in terms of others.

At least that is the case with most Americans. For some, one identification overrides all others—black militants respond to all issues in terms of racial identity, militant members of women's liberation groups in terms of sexual identity, and so forth. The results for political life are important. If a citizen has a variety of identifications, he is likely to hold none as strongly as the citizen who puts all his energy into one. The citizen with many identifications is more willing to compromise, less firm in action. The "single-identity" citizen is likely to be more militant, firmer, less compromising.

Crosscutting vs. Reinforcing Identifications

An important characteristic of group identifications in America is the extent to which they *crosscut* rather than *reinforce* one another.

Let us explain what we mean by these terms, since they help us understand how political conflict in America works itself out. Imagine a society where people are divided by religion (into Catholics and Protestants), by occupation (into workers and managers), and by place of residence (into suburban and central-city residents). If these three divisions of society were reinforcing rather than crosscutting, one would find that all citizens who were similar on one characteristic would be similar on the other two. The society might be divided in this way:

| Catholic workers living in the central city | Protestant managers living in the suburbs |

And insofar as there were interests associated with these identifications, the society would be divided into two groups with conflicting interests. Catholics want aid to parochial schools; Protestants do not. Workers want controls over profits; managers want controls over wages. City dwellers want suburban residents to share in the cost of urban services; suburban residents do not. Thus the society would be divided into groups with the following interests:

One group would be	*The other group would be*
a. in favor of aid to parochial schools.	a. opposed to aid to parochial schools.
b. in favor of control over profits.	b. opposed to controls over profits.
c. in favor of taxing the suburbs to pay for city services.	c. opposed to taxing the suburbs to pay for city services.

Such a situation is likely to be one of high political tension. The two groups have nothing in common. They are divided on every issue. If government power were in the hands of the Protestant managers who live in the suburbs, the city-dwelling Catholic workers would have little reason to believe their interests would be protected—for the group in power would differ from them in every way.

But suppose the identifications were crosscutting, not reinforcing. In this case some workers would be Protestant and others Catholic; some would live in the suburbs and some in the city. The important point here is that citizens divided on one interest would be united on others. The Catholic worker would disagree with the Protestant worker on aid to parochial schools but agree with him on controls over profits. If he lived in a suburb, he would share interests with Protestants who lived there as well as with managers who lived there. And in his church he would meet (maybe not socialize with, but at least see) people of different economic backgrounds.

In general, American politics is characterized by crosscutting patterns of group identification. Catholic workers join with Protestant workers on some issues (economic ones) and with Catholic businessmen on others (parochial schools, perhaps). These patterns have an important impact on American politics, since they affect the political coalitions that can be formed. People have often talked of forming a liberal (or radical) coalition in the United States, bringing together all who are interested in major changes in the social and economic systems. But such a coalition is very difficult to build, for any such group will contain people with very different views on some issues, much as they may agree on others.

Take a simple example: One of the major positions of a liberal or radical coalition is likely to be tax reforms that increase taxes on higher-income groups and eliminate many of the loopholes in tax laws that benefit such groups. Such a position would find agreement among many of the groups that would form the core of a liberal or radical coalition—blacks, white workers, middle-class liberal intellectuals. But those three groups would differ when it came to other issues. The blacks and the white workers might differ on matters of integration; both might differ from the middle-class intellectuals on matters of civil liberties. Such a coalition would obviously be hard to hold together.

Patterns of Division and Competition

We have described the politically relevant groups in American society at some length because it is around such groups that the political struggle takes place. These groups have different interests and therefore make different claims on the government. Each seeks policies that benefit it and, in so doing, often comes into conflict with other groups.

The wide range of groups in America, the variation in the in-

Figure 7.1
Scale of Political Positions

Strongly Favor A	Mildly Favor A	Indifferent Between A and B	Mildly Favor B	Strongly Favor B

tensity of concern citizens have with one set of interests rather than another, and the fact that groups crisscross one another all suggest that no single pattern of division and competition is found in America. From issue to issue, from group to group, the way parts of the society compete with each other may differ. But the major divisions may be changing as well. As we saw in the last chapter, the political beliefs of Americans have been changing somewhat. More and more citizens are developing consistent political beliefs on a number of issues. How far this movement will go is uncertain. The following section discusses the implications for conflict in the United States of different patterns of political belief.

Different Patterns of Political Belief: Implications for Conflict

It will be useful to sketch a variety of patterns of competition or conflict among groups, along with some examples. The reader will understand a good deal about any particular issue or conflict in America if he can fit it into one of these patterns.

Scale of Political Positions   Political conflict begins with conflicting interests. One group of citizens prefers one policy (we can call it A); another prefers an alternative policy (call it B). In addition, some citizens feel strongly about the issue, others feel less strongly, and some are indifferent. Thus we can put various citizens and groups somewhere on the scale, as shown in Figure 7.1. "A" might stand for a hawkish position on Vietnam; "B" for a dovish one. Or perhaps they stand for being for or against integrated housing, or for or against gun control, or for or against various welfare programs. Some citizens will support A or B strongly, some more mildly, and some not at all.

If we convert the scale of political positions into a graph, with the amount of space under the curved line indicating how many people hold that position, we can see a variety of patterns of competition. Consider Example 1. Here the largest group of Americans don't care about A or B, and those who do have a position hold that position rather mildly. Furthermore, the figure is quite symmetrical—the numbers of citizens on either side of the issue are about equal. Many issues take this form, and for obvious reasons they tend to be those on which there is little conflict, little excitement, and perhaps no governmental activity. It will make little difference what action the government will take, because there is little concern on either side. With a pattern like this, government officials are fairly free to do any-

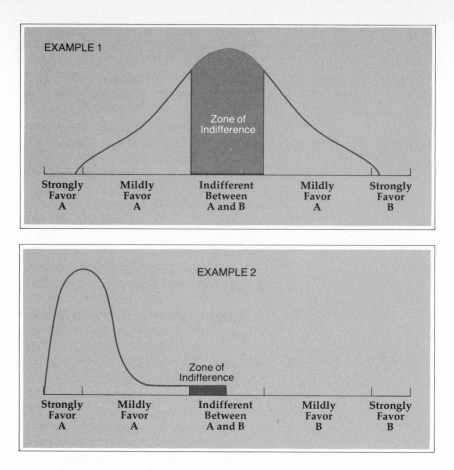

EXAMPLE 1

Zone of Indifference

| Strongly Favor A | Mildly Favor A | Indifferent Between A and B | Mildly Favor A | Strongly Favor B |

EXAMPLE 2

Zone of Indifference

| Strongly Favor A | Mildly Favor A | Indifferent Between A and B | Mildly Favor B | Strongly Favor B |

thing they want about the issue—if they want to do anything at all.

Example 2 shows a different pattern of interests or preferences. Like Example 1, it is a situation where one would expect little conflict or competition, simply because all citizens seem to agree in their strong support for position A.

Examples of such a situation might be the attitudes of Americans toward the enemy in most wars before Vietnam. Most Americans were strongly antagonistic to the enemy. Such a pattern does not lead to internal conflict. It can be a strong political force, a resource used by government leaders if they want public support for an all-out war effort. Or it can greatly limit their freedom of action if, for instance, they want to pursue a more conciliatory policy toward the opposing group.

A pattern of interests of this type, however, can have dangerous results for democracy—woe to the few citizens in favor of policy B! Even those who don't care may be in trouble. Free speech or rights of political association have been most severely limited when American opinion is shaped as in Example 2. Thus in wartime we have often seen the suspension or diminution of the freedoms guaranteed in the First Amendment.

Figure 7.2
Attitudes on Medical Care

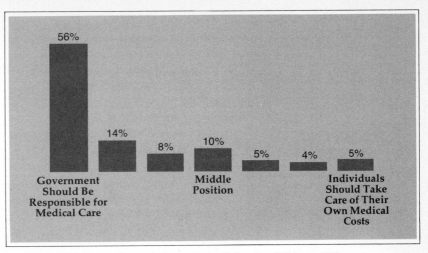

Source: National Opinion Research Center study, University of Chicago, 1973.

This same pattern arises when an issue in American politics is "settled." For instance, there used to be sharp controversy over the degree to which the government should pay for medical care. After the medicare plan was passed, the issue became less controversial. Look at the data in Figure 7.2, which shows the responses people gave to a question asked in 1973. They were asked to place themselves on a scale showing whether they felt government had a responsibility to help people pay for medical care. Most agreed that the government had such a responsibility.

Example 3 is very different from the first two. It shows a major division—about half the citizens strongly prefer A and about half strongly prefer B. Very few are in between. It is obvious that a population divided in this way—especially if the choice between A and B is an important one—is deeply divided indeed. This may describe the United States just before the Civil War.

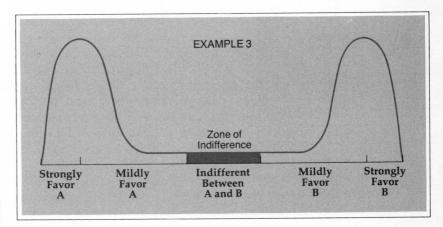

Figure 7.3
Positions on Vietnam

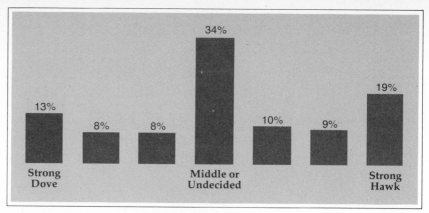

Source: Based on data from an unpublished study on Vietnam and the urban crisis by Richard Brody, Benjamin Page, and Sidney Verba, 1968.

The point to be made, though, is that this pattern has been relatively rare (though a variation on this pattern, which we discuss later, is becoming more common), simply because issues as sharply defined as in Example 3 that split the population down the middle have been infrequent in America. Consider two of the most important recent political controversies: Vietnam and the racial issue.

At the height of the controversy over what to do about Vietnam, citizens were asked to place themselves on a scale showing their policy preferences. They could place themselves at an "extreme dove" position, which meant they wanted to withdraw immediately from Vietnam no matter what; they could place themselves at an "extreme hawk" position, which meant they wanted to use all force to win. Figure 7.3 shows where they placed themselves. Some citizens took strong positions at either end of the scale. But the largest group is found in the middle, and many others took mild positions on one side or the other.

Or consider a similar scale of opinions on what to do about the

Figure 7.4
Positions on the Urban Crisis

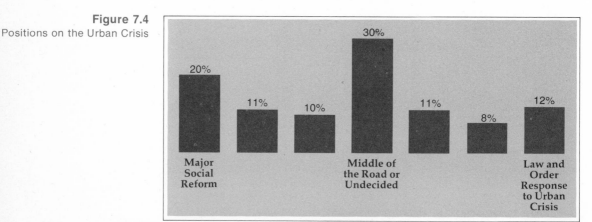

Source: Based on data from an unpublished study on Vietnam and the urban crisis by Richard Brody, Benjamin Page, and Sidney Verba, 1968.

Figure 7.5
Positions on Liberalism
and Conservatism

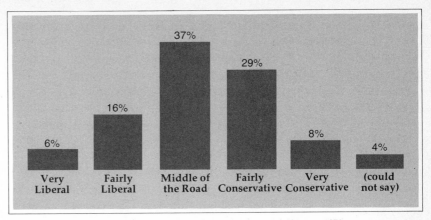

Source: National Opinion Research Center study, University of Chicago, 1973.

"urban crisis." Citizens were asked to place themselves on a scale from favoring major reform to deal with the social and economic issues underlying urban unrest to favoring maximum "law and order" to stop urban unrest. (See Figure 7.4.)

As with the Vietnam issue, one found many Americans in middle positions. Thus on two of the most controversial issues of the day citizens were not divided into two opposing camps.

Indeed the general position of Americans on a broad scale ranging from liberal to conservative is probably reflected in the results of a 1970 Gallup poll. (See Figure 7.5.)

The results differ slightly from what the Gallup poll found in previous years—largely in that the conservative group has become somewhat larger than the liberal. This may be due to a movement of the American people in that direction or, perhaps, to a redefinition of conservatism to stress such issues as sex, pornography, and drugs rather than economic issues.

But the most important point is that opinions tend to lie near the center. In fact the pattern of citizen preferences in America when looked at across a number of issues may often take such a form. It can be seen in Example 4.

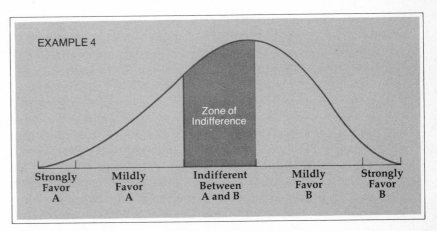

This situation represents a slight variation on Example 1. There is little intensity of political opinion, but what there is seems to favor B. Many ordinary political issues take this form—a fairly large portion of the population mildly favors one alternative; another group, not quite as large, favors the other. And in between is a large group that doesn't care. Policy B stands a good chance of getting favorable action, though it is by no means certain. Those holding position B may have no organization or leadership; or they may need to win the support of some of those who don't care, and because they feel mildly about the issue they may not try hard enough. In any case, if they succeed, it will cause little conflict because both groups are not strongly committed.

This pattern is a fairly good illustration of one major division of the American population—into Democrats and Republicans. Most Americans have one identification or the other; some are independent. But few Americans hold their partisan identification so intensely that they would be fundamentally opposed to having members of the other party in leadership positions (or else elections would be potential civil-war situations). Over the years more citizens have identified with the Democrats than with the Republicans. But this does not mean a Democrat in the White House at each election. Since these identifications are not very strong, many citizens can be swayed from one side to the other. And as we shall see in Chapter 9 on parties and elections, election victory often depends on the pull of many forces besides those that identify a citizen with a party.

In general, the pattern of division in the United States has tended to resemble Example 4. This situation has often been praised by students of American politics because such a situation makes for stability. Granted, a society that resembles Example 3 with citizens far apart and hostile is more likely to fly apart. But the pattern shown in Example 4 means stability in another sense of the word—nothing changes. And it is just this tendency—when one considers the nation as a whole—that may lead to stagnation in governmental policy.

The extent to which the pattern found in Example 4 will remain the dominant one in America is uncertain. In the previous chapter we showed that the American public has changed over time in terms of consistency of political attitudes. More Americans now have consistently conservative or consistently liberal attitudes. And this implies that patterns of division may be moving from the near consensus of Example 4 to the strong division of Example 3. The extent to which that will happen is uncertain as we write this book, but the citizen who wants to understand the patterns of American politics would be wise to follow this development closely.

Furthermore, there are two other patterns that are relevant in America—one a traditional one that has applied to many issues, the other one that is becoming more apparent in recent years. Consider Example 5. Here is a small group of the population strongly in favor of a particular position, faced by the bulk of the population that

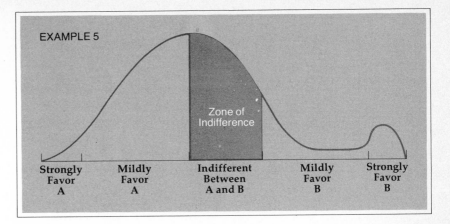

EXAMPLE 5

| Strongly Favor A | Mildly Favor A | Indifferent Between A and B | Mildly Favor B | Strongly Favor B |

Zone of Indifference

either does not care or is mildly on the other side. That such a pattern of preferences is common is suggested by the generalization presented earlier—different problems are of different degrees of concern to different groups of citizens. Drug manufacturers care intensely whether the government regulates the manufacture or sale of their product, since such regulations may cut into their profits. Citizens who do not use many drug products won't care. Citizens who use a lot would prefer such regulations but will care far less intensely than the manufacturers.

The situation in Example 5 repeats itself in many areas. The special role of the medical profession in medical legislation is like this; so is the special importance of hunters and sportsmen in gun control. As we have seen, about 70 percent of the American public favor gun control. The opposition is small, but it is intense. The pattern of Example 5 can produce pressure-group politics, which we discuss later. The main characteristic is that the intense minority is, under such circumstances, likely to win the day. They are more likely to be vocal and to be organized. What they lack in numbers they make up for in intensity.

Let us look at one last example (Example 6). Here we see an intense minority faced by an opposing but also intense majority. Such

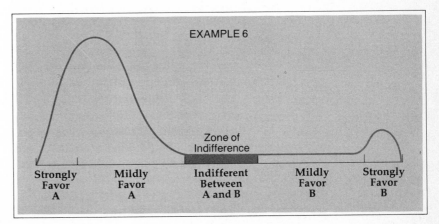

EXAMPLE 6

Zone of Indifference

| Strongly Favor A | Mildly Favor A | Indifferent Between A and B | Mildly Favor B | Strongly Favor B |

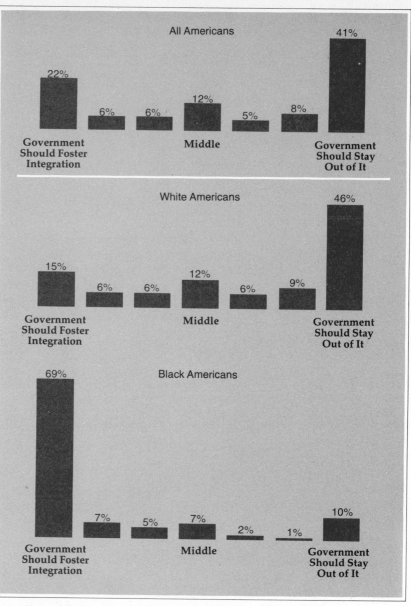

All Americans

22%

6%   6%   12%   5%   8%

41%

Government
Should Foster
Integration

Middle

Government
Should Stay
Out of It

White Americans

46%

15%

6%   6%   12%   6%   9%

Government
Should Foster
Integration

Middle

Government
Should Stay
Out of It

Black Americans

69%

7%   5%   7%   2%   1%

10%

Government
Should Foster
Integration

Middle

Government
Should Stay
Out of It

Source: National Opinion Research Center study, University of Chicago, 1973.

a situation would exist if there were groups in society that were severely deprived but were cut off from the rest of the population by a set of reinforcing divisions. Consider the situation in many of America's metropolitan areas. In the decaying central city lives a population that is poor and black; surrounding them are the suburbs, rich and white. They are divided by race, economic condition, and place of residence. And therefore they have very few common interests. The central-city residents want social services and want the costs shared by those outside the city; they want access to better schools; they want chances for housing outside of the cities. Those in the suburbs differ on all these issues. Further, they have few social ties with those in the cities; they differ in all respects.

We illustrate this division of opinion in Figure 7.6. In 1973 citizens were asked how they felt about housing integration: Should the government see to it that blacks can buy houses in white neighborhoods if they want to, or should it stay out? The answers show that most Americans took positions at one or the other end of the scale—they either felt strongly that the government should see to it that blacks can buy houses in white neighborhoods or felt strongly that the government should stay out. Those who felt that the government should stay out of this outnumber the others by two to one.

The degree to which this issue "polarizes" our society is seen more clearly if we look at white and black opinions separately. We do this in Figure 7.6 as well. There are some whites who strongly favor housing integration, but the bulk of the white population is at the other end. They want the government to stay out. The bulk of the black population wants the government to foster integration. A pattern like that in Figure 7.6 leads to conflict. And that, of course, is the situation on this issue.

Conclusion

There are many patterns of division in America. On some issues there is wide agreement among almost all Americans, on others the public may form two hostile camps, and on other issues an intense minority may face a less intense majority. We cannot predict the specific issues that will arise. But the patterns we have described should be helpful in understanding the nature of new issues and the impact they are likely to have on the political process.

Controversy

The majority of income in America is earned by a minority of families. For instance, the richest 49 percent of Americans earn about three-quarters of the income. Why does not the other 51 percent organize politically to change that situation? They are, after all, a majority of the citizens.

Yet American policy has rarely been organized into a struggle between the haves and the have-nots as many radical Americans have hoped and many conservative Americans have feared. Political conflict in America has never involved all the wealthy vs.

all the less wealthy. Most observers agree on this. But there is controversy over why this is true and whether politics should be organized this way.

One Side

What is needed in America is a poor people's coalition, a union of all those who do not receive the full benefits of American society. Such a union of poor people—the blacks, Chicanos, and other minority groups; the factory workers; the low-paid clerks; the small farmers; old people living on pensions—could elect a government that would equalize the wealth in America. And such a coalition is "natural." Pocketbook issues are of greatest concern to Americans; such issues could overcome other differences among the poor. If this part of the population has not been aware of its common interests, it is because it has lacked political leadership.

The Other Side

The reasons why America won't be divided into the haves and the have-nots in the future are the same that have prevented the growth of coalitions of the poor in the past. The only thing the poor have in common is low income. They do not think of themselves as members of the same group—the white unskilled laborer identifies with neither the white farmer nor the black unskilled laborer. Nor do they have the same objective interests. They have a common interest in higher income. Who doesn't? But there is so much else that divides them; race, region, sex, and age are only a few of the characteristics that *divide* rather than unite the poor. They are unlikely ever to put a movement together. And it is a good thing too. If the nation were divided into the haves and the have-nots—if, that is, the other bases of political conflict were irrelevant—the possibility of severe domestic conflict would be very great.

8

Interest Groups in America

As we saw in the previous chapter, the United States is divided into many groups with different interests. We considered the reasons why some groups become politically powerful while others do not. Groups that are organized are likely to have a greater effect on governmental policy than those that have no organization. In this chapter we look more closely at political organizations: organizations that try to influence governmental policy. How many interest or pressure groups are there in the United States? How powerful are they? What makes some powerful and others not?

The Role of Interest Groups

There is disagreement about the power of interest groups. Some students of politics have argued that all one needs to know about American politics can be learned by studying the role of such groups. Congress and the President, they argue, do not initiate policy. Rather, they respond to the demands of lobbies and organized interests. At best the government acts as a "broker" among such interests—seeing that each organized interest gets a little something in response to its demands. Thus the conflicting pressures from organized groups determine governmental policy.

Most writers on politics think this is an exaggeration. Governmental policy is not merely the sum of interest-group pressures. Yet there is some truth to the view. Organized groups are not all-powerful. But interests represented by well-organized pressure groups are better able to pressure the government than unorganized interests. And this is important in determining who will benefit from governmental policy.

Observers also disagree as to whether the activities of such groups hurt society as a whole. Pressure groups serve the "selfish" interests of particular groups of citizens. Organizations lobby for the interests of clothing manufacturers, doctors, farmers. Nor are such "selfish" interests limited to the wealthy trying to get an even bigger share of the economic pie. Organizations press the claims of blacks, welfare mothers, labor. Their interests are "selfish" not because their demands are not justified but because they represent the specific interests of each group and do not take into account the needs and problems of other groups. Each group is out to "take care of its own."

Critics of pressure groups argue that they achieve their selfish interests at the expense of the society as a whole. Pressure groups compete for the attention of government officials to obtain some benefit for their group. In this way the broader public interest is ignored. No one plans for the problems of the society as a whole. Such a view of interest groups is reflected in the "muckraking" of writers like Lincoln Steffens at the beginning of the century. Such literature has revealed many cases of close association of specific interests with the government. Out of such close association comes a governmental policy that benefits particular interests and may hurt the rest of society. This position is strongly held by a number of the most serious students of American politics.

These critics make a further point. It is not only that the pressure-group system ignores the interests of the nation as a whole in favor of particular selfish interests. It is also a fault of the pressure-group system that only certain interests are communicated. In general, they agree, the interests of business and of the wealthier members of society are communicated in this way.

A different argument is made by other observers of American politics, that there is no conflict between the selfish interests of particular groups and some more general public good. Indeed the public good, the argument goes, does not exist outside of and separate from the specific interests of groups of citizens. Rather, the public good represents the sum of the desires of these various groups, and out of the clash among these groups comes the most effective and responsive public policy.

Although those who defend the interest-group system admit that not all groups are equally represented, they argue that the answer is more, and more equal, group representation. If some interests are well represented by interest groups and others are not, then the others should organize as well.

Does competition among organized interests hurt the general public interest? Or is it the most effective way of seeing that citizen interests are communicated to the government?

We will return to these questions later in this chapter, after we have discussed the role of organized groups in American politics.

How Much Organization?

America has often been called a society of joiners; foreign observers have been struck by the ease with which Americans form organizations and by the great numbers and far-ranging concerns of such organizations. And when we compare the United States to other nations, we find a somewhat higher percentage of organization members here than elsewhere. Current figures indicate that about six out of ten adult Americans belong to some organization, a figure higher than in comparable countries, where a little less than half the adult population is likely to belong to some organized group.

Who Are the Members of Organizations?

Does the figure "six out of ten" mean most Americans have some organization that takes care of their political interests? The answer is unclear. Although the data show that a majority of Americans belong to some organization, they also show a large minority—four out of ten—with no affiliation. More important, perhaps, is that all social groups are not equally likely to be members of organizations. As we

Table 8.1
Types of Organizations
to Which Individuals Belong

Type of Organization	Percent of Population Reporting Membership
Political groups such as Democratic or Republican clubs, and political action groups such as voters' leagues	8
School service groups such as PTA or school alumni groups	17
Service clubs such as Lions, Rotary, Zonta, Junior Chamber of Commerce	6
Youth groups such as Boy Scouts, Girl Scouts	7
Veterans' groups such as American Legion	7
Farm organizations such as Farmer's Union, Farm Bureau, Grange	4
Nationality groups such as Sons of Norway, Hibernian Society	2
Church-related groups such as Bible Study Group, Holy Name Society	6
Fraternal groups such as Elks, Eagles, Masons, and their women's auxiliaries	15
Professional or academic societies such as American Dental Association, Phi Beta Kappa	7
Trade Unions	17
School fraternities and sororities	3
Literary, art, discussion, or study clubs such as book-review clubs, theater groups	4
Hobby or garden clubs such as stamp or coin clubs, flower clubs, pet clubs	5
Sports clubs, bowling leagues, etc.	12

Source: Based on data from Sidney Verba and Norman H. Nie, *Participation in America: Political Democracy and Social Equality* (New York: Harper & Row, 1972.)

saw in Chapter 4, it is the upper-status citizens who are more likely to be organization members. If you are wealthy, if you have a college education, if you are white rather than black, you are more likely to be an organization member. Thus not only is membership not universal in the United States, but what membership there is, is not spread equally across the society.

Political and Nonpolitical Interest Groups

Furthermore, not all organizations citizens belong to have been formed to express political interests. (See Table 8.1.) Only 8 percent of the citizens belong to specifically political groups — political party clubs; nonpartisan political groups like the League of Women Voters; and groups like the NAACP, whose purpose is to pressure the government. Rather, most organizations are formed for other purposes. They are related to recreational interests (fraternal groups, sports and hobby clubs); economic interests (unions, professional associations, farm groups); particular community concerns (parent groups, service clubs); or specific citizen identifications (nationality groups, religious groups).

Many groups are nonpolitical,
but sometimes even these
become involved in politics.

But it would be a mistake to think only groups with a political purpose communicate citizen interests to the government. All these types of groups may become politically active, and some are all the time. Indeed it is hard to draw the line between political and nonpolitical organizations. Since all groups may at times be affected by governmental activity or require some governmental response, any group may become politically active. A good example is the National Rifle Association. Essentially organized as a recreational group for hunters and sportsmen, it became a major political force when it felt its interests challenged by supporters of gun-control legislation. And the same can be said for every other type of group. Church-related groups do not have political goals, but they become involved in conflicts over issues they see affecting their interests—abortion laws, school prayers, or any other issue they take seriously. And groups representing economic interests are constantly involved with the government.

Lobbies

Some organizations are more active in trying to influence the government than others. They have offices in Washington or in state capitals, and they have professional staffs that have close contact with the government. The range of organizations that are active in this way may be seen in Table 8.2, taken from a congressional report on lobbying organizations. Of the hundreds of such groups registered in Washington, it lists those that report the largest expenditures to influence Congress.

The data do not necessarily show which groups are most active in Washington; the Lobbying Act is vague in stating who has to reg-

Table 8.2
The Top Twenty-Five
Spenders[a]

Organization	1973	1972
Common Cause	$934,835	$558,839
International Union, United Automobile, Aerospace and Agricultural Implement Workers	460,992	[b]
American Postal Workers Union (AFL-CIO)	393,399	208,767
American Federation of Labor-Congress of Industrial Organizations (AFL-CIO)	240,800	216,294
American Trucking Associations Inc.	226,157	137,804
American Nurses Association Inc.	218,354	109,642
U.S. Savings and Loan League	204,221	191,726
Gas Supply Committee	195,537	11,263
Disabled American Veterans	193,168	159,431
The Committee of Publicly Owned Companies	180,493	[b]
American Farm Bureau Federation	170,472	180,678
National Education Association	162,755	[b]
National Association of Letter Carriers	160,597	154,187
National Association of Home Builders of the United States	152,177	99,031
Recording Industry Association of America Inc.	141,111	88,396
National Council of Farmer Cooperatives	140,560	184,346
American Insurance Association	139,395	82,395
The Farmers' Educational and Co-operative Union of America	138,403	113,156
Committee of Copyright Owners	135,095	[b]
National Housing Conference Inc.	125,726	77,906
American Petroleum Institute	121,276	38,656
American Medical Association	114,859	96,145
Citizens for Control of Federal Spending	113,659	[b]
American Civil Liberties Union	102,595	73,131
National Association of Insurance Agents Inc.	87,422	50,924

[a] The top 25 spenders of the organizations that filed lobby spending reports for 1973, with the amounts they reported spending in 1973 and 1972.

[b] No spending record.

Source: *Congressional Quarterly Weekly,* July 27, 1974. (Reprinted by permission.)

ister and is not firmly enforced. Indeed published reports of organizational spending are usually described as the "tip of the iceberg." Some have estimated, for instance, that the AMA spends about $8 million a year on its political activities, well above the $114,859 listed for 1973. Common Cause, the "public-interest lobby," comes out on top of the list in Table 8.2, not because it spends the most but because, since it favors greater control over lobbying, it feels a responsibility to list its spending fully.

But the list does show the types of organizations that are active. Some organizations represent particular parts of the business community: truckers, the home building industry, the oil and gas industries, insurance companies. Some represent professional groups with particular interests, like the AMA or the National Education Association. Groups of workers are represented by their unions: postal clerks, letter carriers, automobile and aerospace workers. And some organizations represent groups of citizens who are interested in particular political principles. Common Cause, for example, is a liberal group interested in environmental protection, social-welfare legislation, and government reform. The Citizens for Control of Federal Spending is a more conservative group interested in keeping taxes down.

The list shows the wide range of groups that try to influence the government. It also illustrates the main principle that explains why some groups are active while others are not: Groups become politically active when governmental policy affects them, that is, when they want the government to stop some activity they feel is harmful or to take some action they feel is beneficial. Thus it is no wonder some of the most active groups are the ones that depend on government because they are direct employees of the government (postal clerks, letter carriers, teachers). Nor is one surprised to find such businesses as truckers, savings and loan associations, or insurance associations on the list, since they are heavily affected by federal and state legislation. Where government activity is important, citizens and groups are likely to be active.

Business Lobbies Probably the main lobbying activity in Washington comes from business organizations that have full-time staffs in Washington to deal with government and public affairs. The major defense contractors and large multinational corporations are quite active.

In addition, there are a large number of trade associations. These include organizations for industries dominated by a few large firms, such as the oil industry, as well as organizations like the National Association of Retail Druggists, which represents tens of thousands of drugstores around the country. There are also large "peak" associations that try to organize many different kinds of businesses. The most important are the NAM (National Association of Manufacturers) and the U.S. Chamber of Commerce.

These organizations focus on specific interests: The representatives of the oil industry worry about oil imports or regulation of offshore drilling; the representatives of textile manufacturers are active when it comes to tariffs on foreign textiles. But some of the groups take stands on more general issues. The NAM, for instance, has been active against welfare legislation.

Labor Unions Traditionally the American labor movement has been less "political" than those in other nations. In the United States unions are not formally affiliated with political parties, as they are in many European countries, and they put most of their energy into collective bargaining with employers for better wages and working conditions, rather than into political activity. But unions are major political factors as well. Their economic goals depend on government policies that protect their ability to bargain effectively with management and policies that affect their members directly.

Some unions, such as the United Automobile Workers and the United Steel Workers, have been particularly active in politics. The AFL-CIO has a large staff in Washington that lobbies on matters concerning its members, such as the wages paid on federal projects, as well as things like trade, tariffs, and welfare legislation. A branch of the AFL-CIO—the Committee on Political Education (COPE)—is active in political campaigns.

Professional Associations   Most of the major professional groups in the United States—doctors, dentists, lawyers, teachers, scientists, and so forth—have professional organizations that spend a lot of time and effort lobbying for their members. The AMA is perhaps the best known of these because of its long opposition to federal medical-care programs, an issue on which it began to change its views in 1975. In addition, the National Education Association lobbies for more spending on education, and the American Association for the Advancement of Science lobbies for more spending on scientific research.

Citizen and Consumer Lobbies   It used to be said that interest groups representing producers were better organized than those representing consumers. Oil companies were well organized and represented by professional lobbyists; drivers and homeowners who heat with oil were less well represented. The milk producers were better represented than the milk consumers. The reason, again, is intensity of concern. For the milk producer the price of milk is of great concern; his economic well-being depends on it. The price of milk is important to the consumer as well, but milk is only one of many items in a consumer's shopping basket. The average consumer is more likely to be active and concerned as producer than as consumer—trying to raise his or her income rather than lower the prices in the supermarket.

The same is true of environmental interests. Many citizens want to preserve open spaces and forests for recreation, but these con-

sumer interests are rarely as intense as those of producers—the lumber or paper or mining interests that want to use these natural resources in their businesses. Similarly all citizens might be affected as "consumers" of polluted air, but their concern is less intense than those of the manufacturing firms whose profits may be reduced if they have to invest in pollution control.

In recent years, though, consumer groups and "citizens' lobbies" have become important. The largest such group is Common Cause, which has 323,000 members. It is active in a large variety of areas ranging from consumer protection to reform of campaign financing. In addition, there are groups such as the Sierra Club and those organized by Ralph Nader that have become active on many governmental policies that used to be the subject of more one-sided lobbying. With their professional attitude and willingness to pursue the battle in Congress and in the courts, these organizations have been quite successful.

Are these new organizations, representing consumer interests, environmental concerns, and other noneconomic interests, unlike other pressure groups in that they work not for narrow, selfish interests but for the public welfare? Or are they different from other pressure groups only in that they lobby for a different set of selfish interests—consumer interests rather than producer interests, scenery-lover interests rather than mining interests?

Here is how one American business leader described environmentalists and consumer groups:

> The political system is out of balance. . . . We find our fate increasingly in the hands of a few relatively small but highly vocal, selfish, interest groups. . . . These groups . . . pursue their own interests with complete disregard for the impact of their wants on the rest of the economy. . . . And while they shout about the environmental impact of almost everything, they have no concern whatever for the economic impact of their corrective legislation.[1]

Citizen groups describe the business lobbies in the same words. Whether these groups represent a new type of selfish interest or the broader public interest is unclear. But in either case the citizens' lobbies are a new addition to the system of organized groups in America.

Beneficiary Groups Whenever the government helps one group or another, it creates a number of "beneficiaries." Members of such groups have an interest in seeing that government support and aid are continued and perhaps increased. Many of the organized groups that try to influence the government are of this sort: Farmers lobby for price supports or import controls; veterans lobby for veterans' benefits; welfare recipients press for continued or increased welfare benefits. In this way these groups act like business lobbies. (Indeed we could have listed the farmers with business groups.)

[1] *Consumer Reports*, January 1975, 53.

Special-Interest Groups Many organizations have a particular policy goal: civil liberties, civil rights, opposition to abortion, support for abortion laws, and so forth.

Organizations as Pressure Groups

That there is much organized activity in America is clear. But how does this activity affect governmental policy? Does it have any impact? And if so, who benefits from that impact?

Putting pressure on government is of course the best-known role of organized interests; they act as lobbies in Washington, in state capitals, and in local governments. Observers of the activity of lobbyists have sometimes concluded that the government is dominated by lobbies. They describe governmental policy as if it were the mechanical result of a "parallelogram of forces," the forces being pressures placed on the government by organized groups. In such a situation the public as a whole plays no role. Nor does the government itself. The role of government is merely to react to group forces or, at most, to act as a broker among them.

Such a description of policy making—in Washington or in state capitals—greatly exaggerates the power of organized groups and plays down the other forces acting on the government. One close study of Washington lobbyists concludes that "there is relatively little influence or power in lobbying per se. There are many forces in addition to lobbying which influence public policy; in most cases these forces clearly outweigh the impact of lobbying."[2] These other forces include public opinion and the congressman's feelings about the next election. Above all, one must note the dominant role of the executive branch of the government. Furthermore, as one congressman points out in the study, congressmen have their own opinions. They like to hear the views of lobbyists, but are not necessarily moved by them.

Organized interests are not all-powerful. But they are far from weak. Groups vary in their degrees of effectiveness. Thus it is useful to consider what kind of group is likely to be effective, on what issues, and where.

Organizational Resources

Organizations are effective when they have the resources to influence the government. What are some of these resources?

Financial Resources Lobbying is expensive. The major lobbies have large, full-time staffs in Washington and in state capitals. They sometimes conduct expensive campaigns to influence Congress or the public. During its campaign against President Johnson's medicare

[2] Lester W. Milbrath, *The Washington Lobbyists* (Chicago: Rand McNally, 1963), p. 54.

legislation, the AMA spent over $1 million in three months. One of the major areas of organizational spending is political campaigns. The milk producers' lobby was severely criticized when the Watergate investigations showed that it had contributed heavily to President Nixon's 1972 campaign in return for an alleged agreement to raise price supports for milk. This did not stop the milk producers from giving $2,200,000 to 1974 congressional campaigns.

People Organizations with a mass membership that can get their member: involved in political activity are also likely to be effective. The number of members is not as important as is their willingness to give time and effort to the organization. An organization with members who pressure government officials, can be very effective.

One of the strongest lobbies is the National Rifle Association. It has blocked gun-control legislation for many years. It has 1,050,000 members in 12,000 state and local gun clubs across the country. (It also has at least 35 congressman members.)

The effective lobbying of the National Rifle Association has helped block gun control.

A collection of hand guns inspected by supporters of gun control legislation.

Memphis police throw illegal guns in the Mississippi River.

A gun store in Pennsylvania.

A million members is a large number, but not all that large. Public-opinion polls show that about four out of five Americans favor some kind of gun control; this means the NRA members are outnumbered by over 100 to 1. The effectiveness of the NRA comes from the fact that its members really care about the issue, while the majority that favors gun control is weaker in its concern. The NRA keeps its members informed about gun-control activities through its monthly *American Rifleman* and separate mailings of legislative bulletins. For example:

> If a state legislative committee, for instance, plans a hearing on a gun control bill, every NRA member in that state will receive a bulletin with the time and place of the hearing, the text of the proposed measure, and the name and home cities of all the legislators on the committee.[3]

As a result the hearings are jammed with NRA members.

Expertise   Lobbies have one important resource that ordinary citizens or even members of Congress don't usually have. They have full-time skilled staffs who specialize in the subject the lobby is interested in. Thus they often have much greater technical knowledge than congressmen, who have many other problems and issues to consider. The National Education Association has all the relevant information on educational finance and research on new teaching methods. Representatives of the textile industry know the number of yards of goods imported from Hong Kong each month. The National Association of Retail Druggists can tell you the rate of failures among drugstores. These groups have a special voice in policy making because they know what policies they want to influence and what changes are important to them. Furthermore, they often have more information than the government officials involved. Government officials often depend on these organizations for basic information.

This is one of the reasons why producer interests tend to be better represented than consumer interests. Producer groups—business organizations in one field or another—have full-time professionals whose job is to know about the laws affecting their industry. Consumer groups tend to be "amateurs," working in their spare time and without the knowledge of the professionals. The new "citizens' lobbies" try to get full-time professionals working on the other side.

A good example of this is recent activity in environmental issues. Most citizens have some interest in preserving natural beauty or open park lands or clean rivers. But when it comes to decisions on the development of public lands, the groups that can put in a lot of time and energy usually carry the day. And these are usually the business interests who favor a particular use for public lands—for mining, for private development, for cattle grazing. These groups are professionally concerned; they have the skills to use government agencies

[3] *The Wall Street Journal,* May 24, 1972.

and the courts for their purposes, and, because it is their job to do so, they put in the time and energy needed to be effective. An unorganized public is ineffective against them. What organizations like the Sierra Club do is put professional skills and energy on the other side by having a full-time legal staff whose job is to fight against private development of public lands.

Access There is another resource organizations may develop that can make them particularly effective: access to government officials. All citizens have the right to contact their representative in Congress or to write a letter of complaint to a government office. But full-time professional lobbyists can develop close ties with government officials who are particularly relevant for their concerns. Their knowledge helps in this, and they work at it very hard. The job of the lobbyist is made easier by the fact that he or she may have to work with only a small number of government officials. In Congress most business is done in committees. The good lobbyist develops a close relationship with the chairman and a few key members of the relevant committee, as well as with the government agencies active in his area.

Mobilizing Their Members

The effective pressure group must be able to depend on its members. For one thing, they must maintain their membership. Not all doctors belong to the AMA; in fact only about half of them do. Similarly only about half of the lawyers in America belong to the American Bar Association. An organization that tries to speak for a group will want to have a fairly high portion of that group as members. Furthermore, it needs membership dues to carry out its many activities. And if it can get its members to be active—to write to the government, to campaign for the candidates it prefers—it can increase its influence.

Those organizations are likely to be most effective that offer many rewards to their members. Some people join a group because of their interest in its policy goals, that is, the policies the organization tries to get the government to support. But, as we saw in the last chapter, this may not be enough. Most successful organizations offer many other things to members. Business and professional organizations offer their members technical publications, insurance programs, and many other services. Doctors do not join the AMA because they believe in the policies the AMA supports (though they may), but because the AMA gives them services such as aid in malpractice suits and sends them medical publications. Or consider the American Bar Association. The following are benefits available to its members:

- lawyer placement service
- retirement income plans
- group life insurance program
- dependents' life insurance program

- group disability insurance program
- in-hospital insurance program
- specialized information on all sections of the law
- legal publications and reports, and the *American Bar Association Journal* and the *American Bar News*

Services of this sort are important in keeping members in such organizations. (One of the authors of this book joined the American Association of University Professors so he could take its reduced-fare flights to Europe.) And members who join for these reasons provide the base for a politically powerful organization.

Issues on Which Organizations Are Effective

The narrower and more technical the issue, the more effective organized groups are likely to be.

The Two Levels of Policy Making The policy-making process—a subject we will deal with more fully later—goes through many steps. On the one hand, there is the making of general policy, which is done in Congress and results in broad policy guidelines. But much of this policy making has symbolic meaning.[4] It sets a general direction for policy, but the actual policy depends on specific features worked out in congressional committees and subcommittees, in the application of the legislation by government officials, or in the interpretation of the legislation in the courts.

The point is that while the broad guidelines of legislation seem to be the most important, it is often the specific way the law is administered or the courts' interpretation that really counts. The rules set down by Congress are so general that they have little impact until the details of the law have been settled.

In the struggle for major legislation, pressure groups are active, to be sure, but they are not at their greatest advantage. Congress, in such public activities, must keep its eye on the public, and in turn, the mass media are keeping their eye on Congress. But the specific details of a bill—worked out in committee or in some agency of the executive branch—are a better place for pressure groups to work. In such cases they can use their professional knowledge and access to government officials.

Tax Legislation A good example of the two levels of policy making—the broad statement of principles and the detailed working out of practices—is found in tax legislation. The principle of progressive tax legislation is found in the Sixteenth Amendment. The idea is to tax those who can pay more at higher rates. This could have major effects on income distribution in America. Few argue with the general principle of a progressive tax. And there is no need to argue, because the principle is hardly ever applied.

[4] See Murray Edelman, *The Symbolic Uses of Politics* (Urbana: University of Illinois Press, 1964).

Although attempts have been made to reform income-tax laws several times in the past few decades, the results are almost always the same. Congress sets some broad guidelines, and then the House Ways and Means Committee or the Senate Finance Committee (the committees in which tax legislation is worked out) approve a number of exemptions. These range from attempts to help a particular individual (the famous Louis B. Mayer amendment was designed to help the aging movie magnate protect his retirement benefits) to broader exemptions (such as the even more famous 22 percent depletion allowance for oil compaines, which gave oil producers a big tax benefit). At the hearings on the major tax bills, one will find hundreds of groups making statements on what seem to be very small issues, but they are issues that affect them closely. On each specific issue there is no one to oppose them.

The result of course is that though there is never any direct challenge to the principle of a graduated tax that falls most heavily on the wealthy, tax policy does not work out that way in fact. As many have noted, the tax law allows for a maximum rate of 70 percent. Few pay as much as 50 percent.[5] This is not the result of a decision by some government body—say, Congress or the Treasury Department—that a rate of 70 percent is too high. Rather, the principle of steeply graduated taxes holds, but the practice is to allow so many exemptions—for tax-free municipal bonds, depletion allowances, capital gains, real-estate transactions—that the principle never takes effect.

Tariff Legislation and Business Regulation This pattern of principle and practice in policy making can be found in many fields. Tariff legislation has long been an area where general tariff bills are watered down by a variety of decisions on specific goods. Another example is business regulation. Congress will enact general legislation to regulate some business practices, such as the quality of food products, the amount of pollutants allowed into waterways, and the flameproofing of fabrics. The general principle will be clear—Sell pure food, don't pollute, manufacture only fireproof fabrics. But the details of the regulation—How pure? Is a little pollution all right? What about slow-burning fabrics?—are usually worked out with representatives of the businesses to be regulated. This is not necessarily a bad thing, since only the businesses involved have the necessary information on which the detailed regulations have to be made. But it does give businesses a special voice in setting the terms of their relationship with the government.

One of the reasons for this is seen if we return to some of the patterns of division described in the previous chapter. When it comes to broad issues in which a group with a specific interest wants something that many other citizens oppose in principle, the pattern of division will look something like Figure 8.1. On the right—

[5] See William L. Cary, "Pressure Groups and the Revenue Code," *Harvard Law Review*, 68 (1955), 745–780.

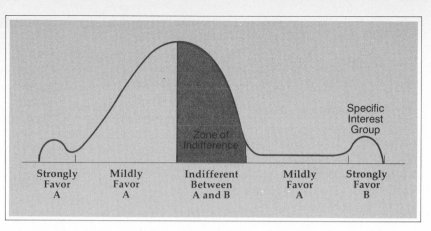

strongly favoring position B—would be the specific interest group, small in number but firm. On the left would be the people generally opposed to the principle that the small interest group wants, and they will probably include a number of citizens who feel strongly about the principle. In such a case the specific group wanting B could win only after a public fight. And it would probably lose, since most of the citizens could become involved. Congressmen might listen to the interest group, but they listen more closely to election predictions.

If, for instance, representatives of top management in large corporations tried—through the National Association of Manufacturers or the U.S. Chamber of Commerce—to have Congress pass a law severely reducing their rate of taxation, and made statements criticizing the principle of a graduated income tax, they would face strong opposition and would probably lose.

If, on the other hand, the House Ways and Means Committee approves a stock option plan in which profits from sales of stock received under such plans can be treated as capital gains if they are sold at least two years after the grant of the option and six months after the transfer of the stock, the public is unlikely to be aroused. As one observer noted after looking at many examples of tax exemptions won by specific interest groups, "in each instance the character of the relief afforded is so technical as to make a simple explanation impossible. Being obscure or downright incomprehensible to the layman, it is not recognized as an outright favor to one individual or a highly selected group."[6]

When it comes to a technical issue, the pattern of division is likely to be as shown in Figure 8.2. A deeply interested and technically skilled group favors a position. The position looks like a technical issue about which the public has little knowledge or concern. Thus there is no opposition. In such circumstances the specific interest group can be quite effective.

[6] Ibid.

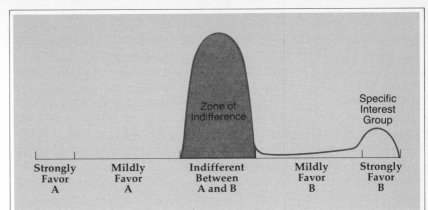

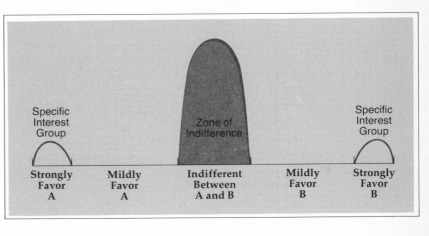

Citizens' lobbies try to convert the situation shown in Figure 8.2 into that shown in Figure 8.3. One lobby opposes another. The knowledge and activity of, say, the timber interests is offset by the professional staff of an organization like the Sierra Club. It is hard to know how many situations in the United States resemble Figure 8.2 and how many resemble Figure 8.3. Despite the rise of the new citizens' lobbies, it is likely that the situation in Figure 8.2, where an interest group is not opposed by any other group, is still a dominant pattern.

Where Are Pressure Groups Active?

Our discussion of the kinds of issues on which pressure groups can be most effective also tells us something about where they are most likely to be effective. One way they are active is in trying to arouse the public through campaigns in the media or through support of candidates in elections. In this way they try to influence public policy at the most general level—by affecting what the public wants and who is elected to office.

Congressional Committees

Interest groups are probably much more active and more effective in dealing with specific committees of Congress. Here they can develop close relationships with specific congressmen—who often come from districts where that particular interest is well represented—and the committee staffs. They often provide the information needed to draft specific bills.

The Executive Branch

Interest groups may develop close ties with the agencies of the executive branch that regulate their affairs: farm interests with the Department of Agriculture, businesses with the Department of Commerce, labor unions with the Department of Labor. In particular, quite close ties may be formed between independent regulatory agencies and the businesses they are created to regulate: trucking interests with the Interstate Commerce Commission, radio and television interests with the Federal Communications Commission, airlines with the Civil Aeronautics Board.

The Court System

The real impact of governmental policy is often felt through the interpretation of laws or the Constitution by the courts. And interest groups have been active in this area as well. Organizations provide the attorneys and professional skills to prepare cases; they often carefully choose the test cases; and they appear in the cases through the filing of *amicus curiae* briefs. Perhaps the most dramatic example is the long series of cases prepared and carried through by the NAACP, the school segregation cases being the best known. Besides the Supreme Court case of *Brown* v. *Board of Education of Topeka* (see Chapter 11), the NAACP was involved in dozens of cases preceding and following it—in lower courts as well as in the Supreme Court—that round out that decision.

Groups whose interest is in some right they believe is guaranteed by the Constitution—civil liberties, civil rights, or the separation of church and state—are particularly active in the federal courts. (See Chapter 12.) Thus one finds such groups as the American Civil Liberties Union, the Emergency Civil Liberties Committee, the NAACP, the Congress of Racial Equality (CORE), the Protestants and Other Americans United for the Separation of Church and State most active in this way.[7]

Economic organizations play a similar role, sponsoring and supporting litigation on matters of concern to them. Again we see the way particular interests can be most effective. Litigation is a slow, costly, and technically difficult process. We hear of major court decisions, but the real impact of court action often comes through a large number of narrower cases in the lower courts. And it is here

[7] See Clement E. Vose, "Interest Groups, Judicial Review and Local Government," *Western Political Quarterly*, 19 (March 1966), 85–100.

that specific interest groups can be effective because they have the necessary interest, skill, and staying power.

Election Campaigns

Organized groups are also very active in election campaigns, supporting candidates they believe will favor them. We have mentioned the large-scale campaign contributions of the milk producers in the 1972 Presidential race and in the 1974 congressional races. As the president of the Mid-American Dairymen put it, "I have become increasingly aware that the soft and sincere voice of the dairy farmer is no match for the jingle of hard currency put in the campaign funds of the politician."[8]

Many interest groups have special branches for campaign activity. The AFL-CIO makes campaign contributions through COPE; the AMA through AMPAC (the American Medical Political Action Committee); the milk producers have C-TAPE (Committee for Thorough Agricultural Political Education). In each case large sums of organizational money are given to favored candidates. The groups listed are but a few who make big contributions; among the agricultural interests, besides milk producers, cattle, rice, cotton, and soybean interests also have political action groups.

Interest Groups as Quasi-Governments

There is one last, and important, way private interest groups play a political role in America. This is by taking on directly the functions of government. Government, as we said in the introductory chapter, exists whenever binding decisions are made for a collectivity, that is, decisions that have the force of law and about which citizens have no choice. This definition is useful because it allows us to see where private organizations perform the governmental function of making such binding decisions.

Private organizations are often given the power to make such decisions in their area of concern.

Controlling Entry into a Profession

Many professional and craft groups control entry into the occupations they represent. Medical associations have control over examinations and accreditation, bar associations over the bar examination, craft unions over apprentice programs, educational associations over accreditation. Furthermore, these associations may control access to important facilities such as hospitals, labor exchanges, and so forth.

This activity is control in the governmental sense in that it is binding on citizens. One cannot practice law or medicine without accreditation; one cannot get work as a plumber without union membership (and that, in turn, requires completion of an apprenticeship

Professional associations often set standards for entry into the profession.

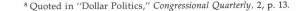

[8] Quoted in "Dollar Politics," *Congressional Quarterly*, 2, p. 13.

program). In this sense the private associations that control entry into the profession act as governments.

Much of this activity, one can argue, is merely technical. Everyone wants a way to accredit doctors or lawyers, some way to judge them as professionals so people who need medical care or legal advice can trust them. And who but the profession itself can judge?

But control can be used for other purposes as well. It can be used to keep members of a profession in line with policies favored by the leaders of that profession. The fact that the AMA controls entry into the medical profession and, often, access by doctors to hospitals, means it could control the behavior of doctors. It could, for instance, discourage group and cooperative practices it did not like. And the AMA has used its power to keep doctors in line behind its policy on national medical care.

Similarly becoming a lawyer depends on passing a bar examination in each state. The examination, particularly the part that deals with "character," has been used in various states to keep out people with radical outlooks. And craft unions—plumbers, electricians, and the like—have used their control over accreditation to keep out blacks.

Citizens who oppose these controls can of course challenge them in the courts or appeal to Congress or state legislatures for a change. But this does not change the fact that they have the force of law.

Controlling Standards and Making Regulations

In a variety of fields the power to set industry-wide standards is given to a trade association or some other private group. Again the logic is that such regulations require the skill and knowledge of those most involved. Furthermore, those most involved and likely to be most affected are given a bigger voice. But it also turns over control to those who are supposed to be controlled.

Controlling Allocation of Public Funds

Many public programs are carried out by private groups that allocate government funds. Of course the government sets broad guidelines, but the control is essentially in the hands of the private group; and the guidelines are often so vague that the private group is fairly free to do as it sees fit.

There are many examples from all fields of government activity. Urban renewal funds are often controlled by private developers, funds for hospitals and other welfare activities are often controlled by private charitable groups, and funds for much of the poverty program were controlled by local groups.

This setup involves the participation of many more citizens who are familiar with local conditions. But it also gives private groups—which are not as accountable to the public as government officials and may not really represent the people they are supposed to represent—day-to-day power over government resources.

For Whom Do Interest Groups Speak?

Formally organized interest groups can be most effective—in certain circumstances—in pursuing specific interests. But it is not completely clear whose interests these are. Do such organizations pursue the interests of their members?

Interest Groups and Their Membership

When an interest group takes a position, it is said to be that of the members of the group—the AMA claims to speak for doctors and the National Education Association (NEA) for teachers. Do they in fact do so? We often do not know. Early in this century Swiss sociologist Roberto Michels wrote of the "iron law of oligarchy," by which he meant the tendency for organizations to be run by a small group of leaders unresponsive to the demands of the members. This may not be an "iron" law, but the tendency is seen frequently.

Most organizations are run by a small number of members who give the time and effort to organizational activities. These members, furthermore, tend to become a special group—professional leaders. Trade union officials are professional officials, not workers who just happen to become leaders. AMA executives are professional officials, not practicing physicians. Indeed the AMA is a classic case of an organization closely controlled by a leadership group.

Opponents of the AMA claimed it did not speak for the medical profession; the AMA claimed it did. In fact it is unclear for whom the AMA spoke, since the profession as a whole was not active in Washington. And this is true of most associations. The members meet rarely, if ever, and control over the activities of the association lies in the hands of a few elected officers—a board of directors—and, above all, a professional staff.

That organizations are generally controlled by a small group leads one to question whether they represent the interests of their members. On the other hand, central control enables organizations to plan campaigns with a specific purpose, so that when they *do* speak for their members they can speak more effectively.

Furthermore, central control of an organization often develops because the members are not interested enough. When some group wants to challenge the leaders, it can often have quite an impact. In recent years, for instance, the conservative leaders of the AMA have been challenged by younger, more liberal doctors. The latter have not taken over the organization, but they have had an impact.

How Powerful Are Interest Groups?

Some observers of American politics, as we have pointed out, claim public policy is simply a reflection of what organized interests want. They talk of a "hidden government," meaning interest groups dominate all decisions. A close look at the way government policies are made will show that this is an exaggeration. Interest groups are not all-powerful. But they are not weak, either.

Interest groups are most powerful when they operate quietly on issues that do not arouse public concern. But when it comes to major clashes over public policy, they become only one voice among many. Lobbies may support candidates, but congressmen do not respond only to particular interests. And the media often arouse the public and Congress when interest groups get too much power.

Consider the AMA and medicare. If the AMA were all-powerful, we would not have a medicare program, because the AMA was firmly opposed to it. We do have such a program. Yet the AMA was successful in delaying medicare. The United States was many years behind comparable societies in setting up a national health system, and the AMA also played a major role in shaping the program.

We will look more closely at the way policy on medical care is formulated, as well as other policies, later. When we consider all the forces that go into policy making, we will find that interest groups are but one of many forces—a force to be reckoned with, but not always dominant.

Controversy

The extent to which interest groups contribute to the public good is problematic—meaning that the issue is unsettled.

One Side

Interest-group politics communicate specific citizen interests to the government. Without such groups policy makers would not have the information they need to be responsive to them. Such activity, particularly when it works at the level of interpretation or application of policy, allows governmental policy to be "fine-tuned" to specific circumstances. In a society as complex as ours, this is needed if government policy is to take account of the great variety of citizen needs.

Pressure groups do not discriminate against any particular group of citizens. It is true that all are not equally organized or equally active, but all have the right to organize and to petition the government. The fact that a group is organized and active indicates that it has interests it is serious about. If other groups do not organize to pressure the government, it means they do not really care enough.

Some claim that interest groups generally represent big business, rarely ordinary citizens.

The close ties between government and interest groups are a way of applying the skills and energy of professionals to the formation of government policy. In this sense the quality of policy improves.

Further, when citizens voluntarily work with the government in formulating regulatory policies, it follows that they will voluntarily comply with those policies. This is all to the good—the less force is used, the better off everyone is.

Finally, the policy that results from the clash of specific interests does not hurt the common good—for the common good is the sum of the interests of specific groups.

In short, interest-group politics produces the best overall governmental policy. It represents the views of specific groups and best serves the needs of the country as a whole.

The Other Side

Interest-group politics does not always represent the most important interests of citizens. Many groups with serious needs are unorganized. It is not necessarily lack of interest that keeps particular parts of the society inactive; they may lack the resources to organize. As a result the interests that are represented are those of upper-status groups, particularly those of the well-organized business community. And the interests of other groups are represented to varying degrees; unionized workers do better than non-unionized ones, though the latter may need government protection more. The result is a conservative tendency in governmental policy; policy tends to aid the privileged. This situation is made worse when power is given to those the government should be regulating, making the regulation less effective.

Interest-group politics may be voluntary, but progress and social change may require force—at least they may require that citizens be forced to accept changes they do not want. A major change in American society—a change that many feel is needed—requires stronger action by the government. And it is in this area that interest-group politics is weakest; no one is concerned with a broader public interest, which is not simply the sum of the interests of specific groups. To solve the serious problems facing American society, the government will have to listen to other voices besides those of narrow, selfish interests.

Which side is right? This question is fundamental to the way politics works in America. And whether one believes interest-group politics benefits the general public or not, it is a current fact of American political life.

9

Political Parties and Elections

The past decade and a half was a complicated and troubling period in American political history. In the mid-1960s Lyndon Johnson was President of the United States. He and his advisers were sending billions of dollars and thousands of troops to Vietnam, and they were planning some of the most significant social programs ever undertaken by the federal government. A few years later Johnson was tending his ranch in Texas and writing his memoirs in his spare time. The White House belonged to Richard Nixon and his advisers, who were trying to withdraw from Vietnam ("Peace with Honor") and trying to replace Johnson's Great Society with their social programs. By 1975 Richard Nixon was a lonely, sick man living in semi-isolation. His Vice-President, Spiro Agnew, had preceded him into political disgrace, and Nixon's close advisers were in criminal courts trying to explain why they should not be in jail; indeed, some were already there. Vietnam was in shambles. The U.S. economy was in a recession.

A scorecard will help straighten out the players and their teams during this complicated political period. The scorecard will help in this chapter, where political parties are discussed, and also in Chapter 11, where Presidential campaigns are reviewed. First a few basic facts.

There is a Presidential election in November every four years. A "typical" Presidential election year begins in the Spring when either or both major political parties hold primary elections (special party elections to see who the party voters prefer as the Presidential nominee for that party). Later in the summer the political parties hold separate nominating conventions where they officially select a person to run as President and another to run as Vice-President on the party ticket. Following a two- to three-month campaign for votes, one of the tickets wins in the November election. The presumption is that the winning President and Vice-President will remain in office for four years. A President may succeed himself once. A past Vice-President can be nominated as a candidate for the Presidency, but there is no guarantee of this.

At the time the voters choose a President, they also select all members of the House of Representatives and one-third of the members of the Senate. (They also elect some governors, other state officials, and state legislators, but these offices do not concern us for the moment.) In addition to the Presidential election every four years there is another type of national election, the *mid-term* election (also called an off-year election), which takes place midway through the Presidential term. Thus there was a Presidential election in 1972, a mid-term election in 1974, a Presidential election in 1976, followed by another mid-term election in 1978. At a mid-term election all seats in the House of Representatives are again open to contest (thus members of the House serve only two years between elections), and a different third of the senators must stand for reelection or give up their positions to newcomers (any given senator serves six years before seeking reelection).

The following chronology is limited to Presidential election years, starting with 1960, or other years in which the control of the White House was affected by events.

1960　The Presidential contest was between John F. Kennedy, the Democratic party nominee, and Richard Nixon, the Republican party nominee. In an extremely close election Kennedy won.

1963　Kennedy had chosen Lyndon B. Johnson, powerful Senate leader from Texas, as his Vice-Presidential running mate. Dramatically, unexpectedly, and tragically, Johnson became President on November 22, 1963, the day President Kennedy was assassinated in Dallas.

1964　During the remainder of the Presidential term Johnson carried on Kennedy's policies. Johnson was nominated by the Democrats to be the Presidential candidate in 1964; Hubert Humphrey was the Vice-Presidential candidate for the Democrats. Senator Barry Goldwater, conservative from Arizona, was the Republican candidate. He was easily defeated, as many traditional Republican voters refused to support him because they considered him too conservative. (Ironically, voters also feared his policies might lead to American involvement in a Vietnam war, which Johnson pledged to avoid.)

1968　The Presidential election year of 1968 was a difficult one, especially for the Democratic party. Johnson's term as President was marked by growing discontent with his Vietnam policies, especially on college campuses. The mid-1960s was also a period of "demonstration politics" by blacks (the black power movement) and women (the women's liberation movement).

In the spring of 1968 opposition to Johnson's Vietnam policies began to be voiced openly by a few leading Democrats. Chief among the dissenters was Senator Eugene McCarthy, who challenged Johnson in an early Democratic party primary election (in New Hampshire). McCarthy's moderate success led another antiwar senator to declare himself a candidate for the Democratic party Presidential nomination: Robert F. Kennedy, younger brother of the assassinated President.

Shortly thereafter Johnson announced that he would *not* be a candidate for his party's nomination in 1968. His Vice-President, Hubert Humphrey, quickly entered the race. The three-way contest between McCarthy, Humphrey, and Kennedy appeared to be favoring Kennedy, especially in California when Kennedy won the last and largest of the Presidential primary elections. The night of this victory, in a Los Angeles hall crowded with his supporters, the second Kennedy was assassinated.

A few weeks later the delegates to the Democratic party nominating convention came to Chicago to choose between Humphrey and McCarthy. Thousands of anti-war demonstrators also came to Chicago, but while the demonstrators were in the streets showing their support for the anti-war candidate McCarthy, the delegates inside the Chicago amphitheater were nominating Humphrey.

Meanwhile Richard Nixon was winning the Republican nomination for the second time; he selected Spiro Agnew, governor of Maryland, as his Vice-Presidential candidate.

The political plot thickened when Alabama's populist governor, George C. Wallace, left the Democratic party to run for President under the label of the American Independent party. Wallace attracted 13 percent of the popular vote, an unusually large percentage for a third-party candidate.

The remainder of the voters slightly favored the Republican ticket, and Richard Nixon moved into the White House.

1972   Nixon and Agnew were renominated by the Republican party. The Democrats chose George McGovern, a vocal anti-war candidate and member of the liberal wing of the Democratic party. McGovern had been bitterly opposed by many Democrats, including George Wallace, who this year had decided to remain in the Democratic party. An attempt on Wallace's life crippled him, however, and he was not well enough to play a leading role in the nominating convention, despite having won more primary votes than McGovern. Wallace supporters and many other leading Democrats, especially in the labor movement, refused to support McGovern. The Nixon-Agnew ticket won an overwhelming victory.

1974   The year of Watergate, a story well known and discussed at various places in the text. Here only the barest of facts. Though the break-in at the Democratic party headquarters, then in a Washington hotel called Watergate, took place in 1972, the impact of the incident on Presidential politics was not forcefully felt until 1974.

That complicated year began with Nixon and Agnew in the White House and ended there with Gerald Ford and Nelson Rockefeller. Agnew left first, in disgrace, after he had pleaded no contest to a federal charge of accepting bribes while governor of Maryland. It took much more pressure before President Nixon was to resign. But he finally did, rather than face certain impeachment and probable conviction in Congress. The telling evidence of his involvement in the Watergate cover-up was revealed in the White House tapes he had recorded.

Nixon had nominated Ford to become Vice-President when Agnew resigned; thus Ford became President when Nixon resigned. Ford in turn chose Rockefeller to fill the then-vacant Vice-Presidential position.

Managing the Transfer of Power

The chronology just reviewed reveals one of the really tough issues for any political system: how to manage the transfer of power. From Kennedy to Johnson—from Johnson to Nixon—from Nixon to Ford. How is power to be passed from one to another? In the United States the political parties do this job, and under the best of circumstances it is not easy. The Vietnam war of the 1960s and the Watergate scandal of the early 1970s were hardly the best of circumstances. Our political institutions have been under great strain in the past few years. The two major political parties have been hit especially hard. In this chapter we ask how well the parties have stood up under the pressure. But first we must deal with some of the important features of the parties themselves.

American Political Parties: Organization and Program

If you have studied comparative politics, you know political parties in some societies effectively involve the masses in the political life of their nation. For instance, some parties add to the formal educational system. They organize lectures and programs to inform the public about political issues; they print booklets that explain policy questions and invite the public to take stands on these questions. Parties in many societies have youth groups and similar organizations. They have a chain of command that links local units with district headquarters and national officers.

None of these activities is common in the United States. Indeed, in contrast to parties elsewhere, the Democrats and the Republicans do not even have formal members. It is rare for a citizen to actually "join" a political party, and few pay dues regularly.

It is hard to think of our political parties as mass based in the sense just described. Our parties hardly ever meet, and when they do the meetings involve very tiny portions of the possible party membership. Almost all party meetings—whether precinct, county, state, or national—take place around election time to nominate candidates and plan campaign strategy. We would be surprised indeed to hear that the Santa Clara County Democratic party is meeting to discuss tariff policy or school busing, and that it intends to give its opinion to government officials in Sacramento or Washington, D.C. And we do not expect the Republican party of Illinois to organize a series of public forums so citizens can voice opinions about issues facing the Illinois legislature.

Decentralized Political Parties

Variety of Viewpoints Each of the major parties is a collection of different and often disagreeing groups rather than a single-minded organization. In the first place, there are a variety of political viewpoints within each party. The Democrats and the Republicans each include a "conservative wing" and a "liberal wing." This is largely a result of historical development. Each party has attracted supporters in a way that creates such differences. The clearest example is the Democratic party. It is the party of the conservative South (conservative on civil rights and social welfare issues) because it was a northern Republican President, Lincoln, who signed the Emancipation Proclamation. The solid support of the Democratic party in the South is only now beginning to weaken, more than a century after the Civil War. But the Democratic party got support from new and very different social groups during the depression in

American parties hardly ever meet. One time they do is to nominate candidates.

the early 1930s. Franklin D. Roosevelt and his party chiefs won the loyalty of ethnic workers, blacks, and the urban poor for the Democratic party by pushing such programs as unemployment insurance, public-works jobs, and social security. The post-Civil War events and the Democratic coalition of the 1930s have resulted in the mixture of a liberal, northern, urban group with a more conservative, southern, rural group in the Democratic party.

The Republican party has also been shaped by history. Partly because it was the party of the North immediately after the Civil War, it became the party of the commercial and industrial class in the Northeast. But the Republican party also won the support of Main Street America and the frontier West, and thus today the Republicans include liberal northeastern business interests (e.g., Vice-President Nelson Rockefeller) as well as more conservative midwestern and western interests (e.g., Senator Barry Goldwater of Arizona).

The historical growth of each party and the resultant variety within each put large barriers in the way of cohesive, party-based programs. The issue that most unites Republicans is the desire to defeat Democrats, and vice versa. Yet the nomination of McGovern in 1972 led many Democratic leaders to sit out the election or even to support Nixon. And between elections the possibility of party unity is much less. Each party tolerates many viewpoints, and little attempt is made to formulate a cohesive party program. Conflicts *within* the parties can be as sharp and divisive as struggles *between* the parties.

Organizational Fragmentation The federal structure of American politics has had a lasting effect on the parties. There are in fact 50 separate Republican parties and 50 separate Democratic parties, more if we include some of the strong and nearly independent organizations at the county or city level. The state and local level parties are loosely linked together by a national committee, but the organizational charts that show lines of communication from precinct to ward to county or district to state to national headquarters are misleading.

National party headquarters has little control over what is done in its name at the state or local level. Party control is decentralized. The active units of the party, where there *are* active units, are at the local level. This contributes to variety—the Democratic party of Biloxi, Mississippi, is a different political animal from the Democratic party of Palo Alto, California. Within the party a process of compromise and negotiation goes on whenever a decision affecting the party as a whole must be made, such as the nomination of a Presidential candidate. On other types of decisions each unit goes its own way, not worrying about what another county or state party might be doing. For example, the nomination of congressional candidates is entirely under the control of the local activists, or perhaps the local voters if they participate in a primary. There is no effective chain of command with instructions and policies formulated at the top and passed down the line. Even fund raising is mostly a local affair; national headquarters funds the Presidential campaign, but state organizations concentrate on statewide elections and district and local organizations raise funds for their candidates.

The powers of state and local party units are related to federalism in the formal governmental structure. There is only one national elected office, but there are hundreds of state and local offices. This is where the action is, even more now that the mass media have taken over the Presidential campaign, leaving less and less for the local organizations to do. And this is bolstered by the principle of states' rights, particularly important to southern Democrats, who resist any attempt to limit their congressional power by including them in a centralized Democratic party under the control of northern liberals.

When we call the United States a two-party system, we do not mean there are only two major party *organizations*. Rather, we mean there are only two major party *symbols*. Elections take place between one group of candidates and their personal organizations under the symbol of the Republican party and another under the symbol of the Democratic party; elections do not take place between two unified organizations. Each party is a loose coalition with the common goal of gaining office under the party label but without a cohesive program for society.

Parties Without Programs

Neither the Republicans nor the Democrats have a general program agreed to by most of the party officials. From time to time a party attempts to state a general program, but even these efforts usually come from a group that is bothered by what another group is doing in the party's name. For example, Republican governors might meet to formulate a program for revenue sharing between federal and state governments because they think Republican congressmen are acting too slowly on this issue. These are of course piecemeal attempts, touching only one of the many policy questions facing the government at any given time.

There are two documents proposed as party programs, but neither need be taken seriously. The first is the party platform, formulated at Presidential nominating conventions. Platforms are campaign documents put together for the benefit of the Presidential nominee. They are not binding on party leaders, not even the nominee himself. The second is the package of legislative proposals announced by the President in his State of the Union Address, Budget Message to Congress, and other speeches. However important these proposals may be, they are not really a party program. The President's proposals are not formulated by his party, not even the congressional members of his party, let alone governors, state legislators, local officials, or party professionals. It is easy to see why. Imagine the difficulties for the Democratic party of putting together a program on, say, civil rights if the drafting committee included Shirley Chisholm, a black congresswoman from New York, and George Wallace, segregationist governor of Alabama.

Summary

American parties lack many things. They lack a mass base and a regular dues-paying source of support. They lack an effective central organization. They lack linkages across the many state and local party groups. They lack a unified program voters can respond to. They lack means of controlling what officeholders elected as Republicans or Democrats do once they are in office. Without these resources, how can they count for much on the political scene? Yet the political parties are powerful. They have been around a long time. Their position in American politics rests on a simple fact already noted: The political parties manage the transfer of power; they control the routes to political office.

Political Parties and the Selection of Political Leaders

In November 1974 the American voters elected 435 people to the House of Representatives and 34 to the Senate. There were also 35 governorships at stake in the 1974 election. In these elections nearly 350 independent and minor-party candidates tried to defeat candidates from the two major parties. Only one succeeded: An independent candidate became governor of Maine. All told, 100 percent of the current members of Congress and 98 percent of the current governors, as well as the vast majority of state legislators, were elected under the label of the major parties.

Was the 1974 election unusual? Not at all. Recruitment to national and state office (and to many local offices as well) is "reserved" for those nominated by a political party. This is not a matter of law.

The Constitution does not declare that political offices shall be held only by members of this or that political party. Indeed the Constitution is silent about political parties. But what is not a matter of law is very much a matter of tradition, custom, and practical politics. Almost from the beginning, the contest to control the government of the United States has been a party contest.

Two factors explain why political parties control the routes to public office in the United States: (1) the large number of party members and (2) the costs and difficulties of organizing a campaign.

Party Members

As discussed in Chapter 4, each of the two major political parties has the loyalty of millions of voters. They identify with one of the major parties the way people identify themselves with a particular religion. Here is a Republican with a strong party identification: "I'm a born Republican. We're all Republicans from start to finish, clear back on the family tree. I won't weaken my party by voting for a Democrat."

People support their party by always voting for the candidates chosen by the small group of party activists.

If candidates didn't have party labels (no matter who is running the campaign), the typical American voter would be confused. Voters *expect* candidates to be supported by one of the major parties. Indeed a "major candidate" is one who has the Democratic or Republican nomination. The typical voter may know next to nothing about how the party is organized, how it goes about nominating its candidates, how it raises money, and how it campaigns. But he does know one thing. One candidate is a Democrat and the other is a Republican, and this fact more than any other helps him decide how to vote. This is the significance of the party: It approves the candidates. The typical American election is a process in which the *party* preferences of voters are translated into winning and losing candidates. This helps explain why the political parties maintain control over the routes to public office.

In Chapter 4 it was noted that the number of voters who refuse to identify themselves with either of the major parties has recently increased. The "independents" claim that no party can count on their loyal support. As Table 9.1 makes very clear, the number of independents has almost doubled in the past two decades. The Republican party has been the big loser, largely because of the Water-

Table 9.1 Party Identifications Among Americans		*1952*	*1960*	*1968*	*1972*	*1974*
	Democrats	47%	46%	45%	41%	41%
	Republicans	27%	27%	24%	23%	18%
	Independents	22%	23%	29%	34%	40%

Source: Based on data from Survey Research Center study, Institute for Social Research, University of Michigan.

gate scandal. But even the Democratic party does not have as many supporters as it did twenty years ago.

If this trend continues, party control over public office is sure to decline. No longer will 100 percent of the members of congress or 98 percent of the state governors be chosen by one of the two major parties. However, the American people are still electing Republicans or Democrats to office. It is far too early to pronounce the end of the party system. It is not too early to wonder what the weakness of the Republican party might mean for American politics. This question is discussed later in the chapter.

Organizing and Paying for Political Campaigns

Political parties traditionally have controlled recruitment to public office. One reason is the large numbers of voters who use the party label in deciding how to vote. The second reason is that political parties help get the name of a candidate to the voters. And this is important. No matter how intelligent and innovative and responsible a political candidate might be, the voters must know who he or she is.

Campaign Organization   The candidate for office must somehow convince thousands or even millions of voters that he or she is the best person for the job. How to make the case? Either the candidate himself or campaign workers must see that speeches are planned, publicity material distributed, advertisements put in newspapers, radio and TV announcements made, and, when possible, individual voters contacted. Political campaigning is very complicated. It can also be expensive.

The political parties provide a skeleton organization that comes to life around election time. "Coming to life" means party officials open temporary election headquarters, volunteer party workers come in and lick stamps, and contributors are asked to write checks. The *Democratic Party Manual* of 1972 lists some of the major campaign tasks: Methods of Raising Money, Research, Coffee Hours, Polling, Use of Computers, Voter Registration, Buttons, Bumper Stickers. And here are some of the people who will be involved: Campaign Director, Director of Communications, Telephone Volunteers, Research Staff, Canvassers, and Bell-ringers.

The independent candidate would have to build the election organization that works for the party nominee. And this will cost the independent candidate money and time that would otherwise go into trying to defeat his opponents. There are reasons, therefore, for the facts noted earlier: The political parties control the routes to office and thereby manage the transfer of political power.

Campaign Costs   "Money is the mother's milk of politics." A California Democrat, Jesse Unruh, made this comment, but he was speaking for all the would-be officeholders who have been kept from

Parties "come to life" at election time.

winning office by lack of campaign funds. Buttons and bumper stickers cost money, to say nothing of TV time, newspaper ads, and jet planes. And campaign costs have gone up and up. In 1952, campaign costs at all levels totaled less than $150 million; in 1964, the approximate figure was $200 million; by 1972, the costs of political campaigning exceeded $400 million.

Much, though not all, of the funds used in campaigning are collected by the political parties. This is another major reason why the parties play such an important role in determining who holds public office. A person seeking office independently of the parties would have to be very rich or have the backing of others who were rich. In a large state like New York or California, a candidate for senator can spend as much as $1 million. Even a candidate for the House of Representatives can spend as much as $100,000. It takes organization to collect this amount of money. The candidate going after local or state or national office outside the party structure faces an uphill battle. He or she must convince contributors that victory is possible despite lack of party support. This is hard to do; history tells of many attempts by independents and third-party candidates to win office, but few successes.

Political Parties and Election Results

For several reasons different branches of government (executive, legislative, and judicial) and different levels of government (national, state, and local) are rarely under the control of the same party. One reason is that voters can vote a "split ticket." A voter may choose a candidate of one party for President, switch to the other party's candidate for state governor, and then switch back for congressman. Not all voters do this, but enough do so that the party controlling the White House need not control Congress. For example, after Republican Nixon's landslide victory in the 1972 Presidential election, the Democrats still controlled both the House of Representatives and the Senate. Even when voters do not split tickets, different parties can control different levels of government. For example, Rhode Island voted Democratic in 1968, voting for Hubert Humphrey for President and electing a Democratic governor. Humphrey lost. Thus while there was a Republican in the White House, there were Democratic governors in Rhode Island and in many other states.

Even though the different branches and levels of government may not be controlled by the same party, they still must cooperate. A Republican President cannot ignore congressional leaders just because they happen to be Democrats, and congressional leaders cannot ignore the executive branch just because it happens to be controlled by Republicans. Cooperation among governing units is necessary, and this often means cooperation across party lines. A loosely organized, decentralized party system fits in well with the fragmentation of governing authority. Parties with strong, inflexible programs would make governing very difficult when Congress and the White House were controlled by different parties or when one level of government was primarily Republican and the other primarily Democratic.

Elections and Social Change

No society stands still. Citizens become concerned about new social problems and make new demands. Many of the problems that trouble us today — abortion, drug control, environmental pollution, street crime — were not important a couple of decades ago. In the 1950s, there was little attention to space exploration; in the 1960s, "putting a man on the moon" got public attention and funds; in the 1970s, the space program is being quietly set aside.

Related to changes in the political agenda are changes in the kinds of social groups active in politics. No one thought of "youth" as a separate political group twenty years ago, but in recent years the youth movement has been something to be taken seriously in American politics. Women's liberation has become a political issue, and very many active groups are concerned with the rights of women; this was not the case even a few years ago.

Is the political-party system responsive to such social change? Do the major parties provide a way of communicating new social concerns, a home for new types of groups? We can try to answer these questions by looking at protest movements and electoral coalitions.

Political-Protest Movements

From time to time political-protest movements arise among those who feel that social change is necessary. Such movements, which arise outside the political parties, bring up new issues or express old ones in new ways.

There have been five serious political-protest movements in the past decade: (1) the black protest movement, expressing the deprivations of centuries; (2) the youth protest, sparked by anti-war sentiment and fueled by the 1968 political campaign of Democratic challenger Eugene McCarthy; (3) "Nader populism," a middle-class movement concerned with environmental issues and consumer protection,

George Wallace campaigning.

hostile to big business, big labor, and big government; (4) the women's liberation movement, attempting to gain basic economic and political rights for women; and (5) a protest led by Alabama Governor George Wallace, based in the South but supported by northern working-class people and some white ethnic groups. The Wallace movement opposes the national leaders who have "given in" to black demands. In addition, it speaks for the "little man" against the "power bosses."

At the outset none of these movements depended on either of the two parties. Take the anti-war movement. Those who disapproved of American policy in Vietnam did not turn to the political parties to express their discontent. Rather, they communicated through the media, in universities and churches, and in the streets. The other protest movements have also operated outside the two major parties. The Wallace-led protestors used a third party in 1968. In that year the American Independent party received a total of 10 million votes. In 1972 Wallace decided to run in the Democratic primaries, and though he won many primary votes and was not far behind McGovern, the nominating convention paid little attention to his platform. He was crippled in an assassination attempt before the convention.

Consumer-protest and conservation movements, too, have been organized almost entirely outside the political-party system, as has women's liberation. Of the major protest movements in the 1960s, only the black movement got any party support. Throughout the 1960s and early 1970s, the Democratic party tried to respond to some of the pressing black demands.

People involved in protest movements sometimes say the two-party system is too inflexible for political protests. However, the events of the past few years show that this is not quite true.

Let us look more closely at the anti-war movement. Its leadership was totally frustrated at the 1968 Democratic Presidential nominating convention in Chicago, and much talk was heard about the inflexibility of the party system. After all, the anti-war movement had led to the decision of incumbent President Lyndon Johnson not to run for reelection, and yet here were the Democratic regulars nominating his Vice-President, Hubert Humphrey. But only four years later the Democratic party invited into the convention hall in Miami exactly the same protest groups that had demonstrated in the streets of Chicago in 1968. The convention nominated a strong anti-war candidate, Senator George McGovern. Thus in only four years the anti-war groups had a clear opportunity to take their case to the American electorate. That the results favored McGovern's Republican opponent, Richard Nixon, does not prove the inflexibility of the party system. It simply shows that a majority of Americans did not support George McGovern and his policies.

Indeed, all of the major protest groups of the 1960s—blacks, doves, women, Nader populists, and Wallacites—were in the 1970s receiving some sort of accommodation by the major parties.

Minor Parties

The absorption of protest movements and minor parties into the dominant two-party system is an old theme in American politics. Third parties have often been formed to challenge one or both of the dominant parties. And though these third parties disappear with time, they usually have some impact. One variety of minor party is the protest group, such as the Populist party in the late 1880s, which expressed discontent with monopolies and trusts. It also successfully agitated for direct election of senators, the primary system instead of the convention method of nominating candidates, women's suffrage, and other political reforms. With time these all became law.

Another type of minor party breaks away from one of the major parties when compromise fails to hold together the many factions that make up any large party. Theodore Roosevelt's Progressive party of 1912 was a secessionist party resulting from a split in the national leadership of the Republican party. More recent examples are the largely regional parties of the South, often led by "states' righters" within the Democratic party. Strom Thurmond (now Republican

Minor party candidates in 1972: (*Top, l. to r.*) Linda Jenness, Socialist Workers Party; E. Harold Munn, Prohibition Party; John C. Schmitz, American Party. (*Bottom, l. to r.*) Dr. Benjamin Spock, People's Party; Gus Hall, American Communist Party; John Hosper, Liberation Party.

234

senator from South Carolina, having switched parties) led the Dixie-crats in 1948, a group of southern Democrats dismayed at the nomination of Harry Truman. Wallace's American Independent party was a secessionist group breaking away from the liberal northern wing of the Democratic party that nominated Humphrey to stand against Nixon.

Not all minor parties have resulted from splits within a major party. The Socialist party is generally outside the policy framework that guides the Republicans and the Democrats. Such a party will outlast secessionist parties but will not usually have as much influence on public policy.

The chief function of minor parties has been to bring new issues, or new ways of looking at old issues, to the political agenda. As they succeed in forcing new policies on the established parties, they tend to disappear. What we see in the 1970s, then, is a repeat of previous history. As the Democrats and Republicans absorb into their ranks the followers and goals of the protest groups of the 1960s, they are doing what major parties have always done. It is one way the party system stays alive and responds to changing conditions and issues.

Maintaining, Deviating, and Realigning Elections

We are about to discuss elections in a way that is probably unfamiliar to you. Usually we focus on whether our candidate won, whether he won by a landslide or just squeaked by, or whether there were dirty tricks in the campaign. Here we are going to discuss three types of elections—maintaining, deviating, and realigning elections—in terms of the ways they affect the electoral coalitions that give structure and stability to the American electoral process.[1]

We have mentioned several times the strength of many people's voting habits. The majority of American voters tend to identify with one or the other of the major parties. They give stability to party politics. They become part of coalitions that persist over a series of elections. For example, in most elections between 1932 and 1968 the Democratic party could depend on urban, working-class voters, and the Republican party could count on small-town, middle-class voters. When voters follow their usual party preferences, they are, without knowing it, maintaining the existing balance of forces. Most elections are of this kind and are called *maintaining* elections.

From time to time, however, issues relevant only to one election upset the existing balance. Voters leave their party to vote for an especially attractive candidate of the other party or to reject an especially unattractive candidate of their own party. Many different things can lead citizens to cross party lines. Eisenhower was suc-

[1] The discussion draws upon studies conducted by the Survey Research Center, University of Michigan. See especially Angus Campbell, Philip E. Converse, Warren E. Miller, and Donald E. Stokes, *The American Voter* (New York: Wiley, 1960), and by the same authors, *Elections and the Political Order* (New York: Wiley, 1966).

cessful in 1952 and 1956 because many Democratic voters simply "liked Ike." In the 1960 Presidential election, religion acted as a short-term electoral force. Kennedy, a Roman Catholic, gained a few Catholic voters who normally would have supported the Republicans, but he lost many more traditionally Democratic Protestants to Nixon, the Republican candidate. In 1964 Goldwater, the Republican candidate, was much more soundly defeated than would have been expected on the basis of the normal strength of the two parties. His conservative philosophy, which pushed many of the more liberal Republicans into the Democratic camp, acted as a short-term electoral force.

Sometimes a large enough number of the citizens identified with the majority party respond to short-term forces and vote for the candidate of the other party so that the majority party loses. Such elections are called *deviating* elections. The elections of 1952 and 1956 were of this sort. There were fewer Republicans than Democrats, but enough of the latter voted for Eisenhower so that he won. The important thing about such deviations is that they are only temporary. The usual balance of forces is regained in the following election.

A third type of election is the *realigning* election. In such an election party loyalties are changed. Some people who have been loyal Democrats become loyal Republicans, and vice versa. This is different from a deviating election, in which a party member switches his vote for a single election in response to short-term forces. In a realigning election voters change their party loyalties more or less permanently. Thus the composition of one or both parties is greatly changed. Between 1932 and 1936 the Democrats put together the coalition that has dominated American politics almost up to the present day. They did this by attracting new kinds of voters—especially immigrant groups—and many traditional Republican voters. Black voters are an example. They had stayed with the party of emancipation, the Republicans, until it was obvious that the party that supported the needs and rights of the less advantaged was the Democratic party. Then they switched.

Such realigning elections, sometimes called *critical* elections, help effect social change, bringing new groups and issues to the political scene. Groups that have been in power drop into the political background; other groups become important political forces. For example, with the electoral realignment of the 1930s came an important shift in the political role of labor. As the party support changes, so does the political agenda. New issues arise and old ones fade. Again the 1930s present a clear example. Programs like social security, unemployment compensation, and public welfare simply were not political issues during the 1920s. However, the realignment of the 1930s put these issues on the political agenda.

Throughout American history realigning elections have occurred periodically. This suggests that the party system is at least partially

Figure 9.1
The American Electorate

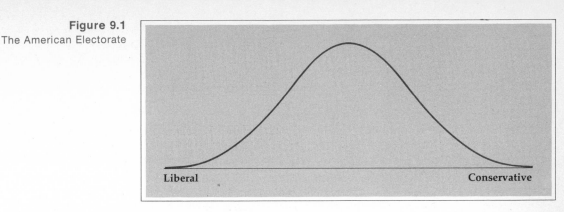

Liberal   Conservative

responsive to changing popular preferences and social needs. Such elections bring new social groups to power and put new issues on the political agenda.

How Different Are the Two Major Parties?

Observers of American politics are unable to agree on whether the two major parties are essentially the same in political ideology or not. By asking the question, Does it make a difference who wins?—we can perhaps draw some conclusions of our own.

When the conservative senator from Arizona, Barry Goldwater, won the Republican nomination in 1964, he argued that finally the voters would have "a choice, not an echo." Goldwater insisted that the two parties had become so alike in outlook that the American voters had no choice between competing viewpoints. Many agree, claiming that a two-party system actually reduces choice because each party must attract and hold the support of a wide variety of groups and individuals. The parties are coalitions, and coalitions cannot be held together unless they are flexible. Besides, this reasoning goes, the big prize for each party is the White House. Because there can be only one winner, it is natural that each party designs its strategy with that prize in mind. This means they must tend toward the middle, where most of the voters are supposed to be—a pattern described by the normal bell curve in Figure 9.1.

Other observers disagree. In a competitive political party system, they say, the parties reflect the basic conflict between haves and have-nots, between rich and poor, property owners and propertyless, businessmen and workers, producers and consumers. The democratic class struggle plays itself out through electoral competition.

The "democratic class struggle" was foreshadowed in 1787 in *The Federalist* (No. 10):

> The most common and durable source of factions [political parties] has been the various and unequal distribution of property. Those who hold and those who are without property have ever formed distinct

interests in society. Those who are creditors, and those who are debtors fall under a like discrimination. A landed interest, a manufacturing interest, a mercantile interest, a moneyed interest, with many lesser interests grow up of necessity in civilized nations, and divide them into different classes, actuated by different sentiments and views.

Early political history showed this to be true. The first political parties, or factions as Madison called them, were organized around conflicting economic interests. Under the leadership of Hamilton the Federalist party protected the interests of commerce, business, and hard money, while the Jeffersonians were more favorable to the small farmer and the debtor class. Class differences in the party system have been traced through nearly two centuries of party changes and, according to some observers, may be seen today in the Republicans and Democrats.

This suggests the diagram shown in Figure 9.2. Here the parties stand in opposition to each other, with the Democrats getting their support from less wealthy social classes (liberals, presumably favoring a more equal distribution of wealth) and the Republicans drawing their support from more wealthy social classes (presumably favoring a conservative, or status quo, viewpoint).

Which is correct—a picture of the parties as more or less the same in outlook, or a picture of them as reflecting conflicting policies? Let us turn to four kinds of evidence:

1. whether the parties draw electoral support from different social groups
2. whether the parties depend on different sources for campaign funds
3. whether the party leaders differ in their policy views
4. whether support for legislation differs between the parties

Different Social Groups
Support the Two Major Parties

There are differences between the social groups that support the major parties. These can be traced to the coalition formed by Democratic President Roosevelt during the depression of the 1930s. During the Depression the Republican party remained close to its traditional principles of fiscal responsibility and individual effort and thus kept the support of business and commercial interests and WASP voters. Meanwhile the Democrats introduced such public-welfare measures as social security, unemployment insurance, and public aid and thus became the party of blacks, immigrant workers, the poor, and the unemployed.

The difference between the class bases of the Republicans and the Democrats can still be seen today. In general, Republicans tend to be of higher socioeconomic status than Democrats. They tend to have higher-status occupations, higher incomes, and more formal education than Democrats. However, the coalitions of the 1930s are not as strong as they once were. Important changes are taking place in the composition of the parties. Workers still are likely to be Demo-

Figure 9.2
Party Differences as Reflections
of Class Antagonisms

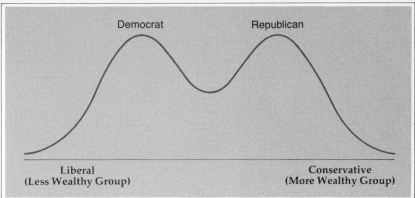

Liberal
(Less Wealthy Group)

Conservative
(More Wealthy Group)

cratic, but now they are more willing to listen to Republican candidates. And across all socioeconomic levels party ties are loosening. This is especially true among the younger voters.

Furthermore, we should be careful not to overstate the differences in social backgrounds of Republican and Democratic voters, for both parties attract voters from a variety of social groups. Factors other than social class affect party identification; regional, ethnic, and religious divisions cut across class lines. That a Catholic businessman is more likely than a Protestant businessman to be a Democrat shows that parties have a religious as well as a class basis.

Voters See Party Differences

The contrast in support given to the Republicans and Democrats is reflected in citizens' images of the parties. Voters are much more likely to view the Republicans rather than the Democrats as the party of fiscal responsibility and as being favorable to business interests. Some voters like the Republicans for this reason: "I like to string along with big business and big money. Well, I'll also tell you under the Republicans the country has prospered." Other voters reject the Republican party because of its close ties with business. A St. Louis policeman says, "Republican leaders are controlled by moneyed men—that's what I don't like about the Republican party—it is run by large corporations."

Very different images are held of the Democratic party, which is thought of as more likely to take care of the working class. The wife of a Connecticut salesman says she likes what the Democrats do for the laboring class: "They try to improve working conditions—work for shorter hours—a higher wage rate—and are more interested in benefits for the working man." This image hurts the Democratic party when the voter is worried about inflation and welfare costs. According to a businessman in Illinois, "the Democrats are a giveaway party. Under their policies there would be no initiative left in the country. Democrats always want to spend more than the government has. Business suffers when the Democrats are in power."

HOW DIFFERENT ARE THE
TWO MAJOR PARTIES?

239

Campaign abuses have led to attempts at campaign reform. Here Congressional leaders sign the Code of Fair Campaign Practices.

Although some of these images are beginning to break down, current economic problems are reminding the voters that the parties do stand for different kinds of programs. President Ford's economic policies include tax benefits to businesses in an effort to get the economy moving by urging business investments and increased production. Democratic leaders responded with programs stressing benefits for the working class, especially the unemployed and the poor, who are hardest hit by inflation and recession.

Differences in Campaign Support

Party differences may also be seen in the different groups that give money to the major parties. A very high portion of Republican party money comes from wealthy individuals and the business community. On the other hand, a very high portion of Democratic party money comes from organized labor and liberal interest groups. For instance, in 1968 national labor committees spent $7.1 million in political campaigns, an average of five or six cents per union member, and nearly all of this went to Democratic candidates. Common Cause, a liberal public-interest group, spent nearly $400,000 in 1972 on House and Senate candidates; all but five were Democrats or independents.

Campaign Funding Abuses   Wealthy individuals and large corporations can buy political favors with campaign money. This was illustrated when investigators, spurred by Watergate, looked closely at campaign giving for the 1972 Presidential election. A large percentage of the money from the business community went to the committee to reelect Nixon and other Republican party campaigns.

Direct contributions from corporate funds, unlawful since 1907, were among the abuses discovered in the Watergate investigations. Corporation executives were pressured by leading members of the Nixon administration. Claude C. Wild, former vice-president of Gulf Oil Corporation, who pleaded guilty to making an illegal contribu-

Table 9.2
Campaign Contributions (1972) from Officials of Corporations with Large Federal Contracts

Corporation	Contributions to Republicans	Contributions to Democrats
Litton Industries	$277,709	$ 500
Hughes Aircraft	248,500	5,700
AT&T	132,560	103,991
Northrop	197,500	3,000
RCA	191,352	8,148
Westinghouse Electric	183,850	3,800
LTV	139,142	16,250
General Dynamics	149,906	750
Ford	112,176	36,620
General Motors	127,628	6,207

Source: Based on data from *Dollar Politics*, vol. 2 (Washington, D.C.: *Congressional Quarterly*, 1974).

Country	Ambassador	Contribution
Great Britain	Walter H. Annenberg	$ 250,000
Switzerland	Shelby Davis	100,000
Luxembourg	Ruth L. Farkas	300,000
Belgium	Leonard K. Firestone	112,600
Netherlands	Kingdon Gould	100,900
Austria	John F. Humes	100,000
France	John N. Irwin II	50,500
France	Arthur K. Watson	300,000
Ireland	John D. Moore	10,442
Total		$1,324,442

Source: Based on data from *Dollar Politics,* vol. 2 (Washington, D.C.: *Congressional Quarterly,* 1974).

tion of $100,000 to the Nixon campaign, told the Senate Watergate Committee: "I consider it considerable pressure when two Cabinet officers [Attorney General John Mitchell and Commerce Secretary Maurice Stans] ask me for funds—that is just a little bit different than somebody collecting for the Boy Scouts." By late 1974 thirteen corporations had admitted making illegal contributions to the Nixon campaign, including American Airlines, Associated Milk Producers, Goodyear Tire, Minnesota Mining and Manufacturing, and Northrop.

The Republican party has also received major support from officials of corporations with large federal contracts. Table 9.2 lists 1972 campaign giving by officers and directors of various corporations heavily involved in Department of Defense, Atomic Energy Commission, and National Aeronautic and Space Administration (NASA) contract work. The advantage of the Republican party is clear.

Ambassadorships for Sale One way both parties raise campaign support is by "promising" attractive ambassadorships to large contributors. This of course is illegal, but was not brought to public notice until the Watergate scandal. The Senate Watergate Committee, however, looked into contributions by people later given ambassadorships by the Nixon administration and concluded: "At the very least, a number of persons saw the making of a contribution as a means of obtaining the recognition needed to be actively considered." Nixon denied the accusation, declaring at a news conference in early 1973 that "ambassadorships have not been for sale." Exactly a year later Nixon's personal attorney, Herbert W. Kalmbach, pleaded guilty to having promised an important European ambassadorship in return for a $100,000 campaign contribution. As Table 9.3 shows, more than $1 million was given to Nixon's 1972 reelection campaign by people with western European ambassadorships.

Campaign Funding Reform The abuses revealed by the Watergate investigations led to major legislation in 1974 that tried to control

Figure 9.3
Major Provisions of Campaign
Finance Reform

Contribution Limits. $1,000 per individual for each primary, runoff and general election, and an aggregate contribution of $25,000 for all federal candidates annually; $5,000 per organization, political committee and state party organization for each election.

Candidate's and his family's contributions: $50,000 for President; $35,000 for Senate; $25,000 for House.

Individual unsolicited expenditures on behalf of a candidate limited to $1,000 a year.

Cash contributions of over $100 and foreign contributions barred.

Spending Limits. Presidential primaries—$10-million total per candidate for all primaries.

Presidential general election—$20-million.

Presidential nominating conventions—$2-million each major political party, lesser amounts for minor parties.

Senate primaries—$100,000 or eight cents per eligible voter, whichever was greater.

Senate general elections—$150,000 or 12 cents per eligible voter, whichever was greater.

House primaries—$70,000.

House general elections—$70,000.

campaign funding. There are three main parts to the legislation: (1) limits on the amount of money an individual or an organization can give; (2) limits on how much candidates for various national offices can spend; (3) provision for public funding of Presidential elections (discussed in Chapter 11). Figure 9.3 shows the limits on contributions and spending.

Party Leaders Differ in Political Philosophy

Studies confirm that Democratic party leaders usually take a more liberal position than Republican party leaders. Democratic leaders are more egalitarian in social philosophy and more willing to expand the social services of the government. They are more critical of big business and normally favor a more progressive income tax. In contrast, Republican leaders oppose many egalitarian programs and believe the government's role in social services and welfare should expand either slowly or not at all. Republicans have a tendency to fear the influence of trade unions and to resist an excessive amount of business regulation.

The political opinions of delegates to the Presidential nominating conventions in 1956 were studied, and here is what the authors concluded: The Democratic party "is marked by a strong belief in the power of collective action to promote social justice, equality, humanitarianism, and economic planning, while preserving freedom." The Republican side "is distinguished by faith in the wisdom of the natural competitive process and in the supreme virtue of individuals, 'character,' self-reliance, frugality, and independence from government." Although the fit is not perfect, "the American parties

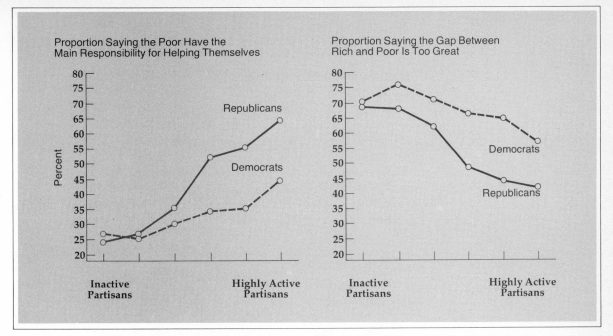

Figure 9.4

Welfare Attitudes of Democrats and Republicans at Various Activity Levels

Source: Based on data from Sidney Verba and Norman H. Nie, *Participation in America: Political Democracy and Social Inequality* (New York: Harper & Row, 1972).

do tend to embody these competing points of view and to serve as reference groups for those who hold them."[2]

A survey ten years later had similar results. Evidence from two questions on social egalitarianism is presented in Figure 9.4, where we see that politically active Democrats are less willing than active Republicans to say the poor have the main responsibility for helping themselves, and Democrats are more likely than Republicans to think the income gap between rich and poor is too great. These data reveal two additional points of interest. First, the more active party members differ much more sharply than the less active members. Activists are more likely to spend their time with people who share their political outlook than the average voter. Moreover, the activists are attracted to politics by policy matters, whereas the average voter is often voting in a family tradition or out of habit.

Second, Democratic party activists are actually more conservative than rank-and-file Republicans. One important reason is that Democratic leaders are largely middle class in social origin and in occupation. But the voters of a party are much more varied in background, and thus even the Republican party will include voters drawn from the working and lower classes. This has the result of sometimes

[2] These findings are taken from a study of the delegates to the 1956 Presidential nominating conventions of both parties. These delegates come from every part of the country and from every level of party and government. For a full report see Herbert McClosky, Paul J. Hoffmann, and Rosemary O'Hara, "Issue Conflict and Consensus Among Party Leaders and Followers," *American Political Science Review*, June 1960, 420.

pushing *both* sets of party leaders to the more conservative side of a question and leaving *both* sets of voters favoring more liberal policies.

Democratic and Republican
Congressmen Support Different Legislation

Shortly we will see that Democratic and Republican congressmen do not support the same legislative proposals, but first a word about political parties in Congress. Neither of the parties can enforce strict party loyalty or impose a party program on its representatives in Congress. For reasons already outlined, the parties are loose, regionally based coalitions, not centrally organized or directed parties with cohesive programs. Although congressional leaders and the President can put pressure on party members, they can go only so far. The Republican or Democrat in Congress is more independent of his party than of his group supporters, the voters back home, his financial backers, and his own philosophy. If, then, differences between the parties in congressional votes are found, these reflect major differences in philosophy between the parties.

Political scientists have studied how the parties vote in Congress and have reached two conclusions: (1) There is much cohesion within each party and major policy differences between the parties, and (2) deviations from these patterns are almost entirely due to voter preferences. Thus if a Democrat votes differently in Congress from his fellow Democrats, it is usually because of particular pressure from the voters back home or, more likely, from an important interest group in his home district.

Differences in voting records between the two parties may be seen in roll-call votes in the House of Representatives. Table 9.4 lists votes on selected legislative proposals over the past quarter-century; the striking contrast between Republicans and Democrats confirms party differences. On balance, the Republicans have been economic protectionists and the Democrats economic protestors. The Republican party has opposed government regulation of the economy, income-equalization and social-welfare programs, and has favored policies that create jobs and economic growth through free enterprise and private initiative. The Democrats introduced Keynesian economics, with its emphasis on greater government intervention in the economy; they have tried to reduce income differences through tax reform; and they have favored social-welfare policies.

While this description is accurate, it is certainly not complete. *Each* party can alternately be seen as protecting conservative principles *and* calling for reform. The first major attempt to regulate commercial trusts and financial empires belongs to a Republican President, Theodore Roosevelt (1901–1909), who so disagreed with the conservative faction within his own party, a wholly pro-business and antilabor faction, that he formed the Progressive party, under whose banner he unsuccessfully ran for President in 1912. (He split

Table 9.4
Party Differences in the House
of Representatives, 1945–1974

Year	Selected Legislation	Democrats in Favor	Republicans in Favor
1945	Full Employment Act	90%	36%
1947	Maintain Individual Income Tax Rates	62	1
1954	Increase Unemployment Compensation	54	9
1961	Emergency Educational Act	67	4
1964	Antipoverty Program	84	13
1969	Tax Reform	86	22
1971	Hospital Construction	99	41
1973	Increase Minimum Wage	88	27
1974	Federal Aid to City Transit Systems	81	23

Source: Based on data from Robert A. Dahl, "Key Votes, 1945–1964," *Pluralist Democracy in the United States* (Chicago: Rand McNally, 1967), pp. 238–242; *Labor Looks at the 91st Congress,* an AFL-CIO Legislative Report, 1971; *Labor Looks at Congress 1973,* an AFL-CIO Legislative Report, 1974; *Labor Looks at the 93rd Congress,* an AFL-CIO Legislative Report, 1975.

the Republican vote, and the election went to Democrat Woodrow Wilson.) The Democratic party has not always been reform minded. Certainly the Democratic party within Congress, dominated by southern conservatives, has blocked social-welfare policies, especially when these policies are connected with civil rights. The liberal-labor coalition within the Democratic party is only one faction, and not always the one that controls legislation.

Still, various types of evidence show meaningful differences between the two major parties, differences at least partially rooted in conflicting class interests. The argument that the Republicans and Democrats present "no choice" to the voters doesn't hold up; nor does the argument that it makes no difference which party controls Congress.

Political Parties and Foreign Policy

There really are two types of foreign-policy issues: those in which the political parties play a role and those in which they do not. Among the first are tariff policy and foreign aid. It is clear that these are as much domestic as foreign issues. Thus tariff policy reflects the interests of business and labor groups; on balance, the Republicans have been more protective of home industries and have favored high tariffs, whereas the Democrats have called for lower tariffs and free trade so consumer products could be made as cheap as possible. This difference is breaking down, however, as the international business community (largely Republican) presses for less restrictive trade so it can market overseas, and some labor unions (largely Democratic) favor high tariffs to guard against competition from "cheap labor" in other countries that results in unemployment at home.

Foreign aid is more strictly a foreign-policy issue, but it is never separate from domestic issues. Those who want to balance the budget (mostly Republicans) conflict with those who want to increase foreign aid (mostly Democrats); conflict also arises because of the strong ties between domestic pressure groups and other nations. Aid to Israel has always been connected with the Jewish vote in the United States. Black Americans are beginning to press for more favorable treatment of black African nations and for greater opposition to white-controlled African nations such as South Africa.

In many other foreign-policy issues, political parties play a minor role. These are the issues of war and peace, national security and defense. Here both parties accept the leadership of the President and his executive advisers. This is a *nonpartisan* issue; major foreign policy since World War II has been made by a small group of experts isolated from serious party politics. This is evident in a long list of major foreign policy decisions, which would include, besides the Vietnam war, involvement in military alliances such as NATO, participation in the arms race and nuclear stockpiling, the deployment of armed forces around the world, and the use made of the United Nations for foreign-policy concerns. These policies have not been made by political party leaders getting together to formulate a bipartisan role for the United States in world affairs. They have been made by the President, speaking as leader of the nation rather than as head of his party, on the advice of trusted advisers from universities, major corporations, large law firms, the State Department, and the Pentagon.

Nothing so clearly illustrates the irrelevance of the parties to foreign policy than the divisive events of the 1960s and early 1970s, as the public became disillusioned with the Vietnam war. There was a split between hawks and doves within the government, but it had little to do with party politics. It led to a battle between Congress and the Presidency over who should control foreign policy. The main opponents, Senator Fulbright and President Johnson, were both Democrats.

Summary

The discussion of the role of political parties in American politics suggests several major themes. First, it is the political parties that manage the transfer of power in American politics. They do so despite lack of internal organization and a cohesive program. Indeed the decentralization of the political parties makes it possible for them to manage the election of political leaders ranging from the President of the United States to the mayor of a small town. Second, the control of the parties over political office is not constitutional or legal in any strict sense. There is nothing to prevent people from winning public office completely outside the party system. But this is not easy, because millions of voters habitually support candidates who are nominated by the parties. Furthermore, the parties provide campaign help in the form of organization and money to the people they nominate.

Third, the relationship between political parties and election results is complex. A major challenge facing the parties is to make room for new ideas and new groups. Sometimes these new ideas or groups cannot find a home in the Democratic or Republican parties and turn, instead, to a third-party movement to voice their demands. When voters give support to a third party or a minor party, the leaders of the major parties worry. And a major party will often change its policies and programs to attract the voters back, or perhaps to attract voters from the other major party. Of course it is possible that a party could lose so much support that it simply disappears. This happened to the Whig party before the Civil War. Some observers feel that the Republican party is threatened in this way; we discuss this in the next section.

The fourth major theme discussed in this chapter is the difference between the two parties. Various kinds of evidence leads to the conclusion that it makes a difference who wins elections. Policies and programs differ depending on which party is in control.

The Future of the Two-Party System

It is difficult, perhaps impossible, to imagine American politics without the Democratic and Republican parties as we know them today. But there are factors at work suggesting that the party system, along with other institutions in American politics, is undergoing some major changes. And it is very hard to figure out where these changes might take the party system.

The variety of political movements in the past few years indicates that "politics as usual" will no longer work. This has put the party system under some strain. New groups—blacks, women, ethnics— are demanding greater voice in political affairs. Certainly one demand is for more open politics, which means the established party leaders will be called upon to share some of their traditional powers. Already this is changing the kinds of candidates who run for public office. For example, in the 1974 congressional races six winning candidates were under 30.

Along with these pressures for change has come a decline in party loyalty. This we see in two ways: (1) the increasing numbers of voters who call themselves independents, indicating a large minority available to support either party, and (2) increased ticket splitting, showing a weakening of party loyalties even among those who continue to identify with a party.

The strongest evidence that major changes are taking place is the actual voting behavior of citizens. In the 1972 Presidential race there were dramatic switches of normally Democratic voters into the Republican camp. Large numbers of blue-collar Catholics and ethnics switched from the Democratic ticket in the traditionally Democratic industrial states of the North; the Jewish vote remained Democratic,

but only barely so, whereas it traditionally has supported the Democratic ticket by a 9-to-1 ratio; the southern support for the Democratic party continued to weaken; and the youth vote, which some had felt would strengthen the Democratic party, favored Nixon.

Yet not all the evidence points toward realignment. If groups are indeed changing party loyalties, this would be reflected in congressional, gubernatorial, and local elections as well. But in all but the Presidential race the results of the 1972 election were fairly typical. The Democratic party did not lose its majority in Congress, nor its edge in governorships, nor control of the state legislatures it traditionally dominates. Perhaps, then, the 1972 election was a deviating election rather than a realigning one. If so, the Catholics, the workers, the ethnics, the Jews, the southerners, and other traditionally Democratic voters would return to their habitual party at the next election, and the balance we have known since 1932 would reestablish itself.

This appeared to have happened in 1974, when the election results so favored the Democratic party that party leaders worried about the future of the Republican party. Many of the election defeats suffered by Republicans in the fall of 1974 were a direct result of Watergate. A Republican President, Nixon, had just left office in disgrace, the first President to resign in the history of the nation. And many voters, including traditional Republicans, showed dissatisfaction with the Nixon administration by voting against all Republicans, whether they were candidates for governorship, Congress, or local office.

It is doubtful that this will happen again in the 1976 election. But this does not mean the Republican party will have regained its former strength. As Table 9.1 indicated, the decline in support for the Republican party began before Watergate. Many voters are deciding that the Republican party no longer has a meaningful program for the kinds of problems facing American society.

A large number of citizens have withdrawn from any kind of electoral participation. Barely more than a majority of the eligible citizens even bothered to vote in 1972; in the 1974 congressional contests the number voting dropped to less than 40 percent. This low voting turnout is certainly a sign of dissatisfaction.

The American public is showing displeasure at the ways the two parties have responded to the social problems facing the country. The major parties will attempt to accommodate themselves to the new groups on the political scene. They will try to deal with the political agenda of inflation, recession, consumer protection, tax reform, social welfare, and street crime. They will not remain unchanged. And if they cannot absorb the new groups and deal with these issues, the two-party system as we have known it will fade. The inflexible party is a doomed party. But historically the party system has more than once shown flexibility.

Controversy

In choosing its Presidential ticket should a political party concern itself primarily with winning or should it stress the differences between the two parties? More often than not the two major parties nominate "centrist" Presidential candidates; that is, they nominate candidates who can appeal to the middle ground in American politics. In doing so they smooth over important differences in political outlook between the Republicans and the Democrats. Most of the time the major parties purposely provide more echo than choice.

One Side

The American voters respond favorably to Presidential candidates who stand midway between a broadly conservative and a broadly liberal outlook. Since it is the job of political parties to win elections, they should give the voters what they want. Recent nominations of "extreme" candidates have resulted in serious defeats. In 1964 the Republican convention nominated Senator Barry Goldwater, spokesman of the conservative wing of the party. Goldwater led the Republican ticket to a major defeat as the Democratic nominees, Johnson and Humphrey, won more than 60 percent of the Presidential votes. Election year 1972 was a repeat performance, except this time the Democratic party chose a candidate, Senator George McGovern, who spoke for its liberal wing. McGovern's defeat by Nixon and Agnew was similar to Goldwater's defeat eight years earlier—and for many of the same reasons. A Presidential candidate well to the left or right of center leads many voters to switch to the other party. This shows that voters prefer candidates, at least Presidential candidates, who are middle-of-the-roaders.

Besides, crushing defeats like those suffered by Goldwater and McGovern can have unfortunate results if the winning party feels that the landslide victory gives it the right to do whatever it wants.

The Other Side

While it is true that voters seem to prefer middle-of-the-road candidates, the major parties have a responsibility to values other than winning. They should give the voters a clear choice and use the Presidential election as a chance to express different goals and policies for the nation.

Such a choice is especially important in a Presidential campaign. Most American citizens pay attention to politics only at this time. If there is to be meaningful participation by the typical citizen, it can best occur during a Presidential election year. If the typical citizen is going to think seriously about the alternatives facing society, he will do so in response to debates between Presidential candidates. When the Presidential campaign smooths over major differences about how to handle the problems of the nation, the democratic process is not working. The "me-too-ism" of most Presidential campaigns denies the opportunity for a national debate about significant issues.

A candidate who clearly differs from his opponent plays an important educating role, even if he loses. He reminds the nation that alternative policies are possible. This is part of the responsibility of leadership. In 1972, for instance, McGovern's strong anti-war stand might have contributed to his defeat, but perhaps it also contributed to the urgency with which the Nixon administration pursued peace negotiations that year. McGovern himself saw it this way: "There can be no question at all that we have pushed this country in the direction of peace, and I think each one of us loves the title of peacemaker more than any office in the land."

When the political parties fail to provide alternatives, they fail to provide leadership, and in this way they fail the American public.

How Institutions Work: II
How Our Political Parties Are Organized

What is the organizational basis of American political parties?

Our political parties can be thought of in terms of layers of organization. Each layer—city or county, state, and national—is concerned chiefly with elections within its own area. The ties that link party organizations across these layers are more formal than real. Party structure is most often described as *decentralized,* which means the parties are less organized at the state level than at the local level and least organized at the national level. Indeed so decentralized and fragmented are the parties that, depending on time and place, they may hardly be organized at all.

How are the parties organized at the national level?

The highest-level body of each party is its national committee. It consists of one man and one woman from each state, the District of Columbia, Puerto Rico, and certain of the territories. The Republican national committee also includes state chairmen from states that voted Republican in the last state or national election. Committee members are chosen in various ways in the states and rarely meet as a group. In fact the national committee amounts to little more than the national chairman and the party staff in Washington.

What role does the national chairperson play in party affairs?

Although formally elected by the national convention, the national chairperson is really the choice of the party's Presidential nominee. Thus Jean Westwood was named Democratic chairperson by candidate George McGovern in 1972, but she was replaced in the power struggle that followed McGovern's defeat. This points to the national committee's primary purpose as one of raising money and helping coordinate the Presidential campaign every four years. But even this role is small, since Presidential candidates usually either take over the national machinery and make it their own or, like Nixon in 1972, may create a separate organization such as the Committee to Re-elect the President and use it to run the campaign.

Are there any other party structures at the national level?

Both Republicans and Democrats have congressional and senatorial campaign committees chosen by the party members in each branch. They are independent of the national committee and serve to channel money and assistance to House and Senate candidates.

What is the shape of party organization at the state level?

At the top of the state structure is each party's state central committee. Its members are chosen locally in counties or other election districts and serve to organize state party conventions, coordinate campaigns, and raise funds. Like the national committees, state organizations tend to be weak except when a dominant leader—the governor or a big-city mayor—is able to attract organized support. Even in these situations the basis of strength is usually personal and cannot be translated into an ongoing political organization.

Patterns of political strength at the state level vary widely. It is estimated that there is serious competition between the parties in about half the states, with the others having either one-party or modified one-party systems. And even where there is two-party competition the pattern of organization may be very uneven. In Michigan, for example, the Democratic party organization is highly centered in Detroit and Wayne County, while Republicans dominate much of the remaining state.

What makes some party organizations operate successfully?

Successful party organization in America takes place at the local level. The basic unit is the precinct or election district, containing from 300 to 1000 voters. The key position is that of the precinct captain responsible for turning out the vote; the captain and the ward leaders may be volunteers or may be chosen in the same primaries in which candidates for office are nominated. In any event they serve as the building blocks of the larger district, city, and county organizations that make up the local layer of party structure. Such political "machines" are rare today, though the Democratic Cook County organization continues to function in this way. Generally speaking, areas where local political units are well organized tend to be dominated by one party—and for good reason. Effective party strength depends on money, organizational skills, many hours of work, and in some cases political control over jobs. These are scarce resources that usually can't support two well-organized parties within the same political space.

10

Congress: Representation and Legislation

Article 1, Section 1, of the U.S. Constitution declares:

> All legislative Powers herein granted shall be vested in a Congress of the United States, which shall consist of a Senate and a House of Representatives.

Thus was created Congress, and in the remainder of Article I the duties, powers, and responsibilities of that body are given in detail.

The Roots of Congress

In creating a Congress the writers of the Constitution followed an ancient practice. In pre-Christian Greece and Rome special assemblies were chosen to make laws for the entire community. And if we stretch the language a bit, the tribal elders gathered around the chief resemble the legislative assembly. Americans, however, trace their legislative assembly to medieval British parliaments, the true ancestors of modern-day legislatures. In these medieval parliaments a selected few noblemen and clergymen met with the king to present the complaints of the estates for which they spoke. In its earliest days parliament was only a representative assembly: It *re*-presented the viewpoint of the important groups in society to the king. But it did not take part in lawmaking. The lawmaking powers remained with the king and his advisers. Parliament did not become a legislative assembly until later, and this role was not firmly established until the eighteenth century.

By the 1780s, however, the American colonies had a lot of experience with their own legislative assemblies. And they liked what they had. The attempt of King George to whittle away the authority of these legislatures spurred the independence movement, for in the eyes of the colonists the royal governors (appointed by the king) in each colony were being given too much control, especially over economic affairs. Thus was born the effective political slogan "No taxation without representation." At first this was a rallying cry only for those who were demanding greater representation in the Parliament of England and greater independence for the colonial legislatures. When these demands were rebuffed, the rebel movement became an open demand for independence.

After the war was fought and won, the new nation had to set up political institutions that would avoid the excesses and arbitrariness of executive authority, whether that authority was a king or a governor or a president. The so-called separation-of-powers system, in which Congress cooperates with the executive but also stands against it, was the result. The power of political executives, thought the founders, is too often arbitrary and antidemocratic. A Congress would institutionalize a "counterelite," an independent group of leaders who would owe their careers and authority to popular election. This counterelite would check the excesses of executive power while at the same time remaining close in its thinking to the voters it represents.

Representative Assemblies in the United States

"Representation is the grand discovery of modern times," wrote the Scottish philosopher James Mill, and his feeling is widely shared. Political representation is seen as a happy, workable compromise between the dangers of hereditary leadership and the difficulties of participatory democracy. This compromise is based on a belief in popular rule but recognizes that the people cannot actually govern themselves. Thus, as stated in *The Federalist*, political representation is an efficient "substitute for the meeting of the citizens in person."

Not all citizens are equally fond of politics. Some would just as soon not be bothered with the detailed, or even the broad, issues of public policy. Such citizens demand the right to be apolitical, or to become political animals as infrequently and painlessly as possible (voting every two or four years). But if many citizens do not wish to be involved, neither do they wish to feel powerless. Political representation comes to the rescue. It allows a compromise between political indifference and activism.

The Popularity of Representative Groups

For these reasons representative assemblies have been popular in the United States. In addition to Congress we have state legislatures, village, township, and city councils, school boards, special district commissions, and various county-level boards and commissions. All told, there are about 80,000 representative assemblies in the formal governmental structures in America. More than a half-million American citizens hold office as elected representatives. Representative principles have spread well beyond formal government. We find them throughout our economic and social life. Stockholders elect a board of directors to represent them and protect their interests against the managers of the firm. Union members elect officials who are supposed to govern the union in a manner that reflects member preferences. Voluntary associations in the thousands are led by elected representatives. We are introduced to political representation at an early age, as when we elect classmates to represent the homeroom on the student council, elect the officers of the school patrol, or choose cheerleaders. No political ideal, with the exception of majority voting perhaps, is as deeply a part of our political culture as is the principle of representation itself.

Congress: The Responsive Branch

Of the three major branches of government—executive, legislative, judicial—the legislative branch, Congress, is supposed to be the most responsive to the public. Consider the Supreme Court. It has only nine members, who are appointed for life. It meets in secret; it is guided by the Constitution and by legal precedent; it announces major decisions in a technical language. The Supreme Court is remote from the hustle and bustle of everyday politics.

The executive branch is not as remote as the Supreme Court, but it is not completely accessible. It is often mysterious to the common citizen. The most visible and most powerful part of the executive branch, the White House, keeps its distance. There is no visitor's gallery, as there is in Congress, where any citizen can walk in and watch the President and his advisers in action. Press conferences are held when the President wants to hold them. Under Nixon the White House staff became known for its arrogance, and when President Ford replaced Nixon he had to promise the nation that government would be more open than in the past. This promise has been hard to keep. It still takes a lot of attention by the press, members of Congress, and citizen groups to find out what is going on inside the White House.

Congress is very different from the Supreme Court and the White House. It is not nearly as solemn as the Court nor nearly as bureaucratic as the Presidency. It is made up of 535 men and women, all of whom want to be in the news. They come from every corner of the nation, and they carry with them the concerns and demands and hopes of a very complicated society. Congress is anything but remote from the hustle and bustle of everyday politics. It is at the center of those politics, the meeting place of journalists and lobbyists and protestors and plain citizens.

Congress and Democracy

The burden of protecting the basic principles of democracy falls mainly on Congress. It is a big job. In the social and economic conditions of the twentieth century, the ideas of popular rule are difficult to maintain. Huge nation-states, big defense budgets, industrialization, the mass media, and complicated social and economic issues make nonsense of the claim that people can govern themselves. At least, democratic principles have been undermined by the growth of huge bureaucracies and the steadily growing role of the state in organizing and regulating (and manipulating) social life. The fascist governments of Europe shattered the belief that democracy was safe from tyranny. Stalinism killed the hope that communism as an economic system would somehow protect democracy where capitalism had failed. And the growth of the military-industrial complex has caused many in the United States to question whether our political arrangements can keep power from shifting to a small number of men who manage the giant economic and political bureaucracies. Centralized organization and concentrated powers can too easily produce mass manipulation; democracy becomes the façade behind which the few direct the society. These are

not groundless fears. Political representation is a major weapon against this tendency. If a democratic nation can protect its representative assembly, then the trend toward concentrated power is checked. The legislature is rooted in popular choice. If we cannot have government by the people, at least we can have government of and for the people.

How well is Congress doing its job? Many feel that Congress is failing.

Congress Under Attack

Congress has received more than its share of criticism in recent years. Lethargic, labyrinthine, parochial, reactionary, inefficient, powerless, misguided, undemocratic—this is how Congress is described. As one of its own members has complained, it is in the legislative branch of government that "political lag remains triumphant." Senator Joseph Clark is not alone in making this charge; many observers feel that Congress is not yet part of the twentieth century.

A Local Institution
Dealing with National Issues

Dissatisfaction with Congress seems to be based on the complaint that the *institution* has not kept up with the *issues*. The issues with which the American government must deal are national in scope; Congress is essentially a local institution.

American society has become a national society. The issues that count are those that affect the whole society. Transportation and housing and legal justice and national security and education affect the whole society. The nationalization of issues has occurred hand in hand with the nationalization of social institutions. Consider the institutions that matter in our society: the *National* Council of Churches, the *National* Baseball League, the *National* Association of Manufacturers, the *National* Education Association, the *National* Federation of Independent Business, the *National* Broadcasting Company. The Main St. Methodist Church remains, like the community baseball team, the local shoe factory, the Horace Mann PTA, the corner drugstore, and the town's radio station, but such local institutions have nowhere near the political importance of the huge national organization, a product of the twentieth century.

The federal government has both encouraged and suffered from the trend toward nationalization. Federal agencies and activities have grown in response to social problems that are national in scope. As transportation has become *trans-* and even *inter*national, the government has had to organize agencies such as the Federal Aviation Administration (FAA) to protect the safety and well-being of users. Medical research has implications for the entire nation, so the government has created the National Institutes of Health and the National Science Foundation to fund and regulate this research. For every important issue one can think of—fiscal policy, unemployment, civil rights, highway safety, consumer protection—there are federal agencies and programs.

It is often said that Congress is ill equipped to play a serious role in formulating *national* programs. Yet Congress is supposed to represent and legislate for the American public. When you are bothered about the quality of life in America—traffic congestion, consumer prices, racial injustice, polluted rivers, street crime, mediocre schools, war spending—you in fact are bothered about issues that Congress has the constitutional authority to deal with.

The Congressman's Career

Although serving in national office, congressmen are closely tied to one particular part of the country. The typical congressman has lived his entire life in the district or state he represents. His education was in a local college or the state university. And if he went to law school, as more than half of the congressmen have, it was often to a local institution. If his career was business, it was not as an executive of a national corporation who was often transferred but, rather, in a business headquartered in his hometown.

The typical congressional career involves working through local office and perhaps the state legislature. At the turn of the century, three-fourths of congressmen had held state or local office before moving to Congress; six decades later, despite the great changes in American society over the period, this career pattern was still true of two-thirds of the congressmen. In contrast, while in 1900 about one-half of the top administrative leaders had held state or local office, in 1960 fewer than one-fifth of them had.

If recruitment stresses local ties, so does the continuing career. A member of the House of Representatives must stand for reelection every two years. He is hardly off to Washington before it is time to come home and campaign again. As the writers of the Constitution intended, this makes sure the representative will not quickly forget his election promises. It also keeps him in close contact with local interests and his local campaign organizations. Actually, however, members have rather long careers in Congress. Nine of every ten who stand for reelection are successful. Being a representative or a senator is a career in itself; some people serve for their entire adult lives. Thus at any given time Congress is made up mostly of veterans.

This pattern, it is claimed, contributes to the isolation of Congress from the changing issues of society. It leaves Congress under the control of people who first put together their winning coalition two or more decades ago. As long as these veterans continue to satisfy the narrow interests of a few key groups in their home districts or states, they can continue their congressional careers. The longer they stay, the easier it is to take care of voter interests, for it is the old-timers who, because of the seniority system, control the allocation of defense contracts, federal loans, funds for road construction, and similar "pork barrel" items. This leads to further isolation from national problems.

As summarized by Senator Richard Neuberger, "If there is one maxim which seems to prevail among many members of our national legislature, it is that local matters must come first and global problems a poor second — that is, if the member of Congress is to survive politically." A member of the House says, "My first duty is to get reelected. I'm here to represent my district. . . . This is part of my actual belief as to the function of congressmen. . . . What is good for the majority of districts is good for the country. What snarls up the system is these so-called statesmen-congressmen who vote for what they think is the country's interest. . . . We aren't . . . paid to be statesmen."[1]

A Middle-Class Body

Recently a Democratic congresswoman from New York, Rep. Bella S. Abzug, in a speech to the National Women's Political Caucus, insisted that a representative Congress would have half women, 11 percent blacks, more younger and more working-class people, and greater numbers of teachers, artists, and similarly un-

[1] The quotation from Senator Neuberger appears in Samuel P. Huntington, "Congressional Responses to the Twentieth Century," in David B. Truman, ed., *The Congress and America's Future* (Englewood Cliffs, N.J.: Prentice-Hall, 1965), p. 15. The second quotation appears in Lewis A. Dexter, "The Representative and His District," as reprinted in Theodore J. Lowi, ed., *Legislative Politics U.S.A.*, 2d ed. (Boston: Little, Brown, 1965), p. 86.

represented occupations. She correctly described Congress as dominated by men, mostly white, who have much higher education than the general population and are either from the professions (mostly law) or from the business and commercial sectors of society.

This has long bothered critics who speak in the populist tradition. Why should Congress have only 3 percent women members when women make up 51 percent of the population? Why should there be so few black or Chicano congressmen, although minority groups make up 11 percent of the total population? (See Table 5.1 for black and women members of Congress.)

What the reformer counts on is the likelihood that changing the composition of Congress will change the social policies it pursues. When civil rights organizations campaign for black candidates, it is because they think blacks can best speak for the concerns of racial minorities; when the Women's Caucus demands more congresswomen, they assume that the feminist viewpoint can be more forcefully presented by females than by males; when the U.S. Chamber of Commerce organizes political action groups, it is because it feels that businessmen in Congress will favor commerce.

But just because a man works in a factory does not guarantee that he has the interests of the working class at heart; not all women believe equally in the feminist movement; and a black skin covers the political views of an Uncle Tom just as it does those of a Black Panther. Conversely, being born of the middle class does not always mean hostility toward the working class; not all men don't care about women's liberation; some whites, including white congressmen, have been active in the civil-rights movement.

In recent years Congress has been undergoing steady, if gradual, change. It now has more women, more blacks, and more younger people than ever before. The results will be discussed later in the chapter.

It is true that Congress, with its local roots, has difficulty dealing with broad national issues. And it is true that the views of certain social groups have traditionally been unrepresented. Yet the criticisms overlook some of the important ways Congress does act as a representative assembly.

The Member of Congress as a Representative

Political representation is a complex issue. Is the representative to carry out the wishes of those who elected him, or is he to use his independent judgment? One view holds that a representative who does not closely follow the instructions of his constituency is not a representative at all. The opposing view asks: If every representative is bound by the instructions of his constituency, why bother to have a legislature? Why not simply decide public policy by public vote? But democracy by public-opinion poll would be foolish; it would ignore the benefits of an assembly that can formulate a policy representing the general interest rather than being a hodgepodge of disconnected and local concerns.

The case for the legislator as an elected but nevertheless independent agent was forcefully presented by Edmund Burke two centuries ago:

> Certainly, gentlemen, it ought to be the happiness and glory of a representative, to live in the strictest union, the closest correspondence, and the most unreserved communication with his constituents. . . . It is his duty to sacrifice his repose, his pleasures, his satisfactions, to theirs; and, above all, ever, and in all cases, to prefer their interest to his own. But, his unbiased opinion, his mature judgment, his enlightened conscience, he ought not to sacrifice to you, to any man, or to any set of men living. These he does not derive from your pleasure; no, nor from the law and the constitution. They are a trust from Providence, for the abuse of which he is deeply answerable. . . . Parliament is not [where] local prejudices ought to guide, but the general good, resulting from the general reason of the whole. . . .[2]

In fact most congressmen steer a middle course between the two viewpoints. They either mix them depending on the issue at hand or they lean toward the independent position, except in cases that clearly affect the well-being of their home area. This can be seen by considering how the congressman represents individual citizens of his home area, how he represents the voters, and how he represents organized interests.

Representing the Individual Citizen

Some descriptions of Congress picture the interested citizen with a problem he expects his elected representative to solve. This mythical citizen writes, calls, or visits his congressman, and the latter tries to take care of the citizen's need, not only because the citizen represents a vote but because such efforts are his duty. Unrealistic as this picture appears, it holds a great deal of truth.

The reason is simple. The federal bureaucracy touches the life of the individual citizen in dozens of ways: military draft, social-security payments, income-tax laws, small-business loans, medicare, public employment, regulation of working conditions, consumer protection, and so forth. When the citizen is mistreated by an executive agency or needs some government service, he turns to his congressman for help. So a congressman's work includes running errands for citizens or acting as an intermediary between citizen and bureaucracy. It is difficult to judge the amount of time a representative or a senator spends in this way, though some estimates go as high as 50 percent. It is certainly true that a congressman's staff spends much of its time on these individual problems.

Senator Vance Hartke, Democrat from Indiana, once inserted the following statement in the *Congressional Record* (no doubt so he

[2] Edmund Burke, "Speech to the Electors of Bristol" (1774), *Works*, II, 11.

could have it copied and mailed to Indiana voters):

> My office in Washington is a Hoosier headquarters. We receive an average of 275 phone calls a day, most of them from Indiana. We had nearly 6,000 visitors during the past year. . . . We received 45,938 letters and mailed out 50,678 letters. . . . We had 300 inquiries from people from Indiana who work for the Federal Government and wanted assistance with something pertaining to their jobs.
>
> The defense buildup has resulted in a great number of service and veteran problems. Since January 1, we have handled 709 of these problems, with the number growing daily. We assisted 261 Hoosiers with social security problems, 27 with draft board problems, 18 with railroad retirements, and 711 who sought patronage employment.
>
> I have helped also with 61 immigration cases who could be helped within the framework of the present law. Fifteen private immigration bills were introduced to assist those people who were worthy and who could not be helped through existing legislation. . . .
>
> It is my sincere conviction that I am in Washington to serve.

There is some concern that errand running takes up so much energy and time that Congress may be swamped and could decline as a legislative assembly. Rep. Reuss makes this point when he describes a congressman as a harried man and remarks that "the days are hardly long enough for him to think and act soundly on all the great issues of war and peace, national prosperity and civil rights," especially when the days are shortened by "the requests and demands from voters that require him to serve as their mediator with the Federal Government."

Few congressmen neglect these requests, however. Reelection can depend as much or more on your reputation as "available and helpful" than on your votes in Congress. Errand running creates a bond between citizen and legislator, but a bond that has relatively little to do with public policy. A request for help in dealing with the Internal Revenue Service need have nothing to do with tax reform or income distribution; a request for help in getting a small-business loan need have nothing to do with government fiscal policy.

The gap between citizen request and public policy can lead to a great deal of independence for the congressman. If he solves the citizen's problem, he can be reelected, however he votes on tax reform or fiscal management. Thus while the congressman is paying very close attention to the citizen's *problems,* he is paying less attention to the citizen's *viewpoints.* Of course the congressman is aware of the general viewpoint of his state or district, but as we will see in the next section, there is little reason to think this has a strong effect on his actions.

Representing the Voters

It is often hard for a congressman to represent voters accurately. When he was a senator from Massachusetts, John F. Kennedy wrote: "In Washington I frequently find myself believing that forty or fifty letters, six visits from professional politicians and lobbyists, and three editorials in Massachusetts newspapers constitute public opinion on a given issue. Yet in truth I rarely know how the great majority of the voters feel, or even how much they know of the issues that seem so burning in Washington."

This feeling has been called *mandate uncertainty*. Most congressmen are very uncertain about how to interpret election victory. Partly this is because voters do not have very well-informed viewpoints and do not participate in politics in great numbers. (See Chapter 4.) On the average, fewer than half the eligible voters bother to vote in congressional elections. Turnout is especially low in "off-year" elections. It takes a Presidential campaign to attract attention even to Senate contests. How can the successful congressional candidate interpret his victory if less than one-quarter of the eligible voters in his district supported him? This situation is made worse by how little the average voter knows about his representative. Even in competitive congressional races fewer than one-fourth of the voters know *anything* about either of the candidates and almost none knows anything about the policy positions.

Mandate uncertainty is also caused by the large number of issues in any campaign. A candidate declares himself for or against a lot of separate policies. He supports a negative income tax and revenue sharing with the state government, he opposes continued space exploration and federally funded cancer research, and he is largely silent on foreign policy issues. Did he win because of the issues he supported? Or did he win because he came out against certain policies? Or because he veered away from foreign policy and concentrated on domestic questions? Maybe the winner did not gain votes by his stands as much as his opponent lost votes by *his* stands.

Members of Congress represent the blocs of voters in their district. Manhattan Congresswoman Bella Abzug joins a protest parade.

In addition to mandate uncertainty, the sheer pressures of time and the complexity of congressional business make it impossible for the elected representative to translate voter preferences into public policy. The range of issues before Congress is huge: fiscal matters, civil rights, foreign treaties, funds for space exploration, wage and price policy, welfare programs, revenue sharing, tax reform, energy programs, and so on. No senator or representative checks with his constituency before every roll-call vote, and of course none checks before a vote in committee or subcommittee, where most legislation is actually written. Only a tiny fraction of the voters will have the vaguest idea about the bills pending in Congress, let alone any information about what their particular representative is doing.

Still, it is wrong to conclude that the policy views of his electorate have *no* bearing on how a congressman votes. Citizens may not have detailed information about specific legislation, but they are not usually neutral about the major issues of war and peace, inflation and unemployment, civil rights, and so forth. The general tendencies in a district or state are known to the congressman and put limits on policies he supports. The civil-rights voting record of Shirley Chisholm, liberal black congresswoman from New York, is very different from the voting record of William Poage, ultraconservative Texas congressman, but a person with Chisholm's views would not be elected in Poage's district in Texas, nor would someone with Poage's views stand a chance of being elected in Chisholm's district.

Unfortunately we have very few studies comparing the policy views of a congressman with those of the voters he represents. One such study, however, shows a high correlation between the way congressmen vote and the preferences of their constituencies on bills having to do with civil rights and race relations.[3] The study found that congressional districts with a population generally liberal on civil-rights issues are represented by congressmen who vote in favor of civil-rights measures, and that districts with a more conservative population are represented by congressmen who oppose such measures.

This can be explained in two different ways. The congressman's own attitudes may be nearly identical to those of the voters, in which case he need pay no attention to voter preferences. Or perhaps the congressman may not always see eye to eye with the voters but fears to differ with them, at least on an issue as major as civil rights and race relations. The evidence shows that the latter explanation is more nearly the case: Congressmen appear to change their own views about race questions to accord more with the views of their constituency. Furthermore, congressmen are quite accurate in judging what the voters feel about civil rights.

This study confirms that the broad view of the constituency is translated into a vote pro or con in Congress and shows that the

[3] The study cited here and in the next two paragraphs is from Warren E. Miller and Donald E. Stokes, "Constituency Influence in Congress," *American Political Science Review,* 57 (1963), 45–57.

notion of mandate uncertainty may have been exaggerated. But recall that the research found this pattern only in the area of civil rights. When voters and congressmen were asked about foreign policy and social-welfare issues, it was apparent that the attitude of the congressmen was not often in accord with that of their constituencies. On foreign policy in particular, congressmen seem not to be affected by the viewpoint of their voters. Perhaps congressmen sense that voters feel less secure in their views about foreign policy and are willing to give Congress and the Presidency much more leeway.

Representing Interest Groups

Although a congressman may be uncertain about the views of the several thousands and even millions of individual voters in his district or state, he is not as uncertain about the views of the major groups back home, especially when legislation is pending that directly affects the interests of those groups. The contact congressmen have with their constituents is most often with the active and organized parts of the community: the interest groups.

Blocs of voters are more critical than the individual voter. The representative aiming at reelection must keep in mind the general policy preferences of groups that represent sizable voting power. And he does not have to work hard to learn those views. Organizations with a standing interest in legislative matters support a full-time staff in Washington whose job begins and ends with lobbying congressmen. Such organizations inform, persuade, and sometimes threaten in order to get favorable treatment from "their representative in Washington." What they offer of course is electoral support, either campaign contributions or votes. It is generally accepted, though, that group leaders cannot easily control the voting choices of group members. But they do control campaign funds, and they distribute publicity to group members about the area's congressmen. Nearly all political pressuring in Washington comes through organizations. If the congressman receives a mass mailing on a labor issue, it is because the union has organized that mailing; if the congressman is asked to speak to parents concerned about school busing, it is because a civic group has organized the meeting; if the congressman is asked to let a group of farmers present a petition on wheat prices, it is because a farmers' association has collected the signatures. This type of pressure-group activity is particularly important if there are only one or two major interests that dominate the district or state. Thus automobile manufacturers and the auto unions are listened to carefully by congressmen from Michigan; a citrus growers' association will be especially important to a Florida congressman.

A Difference Between House and Senate One of the important differences between the Senate and the House of Representatives is suggested by this point. The constituency of a senator is nearly always more varied than that of a representative. Seldom will a single interest so dominate a state that its senators are in effect representatives only of that interest, though the influence of oil in Texas and of mining in Utah has at times been almost that strong. For the most part a senator will build a winning electoral coalition from a variety of groups and interests. It is for this reason that the Senate is said to have a constituency similar to that of the President. The constituency of a senator, especially from a populous, urban state, is closer to that of the entire nation than that of a member of the House. Few senators will not have labor unions or civil-rights groups among the organizations they deal with, but many representatives are selected from districts without unions or minority groups. Any given representative deals with a narrower range of constituency pressures than nearly any senator (though a representative from New York City has a more varied constituency than a senator from Montana).

Two Forms of Group Politics In one respect this discussion of group politics and representative behavior is somewhat misleading. Organizations are active in two ways. First, as we have suggested, they are active as local pressure groups attempting to persuade a congressman to support legislation that will benefit his area. This is the case of the businessmen of a community trying to control the route of a federal highway, the case of a trade union trying to get a big contract for a local industry, the case of a large university trying to obtain a federal research center, the case of a farmers' association trying to get more favorable soil-bank terms. These are specific groups using political influence to direct benefits to their area. They do not compete with any other interest in the area, and they usually have no difficulty getting the help of their congressman. The struggle takes place *within* Congress, because more than one part of the country wants to affect the route of the highway, wants the same defense contract, wants the same research center, or wants favorable treatment from the Department of Agriculture. Congressmen are judged by how successfully they negotiate within the federal government on such matters. Listen to no less an authority than President Johnson:

> At the March 2, 1968, rollout ceremony for the giant C-5A cargo aircraft at the Lockheed Aircraft plant at Marietta, Ga., President Johnson warmly complimented the Georgia congressional delegation for helping to land the contract for their state. "I would have you good folks of Georgia know that there are a lot of Marietta, Georgias, scattered throughout our fifty states," the President said. ". . . All of them would like to have the pride [and cash inflow, we might add] that comes from this production. . . . But all of them don't have the Georgia delegation."

In contrast, groups can also compete with different groups, both of them trying to influence broad legislative policy or bills that may affect the well-being of an organization with a national membership. For example, congressmen often hear from such powerful national organizations as the political agencies of the AFL-CIO, the AMA, the American Farm Bureau Federation, the American Legion, and the National Association of Manufacturers. These organizations claim to speak for members across the entire nation. With less cause, they claim to speak in the national interest.

When the national headquarters of mass organizations try to affect legislation, the results are very different from those that occur when a local interest group contacts its congressmen, because the issues that involve the national organizations are nearly always divisive in one way or another. As the battle shapes up between business and labor, between farmers and consumers, or between minority groups and states' rights organizations, Congress itself is the battlefield, and congressmen are pressured from both sides.

Group Politics and Geographic Representation

The national organizations influence the congressional process in many ways, but here we are interested primarily in how they affect political representation. What seems clear is that national organizations have a large impact on a representational system formally based on geography. The Constitution makes residence the basis for electing members of Congress, but geographic representation has its drawbacks. Doesn't the doctor in St. Louis have more in common with his fellow doctor in Dallas than with his next-door neighbor, a grocery-store owner? It depends on the issue. Politics is such a complex mixture of interests and issues that any election arrangement will sometimes make odd bedfellows.

Consider the alignment of three citizens on issues:

	Citizen A	Citizen B	Citizen C
Residence	Chicago suburb	Chicago suburb	Small town in Kansas
Occupation	Retired military	Public-school teacher	Shop owner
Race	White	Black	White

On an issue directly related to residence, we would find Citizens A and B aligned against Citizen C, but on other types of issues the alignment might well shift. For instance, it might look like this:

Issue	Alignment of Citizens
Federal support for urban transit	A and B vs. C
Increased veteran benefits	B and C vs. A
Compensatory hiring of minority races	A and C vs. B

In this hypothetical case residence aligns citizens in a meaningful way on the issue of federal support for urban transit but not the veteran-benefits or racial issues. By the same token, representation based on occupation does not make much sense on issues that directly benefit particular sections of the country or on issues having to do specifically with race. And race is inappropriate as a basis for representation on issues that involve residency or occupation.

In any case the election of representatives on a geographic basis is a permanent part of our politics. No alternatives have been given serious attention. Bearing this in mind, we can see the great importance of national organizations in the legislative process. On many issues they crisscross arbitrary geographic boundaries and provide an umbrella under which citizens may gather on issues that affect them in their occupational roles or because of their sex, age, race, background, language, or social outlook. The AMA collects the energies, resources, and viewpoints of doctors from Honolulu to Huzzah, from Mississippi to Maine. The National Council of Senior Citizens does the same thing for older citizens, no matter where they live or what their sex or race. The memberships of such organizations are in one way narrow, focused on a single set of issues, but they are broad in their national base. This combination adds strength to national organizations.

Organizations with national memberships introduce an element of functional representation that cuts across sectional boundaries and counteracts the local focus that results from purely geographic representation. Insofar as Congress is responsive to national organizations on national issues, it is being much less local in outlook than some critics have claimed.

Summary

Critics say Congress is not fulfilling its representational responsibility. It is too much an institution of the nineteenth century, whereas the problems of the society belong very much to the twentieth century. Congress is local, middle class, conservative, and cautious — unable to play a creative role in formulating national programs. There is some truth to these criticisms. But they do not take full account of the many ways congressmen do represent. As a direct result of growing federal programs and activities, individual citizens make a large number of requests to their congressmen, who (with their staffs) respond enthusiastically. Moreover, in a general if vague manner congressmen do pay attention to what they believe the voters think about major policy questions. Certainly there is no one-to-one correspondence between congressional voting and voter viewpoints, but voter preferences are not ignored. Finally, congressmen are responsive to organized pressure. They try to satisfy important groups in the district or state, at least on matters directly affecting them. And in a broader sense legislative policy on national issues partially reflects the preferences of national organizations.

Congress: The Legislative Branch

Richard Bolling, a Democrat from Missouri, has been a member of Congress for 26 years. He wonders if Congress can do the job given it by the Constitution:

> In the many years that I have been a member of Congress, the House has revealed itself to me as ineffective in its role as a coordinate branch of the Federal Government, negative in its approach to national tasks, generally unresponsive to any but parochial economic interests. Its procedures, time-consuming and unwieldy, mask anonymous centers of irresponsible powers. Its legislation is often a travesty of what the national welfare requires.[4]

Strong words, but particularly important because they come from a member of Congress. Representative Bolling is among a group of reformers who believe the House of Representatives, and more generally Congress, is an organizational mess. This fact as much as anything else keeps Congress from being the effective legislative body it should be.

Two separate questions are being asked. First, what are the organizational problems that reforms are supposed to cure? Second, is it true that a reorganized Congress would be an effective legislative body?

The Organization of Congress

The Constitution separated Congress into two houses, the Senate and the House of Representatives. But the Constitution is silent on how the two houses should organize themselves. How Congress selects its leaders, divides responsibilities and duties, debates and votes on issues, and manages its affairs are matters to be settled by the members.

Senate and House Differences

Size   The Senate is the smaller and more prestigious group. Numbering only 100 people, two elected from each of the 50 states, it has a more informal way of working than the House. "The Senate of the United States is a small and special world," writes one student of Congress. "The chamber is quiet. It must be, because there is no public address system and business is conducted in conversational tones. It is dignified: somber-suited men, a few quite old, move in the perpetual twilight of its high ceiling lights." This small and special world is "ingrown and not wholly immune from narcissism, yet its nerve ends are in the great world outside, and its reaction to events can be instantaneous."[5]

[4] Richard Bolling, *House Out of Order* (New York: Dutton, 1965), p. 17.
[5] Ralph K. Huitt, "The Internal Distribution of Influence: The Senate," in Truman, p. 77.

In contrast, there are 435 members of the House of Representatives, the number from each state depending on its population. The most populous state, California, has the largest delegation, 43; a half-dozen small states send only one representative each. Legislative business in the House is carefully regulated by a complex set of procedures, and power is concentrated in a small portion of its membership. As few as 10–15 percent of the House members control the flow of legislative business. Many members, especially those fairly new to Washington, have no effective power at all. One newcomer to Congress announced his retirement after serving only one term: "I could see I wasn't going to get any place. These old men have got everything so tied down you can't do anything. There are only about 40 out of the 435 members who call the shots. They're the committee chairmen and the ranking members and they're all around 70 or 80."[6]

Prestige The Senate is more nearly a club of equals. The senator's term of office is six years, in contrast to only two for the representative, and thus even a new senator will be in Washington long enough to be noticed. The House member needs to be reelected several times before he begins to be noticed. Many senators are as well known as state governors, and a few are nearly as well known as the President himself. Indeed four of the past six Presidents were at one time senators: Truman, Johnson, Kennedy, and Nixon. Only in very unusual circumstances will a member of the House gain a national reputation, though it can happen, as in the long, powerful career of Speaker Sam Rayburn of Texas.

The Senate is generally more visible to the public. Senate debate, for example, receives more attention from the press and TV than House debate. This is partly because Senate debate is unlimited except when closed by the members themselves, and the practice of *filibustering*, in which a tiny group can hold up Senate business for as long as it can talk, sometimes can extend debate on a single issue over days or even weeks. The legislative debate in the House is much less dramatic; the time given any individual is sharply limited, usually five minutes, and only a certain number of pro and con

[6] W. Burkhalter, as cited in the Washington *Post,* April 3, 1964.

speakers will debate a particular issue. The daily workings of the House have much less flair and drama than those of the Senate.

Powers Although individual senators have on the average more power and prestige than individual representatives, this does not mean that the House as a collective body is less powerful than the Senate. Both parts of Congress share fully in the power to legislate, and bills must receive the stamp of approval in the Senate and the House before passing into law. There are certain powers assigned to only one of the houses. Most notable among these are the power of the Senate to confirm such Presidential appointees as Supreme Court justices (thus the involvement of the Senate in the defeat of two controversial Nixon appointees) and ambassadors and heads of major executive agencies, and the power of the Senate to ratify treaties. These special Senate powers are more than compensated for by the power of the House to originate all money bills, including those by which revenue is raised (tax bills and tariff legislation, for instance) and those by which money is appropriated to run the federal government. The "appropriation power" as it is sometimes called is only the power of initiation, for even revenue raising and appropriation bills must pass the Senate as well as the House. But the power to originate is the power to set the agenda, giving the House considerable influence in this, perhaps the most significant aspect of legislation.

Leadership in the House

The member of the House with the greatest formal power is the Speaker, currently Carl Albert. The Speaker presides over floor debate and can sometimes influence legislation by recognizing or ignoring particular members. He also appoints members of select committees that do special jobs. However, the Speaker does not appoint members of standing committees, a power lost in a major reform in 1910. The result was a strengthening of the committee system, which is now under attack from a group of reformers.

The Speaker is always a member of the majority party. Indeed he is the recognized leader of the majority party. This, more than formal powers, is what gives the position influence and authority in House politics. The Speaker is chosen at a meeting, often called a *caucus*, of the majority party before the official opening of a new congressional session.

Working closely with the Speaker is the majority party floor leader and the majority party whip, who help plan strategy for getting bills through the House. The floor leader negotiates with congressional chairmen and with members of the House Rules Committee. This committee controls what bills will be brought before the House; no bill can be debated without a "rule" that specifies how much debate will be allowed and whether amendments can be added. Assisting the floor leader is the party whip, along with deputy whips, who are responsible for knowing how many party members are likely to

support particular legislation. The whips also try to round up members in time for important votes. (In English fox hunts the man who is supposed to keep the hunting dogs from straying is called a "whipper-in," from which comes the term *whip* in legislatures.)

Leadership in the Senate

According to the Constitution, the person who presides over the Senate is the Vice-President, but it is an unusual day when the Vice-President appears in the Senate. In his absence the formal leadership in the Senate belongs to the president pro tempore, but this position is more ceremonial than powerful.

The Senate majority leader, elected by the majority party, is the recognized leader of the Senate. His powers derive from a position as head of the party as well as whatever personal skills he brings to leadership. The present Senate majority leader, Montana Democrat Mike Mansfield, does not push his views on his colleagues. When some senators complained that he was not forceful enough as a leader, Mansfield responded: "I am neither a circus ringmaster, a master of ceremonies of a Senate nightclub, a tamer of Senate lions, nor a wheeler and dealer."

His predecessor, Lyndon Johnson, was a bit of all those things Mansfield claimed not to be. Johnson was a forceful leader. He persuaded and threatened, traded and compromised, and most of all, counted votes. He knew who might support what version of which bill. And he used his knowledge and resources to shape legislation.

The contrast between Mansfield and Johnson holds an important lesson. It is often not the formal position but the personality and the drive of the person in the position that determines how much leadership will be exercised. This is especially true in a group of only 100 people, where power is exercised, if at all, in face-to-face settings.

Minority Party Leaders

In both the House and the Senate, the leadership structure of the majority party is matched by leadership in the minority party. At present the Republican party is the minority party, but it has its own leaders and its own whips. One important role played by minority party leadership is linkage with the White House when the President belongs to the party not in control of Congress. The Senate minority leader, for example, is Republican Hugh Scott. Senator Scott frequently confers with President Ford, as he previously did with President Nixon, about Republican party strategy in a Congress dominated by the Democrats.

Legislation by Committee

It is impossible for 535 people to come together, debate dozens of complicated issues, and easily reach a collective decision. Even separating these people into two groups, one of 435 and one of 100, does not solve the problem. Even if all their other commitments (running errands for constituents, ceremonial functions, meeting with organization leaders, electioneering, and political party work) allowed enough time for the legislators to meet and discuss each bill, no one of them could be even reasonably informed about the variety of things that require congressional action. How, for instance, is the single legislator to learn enough about each subject to be able to deal, in turn, with a flood-control system for the Northwest, tariff policy on textile imports, wiretapping by the FBI, immigration quotas for Asian nationals, and a mutual defense treaty with Canada? To make matters more complex, each of these broad issues can be subdivided into dozens of small but important questions: Should the flood-control program be tied in with an irrigation project in the Southwest? Should there be matching funds from the various states, or should it be wholly federally financed? Is it the case, as the conservationists have claimed, that the proposal made by the Army Corps of Engineers will destroy a wildlife habitat?

Standing Committees of Congress

The more complicated the policy issue, the more complicated must be the legislation that deals with it, and the more necessary it is to give the drafting of the legislation to a small group of experts. Of this necessity was born the *standing committee* of Congress. When a situation calls for division of labor, the typical response is the committee. And this has been the response of Congress.

Standing committees in both houses have stated areas of responsibility. These responsibilities include reviewing all bills referred to the committee, consulting relevant executive agencies about possible effects of the bills, writing and rewriting the actual legislation, holding public hearings if necessary, and finally, sending the "finished" bill to the House or Senate *with the committee's recommendations*.

The committees are where legislation takes place and where proposals for legislation are blocked. Insofar as Congress does govern the nation, it does so through committees. Table 10.1 lists the standing committees of Congress, ranked according to their importance.

Subcommittees of Congress Because the responsibilities of any single committee can include many issues and because the membership of even the committees themselves can be so large (the House Appropriations Committee has 50 members), there is need for a subcommittee structure. Indeed subcommittees have grown in importance over the past several decades, and there now are nearly 250 subcommittees in Congress. Table 10.2 lists the subcommittees of the Senate Committee on Foreign Relations and those of the House Committee on Appropriations.

Committee Assignments

In the House of Representatives each member is normally assigned to only one standing committee, although he may serve on

Table 10.1
Standing Committees
of Congress (Ranked in
Groups, by Order of Importance)

	Senate (18)	House (22)
I	Appropriations Finance Foreign Relations	Appropriations Rules Ways and Means
II	Agriculture and Forestry Armed Services Budget[a] Commerce Judiciary	Agriculture Armed Services Budget[a] Government Operations International Relations Interstate and Foreign Commerce Judiciary
III	Aeronautical and Space Science Banking, Housing and Urban Affairs Interior and Insular Affairs Labor and Public Welfare Public Works	Banking and Currency Education and Labor Interior and Insular Affairs Public Works Science and Astronautics
IV	Government Operations Post Office and Civil Service Veterans Affairs	Internal Security Merchant Marine and Fisheries Post Office and Civil Service Standards of Official Conduct Veterans Affairs
V	District of Columbia Rules and Administration	District of Columbia House Administration

[a] New committees with important formal powers but not as yet clearly established policy influence.

Source: Rankings based on data from several sources, including Donald H. Matthews, *U.S. Senators and Their World* (New York: Vintage, 1960); and H. Douglas Price, as cited in Stephen K. Bailey, *The New Congress* (New York: St. Martin, 1966).

several subcommittees. Senators, in contrast, will have at least two committee assignments and from seven to ten subcommittee assignments. This, by the way, increases the influence of the House because, being so much larger, it can divide up legislative tasks more effectively than the smaller Senate. As a result House members often develop great expertise in a legislative area—fiscal policy, say, or farm price supports. The harried senator is less likely to be a subject-matter expert, having to rely more on his staff than the representative. The greater expertise of the House member is particularly valuable in conference committees, which are joint House-Senate committees to negotiate an agreed version of a bill that has passed both houses, though in different forms.

Committee assignments are made by the party leaders of the Senate and the House, and committee seats are assigned according to the relative strength of the two parties. Thus if two-thirds of the senators are Democrats and one-third are Republicans, each committee (and, less exactly, each subcommittee) will be about two-thirds Democrats and one-third Republicans.

Positions on the more powerful committees are highly prized. This gives party leaders one of their major sources of power. Assign-

Table 10.2

Subcommittees of the Senate
Committee on Foreign
Relations and of the House
Committee on Appropriations

Senate Committee on Foreign Relations	House Committee on Appropriations
African Affairs	Agriculture
American Republics Affairs	Defense
Canadian Affairs	District of Columbia
Disarmament	Foreign Operations
Economic and Social Policy Affairs	Independent Offices
European Affairs	Interior and Related Agencies
Far Eastern Affairs	Labor, Health, Education, and Welfare
International Organization Affairs	Legislative
Near Eastern and South Asian Affairs	Military Construction
State Department Organization and Public Affairs	Public Works
	State, Justice, Commerce, and the Judiciary
	Treasury, Post Office, and Executive Office

ing freshmen to committees and filling committee vacancies gives party leaders a chance to reward those they approve of and punish those who don't play by the rules. Newcomers to the House have difficulty getting appointed to the important committees. "It would be too risky to put on a person whose views and nature the leadership has no opportunity to assess," said one veteran. A freshman representative lucky enough to be appointed to the powerful House Appropriations Committee recalled how it happened: "The Chairman I guess did some checking around in my area. After all, I was new and he didn't know me. People told me that they were called to see if I was—well, unstable or apt to go off on tangents . . . to see whether or not I had any preconceived notions about things and would not be flexible—whether I would oppose things even though it was obvious."[7]

Reelection to Congress can often depend on one's committee assignment. Thus a congressman from a rural district tries to get a seat on the Agriculture Committee, the better to serve his area and keep a watch on the Department of Agriculture. It is not uncommon for a congressman to claim that his seniority on a committee that directly benefits the home area is itself a good enough reason to return him to Washington. His opponent, he adds, would go to Washington as a powerless and inexperienced freshman. Such campaign claims reflect considerable truth.

Committee positions become the basis of power within Congress, as illustrated in the career of the late Senator Robert S. Kerr, Democrat from Oklahoma. Although not a formal leader in the Senate, Kerr was certainly one of its three or four most powerful members.

[7] Cited in Richard F. Fenno, Jr., "The House Appropriations Committee as a Political System: The Problem of Integration," as reprinted in Leroy N. Riselbach, ed., *The Congressional System* (Belmont, Calif.: Wadsworth, 1970), p. 194.

The base of Kerr's power was never his major committees. Rather, it was his chairmanship of the Rivers and Harbors Subcommittee of the Public Works Committee, an obscure post that makes few national headlines, but much political hay. Kerr not only used it to consolidate his position in Oklahoma by festooning the state with public works but placed practically all Senators under obligation to him by promoting their pet home projects. He never hesitated to collect on these obligations later, when the votes were needed.[8]

Of course party leaders can try to hurt congressional careers by purposely assigning "unwanteds" to committees that isolate them from the concerns of their constituents. Freshman Representative Herman Badillo, from the Bronx, was initially appointed to the Agriculture Committee, where he felt unable to do much for his urban supporters. As he told Speaker Carl Albert, "There isn't any crop in my district except marijuana." Outspoken liberal Shirley Chisholm, black congresswoman from Brooklyn, also was initially assigned to Agriculture. She remarked that "apparently all they know here in Washington about Brooklyn is that a tree grew there." Both of these appointments, however, were changed upon pressure from the New York delegation.

The request of a senator or a representative to serve on a committee related to the concerns of his constituents is reasonable, but it does contribute to the local outlook that critics complain of. There is a price to pay for appointing lawyers to Judiciary, farmers to Agriculture, businessmen to Banking and Currency, urban dwellers to Education and Labor, or westerners to Interior. Committees become the property of specialized interests, and public policy making the result of compromises among small groups more concerned with satisfying narrow constituencies than dealing with national issues.

The Agriculture Committee of the House of Representatives is a good example of the tension between particular voter preferences and broader national programs. The Agriculture Committee, until recently chaired by a conservative rural Texan, W. R. Poage, has long been dominated by representatives from the nation's farm belt. People elected from rural districts wanted seats on the Agricultural Committee, and, as we just saw, people from urban districts fought to stay off the Agriculture Committee. But the Agriculture Committee has jurisdiction over proposed legislation of concern to more than farmers. In recent years, for example, this Committee has heavily influenced federal school lunch and food stamp programs. Such legislation has not been to the liking of members of Congress from urban districts, where there is greatest need for hot school lunches and food stamps.

It finally became clear to the liberal, urban representatives that the House Agriculture Committee needed a very different outlook if food and farm programs were to benefit consumers as well as

[8] Cited in Nelson W. Polsby, *Congress and the Presidency* (Englewood Cliffs, N.J.: Prentice-Hall, 1964), p. 38.

Chairman Al Ullman of the House Ways and Means Committee chats with Treasury Secretary Simon before a committee session.

producers. In a major effort at reform, the Democrats in the House voted to remove Poage from the chair of the Agriculture Committee, despite his seniority. Moreover, twenty new members came on to the Committee, many of them liberal and consumer oriented.

Bases of Committee Powers

Committee powers come from four factors: (1) their control over the flow of legislation, (2) the expertise of members and the division of labor among committees that results, (3) the ties committees have with executive agencies and interest groups, and (4) public hearings.

Control over the Flow of Legislation   The first of these is a direct result of congressional rules as well as custom. It is the factor most often attacked by congressional reformers, but generally to little effect. What Woodrow Wilson observed 90 years ago needs only a slight change to be equally correct today: ". . . The practical effect of this Committee organization of the House is to consign to each of the Standing Committees the entire direction of legislation upon those subjects which properly comes to its consideration. As to those subjects it is entitled to the initiative, and all legislative action with regard to them is under its overruling guidances."[9] Today the legislative agenda is largely set by the executive branch, but Wilson's description of committee control over the flow of legislation is still accurate.

Expertise   The second base of committee power, expertise, is a natural outcome of the committee structure itself. Any organization that subdivides itself into working committees is simply recognizing the need for such expertise. Because all members cannot be equally informed about all issues, this is a practical arrangement. If, as in Congress, these working committees are permanent and the same

[9] From Woodrow Wilson, *Congressional Government,* first published in 1884.

people remain on them for a long time, then it is hardly surprising that each committee develops considerable expertise in its area. This is true as well of the subcommittee structure; thus the Foreign Relations Subcommittee on African Affairs will develop extensive knowledge of that continent but have only slight understanding of issues in Canadian-American affairs. On many matters of public policy, a system of division of labor among committees and subcommittees develops. A congressman goes along with the recommendation of a committee with the comment, "They are the experts in this field, and usually know what they are doing." In the great majority of cases, the recommendation of the subcommittee is accepted by the full committee and the recommendation of the full committee is accepted by the House or Senate. It is inside the committee, or even subcommittee, that one must look for sharp debate, lobbying, negotiations with the executive agency, and the final shaping of legislation.

Relationships with Interest Groups and Executive Agencies   The third base of committee power is the ties it forms with relevant interest groups and executive agencies. The fact that the committee is concerned with a certain subject and some of its members (the more powerful ones) stay on the committee for a long time makes it easy to form close ties with the groups in society most affected. The two Agriculture Committees, for instance, will be led not only by congressmen from rural states but probably by congressmen who have long received campaign and electoral support from the American Farm Bureau Federation. The bond is made stronger by a close relationship with the Department of Agriculture. Each of these three partners is attentive and supportive toward the other two, protecting them from "enemies" who might threaten their power either individually or collectively. Similar arrangements are common in the committees on labor, commerce, finance, welfare, education, space, defense, and nearly every other area of American life.

The three-way partnership among congressional committee, executive agency, and pressure group strengthens the control of committees over legislation. Programs formulated in this way are not likely to be overridden on the floor of Congress.

Public Hearings   Congressional committees and subcommittees can hold public hearings on legislation under consideration. These hearings perform several broad functions. First, they help congressmen collect information and opinions from interested groups. This helps Congress in formulating legislation, and it gives groups and individuals a way to try to influence policy. A public hearing on, say, price controls will call a large number of "expert" witnesses. Of course testimony will clash, but congressmen, often being lawyers, use conflicting testimony much as a judge or jury uses it in a court case. Thus one expert may argue that price controls will hurt the economy, while another will claim that controls will halt inflation and thus benefit the economy.

Sam Ervin, Chairman of the Senate Watergate investigation, confers before testimony.

Televised hearings, as these of the Watergate investigation, can educate the public.

Witnesses before congressional committees often represent an executive agency, perhaps one of the President's senior economic advisers. They may also speak for major interest groups affected by the proposed legislation. Sometimes a committee wants testimony from an individual who does not wish to appear. In such cases the committee can issue a subpoena.

One of the most complicated issues of the 1970s is whether the executive branch can claim "executive privilege" and thereby refuse to testify before Congress. This issue was brought into sharp focus during the Watergate hearings. The special Senate committee on Watergate received wide press coverage, including live television. This had the purpose of educating the public about the need for reform of laws regulating political campaigning, but it also dramatized the issues that separate Congress and the Presidency. Such public hearings can add to the influence of a congressional committee and, as in the case of Watergate, contribute to the power of Congress as a whole. We return to this issue in Chapter 14.

Committee Chairmen

Within the congressional committee the most powerful person is the chairman. Traditionally his formal and informal powers cover such matters as appointing subcommittee members, hiring and firing committee staff members, supervising the activity of the committee staff, calling committee meetings, determing the order of business and the agenda, deciding whether to hold public hearings, managing the floor debate, consulting with the executive branch and chairmen of other committees, and, when necessary, serving on the House-Senate conference committee, which irons out differences between the House and Senate versions of a bill.

The Seniority Rule

The standard method of reaching the chairmanship of a committee is simple. A member of Congress should get reelected, continue to serve on the same committee, and wait for his party to become the majority party. Until very recently committee chairmen were selected according to *seniority*. The ranking member on a committee of the majority party in Congress is the chairman. The ranking minority party member is the "shadow chairman," and in this role has some say over the committee's staff and the appointment of his party's members to subcommittees. But his influence is always much less than that of the chairman himself, though he is in line for the chair if in the next election his party becomes the majority party.

Criticisms of the Seniority Rule

Many arguments are made against the seniority rule. There is, first, the complaint that the seniority system passes over ability for length of committee service. This is recognized in a revealing comment by Senator Byrd of Virginia: "Seniority of service and committee rank have importance over and above the capabilities of the members." (A congressman gains seniority through committee service and not how long he has been in Congress, a fact that strengthens the tendency of congressmen to burrow deeper and deeper into a single legislative area rather than change committees.) Seniority rewards age as well as long service, for the two cannot be separated. Congressional power passes into the hands of men in their sixties and seventies, many of whom built their winning coalitions around the issues of the 1930s. Sometimes these men grow with the times, adjusting to new groups and new issues. But sometimes they do not. Reelected from one-party, safe districts, they can easily ignore a changing national political agenda. William Poage, a Texas congressman in his mid-seventies, was until 1975 chairman of the House Agriculture Committee. In committee hearings on a food stamp program for the poor, he asked a witness from the liberal Urban Coalition why he was "so concerned in maintaining a bunch of drones. You know what happens in the beehive? They kill those drones. That is what happens in most primitive societies. Maybe we have just gotten too far away from the situation of primitive man."

Reform of the Seniority Rule

Representative Poage is no longer chairman of the Agriculture Committee. This is not because he lost an election to the House or because he has retired. It is because the Democratic members of the House removed him from the chairmanship. Poage was not the only chairman to lose his powerful position. F. Edward Herbert of Louisiana was removed as head of the Armed Services Committee, and Wright Patman of Texas, 82 years old and a congressman with 46 years of service, was stripped of his powers as head of the Banking and Currency Committee.

Not since 1925 had anything like this happened. It is clear that major reform is under way. The first step took place within the Republican party in 1970, when the Republicans in the House decided to use secret ballots to determine the highest-ranking Republican on each House committee. But because the Republican party does not control the House, this reform did not affect selection of chairmen.

In January 1973 the Democratic party used a similar method, but no committee chairmen lost their positions. The seniority rule was not broken until after the congressional election of 1974, the first election after Watergate and the fall of Nixon.

The 1974 election brought to Washington the largest number of newcomers in many years: 92 freshman representatives. Because Democrats could take advantage of voter anger at Republicans, the majority of these freshmen were Democrats (75). They provided the votes that led to the downfall of once-powerful committee chairmen.

Reforming the Committee System

Criticisms of the committee system go beyond how chairmen are selected. A reform-minded caucus of House Democrats is not likely to be satisfied just because the seniority rule has been bent.

A major problem of the committee system is the question of which committee has control over what issues. The basic arrangement of committees has not been revised since 1946. (See Table 10.1 for list of committees.) But in 1946 there was no international monetary crisis, no complicated cluster of urban problems, and no shortage of energy sources. Which House committee, for instance, should take charge of energy policy? A good energy policy will provide for new tariff and international trade arrangements, new antitrust investigations, a revised tax structure, regulations affecting mining and nuclear plants, and research on new sources of energy. As many as a half-dozen different House committees (and the same is true in the Senate) claim that energy policy is in their area.

This situation has resulted in a committee to study committees, led by reformer Richard Bolling. If Bolling can persuade his fellow congressmen to accept a different, more rational committee arrangement, it will affect much more than the seniority system. A different committee structure could greatly improve the ability of Congress to match the executive branch in the formation of national policy. This issue is further discussed in Chapter 14, where we review the politics of separation of powers.

How Legislation Is Passed

How is a bill passed? As shown in Figure 10.1, a bill must first be introduced in both houses of Congress; it is then referred to committee. The committees, and perhaps the relevant subcommittees,

Figure 10.1
How a Bill Becomes a Law

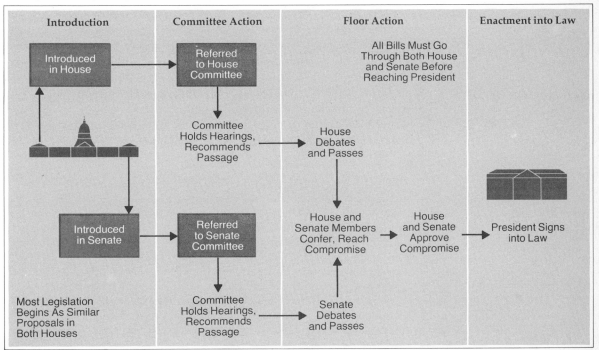

Introduction	Committee Action	Floor Action	Enactment into Law
Introduced in House	Referred to House Committee	All Bills Must Go Through Both House and Senate Before Reaching President	
	Committee Holds Hearings, Recommends Passage	House Debates and Passes	
Introduced in Senate	Referred to Senate Committee	House and Senate Members Confer, Reach Compromise	House and Senate Approve Compromise	President Signs into Law
Most Legislation Begins As Similar Proposals in Both Houses	Committee Holds Hearings, Recommends Passage	Senate Debates and Passes	

hold hearings and then do the work of detailed formulation of legislation. If a committee "reports out" a bill, it is placed on the legislative agenda. It is then debated, perhaps amended, and passed or defeated. If both the House and the Senate pass similar versions of a bill, a conference committee consisting of members from both houses of Congress works out a compromise bill. If this compromise version is passed by both the House and the Senate, the bill goes to the President. If he signs it, the bill becomes law. If he vetoes it, the bill can still become law if it is passed once again by a two-thirds majority of both houses of Congress. If the President fails to act for ten days, the bill automatically becomes law—if Congress is still in session. If, however, Congress has adjourned, the bill is not enacted, having become the victim of a "pocket veto." This may seem a mere technicality, but since a great deal of legislation is passed in the hectic days before adjournment, the pocket veto is important.

Thus a bill faces many barriers. It might be referred to an unfriendly committee, where it will be watered down or simply left to die; it might get bottled up in the all-important House Rules Committee, which must pass on legislation before it can be acted upon by the House; or it might be subjected to a Senate filibuster, that is, killed by prolonged debate.

There are many points at which a bill can be killed, but the real moment of truth is when it is put to a vote. Thus if we are to understand how Congress works, we must consider the various factors that influence a congressman's vote.

Factors Affecting Congressional Voting

Many things affect congressional voting: prior agreement with an executive agency, or fear of Presidential anger; career hopes both inside and outside Congress; the congressman's principles; instructions from party leaders; campaign promises; favors owed to lobbyists; thorough staff briefings; friendships; bargains and compromises negotiated; guesses as to probable voter responses; and, of course, committee loyalties.

Sometimes the outside observer is dismayed at the seeming casualness of it all, of great issues of state being decided on what appear to be the flimsiest of reasons. Here is one description:

All but four of the one hundred senators' desks are unoccupied this afternoon. The debate on the pending amendment is sputtering along. In the visitors' galleries, groups of tourists, initially awed, then perplexed, have been filing in and out at the 15 minute intervals prescribed by the attendants. Now, after whispered consultations below, the debate ends and the voting bell sounds, reverberating through the vast Senate complex of Capitol Hill buildings. Scores of senators begin to converge upon the chamber.

Possessed of the prima donna's disdain for peers, compelled by their profession to fight one another on issues, they have often measured each other as enemies. But they are conscious, too, that they are brothers, that ambition makes them endure the same indignities, wage the same lonely struggle for career survival. And so they compensate for the mutual hostility inherent in their situation with the kind of exaggerated cordiality that is evident as they enter the doorways together.

But, as the senators approach their desks, the cordial glow is fleetingly interrupted by a look of perplexity—what the hell is the vote about this time? . . . To men so skilled, the minute remaining before the roll call should be adequate to identify the issue and divine the safe vote.

Covertly, they case the situation through the particular stratagem each has worked out over the years. Some have aides who now come forward to whisper a 30-second summary of the 3-hour debate. Some just follow their party leader, who has minions stationed about the floor to pass the word "aye" or "nay" to the faithful. Some, who are not faithful, follow the lead of their particular Senate guru. . . . Some, particularly those who are committee chairmen or near-chairmen, automatically support the position of the chairman who has jurisdiction over the measure—for they expect the same hierarchial support when they are piloting their own bills through the Senate.

And, too, there is a last-second vote hustling on the floor. "Give me a vote, Bill, if you can," the sponsor of the pending amendment will say to an undecided senator he has given a vote to in the past; and, if this is not one of those red-flagged issues of particular interest back home, the vote may well be given for "friendship's sake," with the donor carefully filing the incident away in his memory for future repayment.

Thus, by a variety of means most of them substitute for personal study and decision, the senators work their will, and the votes are counted.[10]

Although this is a good description of much congressional voting, there are times when an issue is debated and investigated by all members. One such occasion was the Senate vote in 1969 on President Nixon's plan to deploy the Safeguard antiballistic missile (ABM). A marathon debate, lasting nearly five months, involved dozens of congressional witnesses, extensive media coverage, serious study by many senators, intense lobbying on both sides. The critical vote was a 50–50 tie, allowing Spiro Agnew (who as Vice-President officially presided over the Senate) to vote in favor of the administration's proposal. A few days before the vote Senator Pearson, a Kansas Republican, said, "You know, this issue will come as close as any to turning on the quiet conscience of the individual senators. The Senate would be a powerful instrument if all the issues were debated in this manner."[11]

Harried men and women, having to consider dozens of major bills and hundreds of minor ones, seldom can afford the time for thorough debate. What are some of the factors that influence voting?

[10] James Boyd, "A Senator's Day," in Charles Peters and Timothy J. Adams, eds., *Inside the System* (New York: Praeger, 1970), pp. 101–103.
[11] Cited in Nathan Miller, "The Making of a Majority: Safeguard and the Senate," in Peters and Adams, p. 158.

Bargaining Often a vote reflects outright bargaining: "You help me this time, and I'll give you a vote when you need it." Here is an exchange that took place during a 1956 debate on support for burley tobacco:

> MR. LANGER (North Dakota): We do not raise any tobacco in North Dakota, but we are interested in the tobacco situation in Kentucky, and I hope the Senator will support us in securing assistance for the wheat growers in our state.
> MR. CLEMENTS (Kentucky): I think the Senator will find that my support will be 100 percent.
> MR. BARKLEY (Kentucky): Mr. President, will my colleague from Kentucky yield?
> MR. CLEMENTS: I yield.
> MR. BARKLEY: The colloquy just had confirms and justifies the Woodrow Wilsonian doctrine of open covenants openly arrived at. (Laughter.)[12]

Friendship Friendship also helps build winning coalitions. In August 1971 the Senate prepared to vote on a bill to bail Lockheed Aircraft Corporation out of its financial difficulties by giving federal guarantees to a huge loan. One senator determined to vote against the bill was Lee Metcalf, a Montana Democrat, who had told his staff he was against "big-business slush funds." "But as he approached the floor he was cornered by his friend Alan Cranston of California, home of potentially unemployed Lockheed workers. Senator Cranston beseeched his Democratic colleague not to throw thirty thousand people out of work. Metcalf, weakened, finally chose employment over ideology and voted for the Lockheed loan, which slipped by the Senate 49–48."[13]

Economic Interests Some congressmen of course are interested in the legislation at hand. Mississippi Democrat James Eastland sits on the Agriculture Committee and repeatedly votes against ceilings on farm subsidies. Perhaps it is not a coincidence that in 1971 his wife received $159,000 in agricultural subsidies for farm land held in her name. Russell Long of Louisiana, chairman of the Senate Finance Committee, takes his stand against any changes in oil depletion allowances. Well he might. Between 1964 and 1969 his income from oil was $1,196,915, of which more than $300,000 was tax free. Reasons Long about the possible conflict of interest: "If you have financial interests completely parallel to [those of] your state, then you have no problem." In 1969 the *Congressional Quarterly* estimated that 183 congressmen held stock or other financial interests in companies doing business with the federal government or subject to federal legislation.[14]

[12] *Congressional Record,* February 16, 1956, pp. 2300–2301.
[13] Mark J. Green, James M. Fallows, and David R. Zwick, *Who Runs Congress?* A Ralph Nader Congress Project Report (New York: Bantam, 1972), p. 211.
[14] Evidence for this paragraph comes from ibid., p. 140.

President Ford signs the Energy Bill.

Committee Recommendations Bargains, friendships, and economic interests undoubtedly influence some of the votes some of the time. But in the long run the most effective factors are committee recommendations, political party affiliations, and voting constituencies. A careful study of the 84th Congress found that if a large majority of the committee in charge of a bill support it, then its chances of full Senate approval are nearly perfect. Indeed 51 bills received at least 80 percent support in committee; every one of them passed. In 37 cases, committee support was between 60 percent and 80 percent; 32 passed. A recommendation from a divided committee passes only about half the time.[15]

Party Ties It has often been said that our congressional parties are "undisciplined," which means individual party members are free to vote against the wishes of party leaders. In this way our political parties are very different from, say, those of Great Britain, where disloyal voting by party members is a vote of no confidence in leadership and can bring down the government.

The lack of party discipline in the British sense does not mean there is no relationship between party identification and congressional voting. This we already saw in Chapter 9, where Democrats and Republicans in the House are compared on major legislative issues spanning a quarter-century. All things being equal, which they seldom are, congressmen prefer to vote with their party rather than against it. Usually this means the congressmen of the same party as the President try to support administration programs, while the "opposition" party attempts to block those programs. Northern Democrats in the House, for instance, supported President Kennedy on 84 percent of the domestic legislation he favored. Southern Democrats were not quite as enthusiastic, giving him 57 percent support. Republicans, however, trailed with 34 percent.[16] Students of Congress have concluded that party pressure, whether direct or indirect, is the most effective pressure on congressional voting.

Voters Back Home When congressmen regularly vote against their party, the reason is usually to be found in *perceived constituency* preferences. We have stressed that citizens know little about their senator or representative, let alone how he might be voting on a complex tariff amendment in a subcommittee meeting. Yet there are times when voters do know a great deal about the stands taken by their congressmen. A representative from Seattle, where many people depend for employment on the Boeing Aircraft Company, would not have been likely to vote against federal funding for the supersonic-transport plane once being built there. No senator dependent on his state's labor unions for campaign funds and workers would

[15] Donald R. Matthews, *U.S. Senators and Their World* (New York: Vintage, 1960), p. 170.
[16] See Lewis A. Froman, Jr., *Congressmen and Their Constituencies* (Chicago: Rand McNally, 1963), Table 7.1, p. 91.

support a bill that outlawed the right to strike. A congressman from a white, rural Alabama district need not ask what his constituents feel about compensatory hiring of blacks; he knows what they feel and he knows how he will vote on any such bill.

Thus constituency opinion does matter—not always, not even usually. But it seems to matter most on the questions that matter most to the people back home.

Summary

Our discussion of Congress has covered much ground for good reason: Congress is at the center of our representative form of government. Some observers are unhappy about this, for they see in Congress the bankruptcy of democracy. Other observers believe the critics exaggerate the weaknesses and overlook the strengths of Congress. In this book we can give no final answers to our two major questions: How well does Congress represent? How well does it legislate? But the reader should think about these questions in the light of the information in this chapter. More analysis is to come on the second question; we discuss the President as legislator. And on the first issue—How well does Congress represent?—we present a controversial question to help you think through your own answer.

Controversy

There has been much debate over *whether* Congress represents, but this misses the point. When congressmen try to get a pork-barrel federal program for their district, they are representing. Even when they favor policies that give tax advantages to wealthy constituents, they are representing. At issue is not whether Congress represents but whether congressmen should represent the interests of those who support and send them to Washington or the broader public interest.

One Side

Congressmen should vote for their constituency's interests, at least insofar as they know what they are on a particular bill. Not only should they concern themselves with the voters back home, they should try to represent the groups and organizations that supply them with campaign funds. Someone who represents a wealthy community should try to whittle away at the progressive income tax, just as his colleague whose district is crowded with the poor should try to make taxes more progressive. If funds for the supersonic transport brings employment to your home state, your job is to fight for those funds. No one expects a black congresswoman from a northern city to prefer farm subsidies for Montana wheat growers over an educational head-start program, and no one should expect her Montana colleague to favor the head-start program over wheat subsidies. A senator who receives campaign funds from the AMA should oppose medicare, just as a representative who accepts campaign help from the Senior Citizens should favor medicare.

Take the case of Jamie Whitten, Democratic representative from the hill country of northern Mississippi. He is the powerful chairman of the House Appropriations Subcommittee on Agriculture. From this strategic position he forced the Department of Health, Education and Welfare (HEW) to leave Mississippi out of the National Nutrition Survey, the first effort by the federal government to investigate malnutrition in the United States. He has delayed and blocked various programs that would provide surplus food to schoolchildren or other hungry citizens. He opposes any attempt to study how technological changes in farming might affect the livelihood of farm workers or sharecroppers. His record as an opponent of social-reform measures is consistent. And his record seems to impress the constituents, for he has been reelected sixteen times.

Reelection—this is the true test of democracy. Congressmen are supposed to seek reelection, for this is the major check voters have over them. To seek reelection is to favor policies of direct benefit to local constituents or of particular concern to groups providing campaign funds. But this is what an elected representative assembly should do—represent those who send you to Washington.

The Other Side

Not all agree with the congressman who insists that he isn't paid to be a statesman. The argument against representing narrow constituency interests was effectively voiced two centuries ago by Edmund Burke in a famous speech to the Electors of Bristol:

> Parliament is not a [collection] of ambassadors from different and hostile interests, which interests each must maintain, as an agent and advocate, against other agents and advocates; Parliament is a deliberative assembly of one nation, with one interest—that of the whole—where not local purposes, not local prejudices, ought to guide, but the general good, resulting from the general reason of the whole. You choose a member, indeed; but when you have chosen him, he is not a member of Bristol, but he is a member of Parliament.[17]

Burke's observations deserve careful reading. He believed there is more to representative democracy than satisfying the immediate needs of your supporters. Someone must be thinking about the

[17] Burke, *loc. cit.*

whole picture. Someone must try to figure out which policies are best for the entire nation. The best place for this to happen is in an elected, deliberative assembly. In our government this would be the U.S. Congress.

Let us again consider Jamie Whitten. During World War II some people in the federal government began to ask how the black GI returning from the battlefields would adjust to conditions in the South. They thought it would be useful to plan a study that would help the government prepare for the range of social and economic difficulties likely to be faced by the returning war veterans. Jamie Whitten killed this proposal. As he saw it the Department of Agriculture's job was to help the cotton planter and his crop, not to help the rural poor. His view no doubt reflected the feelings of his supporters.

But in killing the proposed study and blocking many similar ideas, Whitten may have contributed to the massive rural-urban migration that has changed American society so much since the immediate post-World War II years. Northern cities, unprepared for the inflow of rural poor and southern blacks, have faced the huge problems of urban decay and have not had the resources to handle those problems.

It would be foolish and incorrect to say that Jamie Whitten somehow "caused" the urban crisis of the 1960s. It is not foolish and not incorrect to say that creative government programs started in the 1940s but looking toward the 1960s might well have eased the sufferings caused by the rural-urban migration. A Congress full of representatives concerned primarily with narrow and immediate constituency preferences is not likely to think up and fund such creative programs. But this is what a truly representative legislature would do.

How Institutions Work: III
A Bill Becomes a Law

Where do bills originate?

Any member of the House or Senate may introduce a bill, except that all revenue bills must originate in the House. Because no bill can become law unless passed by both House and Senate, the general procedure is for identical bills to be introduced at about the same time in both houses of Congress.

What is the difference between a "public" and a "private" bill?

A public bill affects general classes of citizens, while a private bill is for the relief of individual citizens.

What is the next step after a bill is introduced?

The bill is referred to the appropriate committee, depending on the subject matter involved. Private bills, however, are referred wherever their sponsors indicate.

Why is the committee so important to the life of a bill at this point?

As the figures in Table 10.3 indicate, each session of Congress faces far more bills than it can possibly handle. So do most committees. It is the committee chairmen who decide which bills the committees will take up. And it is at this point that 80–90 percent of all bills introduced in Congress die without any action having been taken on them. Committees eliminate far more bills by

ignoring them than by voting them down. Bills that have been set aside in committee are said to have been "pigeonholed." They can be rescued by a discharge petition signed by a majority of House members or by a special resolution of the Senate, but such attempts are rare.

If a committee does decide to take up a bill, what are the stages that follow?

The bill is first scheduled for consideration by the committee or sent to a subcommittee. It is then studied and, if it is important enough, hearings are held. These may be either public or private. The subcommittee then amends, rewrites, or "marks up" a bill and sends it back to the full committee. The committee then votes on whether to report the bill to the House or Senate. This is another critical stage in the life of a bill, because the committee can effectively kill a proposal by an unfavorable vote or by simply not acting at all.

If a bill is favorably reported by a House committee, how is it then brought to the floor for a vote?

Procedures used in the House at this stage are somewhat complicated. A bill coming out of committee is placed on one of several legislative calendars. Bills coming out of a certain few committees (Appropriations, and Ways and Means, for example) are given privileged status and can be reported to the full House at any time for action. All other important public bills are assigned to

Table 10.3
The 90th Congress,
Both Sessions

	House of Representatives	Senate	Total
Bills introduced and referred to committee	20,587	4,199	24,786
Bills reported by committee	1,319	1,403	2,722
Bills enacted into law	1,133	1,286	2,419

Source: Adapted from Nelson Polsby, *Congress and the Presidency* (Englewood Cliffs, N.J.: Prentice-Hall, 1971), p. 90.

the House Calendar. They need a "special rule" from the House Rules Committee before they can be sent to the floor for debate.

Why is the Rules Committee so important in conducting the business of the House?

The role of the House Rules Committee has been compared to that of a traffic cop directing the flow of pending legislation. It not only determines the order in which bills get to the House floor but also sets the conditions under which they will be debated. The process works as follows: Normally when a bill is voted out of a House committee and entered on the calendar, the next step is for the committee chairman to request the Rules Committee for a special rule taking the bill off the calendar and putting it before the House. The Rules Committee usually holds hearings on this request, at which both the managers and the opponents of the bill in question argue for or against the granting of a special rule. The question of a special rule is not just a formal procedure; members of the Rules Committee consider bills on their merits and with an eye toward party strategies. Any bill that fails to clear the Rules Committee has probably been derailed for good.

Is there no way a bill can be brought to a vote if it is blocked by the Rules Committee?

There are several maneuvers, including the discharge petition, by which the Rules Committee can be forced to send a bill to the floor. But they are seldom used.

It should be pointed out that although the Rules Committee does sometimes block important legislation, the majority of bills killed by the Committee are not of major importance. The Rules Committee does not control all bills reported from House committees. Most measures brought to the floor each session are noncontroversial and are handled in routine fashion via the "consent" and "private" calendars. Here the Rules Committee plays no part. There are perhaps only 100 bills each session of Congress that are controversial enough to warrant at least moderate debate on the House floor. It is for these bills that the Rules Committee is important.

If a bill is reported by a Senate committee, how is it brought to the Senate floor for a vote?

There is only one legislative calendar in the Senate, so bills reported out of Senate committees are all placed on the calendar of business. And in the Senate the power to schedule floor action is held by the majority party's Policy Committee.

These more simplified procedures for getting a bill onto the agenda illustrate one of the major differences between House and Senate: The House, a large, unwieldy body, operates according to rigidly defined schedules. The Senate, on the other hand, conducts its affairs less rigidly and with more room for informal agreements on procedure.

What are the rules by which floor debate is carried out?

The ground rules for House debate are usually laid down in the special rule that has come out of the Rules Committee. This states how long a bill may be debated and whether it may be amended on the floor. If floor amendment is not allowed, the bill is considered under a "closed rule," which permits only members of the committee that reported it to make any changes in language. When amendments are allowed from anyone on the floor, this is an "open rule."

As might be expected, debate in the Senate is less restricted. Senate debate is allowed to run far off the legislative track. Debate is usually unlimited, a tradition that has given rise to the filibuster, when senators opposed to a given bill engage in marathon speech making to tie up the Senate for days or weeks in order to stall action on other legislation. The hope is to force concessions on the bill the filibuster is directed against or to get the bill set aside. Filibusters can be broken only by a two-thirds vote of senators present, and although filibusters are infrequent, successful attempts to end them are even rarer.

What happens if the House and Senate pass different versions of a bill?

If the differences are slight, one may simply agree to the other's version. But if the differences are great, it is necessary to appoint a Conference Committee staffed by interested senior members from both the House and Senate committees that managed the bill. They work together to iron out language acceptable to both, but a majority vote of each group is needed for approval. If the Conference is successful, the final text of the bill must still go back to each body for final approval.

After a bill has been passed by Congress and sent to the White House, what choices does the President have?

The President is faced with four possibilities. He can simply sign the bill. Or if he fails to sign it within ten days and Congress is in session, the bill becomes law without his signature. However, if Congress has adjourned, the President's failure to act constitutes a "pocket veto" and the bill does not become law. Finally, the President can veto the bill by refusing to sign it and returning it to Congress. Congress can then reconsider the bill but must pass it with a two-thirds majority in both houses for it to become law. Otherwise the bill dies.

What does the series of steps necessary to make a bill into a law tell us about power in Congress?

Power in Congress is essentially negative. Any bill introduced must get over a series of hurdles. If a piece of legislation stumbles at any point along the way, it is very likely out of the running:

You can clear the first five tests, fail on the sixth, and thus lose the entire effort. The result of such a system is that interest groups and political opponents have numerous points of access to the legislative process. They can tie up, rewrite, or defeat a bill at many points along the way, adapting their strategies and shifting their forces accordingly. As a result the kind of power required to maneuver a bill through Congress is the power to shape formulas acceptable to the majorities in subcommittee, full committee, on the floor, and in conference. It is the power to combine politics with procedure without one strangling the other, and it rests largely with the President and his congressional supporters, with the leadership of the House and Senate, and with the managers of bills in committee.

The Presidency

Shortly after winning the Presidency in 1960, John Kennedy gave his view of the American President: "The history of this nation—its brightest and its bleakest pages—has been written largely in terms of the different views our Presidents have had of the Presidency itself." Perhaps this claim is exaggerated; a good deal more has gone into American history than how three dozen men have defined their duty. But some truth remains in Kennedy's comment. More than other men, by a wide margin, the President of the United States can affect—though not control—history. What else did Kennedy think about the Presidency? Here are some excerpts from his speech:

> He must above all be the Chief Executive in every sense of that word. He must be prepared to exercise the fullest powers of his office—all that are specified and some that are not. He must master complex problems. . . . He must originate action. . . . It is the President alone who must make the major decisions of our foreign policy. That is what the Constitution wisely commands. And even domestically, the President must initiate policies and devise laws to meet the needs of the nation. And he must be prepared to use all the resources of his office to insure the enactment of that legislation. . . .
>
> No President, it seems to me, can escape politics. He has not only been chosen by the nation—he has been chosen by his party. And if he insists that he is "President of all the people" and should, therefore, offend none of them—if he blurs the issues and differences between the parties—if he neglects the party machinery and avoids his party's leadership—then he has not only weakened the political party as an instrument of the democratic process—he has dealt a blow to the democratic process itself.
>
> But the White House is not only the center of political leadership. It must be the center of moral leadership—a "bully pulpit," as Theodore Roosevelt described it. For only the President represents the national interest. And upon him alone converge all the needs and aspirations of all parts of the country, all departments of the Government, all nations of the world.

The Constitution and Presidential Powers

Kennedy, an energetic President, undoubtedly claimed more powers for the Presidency than the Constitution intended. This is in the tradition of such strong nineteenth-century Presidents as Jefferson, Jackson, and Lincoln, a tradition carried on in the twentieth century by Wilson, both Roosevelts, Truman, Johnson, and Nixon. These men have poured much meaning into the ambiguous language of Article II of the Constitution: "The executive power shall be vested in a President of the United States of America."

The Growth of Presidential Powers

The Constitution does more than assign executive powers to the Presidency, though not much more. In Section 2 of Article II, it is stated that the President shall be Commander-in-Chief; in Section

3, the President is told to inform Congress on the state of the union and to recommend legislation. These duties have been the basis for the huge growth of the executive branch of government. At the center stands the President, who, along with close advisers and department heads, has control over the extensive military, economic, and personnel resources of the executive branch.

The President as Commander-in-Chief

In 1957 a federal court order directed the Little Rock, Arkansas, school system to desegregate its public schools. The white citizens of Little Rock, the school officials, and even the governor of Arkansas refused to obey. When a federal court order is disobeyed, what is the President to do? In this case the President acted as Commander-in-Chief. Eisenhower sent federal troops to Little Rock. In a radio and television address to the nation, he explained his action.

> Good Evening, my Fellow Citizens:
> For a few minutes this evening I want to speak to you about the serious situation that has arisen in Little Rock. . . . In that city, under the leadership of demagogic extremists, disorderly mobs have deliberately prevented the carrying out of proper orders from a Federal Court. Local authorities have not eliminated that violent opposition and, under the law, I yesterday issued a Proclamation calling upon the mob to disperse.
> This morning the mob again gathered in front of the Central High School. . . . I have today issued an Executive Order directing the use of troops under Federal authority to aid in the execution of Federal law at Little Rock, Arkansas. This became necessary when my Proclamation of yesterday was not observed, and the obstruction of justice still continues.

The President reasoned that it was his responsibility to uphold the law:

> Unless the President did so, anarchy would result.
> There would be no security for any except that which each one of us could provide for himself.
> The interest of the nation in the proper fulfillment of the law's requirements cannot yield to opposition and demonstrations by some few persons.
> Mob rule cannot be allowed to override the decisions of our courts.

The same powers and responsibilities were cited five years later by President Kennedy in response to a threat from outside the nation's boundaries. In October 1962, as Kennedy was having breakfast, his chief of staff for national security affairs arrived with bad news. The Central Intelligence Agency had evidence that the Soviet Union was arming Cuba with intermediate-range ballistic missiles that could destroy nearly any city in the United States. A week of intensive and very secret meetings between the President and his advisers resulted in the Cuban blockade, a military act that prevented Soviet ships from landing and installing the missiles. The President went on national television to announce his decision:

Whereas the peace of the world and the security of the United States and of all American states are endangered by reason of the establishment by the Sino-Soviet powers of an offensive military capability in Cuba, including bases for ballistic missiles with a potential range covering most of North and South America. . . .

Now, therefore, I, John F. Kennedy, President of the United States of America, acting under and by virtue of the authority conferred upon me by the Constitution and statutes of the United States . . . do hereby proclaim that the forces under my command are ordered . . . to interdict, subject to the instructions herein contained, the delivery of offensive weapons and associated material to Cuba.

War Powers

The wisdom of sending troops to Little Rock or blockading Cuba might be questioned. The authority of Eisenhower and Kennedy to act as they did is not questionable, for clearly the Constitution states that the President is Commander-in-Chief of the armed forces.

But there is a paradox here. The Constitution gives Congress the right to declare war. It might be supposed, then, that the President's authority as commander of the armed forces would come into play when a war has been declared. This is not the case. There was no war in Little Rock when Eisenhower sent in troops. And we were not at war with either Cuba or the Soviet Union when Kennedy ordered the blockade.

Thus the President's powers as Commander-in-Chief are very much greater than might be suspected. The President can act militarily whether there is a declared war or not. Indeed Congress has declared war only five times since 1789: the War of 1812, the Mexican War, the Spanish-American War, World War I, and World War II. And during this time U.S. forces have been involved in overseas military action more than 150 times. William Rehnquist, now an associate justice of the Supreme Court, wrote in 1970:

It has been recognized from the earliest days of the Republic, by the President, by Congress and by the Supreme Court, that the United States may lawfully engage in armed hostilities with a foreign power without a congressional declaration of war.

This view has been challenged by members of Congress. Recently congressional resolutions on Cambodia and Vietnam have limited the kinds of military action President Ford is allowed to take. But these resolutions have not changed the basic fact that military action and war can have separate constitutional status.

The distinction between military action and war has been basic to the growth of Presidential powers in the twentieth century. President Roosevelt drew on this doctrine in 1940, when he gave military protection and supplies to Britain in the months before Pearl Harbor. The United States was formally neutral at the time but was clearly aligning itself with Britain against Germany. Other cases are the military action in Korea in 1950 and the stationing of seven U.S.

The President can affect—
though not control—history.

divisions in Germany in 1951, actions taken by President Truman without a declaration of war by Congress.

More recently we have had the Bay of Pigs invasion of Cuba (under Kennedy), the marine military action in the Dominican Republic and the attacks on North Vietnam (under Johnson), and the bombing and invasion of Cambodia and Laos (under Nixon). The history of the twentieth century makes it clear that the Presidential power as Commander-in-Chief is in fact the power to make war, and that this power has greatly increased the role of the President in domestic and international affairs.

The President as Chief Diplomat

Tradition as well as the Constitution have made the federal government the sovereign power in foreign affairs and have established the President as the chief diplomat. Early in our history, however, these issues were matters of debate. Daniel Webster argued that the legislatures of the individual states could contract loans and make other agreements with foreign nations: "Every state is an independent, sovereign political community." The contrary opinion was voiced by Chief Justice Taney, who in 1841 argued that it was unconstitutional for the governor of Vermont to surrender an alleged fugitive to the government of Canada. "All the powers which relate to our foreign intercourse," wrote the Chief Justice, "are confined to the general government." The writers of the Constitution intended "to make us, so far as regarded our foreign relations, one people and one nation; and to cut off all communications between foreign governments and the several state authorities."

Chief Justice Taney took certain liberties with the Constitution. A close reading does not prove beyond a doubt that all powers in foreign matters were denied to the individual states. But the Taney doctrine has prevailed. And as a result the relations this country has with another are all channeled through the federal government.

This sets the stage for the President to become the chief diplomat. But this did not happen automatically. Whether foreign-policy powers rest chiefly with the President or with Congress has long been debated, most recently in the 1960s and early 1970s in the struggle over who would control the direction of the Vietnam war.

Chief Justice John Marshall foresaw this situation as early as 1799. He asserted that "the President is the sole organ of the nation in its external relations, and its sole representative with foreign nations." The Constitution appears to confirm this judgment. Treaty-making powers are specifically assigned to the President, as is the responsibility to send and receive diplomatic messages and messengers. Yet the Constitution says foreign treaties must receive the support of two-thirds of the Senate, and that the appointment of diplomats is with the advice and consent of the Senate. Most important, the power to declare war is a legislative and not an executive responsibility. It is possible that the founders intended the President mainly to act as a messenger between Congress and foreign countries. If this were the case, the President would be instructed by Congress in his conduct of foreign affairs.

The President's Foreign-Policy Powers

If it is hard to decide what the legal situation is, there is little doubt about what has happened in practice. Foreign policy has been carried out by the Presidents, especially in the last half-century. Only the President is in "continuous session," and for this reason, if for no other, many foreign-policy powers are his to claim. It is often said that the world has shrunk in the twentieth century. Things happen quickly, and what happens in one part of the world affects what happens elsewhere. The business, military, and diplomatic empire of the United States is scattered around the world. Our military presence includes over 2000 bases on foreign soil; U.S. government aid programs are in more than 80 different countries; and private economic investments abroad total more than $110 billion. A language riot in India, a border incident in Latin America, a monetary crisis in Europe, a new security pact in the Arab world—these and thousands of other happenings affect American programs and people. They require quick attention and action.

The President is in a position to act. He has authority over the network of ambassadors and consulates and technical aid offices throughout the world; he is responsible for military forces; he has direct access to a huge international intelligence operation that provides the information on which foreign policy is based. In his actions as Commander-in-Chief and chief diplomat, the President cannot avoid making policy. Nixon's dramatic visit to China in 1972 is a case in point. This visit was planned in strict secrecy. Congressional approval was not necessary. The American public was not informed until final arrangements were made. Yet the policy significance of this visit was perhaps greater than any other single action by Nixon in his first term. The visit had an immediate effect on China's admission into the United Nations, on U.S. military and technical aid policy toward India, on security pacts with Japan, and on summit talks with the Soviet Union later in the year. The visit had longer-term effects on our trade and tariff policies, our nuclear strategy, and our balance of payments.

But we do not react with surprise on learning that the President can change our military stance and our foreign relations. After all, this role is assigned him by the Constitution. Most modern-day Presidents have been only too willing to engage in summit politics. Few seem able to resist the temptation to "remake" the world, or at least to make sure that the enormous military, economic, and diplomatic resources of the United States are felt worldwide.

Executive Agreements   The President does not have unlimited control over foreign policy. Congress periodically tries to assert its influence, primarily by threatening to shut off funds for foreign programs it disagrees with. It can also refuse to agree to treaties, but the President has a way to get around this congressional power. *Executive agreements* between the United States and another nation are formulated by the State Department and put into effect by the President. Executive agreements need no congressional approval, and they can include such major arrangements as location of military bases and types of technical and military aid programs.

The President's Legislative Program

The constitutional doctrine of separation of powers makes a clear distinction between the branch that legislates, Congress, and the branch that puts the laws into effect, the executive. This distinction is nowhere near as neat in practice. Historically separation of powers has meant struggle for power. And in this struggle both the legislative and executive branches have devised numerous strategies not mentioned in the Constitution.

Chief among these strategies on the executive side is the President's legislative program. The Constitution says the President "shall from time to time give to the Congress information of the State of the Union, and recommend to their consideration such measures as he shall judge necessary and expedient." On this basis all forceful Presidents have announced their own legislative programs: Franklin Roosevelt's "New Deal," John Kennedy's "New Frontier," and Lyndon Johnson's "Great Society" are examples. Legislative proposals are put forth in the State of the Union Address, the Budget Message, and the Economic Report. President Nixon added a State of the World Message in which he outlined his foreign-policy goals. In addition to these formal speeches, the President can and does send special messages to Congress at any time, as President Ford has done in the case of energy policy and economic programs.

State of the Union Address   The annual State of the Union Address is most often used to announce a Presidential program. A good example is Nixon's 1972 address, in which he proposed specific legislation in eighteen different policy areas: technology, trade and monetary affairs, welfare reform, social services, environment, health care, hunger and nutrition, aging and the elderly, civil rights, women's rights, veterans' benefits, youth, farmers, the cities, transportation, fighting crime, consumer protection, and school financing. In each area he referred to legislative proposals made in his first administration or promised specific proposals over the course of the coming year. Here, for instance, is one paragraph from that speech:

> I shall soon send to the Congress a special message proposing a new program of federal partnership in technological research and development with federal incentives to increase private research, federally supported research and projects designed to improve our everyday lives in ways that will range from improving mass transit to developing new systems of emergency health care that could save thousands of lives annually.

Presidential proposals and special messages become the legislative agenda. In one year, for instance, President Johnson asked for congressional action on 469 separate proposals. Approximately 80 percent of all major laws passed in the last two decades have started in the executive branch. Here is what one Republican congressman told a member of President Kennedy's Democratic administration: "We're not supposed to draw up these bills—that's your job, and then you bring them to us."

President Ford meets with his Secretary of Agriculture.

Staffing and Managing the Presidency

Where do administration proposals come from? Certainly not entirely from one person. The ideas and efforts and responsibilities of the President are in fact those of a network of Presidential advisers and assistants. This is the group that largely plans and carries out the Presidential program and tries to organize a strategy for dealing with the several important groups—Congress, the bureaucracy, the public—that will determine its success or failure.

The growth of the Presidency during recent administrations is one index of the increasing importance of the executive branch. As recently as the turn of the century, the President carried out his duties with the help of a secretary, someone to carry messages, and a few clerks, all paid from the President's personal funds. The modern Presidency actually dates only from the administrations of Franklin D. Roosevelt in the 1930s and 1940s. But even then the staff numbered only in the dozens, though during Roosevelt's administrations there was a separate budget to pay the salaries of the White House staff. The last 30 years have seen great expansion. The total payroll for the executive office in fiscal 1973 was more than $60 million, and Nixon's staff was estimated at more than 2000.

The quality of leadership provided by the White House is largely determined by the President's staff. This is what is meant by "Ford's administration" or "Kennedy's team." An important job for any new President is to find the right people for these positions and to make the most of their skills.

Every President approaches the task of staffing and managing the Presidency somewhat differently. FDR encouraged overlapping lines of communication and jurisdiction, sometimes giving the same job to two separate agencies. He did this to keep close control over the separate units of the Presidency. Eisenhower organized the Presidency in almost the opposite way. Drawing on his military experience, he established a firm hierarchy of responsibility; only the most important issues were supposed to reach his desk. Kennedy had the habit of calling small, informal groups together to work on particular issues until a decision was reached or a program formulated. Nixon relied heavily on a few key advisers.

Although there are differences of style from one President to the next, there are certain common problems in the relationship between President and staff. To get information and intelligent advice on dozens of matters, the President surrounds himself with experienced advisers. It is natural to expect that these advisers have firm ideas of their own. Yet the temptation to say what the "Chief" wants to hear is very great indeed. For at the same time that the President expects independent ideas from his staff, he expects loyalty to himself and the administration's program. From the President's point of view, his strong-minded staff must never undermine the policy goals he has set. Early in his first term Nixon fired a Cabinet member, Walter Hickel (Secretary of the Interior), for writing a letter complaining that the Nixon administration was not sensitive to the demands of college youth. As far as Nixon was concerned, the line between loyal dissent and disloyal opposition had been crossed by a member of the team, and off the team he went.

How Proposals Originate and Are Routed

The White House staff does not have sole responsibility for the Presidential program. A specific proposal can come from a variety of sources within the executive branch—and can be greatly modified or even blocked long before it reaches the President and his closest advisers. Although no overview can describe how the executive program comes to be, here is one fairly common route.

A department or agency within the executive branch begins to formulate a new program or modify an existing one. It may consult with a relevant congressional committee even at this very early stage, though this step is mostly informal. The agency might also check with any interest groups that normally have a position on such programs. If the Department of Health, Education and Welfare has a group working on a program for federally financed university scholarships, for example, it is likely that they would be in touch with the staffs of congressional committees that normally handle bills on education. They would also be in touch with relevant organizations such as the American Association for the Advancement of Science. The program would begin to take shape, including some provisions (low-interest loans, perhaps) but dropping others (support for graduate teaching assistants) in response to actual or imagined opposition. As the proposal is taking shape, it would be sent to the Office of Management and Budget (OMB).

This is the chief clearinghouse, responsible for coordinating the hundreds of programs annually proposed by various executive agencies. It also has the power to suggest to the President or his staff advisers that a proposed program cannot be fitted into the budget this year. A proposal that does not pass through the OMB has very little chance of reaching the President's desk, let alone becoming law. And the OMB is in constant contact with congressional leaders, keeping informed of what legislation might be developing in a particular committee. Sometimes the OMB will advise an executive agency to shelve its program because a group on Capitol Hill already has congressional support for a similar project.

Even when an agency proposal gets through the OMB, it will not necessarily become part of the President's own legislative program. The executive agency may, however, be given the green light to try to get congressional action on its own. Franklin D. Roosevelt did this as early as 1935. To protect his own programs from various agencies in the federal bureaucracy, and to protect agencies from sniping at one another, he divided proposals into three categories:

First, the kind of legislation that, administratively, I could not give approval to — [clearance] will eliminate that; secondly, the type of legislation which we are perfectly willing to have the department or agency press for, but at the same time we do not want it put into the [third] category of major Administration bills. Obviously I have to confine myself to what the newspapers called last year "the comparatively small list of *must* legislation." If I make every bill that the the Government is interested in *must* legislation, it is going to complicate things . . . very much; and where I clear legislation with a notation that says "no objection" that means you are at perfect liberty to try to get the thing through [Congress], but I am not going to send a special message for it. It is all your trouble, not mine.[1]

Of course from the President's viewpoint there is *must* legislation, and it is these proposals that receive his attention and effort. Yet we should not attribute too much of the President's legislative program to his own ideas. For the most part a President's personal policy views are only vaguely formulated. He does not have the time to think through all the details of legislative proposals. However, his advisers, staff, party leaders, and executive heads do have strong interests in specific policies. Most of the White House proposals to Congress came from these sources. And these "high-energy" advisers are themselves in touch with a larger network that includes congressmen, governors and other state officials, big-city mayors, powerful interest-group leaders, and media people. Presidential proposals, then, reflect at least some shared outlooks.

This again shows the importance of the types of men and interests that a new administration brings to Washington. A President understandably wants to make a place in history. To do so, he depends heavily on a staff that can shape a set of legislative proposals likely to receive support in Congress. Nixon entered the White House after eight years of Republican exile from power. He immediately organized interagency committees to deal with specific policies, such as health care, the environment, and long-term strategic planning. Commenting on these "project teams," *Science* magazine wrote:

The basic political drive behind all this planning activity is Nixon's need to fashion a distinctive and creative Administration. . . . The rhetoric of his State of the Union and State of the World speeches, as he enters his second year, suggests that his ambition is to mold the

---

[1] This statement was made at a meeting of the National Emergency Council, as recorded in the *Proceedings of the Twenty-Second Meeting,* January 22, 1935, p. 2.

politics of the next 20 or 30 years, as Franklin D. Roosevelt set the context for domestic policies for the last 35 years, or as Harry S Truman defined the basic foreign policies of the last two decades.[2]

What a President sets out to get and what he actually gets are not the same thing. It is true that the chief executive and his staff have many resources. Some of these we have named: executive agreements in foreign policy, party leadership and control over jobs, a huge bureaucracy to give him information and proposals, the status of Commander-in-Chief, and ready access to the news media.

Tactics for Enactment of Programs

In addition, the President can put pressure on important congressmen. Johnson and Kennedy, who had both served in the House and Senate, relied heavily on this tactic. Johnson was in close contact with congressmen when Presidential measures were at stake. Here is how one influential member of the House Rules Committee commented on a telephone call from the President:

> What do you say to the President of the United States? I told him I'd sleep on it. Then the next day I said to myself, "I've always been a party man, and if he really wanted me of course I'd go along even if the bill wasn't set up exactly the way I wanted it." Probably I took half a dozen guys with me. We won in the crunch by six votes. Now, I wouldn't have voted for it except for this telephone call.[3]

In a second way Presidents use the prestige of the office to put pressure on Congress. They sometimes go on national radio or TV to speak directly to the public, and to urge the public to pressure Congress on behalf of Presidential programs. Franklin Roosevelt did this in his famous fireside chats. Here is Roosevelt in 1942 asking for price controls:

> Today I sent a message to the Congress, pointing out the overwhelming urgency of the serious domestic economic crisis with which we are threatened. . . . I have asked the Congress to pass legislation under which the President would be specifically authorized to stabilize the cost of living, including the price of all farm commodities.

Franklin D. Roosevelt used radio to carry his Presidential programs to the people. Today television serves the same purpose.

Roosevelt expected action within three weeks. If Congress didn't act, he pledged to act anyway, giving the war as a cause. "In the event that the Congress should fail to act, and act adequately, I shall accept the responsibility, and I will act. The President has the powers, under the Constitution and under Congressional Acts, to take measures necessary to avert a disaster which would interfere with the winning of the war." Whether Roosevelt actually had those powers was never tested in the courts, for Congress acted. Recent Presidents have followed Roosevelt's lead. Nixon was under congressional pressure to deescalate the Vietnam war when he sent

THE GROWTH OF
PRESIDENTIAL POWERS

[2] *Science,* 167 (February 27, 1970), 1232.
[3] *Newsweek,* August 2, 1965, p. 22.

troops into Cambodia (1970) and later mined the harbor of Haiphong (1972). Both times he went on national television to plead for public support. Nixon later used television in an attempt to sway public opinion during the Watergate affair. In this attempt he was quite unsuccessful; his popularity rating had fallen to an all-time low for Presidents just before he resigned.

The Presidential Program: Restraints

To review the role of the Presidency in formulating programs is not to say that Presidents always, or even usually, get what they want. As we shall see in Chapter 14, the separation-of-powers system functions, but in a very different way from how the Constitution intended. The President is restrained because he shares powers with Congress. More than this, he is restrained by the difficulty of starting new programs and, even more important, by the difficulty of stopping old programs.

Difficulty of Starting New Programs   When Ford became President he inherited serious economic problems: unemployment, recession, and steep inflation. Central to these problems was the rapidly increasing cost of energy, which accounted for about 50 percent of the annual increase in the cost of living. Energy costs were linked to great increases in the price of imported oil. In just one three-month period (October–December 1974), the price of imported oil had increased by 400 percent.

It was a difficult time to become President. Shortly after taking office Ford spoke to a world energy conference: "It is difficult to discuss the energy problem without unfortunately lapsing into doomsday language," he said. "Exorbitant prices can only distort the world economy, run the risk of worldwide depression and threaten the breakdown of world order and safety." Ford's Secretary of State, Henry Kissinger, used similar language in the United Nations: "The complex, fragile structure of global economic cooperation required to sustain national economic growth stands in danger of being shattered."

With such big problems we might expect a wide range of innovative economic policies and energy programs. Nothing of the sort emerged in the first six months of the Ford Presidency. Why not? Because innovative policies and programs are not easy to think up, and when thought up they are not easy to put into effect. Even the powers of the Presidency and the prestige of the White House cannot always attract exactly the right talent, let alone ensure a cooperative approach. And if an innovative policy is formulated, it is not easy to put into effect. A program as sweeping as would be necessary to solve the energy problems would necessarily affect the habits and well-being of millions of people, thousands of businesses, and dozens of already functioning government programs. In a later discussion (Chapter 16), we will give more attention to the difficulties of formulating and putting into effect major public programs. Here we stress that the President's powers are great, but not so great that he can easily cut through the barriers between a major problem and a workable solution.

Difficulty of Stopping Old Programs If things are hard to start, they are often even harder to stop. Government programs have great momentum, for careers and vested interests are always linked to any ongoing program. Just because a new President comes to town, there is no guarantee that established programs can be easily changed. Most policy is made by adding to or subtracting from what has gone before. Every President wishes to leave his mark on history, but every President must adjust to the personalities, quarrels, values and commitments, and inertia of the present day.

Eisenhower, the Republican, did not dismantle the New Deal programs begun by Democratic administrations from 1932 to 1952. Nor did the eight years of Democratic control of the White House following Eisenhower's eight years in office represent a sharp break in public policy—though many new programs were added. President Nixon tried to cut spending for programs started in administrations before his, but the job was nearly impossible. Here is his campaign pledge in 1972:

> We would like to operate the Federal Government at less cost, and we think we know how to do it. . . . We are for lower costs, for less function in the Federal Government. . . . My goal is not only no tax increase in 1973, but no tax increase in the next four years.

As one commentator observes:

> But where can the Administration cut enough to make its next budget consistent with this pledge? Roughly 40 percent of the projected budgets are allocated to defense, space and related activities—and it is clear the Administration does not want to cut here.
>
> Of the domestic budget, well more than half goes directly to people, either in cash benefits (Social Security, unemployment insurance, veterans' pensions, welfare, civil-service retirement, etc.) or in kind (Medicare, Medicaid, public housing). These people have real needs, real votes and real representatives on Capitol Hill. It is inconceivable that the President would propose legislation to cut these benefits back or that the Congress would pass it.
>
> Contractual obligations of the Government, such as interest on the debt, cannot be tampered with, and no one really wants to cut out such services as national parks or fish and wildlife preservation.
>
> This leaves grants to state and local governments as the prime candidates for cuts. . . . In practice, however, it has so far proved . . . impossible to cut the total funds. . . . Each program brings identifiable benefits to a particular group which is aware that the program exists and resists its elimination. Moreover, and perhaps more important, most of these programs support the services of particular professional groups—librarians, vocational-education teachers, veterinarians, psychiatric social workers, sanitary engineers. Each of these groups

Figure 11.1
The Federal Budget Under Six
Presidents

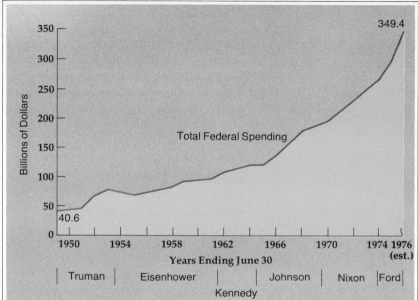

Source: U.S. Office of Management and Budget.

believes it is doing something important and useful—and it doubtless is—and fights to preserve and expand the programs it knows will support its activities.

Moreover, a Congressman likes easily identifiable programs and projects that he can point to with pride in an election year—a new hospital wing, a bridge, or a research center in his district.[4]

Nixon did reduce federal spending on certain social-welfare programs, but, as Figure 11.1 shows, the trend toward more spending was not halted. The growth of the federal budget has continued whether the President is a Democrat or a Republican. Once they are started, it is very hard to stop federal programs.

The President as a Symbol

The government is a collection of institutions, organizations, laws, and policies. The nation is more than this. It includes the idea of political community. The members of the community share a "we feeling," as in "We are all Americans." This sense of shared community cuts across differences of opinion about particular policies or personalities. To see oneself as an American is to be psychologically separated from citizens of other nations, just as they are separated from Americans by their own sense of political community.

The political community of any nation is felt through symbols and ceremonies, a shared past and common heroes, public holidays and public monuments. Our 1976 bicentennial (200th birthday) celebra-

[4] Alice M. Rivlin, "Dear Voter: Your Taxes Are Going Up," *New York Times Magazine*, November 5, 1972, pp. 113–114.

The President is the primary symbol of the political community.

tion is an expression of the symbols and ceremonies that try to capture what we mean by the political community.

The President is the primary symbol of the political community and the main actor in many public ceremonies. It is the President who proclaims National Codfish Day, who dedicates a National Arts Center, who is the central figure in bicentennial celebrations, who annually speaks on the State of the Union, and who toasts foreign dignitaries in the name of the United States. In these ways the President shows that he can speak for the entire political community. And he is looked upon in this way by the American public. Most of us first experience our nation in terms of its most dramatic personalities, and the most dramatic of all personalities is the President. The big social and economic changes that took place in the 1930s are summarized as Roosevelt's New Deal. In the same way we refer to Johnson's Great Society and Nixon's New Economic Policy.

In the speech by President Kennedy quoted at the beginning of this chapter, the White House was compared to a pulpit. This would make the President a minister, priest, or rabbi. These are not far-fetched analogies. When Richard Nixon became President in 1969, he called our national difficulties a "crisis of the spirit" and promised that his administration would meet that crisis with an "answer of the spirit." Somewhat later the widely read newspaper columnist James Reston commented on American society in similar terms. He presented a bleak picture of America as "a divided and selfish nation, dominated by powerful special interest groups that have no common concern for the national interest." He then wrote:

> In such a situation, the role of the Federal Government, and particularly of the President, is critical, for in a secular society that is full of doubt about the church, the university and the press, the White House is still the pinnacle of our civil life and the hope of some moral order and presiding national purpose. . . . More than anybody else, the President has the power to establish the standard and set the model, to direct or manipulate the powerful forces of the nation, to encourage the best in us. . . .

The Watergate affair dramatically raised the issue of moral leadership. The President of the United States, revealed as foul-mouthed, tolerant of petty criminal activity, and a participant in discussions that led to criminal convictions of close associates, clearly had let the country down. Not because his policies were failures, but because he failed to measure up to the moral standards imposed on the major figure in the American political community. Confidence in Nixon declined rapidly as the Watergate scandal unfolded. Figure 11.2 shows how sharply his popularity dropped during this period. It is no coincidence that over the same period the American people increasingly came to distrust all government leaders and even to lose confidence in nongovernmental institutions (see discussion in Chapter 6).

The Watergate affair showed that for better or worse the President is the focal point of political hopes and fears. The President

THE PRESIDENT AS A
SYMBOL

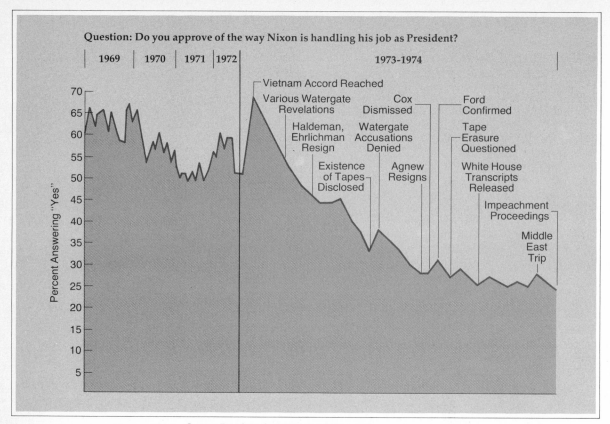

Question: Do you approve of the way Nixon is handling his job as President?

1969 | 1970 | 1971 | 1972 | 1973–1974

Percent Answering "Yes"

- Vietnam Accord Reached
- Various Watergate Revelations
- Haldeman, Ehrlichman Resign
- Existence of Tapes Disclosed
- Cox Dismissed
- Watergate Accusations Denied
- Agnew Resigns
- Ford Confirmed
- Tape Erasure Questioned
- White House Transcripts Released
- Impeachment Proceedings
- Middle East Trip

Figure 11.2
Nixon's Popularity

Source: Based on data from the Gallup poll.

is the one political figure who dramatizes the nation to its members. When the drama is a noble one, national confidence increases. When the drama is a sordid one, confidence drops.

The Road to the White House

Parents and teachers are fond of stories with a "log cabin to White House" theme: stories that contribute to the democratic myth that anyone can grow up to be President. Yet it is the son, not the father, who has the political insight in the following exchange:

> FATHER TO SON WATCHING TV: Why aren't you studying? When Abe Lincoln was your age he was reading law by the flickering light of the log cabin fire.
> SON: And when he was your age, he was President.

Truly it is said, "Many are called but few are chosen." Only 37 people have made it to the White House so far.

Presidential Hopefuls

If every 10-year-old hopes someday to become President, this is not true of every 50-year-old. Only a very small number in the suitable age bracket seriously hope to become President. Presidents have been and will continue to be chosen from a small set of already powerful, visible people in national political life. Governors of large states, especially New York, Pennsylvania, Illinois, and California, fall into this small group. So do forceful, articulate senators. Popular war heroes, if the war was a popular one, might count. A widely known college president might be mentioned but is not likely to be nominated unless there also was an important government position somewhere in his career. And of course Vice-Presidents are in the pool, a special group about which we will have more to say.

The Presidential selection process starts with a group of "eligibles," eligible because they are of the right age group, the right sex, the right race. But more important, eligible because of their positions and accomplishments in national political life.

How many from this eligible group really hope to become President? The answer will vary depending on important conditions, mainly, who is currently in the White House.

Members of the "In-Party"   It is convenient to call the political party of the current President the "in-party." Ford is a Republican, so the Republican party is the in-party even though it is the minority party in both houses of Congress, controls only 13 governorships, and controls both houses of the state legislature in only 4 states. The great importance of the Presidency is shown by the fact that even under these conditions the party of the White House is the in-party.

The number of Presidential hopefuls within the in-party varies, of course, depending on whether the current President can succeed himself. Presidents are limited to two terms by the Twenty-Second Amendment (passed after Franklin Roosevelt had been elected to the Presidency four times). If the President cannot succeed himself, then the field is open, unless a particular person, such as the Vice-President, is clearly the front runner. The most recent case of a President serving out his two terms was Eisenhower in 1960. And in that year Eisenhower's Vice-President for eight years, Richard Nixon, had almost no serious challenge for the Republican party nomination.

Traditionally the current President is renominated by his party without serious opposition. But one of the most fascinating things about American politics in recent years is the crumbling of this tradition. In 1968 Democrat Lyndon Johnson was President; legally he could serve another term. Yet he was challenged within his own party in primary elections. First Eugene McCarthy and then Robert Kennedy openly declared themselves candidates for the Democratic party nomination. They gained such support that Johnson declared he would not seek renomination. A President had been forced from office by a serious challenge within the ranks of his own party. Still, the Johnson case was thought to result only from the very unusual conditions of the unpopular Vietnam war. The President was still considered safe, at least within his own party.

Public Financing   Something has happened that puts the question of "safety" in an entirely new light. The campaign-finance legislation passed in 1974 provides for public financing of Presidential primaries (see Chapter 9). A challenger within the President's own party now has funds that do not come from the party itself. The advantage of being President, with control over the party and party funds and influence over potential political contributors, is lessened. In early 1975 a Republican senator with Presidential ambitions, Howard Baker of Tennessee, was quick to point out the implications:

> The value of incumbency has been greatly diminished by public financing and subsidies for primary candidates. You're likely to see a lot more people run against a sitting President.

The 1976 election year may be a turning point in Presidential selection politics. If Baker is correct, serious challenges within the party of the current President will become more frequent. A state governor or a senator who feels that the current President's policies are wrong-headed or inadequate to the country's problems will declare himself available. If supporters rally around and leading party figures endorse him, he will become an active candidate.

Members of the "Out-Party"   In the party that has no current President, the number of people who will seriously hope to become President can grow to a dozen or two. In 1975 the Democratic party found itself in this position. By early 1975 there were eight people running: two senators and two ex-senators, one member of the House of Representatives, one governor, and two former governors. In addition, another ten people had expressed open, positive interest in the Presidency, including six more senators, three more governors, and one big-city mayor.

These declarations of availability were taking place more than a year before the first Presidential primaries. Of course not all these people will remain candidates throughout the year. Some will realize that their candidacy is hopeless or too costly and will take themselves out of the race. Indeed by early 1975 four Democratic senators had announced that they definitely would not be candidates (though minds can be changed)—including previous candidates Hubert Humphrey and Edward Muskie, as well as Edward Kennedy. And there is no guarantee that the list of hopefuls in the winter of 1975 includes the name of the person who will be nominated by the Democratic party in the summer of 1976.

Strategic Considerations

Whether Republican or Democrat, the Presidential hopeful must develop a complex plan of action. Hundreds of circumstances must be taken into account, most of which lie beyond the control of the candidate and his advisers. Two students of American electoral politics summarize these as follows:

Some of these circumstances are contingent and relate to the strategies being pursued by other active participants in the election process and to the resources at their command. Other circumstances are more stable and have to do with features of the American political system that have persisted over time. These features provide advantages and handicaps differently to Democrats and Republicans, to incumbent Presidents and challengers.[5]

Thus a Presidential hopeful faces a series of barriers. First of all, of course, he must get his party's nomination. This involves a strategy aimed at the nominating convention, and perhaps the primaries that precede it. To be nominated is only the first step. Election victory is the next goal. The Presidential campaign involves a lot of major decisions: where to campaign, on what issues, with what emphasis, using how much of which resources, and so on. We will take up in turn the problems of nomination and election.

Nominating a Presidential Candidate

We emphasized in an earlier chapter that the route to public office in the United States detours through some sort of political party nomination process. This has been the case for nearly two centuries, though the way the nomination process worked in 1800 was very different from how it works today.

King Caucus   The earliest political parties were nothing more than small groups of men gathered into party "caucuses" controlling who became candidates. Nominating caucuses for governorships and other state offices were generally made up of like-minded party members in the state legislatures. Congressional caucuses nominated the Presidential candidates, who then took their case to the voters, who were still a minority of male adult members of society (see Chapter 3).

"King Caucus," as this system was called, did not last long, but it was the first step in the process leading to party domination over access to public office. The second step also has to do with nominating candidates. Jacksonian popular democracy, a social movement of the 1820s taking its name from Andrew Jackson (the seventh President), attempted to broaden the bases of participation in American politics. One of its notable successes was replacing the caucus system of party nominations with conventions. Conventions were made up of delegates selected by state and local party organizations and, thus, were supposed to be more broadly representative than caucuses.

Primary Elections   Throughout the nineteenth century nomination for nearly all public offices was done by party conventions. Today nominating conventions are important primarily for Presidential

[5] N. W. Polsby and A. B. Wildavsky, *Presidential Elections* (New York: Scribner, 1964), p. 5.

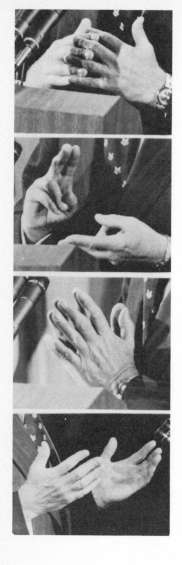

candidates. Candidates for most governorships, state and national legislatures, and many local offices are now nominated in direct primaries. Primaries—party elections that precede the general election—were introduced to reform "nondemocratic" politics. At the turn of the century various reform groups charged that party conventions had come under the control of political bosses and that candidates were controlled by special interests. The reformers felt that a larger dose of democracy would cure this ill, and proposed primary elections.

Primary elections are a means of involving the party followers in the nomination process. From among numerous candidates of the same party, the supporters of that party choose the person best qualified for the forthcoming general election. At least this is the theory. Some form of primary elections have now been adopted in every state, though the form and importance of primaries vary considerably from state to state. We cannot review all the different kinds of primaries; instead, we must satisfy ourselves with two very general conclusions.

On the negative side, the primary as a means of nominating candidates has many flaws. Voter turnout is always low. The choices presented are often not clear, resulting in considerable confusion among voters. At the same time, the costs in campaign funds and effort can be very high, using up resources the party needs for the general election. Certainly the primaries have not brought about mass political participation in the nomination process. On the positive side, the primaries have lessened the control of a small group of people over nominations. They provide a channel by which an opposing group can put forward a candidate.

Presidential Primaries   Presidential primaries have been growing in importance in recent years, especially for the Democratic party. In 1968 Senator Eugene McCarthy decided to challenge President Johnson, largely because McCarthy was so strongly opposed to Johnson's Vietnam war policies. As noted earlier, Johnson later removed himself from the contest for the Democratic party Presidential nomination. Certainly one of the things that helped convince him not to run was McCarthy's showing in a Presidential primary in New Hampshire. McCarthy's success in the primary also played a role in Robert Kennedy's strategy. Kennedy recognized from the New Hampshire primary results that the current President could be defeated in the primaries and declared that he, too, would become a candidate for the Democratic party nomination.

Presidential primaries were even more significant in the 1972 nomination of Senator George McGovern as the Democratic party candidate. McGovern, a strong anti-war candidate, was an insurgent within the Democratic party. The party professionals, especially labor leaders, made it clear that they preferred Hubert Humphrey. McGovern took his case to the voters in a series of primary campaigns, starting with New Hampshire in March and ending in Cali-

fornia in June. All told, there were 17 state primary elections in which some combination of the major candidates campaigned (major candidates in 1972 being McGovern, Humphrey, Senator Muskie, and Governor Wallace). McGovern won more than any other candidate (7 primaries), including California, usually a critical primary because it comes near the time of the national convention and because California sends such a large delegation to the convention. These primary victories helped immensely in gathering the delegate strength needed to win the Democratic party nomination in 1972.

McGovern was aided by the "unit rule" followed in many states. Under this rule the primary candidate who gets the greatest number of votes in the primary election gets *all* of that state's delegates to the nominating convention. For example, in 1972 McGovern received 45 percent of the votes in the California primary election and Humphrey received 40 percent, the remainder being divided among other candidates. But McGovern won all 271 delegates. It was a winner-take-all election.

The Democratic party has now declared the unit rule illegal. Delegates are supposed to be divided according to the voting strength of the several candidates. Had the new rule been in effect in 1972, for example, McGovern would have won only 122 delegates from California and Humphrey would have won 108. On balance, the absence of the unit rule will favor "minority candidates" such as George Wallace. Wallace has some strength in many states, but not usually enough to lead all other contenders. Under the new rules he would win delegate support in proportion to the number of primary votes he gets.

Presidential primaries have not played as big a role in Republican party politics as they have for the Democrats. But as noted earlier, this may be changing. A greater number of primaries, being planned in as many as 30 states in 1976, along with the availability of public funds for primary contests, may attract more people into the race for the party nomination.

Presidential Nominating Conventions

Every four years the Democrats and the Republicans, as well as lesser parties, meet in convention for the purpose of nominating a Presidential ticket. Party conventions are remarkable gatherings; they provide hours and hours of TV entertainment for the American public. Several hundred party members meet in a city selected by the national party organization (in close consultation with the television networks) to debate and formulate a "party platform" and choose a Presidential nominee. When the two party conventions have finished their business, two men from an adult population of more than one hundred million Americans are serious contenders for the White House. In this sense the choice of President is predetermined. Only the two nominees of the major parties have a realistic chance. Yet at the same time the choice is meaningful, for the party nominating process has given the electorate manageable alternatives.

THE ROAD TO THE WHITE HOUSE

How Delegates Are Selected Delegates to the Presidential nominating convention are selected in a variety of ways. Some states have Presidential primaries that bind the delegates to the candidate winning the primary election; other states have primaries that allow the voters to show their preferences but still leave the delegates some independence. In yet other states the primary election chooses unbound delegates. In some states the voters choose some delegates, but other delegates from that state are chosen by district or state party committees. All told, the use of some form of Presidential primary accounts for the selection of only a minority of delegates to either of the nominating conventions. The great majority of states rely on party committees or conventions to select convention delegates.

During the preconvention politicking the states with primary elections receive the greatest news coverage and public attention. But the candidate who is seriously trying to win nomination will use many of his organizational resources to influence delegate selection in the nonprimary states as well. In 1960 John F. Kennedy combined primary victories with careful delegate selection in nonprimary states and won his party's nomination on the first ballot. In 1964 Barry Goldwater earned the Republican nomination by quietly influencing delegate selection in party conventions throughout the country. And in 1972 George McGovern surprised observers by his victories in several key Presidential primaries. Building on these victories, he was able to attract enough delegate strength from other states to ensure his first-ballot nomination at the Democratic convention.

Who Are the Delegates? Convention delegates are a cross-section of the political party. Included among them will be many officeholders, congressmen, governors, mayors, state legislators. There will be party activists and contributors. In both major parties the delegates have tended to be white, male, and wealthier than the general population.

Both parties, though especially the Democratic party, have reformed delegate-selection practices in recent years so as to provide a more balanced convention. In 1970 a report of the Democratic party reform commission (headed at first by George McGovern, who was to benefit from the reforms at the 1972 convention) reported that too many delegates were selected at "secret caucuses" and "closed slate-making meetings." It also reported that minorities, especially blacks, Chicanos, women, and youth, were discriminated against. The report suggested guidelines that would result in greater minority representation. Table 11.1 shows that this happened; the number of minority delegates to the Democratic party convention in 1972 showed a marked increase from 1968. This was at the expense of the party regulars, who were forced to sit home and watch the convention on television. (Nearly 80 percent of the 1972 delegates

Table 11.1
Delegates to the Democratic
National Convention:
1968 and 1972

	Blacks	Youth[a]	Women	Chicanos and Others
1968	5%	4%	13%	—
1972	15%	21%	38%	5%

[a] Less than thirty.

Source: *The Party Reformed,* Final Report of the Commission on Party Structure and Delegate Selection (Washington, D.C.: Democratic National Committee, 1972), pp. 7–8.

were attending a convention for the first time.) Although the newcomers gave the nomination to McGovern, freezing the party regulars out of the convention hurt McGovern's campaign. Many important Democrats, such as Chicago Mayor Richard Daley and labor leader George Meany, refused to support the McGovern campaign. The size of the victory margin of the Nixon-Agnew ticket over McGovern in the 1972 general election was certainly related to the anger of the Democratic party regulars at being shut out of "their" convention.

The Convention Chooses In 1972 the Democratic party held its convention in Miami in July, followed by the Republican party in August. When the conventions were over there were two national tickets. But did the delegates who poured into Miami during the summer of 1972 actually decide anything? Or were they only there to confirm what had already been decided? If so, who decided what was to be confirmed? As a matter of fact the 1972 conventions did confirm the obvious. Certainly on the Republican side the renomination of Nixon and Agnew was taken for granted. And even at the Democratic convention McGovern was an easy first-ballot winner, despite the fact that Humphrey was still an active candidate.

It has not always been so. Past conventions have been meetings in which negotiating, compromising, and "deals" have resulted in an unexpected nomination. And other conventions have seen intense factional battles, with the outcome depending on how the undecided delegates finally voted.

Today, however, much of the struggle that used to occur in the conventions has been shifted to the preconvention period—the Presidential primaries and the state and local meetings where delegates are selected. This is the conclusion of a study of Presidential nominating politics by the Brookings Institution, a prestigious research organization. This study continues, "with the great modern access to information about delegate commitments and intentions, most of the losers in recent times have probably known that they were beaten before the convention opened."[6]

But if the preconvention politicking fails to produce a clear front

[6] Paul T. David, Ralph M. Goldman, and Richard C. Bain, *The Politics of National Party Conventions,* ed. by Kathleen Sproul (New York: Vintage, 1964), p. 324.

runner, it will be at the convention itself that the party will choose its nominee. The politics of Presidential nomination is in the paradoxical situation of giving increasing emphasis to Presidential primaries *and*, perhaps, to the convention. For if the party is fragmented and there are many candidates fighting it out in the primaries, probably by convention time no single person will dominate.

The Presidential Campaign

Two major Presidential candidates, and their Vice-Presidential running mates, will be left in the race at the end of the party primaries, delegate-selection conferences, and nominating convention. Now starts the great democratic ritual in American politics, the Presidential campaign.

If anything political attracts the attention of the American public, it is the Presidential campaign every four years. The image and the voice of a candidate bombards the citizen in billboards, bumper stickers, newspaper advertisements, radio spots, and most of all, television. A citizen may not care about the results, but it is not easy to avoid the campaign. Walk past a newsstand, and a half-dozen different pictures of one or both of the candidates will smile out from magazine covers. Turn the television on, and sooner or later comes a spot announcement telling the viewer how much *this* election means and how the candidate can solve the country's problems.

More than national holidays, more than public ceremonies, more than patriotic songs and speeches, the Presidential campaign is the event that reaffirms what a democracy is supposed to be about.

Campaign Strategy: Appeals to Party Members Among other things, the Presidential campaign focuses the energies of party members. The contest is, after all, between Democrats and Republicans and perhaps, as in 1968, an important third party as well. These energies are most evident in the final month before election day, when both candidates (as well as minor-party candidates) scurry around the country praising their own value and criticizing their opponents. Depending on the personalities of the candidates and the mood of the country, this debate can get rather vicious. Sometimes the Presidential candidates themselves will refrain from mudslinging, but lesser figures, maybe a Vice-President, will let the opponent have it. Spiro Agnew, Vice-President under Nixon, was fond of casting doubt on the patriotism of Democrats who objected to Nixon's policies in Vietnam. When McGovern was nominated by the Democratic party in the summer of 1972, Nixon was discreetly silent, but Agnew accused McGovern of giving aid and comfort to the enemy, and other spokesmen for Nixon labeled McGovern a socialist.

Attacks on the personal virtue of one's opponent are less significant than the legitimate debate that goes on between leaders of opposing parties. This debate is necessarily partisan. It claims that one side has more leadership, wisdom, and talent than the opponents. It indirectly calls into question the judgment of every voter who would be so foolish or shortsighted as to support the other party. Actually the Democratic party is normally more partisan in its appeals than the Republicans. The Democrats enjoy the status of majority party (more loyal followers than the Republicans) and thus need only attract traditional supporters. The Republican candidate heads the minority party; fewer citizens view themselves as Republicans. The Republicans therefore will more often make nonpartisan appeals, stressing that the voter should support the best man rather than a particular party. Nevertheless the Presidential campaign intensifies partisan differences.

Campaign Strategy: The Electoral College   A candidate for the Presidency must decide where to put his time and effort. Should he campaign in every state? Should he concentrate on the most populous states? Or should he concentrate on states where the election is going to be close?

These are exactly the kinds of questions that must be answered by the campaign strategy. The reason for their importance is found in something called the electoral college. The electoral college, as set down in the Constitution, was a method of choosing a President and Vice-President by a small group of respected citizens. Alexander Hamilton, in *The Federalist* (No. 68), states the case: The choice of a President "should be made by men most capable of analyzing the qualities adapted to the station. . . . A small number of persons, selected by their fellow citizens from the general mass, will be most likely to possess the information and discernment requisite to such complicated investigations." This small number of persons, the electoral college, was to be chosen by the state legislatures.

This ancient institution still plays a major role in Presidential selection, but not the one the founders intended. It has become an institution of popular democratic control. Each state has a number of electoral votes equivalent to the size of its congressional delegation. Figure 11.3 shows that at present electoral votes vary from 45 (California) to 3 (6 small states plus the District of Columbia have only 3 votes each). Electoral votes are bound by the unit rule; that is, all of the electoral votes of a state go to the Presidential candidate who wins a plurality of the votes in that state. This rule makes the largest states—the urban, industrial states—most important politically. For instance, the candidate who can win the two largest states (California and New York) has nearly a third of the total electoral votes needed to win the Presidency (96 out of 270).

This situation has had a major impact on twentieth-century politics. Because large states can be so much more important than small ones (the electoral vote of California is worth the combined electoral votes of 13 small states), the large states tend to dominate the nomination process. This bias carries over into the campaign, as both parties concentrate on winning the large states.

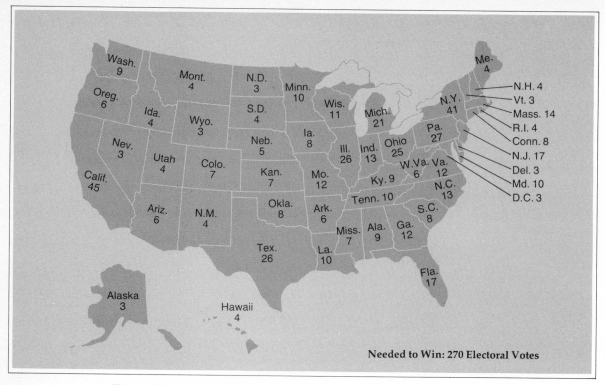

Washington 9, Montana 4, North Dakota 3, Minnesota 10, Oregon 6, Idaho 4, Wyoming 3, South Dakota 4, Wisconsin 11, Michigan 21, New York 41, Maine 4, Nevada 3, Utah 4, Colorado 7, Nebraska 5, Iowa 8, Illinois 26, Indiana 13, Ohio 25, Pennsylvania 27, West Virginia 6, Virginia 12, California 45, Arizona 6, New Mexico 4, Kansas 7, Missouri 12, Kentucky 9, North Carolina 13, Oklahoma 8, Arkansas 6, Tennessee 10, South Carolina 8, Mississippi 7, Alabama 9, Georgia 12, Texas 26, Louisiana 10, Florida 17, Alaska 3, Hawaii 4, New Hampshire 4, Vermont 3, Massachusetts 14, Rhode Island 4, Connecticut 8, New Jersey 17, Delaware 3, Maryland 10, District of Columbia 3

Needed to Win: 270 Electoral Votes

Figure 11.3
Electoral Votes for Each State

Campaign Costs Campaigns involve many activities—travel and speeches, publicity and polls, television shows and radio spots, voter registration and voter mobilization efforts, telephoning and mailings. These activities cost a lot. Officially the Presidential campaign in 1972 cost the candidates and the parties more than $100 million; unofficially it cost much more. Add to this the costs of preconvention and primary spending as well as the costs of congressional and statewide campaigns, and the amount spent in 1972 totals more than $400 million (the approximate cost of a five-year federal government heart disease prevention program).

Traditionally the source of campaign funds has been individual gifts and interest groups. Before the campaign reforms now in effect (see Chapter 9), some individuals gave very large contributions. At least a half-dozen individuals, for example, gave more than a quarter of a million dollars apiece to the 1972 Nixon campaign. One of McGovern's contributors gave nearly three-quarters of a million dollars. Perhaps the record for individual political contributions goes to Nelson Rockefeller, whose gifts over the 18-year period before he became Vice-President are listed in Table 11.2.

Though they stand out, large contributors do not really dominate campaign giving. A large portion of campaign money has come from small gifts of less than $100 requested through direct mailings, television appeals, and at political rallies and dinners. Also important are special-interest groups that collect money from their members

Table 11.2
Political Contributions
by Nelson Rockefeller,
1957–1974

Personal Presidential campaigns	$1,000,228
Republican party clubs, committees, and congressional, local, and state candidates in New York state	1,443,603
Republican party national committees, clubs, and candidates.	347,224
Winthrop Rockefeller (brother) team Arkansas gubernatorial campaigns	274,000
Out-of-state Republican party clubs, committees, and candidates	119,720
Rockefeller team New York state campaigns	80,599
Total (18 years)	$3,265,374

and give it to political candidates. The political action committee of Associated Milk Producers was a very big contributor to Nixon's 1972 campaign. Other important givers were political action groups of the AMA, the AFL-CIO, and the National Education Association.

The abuses revealed in the Watergate investigations along with the sheer costs in campaigning have led to major reforms in the funding and spending of Presidential campaigns. Some of these reforms were reviewed in Chapter 9, where we learned that there are now limits on contributions as well as spending limits.

The Presidential Election Campaign Fund   One result of the reform legislation was the setting up of a special federal fund to be paid for through taxes. Each year the taxpayer can specify that $1.00 of his or her tax money is to go into the Presidential Election Campaign Fund. The money raised in this way is then given to Presidential candidates, presumably making them less dependent on wealthy contributors and special-interest groups.

Approximately 15 percent of the nation's taxpayers contributed a dollar of their tax money in 1974; it is estimated that this percentage will double by 1976 and then level off. By July 1974 nearly $30 million had been collected toward the 1976 Presidential campaign; it is hoped that this figure will approach $42 million, which is what the General Accounting Office (responsible for administering the fund) considers necessary for the 1976 campaign.

A candidate can choose to take advantage of public financing or to rely only on private financing. If he chooses public financing, he is

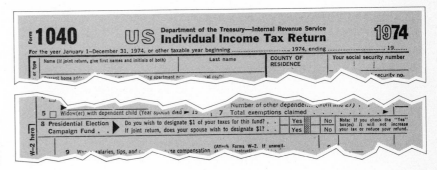

limited to spending no more than 15¢ for each voting-age person in the United States. A candidate relying on public money could ask for private contributions only if the public fund did not cover campaign costs under this rule, and could ask for only enough to make up the difference.

As passed in 1971, the law provides that the Republican and Democratic Presidential nominees would receive money before the campaign. There is also a provision for minor-party candidates according to a formula based on how many votes they receive in the general election. The public funding provisions include money for primaries as well. The amount depends on the number of candidates, the raising of matching money, and the voting strength of candidates.

It is too early to tell how public funding will work out in the United States. But the huge amounts of money spent in 1972 should be reduced. This may, in turn, reduce the role played in party nominations by wealthy contributors and well-funded special-interest groups.

Vacancies in the White House

Nine times in American history a man has become President because of a vacancy in the White House. These men were Vice-Presidents; they stepped into the White House after the death or resignation of the President. Three of these cases are crowded into the years since the end of World War II. Roosevelt was elected to a fourth term in 1944, only to die in the spring of 1945. Harry Truman became President. Then in 1963 Kennedy was assassinated in Dallas, Texas, and his running mate from 1960 became President. Johnson went on to win the Presidency in his own right in 1964.

The most recent case is unique in two ways. Before 1974, all vacancies in the White House had been due to the death of the President. Nixon was the first President ever to resign. And before 1974 all Vice-Presidents who stepped into a vacated office had themselves been elected as Vice-Presidents. The events of 1974 were different. On October 10, 1973, the elected Vice-President, Spiro Agnew, resigned in the midst of charges of bribery, tax evasion, and conspiracy. He was replaced by Gerald Ford under the conditions stipulated in the Twenty-Fifth Amendment. And Ford took over when Nixon resigned. Ford then nominated Nelson Rockefeller as Vice-President, and the nomination was confirmed by Congress. Thus in 1975 the American people had a President and a Vice-President who had not been elected to those positions.

Presidents: What Manner of Men?

When the noise and politics of nominations and campaigns are over, one man, and only one, is suddenly on top. How he handles pressure, how he works with advisers, how he speaks to the public, and how clearly he thinks about problems have a large impact on life in this and other societies. Nixon had the creativity to ease tensions

1963: Lyndon B. Johnson is sworn in as President.

1968: Johnson announces he will not run for reelection.

1968: Nixon and Agnew are elected.

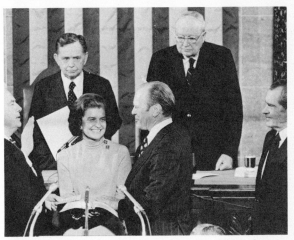

1973: Gerald Ford is sworn in as Vice-President after Agnew's resignation.

1974: Nixon after his farewell address to the White House staff.

1974: Nelson Rockefeller after being sworn in as Vice-President.

with China and the Soviet Union, and thereby increased the chances of peace in the world. He had the arrogance to think he could fool most of the people most of the time on Watergate, and thereby reduced the confidence Americans felt in their government and even in themselves. Johnson had the energy and forcefulness to enact new civil-rights, welfare, and medical care programs, and thereby improved the lives of some of America's poor and oppressed groups. But the same energy and forcefulness led Johnson into the thicket of the Vietnam war, from which neither he nor the American society could escape unscarred. Today President Ford struggles with a recession and an energy crisis, not quite knowing whether a particular tax program or spending policy will increase or solve America's economic problems. If he and his advisers make wrong choices, many will suffer. If they make right choices, fewer will suffer and for a shorter period. The stakes are high.

Only 37 people in America's history have had the chance to make —or avoid—the huge mistakes that our system of government gives to the President. And these 37 people have approached the task differently, depending on the political habits they brought to the office and on their outlook toward their own life. One student of Presidential character has attempted to classify Presidents along these lines, using the term *style* to describe the habits of governing and the term *character* to describe the attitude toward self.[7]

Presidential style can be roughly divided into active or passive. For instance, William Howard Taft, Republican President from 1908 to 1912, took a very restrictive view of his duties as President. "The President," he remarked, "can exercise no power which cannot be fairly and reasonably traced to some specific grant of authority." This reflects the classic passive style of Presidential authority, a style that in many ways was repeated by Dwight Eisenhower, Republican President from 1952 to 1960. Eisenhower disliked much of the nitty-gritty of politics. He was uninterested in using the vast patronage powers of the Presidency; he refused to meddle in congressional politics; he did not like speech making; he ignored the press as much as possible; he avoided summit politics in international relations. On the latter topic, for instance, Eisenhower said: "This idea of the President of the United States going personally abroad to negotiate— it's just damn stupid."

Other Presidents have favored vigorous Presidential action. Kennedy, for instance, viewed the Presidency as the "vital center of action in our whole scheme of government." Rejecting the passive role, he argued that the President must "place himself in the very thick of the fight." Nixon, campaigning in 1968, said: "The days of the passive Presidency belong to a simpler past; the next President must take an activist view of his office. . . . He must lead."

Presidential character refers to whether the man in the White

[7] James David Barber, *The Presidential Character: Predicting Performance in the White House* (Englewood Cliffs, N.J.: Prentice-Hall, 1972).

House seems generally happy and optimistic toward himself and his duties, or moody, irritable, weighed down with the burdens of office. Although it is hard to characterize Presidents in such terms, this kind of analysis is useful if it can uncover something about the personality of the President. Johnson, for example, became increasingly negative and unhappy as opposition to his Vietnam war policies rose, until toward the end of his term he was complaining that "everybody is trying to cut me down, destroy me" and asking, "Why don't people like me?" A sense of persecution was even stronger in Nixon; he became moody, withdrawn, and irritable as impeachment for his role in Watergate became more certain.

Personality: Does It Make a Difference?

The attempt to identify "personality types" in the White House seems fruitless to many observers of American politics. Decisions are made in the context of demanding situations and conditions; no matter who is in the White House, the same decision will be made. It is pointed out, for example, that Johnson was under such pressure to escalate the Vietnam war that there was really no alternative. When Johnson became President there was an existing framework within which foreign policy, including policy toward Southeast Asia, was being made. The assumptions of this framework, shaped by previous Presidents and their advisers, included a belief that saving South Vietnam from communist domination was important to America's national security. This view was shared in 1965 by nearly all of Johnson's advisers, by leading foreign-policy experts both inside and outside of government, and by leading commentators in the universities and the media. Within this context, how could Johnson have acted differently? He escalated the war because that was the logical thing to do if one assumed that South Vietnam was vital to American security.

Such an analysis leaves little room for personality. The President is seen as responding to conditions and pressures. But this poses a different question. Johnson's way of handling the war—his choice of bombing targets, his dealings with congressional critics, his secretiveness, and his response to the anti-war movement—allowed for variation. And even small variations (refusing to meet with congressional critics) could take on great political significance. As these variations take on political meaning, we begin to see the importance of the character and personality of the man in the White House.

Watergate brings this lesson home with a force unimagined even during the difficult days of Vietnam. Nixon's secrecy and isolation and moodiness made him a target for those determined to get to the bottom of Watergate. If early in the cover-up he had simply confessed the poor judgment of his advisers and the lack of candor he had shown in earlier statements, it is likely that he would have been forgiven. But Nixon saw himself as a fighter against huge odds. He paid a high cost. So did society, showing once again that it is the President who stands at the very center of American politics.

The White House
Washington

August 9, 1974

Dear Mr. Secretary:

I hereby resign the Office of President of the United States.

Sincerely,

/s/ Richard Nixon

The Honorable Henry A. Kissinger
The Secretary of State
Washington, D.C. 20520

How Institutions Work: IV
The Nomination, Election, and Replacement of a President

How are Presidential candidates chosen?

Since 1832 candidates for President have been nominated by their party's national conventions, held for that purpose every four years. Several thousand party members meet at the convention, and nomination of a candidate is by majority vote among the delegates.

How are delegates to the national convention chosen?

Procedures vary widely from state to state. Commonly used selection methods are: (1) election of delegates at primary elections, (2) selection by state or district conventions, and (3) selection by the state committees of the parties. There is currently an effort by both Republicans and Democrats to make procedures for selecting delegates more democratic and to ensure more equal representation for women and minorities.

What determines the size of each state's delegation to the convention?

This is determined by each party's national committee through a complex formula based on population as well as on how successful the party has been in that state's most recent statewide or congressional election.

When is the Presidential election held?

Every four years on the Tuesday after the first Monday in November.

What role does the electoral college play in a Presidential election?

The Constitution does not provide for popular election of the President. Instead, the legislature of each state is to appoint electors equal in number to that state's senators and representatives in

Congress. Technically speaking, then, the voter is not voting directly for a Presidential candidate but for the slate of electors pledged to that candidate. Most voters are unaware of this, because in most states the names of the electors do not appear on the ballot.

The slate that gets the most votes in the general election then meets as a "college" in December of a Presidential year and casts its ballots. The ballots are then sent to Washington, where the electoral votes are officially counted in a joint session of Congress on January 6. The candidate with a majority of the electoral votes (or 270 out of 538) is formally elected President.

Must an elector vote for the candidate to whom he is pledged?

There is no legal obligation to do so, although desertions are rare. In 1968 Nixon carried North Carolina, but one of the electors pledged to him voted for Wallace.

What happens if no candidate wins a majority of the electoral votes?

In that case the House of Representatives must choose the President, with each state delegation in the House having one vote. Two Presidents have been elected by this procedure: Jefferson in 1801 and John Quincy Adams in 1825.

Can a President be legally removed from office?

Yes. The Constitution provides that a President may be removed from office upon impeachment for and conviction of treason, bribery, or other "high crimes and misdemeanors," generally understood to include gross abuse of authority or failure to uphold the oath of office. The House of

Representatives has the sole power to vote charges of impeachment, in which case the Senate sits as a trial body and decides whether or not to convict. A two-thirds vote is necessary for conviction. Only one President, Andrew Johnson in 1868, has been impeached by the House, but he was acquitted in the Senate by a margin of one vote. The House Judiciary Committee voted articles of impeachment against Nixon in 1974; he resigned prior to a vote of the full House.

What happens if the office of the Presidency becomes vacant or the President is unable to carry out his office?
Although no President has been impeached and removed from office, eight have died in office and one has resigned. The Constitution provides that in the event of a vacancy the Vice-President becomes President. The assassination of President Kennedy alerted the nation to the potentially dangerous constitutional void that occurs when the Vice-President becomes President, leaving the office of Vice-President empty. Congress accordingly proposed and the states ratified the Twenty-Fifth Amendment to the Constitution, which specifies the procedures to be followed when the Vice-Presidency becomes vacant. In such a case the President is required to nominate a Vice-President, who takes office if he is confirmed by a majority vote of both houses of Congress. Under the Twenty-Fifth Amendment Gerald Ford replaced Spiro Agnew in 1973 as Vice-President, and Nelson Rockefeller was confirmed as Vice-President in 1975 to fill the vacancy created by Ford's becoming President.

The Twenty-Fifth Amendment also specifies how the Vice-President temporarily assumes the duties of the President if the latter becomes seriously ill or unable to carry out his office.

What happens if offices of both President and Vice-President become vacant at the same time?
In such a case the Presidential Succession Act of 1947 provides that the speaker of the House would become President.

12

The Supreme Court in American Politics

Separation of powers is a central idea in our form of government. There is to be a legislature that makes laws, an executive that carries them out, and a court that passes judgment when conflicts arise over the meaning and application of laws. We will have many chances to see that such tidy distinctions rarely work out in practice. Separation of powers is actually a sharing of powers and, therefore, a struggle for power.

Nevertheless, there is something called *legislation,* and it occurs mainly in Congress; there is something called *execution,* and it occurs primarily in the executive branch; and there is something called *adjudication,* and it is the job of the court system. In this chapter we discuss adjudication, especially in the United States Supreme Court. Because adjudication is not well understood, at least not nearly so well as legislation and execution, it is useful to start with a description of how courts operate.

What Do We Mean by Adjudication?

Courts differ from legislatures or executives in the way they establish new policies. Courts do not undertake action; rather, they wait until a case comes to them. A case becomes a chance for a court to declare a general rule.

To understand this it is necessary to be clear about the roles of the participants. American courts will hear only cases in which there is a genuine controversy between two parties—a plaintiff and a defendant. Courts in the United States consistently refuse to supervise friendly, nonadversary proceedings whose object is to get a declaration of policy on a general social issue. The courts rule only if there is a genuine controversy, that is, if there is need to find a principle to resolve an issue in the case before them.

For the same reason, the courts generally will not supervise cases in which the injury is merely a future possibility. American courts are not a forum in which to discuss the probable benefits and costs, the apparent wisdom or absurdity, of a public policy or private course of action. They exist to cope with the legal issues involving the suffering, or alleged suffering, of one party at the hands of another. Unless the courts can determine the actual injury one party has already suffered—or can be foreseen if the court doesn't issue an injunction—they cannot know what remedy will remove the injustice. This underlies the great importance assigned by the courts to the seemingly technical question of whether an individual plaintiff has "standing to sue." To have "standing," one must show that one has suffered some wrong the courts can conceivably right through their judicial power.

The court then presides over an adversary proceeding between two parties. If the case involves a challenge to an act of the government, one of the adversaries is the challenger: the convicted criminal who claims that he was not given the right to a fair trial guaranteed by the Constitution; the businessman who claims the government exceeded its authority in regulating his business; the schoolchild who claims he or she is not getting equal protection of the law by being sent to a segregated school. The other adversary is the government: a state government if it is a state criminal proceeding that is challenged; the federal government if a federal regulatory act is being challenged; a local school board if it is the subject of the desegregation suit.

This same contest between adversaries applies to all court proceedings: the divorce contest, where one adversary sues the other for divorce; the civil suit, where one party accuses the other of injuring it; the criminal prosecution, where the government prosecutor faces the lawyer of the accused. Because the outcome depends on this adversary proceeding, we will look more closely at it.

The Role of the Lawyer

We begin with the lawyer. The role of the lawyer is often misunderstood. Lawyers do not necessarily sympathize with the goals of their clients. They may even strongly dislike the people — or goals — they defend. But it is central to the lawyer's creed that his client receive the most forceful representation of his interests possible. Even accused criminals whom the lawyer himself believes guilty are entitled to such representation.

The lawyer does not search on his own for "justice" or the "truth." These values will be secured, he believes, if lawyers on each side of the case present the strongest arguments they can. Lawyers are also "officers of the court." They state the claims of their clients in such a way that the issue can be resolved within the terms of the law: what specific interests are at stake; what legal remedies are sought; what facts and principles are to guide resolution of the conflict.

The Role of the Judge

The role of the judge, too, is often misunderstood. Unlike continental European judges, the American judge is not expected to investigate on his own: to decide which allegations are true, which false, and which facts are being suppressed or overlooked by both parties to the controversy. On the contrary, he is expected to base his decision — or to instruct the jury to base theirs — solely on arguments and evidence presented to him in open contest. His responsibility is to make sure a proper adversary proceeding is carried out: that legally correct claims and charges are entered; that each party is given a chance to present his case; that irrelevant testimony is kept off the record; that illegally obtained evidence is not used.

This description of adversary proceedings is short and incomplete. And in fact many court proceedings depart somewhat from these norms. They are sometimes arranged to speed a divorce or to test the constitutionality of a law. Poor clients sometimes receive less than full support from their lawyers. Some judges reach well beyond the needs of the case at hand to make general statements on public policy. Yet the general norms of adversary proceedings help explain the moral force court judgments have in this country.

The Advantages of Adjudication

Why are such proceedings felt to be better than rule making by a single disinterested body? For one thing, adversary proceedings reveal the specific interests actually affected by public policy. The most careful legislator cannot foresee all the future circumstances to which a general law will apply. Adjudication lets those actually affected by a law state their case and ask for a reasonable interpretation of the law in the light of those problems. Moreover, the adjudication process harnesses self-interest to the search for the public interest by giving the participants a strong incentive to bring in all the arguments they can. Legislatures may casually vote through laws they half understand; they may be swayed by superficial arguments, by time pressure, by general principles unrelated to the actual costs their decision imposes. Adversaries in an adjudicatory proceeding cannot afford to be casual.

Adjudication also brings out questions of fact and principle. This may seem unlikely in an adversary proceeding. But the motives of the participants should not be confused with the terms on which their arguments become effective. To win in court one does not have to show that public support is on one's side. Rather, the participants must disprove charges or make claims based on rights they are guaranteed by the rules under which they have agreed to live. Arguments focus on the neutral principles of justice. To win it is necessary to show that the claim is just or that an indictment is true.

This nonpolitical concern for fact and principle creates a third advantage of adjudication. It provides legal channels through which minorities can maintain their rights against majority preferences. The minorities that have thus benefited include unpopular citizens accused of crimes, blacks, the very wealthy, Jehovah's Witnesses, birdwatchers, corporations, and communists. What these disparate groups have in common is that none would fare very well in an egalitarian democracy wholly controlled by majority rule. In acting on behalf of minorities, courts sometimes have blocked efforts at social reform by legislative majorities. They did so between the end of the Civil War and 1937, when they protected the giant corporations from government regulation. In these circumstances it is easy to see the courts as the defense of special privilege against the people's will. However, if at times the courts have protected privileges, they have also defended the rights of less privileged minorities. Blacks were long ignored by alternately indifferent and fearful legislatures; only a series of landmark judicial decisions has begun to right the wrongs of racial discrimination.

The Disadvantages of Adjudication

Against the advantages of adjudication must be placed its dis-advantages. The case-by-case method of evolving a public policy may, while directing attention to the impact of a general rule on specific interests, also prove slow, cumbersome, and internally inconsistent as a way to regulate society. Judges in court face a dilemma: If they confine their decisions to the points that need resolution in the case before them, they risk adding a partial solution to a complex problem demanding more uniform treatment; yet to the extent that they go beyond these limits they reduce the validity and moral force of their decision. The logic of the adversary process, moreover, encourages intense, unqualified statements of principle implying that only two possible points of view of the controversy exist and that only one is right.

We have already noted that adjudication coexists uneasily with majority rule in this country. The strength of adjudication is that it helps minorities and the individual claimant. Now we must add that some of the "minorities" whose rights are upheld by the courts are often those who can pay for this protection. Adjudication is expensive, especially the cost of a lawyer. The procedures of the courtroom are complex and often cumbersome, and without a skilled lawyer one risks losing simply by not knowing some highly technical requirement. But a trial involves many other costs—courtroom fees, the cost of a delayed settlement, the expense of a transcript if one wishes to appeal the decision. Defendants in criminal cases who are too poor to hire a lawyer may have one assigned, but even the best assigned counsel is handicapped if he lacks funds to turn up the evidence he needs to win in court. Of course one may lose the case and, thus, lose not only the initial investment but also such additional damages and court costs as the judge may require. It is not surprising that many who are sure their rights have been infringed nevertheless fear to go to court.

There are still subtler barriers for disadvantaged minorities. Because the courtroom is dominated by those who can pay, corporation lawyers, bankers, realtors, insurance agents, and automobile dealers are generally well informed of their rights under the law and are quick to take legal action when it is to their financial advantage to do so. They mingle freely as social equals with judges and other lawyers, who share their interest in "practical" affairs and who—taken as a whole—have benefited from a longer and more expensive education than the general public. With good reason, the poor, the less well educated, and certain minorities feel out of place in court. They appear most often before the bar to meet charges of defaulting on contract or as defendants in criminal proceedings. Civil law is seldom written to benefit them, and they are less likely to know how to turn the law to their advantage. They know that most judges and lawyers regard them as socially inferior, and that (until recently) juries in their cases will come largely from the white middle classes.

The Effectiveness of Adjudication in Social Reform

How effective is adjudication in social reform? It is sometimes argued that a single, decisive ruling by the courts may gain a reform far quicker than years of frustrating lobbying with an elected legislature. Lobbies to repeal antiabortion statutes, for example, now concentrate on bringing test cases to the courts. Environmental protection groups, discouraged by the slow progress of antipollution and land-use control bills through the state legislatures, have tried to short-circuit the process by getting favorable court rulings. Yet this increasingly popular strategy is open to question.

Democratic government rests heavily on persuasion and on community consensus. Judicial rulings offer a tempting short cut, particularly because they often have a legitimacy not given to more overtly political solutions; but this is easily strained by overuse.

The Supreme Court

This tension between courts and legislatures—more generally, between the legitimacy of adjudication and of mobilized popular support—may be seen in the central processes of American constitutional democracy. Its chief symbol is the United States Supreme Court. No other court in the world has remained so dramatically in the public eye; none has as decisively and as repeatedly checked the clearly expressed intent of the popularly elected branches of government and yet remained so firmly a part of a democratic political system. Although its nine judges are appointed for life, it has earned its place as a fully coequal branch—and, if public-opinion polls are to be accepted, the most respected of the three branches—of the national government. For most Americans the Supreme Court symbolizes the principle that no government official may act above the law. Because of the Supreme Court's special relation to constitutional government in the United States, we devote most of this chapter to discussing it. The reader should, however, keep in mind that the Supreme Court is part of a larger system of federal, state, and local courts, which are discussed briefly at the end of the chapter.

The Supreme Court and the President

The Case of the Cherokee Nation

At the beginning of the nineteenth century, the Cherokee Indian tribe was the largest and most important tribe in the southeastern United States. Its settled, advanced culture was based on agriculture; its members communicated through a written language of their own; its government was based on an elective chief and a two-chamber legislature. Although it had sided with Great Britain in the War for Independence and had continued the struggle with the ex-colonial "borderers" until 1794, it negotiated a peace treaty at that time that it scrupulously observed for the next three decades.

Then in 1828 the Cherokee Nation suffered two disasters at once. Gold was discovered on Cherokee land by a prospecting white man. At about the same time, Andrew Jackson, himself a "borderer" and famous Indian fighter, was elected President of the United States. Immediately a process now drearily familiar was set in motion. One of Jackson's first acts was to push through Congress the Indian Removal Act, which granted the President authority to drive all Indian tribes west of the Mississippi. Following Jackson's lead, the Georgia legislature declared all treaties with the Cherokee Nation null and void. Former Cherokee lands were then given to interested whites through a lottery system.

John Ross, the tribal chief, appealed in vain to President Jackson to halt the seizure. Appeals to other popularly elected public officials proved equally futile. But the Cherokee Nation still retained one last defense. The Georgia legislature's action was an outright violation of the Cherokees' treaty with the federal government. It also violated the Fifth Amendment's prohibition against deprivation of property without due process of law. On these grounds the Cherokee Nation carried its case to the United States Supreme Court. The Court tried to duck the issue but was eventually prevailed upon to hear the case. In a statement affirming the "original natural rights [of the Cherokees] . . . and the settled doctrine of the law of nations," it made the actions of the Georgia legislature legally void.

President Jackson was furious. "John Marshall [the Chief Justice] has rendered his decision; now let him enforce it," he said. As Jackson knew very well, this was impossible. A court of elderly jurists, without executive support, could never hope to reverse the actions of a popularly elected legislature. The Court and the Constitution had not stopped a determined legislature and a determined executive. In short order a new federal treaty was signed with an unrepresentative small group of the Cherokee Nation, gold prospectors and other

Steelworkers hear President
Truman's announcement of the
government's seizure of the
steel mills.

settlers poured in, and General Winfield Scott was sent to drive the Cherokees off their ancestral lands and burn their houses. Thus began the long march along the "trail of tears" to Oklahoma—a march during which 4,000 of the 14,000 tribesmen perished.

Truman and the Steel Seizure Case

Somewhat more than a century later, President Truman found himself in an awkward, even alarming, position. American troops were jointly engaged with South Korean troops in a desperate effort to hold the line at the 38th parallel against North Korean and Chinese communist troops. In this effort they depended on steel for helmets, shells, battleships, and warplanes. Yet federal arbitration boards had twice unsuccessfully attempted to mediate a wage dispute between the major steel companies and their employees, and the United Steelworkers of America had announced a strike to enforce its demands. The walkout was set for April 9, 1952.

In the hours before the threatened strike was to begin, the President reviewed his remaining options. Allowing the strike to occur was politically and morally unthinkable in time of war. Further attempts at mediation were clearly futile. The Taft-Hartley Labor Disputes Act of 1947 had given him the authority to order striking workers back to work for an eight-day "cooling off" period if their strike would seriously endanger the public welfare. But Truman, who had centered his 1948 Presidential campaign as a Democrat on the "antilabor" features of the Taft-Hartley Act, could not bring himself to do this. Relying instead on his constitutional responsibility to maintain the security and welfare of the nation, he ordered his secretary of commerce to seize and operate the steel mills in the name of the federal government pending settlement of the dispute.

The mills tried to get a federal court injunction against Secretary Sawyer. Because the dispute raised issues of national importance, the Supreme Court accepted an appeal from the district court with unusual speed. On June 2 it ordered President Truman to return the mills to their former owners. The President promptly complied.

Public opinion was favorable to the outcome, and editorials echoed popular sentiment in calling the Court's decision a reaffirmation of the principle that even the President is firmly bound by the Constitution.

Largely obscured by the excitement of the case was its most significant feature. Despite the national emergency, despite his political embarrassment, President Truman unhesitatingly complied with the Supreme Court. On all sides it was simply taken for granted that as the Court spoke, so would the President act.

This assumption is itself remarkable. As we have seen, President Jackson's violation of the Constitution a century before was far worse, but he was strongly supported by public opinion. In the early nineteenth century, the President could argue that his interpretation of the Constitution was as valid as the Court's. By the mid-twentieth century, this argument was unthinkable. Not only were Presidents to be bound by the Constitution; the Supreme Court alone could interpret what it specified. This was the most significant element of the case: that a tribunal of nine men—having neither Congress' power of the purse, nor the President's control over the military, nor the mandate of popular election that both Congress and the President possess—could become the final authority on the interpretation of the Constitution.

To understand how the Supreme Court has won this authority, it is necessary to go back to the cases in which the power of judicial review was first established.

The Supreme Court and the Constitution

The Right of Judicial Review

In what is known as the supremacy clause, the Constitution declares:

> This Constitution, and the Laws of the United States which shall be made in pursuance thereof . . . shall be the supreme Law of the Land; and the Judges in every State shall be bound thereby, any Thing in the Constitution or Laws of any State to the Contrary notwithstanding.

In this clause the founders were saying that in conflicts between state laws and laws of the federal government, federal laws were to be binding.

One might expect, therefore, that they would have said *who* was to interpret the Constitution and decide when various laws were in conflict with it. But they did not. In particular, they did not explain the role of the Supreme Court in judicial review.

This may have been done on purpose. The founders knew that not all controversial questions could be settled at a single convention.

Had the delegates at Philadelphia proposed giving a group of nine judges appointed for life the authority to veto all legislation contrary to their interpretation of the Constitution, the convention would almost certainly have broken up. States' righters and populist Democrats would have objected strongly. However, if they had failed to provide for a federal Supreme Court of broad, if vague, responsibilities for guarding the Constitution, the Federalists and Constitutionalists would not have been satisfied. All things considered, the best solution was a guardian agency of great but uncertain potential, to be defined in the political conflicts of the future.

Hamilton's Support of Judicial Review

If the Constitutional Convention remained silent about judicial review, not all of the delegates themselves did so. Alexander Hamilton used *The Federalist Papers* to describe the role of the Supreme Court. His argument was that the idea of judicial review by judges appointed for life was not inconsistent with majoritarian democracy. Two assumptions support his position: First, all men are subject to shortsighted ambition and self-interest; second, the Constitution reflects the fundamental will of the American people, whereas acts of a legislature represent the preferences of temporary majorities.

Given these assumptions, Hamilton had little trouble showing that a constitutional government cannot depend on legislators' judgments of the constitutionality of their own acts. Self-interest will blind them to discrepancies between what they want and what the Constitution permits. A disinterested body outside the legislature — such as the Supreme Court — is needed. Only thus can the American people be assured that their will, as set forth in the Constitution, will remain supreme over the will of their temporary representatives in Congress.

Hamilton's first assumption might seem to say *no* group of men can judge the constitutionality of an act of government. What makes the Supreme Court a more disinterested judge? Hamilton answers this question squarely. Supreme Court judges, he admits, are no different from legislators and executives in their motives. They are, however, less to be feared. Lacking "influence over either the sword or the purse," the Court has "no direction over either the strength or the wealth of the community." It can use "neither FORCE nor WILL but merely JUDGMENT" in reaching a decision; it must judge "in accordance with rules that other agencies have prescribed," and must ultimately "depend upon the aid of the executive arm even for the efficacy of its judgments."

From these arguments Hamilton's conclusions follow. The "least dangerous" branch of government offers no serious threat to the other two branches or to the public generally. The dangers are quite different — that the judiciary will lose its independence, becoming absorbed into one of the other two branches, or that, in its isolation, it will be ineffective in maintaining the rights of the citizens under the Constitution. Independent life tenure for the justices thus strengthens this "weakest of the three departments of power." The Constitution is intended to protect the enduring interests of the American people, but the Court will be unable to uphold minority rights and basic freedoms if its members can be changed with every change in the mood of the electorate or its representatives in the government. Hamilton goes on to say that the knowledge that a politically independent body of learned and honored men will refuse to enforce unconstitutional statutes will keep the other branches of the government within constitutional bounds. Judicial review, he concludes, is a necessary balancing tool for any popular government. *Elected* legislatures and executives are needed to ensure a government responsive to the short-term preferences of the people; but an independent body is needed to guard the more lasting principles.

Hamilton's view prevailed, but not until two explosive political issues were settled. Opposed to Hamilton's position were, first, those who felt that Congress, as the constitutionally established legislature for the Republic, was the institution best suited to pass final judgment on the meaning of the Constitution, and second, those committed to state "sovereignty," who believed the state supreme courts were fully empowered to interpret the Constitution in relation to the laws of the various states. Two issues had to be resolved, one stemming from the ambiguities in "separation of powers" and the second stemming from ambiguities in "federalism." The first was resolved in favor of the Court over Congress, the second in favor of the federal government over the states. Let us look at the two landmark decisions.

Establishing the Right to Decide

As early as the mid-1790s two factions were trying to win the Presidency. One faction, the Federalists, was led by John Adams (who became President in 1796), and the other was led by Thomas Jefferson. The Supreme Court was caught up in this bitter fight. During the election contest between Adams and Jefferson in 1800, several justices used their position to speak for Adams and the Federalist party.

The Marbury Case

The huge popular endorsement of the Jeffersonian party in the 1800 election threatened the Supreme Court as an independent institution. The challenge was raised when outgoing President Adams, who had appointed as Chief Justice the outspoken Federalist John Marshall, rushed through a series of "midnight appointments" of new federal judges. Adams was accused of trying to entrench in the judicial branch of government the Federalist views he had been unable to sustain in its elected branches.

It was clear that there would be a contest between the President,

John Marshall, Chief Justice of the United States Supreme Court, 1801–1835.

controlled by the Jeffersonians, and the courts, controlled by the Federalists, and an issue was soon found: In its last-minute haste to pack the judiciary with Federalists, the Adams administration had neglected to deliver to William Marbury his commission as justice of the peace for the District of Columbia. President Jefferson's Secretary of State, James Madison, refused to deliver the commission, and Marbury sued for a writ of mandamus compelling him to do so. This suit placed the Marshall Court in an awkward position. The justices knew Madison had no intention of delivering the commission to Marbury, and if the Court issued a writ of mandamus it would mean an open struggle with the executive branch responsible for enforcing the writ. This tension between the executive branch and the judiciary would merely expose the Court's weakness. Yet to concede Madison's right to deny Marbury his commission would be a humiliating surrender.

Chief Justice Marshall was equal to the challenge. In an opinion that laid the cornerstone of judicial review, he granted Jefferson his momentary objective while establishing a precedent of greater long-term importance. Jefferson's and Madison's refusal to deliver the commission to Marbury, he wrote in his opinion, was illegal. The Supreme Court, however, lacked jurisdiction in this case. For although Congress, in the Judiciary Act of 1789, allowed the Court to issue writs of mandamus, that section of the law was contrary to the Constitution and thus was invalid.

As a masterpiece of judicial strategy, *Marbury* v. *Madison* (1803) has never been equaled.[1] Marshall managed to divert the attention of both parties from what was certainly the most significant element in the decision—the bold assertion that the Supreme Court, on the basis of *its* interpretation of the Constitution, could set limits on Congress.

From the perspective of the twentieth century, *Marbury* v. *Madison* decisively established the Supreme Court's right to define the limits of governmental activity. This power of the Court has been used sparingly, however. Only 85 acts or parts of acts have been declared unconstitutional in the 170 years since *Marbury* v. *Madison*. Some of these acts have been very important ones, but most constitutional scholars believe the significance of judicial review is not so much in the statutes declared unconstitutional as in the threat of a Supreme Court veto.

Marbury v. *Madison* served a second important purpose. In 1800 localism was still powerful in the new nation, and the Federalists saw in the Supreme Court a potential tool for cementing national unity. By bringing a certain amount of uniformity to judicial interpretations of federal law and the Constitution, and through a broad interpretation of the constitutional powers of the federal government, they hoped to offset what they saw as dangerous tendencies

[1] *Marbury* v. *Madison* 1 Cranch 137 (1803).

toward secessionism. The Marbury case was an important step toward this end, for if the Court could veto the legislation of a co-equal branch of government, it could certainly do the same to state legislation. But the contest between nationalist and localist forces was too explosive to be settled by a single judicial decision, and Marshall knew the Court was still too shaky to try to settle it at that point.

By the end of President Madison's second term, however, Marshall felt ready to lead the Court in his chosen direction. There followed a series of landmark decisions in which the full weight of the Court was thrown behind the expansion and consolidation of the federal government's powers. We can here consider only one— *McCulloch* v. *Maryland* (1819)—John Marshall's greatest decision and possibly the Supreme Court's most important statement about the relation of the Constitution to the organization of the American government.[2]

The McCulloch Case

The McCulloch case arose from the efforts of the Maryland state legislature to protect the banks it had chartered against "outside" competition by imposing a tax on other banks. Of the competing banks, the most feared was the Bank of the United States, set up by an act of Congress in 1816 to help finance the growth of the nation. McCulloch, cashier of the Baltimore branch of the Bank of the United States, refused to pay a $15,000 annual fee to the State of Maryland or to put Maryland tax stamps on the bank notes he issued. Maryland won a judgment against McCulloch in one of its county courts, arguing that within its own borders it could tax as it pleased—even a bank founded by the U.S. Congress. The Bank's lawyers replied that Maryland's claim would hopelessly restrict the federal government's economic powers. The Maryland State Court of Appeals rejected their argument, so the Bank appealed to the United States Supreme Court. Here was a clear clash of federal vs. state power.

Marshall, who fully agreed with the Bank, rejected the argument that the powers of the federal government had been delegated to it by the states. Marshall wrote that the Constitution came into being as an act of a *sovereign people* and that all levels of government— state and federal—derived their authority from it. No one level of government can therefore claim a natural supremacy over the others, he said; all depend on a single expression of the collective national will. But precisely because this expression of national will happened rarely, it must not be narrowly interpreted: "We must never forget that it is a *constitution* we are expounding," he said.

We are wrong, Marshall held, if we think that because a specific power is not listed in the Constitution, the national government lacks the constitutional authority to adopt necessary measures. A

[2] *McCulloch* v. *Maryland* 4 Wheaton 316 (1819).

document "adapted to the various crises of human affairs," flexible enough to accommodate an uncertain future, will contain no such listing. The Constitution empowers Congress "To make all Laws which shall be necessary and proper to carrying into Execution the . . . Powers vested by this Constitution in the Government of the United States." This clause, Marshall argues, gives the federal government broad powers:

> Let the end be legitimate, let it be within the scope of the constitution, and all means which are appropriate, which are plainly adapted to that end, which are not prohibited, but consistent with the letter and spirit of the constitution, are constitutional. . . .

The Maryland tax, which carries with it "the power to destroy," stands in the way of an agency related to the goals of the federal government; therefore it is constitutionally invalid.

The McCulloch opinion is an important landmark in the creation of the unique place of the Supreme Court as the interpreter of the fundamental law of the Union. The Supreme Court, in the McCulloch case, justifies both the growth of federal power and the role of the Court in adjudicating disputes between the states and the federal government.

The Struggle for Judicial Supremacy

Throughout much of its history the Supreme Court has been a center of controversy. All adversary proceedings result in some loss to someone, and the natural impulse of the loser is to turn on the institution that gave the verdict. By all odds, however, the most sustained, serious, and widely supported challenge to the power of the Court occurred in 1937, at the beginning of President Roosevelt's second term of office. Not since the opening days of the Marshall Court had judicial independence been in such danger.

At the close of the Civil War, Marshall's vision of one nation united under a federal constitution and a vigorous national government had become a firm reality through force of arms. The Supreme Court was now free to turn its attention to another concern: the relationship of the government to the economy. For the next seventy years the Court saw as its main responsibility the maintenance of legal conditions favorable to the rapid growth of industrial capitalism. Both the federal and the state legislatures were checked if their actions threatened free enterprise. This involved the Court ever more deeply with specific policies of the other branches of government.

As usual, the Court started cautiously. For some time it was distracted by unsolved problems of the Civil War—particularly cases involving the citizenship status of the newly emancipated blacks. In 1883, however, the Court abandoned all efforts to protect blacks from legal oppression and popular prejudice. From then on its major work had to do with the economy, and by 1890 its decisions in economic controversies had formed a consistent pattern. This pattern, briefly described, was the preservation of unregulated free enterprise.

The Due Process Clause Applied to the Economy

The Court held that the U.S. Constitution prohibited both the state and federal governments from interfering with competition in the marketplace. This legal case rested on several arguments. The foremost was the "due process" clause of the Fourteenth Amendment, which provided that "no State shall . . . deprive any person of life, liberty, or property, without due process of law" and was intended to protect emancipated slaves from state action of a kind long prohibited at a federal level by the Fifth Amendment. This clause was almost immediately taken over by powerful corporate interests, whose lawyers urged the Court to interpret it as a constitutional barrier to limitations on profit. At first some justices were surprised at the proposal; at most, a strict reading of the due process clause would seem to require that state governments follow regular legal procedures in regulating private property. But a dominant business opinion supported by well-financed legal arguments reshaped this view. The due process clause became a constitutional guarantee that owners of private property could enter a successful suit in court against almost all forms of state regulation beyond those protecting the health and safety of the citizen.

FDR's Battles with the Supreme Court

In a normal period the Court would perhaps have gone unchallenged. But in October 1929 the stock market collapsed, and with it the economic certainties of American capitalism. The idea of corporate immunity to government control was thrown on the defensive as ruined speculators, bankrupt merchants, unemployed laborers, and farmers facing foreclosure joined in the demand for sweeping governmental action. From this point forward the Supreme Court became the defense against a major coalition calling for a new economic order.

Thus as the economic crisis deepened a governmental crisis grew. The reform administration of Franklin D. Roosevelt introduced laws to deal with the crisis. But these new laws often ran into the roadblock of the Supreme Court. By 1935, the Court was rejecting as unconstitutional most of the major innovations of the New Deal. Between 1935 and 1937, the Court vetoed a total of twelve congressional statutes—nearly one-seventh of all the federal laws it had declared unconstitutional in nearly two centuries. The Court overturned statutes designed to bring relief to the nation's farmers, the oil industry, the coal industry, and the like.

The Court reasoned that it had no choice; these laws clearly went against constitutional provisions. And the Court appeared to be-

Chief Justice Charles
Evans Hughes.

lieve that it could ignore the rising tide of public disapproval, congressional annoyance, and Presidential frustration. In other words, the Court believed it was above politics and merely carrying out the "automatic" task of comparing laws to the Constitution and rejecting those that did not fit the provisions. In fact, as events showed, it was wrong on both counts. It could not ignore political currents, nor were its decisions inevitable. Other justices would see things differently.

Roosevelt's "Court-Packing" Scheme The lifetime appointments of the justices seemed to protect them against popular sentiment; but in the end their power rested on the acceptance of their legitimacy, and this legitimacy was now fraying rapidly. President Roosevelt, fresh from his second election victory, tried to "pack" the Court through a law allowing him to add new justices. This was blocked, but it was a mere skirmish in the larger battle over judicial supremacy. And that battle was lost by the conservatives when the "swing men" on the Court, Justice Roberts and Chief Justice Hughes, decided to make, in the newspaper language of the day, the "switch in time that saved nine."

Laws hardly distinguishable from those found unconstitutional by 6–3 majorities were now upheld by a majority of five justices. On March 29, 1937, while the debate over the "court-packing" scheme was at its height in Congress, the Court found that the Fourteenth Amendment's due process clause no longer stood in the way—as it had in New York barely a year before—of a minimum-wage law in the state of Washington. Two weeks later, Chief Justice Hughes declared that Congress had the right to establish a National Labor Relations Board to deal with conflicts over union organization and collective-bargaining rights. Four dissenting justices pointed out that in a long train of decisions, including several in the past two years, the Court had ruled so sweeping a grant of power to be unconstitutional; but the Chief Justice simply said, "These cases are not controlling here."

The change in the Supreme Court opened the way for wide government regulation of the economy. In a clash with the other branches of the government, the Supreme Court finally backed down. But of course this should not lead to the conclusion that the Court is the weakest branch of the government; it had dominated economic policy making for almost half a century despite the pressures from the elected branches of the government. It is a powerful institution but, as the events of the 1930s showed, not all-powerful.

The Supreme Court and Racial Discrimination

In the years following the Civil War, the Supreme Court's record shows that it did little to end racial discrimination—in fact some decisions reinforced it. In 1876 the Court severely limited a law aimed at the Ku Klux Klan. In the same year it struck down two provisions of an act designed to secure black voting rights under the Fifteenth Amendment.

The most famous case of the post-Civil War period was *Plessy* v. *Ferguson* (1896)—involving a Louisiana law requiring segregated railroad facilities—in which the Court's decision replaced the principle of "equal protection of the laws" with the racist doctrine of "separate but equal."[3] A nearly unanimous Court held that although the object of the Fourteenth Amendment was undoubtedly to enforce the absolute equality of the two races before the law,

> in the nature of things it could not have intended to abolish distinctions based on color, or to enforce social, as distinct from political equality, or a commingling of the races on terms unsatisfactory to either. . . . Legislation is powerless to eradicate racial instincts or to abolish distinctions based upon physical differences, and the attempt to do so can only result in accentuating the difficulties of the present situation. . . . If one race be inferior to the other socially, the Constitution of the United States cannot put them on the same plane.

So for the next half-century the Supreme Court turned its back on America's black minority. The one exception lay in the field of voting rights. Voting had a special status under the specific prohibitions of the Fifteenth Amendment, and the Court did deal with the more flagrant attempts to deny blacks this most basic of civil rights. As early as 1915, the Court invalidated Oklahoma's "grandfather clause," which required a literacy test of all voters but exempted all lineal descendants of those who had voted before January 1, 1866. Some ten years later, it struck down efforts by Texas to bar blacks from voting in the important primaries of the Democratic party. By the end of World War II, the unconstitutionality of laws barring racial minorities from the polls was no longer at issue.

Civil Rights After World War II

World War II greatly changed the status of black Americans, though its effects were not immediately recognized. Blacks moved northward in large numbers from southern tenant farms to get better-paying jobs in the defense industries, and most of them stayed on afterward as semiskilled laborers to become "swing" constituencies in close elections in the northern cities.

Congress didn't respond to these developments, but President Truman, spurred both by personal conviction and by awareness of the strategic importance of black voters in the northern industrial states, desegregated the armed services by executive order, created a new Fair Employment Practices Committee (FEPC) within the Civil Service Commission, and established a Civil Rights Commission to suggest ways to reduce racial discrimination in public life.

THE SUPREME COURT AND
RACIAL DISCRIMINATION

[3] *Plessy* v. *Ferguson* 163 U.S. 537 (1896).

The NAACP's Fight Against Racial Discrimination

The National Association for the Advancement of Colored People, convinced through experience that Congress could not be made responsive to its demands, decided to expand its longstanding fight in the courts by launching a series of carefully chosen suits to widen the range of constitutionally protected civil rights. Elaborate planning was needed, for experience had shown that litigation seldom brought basic social reforms. The plaintiff might run out of funds or lose interest in the case; he might compromise to accomplish his own purposes before the broad constitutional issues had been raised in appellate courts; or the courts, as they usually did, might find nonconstitutional issues on which to settle the case. Even if the cases were won, the courts might define the constitutional issue so narrowly that the individual case would have little effect on the status of 15 million people. Some of the novel tactics—pro-NAACP articles in law-review journals, for instance, tended to create a favorable climate among external groups (including the attorney general's office), who came to regard themselves as "friends of the court" in the matter—created uneasiness among conservative justices who felt that pressure tactics and demonstrations of popular support were out of place. Nevertheless the NAACP was strikingly successful in a number of cases involving state-supported discrimination in public transportation and housing.

The NAACP's Fight for Equal Education

But the biggest battle for the NAACP still lay ahead. Midway through the twentieth century, the schools of all the southern and border states were still segregated by law, and racially segregated housing patterns resulted in de facto segregation in a high percentage of northern schools as well. And education, as every black parent well knew, determined one's chances in life. For this very reason the question of racial segregation in the public schools was the most explosive civil-rights issue that could be placed on the Supreme Court agenda. Not until the constitutional foundations of racial desegregation had been firmly built up in other, less sensitive areas did the Court show a willingness to hear public-school cases on appeal from the lower courts.

At first the question seemed to be one of substantive equality. To meet the requirement that no person be denied the equal protection of the laws, the Court, in *Plessy* v. *Ferguson,* had said "separate" facilities for blacks could be and were in fact "equal" to those provided whites. That such facilities were inferior was common knowledge, but the Supreme Court for half a century had declined to assess the extent to which the facilities were in fact equal.

Sweatt **v.** *Painter* It was a major victory for the opponents of racial discrimination, then, when the Supreme Court agreed to inquire closely into educational conditions for black Americans in state-

The fight against segration was carried on by the NAACP through the courts.

supported institutions. A key case was *Sweatt* v. *Painter* (1950).[4] Sweatt had been denied admission to the University of Texas Law School solely because he was black. A trial court agreed that he had been unconstitutionally denied the equal protection of the laws but continued the case for six months to give the state time to provide equal facilities for blacks. In 1947 Texas opened the doors of a make-shift law school, with a faculty of five and a library of a few thousand volumes, to 23 black students. Sweatt refused to accept this over-night institution as the equivalent of a law school with a student body of 850, a library of 65,000 volumes, and a distinguished faculty. He carried his case to the Supreme Court. The Court had little diffi-culty in finding it a matter of fact that the whites-only University of Texas Law School had much better facilities. In a noteworthy pas-sage, Chief Justice Vinson declared that a

> law school, the proving ground for legal learning and practice, cannot be effective in isolation from the individuals and institutions with which the law interacts. . . . The law school to which Texas is willing to admit petitioner excludes from its student body members of the racial groups which number 85 percent of the population of the State and includes most of the lawyers, witnesses, jurors, judges, and other officials with whom petitioner inevitably will be dealing when he becomes a member of the Texas bar.

"With such a substantial and significant segment of society ex-cluded," said the Chief Justice, no school, whatever its facilities, could offer Sweatt an equal chance to get the experience and social contacts needed for successful participation in a nation dominated by whites.

With *Sweatt* v. *Painter* the long struggle to establish the fallacy of the "separate but equal" doctrine came to a close. It remained only to make clear to the general public how these principles applied to segregation in public schools.

Brown* v. *Board of Education of Topeka The NAACP believed it had at last found the ideal test case in *Brown* v. *Board of Education of Topeka* (1954) for making the Supreme Court speak directly on the constitutional status of the "separate but equal" doctrine.[5] The

[4] *Sweatt* v. *Painter* 339 U.S. 629 (1950).
[5] *Brown* v. *Board of Education of Topeka* 347 U.S. 483 (1954).

schools for black children in Topeka, Kansas, were equal to white schools in all respects—physical plant and equipment, curricula, courses available, qualifications and quality of teachers. Yet the basic difference, and the one to be cited by the Court, was that black children were not allowed to go to school with white children, and of course the opposite held as well. In 1954 a unanimous Court ruled that "in the field of public education the doctrine of 'separate but equal' has no place." The assertion of the Court was that "separate educational facilities are inherently unequal."

With this decision the Supreme Court reshaped the agenda of modern American politics. Racial discrimination could no longer be thought of as consistent with the constitutional principle of equality before the law. For another ten years, however, the judiciary was left to struggle on practically alone with the huge job of implementing the government's newly defined legal and moral responsibility to black citizens. The executive branch did little, and only in 1964 did Congress begin to respond positively.

Desegregation of the schools is a highly sensitive, complicated problem that cannot be easily and readily solved. It is far from being settled, as the Controversy at the end of this chapter makes clear.

The Warren Court: Judicial Activism

Earl Warren was Chief Justice from 1954 to 1969. Following custom, the Supreme Court was known as the Warren Court during this fifteen-year period. It was also known as an activist court, for in many areas the Supreme Court was at the center of major controversies.

We have already noted that the Warren Court made the landmark decision on school desegregation. This was only the first of a series of decisions that tried to reshape race relations in the United States. For instance, in cases affecting voting rights the Supreme Court declared unconstitutional the requirement that a candidate's race be noted on a ballot and the drawing of political districts along racial lines.

One Man, One Vote

Race relations was one area in which the Warren Court took the initiative, replacing both Congress and the Presidency as the agent of reform. Other, perhaps more controversial, areas of reform were the vote and political representation. Before the 1960s state legislatures drew the boundaries of state and congressional districts with little regard for the number of people in a given district. A legislator elected from a rural district might represent only 25,000 voters; one from an urban area might represent ten times that many voters. This struck the Warren Court as unfair. Does the voter who is one of 250,000 have the same voting rights as the voter who is one of 25,000? No, said the Court. In *Baker* v. *Carr* (1962) the Supreme Court held that equal protection of the law is denied when legislative seats are not assigned according to population.[6] If American citizens were moving from the farms and small towns to the suburbs and big cities, then it was only right that the number of representatives to be elected would move likewise. If half the voters of Illinois lived in Chicago, then half the state legislators would come from Chicago, leaving all the rest of the state to be represented by the other half. The "one man, one vote" ruling was extended in the following three cases:

Westbury v. *Sanders* 376 U.S. 1 (1964)
The ruling of *Baker* v. *Carr* applied to election districts for state legislatures. Now the "one man, one vote" ruling is applied to congressional districts, which should have "as nearly as practicable" equal population.

Reynolds v. *Sims* 377 U.S. 533 (1964)
The "one man, one vote" rule applies to both houses of state legislatures, thus declaring unconstitutional the practice in some states of assigning seats in one house according to population size but in the other house according to other criteria.

Of course this ruling could not be applied to the national Congress, for the number of seats in the Senate is fixed at two for each state—no matter how many voters live in the state.

Kirkpatrick v. *Preisler* 394 U.S. 526 (1969)
It is the responsibility of the states to draw election districts with precisely equal populations. If Missouri has ten representatives, then each congressional district should have as close as possible to one-tenth of the population of Missouri. Any deviation from mathematical average must be justified by the state.

Criminal Due Process   Earlier in this chapter we emphasized that justice in the United States depends on an adversary process— someone argues for and someone against the person accused of a crime. The judge, or the judge and jury, are not fact finders; they listen to the facts presented by counsel for and prosecutor against the defendant.

Where do the facts come from that are presented to the judge or the jury? Very often they come from investigations carried out by the police, including questioning (some would say "police grilling") of the suspect. What if the suspect is uneducated and poor, too uneducated to fully understand the ins and outs of the law and too poor to hire a lawyer? The Warren Court considered such a situation in *Gideon* v. *Wainwright* (1963).[7] A majority of the Court felt that the adversary system of justice made no sense if only one party, the police and the prosecution, had the resources to conduct investigations. Moreover, if a criminal suspect answered police questions, he might easily hurt his own case. The Court ruled that if the defendant

[6] *Baker* v. *Carr* 369 U.S. 186 (1962).
[7] *Gideon* v. *Wainwright* 372 U.S. 335 (1963).

is too poor to hire a lawyer, the state must supply him with one. This had led to a great expansion of the public defender system in the United States. There are now more than 700 county, city, and state defender offices that provide legal counsel to the poor.

The Gideon ruling was extended in a series of other cases on criminal justice. Not only was the government responsible to provide counsel in the courtroom; counsel should be provided even at the pretrial and investigatory stages. Even police questioning must be delayed until a lawyer is present, if the defendant requests counsel. And to make sure a suspect knows his rights, the police must immediately tell him he may remain silent until a lawyer is available.

In other aspects of criminal due process, the Warren Court held that no evidence obtained in an illegal search could be used in a federal court, that wiretapping was "search and seizure" and could not be used as evidence unless it had been authorized by a warrant, and put an end to vaguely justified "evidence hunts" by the police.

The Burger Court: Judicial Restraint

The role of the Warren Court in protecting the rights of criminals was strongly criticized in many quarters. There were calls for the impeachment of Chief Justice Warren. A favorite campaign theme of Nixon, seeking the Presidency in 1968, was that he would restore law and order. Nixon attacked the permissiveness in society that, he charged, allowed blacks to burn down ghetto stores, university students to take over campus buildings, anti-war demonstrators to disrupt government business, and criminals to go unpunished. He spoke of the "coddling of criminals" and accused the Supreme Court of "seriously hamstringing the peace forces in our society."

The Burger Court.

Table 12.1
Members of the
Supreme Court, 1975

Member	Appointed by	Year
William O. Douglas	Roosevelt	1939
William J. Brennan, Jr.	Eisenhower	1957
Potter Stewart	Eisenhower	1959
Byron R. White	Kennedy	1962
Thurgood Marshall	Johnson	1967
Warren E. Burger	Nixon	1969
Harry A. Blackmun	Nixon	1970
Lewis F. Powell, Jr.	Nixon	1971
William H. Rehnquist	Nixon	1971

Nixon pledged to appoint to the Supreme Court only judges who would be strictly bound by the Constitution. Shortly after Nixon's election he was given a chance to fulfill his campaign pledge. Warren resigned from the Court, and Nixon was able to choose a chief justice who would reflect his political and judicial philosophy. The appointment of a new chief justice, according to Nixon, was the most important one a President could make. "Our history tells us that the chief justices have probably had more profound and lasting influence on their times and on the direction of the nation than most Presidents have had."

Nixon selected Warren Burger, a man who had clearly spoken out against the activism of the Warren Court. And within the first three years of his Presidency Nixon was able to make three more appointments to the Court. (See Table 12.1.) In every case he chose justices who were conservative in outlook.

And though the Burger Court has been in some ways more cautious than the Warren Court, it has by no means reversed the trends established under Chief Justice Warren. The rulings of the Warren Court in desegregation cases and in criminal law processes have now become precedents. In recent years the Supreme Court has approved the use of busing to integrate schools, has outlawed the death penalty in criminal cases, has rejected the claim of the Nixon administration that it did not have to get Court approval before using wiretaps on suspected subversives, and has ruled against Nixon's claim that the Watergate tapes were protected by executive privilege. The latter ruling was important in Nixon's decision to resign.

The Supreme Court and American Politics

To some observers the Supreme Court has always been an anomaly. What place has a body of officials appointed for life in a government based on accountability through elections? And in a government where one power is supposed to balance another, what place has a body with supposedly "supreme" power over the interpretation of the Constitution? But as the Court's history makes clear, the United States Supreme Court is by no means all-powerful.

Limitations on the Power of the Court

For one thing, the Supreme Court decides on the constitutionality of laws within the framework of the Constitution and the precedents of previous cases. This greatly limits the Court's ability to write into a decision anything it sees fit. Some observers claim that the Supreme Court's activity is therefore automatic; justices merely compare the clear words of the Constitution with the act of Congress or the state legislature that is in question. Justice Roberts of the Supreme Court stated this position:

> It is sometimes said that the court assumes a power to overrule or control the action of the people's representatives. . . . This is a misconception. . . . When an act of Congress is appropriately challenged in the courts as not conforming to the constitutional mandate, the judicial branch of the Government has only one duty—to lay the article of the Constitution which is invoked beside the statute which is challenged and to decide whether the latter squares with the former.

Most observers of the Supreme Court, however, would disagree with Justice Roberts. Indeed this statement was made in one of the most controversial decisions of the Supreme Court, the one that struck down the first Agricultural Adjustment Act, on which the hope of millions of desperate farmers had rested. Comparing the statute being challenged with the Constitution to see if the former squared with the latter was hardly a mechanical act. In fact within a few years the Supreme Court had changed its mind on the issue.

The point is that the Constitution is rarely clear and unambiguous. Indeed it has survived throughout the years largely by being ambiguous—so later generations could interpret it to fit the times. When the Court rules on the constitutionality of a law, it is guided by the Constitution; but it still must *interpret,* and there it uses discretion. At times it has been criticized for interpreting the Constitution too loosely, at other times for not interpreting it loosely enough. These controversies will continue, for the Court's actions are not automatic.

Political Restraint   Another limitation on the powers of the Court is what may be called a political restraint. A widespread misconception about the Supreme Court is that it is isolated from the mainstream of politics or the "real world." In part this is true. The justices are not up for election; they do stay out of party politics; they are not directly visited by lobbyists or constituents. They are, as the founders intended them to be, above politics in this sense.

Yet the justices are by no means cut off from the currents of American politics and from the preferences of the public. For one thing, they are appointed by Presidents interested in certain policies. Franklin D. Roosevelt, thwarted in his attempts at economic reform in the 1930s, appointed justices he believed would read the Constitution permissively when it came to expansion of federal power. More recently President Nixon appointed justices he believed would reverse what he considered overpermissiveness of the Court in matters of criminal prosecution.

Even after appointment justices remain attuned to the "temper of the times." The justices do not just read the Constitution—they read the newspapers as well. It would be an exaggeration to say that the justices write their opinions on the basis of the last election. But there is evidence that they are sensitive to election results. This was seen in the 1930s, when the Court switched from defending free enterprise against government controls to allowing the government to enact a wide range of controls over the economy.

Self-Imposed Restraints   A further limitation on the power of the justices is self-imposed. The Court ignores certain issues, even though they may be of major constitutional significance. For instance, it has rarely taken any position on the powers of the President in the area of foreign and military affairs. During the late 1960s and early 1970s, the question of the constitutionality of the war in Vietnam was raised. There had been no declaration of war by Congress, yet the power to declare war was given to Congress in the Constitution. The Vietnam policies of Presidents Johnson and Nixon clearly raised a constitutional issue. Yet the Court refused to challenge the actions of the government in Vietnam.

Overruling by Amendment and by Avoiding Compliance   The power of the Supreme Court is limited in another way. Even after it has declared an act unconstitutional, the Court can be overruled. One way is through constitutional amendment. This, as we have pointed out, is usually a slow and cumbersome process. But the Sixteenth Amendment directly overruled a Supreme Court decision barring the federal government from levying a federal income tax.

The amendment process is not the only way Supreme Court rulings can be negated. The Supreme Court cannot enforce its decisions. Although government officials usually will not openly disobey the Court, there are many ways they can avoid compliance. In cases where local officials disagree with a Court ruling, they can be very successful in limiting its effect. Two areas of concern where this has been the case involve the Court's decisions on school desegregation and on barring prayers in the public schools. In each case compliance has often been avoided.

Congressional Control over the Court's Powers   Finally, the powers of the Supreme Court are limited by congressional powers to approve appointments and to impeach justices for misconduct in office.

The Court System

We have treated the Supreme Court at length because of its unique role in American politics. But it is actually part of a complex system of federal, state, and municipal courts, as shown in Figure 12.1.

Figure 12.1
The Judicial System

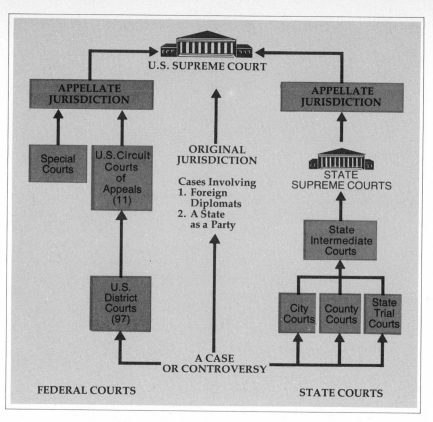

The Federal Judicial System

The federal judicial system has three layers: The Supreme Court is the top layer, circuit courts the middle layer, and district courts the foundation. There are also special courts for cases involving customs, patents, and the military.

The Supreme Court has both original and appellate jurisdiction. To have *original* jurisdiction means that cases can start, or originate, before the Supreme Court. In only two kinds of cases does the Supreme Court have original jurisdiction: (1) cases that involve ambassadors and other public ministers; (2) cases that involve a dispute between states, for instance, a case involving a disagreement over state borders, as when the Court determined which branch of the Red River was the boundary between Texas and Oklahoma.

Appellate jurisdiction means cases come before the Court because they are appealed from lower courts. The Supreme Court hears cases appealed from lower federal courts and from state supreme courts. Certain kinds of appeals from state courts must be heard by the Supreme Court: when a state law has been challenged on grounds that it is unconstitutional and the law has been upheld by the state court, and when a treaty or statute of the United States has been declared invalid by a state court.

Circuit Courts of Appeals Most cases come before the Supreme Court on appeal from circuit courts. There are at present 11 such courts in the nation, each with jurisdiction over a particular area. The circuit courts were created in 1891 to ease the burden on the Supreme Court and to make handling of cases in the federal judicial system easier. These courts have between 3 and 15 judges, depending on the number of cases generally tried in the circuit or region for which the court has responsibility. The circuit courts are called courts of appeal because they have no original jurisdiction; they hear only cases appealed from lower courts. Only the Supreme Court can review the decision of a circuit court.

District Courts Ninety-seven district courts, along with 4 territorial courts (Canal Zone, Guam, Puerto Rico, and Virgin Islands), try the great majority of the cases that enter the federal court system. Populous states like California have as many as four district courts, but the normal arrangement is for a district court to coincide with state boundaries. A large district court might have as many as 24 judges, though the work load would be divided and often only 3 judges will hear a case. District courts hear cases that involve citizens from different states (an automobile accident involving an Iowa driver and an Illinois pedestrian, for instance) or transportation of stolen goods across state lines. District courts also try cases involving violations of federal laws—immigration, counterfeiting, antitrust, food and drug, income tax, mail fraud, and so forth.

State Judiciary Systems In addition to the federal judiciary system, each state has its own judiciary system. Some of these systems are very complicated. State systems are often organized on a county or district basis, which leads to decentralization. Generally, however, a state court can be classified at one of three levels:

1. TRIAL COURTS Called different things depending on the area, these courts try minor criminal cases: traffic violations, disturbing the peace, petty theft. In rural areas, these are the justice of the peace courts, often headed by people without formal legal training. In a city, these lower-level trial courts are called police courts, city courts, or municipal courts.

   More serious crimes are heard in major trial courts, sometimes known as superior courts or county courts. Here the defendant might have trial by jury. The jurisdiction of such courts is normally fixed by state legislatures. Murder, burglary, rape, and other felonies are tried in these courts.

2. INTERMEDIATE COURTS OF APPEALS Larger states have courts of appeal, which review cases from trial courts at the county or municipal level and form a layer between trial courts and state supreme courts.

3. STATE SUPREME COURTS Each state has a supreme court, which plays a role similar to that of the United States Supreme Court. They hear cases on appeal from lower state courts and in some cases have original jurisdiction.

	Democrats	Republicans	Same Party as President
Roosevelt (D)	188	6	96%
Truman (D)	116	9	93%
Eisenhower (R)	9	165	95%
Kennedy (D)	111	11	90%
Johnson (D)	159	9	95%
Nixon (R)	18	220	93%

Source: Based on data from *Nixon: The Fourth Year of His Presidency* (Washington, D.C.: *Congressional Quarterly*, 1973), and updated from the *Chicago Tribune*.

Selection of Judges   Because there are two distinct judicial systems, federal and state, there are two different kinds of judges. All federal judges are appointed by the President, though they must be approved by the Senate. The appointment of federal judges is usually done on a party basis—a Republican President appointing Republican judges and a Democratic President appointing Democratic judges. Table 12.2 shows the percentage of judicial appointments that comes from the political party of the appointing President. As Philip B. Kurland, professor of law at the University of Chicago, says, "The judiciary has long been treated as the place to put political workhorses out to pasture. The great majority of America's judges have their posts because—and only because—of prior services rendered to the dominant political party."

Selection of judges at the state and local levels is done by appointment, election, or both. The most frequent arrangement, found in 38 states, is popular election with terms lasting anywhere from 2 years to life. In other states the judges are appointed by the governor with approval by the legislature. And in some cases the judges are chosen directly by the legislatures. About a dozen states use a combination of appointment and election patterned on the arrangement introduced in Missouri in 1940 and called the Missouri Plan: (1) A nonpartisan commission of lawyers, citizens, and a judge nominate candidates for judgeships; (2) the governor appoints judges from the nominees; (3) voters approve or withhold approval after the judge has served an initial term on the bench.

Few are satisfied with the way judges are selected in the United States, for it seems that no matter what the formal arrangement it is the politicians who in fact select judges. Politically chosen judges, whether or not ratified by voters, are not always respected by citizens. And, as concluded by a Presidential task force on justice, the quality of the judiciary largely determines the quality of justice.

The Politics of a Dual Court System

Federalism imposed on a judicial system results in two sets of courts, federal and state. These courts have overlapping, competing, and sometimes conflicting jurisdictions. It all adds up to a complicated judicial system. But very little has been done to try to straighten it out. One student of the American judiciary writes: "The most important observation about change in court structure is that extraordinarily little of it has occurred in the last century."[8] There are several reasons for this.

Different Courts Service Different Interests   The existence of both a federal and a state judicial system offers alternatives to someone seeking a favorable court ruling. A southern black, for instance, would usually prefer to have a civil-rights case heard in a federal district court than before the local magistrate. Southern judges, especially when elected by white voters, have not welcomed claims for equal treatment by blacks.

The federal system might also be preferred when an interest group wants uniform regulation across the entire country. This goal led business interests to try to get the commerce clause included in the Constitution. If each state regulated the transport and handling of goods differently interstate commerce would be nearly impossible.

But of course sometimes it is to the benefit of a local group to have the case heard in a state court. The state court system has long been used in the struggle to protect state sovereignty. Arizona, for instance, resisted the federal government's attempt to build Hoover Dam without first getting the approval of the Arizona state engineer, though it was overruled by the United States Supreme Court. The states have used their own court systems to adjudicate cases stemming from taxation policies, including state taxes on certain transactions with federal agencies.

The Participants Have a Stake   Any attempt to reform the judiciary system would certainly affect, often negatively, the interests of lawyers and judges who earn their living in the courts. Attorneys, for example, oppose changes in the court structure for fear it will disrupt established routines and contacts. Moreover, they fully recognize that the maze of courts provides many points where they can press the claims of their clients. If a client might suffer in the federal system, they try to get the case into the state system, or vice versa.

Judges, too, often oppose reform. No individual judge can be certain that his or her position would be protected in the event of major changes. Particularly opposed are changes that might take the "politics" out of judicial selection — for this would deny many judges their jobs and take from political parties one of their main sources of patronage.

The Nonspecialized Judiciary   All in all, then, the judicial system struggles to deal with twentieth-century problems with the structures and processes of the nineteenth century. While the executive

[8] Herbert Jacob, *Urban Justice* (Englewood Cliffs, N.J.: Prentice-Hall, 1973), p. 91. The argument in this section also relies on the same author's *Justice in America* (Boston: Little, Brown, 1965), chap. 8.

branch of government has specialized into dozens of departments and hundreds of agencies and the legislative branch has delegated tasks to committees, the judicial branch has been very much the same for nearly a hundred years. Judges are generalists, expected to hear cases ranging all the way from criminal conspiracy to divorce. But in recent years the problems of justice in American society have become great. Pressures for change in the judiciary are stronger now than at any time in the recent past.

Controversy

In the early 1970s the Supreme Court as well as the other federal courts became involved in an explosive controversy over the courts' attempts to have schoolchildren bused to achieve desegregation of schools. *Brown* v. *Board of Education of Topeka* had ruled that legal segregation of the public schools violated the Constitution. But as the years passed it became clear that abolishing legal segregation would not necessarily eliminate segregated schools. The reason was obvious. In many parts of the country, housing patterns had developed in which black Americans and other minority groups lived in separate sections of metropolitan areas — usually in the center of the city — while whites lived in other neighborhoods and in the suburbs. If children went to neighborhood schools, they usually went to schools that were de facto segregated. Some courts, therefore, decided that only by busing schoolchildren from one neighborhood to another, or even from one community to another, could segregation be eliminated.

One Side

Busing schoolchildren is the only way to end de facto segregation. Under the Brown doctrine segregated schools violate the Constitution whether they are the result of state laws or of housing patterns. To put an end to de facto segregated schools, white pupils must be bused into black neighborhoods, or even from community to community, and black students bused into white areas.

There is also the question of which branch of the government should enforce desegregation of the schools. It is the constitutional duty of the courts to do so. The President, Congress, and state legislatures are powerless to act effectively because of the political pressures on them. To be sure, the courts may not be the best place to formulate regulations for school desegregation, but in the absence of action by the other branches of the government, they are the only place where such action can be taken.

The Supreme Court is well aware of the complexity of the problem — it has taken on a big job that it has to do alone, with little aid from the executive and legislative branches of government — and in several cases it has written enforcement decisions on desegregation. Admittedly the Court has not made a definitive decision on desegregation, but perhaps this is due to judicial sensitivity to the complexity of the issue and the intense feelings surrounding it. And it may be that in view of the opposition to busing the Court is following its own directions to the federal district courts in the Brown decision: Require the local state officials to move toward integration "with all deliberate speed."

The Other Side

The only way to end de facto school segregation is to break down the barriers that force blacks and other minority groups to live in separate areas. The solution is to get rid of the ghettos. Under the Brown doctrine de facto segregated schools do not violate the Constitution. Some courts have ruled to this effect: The Brown decision, they have decided, applies only to those cases where segregation is the result of *discrimination by intent.*

The legislature and the executive should enforce desegregation —not the courts. If the courts rule that a local district has to bus children from one neighborhood to another to achieve racial balance—or even from one community to another, as some court decisions that demanded the merging of central-city and suburban districts would have required—the courts are taking over the law-making role of the legislature, ignoring the opinions of the community, and reading the Constitution as they see fit, influenced perhaps by the personal preferences of the justices.

Further, issues such as redrawing school boundaries and making plans for busing children from one area to another are too sensitive and complicated to be handled by adversary proceedings in court.

Besides, court decisions can be avoided. Various members of Congress considered introducing a constitutional amendment barring the busing of children to reduce segregation. Laws were passed, such as the Higher Education Act of 1972, which attempted to restrict the use of busing for desegregation purposes. (The constitutionality of the laws still, of course, requires a court test.) And as might be expected in the light of his views on busing, President Nixon made new appointments to change the direction of Court decisions on desegregation. This made the Court more divided on the issue (though still leaning in the activist direction).

Then there is the role of the Supreme Court itself in enforcing desegregation. Granted, the Court took on a huge job when it made the Brown ruling. This is a sociological decision, and such decisions are hard to enforce; it is not easy to change a person's attitudes, beliefs, and way of living. And if, as some think, the courts are the only place where movement toward desegregation can take place, why hasn't the Court made a definitive enforcement decision rather than, for the most part, leaving the responsibility to the lower courts?

This conflict brings to mind another time when the Supreme Court raised a tornado of anti-Court feelings. In the New Deal era of the 1930s, the Court came under fire when it continued to defend big business against the wishes of the people and their elected representatives for regulation of the economy. Then, sensitive to the climate of opinion, the Court reversed its position. As in the 1930s, the busing issue in the 1970s generated a series of attacks on the Court by many political forces: by Congress, by the state legislatures, by the press, and in political campaigns. And, as in the 1930s, again the cry was "legislative usurpation."

Finally, there are the views of the majority of the citizens. Whether or not the courts are moving against the current of public opinion is not yet clear. If this is the case, we must ask the question, Has the Court the right to enforce busing to integrate the schools if such a policy goes against the will of the majority of the citizens?

How Institutions Work: V
The Judicial Appeal Process

When may a judicial decision be appealed?

Appellate courts hear only cases that are appealed after the completion of a trial. Almost every litigant who takes his case to court has the right to an appeal.

How does an appeals court differ from a trial court?

Appeals courts do not operate under the same rules as trial courts. The appeals court does not retry the case being appealed but, rather, works from the record of the original trial, from the appeal briefs filed by the attorneys, and from the oral arguments presented. To win a case on appeal, a litigant must normally show that the trial court misconstrued the case before it, made procedural errors, applied the wrong legal rules, or drew a clearly mistaken conclusion from the evidence. Besides preventing miscarriages of justice, appeals courts make the interpretation of laws and the administration of justice more uniform.

What is the structure of the appeals court system?

As Figure 12.1 shows, there are two levels of appeals courts, one federal and one state. The eleven U.S. circuit courts of appeals hear all appeals from federal district agencies. The federal appeals courts each operate with from 3 to 15 judges. Unlike trials, appeals are heard by a panel of judges, usually 3. There is never a jury in an appellate proceeding. Although the circuit courts must hear all appeals brought to them from the district courts, only a small portion of cases filed in district courts are actually appealed.

Also part of the appeals structure are several special federal courts, including the Court of Claims, the Court of Customs and Patent Appeals, and the Court of Military Appeals.

The appeals structure of fewer than half the states includes state intermediate courts. All states, however, have a highest court of appeals, usually called the state supreme court. Like the federal circuit courts, most state supreme courts must hear every case brought before them. Procedures used in these courts vary widely across the country, although in all states cases are decided by a majority vote of the justices.

How do cases reach the United States Supreme Court?

As indicated in Figure 12.1, appellate cases may come to the Supreme Court from the circuit courts, from the special courts, or from the state supreme courts. The procedures by which cases reach the Supreme Court from other courts is complex. Generally speaking, two ways are used: appeal or certiorari. The appeal procedure is used when the issue at stake is a jurisdictional one between the states and the federal government. But most cases are brought to the Supreme Court by a writ of certiorari (from the Latin "to be made more certain"). The losing party in a federal court of appeals or in a state supreme court, if his claim involves a question of federal law, may petition the Court to hear his case.

How do the justices decide which cases to take?

Unlike most other appeals courts, the Supreme Court can almost always decide which cases it will hear. After examining the requests for review, the justices vote on each one. If four justices vote in favor, a case is put on the docket; if not, the case is rejected and the decision of the lower court stands.

A case stands little chance of being heard by the Supreme Court unless the issues it raises are major. The justices realize that they cannot correct every judicial error. Instead, the Court serves as the highest judicial vehicle for settling public policy conflicts. This concern with public policy is why the Court often accepts supporting briefs of those who act as *amicus curiae* or "friends of the court" in a particular case. The federal government or private interest groups may seek such status in order to argue the political and social as well as legal implications of a given case.

How many cases does the Supreme Court hear?

Altogether, the Court now receives over 4000 petitions a year. The justices usually agree to hear fewer than 300 of these.

Is the decision of the United States Supreme Court the final judicial action in a case?

It depends. Only when the Court upholds the lower court's action does the litigation cease. When the Supreme Court reverses a lower-court decision, the case may be retried. Litigants who succeed before the Supreme Court may thus win the affirmation of a principle only to lose their case in retrial on the particular evidence in question.

13

The Separation of Powers

The framers of the Constitution faced a dilemma: They wanted to create a national government with the power to act, and they wanted to limit that power. The weak government created by the Articles of Confederation made it clear that more power was needed in the central government. But as a colony under the arbitrary authority of the British Parliament and Crown they had seen that power could be abused unless it was checked.

How does one create power and at the same time hold it in check? In the next chapter we see one way this can be done. The Constitution created a national government capable of passing laws, but it put limitations on the laws it could pass; in particular, it limited the extent to which the government could interfere with the freedom of the citizen.

There is another major way in which the Constitution attempts to limit the power of the government: It restricts the power of any particular branch of the government. Just as the government does not have absolute power over citizens, so no one part of the government has absolute power over any other. This system of *separation of powers* or *checks and balances* works as an internal check on the abuse of power.

As with most constitutional innovations, the system of checks and balances has not worked out exactly as the founders imagined. Yet it has been a major force in American politics.

The Constitutional Framework

The writers of the Constitution knew there could be no nation unless the government had power over the citizens. It needed the authority to tax, to regulate the actions of citizens, to make binding contracts, and to punish offenders. Still, they were cautious about giving these governmental powers to any single group of men, especially because it would necessarily be a small group.

The founders created a complex system of divided powers. Those in one branch of the government were given the constitutional means to resist domination by others, thus keeping any single interest from having complete authority. *The Federalist* (No. 51) remarked that external controls over government by the public are always inadequate. The defect must be remedied "by so contriving the interior structure of the government so that its several constituent parts may, by their mutual relations, be the means of keeping each other in their proper place." Here, then, was the principle of fragmenting authority. And in a passage that clearly expresses the assumptions behind this principle, *The Federalist* (No. 51) continues:

> Ambition must be made to counteract ambition. It may be a reflection on human nature, that such devices should be necessary to control the abuses of government. But what is government itself, but the greatest

of all reflections on human nature? If men were angels, no government would be necessary. If angels were to govern men, neither external nor internal controls on government would be necessary. In framing a government which is to be administered by men over men, the great difficulty lies in this: you must first enable the government to control the governed; and in the next place oblige it to control itself.

Separation of Powers

These internal controls over government were achieved through the famous separation-of-powers system. *The Federalist* (No. 47) proclaims that "the accumulation of all powers, legislative, executive, and judiciary, in the same hands, whether of one, a few, or many, and whether hereditary, self-appointed, or elective, may justly be pronounced the very definition of tyranny." To prevent tyranny the government was divided into three separate branches: one that makes laws, one that executes the laws, and one that hears disputes arising out of conflicting interpretations of the laws.

This separation of the federal government into legislative, executive, and judicial branches was, according to *The Federalist*, to accomplish three goals.

First, the powers of government were to be fragmented. Thus the federal form of government was complemented by separation of powers. The argument is stated clearly in *The Federalist* (No. 51):

> In the compound Republic of America, the power surrendered by the people is first divided between two distinct governments (Federal government and the States), and then the portion allotted to each subdivided among distinct and separate departments. Hence, a double security rises to the rights of the people. The different governments will control each other, at the same time that each will be controlled by itself.

Second, through a checks-and-balances system each branch of government could check the activities of the others. There are many examples. Congress legislates, but the President can veto a law of Congress. Then again Congress can override the veto, though it takes a two-thirds vote. The President appoints judges, but they must be confirmed by the Senate. The judges are appointed for life, unless impeachment proceedings begun in Congress are successful. So it goes throughout the federal government, and every state government as well: a multitude of cross-checking restraints on authority. Table 13.1 shows how often some of these restraints have been used.

Third, the kinds of checks and balances just described mean various units of government must cooperate with one another to reach common goals. A wider range of interests is thereby reflected in governmental policy. Moreover, each branch has its own outlook. The blending of these different perspectives should, in theory, result in better government. The system of separated functions also requires a greater effort at communication among various groups.

Table 13.1
The Use of Checks
and Balances, 1789–1970

> *Between 1789 and 1970*
> _____
>
> There were 2255 Presidential vetoes of congressional acts.
> Congress subsequently overruled 75 of those vetoes.
> The Supreme Court ruled 85 congressional acts or parts of acts
>   unconstitutional.
> The Senate refused to confirm 27 nominees to the Supreme Court (out of a
>   total of 138 nominees).
> Congress impeached 9 federal judges; of these, 4 were convicted. The Senate
>   rejected 8 Cabinet nominations.

Source: *Senate Library, Presidential Vetoes* (New York: Greenwood Press, 1968); *Congressional Quarterly;* and *Current American Government* (Washington, D.C.: *Congressional Quarterly,* Spring 1973), p. 106.

This is more likely to produce a true "national interest" than a government under the control of a single branch.

It cannot be said that each of these goals has always been achieved in American political history. The separation-of-powers system has worked out differently than the founders thought it would. Yet the fragmentation of authority and need for cooperation remain basic features of the government. And over the years the goals of the founders have been remarkably well served.

Separation of Powers in Action

Like all constitutional provisions, separation of powers has undergone constant change. The Constitution never made it completely clear how the various branches were to relate to each other. In Chapter 12, for instance, we saw how the key power of judicial review by the Supreme Court evolved over time in ways not clearly foreseen by the writers of the Constitution.

In one sense the founders' design has been preserved. The three branches of the national government—the President, Congress, and the Supreme Court—remain centers of real power, independent of each other. The relative power of the branches has varied. At times one has appeared to be stronger and the others weaker. But each has played an important role at most stages of U.S. history.

On the other hand, the three branches have not functioned as the founders expected. Each was supposed to do one specialized job: Congress to make laws, the President to execute them, and the courts to interpret them. In fact, the three branches share these functions.

Congress does pass laws, but the executive and judicial branches take an important part in the lawmaking function as well. The legislative power of the President goes well beyond his constitutional power to veto laws. Much legislation begins in the executive departments or is part of the "President's program." Similarly the Court's legislative power goes well beyond the judicial review of legislation. In some fields the courts have made laws that govern

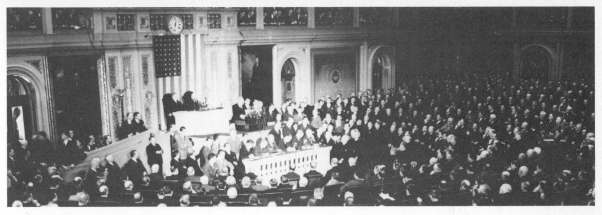

President Roosevelt asking
Congress for a declaration of
war, December 8, 1941.

citizen behavior as much as any law of Congress. School desegregation is one example. Decisions of the Supreme Court and the lower courts have often prescribed general rules for integration of the schools.

Nor is the power to carry out the laws limited to the executive branch. Courts have played a major role in this; along with many of the desegregation rulings, the courts have given detailed instructions on how to administer the ruling, and have followed this up by closely supervising the local school boards. Congress is also involved in the administration of laws. Many of its committees watch very closely over the way government agencies carry out the law.

The present system in the United States has been described as a *system of separate institutions sharing powers* rather than a system of separation of powers. The three branches set up by the Constitution remain strong and independent, but their functions overlap. Perhaps the most important overlap is between the legislative powers of Congress and the President. In recent years legislation has tended to be started in the executive branch. Congress ''enacts the President's program.'' This suggests a passive Congress. But is that the case?

The Battle Between Congress and the Presidency

The press often exaggerates the power of the Presidency in making public policy. It refers to Johnson's War on Poverty or Nixon's Revenue-Sharing Plan. But seldom will a major Presidential program be passed without any changes. An executive proposal sent to Congress is reworked, and the final bill is a compromise between congressional and Presidential wishes.

Influence of Strong Congressional Leaders When Congress doesn't like a President's program, not much of it will become law. Running for the Presidency in 1960, Kennedy proclaimed his New Frontier in speech after speech. Perhaps that slogan helped him win, but it did not affect the victories of a half-dozen conservative southern senators who headed major Senate committees. James Eastland, the powerful Democrat from Mississippi, won his Senate seat with 91 percent of the vote in Mississippi while Kennedy was winning the Presidency by only 0.1 percent. Senators like Eastland had strong positions in Congress and voter support back home. Once in office, Kennedy had little success instituting his New Frontier program against such powerful congressional leaders as Eastland. The President pushed through no civil-rights legislation, for instance, leaving that issue to the law courts and the attorney general's office.

One source of congressional strength, as already noted, is its roots back home. The Washington community, especially the executive branch, is more isolated from "public sentiment" than is generally thought. As one long-time observer of Washington politics concludes,

> congressional sentiment tends to be officialdom's pragmatic substitute for "public opinion" because it is on Congress, not the general public, that officials must depend, day after day, for legislation and for funds to keep programs and personnel alive. And bureaucrats are not the only ones who make that substitution. For comparable reasons it is made, much of the time, by diplomats of many countries, officers of every state, representatives of private interests, local party leaders, and even congressmen themselves.[1]

Congress' Legal Power over the Executive Branch Congress also has very specific legal powers over the executive branch. The four most significant powers held by Congress are the following:

1. ORGANIZATION The departments and agencies of the executive branch are created by acts of Congress.
2. AUTHORIZATION Executive agencies operate within boundaries and on programs established by congressional legislation. The National Aeronautics and Space Administration (NASA) cannot design just any space program it wants to; its programs and its very existence depend on congressional authorization.
3. FINANCING Congress controls the purse strings, and programs that are not funded cannot be implemented. In a bitter battle between the President and Congress in 1970, Congress refused to provide funds for the development of a supersonic transport (the SST), and Nixon had no choice but to let the project drop.
4. REVIEW The executive agencies are subject to inquiry by Congress. Public hearings by a hostile congressional committee can embarrass an agency and do much to change administration policy.

Congress has not, in recent decades, used its powers to the fullest. This has led some observers to conclude that Congress no longer checks the executive. "No matter how hard the Congress may struggle on one issue, it is overwhelmed by the vastly greater forces of the presidency. Whether Congress wins or loses, the President ends

[1] Richard E. Neustadt, *Presidential Power* (New York: Wiley, 1962), p. 89.

up on top," is the conclusion reached by the Ralph Nader Congress Project.[2] There is evidence leading to this conclusion.

For instance, even when Congress passes legislation the President doesn't like, the battle is not over. The President has the power to veto the legislation simply by refusing to sign the bill into law. Veto power was included in the Constitution primarily as a Presidential check on unconstitutional or undesirable legislation. But usage has transformed it into an important policy tool of the President; he can threaten to veto acts of Congress that don't suit the Presidential program. Here is Nixon in a special message to Congress as it prepared to vote on major health and education bills:

> I will simply not let reckless spending of this kind destroy the tax-reduction we have secured and the hard-earned success we have earned in the battle against inflation. . . . With or without the cooperation of the Congress, I am going to do everything within my power to prevent such a fiscal crisis for millions of our people. . . . Let there be no misunderstanding, if bills come to my desk calling for excessive spending which threatens the federal budget, I will veto them.

Congress can override the Presidential veto with a two-thirds vote. Such a majority is not easy to get. Franklin Roosevelt vetoed 631 separate congressional measures; only 9 were overridden by Congress. Eisenhower vetoed 181 bills; only 2 of them were overridden. Recent Presidents have had more effective opposition, though. Nixon vetoed 43 bills, of which 6 were overridden. And in his first six months in office Gerald Ford vetoed 24 bills, of which 4 were overridden.

We discussed the growth of the executive branch in Chapter 11. This growth, coupled with the apparent weakness and disorganization of Congress, has led some to claim that the executive branch is taking over more and more of the legislative initiative traditionally (and constitutionally) belonging to Congress. Yet two things should be kept in mind. First, what Congress gives, Congress can take away. Presidential initiative depends on a large and energetice White House staff as well as executive agencies. Authorization and funds for these come from Congress. Should Congress decide to reassert its full control over legislation, there is nothing the Presidency can do. Students of politics believe the power balance between the legislative and executive branches moves in cycles. It was just a little over a decade ago that critics of the legislative branch were complaining about how *effective* Congress was in blocking the New Frontier legislation of President Kennedy. The tug-of-war between the two branches goes on, and certainly it is too soon to pronounce one branch dead.

There is a second point to keep in mind. The complaint that the executive has supplanted Congress as the major force in American politics comes largely out of a period when foreign-policy questions,

[2] Mark J. Green, James M. Fallows, and David R. Zwick, *Who Rules Congress?* (New York: Bantam, 1972), p. 94.

and especially the Vietnam war, have dominated headlines. It is true that constitutionally the war-making power belongs to Congress. But tradition says otherwise. There is a longstanding, though unspoken, agreement within our national government that matters of defense and national security should be handled by the executive. In matters of warfare, only the executive can act quickly and decisively; in matters of diplomacy, only the executive can act with the necessary secrecy. Congress has had more foreign-policy influence in recent years, but it has rarely managed to substitute its own will for executive leadership.

Congress, on the other hand, plays a bigger role in the bread-and-butter domestic issues. No President, for instance, could expect to push through tax-reform legislation on his own. As columnist Russell Baker has noted, "no power is kept so zealously locked in the congressional safe as the power to decide who gets soaked and who gets the boons on April 15." It is to Congress and not the President that we look for final disposal of domestic welfare questions, such as revenue sharing, an education bill, or a minimum-wage policy.

The President and the Bureaucracy

"Independent institutions sharing powers"—that is how we have described the federal government. The President, Congress, and the courts are each independent of the other. Thus governmental power is dispersed rather than unified. But the dispersal of power into independent institutions goes further than that.

It would be a mistake to think of each of the three branches of the government as unified institutions facing one another. We talk of the executive vs. Congress as if they were two individuals in conflict. In fact, neither the executive nor Congress is a single entity. The executive branch in particular is a huge, sprawling bureaucracy. Within the executive branch are many other independent power centers.

Presidential Control

The federal bureaucracy is a big, complicated organization with layer after layer between the White House and the lowest clerk on the government payroll. The executive branch is crisscrossed by thousands of separate agencies and programs, and by millions of employees.

Bringing order to the federal executive is close to impossible. The 89th Congress alone (1964–1966) passed 21 new health programs, 17 new educational programs, 15 new economic development programs, 17 new resource-development programs, 4 new manpower-training programs, and 12 new programs to aid cities. This was Johnson's "Great Society" legislation, but how was it to be administered? In committee hearings Senator Edmund Muskie looked into federal support for individual states and cities; he reported that there were

The federal bureaucracy is a big and complex organization.

170 different federal aid programs, financed by 400 separate appropriations and administered through 21 departments and agencies, which included 150 Washington-based bureaus and over 400 regional offices to handle applications and distribute funds.

The President is constitutionally in charge of the executive branch, but in practice he is lucky to know what is taking place in even a tiny part of it. Consider the following news item, datelined Notasulga, Alabama, July 27, 1972:

> In 1932, Charlie Pollard, then a 26-year-old Macon County farmer, took advantage of a public health official's offer of a free blood test and was told a few days later that he had "bad blood."
>
> "They been doctoring on me off and on ever since then," Mr. Pollard, now 66, said yesterday. "And they give me a blood tonic."
>
> Mr. Pollard did not know until Tuesday that for the past 40 years he has been one of a constantly dwindling number of human guinea pigs in whose "bad blood" the effects of syphilis have been observed.
>
> U.S. Public Health Service officials revealed Tuesday that under a Public Health Service study, treatment for syphilis has been withheld from hundreds of afflicted Negroes for the 40-year period. For the past 25 years, penicillin has been generally available to treat it. The purpose of the study was observation of the course of the disease in untreated persons over a long period of time.

This study had been carried out by officials of the U.S. government and supported with public funds. It spanned the Presidencies of Roosevelt, Truman, Eisenhower, Kennedy, Johnson, and Nixon, all of whom headed the executive branch, of which the Public Health Service is a small part. Any one of them would probably have stopped the program immediately had it come to their attention. But how can a single man know what is taking place in the name of the U.S. government in hundreds of offices, laboratories, agencies, bureaus, departments, programs, and projects? Kennedy, it is said, was surprised to learn that the U.S. government, represented by the CIA, was planning to invade Cuba. Nixon was surprised to learn that, contrary to orders, U.S. pilots continued to bomb restricted parts of North Vietnam. Here is a snatch of conversation between Franklin Roosevelt and one of his top administrators:

> "When I woke up this morning, the first thing I saw was a headline in the *New York Times* to the effect that our Navy was going to spend two billion dollars on a shipbuilding program. Here I am, the Commander-in-Chief of the Navy having to read about that for the first time in the press. Do you know what I said to that?"
>
> "No, Mr. President."
>
> "I said, ' Jesus Chr-rist!' "[3]

When we think of a top executive like the President of the United States and the bureaucratic agencies under him, we imagine that the President issues orders and the agencies obey. But we forget how

[3] Cited in Sidney Hyman, ed., *Beckoning Frontiers* (New York: Knopf, 1951), p. 336.

dependent top officials can be on their subordinates. The President depends on his subordinates for two important things: information and compliance.

Information   The federal agencies are the only ones close enough to their own field to know what programs are working and what programs are not. Consider foreign policy. The State Department, the CIA, and the military have people on the spot. The President has to rely on them for information. The same is true in domestic affairs. The bureaucrats in the Agriculture Department have the facts and figures on grain production; the officials in the Nuclear Regulatory Commission have the details on nuclear power plant safety.

Control of such information can give subordinates power over their superiors. Information can be distorted to serve the interests of the one sending the information. Agencies of the government that want more money for their programs will give information showing why additional appropriations are needed. Or they can try to make their programs look more successful than they are. The messages sent by field commanders during the Vietnam war made things look a lot better than they were.

Similarly failures can be covered up. An official investigation of the My Lai killings during the Vietnam war—in which a large number of civilians were killed by American troops—found that the number of victims reported became lower as the information was reported upward through the army. By the time it reached the top officials it did not look bad at all.

Bureaucrats have good reason to send distorted information up the executive ladder. Their careers depend on looking good to their superiors. In addition, agencies of the government want to protect their programs; they want to see that they receive enough money each year. They will often adjust their reports to serve these needs.

Compliance   The President is given the constitutional duty to see that laws are "faithfully executed" (Article 2, Section 3). But the actual execution of laws usually takes place at a much lower level. Congressional law directs that there be safety regulation for air travel; the President executes that law. But the detailed regulations are prepared by the Flight Standards Service of the Federal Aviation Administration, which is a branch of the Department of Transportation. The quality of the safety regulation depends more on the rules worked out at the lower level than on the general rules laid down by Congress. Indeed it may depend on how carefully inspectors check aircraft maintenance or pilot qualifications.

One criticism of the "Great Society" programs was that much effort went into designing programs and little into seeing how they were carried out. The result was that many programs were ineffective or had results other than those intended by the President.

Similar problems exist in foreign affairs. The President sets down broad foreign-policy guidelines. But the actual administration of that

Testifying before Congress: (*Above*) Federal Reserve Bank Chairman Arthur Burns before the House Ways and Means Committee. (*Below*) Chairman of the Joint Chiefs of Staff George S. Brown before the Senate Armed Services Committee.

policy takes place at the "country desks" of the State Department (where a government official deals with our policy to Italy or Burma or Kenya) and in embassies around the world.

The size of the government and the fact that the lower levels control a good deal of information make it impossible for the President (or those in the Presidential office) to know what is going on in all parts of the government and to make sure their directives are complied with. Many Presidents have complained that they had no real control over parts of the government: Kennedy complained that he could not count on the State Department to carry out his foreign-policy directives. No matter what he wanted, they acted in their established ways. And most Presidents have made similar complaints about one or another branch of the government.

Congress and the Bureaucracy

The freedom of the bureaucracy from Presidential control is made stronger by the ties various parts of that bureaucracy have with Congress. Government agencies, supposedly subordinate to the President, often establish close working relations with the congressional committees in their area of concern. The various bureaus of the Agriculture Department work closely with the Senate and House Agriculture Committees. The U.S. Corps of Engineers (in charge of flood control on American rivers and other water-resources projects) is famous for its ties with Congress.

Such ties are an excellent example of the way separation of powers works. If the government were divided into the neat branches set down in the Constitution, there would be much more separation between Congress and the bureaucracy. Congress would pass laws; these laws would then go to the President for execution; he, in turn, would direct the bureaus and agencies of the executive branch to carry them out. The connection of the bureaucracy with Congress would be indirect, running through the office of the President. In fact, the connection is often quite direct, bypassing Presidential control.

These direct ties are an important way of developing freedom from Presidential control. The President, for instance, is Commander-in-Chief of the armed forces (Article 2, Section 2). But his control over the armed forces is by no means absolute. The Joint Chiefs of Staff have close ties with the Armed Forces Committees of Congress. They often go directly to Congress if they do not agree with the policies of the White House. The President must take this into account if he disagrees with the Joint Chiefs.

The President's Attempts to Control the Executive

Every President has faced the problem of how to take and keep control of the executive branch. Some have relied heavily on close personal advisers, some on the Cabinet, and some on agencies like the Office of Management and Budget.

Presidential advisors such as
Henry Kissinger play a key role
in the White House.

Presidential Advisers

Presidents often have a few top officials in the White House to
whom they give the job of coordinating domestic or foreign policy.
In the foreign-policy field the powers of such advisers have been
great. Johnson relied heavily on his national security advisers, Mc-
George Bundy and then W. W. Rostow, and Nixon and Ford have
relied on Henry Kissinger.

The problems of coordination through a special adviser are not
simple. At first Kissinger was brought to the White House to give
attention to long-term security and foreign-policy questions. He
was given funds to support a highly professional group of personal
advisers and researchers. His own group numbered about 50 people
chosen on the basis of great achievement in security, military, and
diplomatic matters. Once assembled, Kissinger and his staff were
soon involved in the day-to-day decisions of foreign policy. Kissinger was responsible for setting up the China and Russia summit

meetings, personally negotiated the end of U.S. involvement in the Vietnam war, and took part in Middle East negotiations.

In short, Kissinger became his own state department and sometimes his own defense department. He thus attracted hostility from the groups he upstaged. This hostility was expressed in a rather interesting way during the Pakistani-Indian clashes of late 1970. At a series of meetings of the Special Action Group, a unit of the National Security Council, Kissinger said things that could only be embarrassing if made public. The complete minutes of the meetings were leaked to a newspaper columnist. This leak of top-secret materials must have been an attempt to undermine Kissinger's status.

A similar controversy was generated by Nixon's domestic advisers, H. R. Haldeman and John Ehrlichman. They were given a good deal of power over the various government departments in the domestic field, and their attempt to control governmental programs closely caused tension in the Nixon administration.

This type of tension between the White House staff and the regular government departments was not new with the Nixon administration. Here a very close adviser to Lyndon Johnson explains why Johnson had given control to his personal staff rather than to the Cabinet:

> Power, in the Presidential sense, is a very personal thing. It is invested in one man in the White House. Since power is his greatest resource, it is the instrument by which he works his will. It is not something he is likely to invest in people whose first allegiance is not to him. He is not likely to share what is his most precious resource with people whom he does not know well. Many Cabinet officers are men who are not well known to the President personally prior to his inauguration. They also become men with ties to their own departments, to the bureaucracy, to congressional committees, rather than exclusively to the President, as is the case with White House assistants.[4]

The Cabinet

The preceding quotation points out another institution that might help the President coordinate the executive branch: the Cabinet. But it also suggests why the Cabinet has not been useful in that way. Each Cabinet member is normally in charge of a government department. Thus there is a Secretary of the Treasury, of Commerce, and so forth. The people chosen to head the major government departments usually come from the President's party, they nearly always have had extensive experience, and that experience is normally in the area the department is responsible for. The Secretary of Agriculture, for example, will have long been active in farm matters and will be acceptable to the group his department works with, including the large farmer organizations.

[4] Bill Moyers, taken from an interview conducted by Hugh Sidney, reprinted in Charles Peters and Timothy J. Adams, eds., *Inside the System* (New York: Praeger, 1970), p. 24.

The Cabinet meets.

It is sometimes said that the Cabinet should meet at regular times, coordinate government strategy, and advise the President on policy matters. Few Cabinets have done this. It is rare to find a department head who does not have what a general once termed *localitis:* "the conviction ardently held by every theater commander that the war was being won or lost in his own zone of responsibility, and that the withholding of whatever was necessary for local success was evidence of blindness, if not of imbecility, in the high command."[5] Most Cabinet members struggle to expand programs in their own departments. And though this is expected of department heads, it keeps the Cabinet from becoming a useful advisory group. Most Presidents use Cabinet meetings to inform one department of government what other departments are doing. For actual advice on policy matters, Presidents use smaller, hand-chosen groups.

The Office of Management and Budget

Presidents have tried to coordinate the executive branch through the budget. Each year the President sends a budget to Congress, listing the programs he wants supported and the amount that would be spent on each.

The Bureau of the Budget was set up to coordinate budget requests from the various departments and fit them into the overall Presidential program. During the Nixon administration its name was changed to the Office of Management and Budget (OMB). The purpose of the new agency is to coordinate all parts of the executive branch, not only in the preparation of the budget but in the actual administration of policies.

The OMB gives the executive a new tool. But it will hardly solve all problems of coordination. It has been criticized by particular agencies for interference in the administration of programs. The

[5] This remark is attributed to General George C. Marshall in Arthur M. Schlesinger, Jr., *The Age of Roosevelt: The Coming of the New Deal* (Boston: Houghton Mifflin, 1958), II, p. 520.

bureaucrats in the operating agencies (the agencies carrying out particular programs) claim that the bureaucrats in the OMB are not well informed about the programs they are trying to control. This shows that the struggle in the executive branch between the office of the President and the various departments will continue. The former tries to coordinate, the latter to maintain some independence. It is a struggle that neither side can win, though the balance may shift one way or the other.

Watergate and Presidential Domination

Perhaps no set of events better illustrates the workings of the separation of powers than the Watergate affair. The relative power of the branches of the government has varied over the centuries since the writing of the Constitution. In the nineteenth century, Congress often dominated policy making. From the late nineteenth century to the 1930s, the Supreme Court often played a dominant role, severely limiting the power of Congress and the Presidency to enact social legislation.

In the years since the 1930s, we have seen a great rise of Presidential power. Indeed our era has been considered one of Presidential domination. The growth of Presidential power is not due to power-hungry Presidents. There are many reasons. The Great Depression of the 1930s resulted in an increased role of the federal government in the domestic economy. The executive branch became the "manager" of the U.S. economy. World War II and the resulting deep involvement of the U.S. in the affairs of the rest of the world also increased the President's power. Only the executive branch had the technical skills and organization to formulate the national domestic and foreign policies that were needed.

Presidential Power Under Nixon

President Nixon added further to Presidential powers. But he pushed those powers so far as to come into conflict with the other branches. For example, Nixon asserted the right to "impound" funds, that is, not to spend money appropriated by Congress if he felt the appropriation to be unwise. By impounding funds the President effectively refused to execute laws passed by Congress.

But it was not impoundment of funds or clashes over policy that led to Nixon's resignation. Rather, it was a series of illegal abuses of power that combined to cause that result.

One set of abuses related to the electoral process. The Watergate scandal began with the discovery of an attempt to wiretap the offices of the Democratic National Committee, an attempt that was later linked to the President's own campaign committee. In addition, there was evidence of plans for a number of "dirty tricks" during the campaign. And there was also evidence of campaign contributions illegally solicited in return for favors. These included contributions by

milk producers' cooperatives in return for higher price supports for
milk and from International Telephone and Telegraph in return for
favorable action on an antitrust suit.

It was also revealed that the administration had tried to use the
powers of the executive branch to harass its "enemies." The President and his aides pressured the Internal Revenue Service to audit
the tax returns of people politically opposed to the administration.

Furthermore, the executive powers of the President were used in
an attempt to cover up the Watergate break-in. The President and
his aides tried to manipulate the CIA and the FBI to limit investigation of the break-in.

The Watergate hearings and trials revealed a large number of ways
the Nixon administration had abused executive powers. Evidence
was produced of the so-called Huston plan to keep an eye on domestic radicals. The plan included illegal wiretaps, break-ins, and
disruption of radical organizations. That plan was not carried out,
but later it was shown that the CIA—which is supposed to have no
domestic role—had been checking on radicals.

Finally, the President claimed absolute executive privilege when
it came to the documents and tapes associated with the case. He
claimed that the need for secrecy in executive actions was so great
that only the President could decide what information to reveal to
the public or to the other branches of the government.

High Crimes and Misdemeanors, Not Policy Differences The
abuses we have described formed the basis of the actions against
President Nixon in the courts and by Congress. It is important to
note that the movement to impeach the President did not grow out
of differences between Congress and the President on *policy* matters.
Republican Nixon had been reelected by a large majority in 1972 and
with some definite policy ideas. The Congress that was elected at
the same time had a majority from the Democratic party.

Under such circumstances sharp conflicts over policy are likely,
and there were a number of such conflicts in the second Nixon ad-

THE SEPARATION
OF POWERS

ministration. In a parliamentary system of government, where the executive officer (the prime minister) is elected by the legislature, such conflicts often result in the overthrow of the executive by the legislature through a "vote of no confidence." In our Presidential system, Congress cannot vote a President out of office because it disagrees with his policies. If there is a clash over policy, the result may be stalemate. Congress may refuse to pass laws the President wants, or the President may veto laws that Congress passes. But the President remains President.

The abuses of Presidential power included in the articles of impeachment voted by the House Judiciary Committee were, according to the Committee, illegal actions on the part of the President, not specific policies it disagreed with. The Committee voted down an article of impeachment based on the President's action in ordering the bombing of Cambodia during the Vietnam war. The argument of those who opposed the inclusion of this particular article of impeachment was that the President was carrying out his legitimate function as Commander-in-Chief, and, though they may have disagreed with his action, it was not an impeachable action. (Those who favored impeachment for the bombing of Cambodia agreed with the general principle that the President could not be impeached for carrying out a foreign policy they disagreed with. But they argued that he was acting illegally in this case because he kept the bombing secret from Congress.)

Removing a President from Office

Nixon was reelected by the largest majority in U.S. history. He was head of the most powerful office in the world, the American Presidency. He had under him a huge executive branch whose activities affected all areas of American life. And he was determined to use his executive powers fully (his critics would say ruthlessly) to accomplish his goals. Yet less than two years later he resigned from office under the threat of almost certain impeachment by the House of Representatives and conviction by the Senate. How did this come about?

To find the answer we turn back to the Constitution. As *The Federalist* puts it, we would need no controls over government "if angels were to govern men." But the writers of the Constitution believed our governors were not likely to be angels. Internal and external controls over their conduct would be needed. The Watergate scandal shows how correct their judgment was; the Nixon administration was not run by angels, and the controls devised in the Constitution were put into effect to limit their abuse of power. The Watergate events show clearly how a government made up of *independent* powers can limit abuse by any one branch.

The Role of Congress Our Presidential system of government is, as we have seen, different from a parliamentary system. The head of

SAM J. ERVIN, JR., N.C., CHAIRMAN
RD H. BAKER, JR., TENN., VICE CHAIRMAN
.MADGE, GA.   EDWARD J. GURNEY, FLA.
YE, HAWAII   LOWELL P. WEICKER, JR., CONN.
.TOYA, N. MEX.

SAMUEL DASH
HIEF COUNSEL AND STAFF DIRECTOR
FRED D. THOMPSON
MINORITY COUNSEL
RUFUS L. EDMISTEN
DEPUTY COUNSEL

United States Senate

SELECT COMMITTEE ON
PRESIDENTIAL CAMPAIGN ACTIVITIES
(PURSUANT TO S. RES. 60, 93D CONGRESS) *

WASHINGTON, D.C. 20510

July 17, 1973

The President
The White House
Washington, D. C.

Dear Mr. President:

Today the Select Committee on Presidential Campaign
Activities met and unanimously voted that I request
that you provide the Committee with all relevant
documents and tapes under control of the White House
that relate to the matters the Select Committee is
authorized to investigate under S. Res. 60. I refer
to the documents mentioned in my letter to Mr. Leonard
Garment of June 21, 1973, and the relevant portions
of the tapes alluded to by Mr. Alexander Butterfield
before the Committee on July 16, 1973.

If your illness prevents our meeting to discuss these
issues in the next day or two, I should like to suggest that you designate members of your staff to meet
with members of the Select Committee staff to make
arrangements for our access to White House documents
and tapes pertinent to the Committee's investigation.

I should like respectfully to relate that the Committee's
investigation is on-going and that access to relevant
documents should not be delayed if the Committee is to
perform its mission. May we hear from you at your earliest convenience?

The Committee deeply regrets your illness and hopes
for you a speedy recovery.

Sincerely,

Sam J. Ervin, Jr.
Chairman

the executive branch is not elected by the legislature, nor can the
legislature vote him out of office when it disagrees with him. The
U.S. President is elected by the people. He is not chosen by Congress.

But Article 1 of the Constitution does give Congress the power to
remove a President. The power to impeach a President is given to
the House of Representatives; the power to conduct a trial of the
President after his impeachment is given to the Senate. The Chief
Justice of the United States presides at such a trial, and a two-thirds
vote is needed to convict a President. The Constitution also makes

Senator Sam J. Ervin, Jr., questions the testimony of John D. Erlichman, former assistant to President Nixon, during the Watergate hearings.

clear that such a removal should not be for unpopular policy. A President can be removed only if convicted of "Treason, Bribery, or other high Crimes or Misdemeanors" (Article 2, Section 4).

These terms are ambiguous, and much of the debate over the possible impeachment of Richard Nixon had to do with the interpretation of them. Some people argued that the President had to have committed a crime for which an ordinary citizen would be convicted in court. Others argued that a President could be impeached for gross misconduct in office, even if the acts of misconduct were not in themselves felonies.

The latter position appeared to prevail. The accusations in the articles of impeachment voted by the House Judiciary Committee in July 1974 included not only activities that would have been criminal if committed by a private citizen but also other misconduct—such as failure to supervise the activities of subordinates—that would not be criminal acts.

The constitutional impeachment process was not completed in 1974; Nixon resigned after the House Judiciary Committee had voted three articles of impeachment against him. These were recommendations from the Committee to the entire House of Representatives. The next step in the process would have been a vote by the House on these articles. If a majority of the House had voted for impeachment, the Senate would have tried the President.

Although the impeachment process was never completed, it is clear from the historical record that it was the threat of impeachment that led to Nixon's resignation. It was only when he was sure he would be impeached and convicted that he decided to resign.

The Role of the Judicial Branch   The court system also played a major role in the Watergate affair. Many of the important revelations of Watergate were brought out in the trials conducted by Judge John Sirica of the federal district court.

At times of constitutional crisis the key interpretations are often made by the Supreme Court. Note the important role the Supreme Court played in the Watergate events. A major conflict arose over the tapes of Presidential conversations. They had been subpoenaed as evidence in the trial of some of Nixon's aides who were accused of taking part in the Watergate break-in and cover-up. President Nixon claimed only he could determine whether such Presidential materials would be released to the courts. He cited the doctrine of executive privilege, claiming that the President could not function as the nation's executive head unless he could maintain the secrecy of his records.

The case went to the Supreme Court. The Court ruled that there was indeed an executive privilege; the President could keep secret records if those were needed to carry out his work. But executive privilege was not absolute. If records were needed in a criminal case, the President could not hold them back.

SUPREME COURT OF THE UNITED STATES
Nos. 73-1766 AND 73-1834

United States, Petitioner,
73-1766   *v.*
Richard M. Nixon, President of the United States, et al.

Richard M. Nixon, President of the United States, Petitioner,
73-1834   *v.*
United States.

On Writs of Certiorari to the United States Court of Appeals for the District of Columbia Circuit before judgment.

[July 24, 1974]

MR. CHIEF JUSTICE BURGER delivered the opinion of the Court.

These cases present for review the denial of a motion, filed on behalf of the President of the United States, in the case of *United States* v. *Mitchell et al.* (D. C. Crim. No. 74-110), to quash a third-party subpoena *duces tecum* issued by the United States District Court for the District of Columbia, pursuant to Fed. Rule Crim. Proc. 17(c). The subpoena directed the President to produce certain tape recordings and documents relating to his conversations with aides and advisers. The court rejected the President's claims of absolute executive privilege, of lack of jurisdiction, and of failure to satisfy the requirements of Rule 17(c). The President appealed to the Court of Appeals. We granted the United States' petition for certiorari before judgment,[1] and also the President's

What the Court was saying was that no branch of the government was above the law. It affirmed that the President had wide powers under the Constitution and that he needed such powers. But it also affirmed that those powers were not unlimited.

This decision was an important step in the process that led to the President's resignation. He had resisted a number of efforts to get the tapes, but he could not ignore the Supreme Court. A number of members of Congress made it clear that the President would face certain impeachment and conviction if he defied the Court. (Note how the powers of Congress and the Court combined to limit the power of the President.) When the tape transcripts made clear that the President had known about the Watergate cover-up for a much longer time than he had admitted, he lost the rest of his support in Congress.

The independence of the judicial branch is underlined by the fact that of the eight Supreme Court justices who voted against the President (one justice took no part in the case), three had been appointed by Nixon. The power to appoint justices of the Supreme Court does give the President some control over that body; it is, indeed, one of the ways the Court's power is limited under the system of checks and balances. And the President had used that power to appoint a number of justices whose constitutional views were close to his own. But justices are appointed for life and are not under the control of the President. Throughout history the Supreme Court has acted quite independently of the other branches of the government.

The Fourth Branch of Government *The Federalist Papers* talk of external as well as internal checks on the powers of the government. We have seen how the power of the President was checked by other branches of the government. But outside forces are also important in controlling those who govern. Full public disclosure of the Watergate events would not have been possible had it not been for the relentless digging of a few journalists, particularly from the *Washington Post* and the *New York Times*. Their pursuit of the facts was protected by the First Amendment. In only a handful of nations could newspapers have played as full and aggressive a role. Even in democratic nations like Great Britain, the press would have been legally barred from publicly exposing the details of Watergate.

Watergate and the Constitutional Process

The Watergate affair illustrates some important ways general constitutional provisions such as separation of powers meet new circumstances. As we have seen, there are many silences and ambiguities in the Constitution. These give it the flexibility to adjust to new circumstances.

The process of adjustment is not a mechanical one in which congressmen or Supreme Court justices read the clear words of the Constitution and apply them to the case. The words of the Constitution need interpretation. Such a term as *impeachment* is by no means clear, and executive privilege is not mentioned in the Constitution at all. How do the members of Congress decide the actual

meaning of impeachment? And how do Supreme Court justices decide the actual meaning of executive privilege?

For one thing, they look at the Constitution itself. What does it say on the subject? But where the Constitution is unclear, they look further. They consider the writings of those who wrote the Constitution, as well as the debates at the Constitutional Convention, to see what the founders had in mind. In addition, they consider the earlier historical uses of the word. When the founders used a term like *impeachment,* they were probably influenced by earlier legal practice.

Perhaps most important of all, those interpreting the meaning of the Constitution will consider how others have interpreted it in the past. They will look, in other words, for precedents. How has impeachment been carried out in the past? The members of Congress spent a good deal of time considering the one previous example of a Presidential impeachment: the impeachment and trial of President Andrew Johnson after the Civil War. And the Supreme Court considered the way earlier Presidents and earlier courts had dealt with executive privilege.

Finally, one must mention political forces. Even though the debate over impeachment was conducted in legal terms, the fact that the President was a Republican whose policies were objectionable to many Democrats cannot be ignored. It is hardly accident that the members of Congress in favor of impeachment were more likely to be Democrats, those opposed more likely to be Republicans. And the members of Congress pay attention not only to constitutional precedents but also to the views of their constituents. That Nixon's public support faded during the summer of 1974 probably played some role in their decisions.

THE SEPARATION
OF POWERS

What is the balance between constitutional interpretation and the political calculations of congressmen? Some critics claim it was a purely political process. President Nixon's press secretary accused the House Judiciary Committee of being a "kangaroo court," that is, paying little attention to law or evidence but acting on a political basis. Members of Congress, on the other hand, sometimes talked as if their task were purely legal.

In fact most of the major constitutional crises of our history have combined both forces. The words of the Constitution and constitutional precedents play a role; so do particular political forces. Both could be seen in the Watergate case. But the seriousness of the debate on the nature of impeachment, and the fact that the final pressure for the President's resignation came from conservative members of his own party who decided Nixon's legal position was untenable, suggest that the Judiciary Committee was not a political kangaroo court.

President Ford's pardon of ex-President Nixon.

GRANTING PARDON TO RICHARD NIXON

BY THE PRESIDENT OF THE UNITED STATES OF AMERICA

A PROCLAMATION

Richard Nixon became the thirty-seventh President of the United States on January 20, 1969 and was reelected in 1972 for a second term by the electors of forty-nine of the fifty states. His term in office continued until his resignation on August 9, 1974.

Pursuant to resolutions of the House of Representatives, its Committee on the Judiciary conducted an inquiry and investigation on the impeachment of the President extending over more than eight months. The hearings of the Committee and its deliberations, which received wide national publicity over television, radio, and in printed media, resulted in votes adverse to Richard Nixon on recommended Articles of Impeachment.

As a result of certain acts or omissions occurring before his resignation from the Office of President, Richard Nixon has become liable to possible indictment and trial for offenses against the United States. Whether or not he shall be so prosecuted depends on findings of the appropriate grand jury and on the discretion of the authorized prosecutor. Should an indictment ensue, the accused shall then be entitled to a fair trial by an impartial jury, as guaranteed to every individual by the Constitution.

It is believed that a trial of Richard Nixon, if it became necessary, could not fairly begin until a year or more has elapsed. In the meantime, the tranquility to which this nation has been restored by the events of recent weeks could be irreparably lost by the prospects of bringing to trial a former President of the United States. The prospects of such

trial will cause prolonged and divisive debate over the propriety of exposing to further punishment and degradation a man who has already paid the unprecedented penalty of relinquishing the highest elective office of the United States.

NOW, THEREFORE, I, Gerald R. Ford, President of the United States, pursuant to the pardon power conferred upon me by Article II, Section 2, of the Constitution, have granted and by these presents do grant a full, free, and absolute pardon unto Richard Nixon for all offenses against the United States which he, Richard Nixon, has committed or may have committed or taken part in during the period from January 20, 1969 through August 9, 1974.

IN WITNESS WHEREOF, I have hereunto set my hand this ghth day of September, in the year of our Lord nineteen ired and seventy-four, and of the Independence of the d States of America the one hundred and ninety-ninth.

Gerald R. Ford

Under our uneasy balance of governmental powers, there will be future clashes between the various branches. We can be sure that Congress and the President will differ over their powers in the future, and the Supreme Court may be called on to mediate. When this happens the Watergate decisions will be taken into consideration. Thus Watergate becomes, in turn, a precedent for the future.

After Watergate

Some observers believed the Watergate scandal would lead to a major change in the internal structure of the national government. Some indeed thought it would destroy the Presidency as an effective political force.

The result was not that dramatic. A strong Presidency is needed in the modern world. No sooner had President Nixon left office than President Ford and his administration were managing foreign policy and trying to cope with the domestic economic crisis. The main reason was simply that the nature of the problems required Presidential action and initiative.

On the other hand, the Watergate events seem to have had a profound effect on the balance of powers among the branches of government. For one thing, the crisis reaffirmed the independence of the various branches. Congress called on its ultimate power—impeachment—and the President resigned. The Supreme Court and the President came into direct conflict over the extent of Presidential power. Would the President obey an order from the Supreme Court to turn over the tapes of conversations for which he claimed executive privilege? When Nixon and his attorney were asked this question while the case was before the Court, the answer was usually evasive. But when the Court ruled that the President had to turn over the tapes, he obeyed.

The Balance of Power

Watergate did not "destroy" the Presidency. But it resulted in a more active and independent Congress. As we have seen, Congress overrode President Ford's vetoes more often than earlier Congresses. It took an active role in energy and economic policy. And, in perhaps the biggest shift, it played a larger role in foreign policy making. It explicitly limited U.S. aid to countries such as South Vietnam, Turkey, and Chile, and it was deeply involved in the details of trade negotiations with the Soviet Union and other countries. (In Chapter 17 we will look more closely at some of these policies and see how the role of Congress changed.)

Furthermore, Congress began to oversee government operations more fully. When it was revealed that the CIA had been involved in domestic activities, President Ford appointed a special commission under Vice-President Rockefeller to investigate. But Congress was not content to leave the investigation to the executive branch. Both the House and the Senate set up investigatory committees of their own. More important, perhaps, was the fact that the investigation was not left to the committees that ordinarily dealt with the CIA. In the Senate a special committee was set up under Senator Frank Church. Many senators felt that the Senate Armed Forces Committee, under John Stennis, has not been active enough in watching over the CIA.

It is important to note that Congress was not adding new powers. It was merely using more effectively the powers it always had under the Constitution, such as the power of the purse and the power to investigate. What changed was not the constitutional powers of Congress but the attitudes of the members of Congress toward the use of such powers.

In addition, there was an effort to reorganize Congress so that it could more effectively match the Presidency. In Chapter 10 we discussed the attempt to break the hold of the seniority system on appointments to committee chairmanships. In Chapter 16 we will consider the attempt to set up a more effective budget-making committee. The purpose of these changes is to make Congress more responsive to the need for legislation and more coordinated in handling such legislation.

It is clear that these recent events have somewhat reduced the dominance of the Presidency over the legislative process. But the Presidency remains a powerful independent force—probably, if we could measure such things, the most powerful of the three branches. The same conditions that led to the dominance of the Presidency over Congress still hold. There is still a need for strong, unified authority in dealing with complex domestic and foreign problems. Congress probably can't reorganize itself enough to match the executive in its ability to coordinate policy, nor can it reach the level of expertise of the executive departments. Congress remains, after all, 535 individuals, each with a home constituency and a career to be made. It is not an easy body to coordinate; and an uncoordinated body loses in contests with the executive. As one Congressman put it, "If we all toed the line and did what Carl Albert [the Speaker of the House] said, Carl Albert could go down there and negotiate with the President as an effective opponent. But who wants to do that?"[6]

Even if Congress maintains the will to challenge the President, it may not be able to develop the organizational capacity to do so. A multimember legislative body cannot easily plan and coordinate government policy. It is likely that the new-found strength of Congress will limit the powers of the President to act as independently as before. But control by Congress is likely to be negative, leading the President to modify his program or preventing him from carrying out some programs he favors. Congress is unlikely to take the lead in the development of new legislation.

[6] Quoted in the *New York Times Magazine*, September 23, 1973, p. 88.

Controversy

Should the Presidency or Congress formulate national policy? Because the "Congress vs. President" debate is many sided, it is necessary to make some assumptions in order to state a meaningful controversy: (1) Rather than looking for facts, we debate the "oughtness" of the issue. Relevant evidence is scattered throughout the preceding chapters, and it has been shown that how much power either branch has depends on various conditions. (2) Let us assume that the agenda for public debate and governmental action is best formulated by only one branch of government. This does not challenge the logic of separation of powers. It simply holds that it is more efficient for one branch of government to formulate national policy.

One Side

The Presidency is the appropriate branch of government for formulating national policy. The President is elected by a national constituency rather than by hundreds of localized ones. The Presidential campaign focuses the attention of the nation on broad alternatives for dealing with social issues. Each of the major candidates presents a package of policies to which every region, race, social class, or occupational interest can respond positively or negatively. Individual congressional contests present only partial programs aimed at a particular constituency. A victory or defeat at the Presidential level reflects the majority of the entire society.

Only the executive branch is subject to large-scale turnover of personnel and priorities. When a new Presidential administration comes to power, "a thousand new officials descend on Washington, coming fresh from the people, representing the diverse forces behind the new President and bringing with them new demands, new ideas, and new power. Here truly is representative government along classic lines and of a sort which Congress has not known for decades."[7]

Not only does the Presidency represent national tides of public opinion, it can think and plan on a national level. By careful selection of White House staff, Cabinet officers, and other high executive officials, the President brings together a group unparalleled in experience and talent. Although there will be honest differences within the executive office, there will also be shared vision. Out of

[7] Samuel P. Huntington, "Congressional Responses to the Twentieth Century," in David B. Truman, ed., *The Congress and America's Future* (Englewood Cliffs, N.J.: Prentice-Hall, 1965), p. 17.

THE SEPARATION
OF POWERS

this type of group can come a coordinated national program. Congress represents too many conflicting views to formulate a unified policy.

Finally, the White House has the advantage because it can best bring together international and domestic considerations. Only the executive branch has the worldwide network and information flow necessary to coordinating what goes on at home with what is going on abroad.

In short, the Presidential office is the truly national branch of government, and it has a global perspective. These are the conditions that will make for a meaningful articulation of social priorities and rational strategies.

The Other Side

Congress is the appropriate branch for formulating national policy. Congress has one distinct advantage over the White House. It is in continuous, direct contact with citizens. Congressmen make frequent trips back home. They hear from constituents and lobbyists on a daily basis. The White House, in contrast, is isolated for long periods. There are many bureaucratic layers between the President and his advisers and the public at large. The President deals with the public through the media or his staff; congressmen deal directly with the public. For this reason Congress is best equipped to outline a national program. Consider two points.

A program formulated by Congress will be more "democratic." It will reflect a compromise version of the preferences of citizens spread across the nation. Perhaps Congress is tied to regional concerns, but these are exactly the concerns a government is supposed to service. Citizens want jobs, clean air and water, crime control, social services, and dozens of other specific things. But citizens are not of one mind regarding how much of which of these things they want from government, and at what cost. Only Congress reflects the bewildering and *necessarily* conflicting desires of more than 200 million individuals.

A program formulated by Congress will for this reason be more practical. Congress will come up with a national program that is a compromise of dozens of regional claims and special requests. But such a program is realistic. The contradictions and disagreements within Congress reflect actual contradictions and disagreements within the nation at large. A program that fails to adjust and compromise such real differences is not likely to be accepted. And this is the danger to any highly coherent national program that comes from a star-studded staff of economists, planners, and strategists in the White House.

How Institutions Work: VI
The Federal Budget

What is the significance of the federal budget?

The annual budget serves to order the nation's priorities by establishing how much money the government will spend and for which purposes. Figure 13.1 shows how President Ford's 1976 budget proposes to spend $350 billion. But the budget is also a tool of fiscal policy. The budget may, for example, be reduced to help fight inflation, or a budget surplus or deficit may be planned to slow down or stimulate the economy.

What is the "budgetary process"?

The budgetary process is the ongoing planning, implementation, and auditing of all federal spending. Both the executive and Congress are deeply involved.

Who formulates the annual budget?

The federal government operates for accounting purposes on a fiscal year that starts on October 1 and ends the following September 30. Each spring the agencies and departments begin drawing up their budget requests for the fiscal year starting some 16 months later. These requests are then sent to the Office of Management and Budget, which oversees the executive budget. After review the OMB sends the budget requests to the President, who by now has also been provided with economic forecasts and revenue estimates for the coming year. The President coordinates this information to set budget guidelines. Within these guidelines the individual agencies then submit detailed budget requests, which are analyzed by the OMB and passed on to the President. Although intense bureaucratic in-fighting occurs and although agencies may appeal directly to the President, it is the OMB that largely decides how much money will be spent for each program. The final budget proposal is submitted by the President to Congress, usually in January or February.

What role does Congress play in the budgetary process?

The President's budget proposal is actually only a request, for only Congress can vote to spend federal funds. It does so in a two-step process. First, it enacts *authorizations,* or legislation that authorizes a particular program and puts a ceiling on funds to finance it. Second, it passes *appropriations* bills to grant the actual funds approved by authorization bills. An authorization without an appropriation is meaningless. In fact, however, close to 70 percent of the spending in any fiscal year is locked into the budget by previous congressional decision and is not subject to annual appropriations.

Figure 13.1

The Budget Dollar: Where It Goes (Fiscal Year 1976 Estimate)

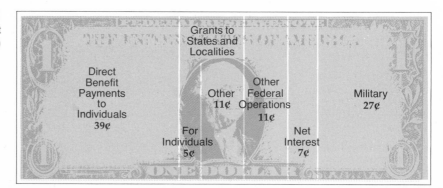

Source: U.S. Office of Management and Budget.

How is Congress organized with respect to budget decisions?

By custom the President's budget requests are considered first by the House Appropriations Committee. After an appropriations bill has been passed by the House, it is transmitted to the Senate Appropriations Committee for similar consideration. Traditionally the Senate has served as a court of appeals for agencies seeking to restore budget cuts made in the House. But there have been obvious problems with this pattern. Congress has typically spent several billion dollars more than the President annually requested, leading to charges of "fiscal irresponsibility." Moreover, the fragmented structure of Congress itself has led to a piece-by-piece consideration of the budget without ever really looking at the budget as a whole. Therefore in 1974 Congress passed legislation designed to reform its budget procedures.

What are the principal changes called for in the budget-reform law?

The reform act creates new House and Senate Budget Committees aided by a new Congressional Budget Office staffed by experts. New procedures call for the Congress to (1) pass a joint resolution early in each session setting an overall target for spending, and then, after the customary appropriations process has been completed, (2) reconcile any differences between the target total and the sum of the parts.

Is there any check on whether the funds approved by Congress are spent as directed and within the budget?

Each executive agency is responsible for making sure its outlays comply with legislation. The OMB also oversees each agency's spending. Congress gets an independent audit of all expenditures through the General Accounting Office.

Does the President have to spend the full amount appropriated by Congress for a given program?

There has been much controversy over this question, especially during the Nixon years, when the executive "impounded" funds for certain programs and refused to spend the full amount intended by law. To avoid long court battles over impoundments, the new congressional budget act requires congressional approval for all Presidential impoundments.

Can the executive get more funds from Congress in special circumstances?

Yes, such requests can be made in the form of supplemental appropriations.

14

The
Individual
and the State

What is a democracy? A democracy is a government that allows individual freedom: Citizens in a democracy are free to speak as they wish and to worship as they wish; they cannot be arbitrarily put in jail for unpopular acts.

What is a democracy? A democracy is a government where the majority rules: Laws and regulations are determined by the will of the majority.

Most citizens would agree that these two answers describe basic democratic principles: individual freedom and majority rule. Yet the two principles are often in conflict. In this chapter we describe the way individual rights and majority rule are balanced.

Majority Rule: Some Modifications

If you asked the average citizen how political decisions are made in the United States, he would very likely answer "by majority vote." In some ways he would be right. A basic "decision rule" of a democracy is majoritarianism. This is a decision rule to which children are introduced very early, often by a homeroom teacher: "Today we must elect someone to represent our class on the student council. We have two nominees, Jennifer and Geoffrey. Write your choice on a piece of paper." When the ballots are counted the teacher announces the results: "Jennifer gets 17 votes and Geoffrey gets 14. The majority decides, so Jennifer is our representative." Although majoritarianism is a basic decision rule in our political life, it is subject to modifications. There are five such modifications.

The Special Majority

There is the *special majority.* Some matters are so important that a "50 percent plus 1" majority is not large enough; a larger majority should favor the decision before it is made. For example, a special majority is required if Congress passes a bill by a simple majority vote, 50 percent plus 1, and the President vetoes it. Congress can then override the veto by a "special" two-thirds majority. The Constitution does not give the President ultimate power over legislation. But it does weigh the President's disapproval seriously, and thus it requires a special majority to pass the bill over his veto.

The Voting Unit

Another modification of the majority rule concerns the choice of the *voting unit.* Federalism, as we shall see in Chapter 15, gives some responsibilities to units much smaller than the entire nation. Which voters should decide if the schools in Richmond, Virginia, are to be integrated—those of the Richmond school district, those of Virginia, those of the southern states, or those of the entire United States? By shifting a choice to the larger unit, you risk an outcome that differs from what would occur in the smaller unit. The battle over states' rights is not over majority vs. minority rule as much as over the geographic area within which majority rule is to prevail. When the decision is left to the local community or to the state, majority rule at the national level may be violated. When the decision is shifted to the national level, the majority preferences of the local community may be swept aside.

Plurality Rule

A third modification of the majority rule is the *plurality rule,* which has an opposite effect from the special majority. Plurality rule allows the opinion of a group less than a majority to prevail, as long as that group is still larger than any other group. In 1968 Nixon got only 43 percent of the popular vote, but this was more than Humphrey got (41 percent) and more than Wallace got (14 percent), so Nixon won the election. Because only 60 percent of the adult population voted that year, Nixon in effect was supported by about 27 percent of those entitled to vote. In fact Presidents are always elected by a minority of the voting-age population. (See Table 14.1.)

The Intense Minority

Another modification of the majoritarian decision rule results less from legal arrangements than from practical considerations. This is the modification introduced by the *intense minority.* Sometimes a small group of citizens feels intensely about an issue, while the large majority doesn't feel as strongly. (See Chapter 7.) Since "the squeaking wheel gets the grease," government officials will often respond to the vocal minority rather than the indifferent majority. In day-to-day politics this informal rule probably prevails more than the constitutional rule of strict majoritarianism.

The Rights of Minorities

There is a final modification of majority rule: *the constitutional rights of minorities.* This modification is so important in American politics that we devote the rest of the chapter to it. The principle of

Table 14.1
Presidents Are Elected by a Minority of the Voting-Age Population

Year	Percent of Voting-Age Citizens Voting	Percent of Popular Vote Received by Victor	Percent of Voting-Age Citizens Voting for Victor
1948	51.4	49.6	25.5
1952	62.6	55.1	34.5
1956	60.1	57.4	34.5
1960	64.0	49.7	31.8
1964	62.9	61.1	38.4
1968	61.8	43.4	26.8
1972	63.0	60.7	38.2

Source: U.S. Department of Commerce, Bureau of the Census, *Statistical Abstract of the United States: 1974* (Washington, D.C., 1974).

minority rights has, since the founding of the nation, been in conflict with majoritarianism. If "50 percent plus 1" were the only rule for democratic decision making, the majority would be free to do whatever it wished to a minority group—it could take away their livelihoods, their homes, their freedoms, even their lives. And it would all be, by definition, democratic.

The "Tyranny of the Majority"

Many writers have warned of democratic tyranny—the so-called tyranny of the majority. In some respects such tyranny is more to be feared than the tyranny of a smaller group. The chances of successful resistance are, of course, less if a minority has a majority united against it. Many foreign observers of life in America have commented on the power of public opinion, particularly over unpopular ideas and behavior. And when public opinion is coupled with the arm of government—that is, when one has a government carrying out the will of the majority—it becomes a force that a deviant minority cannot easily resist.

The writers of the Constitution were, as we have said, concerned with this problem. They designed a government that would curb the power of the majority in many ways. Federalism, checks and balances, and the Bill of Rights all help prevent the concentration of power in the hands of any one group—including the majority. In this, the Supreme Court has been important. It symbolizes the limitations on the majority built into the constitutional framework. In this chapter we look at the role of the Supreme Court and the Constitution in relation to majority rule and minority rights.

Reconciliation of Majority Rule with Minority Rights

The reconciliation of majority rule with minority rights is one of the great dilemmas of democracy. If majority rule is not an easily acceptable absolute principle, neither is minority rights. Give all rights to all minorities—that is, give all minority groups in society the right to disobey the government—and one no longer has a society. Rather, one has a war of all against all. Each of us, after all, is a minority of one.

But where then does one draw the line? What minorities are to be respected and in relation to what rights? Much of the debate on the nature of democracy centers on this question. What rights are so important that they should be protected from the ordinary procedures of democracy whereby the wish of the larger number becomes the rule for all? Historically several kinds of rights have been singled out for protection from the wishes of the majority:

1. The right to free speech, a free press, and freedom of assembly.
2. The right to freedom of religion.

3. The right to have one's property protected from arbitrary acts of the government.
4. The right to have one's person protected from arbitrary acts of the government.

Each of these rights has a somewhat different justification in democratic theory, and each has been given special recognition at one time or another.

Freedom of Speech, Press, and Assembly

Many believe these three rights are the basic ones that must be protected from the majority if democracy is to survive. They are provided in the First Amendment to the Constitution: "Congress shall make no law . . . abridging the freedom of speech, or of the press, or the right of the people peaceably to assemble. . . ." These three rights are what is meant by *civil liberties;* they are also sometimes called First Amendment freedoms. The First Amendment protects these rights against acts of Congress. Over the years the Supreme Court has extended the protection so that state governments are also barred from curtailing them.

First Amendment freedoms are central to a democratic system because they are the key to effective majority rule. Effective majority rule depends on knowledge of alternatives and on the ability of those with minority views to try to convince others. Only if there is freedom to present all sides of an issue can there be a real choice.

And these freedoms are very important to the minority, for a minority cannot expect to carry the day if it is but a small part of the decision-making unit. If majority rule were the only accepted route to decision making, its situation would be hopeless. But the guarantees of free speech, press, and assembly give it a chance to convince others to join with it, thereby forming a new majority. Today's minority can become the basis of tomorrow's majority. Put another way, First Amendment freedoms are supposed to prevent any given majority from becoming "frozen" and therefore too strong. The role of the Supreme Court is important. If the majority tries to put down opposition or outlaw picketing or censor the press, the Court is supposed to block it:

> When the channels of opinion and of peaceful persuasion are corrupted or clogged, political correctives can no longer be relied on, and the democratic system is threatened at its most vital point. In that event, the Court, by intervening, restores the processes of democratic government; it does not disrupt them.[1]

Considerations like these have given the First Amendment freedoms a special place in democratic thought. Some claim they are "absolute" rights, never to be limited by the majority or by the govern-

[1] Robert H. Jackson, *The Struggle for Judicial Supremacy* (New York: Knopf, 1941), p. 285.

Conflict over the limits of free speech arises when speech threatens other values.

ment supposedly speaking for the majority. According to this view, the correction for unpopular ideas or speech is found in the "free marketplace of ideas." No one—neither a minority nor a majority—can legislate truth. Therefore a free society should never bar any group from expressing its views, no matter how unpopular.

Conflicts over the Limits of Free Speech

"Free speech without limitations" sounds like the only acceptable democratic position. But there are arguments against it. For one thing, it clearly violates the idea of majority rule. Suppose a majority of the American people want to bar some form of speech. What is the "democratic" thing to do—bar the speech and thereby violate freedom of speech, or allow it and thereby violate the principle of majority rule? Such a situation is not merely hypothetical. As we saw in Chapter 6, majorities have at times favored the prohibition of speeches favoring communism or atheism. And public-opinion polls on obscenity make it clear that if matters were put to a vote, a majority would oppose the distribution of many books and magazines found on newsstands or the screening of many movies currently in theaters.

These situations help us understand why conflicts over free speech arise. They arise when the speech threatens some other value important to certain groups. Consider some examples.

Libel The right to say what one wants may be a value, but the right of the individual citizen to be protected against unjustified attacks is also a value. Thus limitations of free speech are found in libel laws that protect citizens from such attacks.

But, as in most political issues, the general statement does not go very far in practice. One may agree in principle that speech and the press should be free up to the point where they unfairly offend or hurt some individual. At that point expression should be limited by libel laws. But applying this principle is not so easy. For example, at what point does newspaper criticism of a public official become a libelous attack for which the official can sue the newspaper for damages? These are the issues the courts—including the Supreme Court—are constantly working out.

On the issue of criticism of public officials, the courts have recently leaned in the direction of allowing a wide range of criticism even if it might be damaging. The right to criticize public officials is basic to a democracy. Thus one risks some weakening of the individual's right to be protected from unfair attack in order to make sure the press is free to criticize government activities.[2] And the Court has leaned toward favoring a free press over the protection of the private citizen from libelous statements in the press.[3]

[2] *New York Times* v. *Sullivan* 376 U.S. 254 (1964).
[3] *Gertz* v. *Robert Welch Inc.*

Recent court decisions hold that local standards can determine what is pornography.

Obscenity   Obscenity is another field in which the Supreme Court tries to balance conflicting interests. On one side is the right to publish what one wants (a First Amendment right). On the other side is the right of citizens to protect their children from exposure to material they think will be harmful or to protect themselves from speech they find offensive. On the one hand is the principle that free speech should be limited when it becomes pornographic; that is, all literature and movies ought to be allowed except those that appeal solely to "base or prurient" interests and have no "redeeming social value" or literary qualities. And on the other hand is the principle that all writings and movies should be allowed, regardless of their content.

Most states have some laws banning pornography, but it is hard to define what books and movies fall beyond the line of acceptability. Some people consider many great literary works so damaging to morals that they ought to be barred. In this difficult area the burden falls on the courts to draw the lines.

The Supreme Court has tried for a long time to define what could be barred by state and local pornography laws and what would be protected by the First Amendment. At one time a work could be banned if it had "no redeeming social value." Then the Court proposed that a work that might otherwise be censored as obscene would be saved if it had "serious literary, artistic, political, or scientific value." The problem is that these terms have no clear meaning, and the Court has found itself deciding what is obscene on a case-by-case basis.

In 1973 the Court tried something new. It decided the standards of the local area could apply; what might be pornographic in Kansas would not be in San Francisco.[4] This seemed to clear the way for local censors. But the Court soon made it clear that it had not given up its right to a final say. In a decision overturning a ban in Georgia of the movie *Carnal Knowledge,* the Court made clear that it would continue to see whether local standards were compatible with the First Amendment.

The law is still vague on pornography and obscenity. The Court continues to try to define the boundary between the competing claims of those who would limit pornography and those who claim the right of free speech under the First Amendment.

Free Speech and National Security

The major area of conflict over free speech—and the most important from the point of view of democratic politics—is the conflict between free speech and national security. Free speech is particularly important when it protects those with unpopular political opinions, especially opinions severely critical of government. But the right to express unpopular political opinions may conflict with another right: the right of the society to protect itself.

[4] *Miller* v. *California* 41 LW 4925 (1973).

As with libel and obscenity, it is easier to state principles than to apply them. For instance, the First Amendment guarantee of free speech does not give the citizen the right to commit sabotage or to use violence against government officials, and Congress can pass (and has passed) laws punishing those who commit or try to commit such acts. This principle should be easy to apply, but the boundary between speech and action is by no means clear. Speech, some have argued, can itself be violent. And there is no doubt that speech can be used to incite violent action.

Consider sabotage. The government can arrest and punish those who commit or try to commit sabotage. But:

1. What if I plan an act of sabotage with someone else? I tell him where to plant the bomb and when to do it. I only "speak." He does the actual bombing. Is my "speech" protected by the First Amendment?
2. What if I make a speech at a public meeting saying people should sabotage government operations? After the meeting some of those who heard me speak go out and plant bombs in government buildings. Is my "speech" protected?
3. What if I make a speech like the one described in Example 2, but no one acts? Is my "speech" protected?
4. What if I make a speech that merely says there "are times when it would be justifiable to sabotage the government"? (That is, I do not directly advocate such sabotage.) Suppose someone hears the speech, decides the current circumstances justify sabotage, and attempts it. Is my "speech" protected?
5. Suppose I write a book on the history of sabotage and treat some famous saboteurs sympathetically? Is my "speech" protected?

It should be clear from these examples that the clash between the principle of free speech and the principle that the government can punish action directed against it can arise in many circumstances. And at times it is unclear whether one is dealing with speech or action. For one thing, it is hard to determine when speech directly advocates action and when it does not. In Example 1 it would seem clear that it does; perhaps in Example 2 as well. But what if one says, as in Example 4, "there are times when one must act"? Is that person advocating action?

And it's hard to tell whether the speech in fact leads to action. Again it would seem clear that it does in Example 1. But can we be sure, in Example 2, that the speech led to the action? (What if the action comes a month or so later?)

In Example 1 the "speech" involved would probably not be protected by the First Amendment. It is clearly part of a criminal action and punishable without violating the Constitution.

Example 5 is a fairly clear case of "speech" that is protected under the First Amendment (even though it is possible that someone would read such a book and be motivated to imitate a saboteur).

Examples 2, 3, and 4 lie in between, and it is not clear whether the courts would consider the behavior *speech* protected by the Consti-

Civil liberties have sometimes been suspended in wartime. Japanese-Americans at an Arkansas relocation center during World War II.

tution or *activity* punishable as subversive. At times the courts have seemed to rely on a doctrine of "clear and present danger," first enunciated by Justice Oliver Wendell Holmes in 1919.[5] Under this doctrine speech is punishable only when it may lead straight to illegal action and when the connection between the speech and the illegal action is unambiguous. But the "clear and present danger" doctrine is just another way of stating the problem of deciding where speech ends and action begins. When does such a danger exist? The doctrine is not a clear principle that can be followed by the courts.

Governmental Actions Against Conspiracy and Subversion

Drawing the line between civil liberties and the right of the government to protect itself is made difficult by the fact that attempts to limit these liberties usually take place in times of national emergency—in particular, in time of war. At such times the dangers of sabotage and subversion loom large in the eyes of the government and the public. Civil liberties usually suffer. In the Civil War, for instance, President Lincoln suspended the writ of habeas corpus (a fundamental right guaranteed in the Constitution under which citizens cannot be held in jail without being brought into court or to trial). And in World War II, all Americans of Japanese ancestry, whether or not there was evidence of subversive activity, were moved from the West Coast to "relocation centers" in the Midwest, where they were kept until the war was over.

In both cases the Supreme Court later said the government had acted unconstitutionally, but in both cases the Court decision came after the war was over.

The Smith Act of 1940   In the three decades since World War II, the issue of civil liberties vs. national security has centered on a series of laws aimed at blocking conspiracy and subversion. These

[5] *Schenck v. United States* 249 U.S. 47 (1919).

laws, and the court cases relating to them, arose when the nation was involved in a "cold war" with the forces of communism. The Smith Act, passed in 1940, made it a crime to teach or advocate the violent overthrow of the U.S. government. In 1951 the Supreme Court upheld the conviction of Eugene Dennis, head of the U.S. Communist party, under the Smith Act.[6] Critics of this decision (including the dissenting justices) argued that the defendants were convicted for speech, not action (for "teaching and advocating"), but the Supreme Court majority held that the government had the right to protect itself against the *actions* the defendants taught and advocated. Therefore such teaching and advocacy was punishable.

In later cases the Supreme Court has generally upheld the provisions of the Smith Act. But it has put a heavy burden of proof on the government and has been narrow in its interpretation of the Act. In this way it has limited the extent to which the law can curtail speech, without ever saying provisions of the law violate the constitutional guarantees of free speech.

The McCarran Act of 1950 The Court's indecision is also seen in its interpretation of another post-World War II law — the McCarran Act of 1950 requiring registration of communist and communist-front organizations — which Congress passed at the beginning of the Korean War. The Supreme Court held that although the registration requirements were constitutional, making the officials and other members of the party register would mean they could be required to testify against themselves, and this would violate their freedom from self-incrimination guaranteed by the Fifth Amendment.[7] Thus the Supreme Court did not challenge the constitutionality of the registration requirements, but it did interpret them narrowly so as to limit the extent to which they curtailed freedom of association.

The Antiriot Bill The most recent attempt by Congress to legislate against subversion came in response to the urban unrest and violence of the late 1960s. A 1968 antiriot bill made it a crime to cross a state line to incite riots or conspire to do so. The law was invoked in the trial of the "Chicago Seven," accused of conspiring to incite riots at the 1968 Democratic Convention in Chicago. No conspiracy was proved, but five of the defendants were convicted of crossing a state line to incite a riot. Those convictions were reversed in 1972 by a federal appeals court because of the way their trial had been conducted. But the court upheld the antiriot law itself. As with the Smith and McCarran Acts, the courts provide narrow interpretations that limit the impact of such laws on civil liberties but do not challenge the laws directly (which makes it possible for the laws to be used to limit free speech).

[6] *Dennis et al.* v. *United States* 341 U.S. 494 (1951).
[7] *Communist Party* v. *Subversive Activities Control Board* 367 U.S. 1 (1961).

Symbolic Speech   The Supreme Court has enlarged the definition of speech to include symbolic acts, such as wearing armbands to show protest or hanging the American flag upside-down as a symbol of political distress. In 1974, for instance, it ruled that someone who sewed the U.S. flag on the seat of his pants could not be punished under a Massachusetts law against abusing the flag. The law, according to the Court, was unconstitutionally vague.[8] And it similarly overturned the conviction of a student who protested the war in Vietnam by attaching a peace symbol to the flag and hanging it upside-down. The interest of the state in protecting national symbols from abuse and ridicule, the Court reasoned, was not as great as the interest of society in free political expression.

The Free Press and the Pentagon Papers   One of the most dramatic Supreme Court decisions on matters of free speech grew out of the publication of the Pentagon Papers. The case pitted two of the best-known newspapers in the country, the *New York Times* and the *Washington Post,* against the executive branch of the government. It arose when the government tried to block publication of the Pentagon Papers, papers containing top secret information on the Vietnam war, in which the nation was still involved.

The government was attempting *prior restraint;* that is, it was attempting to block the publication of material in advance. The government claimed publication of the papers would do "grave and irreparable" damage to the national interest. This national security interest was placed against the First Amendment guarantee of a free press. In previous cases the Supreme Court had struck down attempts at prior restraint. And in the Pentagon Papers case it reaffirmed that rule.[9] The newspapers were freed from restraint and continued to publish the papers. The papers revealed involvement in Vietnam by the Kennedy and Johnson administrations long before the public or Congress knew what was going on.

This Supreme Court decision was hailed as a victory for free speech over national security. But such victories are rarely clear-cut. The newspapers were able to continue publishing the Pentagon Papers and the prohibition against prior restraint was upheld. But the nine justices wrote nine separate opinions on the case—six in favor of the newspapers' position and three in favor of the government's. This shows how confused the law is on the subject. Most of the justices said there could be cases in which prior restraint would be allowed if publication of some national security material would "result in direct, immediate, and irreparable damage to our nation or its people." In this case, they found no such damage likely. But the possibility of prior restraint in the future was not removed.

Furthermore, the Court left open the possibility that the news-

[8] *Smith* v. *Goguen* 94 S. Ct. 1242 (1974).
[9] *New York Times Co.* v. *United States* 403 U.S. 713 (1971).

papers would be prosecuted after publication for harm done to the national interest. In fact the newspapers were not brought to trial for this, though Daniel Ellsberg, who had leaked the papers to the press, was prosecuted for violations of national security. (His case, in turn, was dismissed when it was shown that the government had used illegal means to get evidence against him.)

Though the Pentagon Papers case resulted in no clear precedent for future cases, it remains an important example of the way the Supreme Court protects First Amendment freedoms. The administration used its strongest argument—national security—in attempting to block publication of the Pentagon Papers. In most societies (democratic as well as nondemocratic), governments would be able to bar publication for such a reason. In this case, the Supreme Court said the newspapers, not the government, had the right to decide what news to print.

Freedom of Speech: Not an Absolute Right

In sum, the freedoms guaranteed in the First Amendment are real but by no means absolute. Attempts by the federal government to use antisubversive legislation to limit such freedom in the name of national security cannot obscure the fact that in the United States it is legal to express strong criticism of the government. But the antisubversive laws passed by Congress, the enforcement of those laws by the Justice Department, and the interpretation of those laws by the courts make clear that the First Amendment freedoms are not absolute. At times of crisis or political conflict, the government is likely to try to prevent subversive acts and in so doing limit political dissent. The Supreme Court checks these limitations of free speech. But it often does so rather late (when the damage to free speech may already have been done) and usually by restricting the government to narrow limits in its enforcement of these laws rather than by directly challenging their constitutionality.

Freedom of Religion

The same constitutional amendment that guarantees free speech contains the equally basic guarantee of freedom of religion. The First Amendment bars the government from interfering with the religious practices of the American people—either by setting up a state-supported church or by favoring any one religion over another. This may be one of the cornerstones of civil peace in America. In a society with many religions, severe conflict may arise if the government favors one over another. The First Amendment reduces this possibility.

Yet, as with freedom of speech, the wording of the First Amendment does not settle the issue. The famous words of that amendment—"Congress shall make no law respecting an establishment of religion, or prohibiting the free exercise thereof . . ."—are ambiguous. The provision was meant to bar a state-supported religion and permanently separate church and state. But how wide that separation was supposed to be remains unclear.

The government cannot establish a church. But does this mean it cannot give aid to parochial schools? Does it mean it cannot provide buses for children going to such schools? What about policemen to direct traffic outside such schools?

The government cannot prohibit an individual from practicing his religion. But what if his religion involves polygamy or snake-handling? Or forbids him to pay taxes or serve in the armed forces or salute the flag? Are all activities justified if they represent "exercises of religion"? If not, has freedom of religion been limited?

As with free speech, it can be seen that the Constitution leaves unanswered questions. The result is a mixed, inconsistent system under which the government respects the separation of church and state in general, but not completely. It does not (under Supreme Court rulings) give aid to parochial schools, but it is allowed (also under Supreme Court rulings) to provide buses for children going to such schools. Chapel attendance was required at the nation's military academies—West Point, Annapolis, the Air Force Academy —until 1972, when the Supreme Court ruled it unconstitutional. But the federal government still supports chaplains in the armed forces, and the sessions of Congress open with prayer. Those who object for religious reasons can refuse to salute the flag. But citizens cannot refuse to pay taxes for religious reasons.

All these seeming inconsistencies stem from the same general problem—the need to balance one value with other values. Consider the following aspects of church-state relations.

The Right to Worship as One Sees Fit

Freedom of religion is clearly guaranteed in the First Amendment. The government can neither prohibit nor enforce any particular religion. Yet the boundaries of the free exercise of religion become controversial when religious practice would violate some other principle. In the nineteenth century the Supreme Court upheld the government's prohibition of polygamy even though this was a fundamental practice of the Mormon religion.[10] The Court reasoned that polygamy was so contrary to the American moral code that even though it was a matter of religious faith it could not be allowed to continue. One wonders what decision the Court would reach today, when views about the nature of marriage have loosened somewhat. But even if the Court decided polygamy is no longer as shocking as it once was, there are certainly many other practices—such as public nudity—that it would continue to prohibit.

Freedom of Religion in the Field of Education

The field of education offers many examples of the delicate balance between freedom of religion and the requirements of the state.

[10] *Reynolds* v. *United States* 98 U.S. 145 (1879).

The Supreme Court has upheld compulsory education laws even for members of religious groups opposed to education—the Amish, for example. But it has allowed parents to choose religious schools for their children (as long as these schools meet state educational standards). However, religious schools are not able to get government support. Apparently the Court believes, on the one hand, that the interest of society in educating its citizens overrides the objections of some religious groups to compulsory education but, on the other, that there is no overriding need for such education to take place in state-controlled schools.

The attempt to balance the rights of minority religious practices against obedience to general laws is found in the so-called flag-salute cases. The Jehovah's Witnesses—whose firm rejection of secular authority has led to many run-ins with the law and to numerous court cases—oppose the worship of images. They do not allow their children to salute the flag. But laws required a flag-salute ceremony at the beginning of the school day, the justification of such laws being that the state had the right to teach children respect for national symbols.

In 1940 the Supreme Court upheld such a state law, saying Jehovah's Witnesses could be required to salute the flag.[11] Three years later the Court reversed itself—with four justices who had supported the right of the state to require a flag salute now supporting the right of the minority group to refuse to do so.[12] The new reasoning of the Court was that the state's interest in a flag salute was not important enough to override the right of the minority to follow its religious convictions.

Freedom of Religion for Nonbelievers

The provisions of the First Amendment were intended to prevent the government from favoring a particular religion over another. But might not the government favor those who were religious over those who were not? In many ways governmental policy seemed to do this. But in recent years the Court has curtailed such practices. We have mentioned the abolition of compulsory chapel attendance at the military academies. In addition, the Supreme Court struck down a longstanding provision of the Maryland constitution requiring that those holding public office say they believe in God.

Conscientious-Objector Status Similarly the Court has extended the right to refuse to do military service to those who do not belong to an established religion or say they believe in God. Earlier, those who claimed conscientious-objector status had to prove their right to it on religious grounds—usually a membership in some religious group that traditionally opposed military service. But in 1965 the

[11] *Minersville School District* v. *Gobitis* 310 U.S. 586 (1940).
[12] *West Virginia State Board of Education* v. *Barnette* 319 U.S. 624 (1943).

Does prayer in the public schools violate the Constitution? The Supreme Court has said that it does.

Court decided this discriminated in favor of particular religions, and extended the right to conscientious-objector status to those who oppose war on ethical grounds.[13]

School Prayers   Perhaps the most controversial problem of religious freedom is in the area of school prayers. Does it violate the freedom of nonbelievers if the government sponsors prayers in the public schools—even if the prayers are nonsectarian and not compulsory?

Many school systems around the country traditionally opened the school day with some prayer. In 1962 the Supreme Court barred such prayers.[14] It ruled that a school district in New York state violated the Constitution by requiring that classes be started with a nonsectarian prayer composed by the New York Board of Regents. The school board had specifically indicated that pupils could, at the request of their parents, be excused. Yet the Court held that such prayers violated the separation of church and state, since they were required by the government. And in a similar case the Court barred a Pennsylvania law that the Bible be read daily in the schools in that state.

There can be little doubt that the Court was taking the side of a small minority. Public-opinion polls have consistently shown large majorities of the public in favor of school prayers. The parents who objected (and brought the case to the courts) were a small and generally unpopular group.

Here is a clear case where the issue of separation of church and state is far from settled. Critics of the Supreme Court's decisions argue that while the minority who believe in no religion can expect tolerance for their views, such tolerance is adequately expressed in the fact that children do not have to take part in the prayers. Supporters of the Court's position argue that the Constitution requires more than mere tolerance.

Government Aid to Religious Schools

Another major controversy is over government aid to private religious schools. Does it violate the separation of church and state if the government gives support for such schools? The argument in favor of such support is that these schools contribute to society by educating children. And since parents who send their children to such schools are also taxed to pay for the public-school system, parents who choose a religious school, which they have to support as well, are doubly burdened because of their beliefs. Opponents of such aid say such aid would represent a discriminatory support for particular religions.

The Supreme Court has generally opposed support for religious schools. But, as in most of these issues, the position is by no means

---

[13] *United States* v. *Seegar* 380 U.S. 163 (1965).
[14] *Engel* v. *Vitale* 370 U.S. 421 (1962) and *Abington School District* v. *Schempp* 374 U.S. 203 (1963).

firm. The Court has barred aid to religious elementary and secondary schools, but some aid to church-related schools on the college level is allowed. And various forms of indirect aid—such as school buses—is allowed.[15]

The Right to Property

Throughout American history a large share of the national wealth has been in the hands of a fairly small minority. This condition has persisted despite the principle of majoritarianism, which would seem to give to the poorer majority a means of using government to redistribute wealth. As we saw in Chapter 3, this redistribution has not taken place. We reviewed some of the reasons in that chapter. Here we wish simply to stress that the Constitution helps protect the property rights of citizens.

In the 1780s, unlike today, there was no talk of property rights vs. human rights. The rights for which the Revolutionary War was fought were the rights of political liberty and of property. "The true foundation of republican government," wrote Thomas Jefferson, "is the equal right of every citizen, in his person and in his property." This did *not* mean every citizen would have equal amounts of property. The delegates to the Constitutional Convention met not to redistribute property but to protect it.

Protection of Property Rights

Protection of property rights was written into the Constitution and is established in legal precedent. For example, the Constitution prohibits any state from passing a law that would impair the obligations of contract. There is also a just-compensation clause. The founders recognized that privately owned lands might be needed for public projects, but they were concerned that the costs of such a project should be widely distributed. Thus the property owner would be fairly compensated out of the public treasury. Other clauses restrict both federal and state governments from depriving a citizen of his property without *due process of law*. Stemming from these comparatively simple constitutional provisions are laws protecting private property, and standing behind them is, of course, the police.

What is meant by *property rights*? We have in mind the basic right to own something and prevent others from using it. So we put locks on doors. We also mean the right to sell or trade the thing we own, be it tangible property such as a car or house or intangible property such as stocks and bonds. And we mean the right to will property to chosen heirs. But the rights to own, sell, and give are limited. The courts and the legislatures in the United States have put many restrictions on private property, which raise complicated questions about "minority rights" in a majoritarian democracy.

[15] *Everson* v. *Board of Education of Ewing* 330 U.S. 1 (1947).

The Property Owner vs. the Public Interest

Government restrictions on property often rest on the claim that the public interest overrides the rights of property. The owner of a 300-horsepower automobile cannot drive it at its highest speed because he would thereby threaten "the public safety." The home-owner with a diseased elm tree in his front yard is told he must cut it down to prevent the disease from spreading. The contractor building a downtown apartment building has to include parking space to reduce the public nuisance of cars parked on the streets. In each of these cases one might well ask, "Who are they to tell me what to do with my property?" "They" is the government claiming to act in the public interest.

The task of defining and then applying something as vague as "the public interest" is very complex. The definition of public interest varies from one area to another and from one time to another. Take, for instance, billboards. The right of a property owner to lease some of his land to a billboard company was not challenged through much of our history. And thus our public highways are surrounded by private advertisements. But now, spurred by a different concept of "public interest," some local and state governments are beginning to restrict this practice. In this respect the United States is catching up with other nations. You can drive from one end of Canada to the other and never have the scenery blocked by a billboard.

The Property Owner vs. Human Rights

On the 1964 ballot in California, there was a proposed state constitutional amendment guaranteeing the right of any property holder in California to sell, lease, or rent his property to anyone he chose. This seems a reasonable enough proposal and certainly is in line with property rights. The proposed amendment, however, was in fact in response to an open-occupancy bill passed by the California legislature. The open-occupancy law banned racial discrimination in selling and renting property. Here is a clear case of "property rights" (the right of a citizen to do as he wants with his own home) vs. "human rights" (the right of black citizens not to be discriminated against). The voters of California passed the amendment, but it was later declared unconstitutional by the state supreme court, and this ruling was upheld by the United States Supreme Court.

The open-occupancy law in California shows how legislatures and courts restrict the uses of property when these uses violate other constitutional rights—in this case the right of equality before the law. When two constitutional rights are in conflict, it is the courts that must make a final decision. Sometimes this puts the courts on the side of the minority against the majority. Such was the case in California, when both the state and the federal courts overturned the clear majority preferences of the citizens. The property rights of the majority were restricted in favor of the human rights of the minority.

At other times it is the minority whose property rights are restricted in favor of the human rights of the majority. Progressive income taxes and inheritance taxes can be looked at in this light. A portion of the wealth of the richer groups in society is taxed. This leads to some redistribution from a minority to the majority. We saw in Chapter 3 that this does not go very far; it nevertheless shows some attempt to restrict the property rights of a wealthy minority.

But despite limitations on property because of the public interest or because of competing constitutional rights, there remains firmly planted in our heritage a strong respect for the rights of private ownership. It is remarkable that the restrictions on property are so few. In this way majoritarian democracy has been much less of a threat than many feared. John Dickinson, a delegate to the Constitutional Convention, warned that "the most dangerous influence" to public order was "those multitudes without property and without principle with which our country, like all others, will soon abound." But Dickinson was wrong on one very important fact: The multitudes have not been without property and, thus, have not supported any major challenge to the rights of private ownership. Thomas Jefferson saw the importance of widespread ownership of property when he remarked that "everyone, by his property, or by his satisfactory situation, is interested in the support of law and order." The support of law and order meant in Jefferson's time, as it does today, the use of the legal and police powers of the government to protect private property.

The Right of Privacy

Does the Constitution protect the individual citizen from the society and the state when it comes to his or her private life? This is a new and fascinating area of constitutional interpretation. Many states have laws regulating the sexual activities of citizens. At one time or another the laws have made so-called deviant sexual behavior or the use of any birth-control device illegal. In addition, most states have had laws making abortions illegal.

In recent years the Supreme Court has begun to recognize a citizen's right to "privacy"—arguing, that is, that the state has no business regulating the intimate behavior of individuals. The "right of privacy" is not mentioned in the Constitution. But the Court has found such a right to be implied in other rights that are mentioned, such as the Fourth Amendment right against "unreasonable searches and seizures," the Fifth Amendment protection against "self-incrimination," and the broad but undefined "other rights" mentioned in the Ninth Amendment.[16]

The Supreme Court cited these rights to overturn a Connecticut law that made it illegal to use any drug or device to prevent con-

[16] *Griswold* v. *Connecticut* 381 U.S. 479, 490–492 (1965).

ABORTION IS MURDER

In recent years new questions of personal and sexual freedom have been raised before the courts.

ception.[17] Lower federal courts have cited the same right of privacy to challenge Virginia's sodomy statute, broadly ruling that states could not regulate the private behavior of individuals whether married or unmarried. As the Court put it, the right of privacy applies to "intimate sexual relations between consenting adults, carried out under secluded conditions."[18] And a similar decision by a federal district court recently held that a school district violated the right to privacy by barring the hiring of homosexuals. "The time has now come for private, consenting, adult homosexuality to enter the sphere of constitutionally protected interests."[19] In cases of this sort the courts expand the range of private activities that are protected from the control of the state—even though such activities may be looked on with disfavor by a majority of the population.

Abortion   The most controversial issue involving the right to privacy is that of abortion. In an important decision in 1973, the Supreme Court overturned antiabortion laws in forty-six states. It held that the right to privacy included the right of a woman to decide to terminate a pregnancy during the first three months.

Few Court decisions have aroused as much conflict. The Catholic Church opposes abortion, as do many others. The opponents of abortion claim to represent the constitutional rights of another group: unborn children. It is likely that this controversy will continue, for there are deeply felt interests on each side. Some antiabortionists have started to seek an amendment to the Constitution to overrule the Supreme Court. In the meantime the Court ruling tips the scales in favor of the right of pregnant women to choose whether or not they wish to continue their pregnancy.

[17] Ibid.
[18] *Lovisi* v. *Slayton* 363 Fed. Supp. 620, 625–626 (1973).
[19] 41 LW 2691 (1973).

Criminal Rights

The area of criminal rights may be the hardest one in which to balance individual freedom and majority concerns. Crime has grown to huge proportions in American society. The 1969 Uniform Crime Reports listed over 4.3 million crimes against property and nearly 700,000 violent crimes in that year alone, and much additional crime is unreported. A Gallup survey in 1972 showed that 1 out of every 3 center-city residents had been mugged, assaulted, or burglarized in the preceding 12 months.

Many have blamed the growth in crime on Supreme Court decisions "coddling criminals." In 1968 Nixon, campaigning for the Presidency, charged that the Court had put up a "barbed wire of legalisms . . . to protect a suspect from invasion of his rights [and] has effectively shielded hundreds of criminals from punishment." According to this view, if we put fewer restrictions on the police and the prosecutor, we could rid society of more criminals.

Perhaps so, but a democratic society has other values besides protection from criminals. Citizens in a free society are protected from excessive and arbitrary use of police power. This raises the dilemma of buying greater security against crime at the price of greater insecurity against the abuse of governmental power. For example, in the Drug Abuse Act of 1970 Congress authorized the use of "no-knock" search warrants by federal narcotics agents. Agents could break into homes without knocking if they could later show a magistrate that giving a warning would result in, for example, destruction of the drugs as evidence. But the result was that narcotics agents took advantage of the no-knock rule to break into homes in the middle of the night, harass innocent people, and destroy personal property—all without a warrant. Congress accordingly repealed the rule in 1974.

The Focus of Criminal Rights

Like the rights discussed earlier, the rights of criminals are rooted in our constitutional system. Common law assumes that a person is innocent until proven guilty and that the accused has the same rights as all other citizens and is similarly protected against violation of those rights. Here the due process clause of the Fifth Amendment is basic; it affirms not only that government itself is subject to the law but also that citizens cannot be denied legal recourse when their basic rights are violated.

But what are the particular rights at issue? It is useful to distinguish between the *substantive* and the *procedural* aspects of criminal rights. By substantive rights we mean the essence of what is protected: privacy and dignity, freedom of person and property, and protection against "cruel and unusual" punishment. Procedural rights involve the steps and standards the government must follow before imposing punishment. These procedural rights, originally

"Stop and frisk" laws are a subject of constitutional controversy.

applicable only to the federal government, are guaranteed in the Bill of Rights. They have been elaborated by Supreme Court rulings and extended to the states as well. We turn next to a summary of these criminal procedures.

Criminal Procedures

Arrest   To arrest a suspect for an offense, a police officer must have "probable cause" to believe the person has committed or is about to commit a crime. Mere suspicion is not enough, although the line between suspicion and probable cause is not clear. Broadly speaking, the officer must have some tangible evidence. Most arrests are made without a warrant.

Protection against unreasonable arrest was affirmed in a case stemming from the May 1971 Vietnam protests in Washington. Hundreds of demonstrators had marched on the Capitol for a rally. While the protestors listened to the speeches of anti-war congressmen, police arrested 1200 of them and took them to a makeshift detention center. Of all those arrested, only 8 were actually tried, and the charges against them were eventually dismissed. The demonstrators went to court, claiming gross violation of their rights. In 1975 a Washington jury awarded $12 million in damages—roughly $10,000 apiece. It is thought to be the first case in U.S. history in which damages were awarded directly for violations of rights guaranteed by the Constitution.

Search and Seizure   "The right of the people," states the Fourth Amendment, "to be secure . . . against unreasonable searches and seizures, shall not be violated, and no warrants shall issue, but upon probable cause, . . . and particularly describing the place to be searched, and the persons or things to be seized." Interpretation of this right is so dependent on particular circumstances that Supreme Court rulings have varied almost as widely as police practices. In general, the Court has confined the area to be searched without a warrant to the person of the suspect and the immediate area under his control. If the authorities wish to look into a suspect's home or office, they normally must get a warrant. A police officer may carry out a search and seizure without a warrant, however, if there is probable cause to believe a crime has been committed and there is no time to get a warrant, or if it is necessary to seize weapons or to prevent the destruction of evidence. These rules are easy enough to apply in many cases, but situations often arise in which decisions must be made on the spur of the moment and in real danger.

The Court has found it very hard to establish general principles on the application of "stop and frisk" laws in several states. The Court has approved of at least modified searches when there is enough cause to suspect criminal activity but no reasonable or probable grounds for arrest. For example, in 1968 the Court found it reasonable for a detective to question and then search three men he

Telephone box used in an illegal wiretap.

observed repeatedly casing a store. The Court then affirmed their conviction for carrying concealed weapons.[20] On the other hand, the same justices in the same year reversed a conviction on the grounds that the fact that the defendant was seen talking to a number of known drug addicts did not justify his being searched and convicted for possession of heroin.[21]

The Court has also moved to bring electronic eavesdropping within the scope of the guarantee against unreasonable search and seizure, saying such eavesdropping is illegal without a court order.

As a further effort to discourage unauthorized search and seizure, the Court has banned the use in court of evidence gotten in this way. We noted earlier the dismissal of the Ellsberg case when it was shown that the government had used illegal means to get evidence against him.

The Right to a Fair Hearing

By judicial interpretation, conditions necessary to produce a "fair hearing" have been included in the constitutional requirement of due process. Such rights include prohibitions against having to testify against oneself, against unreasonable bail, and against double jeopardy (a defendant can be tried only once for a single act). The Constitution also guarantees the right to a speedy and public trial, to an impartial jury, to be informed of the charges against one, to confront the witnesses against one, and to make favorable witnesses appear in one's behalf (the power of subpoena).

Moreover, as we saw in the previous chapter, the Court has ruled that criminal defendants must be provided counsel at government expense if they cannot afford their own,[22] and that the police must inform the accused of his constitutional rights, including the right to free counsel, before they can begin questioning him.[23]

And though the Bill of Rights does not specifically mention a right to appeal, the federal government and all the states allow at least one such appeal as a matter of legal right. The appellate court examines the trial as a whole to make sure it was fair to the accused in both substance and procedure: to ensure, for example, the judge was unbiased, the jury was not improperly influenced, and a reasonable body of people could have concluded from the evidence that the defendant was guilty. Here too the Supreme Court has ruled that the government must give needy convicts free legal counsel to make good the right to an initial appeal.

Approaches to Criminal Justice

The Adversary Model   As we have observed, in recent years the Supreme Court has moved aggressively to extend the Bill of Rights to cover all criminal proceedings at all stages. The goal has been to

[20] *Terry* v. *Ohio* 392 U.S. 1 (1968).
[21] *Sibron* v. *New York* 392 U.S. 40, 64 (1968).
[22] *Gideon* v. *Wainwright* 372 U.S. 335 (1963).
[23] *Miranda* v. *Arizona* 384 U.S. 436 (1966).

better assure equal treatment for all defendants, rich or poor, particularly by requiring that free legal counsel be provided to the poor. In making such a requirement the Court has not acted out of benevolence to the poor. Rather, it has acted in recognition of the fact that society has deliberately chosen the adversary system. As discussed in the previous chapter, the adversary system assumes that a vigorous clash of opposing sides—the accused vs. the prosecution—is the best means of uncovering the truth. Since this necessarily involves complex rules of procedure and evidence far beyond the grasp of all but trained lawyers, each side must have enough resources to present its case if the truth is to emerge. It is because society—not the individual defendant—has chosen the adversary system that the Court has ensured legal counsel for all those accused. Otherwise the greater resources available to the government would tip the scales of justice hopelessly against many defendants.

The Administrative Model   The fact remains that in the great majority of criminal cases, the adversary model does not come into play. Most cases—about 90 percent—never come to trial. Instead, they are handled according to what can be called the *administrative model* of criminal justice. The administrative model differs from the adversary system in both assumption and purpose.

The administrative system of justice assumes that most defendants are guilty. This is based on the observation that the police do not arrest people at random. The objective therefore is to determine the proper treatment for the defendant. This is done most commonly through "plea bargaining," in which the prosecutor offers to reduce or drop certain charges against the defendant in return for a guilty plea. Thus the defense and the prosecution are not adversaries but negotiators. The overriding concern they share is to maintain a smooth flow of cases and to avoid a breakdown of the court structure. As a Manhattan prosecutor put it, "our office keeps eight courtrooms extremely busy trying 5 percent of the cases. If even 10 percent of the cases ended in a trial, the system would break down. We can't afford to think very much about anything else."[24]

Any defendant can of course insist on a trial. But if he is in fact guilty, he may decide there is little to gain from adversary proceedings. The administrative process encourages guilty pleas rather than requests for trial, notably by setting bail beyond what the accused can pay. The defendant may conclude that he has little to gain from a long delay in jail awaiting trial.

The administrative system of justice lacks formal safeguards for the accused. Whereas due-process rights are at the heart of the adversary process, administrative justice has few procedural restrictions. The important decisions are made in private between the prosecutor, the defense, and the judge. The administrative model

[24] Albert W. Alschuler, "The Prosecutor's Role in Plea Bargaining," *University of Chicago Law Review*, 36 (1968), 55.

is governed by the interests of all the parties involved in disposing of a case so that everybody gains something: a high conviction rate for the prosecutor, a reduction of charge and sentence for the accused, and a more efficient flow of cases through the court system.

It must be remembered that the adversary and administrative models of justice are not found in pure forms. In practice one model may be mingled with the other, and typically they coexist within the same courtroom. Nonetheless they do reflect a basic difference. The administrative process views criminal justice from the standpoint of society's interest in an effective, efficient system of arresting and sentencing criminals. The adversary process views it from the standpoint of the right to challenge before a judge each action of the government. This stress on individual rights is considered necessary to protect society against arbitrary use of police power.

Controversy

The Constitution bars the government from favoring one religion over another. It is supposed to keep the government out of religion and religion out of the government. Yet this barrier has never been absolute. There are chaplains in the military; the sessions of Congress open with prayer; the Pledge of Allegiance was rewritten to read "one nation, under God."

A main area of controversy is prayers in public schools. The Supreme Court has generally ruled that such prayers are unconstitutional, but communities often try to get around these rulings.

One Side

Communities should be allowed to require that school begin with a prayer. Some communities may not want to pass such laws, and that is all right. But some communities are quite religious, and if the local citizens feel that a prayer is a good way to begin the day, they should have the right to require it.

Furthermore, they can allow pupils who do not want to take part in the prayer to leave the room. And prayers can be nonsectarian. Thus no one loses any freedom. On the contrary, when it forbids school prayers the Supreme Court takes away the freedom of local communities to run their schools as they want.

The Other Side

It is true that many Americans want the school day to open with prayer. And in many communities a large majority would favor this. But it is just such majorities against which the minority has to be protected. Prayer in the schools represents a breakdown of the constitutional barrier between church and state. It places the support of the state behind religion.

Nor is it adequate protection for the minority if the child who does not want to join in the prayer can leave the room. The Supreme Court was correct in overturning school-prayer laws even when that protection was built in. The reason is that the child will feel pressure to be like the majority. Prayer does not belong in the schools.

15

White House, State House, City Hall: Federalism in America

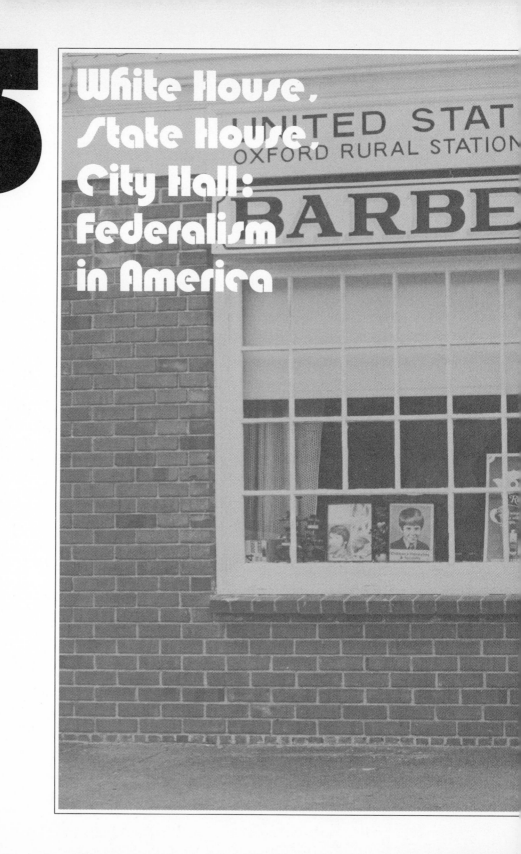

To understand the full complexity of government in America, it is important to note that one must talk not of American government but of American *governments*. A major fact of political life is that there are many governments in America. The federal government in Washington is of course the biggest and the most powerful. But it is just one of a large number of governments; there are also state governments and a great variety of local governments.

Unitary Governments, Confederations, and Federations

A nation may have a unitary government or may be a confederation or federation. A unitary government is one in which all state and local governments are subordinate to the central government; the latter creates and, if it wishes, can abolish local governments. Policies are made centrally. Many European nations, such as France, have such unitary systems. At the other extreme is a confederation. In a confederation the central government is subordinate to the state governments. It has little direct power over the individual citizen; it acts only through the state governments. An example of a confederation is the government established by the Articles of Confederation between 1783 and 1788.

A federal form of government is somewhere between these two types. In a federation neither the central government nor the state governments are subordinate. Neither can abolish the other, and each has a sphere of activity independent of the other. Both levels have direct power over citizens. In short, neither the central government nor the state governments are supreme.

What form of government do we have in the United States? The traditional answer is that we have a federal form of government, in contrast to unitary governments and confederations. But in practice it is difficult to fit the United States neatly into any category. (Note the confusion in our language: When we talk of a "federal form of government," we refer to the relations between the central government in Washington and the states. But the term *federal government* also means the central or national government in Washington.)

If a federal form of government implies that the central and state governments are somehow equal, the United States does not have such a form of government. The state governments are clearly subordinate to the federal government in Washington. If a federal form of government means each level has certain powers that the other level cannot take away, the United States does not have such a form of government. The current interpretation of the Constitution by the Supreme Court is that national laws (that is, laws of the U.S. Congress) are the "supreme law of the land" and override any state laws that interfere. In these ways the United States resembles a unitary form of government.

WHITE HOUSE, STATE
HOUSE, CITY HALL:
FEDERALISM IN AMERICA

But it is far from a unitary government. For one thing, the states are not created by the federal government and cannot be abolished by it. The preservation of the states is, of course, meaningless if all their powers are taken away. But though under present constitutional interpretation the federal government could take over almost all state functions if it wished, the fact remains that it has not and is unlikely to do so. For several reasons state governments remain important and independent centers of power. The federal and state governments can each raise and spend money; each level has important control over our lives.

Can we, then, call the United States a federation? In some ways yes and in others no. It is a federation through the constitutional guarantee of the survival of the states. It is also a federation in the sense that real powers remain in the states. But it resembles a unitary government as well. The central government is clearly dominant and could be more so if it wanted.

Perhaps it is more useful to consider the ways the nation and the states interrelate than to try to label the system. The important questions are: Where are decisions made? How is authority divided? How are the arguments of centralization and decentralization settled?

The delegates to the Constitutional Convention tried to deal with the question of division of powers by naming different areas in which the governments would be active. But there has never been a simple division of labor with the states dealing with some problems, the federal government with others. Rather, the history of the relationship of the states and the nation is one of constant change and complex interaction; it involves shared and overlapping powers more often than separate and distinct ones.

Local Governments

The pattern of government in America would be relatively simple if one were dealing only with the national government and the states. Fifty-one governments are, after all, not that many. But there are many, many more governments in America—county governments, cities, towns, townships, as well as special districts for all sorts of purposes from education to sewage disposal to recreation to mosquito abatement. Indeed, as one can see from Table 15.1, there are almost 80,000 government units in America today: 18,517 municipalities, 16,991 townships, 23,885 special districts, and 15,781 school districts.

Table 15.1
Number and Types
of Local Government, 1967

Counties	3,044
Municipalities	18,517
Townships	16,991
Special districts	23,885
School districts	15,781
All local governments	78,259

Source: U.S. Department of Commerce, Bureau of the Census, *Census of Governments, 1972.*

423

Are these 78,000 units really governments? Some would say no. Only the federal government and the states are guaranteed existence and autonomy by the American Constitution. This means that in certain ways their power is ultimate; it does not come from higher levels of government. The Constitution, on the other hand, does not guarantee the existence of cities or counties—and certainly not mosquito-abatement districts. Rather, these smaller local governments are set up by state governments and, at least as far as the Constitution is concerned, are subordinate to the states.

Yet in fact these 78,000 units have many of the features of government. Some of them have guaranteed existence in state constitutions, though not in the federal Constitution. Many cities have powers clearly given them by home-rule laws. But above all these political units are governments in that they have the power to raise money and to spend it. Sometimes (like city and county governments) they raise funds and spend them on a wide range of programs; sometimes (like the special districts) they deal with specific problems. But even in the latter case the problems are important ones and the districts act as real governments.

Finally, cities, counties, and school districts are real governments because they are part of American political life. The states neither could nor would want to abolish them. Moreover, there is no hierarchy in which local governments deal with the states and the states with the federal government. Local governments deal directly with the federal government, with one another, and with the states. And to complicate things even more, there are also numerous intergovernmental agencies—crisscrossing and combining various political units. The Port of New York Authority crisscrosses two states and seven counties in an attempt to organize some of the complex problems of transportation and commerce in the New York metropolitan area. As any observer of that powerful group can tell you, it is also a quite independent government unit. Problems of pollution or control of water resources have led to many other such intergovernmental agencies in various parts of the nation.

That many local governments are single-purpose governments (set up to control pollution, get rid of mosquitoes, build sewers) does not make them any less real governments. Education is, in terms of spending, the largest domestic governmental activity. Over four-fifths of American public schools are controlled by independent school districts—districts that are independent of other local governments even when they cover the same territory. These districts are run by independent school boards, often elected by the local residents or sometimes appointed by the local town council. These districts can levy taxes and float bonds to build and maintain schools and pay salaries. They have much to say about curriculum and special programs. It is true that they all must operate within guidelines set by the states (and federal guidelines if they have federal funds). But they usually have much discretion. By almost any standard these school districts are real governments.

Thus instead of two levels of government—the federal government and the states—there are several levels covering the same territory and overlapping one another. One estimate is that there are about 1500 government units in the New York metropolitan area. Or consider the number of units in the Chicago suburb of Park Forest: Cook County, Will County, Cook County Forest Preserve District, Village of Park Forest, Rich Township, Bloom Township, Monee Township, Suburban Tuberculosis Sanitarium District, Bloom Township Sanitary District, Non-High School District 216, Non-High School District 213, Rich Township High School District 227, Elementary School District 163, South Cook County Mosquito Abatement District.[1]

These governments vary in size from small districts—with budgets of a few thousand dollars affecting some small part of the lives of a few hundred citizens—to governments like those of New York or Chicago—with budgets larger than those of most of the United Nations.

Why so many governments? Why such a variety? How can they possibly get along with one another?

To answer these questions we will first consider rather generally why one might want a large government (like the federal government or the government of California) rather than a small government (like that of South Royalton, Vermont), and vice versa. And in the light of these general questions we shall consider how the particular pattern of American governments evolved. We can then see how these governments get along (and why they sometimes don't) as well as the results of having so many governments.

Centralization vs. Decentralization

We can understand this issue if we start with the example of a major governmental activity: education. It used to be said that the Minister of Education in France could look at his watch and say with confidence: "At this moment, every sixth-grade child in France is doing the following problem in math. . . ." And he could tell you the exact problem they were working on. The story is an exaggeration, but it shows that French education is a highly centralized system in which schedules, curriculum, standards, and the like are all set by the Ministry of Education in Paris and then carried out in the local schools.

Compare this with the educational system in America. Suppose someone wanted to find out what pupils were doing in the sixth grade in the United States. He could go to the Office of Education in the Department of Health, Education and Welfare in Washington. But he would not find out there. Matters of schedule, curriculum,

[1] Edward C. Banfield and Morton Grodzins, *Government and Housing in Metropolitan Areas* (New York: McGraw-Hill, 1958), p. 18; quoted in Advisory Commission on Inter-Governmental Relations, *Metropolitan America: Challenge to Federalism* (Washington, D.C., 1966).

standards, and so forth are not decided in Washington. The American tradition in education is local control. Such matters are generally in the hands of the states or the school boards of counties, cities, towns, or school districts. If someone wanted to know about sixth-grade curriculum, he might have to visit 15,781 separate school jurisdictions.

The Argument for Decentralization

One can make a strong argument for this diversity. After all, pupils differ in different parts of the country. They have different interests, needs, backgrounds. If some central government official tried to set up a uniform curriculum for the ghetto school in Harlem, the suburban school in Grosse Pointe, Michigan, and the rural school in Towner County, North Dakota, that curriculum would fit no place well. Only the local citizens and their school boards understand the educational needs of their own district and can create programs to fit those needs. And this argument would be made not only by the farmers of North Dakota jealous of their freedom from domination by the big cities or by the wealthy suburban residents of Grosse Pointe proud of their well-funded schools, but also by many of the residents of Harlem eager to have a curriculum focusing on their own particular needs and background.

Local control of the schools allows for variety but also for wide differences in quality.

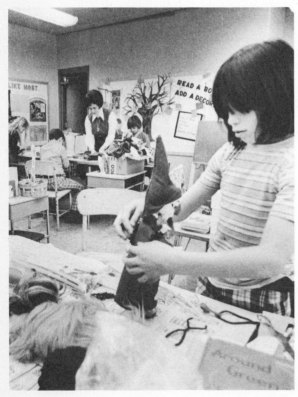
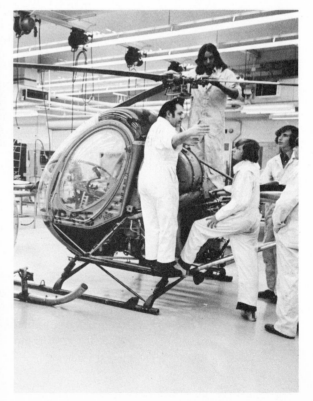

Furthermore, the defender of this system would argue that local control lets the community decide how much it wishes to put into the school system; if the citizens in one community can afford a luxurious school system, shouldn't they be allowed to have it? Isn't that better than a uniform standard across the country? Finally, the defender of the system would point to the huge and complex bureaucracy that would be needed to run a nationwide school system — a bureaucracy that would place the schools beyond the control of the parents. The supporter of localism could cite several studies of the American public showing that the average citizen feels he understands local politics better than national politics, and feels he can have more influence on the local level. And, everything else being equal, citizens are more likely to be politically active where the political unit is small and relatively independent. In short, citizen control may be greater the more local the government.

CENTRALIZATION VS.
DECENTRALIZATION

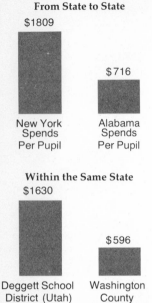

Figure 15.1

Examples of Variations in State Expenditures for Education

From State to State

$1809

$716

New York
Spends
Per Pupil

Alabama
Spends
Per Pupil

Within the Same State

$1630

$596

Deggett School
District (Utah)
Spends
Per Pupil

Washington
County
School District
(Utah)
Spends Per Pupil

Source: Based on data from *Financial Status of the Public Schools, 1974* and *National Education Association and State Review of Government in Utah, 1972.*

The Argument for Centralization

But the defender of a centralized system might argue that a system of local control is chaotic and wasteful. For one thing, there are no national educational standards. And communities vary widely in their ability to provide such an education. The result, he might point out, is that some pupils get a much better education than others who happen to be born in the wrong place. New York spends about two and a half times as much on education as Alabama. In 1973–1974 New York spent $1809 per pupil, Alabama $716. And there are even greater variations within states—wealthy communities spend a lot more per pupil than poorer ones. (See Figure 15.1.)

Furthermore, the defender of centralization might argue that local districts do not have the skills and specialists needed for a modern educational system; these could be provided by a centralized school system. A local school district cannot design a complex new physics curriculum, nor can it always afford laboratory facilities.

The defender of centralization would also say our system is totally uncoordinated. A degree from a French *lycée* (high school) means something specific—you know what the student has studied and what he can do. In the United States, a high school diploma has no standard meaning. In some cases it means a student is prepared for the university, in some cases not. How can you run a complex society that way? And he might point out that many serious urban problems are due to the disparity in school quality. If suburban schools were no different from those in the inner city, we would not face the urban crisis caused by the fact that wealthy citizens often move to the suburbs for the better schools, leaving the cities to the poor.

Finally, the defender of centralization might warn his opponents that they may be mistakenly identifying decentralization with democracy. If decisions are made within a local community, there may be greater control by the average citizen, but this is only potential control. Local government may be democratic, with many chances for citizen participation and control. But it may also be run by a political "boss" or by a small group of wealthy citizens. In such a case more independence for the local community may mean less, not more, citizen control over governmental decisions.

Who Is Right?

It is hard to say who is right. Some may feel that the evidence favors local control; some may feel that the centralized system is better. Few would argue that there is not something to be said for each side. And one can imagine a similar debate about centralized vs. decentralized control over many other matters. On some matters—such as libraries or recreational facilities—the evidence would favor decentralization. On others—transportation facilities that cross borders—more central control would seem desirable. But in all fields there are good arguments on both sides.

WHITE HOUSE, STATE HOUSE, CITY HALL: FEDERALISM IN AMERICA

The Dilemma

There is a real dilemma when it comes to the issue of centralization vs. decentralization—when one argues over federal power vs. states' rights or big government vs. local government. Almost any solution stressing decentralization and local control can be criticized: Coordination is lacking. Almost any solution stressing centralization and federal control can be criticized: It doesn't pay enough attention to local needs and desires. One can see this by supposing one could create a government as big or as small as one wanted. It is clear that any proposal for a government bigger than, say, the small town or the neighborhood can be criticized as too big; there is little chance for effective citizen participation But it is also clear that a government smaller than the whole world could be criticized as too small, for isn't the world one large interdependent system? It follows that any government of intermediate size—say, that of an American city or state, or that of the United States—could be criticized as both too big and too small.

Indeed one can almost predict that a centralized system will come under pressure to decentralize and vice versa. In the United States, with its decentralized school system, there is pressure from many sources for more centralization and coordination. In France, with its centralized system, there is pressure for more local control.

Tension between the two principles is almost automatic. And it may be seen in much of American political history and much of today's American politics. Indeed the crazy-quilt pattern of American governments—the big governments in the state houses and large cities, the bigger government in Washington, the little governments overlapping and crisscrossing these, the intergovernmental agencies—can be viewed as one response to the dilemma of centralization vs. decentralization. If neither solution is right, try both at the same time. In this sense there is reason for the variety of governments in America: some small ones (like school districts) to deal with local problems, some big ones (like the federal or state governments) to coordinate things and deal with problems that require larger government.

The Variety of Governments

The mixed pattern in America does not mean the specific mixture always works. The pattern of central government mixed into local government is not a result of careful consideration of what powers and functions should go to what levels. Rather, it is due to a long historical process, a process dominated less by theories about what form of government best fits what problem than by the *constellation of interests* at the time.

This point is important. The argument over centralization vs. decentralization can be based on general principles: the interdependence of society and the need for coordination, on the one hand, and, on the other, the differences among areas and the desirability of local control. But in any particular circumstances specific interests may lead one group to favor federal and another to favor local control, no matter what their general philosophy about big and little government. If variations among the states in the regulation of commerce hamper business activity, businessmen may argue for uniform federal standards. If on other matters they believe they can more effectively influence state regulatory agencies than federal ones, they will argue for states' rights. Black leaders may want more centralization (federal involvement in local affairs) if they want to challenge the power of white-dominated governments or white-dominated school boards where they are a minority. In neighborhoods where they are a majority, they may call for local control. In general, a group will prefer to see power at the governmental level it believes it can influence most.

The history of federalism, and of local vs. central government, is in large part the history of the clash of real interests. Since interests have pressed in both directions, the result has been the American mixture. To see how this has worked out, we must return to the Constitution.

The Constitutional Evolution

We saw earlier how the authors of the Constitution tried to shift the balance of power between the states and the federal government from the state-dominated system of the Articles of Confederation. They created a federal executive, gave Congress the power to pass laws directly affecting the lives of citizens, including the power to tax and to regulate interstate commerce, and set up a federal court system to adjudicate disputes between the states and the federal government. Thus they created a truly national government. Yet at the same time they balanced the scale by setting limits on the central government such as equal representation for all states in the Senate. In addition, the first ten amendments limited the powers of the government.

The balance seemed a good one, and few criticized it at the time. In fact, however, the division of powers between the central government and the states was still to be worked out in numerous court decisions, in the drift of governmental powers in one direction or another, in the pressures of a changing America, and—in several basic areas—on the battlefields of the Civil War.

But the authors of the Constitution could not foresee these changes; and even if they could, there is probably little they could do about them at the time. The Constitution has lasted partly because things were not finally worked out. The tensions built into the constitutional compromise between nation and states provided a framework within which future generations could work out the specifics of government and, in particular, the role of central vs. decentralized government.

The U.S. Mint: Under the Constitution the states gave up the right to print money.

Why the Delegates Gave Up the Power of the States

Why were the delegates from the various states willing to give up the power held by their states to a central government? This is an important question. It is dangerous to give up power—it may be hard to get back; it may be used against you. For generations people have talked of a world federation, of a federation of Europe, of a federation of African states—new centralized governments that would replace the individual nations. Yet except for unions created by force of arms (in which the various parts do not *give up* their independence but have it *taken away* from them), there are few successful voluntary federations. Why were the states willing to give up their power in 1787? There are several answers.

The States Gained from Union　The first answer has already been suggested. There was something to be gained from union. There had been commercial and administrative chaos under the Articles; trade among the states was hampered; trade with other nations was difficult without a central treaty-making power; the rich new territories on which the states bordered could not be used without some central authority. The delegates to the convention were men of affairs, and their affairs were not running very well. A central government would improve things.

The Society Was Homogeneous　As important as the gains from union was the question of what losses might be suffered. When we discussed problems of conflict and competition among groups in America, we saw that no group is likely to give up power to another—the opposition party, a central government—if it feels that its *vital* interests will suffer. One thing that has prevented the union of nations throughout history is that they have different basic cultures—they speak different languages, follow different religions, have different ways of life. One independent political unit is unlikely to give up its independence to a larger unit if it feels that the latter will not respect these vital interests. If an independent unit has such interests, it will join a larger union only if it can be guaranteed that its interests will be protected, usually by limitations on the power of the new central government to legislate on such matters. And the more extensive such interests are, the more limited the central government and the less meaningful the union will be.

The answer to why the states were willing to join a new central government thus becomes obvious. They had few such vital interests to protect. They had a common language and a relatively common culture; they were not sharply divided on religion. In short, the Union was based on a relatively homogeneous society.

The States' Vital Interests Were Protected　But in areas where there was potential conflict over interests seen by the states to be vital, they hedged the Constitution to protect those interests.

For one thing, the Constitution did not destroy the states. Quite the contrary. Although the founders knew power was being shifted from the state level to the national level, they also saw the Constitution as preserving the independence of the states in many important matters. The states had, after all, existed before the Union.

Small states also feared their vital interests would suffer in a union dominated by a few of the larger, more powerful states. Thus they pushed for a Senate in which each state, no matter what its size, would have equal representation. The convention spent a lot of time worrying about the large-vs.-small-state issue, though this has never become a major conflict in America.

The South's Interests Were Protected The most basic conflict of interest was between the economy and social system of the North and those of the South. The North had a growing economy based on manufacturing. The South had an economy solidly based on the cultivation and export of cotton, and organized around plantation slavery. The South (i.e., the southern delegates representing the white population) had a vital interest that they feared might be hurt by a government dominated by northern states.

To protect these interests certain clauses were included in the Constitution. One barred the national government from taxing exports, since the South depended on finding markets (often foreign ones) for its cotton. Another clause increased the representation of southern states in the House of Representatives by counting slaves among the population (at only three-fifths of their actual number, though many southern delegates would obviously have preferred a full counting). And the Constitution barred Congress from interfering with the slave trade until 1808. This point is a good illustration of what a group may consider a vital interest. The southern delegates would not have compromised on slavery itself; this they considered vital. (In fact there is little evidence that northern delegates were anxious to raise this question anyway.) But the compromise that allowed a future limitation on the slave trade was less vital, since the southern states could breed slaves.

The issue of North vs. South and the related issue of slavery make it quite clear that the Constitution only temporarily settled matters as to the relations of the states and the nation. What the Constitution meant was not settled until the Civil War, and then only partially. Indeed what the Constitution means and how the powers of the national and state governments are to be divided—on racial matters and on other matters as well—remains open.

State and Nation

As with so many other issues in American political life, the Constitution did not settle the issue of federalism. Rather, it provided a framework within which future changes would be worked out. The basic framework was the federal principle: a unified central government and a series of partially independent states. The Constitution established both principles—centralization and decentralization—without facing the fact that they were contradictory. And perhaps this has allowed the evolution of the federal system within the framework of the Constitution. The balance of power between the nation and the states has changed over time, but the framework of a central government and an independent set of states has survived.

The first era under the Constitution—from its writing to the Civil War—points up the tensions between the principles of centralization and decentralization. During this period a series of major Supreme Court decisions firmly established federal power over taxes and interstate commerce and in many other areas.

In 1819 Chief Justice John Marshall, in his decision on *McCulloch* v. *Maryland,* spelled out the doctrine of *implied powers.* Congress, he declared, was not limited in its powers to those *specifically* listed in the Constitution. Rather, it had all the powers *necessary to carry out* the specific powers listed. The decision made clear that the federal government was indeed a government and not simply the creation of the states. At the same time, the Supreme Court established itself as the supreme interpreter of the Constitution.

The Principle of the Concurrent Majority

Meanwhile there was the pull of decentralization that was to lead to the Civil War. The issue centered on the question of the vital interests particular areas wanted to see protected. During this era John Calhoun, a leading southern senator, developed the idea of *concurrent majority.* According to this theory, no mere majority of the citizens of the United States, nor a majority of the states themselves, could tell the others what to do. Rather, policies had to be based on the agreement of majorities *within the regions involved;* that is, each section would have to agree on policies that affected it. As one might expect, this reflected the specific interests of Calhoun's region, interests the South wanted protected from the rest of the nation. The principle was, of course, quite contrary to a strong federal government. Indeed the reader will see that the principle of concurrent majority is very similar to the veto power of members of the Security Council of the United Nations, where any of the major powers can block decisions it does not agree with.

The Civil War partially resolved the tension of centralization vs. decentralization. It settled the issue of secession: Decentralization could never go so far as to let a state or group of states leave the Union. But, as with the writing of the Constitution itself, the war did not settle the issue of the central government vs. the states. Nor did it do away with the issue of the concurrent majority. As we saw when we considered the group process in America, and as we shall see later, the notion of a concurrent majority survives, though described in other terms. Specific groups still have a strong voice—often a deciding voice—over policies that affect them. Often these groups are not specific states or regions but, rather, economic interest groups. But the principle of decentralization remains.

Dual Federalism

In the years from the Civil War to the revolution in constitutional interpretation in 1937, the Supreme Court evolved a doctrine that has been labeled *dual federalism*. According to this doctrine, the states and the national government each had its own area of jurisdiction. The Commerce Clause of the Constitution was interpreted as barring the states from regulating interstate commerce. The Tenth Amendment, on the other hand, was interpreted as limiting Congress by reserving powers to the states.

Dual federalism was a negative doctrine. Its main effect was to limit the power of both the national and state governments. National power was limited to protect state power; state power was limited to protect national power. The result was that the Supreme Court often blocked both levels from carrying out social-reform legislation.

New Federalism

The Supreme Court decisions since the late 1930s have completely changed this balance. The phrase in the Tenth Amendment that spoke of powers "reserved" to the states was dismissed by the Supreme Court in 1941 as a "truism." This meant the states only had whatever powers the national government had not yet taken away.[2] There was no limit on what could be taken away. And in cases since then the Court has laid great stress on the clause of the Constitution that says national laws are the "supreme law of the land . . . anything in the Constitution or laws of any state to the contrary notwithstanding" (Article 6, Section 2).

State courts, on the other hand, have been much more restrictive with local governments. They have tended to follow the so-called Dillon rule (named after a state judge who expounded it most fully). The powers of local governments have tended to be interpreted quite narrowly. If a locality is given a specific power in a state law, it gets that power and nothing more. Thus federal court doctrine has allowed great expansion of federal power, but state courts have tried to hold local powers more closely in check.

Where Does Power Lie?

The Constitution, as currently read by the Supreme Court, does not treat the states and the nation as equals. The laws of the national government are clearly superior. If Congress passes a law that conflicts with a state law, the congressional law prevails. And there is no constitutional limitation on the kind of law Congress can pass.

[2] *United States* v. *Darby* 312 US 100.

The only constitutional limitation on the national government in relation to the states is that Washington cannot abolish the states or change their boundaries without their consent (Article IV, Section 3). But it is clear that Congress could take all effective power away from the states.

The Constitution allows the federal government to expand its powers. Political and social forces since the New Deal era have led the federal government to take advantage of that opportunity. The federal government has become active in many areas where state law once ruled, and in those areas federal law replaces state law. The federal government is the major force in regulating the economy. Its regulations affect business and labor. Matters of ecology were once the concern of the states and local governments (if they were of concern to anyone); the federal government is now active in these fields. Civil rights were once a state and local matter; the federal government is now a major force in this area. Control over voting was once a state matter; federal law now plays a major role here, too.

These are areas that once were largely under state control. The states still play a role, but the federal government has moved in. Add the new programs that have become important since the New Deal—defense spending, atomic energy, the space program—completely run by the federal government, and you can see how the balance of governmental power has shifted toward Washington.

The Financial Crisis of State and Local Government

The weakness of the states and of local governments compared to the government in Washington is increased by the fact that the former cannot raise enough money through taxes to meet their needs. There are three major kinds of taxes that citizens pay in the United States: income taxes, sales taxes (and other taxes on consumer goods), and property taxes. Each of the levels of government tends to rely on one form for most of its revenue. The federal government gets over four-fifths of its revenue from income taxes, state governments get about two-thirds of their revenue from sales taxes, and the localities get almost nine-tenths of their revenue from property taxes.

The federal income tax has a number of advantages over the state and local taxes based on sales and property. First, it provides more money, since it taps personal income directly. Second, it is progressive, since it falls more heavily on the rich—though not by very much. Sales and property taxes are regressive; they fall more heavily on the poorer citizens. Third, income taxes are more flexible; the amount they bring in goes up when the economy expands. Sales and property taxes respond more slowly to the economy.

Finally, sales and property taxes lead to inequality among the states and among localities. This is especially true in the case of property taxes. Wealthy communities or communities with industries located in them can raise much more in property taxes than poorer communities, though the needs of the poorer communities may be greater.

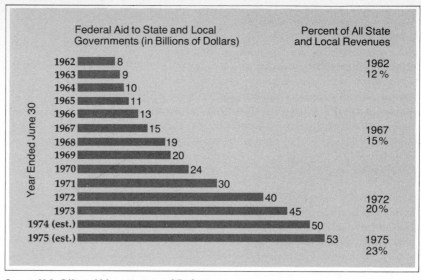

Source: U.S. Office of Management and Budget.

Many states have tried to get around this problem with income taxes of their own. But in most cases political pressures have kept the tax rates very low. State income taxes are unpopular largely because the federal government has already taken such a large bite out of income.

Federal Aid to State and Local Governments

One way the imbalance between the national government and state and local governments is corrected is by the transfer of funds from Washington to the states and localities. State and local budgets have come to depend more and more on federal funds. In the decade between 1962 and 1972, federal aid to the states and localities rose from about $8 billion to over $35 billion per year. (See Figure 15.2.) In 1973, it was estimated that federal assistance provided 22 percent of all state and local revenues. Federal funds are used by the states and localities for a wide range of purposes: welfare programs, education, highways, environmental control, and mass transportation.

There are many forms of federal assistance. The two main forms are grants-in-aid and revenue sharing. The difference between the two lies largely in the strings attached to the aid.

Grants-in-Aid   Grants-in-aid are given for specified purposes; they usually come with regulations as to how the funds are to be used. Grants-in-aid are of two kinds. *Categorical* grants are for narrowly defined purposes. There is usually little or no flexibility in the way the funds can be used. *Block* grants are also for specified purposes, but they are more broadly defined and give the state or locality more power to spend the funds as it wants.

It is clear that categorical grants give more power to Washington.

Improvement of mass transit facilities often depends on federal aid to localities.

Revenue Sharing Revenue sharing goes several steps beyond the block grant in giving states and localities freedom in the use of funds. The program began in 1972 as the cornerstone of President Nixon's New Federalism. Under the program $30 billion is being distributed to the states and to local governments over a five-year period with few strings attached, largely for the states and localities to use as they wish. Local governments are supposed to use the funds in priority areas such as health, public safety, and recreation. But these are general guidelines, and the localities have a lot of flexibility.

Revenue sharing has given states and localities needed funds. But what may be most important is the attitude it reflects. As George P. Schultz, Nixon's Secretary of the Treasury, put it, "revenue sharing is important less for the money it will provide than for the philosophy it contains. Revenue sharing will place the power and the resources back in the state houses and the city halls of this country."[3]

Revenue sharing is clearly an attempt to increase the powers of the states and localities relative to the federal government. And for just that reason it is controversial. Critics of revenue sharing—including some in Congress—claim the local governments do not give funds to important programs like health and welfare. One critic estimates that only 4 percent of the funds go to the poor and aged.[4] Many local governments have not spent the federal funds on new projects, but have used them to replace local funds and have cut taxes. Also, civil-rights groups complain that the program does not include enough protection against racial and sexual discrimination.

In a sense revenue sharing has come under attack because it has succeeded in giving effective power to localities. The critics do not like the way that power is used. Local government officials, they claim, are likely to be conservative and less willing to listen to minority groups or citizens in need of welfare. It is on the national level that such groups have been most effective. To give funds to localities is to reduce the effectiveness of these groups.

The controversy illustrates two important points we have already made about federal, state, and local relations:

1. Where someone stands on the issue of centralization vs. decentralization will usually depend on where he or she stands on other issues. Many local officials prefer revenue sharing because it gives them flexibility. It also gives them a chance to lower local taxes (or to provide more services without raising taxes). And this pleases their most important constituents, the property owners. Some minority groups will prefer tighter national control over spending because they have greater influence on the national government.

2. When one gives power to the states and localities, the results depend on who is in power. Decentralization may or may not increase the power of the ordinary citizen. In some cases citizens are more effective on the national level. In general, some groups will benefit and some lose from such programs as revenue sharing.

[3] Quoted in the *New York Times,* January 3, 1974, p. 30.
[4] Ibid.

In sum, revenue sharing seems to represent a genuine return of power to states and localities. What long-run effects it will have will depend on whether Congress makes a long-term and large-scale commitment to the program and whether Congress begins to restrict the use of the funds. One of the leading experts on federalism has claimed that in the long run revenue sharing will actually decrease the independence of state and local governments. It makes them more dependent on the federal government. As Congress becomes more dissatisfied with the way the states and localities spend the funds, it will put more restrictions on their use. The federal government will end up with even more control.[5]

Clearly state and local dependence on federal funds could lead to further federal domination. But such potential is not always used fully. The states and localities still survive and play important roles.

State and Local Governments in Action

The federal government may be more and more important, but one would not want to write off the state and local units. Counting only domestic programs (that is, excluding spending on defense, foreign affairs, or space programs, which form a large part of the federal budget), states and localities account for most—over 60 percent—of government spending. Moreover, the states and localities still have a lot of power over many of the most important areas of public policy: the protection of life and property; the establishment of domestic or "family" laws covering marriage, divorce, and abortion; the control of land use through eminent domain, zoning restrictions, and so forth. Indeed most government activities that affect our daily lives are under the control of local or state governments. States and localities build highways; they create and maintain most park and recreation facilities. Their decisions affect the environment. And as we have pointed out, the education of children is largely under state and local control. It is true that in each of these areas funds often come from the federal government, and with the funds come some controls. Despite this one can say the states and localities have survived. Indeed they have major legal and financial responsibility over policy areas affecting all members of the political community.

Cooperative Federalism

The complex mixture of federal, state, and local powers is called *cooperative federalism*. There is no clear division of powers; government functions are shared across the several levels. One student of federalism has described it as a marble cake rather than a layer cake.[6]

Consider public education, an area traditionally under state and

[5]Michael D. Reagan, *The New Federalism* (New York: Oxford University Press, 1972), pp. 104–105.

[6] Morton Grodzins, "Centralization and Decentralization in the American Federal System," in Robert A. Goldwin, ed., *A Nation of States* (Chicago: Rand McNally, 1963).

Cooperative federalism: President Ford confers with the governor of New York state and the mayor of New York city.

local control. And so it remains, with most of the funds for education raised and spent locally. Yet the federal government has been involved in one way or another from the very beginning. Before the writing of the Constitution, a 1785 statute provided for federal grants to local government to build schools. Such federal aid continued in the nineteenth century, when, under the Morrill Land Grant Act of 1862, federal land grants were given to the states to set up agricultural land and mechanical colleges. In 1917 the Smith-Hughes Act provided similar grants-in-aid for vocational education.

Since then various federal programs have expanded federal aid to local education. During World War II legislation was passed to help "impacted" areas, that is, places where defense activity (a military base, for instance) put pressure on the local school system because of new population or because federal use of local land reduced the tax base. In such cases federal funds were used to build, operate, and maintain local schools. These programs were continued after World War II. In addition, when the first artificial satellite, Sputnik, was orbited, the federal government decided that a major effort should be made to keep up with the Russians in technological education.

This led to the 1958 National Defense Education Act, which gave aid to local school districts to improve education in mathematics, science, and foreign languages, plus funds to improve school administration. In addition, it provided scholarship and fellowship funds in colleges and universities. The big Elementary and Secondary Education Act of 1965 involved fairly large grants of federal funds to school districts with large numbers of pupils below the poverty line. And in 1974 a General Education Bill extended the 1965 Act. Recent laws have further broadened the federal government's role here.

Sharing Functions The history of government involvement in education illustrates a number of important general points about the way the states and the nation share functions. Despite the growth of the role of the federal government, it is too soon to say state and local power over education has ended. The largest of all government domestic programs is still heavily state and local. During the 1960s the federal government's share of spending on public education almost doubled. But this involved a growth from 6.1 percent in 1960 to 10.6 percent in 1971—showing that most spending for public education remains on the state and local level.

The increased federal involvement in education comes at least in part indirectly, that is, in response to other issues in which the government has always been involved. Thus one main expansion of federal aid to local education derived from concern with matters of defense: The defense system was putting too great a burden on some areas of the country. The educational system could not teach the skills needed for defense. Similarly the most recent expansion of aid to education has been tied to the federal government's involvement in problems such as poverty.

However, one should not take this too literally. In part these bills were passed to aid education per se. But it is usual to justify the expansion of the government in one area in terms of more traditional federal activities.

Federal aid to education also shows how the nation and the states share functions. The federal government itself does not take over schools. Rather, federal involvement is in terms of grants-in-aid to state educational commissions or local school boards. The states and localities continue to control the process of education. Federal aid, though, usually has strings attached, usually in the form of guidelines on educational practices or other issues, guidelines that must be complied with if aid is to be given. How tight these strings are varies from issue to issue, but the guidelines imply some federal involvement in the educational process. However—just to complicate things and illustrate the tug in the federal-state relationship— the federal guidelines are often set up in close consultation with the states and with local school districts, so in part they involve standards the states and localities apply to themselves.

The debate over the role of the federal government in the educational process again shows how the general principles of centralization vs. decentralization interact with more specific interests. Opposition to federal involvement in education is often stated in general terms. One argues that locally controlled education is better than education dominated by a remote Washington bureaucracy, and the argument comes back that national standards and equality of educational opportunity are more important values.

But one's position for or against federal involvement in education often depends not on these general principles of federalism but on where one stands on other issues. Thus federal aid programs to local schools have at times included desegregation requirements. One's position on school desegregation is more likely to affect one's attitude toward federal school aid than the more general principle of central vs. local control.

The result, in relation to education, is a mixed system. The federal government is involved through its grants and guidelines, but the power over the educational system is certainly shared with the states. And this pattern can be found in many fields. The social-security system set up in the 1930s involves a sharing of power and responsibility between the federal government and the states. Consider the program for unemployment insurance: Is it a federal or a state program? In most cases it is a state program; the states levy a payroll tax used to provide unemployment insurance. But the states are required to levy such a tax by a federal law, under which the federal government would levy the tax if the states did not do so. Thus all fifty states levy the tax, since it is to their advantage to do so. Furthermore, though they run their own programs, the states must meet federal standards. But the standards give the states much leeway.

If you are still not sure whether the unemployment-insurance program is a federal or a state one, this is intentional. As with many programs, the actual situation is a complex pattern of shared powers and overlapping functions.

Federal-State-Local Relations What has been said about the sharing of functions between the federal government and the states applies as well to relations between those two levels of government and the more local governments—the cities, counties, towns, school districts. Local governments also share functions with the federal government. In some cases they get federal aid indirectly through the state governments. But in many cases they enter into direct relationships with the federal government, with aid going directly to cities or to school districts. In this sense these local political units are full participants in the federal system.

Why Has the Federal System Evolved as It Has?

No one reading the constitutional provisions that divide power between the federal government and the states—those that give the federal government certain powers and the Tenth Amendment, which seems to limit those powers—would be able on that basis alone to give an accurate description of which levels of government have what powers. This division depended on historical forces. Nor can we give a full analysis of the forces that led to the pattern of federal-state-local relations in every field. But we will discuss two broad aspects of the federal system.

Why has federal power grown so much beyond what the founders imagined? And why, despite the growth of the federal government, have state and local governments remained major sources of power?

Expansion of Federal Power

The answer to the first question lies in the development of America as a nation. The writers of the Constitution wanted to create a unified nation, especially in the areas of interstate commerce and

Federal funds built the interstate highway system.

The Federal Aviation Agency supervises air-traffic control.

foreign affairs. And these were two basic powers, given the way the nation evolved. The more it became a large continental economy and the more it became a world power, the more federal power grew. Consider the federal government's power over interstate commerce. If the United States had remained an agrarian society, that power would have been important, but not nearly as important as it became in a highly industrialized society whose economic growth depended on large internal markets. The more the nation needed a unified economy, the more the role of the federal government increased.

Development of a National Economy The reason is that the development of a national economy makes it impossible for any one state to control it. If a state tries to regulate business and the businesses object to such regulation, they can move to another state. This reduces state control over business and makes federal regulation more likely; indeed regulation of business activities (antitrust legislation, standards for goods, and so forth) has become largely a federal activity.

The major economic problems of the United States are ones that affect the entire nation and need decisions at the national level. Inflation and unemployment do not stop at state borders. The goods in the Chicago supermarket come from all over the country; the energy crisis triggered by Middle East politics touches all parts of America; unemployment rises in Detroit when car sales fall in California, New York, and elsewhere; and unemployment in Detroit, in turn, affects employment in every state. The economy is a tightly interlocked system, and only national policy can deal with it.

The pressure toward federal control may be seen in an area where the drift toward centralization has not gone as far: welfare. If one state sets up a program with much higher welfare payments than other states, it may be swamped by poor families from other states. Yet under the Constitution the state cannot close its borders to citizens moving from other states. The one state that wants a better welfare program is part of the same national economy as the others. What other states do affects its own programs. Under such circumstances pressures build for federal standards.

Growth Through Defense Power   Another source of the growth of federal power is the role of the United States as a world power. Federal power has always grown in wartime, and the seemingly permanent high military budgets maintain that power. This shows why the constitutional definition of the powers of the federal government is not a good guide to its real powers. Imagine that the power over national defense were the only *specific* power given to the federal government. It is easy to see how that power could lead to all the other powers held by the federal government as long as there is a flexible interpretation of *implied* powers. The power to defend the nation is meaningless without the power to raise necessary funds; hence the taxing power. One cannot defend the nation without high technology; hence the federal government's involvement in education. Good defense requires good roads; hence the federal government's multibillion-dollar road-building program. And so forth and so forth.

This hypothetical scheme is not completely imaginary. Federal power has grown over many fields along with defense power. The National Defense Education Act gave large amounts of aid to local school boards in the name of national defense. Federal involvement in transportation, space research, and health programs has often been defense related. The example of defense power also illustrates the more general principle that the specific powers given the federal government in the Constitution can be stretched.

Group Pressures for Equal Treatment   As we saw in Chapter 3, one major issue in American politics is that of equality. Over the years more and more groups have called on the government to enforce equality—between black and white, between the sexes, between the voters in rural and urban areas. The pressure for equality almost always involves federal power. For one thing, the federal courts have greatly limited state and local powers in this area in enforcing the "equal protection of the laws" provision of the Fourteenth Amendment. That provision was used by the Supreme Court to ban school segregation,[7] to equalize voting rights,[8] and in recent cases, by lower federal courts to equalize treatment of the sexes.[9]

[7] *Brown v. Board of Education of Topeka* 347 US 483 (1954).
[8] *Baker v. Carr* 369 US 186 (1962).
[9] See the cases listed in Eduard S. Corwin, *The Constitution and What It Means Today,* revised by Harold W. Chase and Craig R. Ducat (Princeton, N.J.: Princeton University Press, 1974), pp. 645–646, footnotes 235–244.

Furthermore, groups seeking equality have often turned to the national government. Since equality applies to citizens in all parts of the country, federal law is the most likely way to enforce it. And local governments are often more conservative in matters of equality, particularly racial equality. Thus recent decades have seen the growth of federal power in such areas as race relations, equal treatment of the sexes, and voter registration, which were once under state and local control.

What Preserves the States and Localities?

The Constitution puts no limits on federal expansion. The tax structure gives the federal government the resources it needs for continued growth, while the states and localities are financially weak. And more and more problems are national in scope. What, then, preserves state and local governments?

The answer lies mainly in the structure of American politics, particularly the organization of the political parties. If the parties were — like those in some other countries — tightly organized and disciplined, the drift of power into federal hands would have happened faster and more thoroughly. It is possible for the states to be "swamped" by federal power. If the national administration controlled an organized party stretching down to the grass roots, the legal potential would become a political reality.

In fact, as we have seen, the American party system is quite the opposite. The political parties are basically state and local organizations. They may develop national unity when it comes to Presidential elections, but this is only temporary (and not always very united even then). Furthermore, the White House and the state houses (or city halls) are not always controlled by the same party. And even when they are this does not mean the local party is controlled by the party organization in Washington (which in fact hardly exists). In some countries the national party leadership decides who runs under the party label in local elections. If this were the case in the United States, governors and mayors would be under close control by the national party. In fact, who runs in state and local elections — even who runs for Congress — is a matter decided locally, not nationally. And this gives the local party independence from any national control. The result is that states and localities remain independent governments because they have *political power,* not because of the Constitution.

Finances and recent constitutional interpretation would seem to make the U.S. government a unitary system, with the states and localities subordinate to Washington. Political reality tips the balance back and makes the federal government, at least in part, a product of the states and localities. Congressmen are part of the federal government but are strongly aware that they represent particular areas. And even the two officials elected by the nation as a whole — the

President and Vice-President—must be aware of the importance of state parties in the nomination and election process.

Two examples can illustrate this. When the social-security legislation of the New Deal was prepared in the 1930s, the original plan was for a fully federal program. The program had been planned in Washington, and many felt that it would be more effective if administered from there. In fact, the program passed by Congress involved a lot of sharing with the states. Much of the program was administered by the states within the framework of federal guidelines—a pattern found in many other areas. The main reason was that the Roosevelt administration knew Congress would accept only a proposal that provided for the involvement of the states. If there had been tightly centralized party organizations in the United States, President Roosevelt as head of the Democratic party would not have had to worry about the doubts of congressmen; he could have controlled their votes. But these congressmen—though part of the federal government—are elected from their locality, and often act to defend that locality.

To take another example, in 1965 the federal Office of Economic Opportunity (OEO) decided that the city of Chicago was not following federal guidelines on school desegregation. Federal aid to the Chicago school system was needed to keep the system running. This was a case in which federal involvement in local school matters could mean federal control of local school operations. The OEO did cut off school aid to Chicago. But within a few weeks it had backed down. And in the process it had suffered a major blow to its prestige and authority within the government.

Why did this happen? The OEO did not go beyond its legal powers. It would probably have been backed up by the courts, which were pushing in the same direction. And it had the resources to back up its demand on Chicago; the school district could not have functioned without federal aid. These two forces—the absence of court or constitutional limits on government power and its control over revenue sources—make the federal government so powerful.

But the one factor the OEO did not reckon with was the *political power* of the Chicago Democratic organization and its leader, Mayor Richard J. Daley. The Chicago political machine—one of the most effective such organizations in the country at that time—controlled a number of important resources such as the Democratic votes of a major state, numerous members of Congress, and an important bloc of delegates at Presidential nominating conventions. On the basis of such real political power, local government survives.

Of course not all localities are as large as the city of Chicago; nor is it a matter of size alone, for few other cities have local governments as powerful as Chicago's was at the time. Yet the localities—even small ones—have some power over the federal government because of their political independence and because their representatives in Congress will defend that independence.

WHAT PRESERVES THE
STATES AND LOCALITIES?

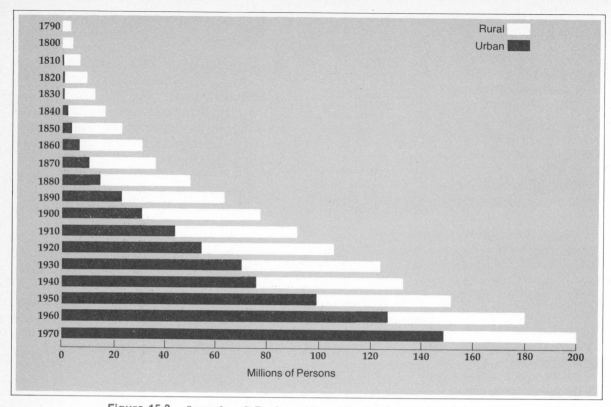

Figure 15.3
Urban and Rural Populations
of the United States, 1790–1970

Source: Irene B. Taeuber and Conrad Taeuber, *People of the United States in the Twenthieth Century* (Washington, D.C.: U.S. Department of Commerce, Bureau of the Census, 1971); and *Social Indicators: 1973* (Washington, D.C., Office of Management and Budget, 1973).

Federalism as an Attitude

We have seen that the fundamental beliefs of citizens help determine what kind of government we have. This is true in relation to the issue of centralization vs. decentralization. It has been argued that Americans "think federally"; that is, they believe in the importance of state and local governments. This is especially true of elected officials, since their voter support is in a particular state or congressional district. Congress often provides for state and local participation in carrying out a law because it believes such participation is a good thing.

Washington, the States, and the Cities

The greatest challenge to the American mixture of governments is found in the large metropolitan areas. Can a constitution written for a small agrarian society deal with the contemporary city? Within the urban areas we see all the problems of central vs. local control, of multiple governments with overlapping functions, of federal-state relations, of federal-local relations. (See Figure 15.3.)

WHITE HOUSE, STATE
HOUSE, CITY HALL:
FEDERALISM IN AMERICA

Metropolitan Areas

Consider the metropolitan areas. Two things are clear: They are socially and economically interdependent, and they are politically divided.

The very definition of a metropolitan area, as used by the Census Bureau, stresses its interdependence: "The general concept of a metropolitan area is one of an integrated economic and social unit with a recognized large population nucleus." And this interdependence takes many forms. People move easily from one part to another; they live in one area (perhaps a suburb) and work in another (perhaps the core city). The various communities in a metropolitan area share roads, public transportation, shopping areas. They are dependent on the same clean water, pure air, space for recreation.

The term *spillovers* is used to describe the activities of one community that affect its neighbors. There are many spillovers. Smoke from a factory in one community pollutes the air of the next community; if one community has an effective mosquito-abatement program but the next does not, the former will still suffer during the summer. If a suburb limits housing to single-family homes on large plots of land, it will effectively keep out poor citizens and, in turn, affect the population of other communities.

There can be beneficial spillovers. One community may provide parks and open them to all metropolitan residents. Or the central city may keep its streets clean, and those streets may be used by commuters who live in the suburbs.

One could go on pointing out areas of interdependence. The major point should be clear: The metropolitan areas are social and economic units sharing problems. But overlaid on this is the disorder of American local government—that curious mixture of local governments with overlapping boundaries, of state government and federal government. As we have pointed out, one estimate is that there are about 1500 governmental units in the New York metropolitan area, and similar numbers may be found in most such areas. There is the government of the central city and separate governments for satellite cities and for small and large suburbs. And these are overlapped and crisscrossed by county governments, special districts, and various state and federal jurisdictions.

The Advisory Commission on Intergovernmental Relations describes the result:

> Fragmentation of this kind may appear to bring government closer
> to the people, but it compounds the difficulties of achieving coordina-
> tion within metropolitan areas. Political responsibility for govern-
> mental performance is divided to the point of obscurity. Public control
> of government policies tends to break down when citizens have to
> deal with a network of independent governments, each responsible for
> highly specialized activities. Even when good channels are developed
> for registering public concern, each government is so circumscribed
> in its powers and in the area of its jurisdiction that important metro-
> politan action is virtually impossible for local governments to under-
> take. If a few governments are prepared to agree on joint or coordi-
> nated programs, their efforts can be blocked by others that are unwilling
> to cooperate.[10]

What this means is that while problems cover a wide area, the solutions take place within small parts of that area. This also often means a wide gap between those who pay for services and those who receive them. The central cities provide clean streets and generally pay for these with taxes raised from their residents. They are then used by suburban residents, who pay their taxes to a suburban government. This helps explain why central cities try to tax suburban residents who work in the city, and since the cities do not always succeed in this, many cities have dirty streets and most do not have good mass-transit systems.

The Crisis in American Cities   Today's urban crisis is due (at least in part) to the fragmentation of government. The situation in the major American cities is by now quite clear. For a number of years the white middle classes have been moving out of the central cities of metropolitan areas into the suburbs. They have been replaced by poor minority groups, mostly black. The 1970 census, for instance, shows that in the 1960s the white population of New York City decreased by 9 percent while the nonwhite population increased by 62 percent. There are many reasons for the movement to the suburbs. Partly it is a desire for fresh air, lawns, and the like. It is also a desire to leave the problems of the cities—especially those of the urban poor—behind and find peaceful, middle-class school districts.

The result is that the urban core of America is decaying, filled with the largely nonwhite poor. The suburbs are white, wealthier—and fearful about the cities. The situation was used in the chapter on

[10] Advisory Commission on Inter-Governmental Relations, op. cit.

Table 15.2
Large Black Student
Population in the Big Cities

School District	Black Enrollment	Percent of All Students
Washington	133,638	95.5%
Atlanta	73,985	77.1%
New Orleans	77,504	74.6%
Newark	56,736	72.3%
Richmond	30,746	70.2%
Gary	31,200	69.6%
Baltimore	129,250	69.3%
St. Louis	72,629	68.8%
Detroit	186,994	67.6%
Philadelphia	173,874	61.4%
Oakland	39,121	60.0%
Birmingham	34,290	59.4%
Memphis	80,158	57.8%
Cleveland	83,596	57.6%
Chicago	315,940	57.1%
Kansas City, Mo.	35,578	54.4%
Louisville	25,078	51.0%

Source: U.S. Department of Health, Education and Welfare, *Directory of Public, Elementary and Secondary Schools in Selected Districts,* all 1972.

group conflict to show how a problem can potentially tear a society apart.

And consider how the overlapping boundaries of governments in the metropolitan area help create this situation. What is important is that the white middle class, when it leaves the city, crosses a political boundary into another community. They no longer vote or otherwise take part in the government of the city; they no longer share its problems; and above all, they no longer pay taxes to the city.

The result is great pressure on the central city to provide services for a growing population that needs such services badly—welfare services as well as the other needs of urban life. But the cities come under these pressures just when the tax base required to provide the services is declining. Furthermore, the school-age population in the central cities includes larger and larger percentages of nonwhites. (See Table 15.2.)

This situation has two effects. It makes it hard to integrate the schools because there are not enough white pupils to go around. It also makes the problem worse as more and more whites flee what they see as ghetto schools.

Suppose the boundaries were different. Suppose the movement to the suburbs did not involve crossing the political boundary to another community. Surely that would not end the problems, but things would look somewhat different. The tax base of the cities would not change as much. The suburbs would still be part of the same district. Similarly it would be easier to integrate the schools if the entire population of the metropolitan area were considered at once, not the core cities and the suburbs separately. And that might weaken the drive among the white middle classes to leave the city—since it would make less difference in the schooling of their children if they did. In short, the cities would still have their problems; the nature of the boundaries does not cause urban problems. But the boundaries would not make the problems worse.

The Supreme Court has considered this issue. A lower court ordered cross-busing between Detroit and its suburbs to achieve racial balance. In July 1974, in what may prove to be a landmark decision, it overturned the lower-court decision by a 5–4 vote. Detroit's schools are about 70 percent black. The lower court reasoned that racial balance could be achieved only by involving the white suburbs. The Supreme Court, however, ruled in favor of another principle: local control of the schools. It is useful to quote the majority opinion, for it shows that centralization (in this case on a metropolitan basis) is far from the only trend in America: "No single tradition in public education is more deeply rooted than local control over the operation of schools; local autonomy has long been thought essential both to the maintenance of community concern and support for public schools and to the quality of the educational process."[11]

The Federal Government and Housing Another solution is greater involvement of the federal government in the metropolitan areas. The federal government has a long history of involvement through its programs in urban areas, mostly in relation to housing. But the nature of that involvement is instructive. The first major federal program was the Housing Act of 1937, which set up the FHA mortgage-insurance program. This allowed many more people to build and own their own homes than would have otherwise been the case. But such a program was of greatest value to middle-class homeowners. And indeed the FHA program helped speed the growth of the suburbs at the expense of the inner city. The FHA program was balanced by federal support for low-rent housing, almost always in the central city. In short, the federal programs have helped create the current urban crisis.

The Federal Government and Urban Renewal Or consider the involvement of the federal government in urban renewal, the major federal urban program of the past few decades. Its purpose was to renew central cities. Local officials were given federal money to buy up blighted property (usually downtown slums inhabited by nonwhites) and to clear the land. It was then sold to others for residential, commercial, or industrial development. The result did not help the poor population of the inner cities. What was supposed to be urban renewal turned out to be black removal.

[11] Quoted in *U.S. News and World Report,* August 5, 1974, p. 24.

The Problem of Local vs. Federal Control The story of urban renewal points up one of the problems of centralization vs. decentralization. When you decentralize power *to whom* do you give it? The federal urban-renewal program was a decentralized one; federal funds were given to local officials, who planned the local renewal schemes. And who benefits from such a program depends on who is in power locally. Our previous discussions of who participates in politics (Chapter 4) and who is chosen for politically important positions (Chapter 5) suggest an answer. It is unlikely to be the urban poor themselves.

A distinguished observer of urban America comments on the effects of local control over federal funds:

> Local communities are allowed great latitude in deciding how federal funds will be spent on the bread-and-butter programs: urban renewal and public housing. If the Main Street merchants are in power, they can use renewal funds to tear down low-cost housing and put up luxury apartments near the department stores—in effect redistributing income from the poor to the well-to-do while reducing the stock of low-cost housing. If more generous souls are in power, the worst housing is torn down to make room for middle- or lower-middle-income housing; the income transfer from poor to not-so-poor is much less, but it is still in the wrong direction. And if the mayor simply is seeking funds with which to run his city in the face of a declining tax base, he discovers that he must join with those who want one of these urban renewal programs because that is about the only way he can get large-scale federal money into his city. He discovers, in short, that he has to hurt his poorest and weakest citizens in order to provide for the general welfare; his only option is to try to do it as humanely as possible. . . . The point is that for almost any legitimate community objective—improving the supply of housing, strengthening the tax base, etc.—urban renewal has in most cases proved to be an unwieldy and costly tool.[12]

This is an important point: Local control means control by whoever controls the local area. Local areas are not homogeneous; they contain both leaders and followers. Citizens often want local control when it means they can control things. If they are not in control locally, they may want outside control. Thus blacks in the inner city sometimes call for local control over schools or the police, for they form a majority and could control these. But where they are a smaller group they may prefer more federal control.

Where does this confusing situation leave us in terms of the "best" boundaries for metropolitan cities? Should they all come under direct federal control; should there be huge metropolitan governments; should there be local governments as there now are; or should there be even more localism involving neighborhood governments?

This book is not intended to suggest solutions to current problems—even if we knew them. These problems would not be solved

[12] James Q. Wilson, "The War on the Cities," *The Public Interest*, no. 3 (Spring 1966), 30–31.

just by changing boundaries. But the situation of the metropolitan areas shows how all governmental units are too big, all are too small. Big units do not easily adjust to the problems of the local citizens, nor do they give them enough control. Small units need to be coordinated with the larger ones.

Let us see how this paradox applies to the cities. Suppose we have federal control or big metropolitan governments. Many of the problems of lack of coordination would be gone and tax bases could be equalized. But could such a government adjust its policies to the needs of citizens in various parts of the metropolitan area? Doesn't each part know best what it wants and have the right to run its own affairs? This question might be asked by a wealthy white suburban resident who would like to ignore the problems of the inner city, but it might also be raised by a black resident of the urban core who wants local control.

But will the opposite solution work — a small, fragmented system of governments like the one that already exists or one divided further into neighborhoods? Certainly this would give the local residents more control over their own lives. Or would it? The problems they would have to deal with — transportation, housing, pollution, even education — extend beyond their neighborhood. Extreme localization of government would give the citizen more control over his government, but it would be over a government that could not deal with today's problems.

The best conclusion is that the dilemma of centralization vs. decentralization is a real one, and the tension between the two principles will continue for many years. What solution is tried at a particular point in time will depend more on the constellation of interests among the participants and their relative political power than on general principles about local or coordinated government.

Controversy

In recent years the issue of where to put the unpopular industries has been raised in many parts of the country. Take the example of oil refineries. They are necessary to the economic well-being of the nation. But they also pollute air and water. The small New Hampshire town of Durham turned down a proposal by a company controlled by the late Aristotle Onassis to build an oil refinery there. The last we heard, the oil refining company was still looking for a place for its refinery.

The people of Durham were pleased to see the refinery people leave. But if all towns took that position, where would oil refineries (or other unpopular industries) go? Many towns have set up barriers to industrial development, but the nation is going to need more factories, power plants, and airports.

One Side

Local governments have the right to control industrial developments within their borders. If they want to preserve their community against noisy or dirty industries, they should be able to. An oil refinery in Durham, New Hampshire, would benefit the economy of all of New England. Why should one small town bear the burden?

The Other Side

Unpopular industries have to go somewhere. And someone has to decide where they go. Local city councils cannot make such decisions objectively; they will always say, "Let them go somewhere else, we don't want it here."

It is up to the federal government to make these decisions if they are to be made. If this means a loss of control by local governments over their industrial development, that cannot be helped.

How Inﬆitutionf Work: VII
The Role and Organization
of ﬆate and Local Government

What is the legal and political framework of state government?

The basic structure of each state government is set forth in a state constitution. All such constitutions are based on the principles of separation of power and checks and balances; all provide for executive, legislative, and judicial branches. The actions of state officials, the laws passed by state legislatures, and the decisions of state courts must conform to the federal Constitution and may be reviewed by the United States Supreme Court.

How are the three branches of government organized at the state level?

Executive

The chief executive in each state is the governor, elected for a two- or four-year term. Like the President, the governor submits the state's annual budget and largely decides the legislative agenda. Most governors can call a special session of the legislature to deal with specific issues, and all but one have veto power. Nonetheless the role of the executive has traditionally been secondary to that of the legislature. And although executive power has been strengthened in most states during the past half-century, the office of governor remains weak in many states.

In almost all cases the governor shares executive power with elected officials other than the lieutenant governor. These typically include the secretary of state, treasurer, attorney general, auditor, and superintendent of education. These other officials may or may not be from the same political party as the governor, and even when they are they may still be political rivals. The result is a weakening of the governor's executive control, a problem made more complicated when there are executive agencies and commissions whose members are not directly responsible to the governor.

Legislative

All state legislatures except for Nebraska's are composed of an upper and a lower house. In accordance with Supreme Court rulings, seats in both houses must be assigned on the basis of population. The size of state legislatures varies widely from fewer than 60 to more than 400 members. As in Congress, the legislatures work through committees, and except in Minnesota and Nebraska, state legislatures are organized along party lines. The quality of the elected legislatures often is not high, for several reasons. Only about half the state legislatures meet on an annual basis, with the others meeting only every two years. Many states also limit the length of legislative sessions, pay low salaries, and provide little staff assistance. The result is that for the majority of state legislators public service is only a part-time job.

Judicial

Although no two states have identical court structures, most state judicial systems are organized along similar lines. At the bottom are justices of the peace and municipal courts; then there is a middle level of county or trial courts and specialized courts that handle juveniles, probate, and the like; at the highest level can be found courts of appeals or state supreme courts. In two-thirds of the states, judges are popularly elected. The other states select judges either by appointment or through a merit system combining both appointment and election.

What are the primary functions of state and local governments?

As stressed in the preceding chapter, the functions of government are increasingly shared by the three levels. But the states have major responsibility for education and public health, transportation, welfare, and the administration of justice.

States also have authority over corporations, public utilities, and financial institutions, as well as in the regulation of political parties and elections. Responsibility for the delivery of these services and the enforcement of state regulations is shared with local governments. Together state and local governments annually spend more than $200 billion and employ over 10 million people.

What is the legal basis of local governments?
All local governments derive their existence and powers from the states. Municipalities have charters granted by the state, while other local units such as counties and special districts are either subdivisions of the state or products of the legislature. They have only the authority granted them by the state. About half the states, however, have "home rule," in which municipalities may run many of their own affairs.

What are the three basic forms of city government?
Most larger cities use the *mayor-council* form of government, in which the mayor shares power with an elected city council. There are strong- and weak-mayor governments, depending on the actual distribution of powers. Council members may be elected in either partisan or nonpartisan elections. A second model is the *commission plan,* which calls for a small board of elected commissioners to serve both as a legislative council and as heads of the city departments. This form is usually nonpartisan and is popular in the West. There is also the *council-manager* plan, which assumes separation of politics from administration. In this form a nonpartisan council hires a professional city manager, who runs the city subject to the council's approval.

What are the other units of local government?
The other units consist of counties, townships, and various special districts. (See Table 15.1.)

Counties
County governments function in all but three states and are the most important unit of local government in rural areas. Intended to serve as administrative and judicial units, counties are usually run by such elected officials as the sheriff, prosecutor, treasurer, and clerk, as well as a board of commissioners.

Townships
Townships are unincorporated, usually rural units of government found in fewer than half the states. The principal governing body is a board of supervisors, but their governmental role has been declining steadily.

Special and School Districts
Unlike the units of local government that are multipurpose in nature, special districts have been created for special purposes. They handle problems that may cut across the boundaries of existing political units. Chief among them are school districts, which can tax, borrow, and spend public funds. There are also over 20,000 special districts to administer particular functions such as soil conservation, fire protection, and recreation.

16

The
Policy
Process

Politics produces policies, and these policies affect the lives of all Americans. What the government does (or does not do) about pollution, the economy, mass transportation, or public safety makes the lives of Americans better or worse. Not that government policies have the same impact on all citizens. Quite the contrary. Some policies make the lives of some citizens better without affecting others. Some make the lives of some citizens better while making the lives of others worse. This differential impact is what much of politics is all about. It makes it important to have access to the government, to influence its policies.

How is policy made in America? Who decides what the government does? Much of our book is about these questions; we have looked at the various actors and institutions in American politics from that point of view. What remains is to tie all this together by looking at the way policy is actually made.

What Is a Policy?

The activity of the government can be understood in terms of *policies* and in terms of *decisions*. Policies are long-term commitments of the government to a *pattern of activity*. Decisions are particular points where that pattern of activity changes. The United States had a *policy* toward China from 1949 to 1971, a rather hostile one stressing nonrecognition, limitations on trade and contacts, and support for the government of Taiwan. In 1971 President Nixon made a *decision* to go to Peking, one that meant a general change in the policy.

In some cases policies continue for a long time while no decisions are made about them. Sometimes policies are maintained through periodic decisions. The decision year after year to oppose the entry of China into the United Nations was part of the overall policy. And sometimes policies are constantly changed by decisions. Government policy on busing to achieve school integration has constantly changed in recent years through decisions by the courts, by the federal executive, and by the states.

How to Understand Government Policy

To understand how government activities affect the lives of Americans, one has to understand the roots of long-term policies as well as the sources of the specific decisions that change those policies. Furthermore, one may have to look quite broadly to see what government policy actually is. We defined a policy as a long-term commitment to a pattern of *activity*. We are interested in what the government actually *does* in a particular area, not just in what it says.

Study the Detailed Provisions Many of the general statements about policy may be hopes rather than descriptions of reality. If Congress passes a law stating that all children have the right to an

equal education, such a law has little meaning without funds to carry it out. Congress often passes laws with a high intent and a small budget. Furthermore, there is often a gap between the general statement of a law and its details. The preamble gives the overall intent of the bill, but the detailed provisions often lead to different results. Tax policy is an example. A major tax bill has general purposes: to raise revenue, control inflation, perhaps redistribute wealth. These are expressed in the preamble of the bill. But the real policy is found in the many specific clauses of the bill, and these may lead to a result quite different from the general statement.

Administration of a Policy In addition, one has to follow a policy from its initial statement right through to its administration. The formal descriptions of American government tell us Congress makes policies and administrative agencies carry them out. But this is not always the way it works, for how the general directives are carried out may determine the effectiveness of a policy. For example, Congress may pass a law to improve inner-city schools; it may even appropriate funds for that purpose. But if the local school officials use those funds for other purposes, the effective policy is not one of helping ghetto schoolchildren. Local school districts have sometimes used funds from the federal government to replace their own contributions to the inner-city school, effectively leaving such schools in the same condition they were in before the law was passed and making more funds available to schools in better neighborhoods.

A similar pattern could be found in urban renewal—as we saw in the chapter on federalism. The overall purpose of urban renewal, as expressed in the preamble to the bill, was to improve conditions in the inner city by replacing slums with better buildings. But how that policy worked depended heavily on how the particular urban-renewal plan developed locally. The specific plan determined who was moved out and where they were moved, what was built in place of the removed buildings, and who ultimately benefited from the program. In many cases it was the builders and the program directors rather than the people themselves who benefited.

The point is that a policy does not administer itself. Someone must carry that policy out. And in the process it can be changed. Congress often passes laws whose meaning is quite vague because it wants administrative agencies to define them more precisely. This increases the need to observe a policy in action rather than the statement of a policy.

It is not unusual that laws passed to achieve high purposes achieve little or nothing. But the failures may not be noticed. Policies are made in Washington with much fanfare; it is big national news when a voting-rights bill or a bill setting up a job corps is passed. The administration of the program in cities and towns all over the country receives a lot less attention. Many of Johnson's Great Society programs were criticized for putting more into development of the general policy than into implementation.[1]

The Supreme Court also makes important statements about policy, and like those of Congress, they do not always automatically go into effect. For example, in a variety of decisions the Supreme Court has cited the First Amendment on the separation of church and state to limit religious activities in the public schools. But individual school districts are sometimes slow to comply and quick to think of alternatives. As one specialist on education and the law wrote, "School systems in virtually every state violate in some way the legal principles concerning religious instruction in the public schools."[2] And if no one minds these violations, little is done.

To take another example, in 1964, 10 years after the Supreme Court's 1954 decision outlawing school segregation, only 2 percent of the black children in the 11 southern states were in integrated schools. Since then, more southern schools have been integrated, but only upon strict enforcement by the Justice Department.

In short, if you want to see government policy in a particular area, you have to see what is actually happening and not what congressional law or Supreme Court decision tells you should be happening.

Implementation   The more complex the process of carrying out a law, the more likely there is to be a wide gap between the intentions of the law and its results. One study of various voting-rights bills passed in the late 1950s and early 1960s illustrates this. A voting-

---

[1] For a dramatic example of failure to implement a program, see Jeffrey L. Pressman and Aaron B. Wildavsky, *Implementation* (Berkeley and Los Angeles: University of California Press, 1973).

[2] Frank J. Sorauf, "*Zorach* v. *Clausen:* The Impact of a Supreme Court Decision," *American Political Science Review,* 53 (September 1959).

rights bill was passed in 1957, another in 1960, and another in 1965. Each had the same purpose: to outlaw voting discrimination against blacks, particularly in the South. The first law had little effect because its implementation required that blacks sue in federal court if they felt their rights were violated. This is a long, expensive, and cumbersome process, and few suits resulted. The 1960 law made things a bit easier: The Justice Department was allowed to bring suits. But this too was cumbersome; each violation had to be taken to court. Few blacks were registered to vote under the 1960 law. The 1965 law, on the other hand, was much more effective. And one of the main reasons for this was that it was easier to carry out—the Justice Department could enforce the law without having to go to court.[3]

Symbolic Response One student of American politics has noted a number of cases in which demand for change—for a decision that would lead to a new policy—has been met by a *symbolic* response. A symbolic response is one in which the government, through a law of Congress or a major statement by the President, states a new policy: "No more rotten meat shall be sold." "Railroads can no longer set fares to discriminate against some customers." "Our rivers and lakes shall be clean." But beyond the broad symbolic statement little is done to carry out the policy. The real policy may look little different from the situation before the new "symbolic" policy was stated. However, such symbols can have important results, particularly if those who want change think such change has in fact taken place. Nothing is different, but they are content. Therefore this scholar calls such policies "symbols of quiescence."[4] This underlines our general point: To understand a real policy one has to look at how it is carried out.

Unintended Results Not all policies work out as those who design or administer them intend them to. Often they have additional results, which follow inevitably from the policy but were by no means planned. Policies of school districts on uniform testing were not intended to discriminate against blacks. But they have a discriminatory effect if the tests ask about aspects of life more familiar to middle-class whites than to blacks or use language more in tune with that used in white homes than in black homes.

Or take the example of the impact on urban America of federal policies on housing, urban development, and roads. These policies were not intended to create a situation in which inner-city ghettos are surrounded by wealthier white suburbs. The Federal Housing Administration (FHA) program was intended to let citizens buy their own homes. In practice, however, it led to white citizens' buying

[3] Frederick M. Wirt, *The Politics of Southern Equality* (Chicago: Aldine, 1970), chap. 3.
[4] Murray Edelman, *The Symbolic Uses of Politics* (Urbana: University of Illinois Press, 1964).

homes outside the city, where land was available and where they believed they would find fresh air and green grass. The FHA did not have a policy against giving such loans equally to blacks. But blacks rarely could afford private homes. And even if they could, the FHA tended to guarantee loans only in neighborhoods that were not likely to become slums. That a black family would want to buy a home in a particular neighborhood (or would be able to) made the agency feel such a neighborhood would not be a safe bet. The purpose of the program: help citizens buy homes. The result: black ghettos.

Unintended results are not always bad. Sometimes a policy with one goal can achieve others at the same time. In response to the energy crisis, speed limits were reduced on the nation's highways. The purpose was to save gasoline. It also saved lives as the accident rate went down.

Limitations on What the Government Can Do

Each of us is, at some point, dissatisfied with some aspect of American society, and we believe it can be improved by government action. We complain that there is poverty in the midst of plenty; that we lack good public transportation; that the schools are failing to educate. We complain of failure of the government to act against these evils: Congress is too disorganized; there are not enough representatives who think the way we do; the President is not providing leadership. The failure lies in the absence of the political will to act.

The complaints are in many cases justified. There are many policy areas in which the government seems unable or unwilling to make policy. But our discussion of implementation should suggest that making broad policy is not enough. There is a long and difficult road between the creation of general policy and the actual results of the policy. Let us consider some reasons why government policy does not always do what it sets out to do.

1. We sometimes do not have clear goals. Policy goals are sometimes vague. Often this is simply because Congress is uncertain as to what it is trying to accomplish. Or the goals of a law may conflict with other goals that are also of value. In recent years there has been a good deal of conflict over the means of achieving school integration, particularly the use of busing. The conflict is not between those favoring integration and those opposed (at least that is not how the conflict is phrased). It is, rather, a conflict between the goal of school integration and the goal of local control of the schools. In the 1973 education law, for instance, Congress tried to achieve both goals at once. But in fact that may be impossible.

Sometimes the conflict between a particular policy and other goals only shows up when the policy is carried out; the result is often a failure to implement the policy. Here is the description of an innovative program to build model communities on government-owned surplus land in metropolitan areas:

> Late in the summer of 1967, the Johnson administration started a program to build model new communities on surplus federally owned land in metropolitan areas. During the next year, the White House and the Department of Housing and Urban Development announced seven projects. Nearly three years later, the program had clearly failed. Three of the projects were dead, and the rest were in serious trouble. Almost no construction had been initiated.
>
> Why would anyone want to look a gift horse in the mouth? Why would anyone reject the benevolent efforts of President Johnson, the White House, and the Department of Housing and Urban Development to offer subsidies on federally owned surplus land in metropolitan areas for the laudable purpose of building new communities joining Black and White, rich and poor, living together in harmony with the new technology? Although initial agreement appeared — at least to the federal officials — to be widespread, disagreements rapidly came to the surface. A number of local groups strongly opposed low cost public housing; local officials preferred kinds of development that would yield more tax revenue; and conservationists were opposed to plans for construction. As apparent agreement rapidly yielded to pervasive disagreement, the program ground to a halt.[5]

2. We sometimes do not know how to achieve our goals. In 1975 the Ford administration proposed a tax cut. The purpose was to increase consumer spending in order to stimulate the economy. There

[5] Pressman and Wildavsky, op. cit., p. 91. The authors draw this example from Martha Derthich, *New Towns In-Town* (Washington, D.C.: Urban Institute, 1972).

were two alternatives: a lump-sum tax rebate or a reduction in monthly withholding. The former gave people a large amount all at once; the latter gave them a bit more each month. Which would lead to more spending (rather than more money being put into savings accounts)? The economic planners did not know. Consumer behavior was not predictable enough.

Take another example: The federal, state, and local governments have put a lot of money and effort into improving education in inner-city schools. Many programs have been tried: innovative curricula, smaller classes, open classrooms, traditional classrooms, and so on. Some programs have been successful; some less so. But we still do not know exactly what makes for successful education and what does not.

3. Some things can be changed more easily than others.   Sometimes the diagnosis of a problem suggests a policy that is fairly easy to achieve; sometimes it suggests changes not so easy to achieve by government action. It is easier to reduce the size of classes in inner-city schools than bring in better teachers (in part because one can measure the size of a class easily, but we are not sure what a good teacher is and how to find one). But it may be easier to improve the quality of teachers than to change the values children learn in the home. If the values learned in the home are the basic factor determining success in school (it is by no means certain that this is the case, though some argue that it is), government programs can do little. Government programs will concentrate on class size, since something can be done about it, even though this may not get to the root of the problem.

4. Things that can be changed cannot always be changed much. Suppose studies showed that smaller class size does improve education. Class sizes can be reduced, but only within limits set by available budgets, teachers, and classrooms. Noticeable effects may come only if classes are reduced from 35 to 20 pupils. But resource limitation means classes are reduced only to 30 pupils. The local school board introduces the "right" policy, but not enough of it. The result is little measurable impact on learning.

5. Well-intentioned policies can fail when other conditions are wrong.   The success of a policy often depends on other conditions that are outside of the control of the policy maker. If the conditions are right, the policy works. If not, the policy fails. In recent years, for example, there has been an increase in government action to end job discrimination on the basis of race or sex. Business firms, universities, and other institutions have been required to take "affirmative action" to open more and better jobs to women and minority groups.

Such programs are easier to carry out in a growing economy where new jobs are constantly being created. The implementation of these

Some problems are easier to solve than others.

programs in the mid-1970s was made more difficult by the economic slump beyond the control of the government officials in charge of carrying out the antidiscrimination laws.

6. It is often hard to tell whether a program succeeds or not. Funds are allocated to a particular program. But is the program successful? It is often hard to tell. The standards of success may be unclear. The government sets up a retraining program so workers laid off from one job can develop skills for a different job. What is the standard for success of such a program? The amount spent on training? The number of people who enroll in the program? The number who complete the program? The extent to which they actually learn new skills? Their success in finding jobs after the program? The permanence of such jobs? A program may be successful by one standard (lots of people graduate from the program) but unsuccessful under another (they cannot find jobs where they can use their new skills).

The problem of evaluation is made harder by the fact that those who carry out the program may have a stake in showing it is successful. And the information that gets to higher officials may be biased to show more success than is actually achieved.

This list of "limitations" is not meant to suggest that all government programs fail. Quite the contrary. Many programs achieve what they set out to achieve, or at least something close to it. The point is simply that planning a policy and successfully implementing it are not the same thing.

Government Action and Nonaction

To understand the full range of governmental policy, one has to consider what the government does *not* do as well as what it does. If the government is inactive in some area, that is a policy as well, though not necessarily a planned one. There may never have been a decision to do nothing. But the lack of action has an impact nevertheless.

A visitor from another country like Belgium or Canada, where there is constant conflict over language policy, might ask about the policy of the American government in relation to the English language. "What do you mean by a language policy?" most Americans would reply. "There is no issue or problem here." Yet it is incorrect to say that we are a monolingual country. Most citizens speak English, but a large minority speak Spanish. The lack of an explicit policy on the subject does not mean there is not an *implicit* policy. It means government business is conducted in English, civil-service examinations are in English, literacy tests for voting are in English, and school teaching is conducted in English. And all of these work to the disadvantage of those whose native language is not English. (Indeed, though formerly the government's language policy was implicit, today a conflict of interests has been recognized—leading to

Even government inaction
represents a policy.

explicit policies in New York city and in California that recognize the multiplicity of languages.)

One could give many examples in which the lack of governmental activity is a policy. What is government's policy on the length of vacations for workers? Surely we do not expect the government to have a policy on this subject, yet some countries do. In the United States, however, vacations are left to bargaining between employers and workers. We may believe vacations are "in the natural order of things" not subject to governmental activity. But there was a time when we believed wages were "naturally" a subject for private agreements among workers and management. Now of course we have many laws affecting wages. For many years the government was inactive in the area of medical care. This had the effect of a policy, for it meant the individual citizen had to pay his own medical expenses.

How Issues Become Issues: Setting the Agenda

The discussion about action and nonaction points to a major factor in understanding the pattern of governmental policies. The first issue may be: What are the issues? The impact of governmental policy on the lives of citizens depends in part on how decisions are made about issues, such as whether the government provides funds for mass transport or for roads. But even more basic may be the question of how the issue of roads or mass transport gets on the agenda in the first place. How do roads become a subject of government decisions? Why should the government have a policy in that area? In understanding government policy we ask why issues become issues.

The first political issue is the choice of issues; the first step in dealing with a problem is to recognize that it is a problem. Once a problem has been raised—"put on the agenda"—citizens can pressure the government; debate can take place in the press, in Congress, in the executive branch; proposals can be made. Remember our stress on government inaction: When the government does nothing (about health care or pollution or vehicle noise), that is in a real sense a policy. And nothing is done when an issue never gets the attention of the American people.

Lack of Procedural Rules

Is there a "proper procedure" for putting problems on the political agenda? When we discussed Congress we dealt with the House Rules Committee, a powerful committee because it controls the agenda of the House of Representatives. It decides what bills come to the floor, and it controls the debate. When it comes to American politics in general, no clear set of rules determines what gets on the agenda. The legal rules on who can bring up an issue are found in the Bill of Rights—they are the right of free speech and the right to

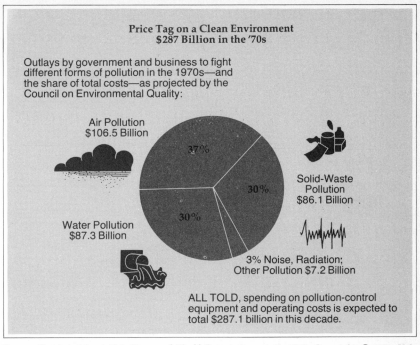

Price Tag on a Clean Environment
$287 Billion in the '70s

Outlays by government and business to fight different forms of pollution in the 1970s—and the share of total costs—as projected by the Council on Environmental Quality:

Air Pollution
$106.5 Billion

37%

30%

30%

Solid-Waste Pollution
$86.1 Billion

Water Pollution
$87.3 Billion

3% Noise, Radiation; Other Pollution $7.2 Billion

ALL TOLD, spending on pollution-control equipment and operating costs is expected to total $287.1 billion in this decade.

Source: Reprinted from *U.S. News and World Report,* August 21, 1972, Copyright © 1972, U.S. News and World Report, Inc.

petition Congress. In this sense anyone has the right to put a matter on the agenda—to write to his congressman saying something should be done. But not everyone does so with equal effectiveness.

The process by which problems come to the attention of the public and the government has not been studied much. One reason is that it is difficult to identify "nonissues," that is, problems that have not yet been recognized. (If it were easy to do so, the problems would be recognized.) Social scientists as well as political leaders have been surprised by the sudden eruption of issues. The women's liberation movement caught most off guard, as did many of the first black protest activities in the 1950s. Looking back, one can say these were "natural" issues certain to arise sooner or later. But that is hindsight.

How Problems Get on the Agenda

Does the Agenda Reflect Reality?   One view of how problems get on the political agenda is that they get on automatically. If the economy is going badly, economic problems automatically get on the agenda of politics; if it is going well, little attention is paid to them. In earlier days, when our rivers and streams were pure, pollution was not on the agenda. Now they are filthy, and pollution is a major political issue. (See Figure 16.1.)

This view has some truth. One cannot imagine pollution as an issue if the air and water is pure. In that sense an objective problem

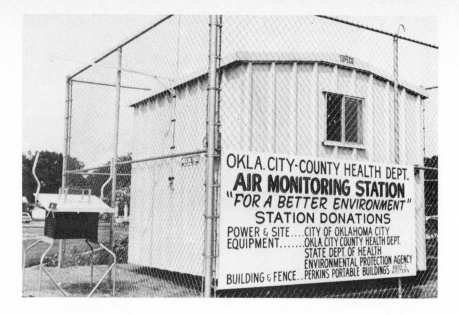

(dirty water) is a *necessary* but not a *sufficient* condition to get a problem on the agenda. The "political" agenda does not merely reflect the "real" problems of a society. Our lakes and rivers were polluted long before the current concern with the problem, well back into the nineteenth century in some cases. Lake Erie became almost hopelessly polluted with little concern. Now that the same thing is happening to some of the other Great Lakes, it is an issue. Surely something besides the objective problem is responsible.

In the 1950s and 1960s the issue of race relations exploded on the American scene. Does that mean there was less of a problem earlier? Quite the contrary. Data show an improvement in the life conditions of American blacks at the same time that their demands for equal rights became stronger. What had to be added to the objective problems was the subjective awareness of them.

There is another reason why the agenda of politics reflects more than the objective problems of society. Each time a new problem arises, it does not push the old ones off the agenda. It is often hard for a new problem to get on the agenda. One political analyst found that the best way to find out what will be on this year's budget is to look at last year's. Just as most organization meetings have "old business" as the first item on the agenda, so does the American political structure. Once a problem has been recognized, it tends to become institutionalized; that is, a government agency is set up to deal with it, it has a place on the government's budget, a congressional committee or subcommittee works on it. It is on the agenda, and year after year it stays there because the government agency and the congressional committee see to it. A new problem has no such support; it may have to wait in the wings for a long time—sometimes years and decades—before it is recognized.

Can Anyone Put a Problem on the Agenda? A second view is that anyone can put a problem on the agenda. In a way this is true, but it is also somewhat misleading. The Constitution guarantees the right to petition Congress or to form a political group. And these things are often done. But not all social groups are equally organized. And unorganized interests have less chance of getting their problems on the political agenda than organized ones.

The fact that a serious problem exists does not make one active in trying to get the government to deal with that problem. This can be seen from a study of political participation that found black Americans more likely than whites saying they had serious problems that could be solved by governmental activity. And the problems blacks mention are serious: adequate jobs, income, housing. Blacks thus recognize their problems as political, that is, problems the government would be most likely to solve. But though blacks are almost twice as likely as whites to say they have problems requiring government action, they are less than half as likely to have contacted an official about such a problem. And when asked why they did not do so, the most frequent reason given by blacks was that they doubted their own effectiveness and the government's responsiveness.[6]

Of course even if a group raises an issue for the political agenda, there is no certainty that it will be given serious consideration. The Constitution gives everyone the right to raise an issue; it does not guarantee a sympathetic reply. Thus just as citizens are not equally likely to raise issues, there is even greater inequality in the response of the government.

Can Any Problem Get on the Agenda? A third point can be made about the political agenda. Just as some people are less likely to put their problems on the agenda, there are certain problems that are less likely to get on the agenda. The "free enterprise" tradition in America makes it unlikely that an issue involving government ownership of industries will be raised or, if raised, will be taken seriously.

There are a number of reasons why such issues might not be raised. Quite simply, they may be considered "so far out of the question" that citizens would not think of raising them. Of course what is "out of the question" may be hard to tell until a question is raised. Many major changes were once considered unlikely or impossible. The notion that some issue is "out of the question" can be a self-fulfilling prophecy. People think some issue is out of the question and therefore do not raise it. In this sense the political agenda has a lot of inertia built into it.

Another reason such issues are not raised is that it may be risky to do so. This is particularly true for candidates for office, as Barry

[6] Sidney Verba and Norman H. Nie, *Participation in America: Political Democracy and Social Equality* (New York: Harper & Row, 1972), chap. 10.

Goldwater learned in his 1964 campaign for the Presidency. The social-security system has become an accepted part of the American scene; no longer an issue for discussion. But in speeches and articles Goldwater had toyed with the idea of modifying social security. It was on this issue that the Democrats chose to "hook and hang" him, observes Theodore H. White in *The Making of the President, 1964.*[7] A television spot in which the fingers of two hands tore up a social-security card was shown over and over again during the campaign. By election day millions of elderly Americans were convinced that as President, Goldwater would abolish social security and cut off their retirement checks. When surveyed after the election, delegates to the Republican Convention that had nominated Goldwater ranked the social-security issue as the second most important reason for their party's defeat.

Who Can Get Issues on the Agenda?

Those who are politically active are more likely to get problems put on the political agenda. The reason is simple. Participation communicates to the government the views of the citizens. If the citizens do not participate, their views remain unknown. One study compared the views of citizens on the major problems of their communities with the problems leaders felt were most pressing and on which they were working. It found that leaders tended to have on *their* agendas the problems expressed by the *active* citizens. Thus the first generalization is that one has to be active to get problems on the agenda.

Activity, however, may not be enough. The same study compared the effectiveness of political activity by upper- and lower-status citizens. Among the active citizens, it was found that those from upper social groups—the wealthy, the educated, those with high-status occupations—were very effective in getting items put on the political agenda. Those lower-status citizens who participated actively were less successful; the agendas of community leaders did not match up very well with the preferences of lower-status citizens.

Why did these lower-status citizens who were active still not succeed in communicating their views on the most pressing problems in the community to their leaders? There are three possible answers, each of which tells us something about setting agendas.

For one thing, the lower-status citizens who were active were socially very different from the community leaders. The leaders tended to be wealthy and well educated; the lower-status activists tended to be poorer and less well educated. These differences may have made the leaders less attentive to them. Second, the problems the lower-status citizens wanted to put on the agenda were different from those the upper-status citizens were interested in. The latter

[7] Theodore H. White, *The Making of the President, 1964* (New York: Atheneum, 1965).

were interested in better community facilities and perhaps also (inconsistently) in lowering taxes. The former wanted basic issues of welfare placed on the agenda. Third, though the lower-status activists were as active as the upper-status ones, there were fewer of them. Thus their views were drowned out by a larger group of upper-status activists.[8]

This discussion should help make clear why some groups turn to more direct, sometimes violent, protest action to bring their problems to the attention of the government. Violent action, as we have suggested, is a *signal,* a way of getting the attention of political leaders. Violent outbursts, whatever their other costs, are effective in calling the attention of leaders to problems they might otherwise ignore. It is a way of getting on the agenda.

There are also individuals and groups in America whose specialty is seeking and publicizing new problems—a long tradition in this country. Around the turn of the century, the muckrakers brought many social problems to public attention and got these problems on the government agenda. Much of the legislation regulating business dates from that time. The job of bringing forth new issues is currently being done by the leaders of the consumer movement, the ecology movement, and the women's rights movement. In addition, investigative reporters often bring new problems to the attention of the public. An example is the revelation in 1975 that the CIA had been investigating the activity of Americans in the United States (by law it is required to limit its activity to foreign countries). The issue was raised by a series of articles in the *New York Times.* Once made public it was put on the political agenda, as Congress and the executive branch set up committees to investigate the charges.

Alternative Modes of Policy Making

Imagine a government official faced with a policy problem. Suppose he is trying to write legislation to deal with automobile pollution. There are two ways he can approach the problem. One we call the *comprehensive* approach, and the other we call the *incremental* approach.

Using the Comprehensive Approach

In using the comprehensive approach the government official will consider all possible ways of handling the issue and all possible effects in relation to other problems. He will very clearly state the goal he is trying to achieve and relate it to other goals he thinks are important. He will then choose the best possible means to achieve the goal.

Let us look at what a comprehensive approach to automobile pollution might entail:

[8] Verba and Nie, chap. 20.

1. THE PAST IS NO LIMIT   The planner dealing with the problem of automobile pollution in a comprehensive manner will not allow himself to be limited by what has been done before. The past design of automobiles, the number of older automobiles on the road, the evolution of the automobile industry, and the pattern of use of the automobile will not interfere with a new comprehensive plan.

2. ALL POSSIBLE POLICIES AND TECHNIQUES WILL BE CONSIDERED   The comprehensive planner will not stop at considering ways to modify current cars; he will consider all possible technologies. Nor will he limit himself to the existing means of transportation. He may very well consider the possibility of replacing the car with mass transit.

3. CONNECTIONS WITH OTHER POLICIES WILL BE CONSIDERED   He will see the linkage of his goal to other policies, and he will not be afraid to plan for changes in those policies if they are related to automobile pollution. Does private ownership of cars lead to greater pollution? Then perhaps private ownership should be barred. Perhaps government ownership of the automobile industry would increase control over pollution. If so, that possibility should be considered as well.

4. ALL VALUES ARE CONSIDERED   The comprehensive planner, however, is not single-minded. He does not consider only how to curb auto fumes. Rather, he is fully aware that we have other values as well as a desire for less pollution. Pollution could be stopped by banning all cars, but that would hurt other values such as a functioning economy and full employment, or our desire to get from place to place.

The comprehensive planner does not ignore these other values but takes them all into consideration. How much do we value curbing pollution? How much do we value curbing inflation? How much do we value full employment? How much do we value limiting government control over the economy? All of these values are related to pollution. A comprehensive planner will weigh them against the gain from curbing car pollution.

5. THE COMPREHENSIVE PLANNER CONSIDERS ALL THE EFFECTS OF HIS PLAN   What effect does it have on jobs, on housing, on other means of transport? Maybe a reduction in pollution will improve health. The planner might even consider the need for new facilities for the aged, who will probably live longer in a pollution-free atmosphere.

Using the Incremental Approach
Consider, on the other hand, the incremental approach to policy making. It differs from the comprehensive approach in every way. (See Figure 16.2.)

1. For the incremental planner, the past is a major constraint. He considers the current situation: how many cars are on the road, their economic importance, current patterns of automobile use. Past policies, such as the policy not to support mass transit, will be considered as "givens"—a framework within which he must work.

2. Rather than considering all possible ways of dealing with the problem, the incremental planner will consider cars as currently designed and the modifications that could fit into current technologies.

3. He will stick fairly closely to the technical problem of standards for automobile pollution and ignore larger changes in the economy. Such

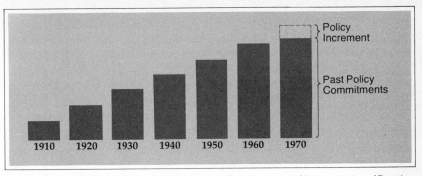

major changes as the banning of the private automobile or the nationalization of the automobile industry would probably not even enter his mind.

4. The incremental planner would not worry much about the effects of his plan in other areas. His area of concern is automobile pollution: Let other governmental agencies worry about inflation or full employment. He will not comprehensively consider all other relevant values and weigh them against that of cleaner air. Rather, he will ignore most other values, and think only of the narrower task at hand.

The results of the two modes of policy making would be different indeed. The comprehensive planner could almost redesign the world from scratch. The incrementalist will create a policy narrowly designed to deal with a specific problem, modifying but not scrapping current practices.

At first glance the comprehensive approach appears much more productive. Piecemeal solutions often accomplish little. And we have seen that failure to consider all the effects of a policy can lead to unforeseen and unwanted results.

The Government Uses the Incremental Approach

Despite the seeming advantages of the comprehensive approach, most governmental policy takes the incremental approach. Policies tend to be based on previous policies and are worked out step by step, narrowly focusing on one aspect of the problem. This is so for the following reasons.

First, comprehensive planning is beyond the ability of planners. To consider all values and weigh one against the other is not possible. There is no precise way of saying (or knowing) how much one values clean air vs. full employment. A plan that covered all relevant values and all possible effects of a decision could not be worked out, even with the most advanced computers.

Second, most government planners are not in a position to consider all aspects of a problem at once. The official who was assigned to work on automobile pollution and came back with a plan that

Once a program is established, pressures grow to keep it. Here government welfare workers call for increased hiring.

required vast funds for mass transit would be told to stick to his job. And that is what most public officials do. Of course there are institutions that are supposed to have a more comprehensive view of all problems: the Presidency and Congress. But even here incremental planning may rule. Congress may make the broadest of legislation, but it itself is organized into committees geared to specific problems rather than planning comprehensively across all fields. And even the President, burdened with particular problems that have to be dealt with at a particular time, may have trouble taking a more general view.

Many Presidents have complained about the lack of time to deal with a problem comprehensively. In the area of foreign policy, for instance, they have complained that the pressure to make decisions on emergency problems makes it impossible to deal with overall and long-term policy. They have often been aware of the problem but unable to deal with it.

Another reason why policy making tends to be incremental is the weight of history. Policy makers cannot avoid past decisions. Once a course is charted, one cannot easily change it without risking severe problems. If a governmental program of one sort has been set up, one cannot come along and start all over again without considering the status and effects of the existing program.

Furthermore, people become committed to existing programs and put pressure on the government to keep them going.

One major study of government spending on various programs asked how one could predict what any state or city would spend on various functions—welfare, health, education, transportation, parks, and so forth. What was the best predictor, the study asked: the party that won the last election? the social makeup of the locality? the changes in the problems the government faced? The answer was no. By far the best predictor of how a government will spend its funds this year is how it spent them last year. Changes there may be, but they will be *incremental* changes. Last year's budget tends to be the starting point for this year's.[9]

The weight of existing programs falls on all governmental levels, high and low. After twenty years out of office, the Republicans elected a President in 1952. The previous two decades had seen the growth of huge governmental programs in the area of social welfare, programs that had been severely criticized by leaders of the Republican opposition. But none of these programs was ended. Some may have been changed somewhat, some cut. But those were incremental changes, not comprehensive ones. The weight of past decisions is also found in foreign policy. Each President inherits the policies of past Presidents. And though each moves in a different direction, this almost always makes a smaller difference than the public (or even the new President and his staff) expect. They may change course by 5, 10, 20 degrees—but rarely by 180 degrees.

The Argument for Incremental Policy Making

Incremental policy making is a fact of American politics. That is how most policy is made. Its defenders argue that it is a most effective way of making policy. For one thing, they point out that such a narrow focus on one aspect of a problem is not a bad way to do things. It is not that other issues and other values are ignored. It is just that there are other government agencies worrying about the other problems. If the official concerned with air pollution does not face the issue of inflation, it does not matter. He would not have dealt with it well anyway. It is not his area and he has other problems to worry about. Let some other part of the government worry about that. And if separate parts of the government worry about separate problems, all problems will be dealt with somewhere.

Furthermore, it is good to make policy without considering all possible effects. Otherwise one would never act; it would take a lifetime of study to consider all the possible effects of a policy.

The argument in favor of incremental planning is not without flaws. It assumes that somehow each possible value has a government agency worrying about it. But of course that is not the case. Certain interests are preserved by certain parts of the government; others aren't dealt with. It is only in recent years that a government agency has been set up to deal with consumer interests, and the organizational power of that agency is much weaker than that of most others. And while it is true that a comprehensive concern for all possible effects might lead to no policy at all, one can find too

[9] Ira Sharkansky, *Spending in the American States* (Chicago: Rand McNally, 1968).

many examples where unintended effects have made the results of a policy almost the opposite of what was planned.

But whether one approves of it or not, one has to understand policy making in America as a process that often goes on in an incremental way. This is reinforced by the tendency to *disaggregate* the policy-making process.

The Disaggregation of Policy Making

A major tendency in American politics is to divide the policy-making process into small units. In part this is reflected in the tendency to decentralize decision making into small government units—states, cities, towns, school districts. More generally it is a tendency to fragment policy making. Policy is made by a narrowly focused government agency for a particular group on a fairly narrow range of issues. Policy is not made for the economy as a whole. Rather, different parts of the government specialize in particular aspects of the economy. The regulation of one part of the economy is done by one branch of the government (a bureau in the Department of Agriculture, the Interstate Commerce Commission, the Bureau of Mines) that works closely with those it regulates (the farmers growing a particular crop, the railroads, the mine interests).

Disaggregated decision making means those who are to be regulated are likely to take part in the regulation. President Nixon's Task Force for Business Taxation, appointed in 1969, was made up of four lawyers from corporate law firms, two New York investment bankers, three representatives of corporate accounting firms, two top officials of large industrial corporations, and three business-oriented economists. Policy is made within narrow limits. Each government agency is concerned with the problems of the particular part of the society whose problems it specializes in. It is not concerned with broader social issues. This disaggregation in the executive branch of the government is paralleled by disaggregation in Congress. The congressional structure of specialized committees and more specialized subcommittees makes for a similar narrow focus on the problems of a particular group.

Consequences of Disaggregated Policy Making

Policy making for narrow constituencies has important results. The top political institutions in the country—the parties, the President, Congress—have (or should have) broad rather than narrow constituencies. Their constituents come from all branches of the economy—workers and management, farms and industries. And they come from all kinds of farms and all kinds of industries, not just wheat farms or the aluminum industry. If policy is made by such institutions, it is likely to take into consideration many sides of a problem. If the constituency is broad, a suggestion for an increase in dairy prices would be considered not only from the point of view of the dairy farmers but from that of the consumers who must pay the prices. But if the constituency is narrow—if policy is made in a bureau of the Department of Agriculture that deals only with dairy interests—policy will more likely be made with only the dairy interests in mind.

How Does Disaggregation Come About?

Disaggregation is in part a result of the organizational structure of the government. It happens when major policy decisions are made by specialized agencies or committees. Disaggregation also results because American political parties do not provide broad programs among which citizens can choose, and it is reinforced by the tendency mentioned earlier for laws of Congress to be general and vague. This leaves a vacuum when it comes to carrying out policy. Someone has to decide how the policy is to be applied, and that is left to administrative agencies with narrower constituencies.

Finally, the disaggregation of governmental policy is supported by a general belief that as much governmental activity as possible should be freed from "politics." The slogan is heard in a number of fields: "Let's keep politics out of the schools!" "The Federal Communications Commission should not be placed under political pressure!" "Don't make medicare a political football!"

Keeping "Politics" Out of Policy Making

The slogans calling for keeping politics out of governmental activity are somewhat self-contradictory, because politics exists whenever binding decisions are made for the society. Whatever the FCC does is, by our definition, political. Medicare, involving federal spending for medical care, is political. Education, the largest domestic governmental program, is political. The confusion lies in the fact that our general "political science" definition of politics isn't what the slogans mean. And to understand that difference is to understand something very important about policy making in America.

When people talk of freeing some area of public concern—schools, communications policy, medicare—from "politics," they generally mean freeing it from *partisan politics.* They think that area should not be the concern of the political parties, with each party trying to use the policy to get votes. Similarly the policy should be removed from the partisan control of Congress. Certain policies, in short, should not be the subject of partisan conflict.

How then should communications, education, or medical-care policy be made? The answer will be that such policies should be impartial, objective, decided by experts. Regulation of the airwaves is a very technical problem. One needs specialists in communications policy. The granting of a new TV license should not be the subject of partisan conflict, with the license going to the side that can get more congressional support. Education of children is a complicated business. It should not be subject to partisan pressures but should be controlled by specialists in education.

This attempt to remove policy making from politics (in the narrow sense of *partisan politics*) is found in the federal administration with its specialized agencies, in Congress with its specialized committees. It is found in the state governments, which have a similar structure. It is found on the local level.

But—and here our broader definition of politics becomes important—to remove some governmental function from partisan politics is not to remove it from politics more generally. The decisions of technical experts remain political as long as they have behind them the force of the government, as long as they involve regulation of behavior or the spending of tax money. What removing a matter from partisan politics means is turning it over to a narrow constituency. Communications policy is not made in a vacuum. Removing that policy area from partisan politics means that the vacuum is filled by the interest most affected—the communications industry. It becomes the constituency of the government agency making that policy. The same is true of education policy. The role of organized educational interests—colleges of education, the educational bureaucracy, teachers' organizations—increases as the pressures of a broader constituency decrease.

Those approving of disaggregated decision making argue that it gives major control over policy to the specific groups most affected. The narrow constituencies closely tied to government agencies or congressional committees are just those the policy affects most. Thus policies can be adjusted to the needs of particular groups.

The argument against such decision making should by now be familiar: Not all constituencies are equally served. Many do not have powerful agencies they can contact. Educational policy may be adjusted to the needs of colleges of education more than those of teachers, and may serve the needs of both better than those of pupils. The education schools are better organized than the teachers; the teachers, in turn, better than the pupils. Furthermore, broad concern with some more general public interest is missing when policy making is disaggregated.

Finally, it should be clear that disaggregation leads to incremental planning. Those who make policy don't take a comprehensive view of social problems. Rather, their attention is focused on the group nearest to themselves—their specific constituency.

Comprehensive and Centralized Planning

As we have often seen in American politics, one tendency is balanced by another: The forces of localism pull against the forces of centralization; Congress pulls against the President; individual liberties pull against national security. The same is true in policy making. The tendency in American politics toward policies that are incremental and disaggregated is in constant tension with attempts to develop more comprehensive and centralized planning.

Both Congress and the executive branch have tried to create institutions for comprehensive policy making, institutions that are more general than the committees of Congress or the departments of the executive.

Comprehensive Institutions

The Office of Management and Budget (OMB)   This agency is directly under the control of the President. It is not a part of any department. Its purpose is to improve the coordination of government policy. It prepares the federal budget and, in so doing, tries to see that the budget proposals coming from the executive departments fit into the President's overall program. In addition, it tries to oversee the way programs are carried out.

The OMB represents an attempt to deal comprehensively with governmental programs. It is a powerful branch of the Presidential office and takes a more comprehensive view than the individual departments do. But often it is involved in a tug-of-war with the individual departments as the latter try to protect and develop their own programs.

The government has been searching for a comprehensive energy program, but it is not easy to find one.

The Council of Economic Advisers   This is a three-member body set up under the Full Employment Act of 1946. Its purpose is to help the President make overall economic policy. The members of the Council tend to be professional economists, but they share the general economic views of the President. In the economic crisis of the mid-1970s, the Council played an increasingly important role in setting general economic policy.

The National Security Council   This body tries to coordinate U.S. foreign policy. It brings together the top officials from the separate departments that deal with foreign affairs: the Department of State, the Department of Defense, and the CIA. Over the years it has grown from a committee of top officials to an agency with a large professional staff. It is an example of the way "coordinating" agencies are created to try to take control of what would otherwise be a disaggregated policy-making process.

Budget Committees in Congress   Congress has also tried to increase its capacity for comprehensive planning. The process of making budget appropriations in the House and Senate has traditionally been incremental and disaggregated. The President would submit his annual budget to Congress. Separate committees worked on separate parts of the President's requests for authority to spend money. There was no committee that looked at the budget as a whole. In 1974 Congress set up new committees on the budget in the House and Senate. These new committees will allow the members of Congress to look at the overall budget, setting target figures before working on various parts of the budget.

COMPREHENSIVE AND
CENTRALIZED PLANNING

The purpose of the new committee is to take a more comprehensive and centralized approach. It is hoped that this will increase the influence of Congress on the budgetary process and make the process less chaotic.

The new committees of Congress are intended to reform its traditionally decentralized ways of doing things. But it is not yet certain how they will work. As the *Congressional Quarterly* (a private magazine that comments on affairs in Washington) put it: "To make the design effective, Congress will have to overcome a lack of budgetary expertise, some committee jurisdictional jealousies, the temptation to waive budget-making deadlines and, occasionally at least, the personal political interests of 100 senators and 435 House members."[10] Or, as one former official of the Office and Management and Budget suggested: "To make it work, Congress and its individual members will have to act a hell of a lot differently than they do now."[11]

Some members of Congress were less pessimistic about the new committees but did agree that it would take several years for them to work properly.

The Actors in Policy Making

Who might be among the influential actors on a particular policy? They can be individuals and groups in the government or outside it.

The Mass Public, Special Publics, Organized Groups One potential actor is the *mass public,* or that part of it called the majority. Its opinion can be expressed in public-opinion polls and in letters to congressmen, perhaps at election time. If public involvement takes a narrower form, *special publics* may be the actors. These so-called attentive publics are likely to have some special interest in a policy: Union members, for instance, are likely to be an attentive public for labor legislation, farmers for farm legislation, doctors for medical legislation. Or the actors may be *organized groups.* And here we can make a useful distinction between groups with a broad constituency and those with a narrower one. A broad constituency would include a wide range of types of citizens and interests; a narrow one would cover a much more precisely defined group. A few examples will make the distinction clear: Groups with broad constituencies include the so-called peak business associations that represent interests from many parts of the business community: organizations like the National Association of Manufacturers or the U.S. Chamber of Commerce representing industry as a whole, or the American Textile Manufacturers Institute representing many branches of a particular industry. In the labor field one would have the AFL-CIO

---

[10] "Current American Government" (Washington, D.C.: *Congressional Quarterly,* Spring 1975), p. 75.
[11] Ibid.

representing unions of all sorts. Other broad constituency groups might include the National Council of Churches (representing many church groups), Common Cause (a lobbying group representing a loose coalition of liberals), or the Liberty Lobby (a parallel group representing conservatives).

More specific groups have narrower memberships. Particular labor unions—the Auto Workers, the Teamsters, the Postal Workers —fall in this category. So do groups representing specific industries or firms. The U.S. Savings and Loan League and the National Association of Retail Druggists speak for narrower interests than those mentioned earlier, as, of course, do U.S. Steel and International Telephone and Telegraph. Groups representing particular kinds of farmers—cotton growers, Wisconsin dairymen—fall into this category as well. We distinguish between interest groups in this way because it makes a difference, in terms of the policy-making process, which kinds are involved. The more disaggregated the policy, the more narrowly based the groups involved.

The Party System   Policy makers who come from the party system might include national party organs such as the National Committee or groups like the Young Democrats or the Ripon Society (a group of liberal Republicans). They might also include state and local party groups.

State and Local Governments   The states, through their governors or other representatives, take part in federal policy making. And so do the cities and other local governments. At times it may be difficult to distinguish a state or local government as actor from a party group as actor. When, as we saw in Chapter 11, Mayor Daley of Chicago used his political "clout" against the Office of Economic Opportunity, was he acting as mayor of Chicago or as head of the powerful Cook County Democratic organization? The answer of course is that he was acting as both, and that is where the "clout" came from.

The Federal Government   The most important actors in the making of federal policy tend to come from within the federal government itself. The office of the President is crucial. This includes the President and his close advisers on the White House staff, as well as government bodies close to the White House such as the OMB, the Council of Economic Advisers, and the National Security Council. The more specific parts of the executive branch—the federal departments such as Agriculture, Commerce, State, and their various bureaus; the independent regulatory commissions such as the Interstate Commerce Commission and the Federal Communications Commission—all take part as well.

This list of actors should be familiar to the reader. It is a summary of the groups we have dealt with so far. Thus we already know a good deal about how they take part in the policy process. But we have dealt with each group separately. To see how they relate to one another, we shall have to see how they interact when making policy. We have introduced policy making in this chapter, but we have dealt with it on a rather general level. To better understand the policy-making process, we turn to some specific areas of policy making in the next chapter.

How We Find Out About Politics: III Policies and Leaders

An earlier discussion of how to study politics focused on the sample survey, which uses interviews and questionnaires. Although the sample survey is a very useful tool for studying the opinions and behavior of the American public, it is not much help in answering many important questions about politics.

In studying public policy—both the institutions in which policy is made and the people who make it—many political scientists do what can be called *documentary research*. This includes a variety of research activities in which the records the government keeps about itself and the records others outside the government publish about government activities and personnel are used to answer questions about politics.

Those who make important decisions in our technological society, whether in the public or in the private sector, need a lot of data if their decisions are to be rational. Therefore much information is gathered and stored in our society. Thus the political scientist doing documentary research can work with a great variety of records about the government and its activities, some of it gathered by the government itself, the rest by nongovernmental agencies concerned about various government activities.

The government describes its personnel, activities, and policies in hundreds of documents and reports. In addition, it describes the personnel, activities, and policies of other areas of American life. You can learn from government documents the number of scientists being trained in various universities, the number of private airplanes sold every year, the number of American businessmen living in Mexico, and the number of beds in private nursing homes. Very few activities in society, whether public or "private," escape the scrutiny of some government agency.

Furthermore, because the government is involved in such a wide range of activities, many nongovern-mental agencies keep records about the government. The AFL-CIO, for instance, publishes the voting records of congressmen on all questions of importance to the labor unions. Also, the American Association for the Advancement of Science, a private, nonprofit professional association, reports the budget and policies of the National Science Foundation in its journal.

Thus there is a large "documentation deposit" that describes in detail the agencies and institutions that make public policy. Although this documentation is extensive, it should be used carefully. There are several things a political scientist who uses these documents should keep in mind.

1. The institutional bias: Many government records are the product of self-reporting. The records of campaign contributions are kept by the political parties that collect the contributions. Crime statistics are made available by the FBI and local police. An evaluation of the Head Start program is published by the Department of Health, Education and Welfare, under whose direction Head Start was begun.

Self-reports are often biased. They exaggerate facts that work to the credit of the reporting agency and underplay facts that would discredit it. For instance, a corporate executive contributes $25,000 to a political party but does so by sending 25 checks of $1,000 each to 25 different committees and candidates. If the party wants to stress that it depends on many small contributions instead of a few large ones, it reports this as 25 separate contributions. A city police department that feels itself short-handed and wants a budget increase might report crime statistics in such a way as to show an increase in crime. Perhaps it calls every loss of property "suspected theft." Another police department that has just had a large budget increase and wants to justify it will report statistics showing a decrease in crime. It reports only cases in which theft clearly took place.

This institutional bias of government agencies is easily understood. To stay in business an agency must show it is doing what it is expected to do and that it could do even better if its budget were increased. But however understandable from a political point of view, the institutional bias poses a problem for the researcher working with public documents. A careful researcher will try to recognize possible bias.

2. Durability: Some records are more durable than others; some last while others are lost or destroyed. The researcher who depends on documents for his data may discover that the records he needs were destroyed in a fire or were never even kept in the first place. Say you wanted to compare turnout in city elections with turnout in national elections for the past 100 years. You would have no trouble finding the data for national elections, but for some communities you might be able to find records of turnout in local elections only for the past 10 or 20 years. Or say you wanted to study colonial regimes in East Africa. It is easy to get records on how England, for instance, administered its colonies in East Africa between 1920 and 1960. It is almost impossible to get records on the many African movements that opposed the colonial government. The records kept by opposition movements of their own activities (their members, their resources, their plans) disappeared as the movements themselves were put down. And the records kept by the colonial government on these movements were destroyed by the colonial officials just before the African nations gained independence.

3. Secrecy: In a democracy the business of government is supposed to be public. And compared to many nations the amount of information the U.S. government makes public about itself is considerable. Yet much government business even in the United States is conducted secretly. This is obviously true—for understandable reasons—in matters involving national security. Governmental secrecy, however, goes far beyond military and security agencies. Nearly everything that goes on inside the White House has traditionally been made public only at the discretion of the President or his staff (except in the dramatic case of the Watergate investigations). Although floor debate in Congress is public, congressional committees and subcommittees often meet in private for the important sessions that finish the drafting of legislation. (Forty percent of all congressional committee meetings were held in secret in 1972.) Supreme Court decisions are of course announced publicly, but the meetings of the justices take place in private. Anyone can read the budget proposed by the OMB, but few can go to the meetings when the arguments for and against particular programs are being considered.

In short, it is much easier to get information on the finished product of the legislative, executive, or judicial agency than to get information on the political process leading to that product. And thus the study of public documents is always to some extent the study of what government chooses to let the outsider know.

Thus although we can learn a lot about the institutions and people of government and about the policies they make through careful study of government documents and similar materials, we must be aware that there are limits to what we can expect to learn from the public record. To give you an idea of the types of studies that can be carried out using these kinds of materials, we list a few examples of such research.

1. Political representation: It is possible to combine several kinds of data to give an overall picture of political representation. Census data can provide a profile of the citizens in a congressional district showing whether they are generally poor or wealthy, generally Catholic or Protestant, generally rural or urban. Using such profiles we could make some guesses about how the elected representative might vote on various public policies. We might guess, for example, that congressmen from rural districts would favor farm subsidies, while congressmen from urban districts would favor rapid-transit subsidies. And of course, because there are records of the actual votes, we would be able to check our hunches. We could enlarge our study by including data—again from the public record—on whether a given district has strong party competition or is generally safe for one or the other of the political parties. Taking these data about the social makeup of the population, about how the elected representatives vote on legislation, and about the strength of the political parties, we could put together a picture of the representation process.

2. The legislative process: Congress is a thoroughly documented institution. A particularly useful source of information about Congress is the weekly *Congressional Quarterly*. It reports the roll-call votes of all members of Congress. It also gives a variety of information about major bills: their subject matter, their sponsors, the content of committee hearings, the action on the floor of Congress, and the results of any Senate–House conferences. It describes who heads various committees, what lobbyists are active on which bills, and how any given legislation fits into the President's program.

This kind of material is valuable for studying a great variety of questions about the legislative process. Is a committee headed by a southern Democrat likely to handle a civil-rights bill differently from a committee headed by a northern Democrat? Which pressure groups are most likely to get legislation favorable to their point of view? Are cohesive subcommittees more successful in getting their bills passed than divided subcommittees?

Political scientists have used documentary data on Congress to study all of these issues. Out of these investigations has come a very detailed understanding of the legislative process. Similar studies have been carried out in state legislatures and even in city councils, though the public record on legislative actions at the state and local levels is not as complete as it is for Congress.

3. The "power elite": For those who want to know about the people who lead our society, a great deal of descriptive material about the social and educational backgrounds and the careers of people who reach the top offices is available. Such biographical information may be found in a variety of publications, such as the *Congressional Directory,* the State Department *Biographical Register, Who's Who in America,* or various biographical directories of special groups such as blacks, lawyers, or corporate directors.

Using such information we could answer several kinds of questions. We could try to figure out how much overlap there is between the various power groups in American society. For example, do the same people who serve on the boards of trustees of large universities also hold major corporate directorships? And are these the same people who move in and out of government, serving from time to time as advisers to important political leaders? Or we could use such information to find out the social backgrounds of leaders. We might want to know, for example, whether a large percentage of congressmen graduated from Ivy League colleges, or whether there are more top diplomats who are black or female than there used to be, or whether the proportion of lawyers in the Senate has changed since the nineteenth century.

4. Priorities in public policy: Government budgets and reports give detailed data about public policy. This kind of information is important, since budgetary data show the priorities given different programs. We know, for instance, that for some time military and security affairs have claimed more than three out of every five dollars spent by the federal government, leaving all other federal programs to be funded out of the remaining 40 percent. We could also use this kind of data to compare priorities across government units. For example, to see whether some states stress elementary education more than others, we could compare the per-pupil spending of different states and the percentage of the state tax dollar spent on elementary education.

5. Correlates of government expenditures: We could also use data from the public record to find out what kinds of political or social factors correlate with different priorities. For example, in the area of elementary education we could try to explain why some cities in Illinois spend more on elementary education than others. Perhaps cities in which businesses pay a large share of the property taxes tend to spend more; perhaps communities in which the citizens are relatively wealthy or well educated tend to spend more. We could find the necessary data to test these hunches in the public record.

We might also look at some political factors to see, for example, whether state spending on elementary education is correlated with voter turnout, party competition, or turnover of elected officials. These data, too, are part of the public record.

Conclusions

These notes touch on only a few of the ways political scientists have used the "documentation deposit" to find out about politics and government in the United States. But they show how much information is available and the importance of this information to systematic study. The sample survey is a powerful research tool but is far too costly to use every time a researcher wants to learn something about government or public policy. Indeed we use the sample survey primarily for studies of the entire population of the country because that is the only way to get data on public opinion or general political participation. But when we turn our attention away from the population at large and concentrate on specific groups or political institutions, the kind of data best suited to research is often found in documents, records, budgets, and the like.

485

17

Public Policies: Domestic and Foreign

In this chapter we present a few case studies of how policy is made. The federal government is active in almost all areas of our lives (and those of people in other countries). To see how policy is made, we might have to look at thousands of issues and at the activities of hundreds of bureaus, committees, and groups. We cannot, of course, do that. We must choose some policy areas to study.

Yet the choice is difficult, for studying the policy process in one area may not tell us much about other areas. How the government makes policy decisions on nuclear weapons may tell us little about how agricultural policy is made.

In this chapter we will consider a range of policies that give some overview of the various ways policy is made and the actors involved. There is no single process by which policies are made, but the categories and distinctions discussed in the previous chapter should serve as a useful framework for analysis.

Government Regulation of Business

Government regulation of business activities illustrates a pattern of policy making common in many areas where the government acts to regulate citizens and organizations. Despite our "free enterprise" tradition the government has been active for many years in regulating business activity. For certain kinds of businesses—public utilities, for instance, and the airlines industry, in which a few firms have a monopoly over a vital public service—the government sets rates. In addition, the government controls certain businesses by granting them limited franchises, by giving a TV license to one firm rather than another, by assigning an air route to one carrier rather than another. For many businesses it sets standards, such as cleanliness for foods, purity for drugs, safety for cars. The government also maintains business competition by enforcing the antitrust laws.

Regulation of business in the United States has tended to be disaggregated and to involve close cooperation between the regulatory agency and the business being regulated.

Laws of Congress are, as we have pointed out, often remarkably vague. They receive meaning only when they are administered. Most of the major laws dealing with the regulation of industry are of this type. They tell the government agency administering the law to grant radio and television licenses according to "public interest and necessity" or to approve applications for air routes on the basis of "public convenience" or to see that public-utility rates are "just and reasonable." These are very general guidelines. What is important, then, is who administers the laws and how.

Independent Regulatory Commissions Many laws regulating business are administered by independent regulatory commissions. The first such commission was the Interstate Commerce Commission

(ICC), created in 1887 to regulate the railroads and other interstate transportation industries. Over the years Congress has created an "alphabet soup" of such agencies to regulate various parts of the business community: the Federal Trade Commission (FTC) to administer the antitrust laws, the Federal Power Commission (FPC), the Federal Communications Commission (FCC), the Securities and Exchange Commission (SEC) to regulate the stock market, the Civil Aeronautics Board (CAB), and so on. (See Table 17.1.)

Although they deal with different areas, the commissions have a number of things in common. They are not directly under the control of the President or Congress. The goal was to make them "non-political" (in the narrow sense of that word as discussed in the previous chapter). These commissions were to be free from partisan politics. Their boards of directors must be bipartisan, and they are appointed for fixed terms so they can't be removed by a change in administration.

Table 17.1
The Independent Regulatory Commissions

Commission	Founded	Number of Members	Length of Term	Function
Interstate Commerce Commission (ICC)	1887	11	7	Sets rates for and regulates railroads, truck lines, buses, shippers, and oil pipelines.
Federal Trade Commission (FTC)	1914	5	7	Administers antitrust laws preventing unfair competition, pricefixing, and deceptive practices.
Federal Power Commission (FPC)	1920	5	5	Regulates and sets rates for utility companies, natural gas pipelines, and hydro-electric projects.
Federal Communications Commission (FCC)	1934	7	7	Licenses and regulates all radio and TV stations; sets telephone and telegraph rates (if interstate).
Securities and Exchange Commission (SEC)	1934	5	5	Regulates the stock market; prevents false or misleading stock rates.
Civil Aeronautics Board (CAB)	1938	5	6	Allocates domestic air routes and sets fares; grants overseas routes subject to Presidential approval.
Federal Maritime Commission (FMC)	1961	5	5	Regulates shipping in foreign commerce.

The stock market is regulated by the Securities and Exchange Commission.

Regulation of business was to be handled as a technical problem for experts, not a political problem for the President and Congress. But as we have argued, the decision to make something "nonpolitical" is itself a political decision in a broad sense. Decisions of regulatory agencies are political in that the power of the government is involved. Separating them from the central decision-making institutions—the Presidency and Congress—does not change that.

Furthermore, instead of serving the general public interest the regulatory agencies have become separate from the rest of the government. They deal only with the industries they regulate—the FCC with the broadcast industry, the ICC with the railroads and truckers, the CAB with the airlines. Over time these industries become the "constituency" of the agency; that is, the agency works closely with the industry it is regulating and gives first consideration to the welfare of that industry. Thus in a way the regulator and the regulated become one and the same.

Regulatory agencies come to depend for information on the businesses they regulate. During a congressional investigation of the regulation of the oil industry, the Department of the Interior admitted it depended on that industry for such important information as production figures. It could neither prove nor disprove that the oil companies were holding back production.

In such cases policy making becomes a totally disaggregated process; policy for each industry is made by a separate agency responsible only for that industry. Congress and the Presidency—the branches of the government that have broad constituencies—are left out. The principal actors are the regulatory agency and the regulated industry working closely together. Often the regulatory agency *responsible for* a particular industry ends up being *responsive to* that industry. The result is usually regulatory policy that favors the industry being regulated. The Civil Aeronautics Board regulates air fares and assigns air routes. The result, according to one economist, is that air fares are 35 percent higher than they would be if the CAB did not set fares and routes to protect the least efficient carriers.

But it is important to note how this happens. When we discussed the potential bases of group conflict in America, we distinguished between divisions over matters of principle and situations involving narrow interests that did not seem to conflict with one another. If, as a general principle, the issue of the public good vs. that of the business community were raised, there is little doubt that the weight of influence would fall on the side of the public good. Who can oppose that? But by disaggregating policy making to specific agencies, each dealing with a specific kind of business, the more general principle is never raised. Rather, policy is made for a particular industry. There are in effect no opponents—no one speaking for a larger public. In such circumstances the important groups are not the broad organizations of the entire business community—the National Association of Manufacturers or the U.S. Chamber of Commerce, for example—but rather the industries and firms being regulated.

This pattern of regulation is found throughout the federal government. We have talked of the independent regulatory commissions, whose legal status, formally independent of Congress and the White House, reflects these tendencies. But the same pattern may be found in the Department of the Interior in relation to regulation of the petroleum industry, in the Treasury Department in relation to regulation of banking, in the Department of Agriculture in relation to farm interests, in the Department of Commerce in relation to the great variety of businesses it deals with. Indeed the same pattern is found in the Department of Labor in relation to regulation of labor unions. In each case the distinction between public and private, between the government agency and the interest being regulated, becomes hopelessly blurred. Industry councils of various sorts, which include representatives of the firms being regulated, take a large part in the writing of the regulations. Such cooperation is of course useful for a federal agency. But it can lead to control of the regulatory agency by the industry that is supposed to be regulated.

Such control over a regulatory agency is made easier by the movement of personnel back and forth between the industry and the agency. When the Federal Energy Office was set up, it was found that 102 of the officials were former oil-industry people, most of them at high levels.

These agencies go through an interesting "life cycle," one that illustrates the process of policy making in many areas of American life.[1]

The Birth of a New Agency   It all usually starts with demand for correction of some abuse. Congress and the public see a need for regulation. Such was the case when the ICC was created (to cope with major abuses by the railroads); it was the case when the SEC was founded (to cope with stock-market abuses). At this stage of a regulatory agency's life, there are many actors involved: the public and the press; specific groups of abused citizens (the farmers who did not like the railroads' rate policy, for instance); the political parties that make reform part of their platform; and the President and Congress, who create the legislation. The business about to be regulated is also, of course, involved. And it may call the intended regulation socialistic. In short, the main elements are many actors, a major public issue, and strong feelings.

At this point the new agency is born. Congress gives it its blessing but little guidance. As we have seen, the statement of purpose is firm but vague.

The Young Agency   At first the new agency is active. The businesses to be regulated resist. The power of the agency is not completely clear, since it was not spelled out by Congress. And often it

[1] The notion of a life cycle is developed by Marver Bernstein, *Regulating Business by Independent Commissions* (Princeton, N.J.: Princeton University Press, 1965).

must wait years for the courts to decide on those powers. The businesses have good technical information and legal advice. Often they are much better staffed than the agencies trying to regulate them.

At this point something else of importance happens. The other actors who were there at the birth of the agency—the President, Congress, the public—fade into the background. For them the battle has been won. A law has been passed to correct the abuse, to regulate the industry. An agency has been set up. And indeed from a *symbolic* point of view all the right things have been done. In fact, however, things may be working out differently. But by now the attention of Congress and the public is elsewhere. The actors have become the agency and the business to be regulated.

The Mature Agency In the end the reforming energy of the agency fades. New personnel come in. The agency becomes the protector of the industry, working closely with it. The regulation is no longer in the public interest but in the interest of the industry itself. The actors have narrowed to those most directly concerned. At this "mature" stage it is easy to see the two features of government regulatory policy: disaggregation of the policy (a narrowly focused agency dealing with a narrow constituency) and cooperation between regulator and regulated.

One reason a close relationship between the regulator and the regulated can occur is that there are no effective "counterparticipants" representing the interests of other groups. In this sense the recent growth of consumer-protection organizations is of great political interest. Public-interest lobbies, such as Common Cause or the specialized groups associated with Ralph Nader, are potential counterparticipants against the informal partnership between the regulating agency and the regulated industry. These relatively new public-interest lobbies have two resources not available to the general public: expertise and staying power. Drawing on these resources, consumer-protection organizations can help make regulation sensitive to needs other than those of the regulated industry. As such, they are an important new actor in this policy area.

Tax Policy

If one wanted to choose the one area of governmental activity that best represents the government in general, one could do no better than to choose the area of tax policy. Taxes are the key to all other government programs, providing the funds for almost everything else the government does. They touch the lives of all citizens. In terms of impact every American is a potential actor on tax policy.

Purposes of Taxation

The main purpose of taxes is to raise revenue. But taxation can have other goals as well.

To Redistribute Income   Taxes can be used to transfer wealth from one group in the society to another. The major way this is done is through the progressive income tax. The logic of a progressive income tax is that those with higher incomes can afford to pay a larger portion of that income in taxes than those with smaller incomes. Look at a federal income-tax form and you will see that income tax varies from a tiny percent of the income of those in low-income brackets up to 70 percent of the income of those earning over $100,000 a year. If these funds are then used for government programs that benefit poorer people more than the wealthy (welfare payments, public housing, etc.), or even if they are used to pay for programs that benefit all citizens equally, it is clear that there has been a transfer of wealth from wealthier citizens to poorer ones.

This has been the goal of much tax policy, particularly the federal income tax. And the evidence is that tax policy does lead to some redistribution of income. Those in lower brackets get more out of the government than they put in; those in higher brackets get out less than they put in. But, as noted in Chapter 3, the extent to which such transfer of income takes place is much less than a quick reading of basic income-tax rates would lead one to believe. If indeed the poor paid only 2–3 percent of their income in taxes while the rich paid 70 percent, there would be quite a bit of income transfer. In fact, the rich rarely pay rates as high as 70 percent of income. The tax laws are full of loopholes—exemption for income from certain kinds of investments, deductions for certain kinds of expenses, lower rates for certain kinds of income. These loopholes tend to be used by upper-income citizens, for two reasons. First, they tend to apply to the kinds of income received by those with higher incomes: to tax-free municipal bonds or capital gains. Second, the upper-income taxpayer is more likely to use professional help in preparing his tax return. The tax laws are very complicated, and only a professional can take full advantage of the many legal deductions and exemptions the laws allow.

Indeed the relative impact of income taxes on rich and poor clearly illustrates two of the principles of policy making we have set forth: (1) To understand a policy you have to look beyond the law as written to how it is applied, and (2) policy making in the United States tends to include those being regulated as active participants.

The first principle is illustrated by the fact that a citizen's actual tax burden is by no means clear from the basic tax bracket in which he falls. One has to look carefully at his income, its sources, and the tax loopholes he takes advantage of. Thus, despite the very high peak rates for taxes, it is estimated that almost no citizens pay an effective rate higher than 50 percent. In 1969 it was discovered that a number of wealthy Americans took advantage of various loopholes to pay no federal income taxes. A "minimum tax" law was passed that year to see that at least some taxes were paid. But apparently some tax lawyer found loopholes in this loophole-closing bill, be-

In 1974 the administration hoped that its tax rebate would stimulate consumer spending.

cause in 1972 there were 500 individuals with incomes over $100,000 who paid no federal income taxes.

The second principle—that those being regulated participate in the regulation—is illustrated by the self-reporting of taxes. In the United States citizens calculate their own taxes, subject of course to audits by the Internal Revenue Service. What this means is that citizens may differ in the extent to which they take advantage of the tax laws. No one has made careful calculations along these lines, but it is likely that many citizens—particularly those who do not get professional help—miss chances to take deductions, while those who get such help (in most cases those with higher incomes) do take advantage of these loopholes. The federal government has tried to correct this situation by simplifying tax returns and offering to calculate the tax. But it is likely that there are great differences among groups in the extent to which they *participate effectively* in the taxing process, that is, take full advantage of the laws as written.

Note that there is nothing illegal here. We are not talking about cheating on taxes. Rather, we are talking about greater or less ability to take advantage of legal tax arrangements.

There is another reason taxes do not redistribute income as much as the basic tax rates suggest they do. Income taxes are but one of the many forms of tax in the United States. They are the main way funds are raised by the federal government, and they are an increasingly important way for states and some municipalities. But there are many other forms of tax, some of them less progressive and some regressive. Sales taxes are a major way funds are raised for state and local governments. And such taxes tend to be regressive, which means those with lower incomes pay a higher portion of their income in sales taxes than those with higher incomes, for the simple reason that poorer citizens spend more of their income on taxable goods. In addition, much local activity is supported by real-estate taxes. These additional taxes greatly modify the extent to which the total tax system redistributes income from rich to poor.

To Regulate the Economy In addition to the raising of revenue and the redistribution of income, taxes can be used for other purposes. Tax policy is used as a means of regulating the economy. Higher tax rates may be used to curb spending in times of inflation or too rapid economic expansion. Tax rates may be lowered to increase spending and stimulate business in an economic slowdown. The administration used a tax rebate in 1974 for this purpose. Tax policy may be used as an indirect means of controlling certain activities. High taxes on alcoholic beverages and cigarettes reflect a governmental policy (not a very strong one) of limiting their use. Taxes on gasoline can be used for the same purpose. Taxes can be used to stimulate particular parts of the economy—by adjusting tax rates so citizens will invest in those areas.

These uses of the tax power are important to keep in mind, because they affect how tax policy is made. They may bring different actors into the field.

How Is Tax Policy Made?

At first glance tax policy doesn't look like a good area for disaggregated policy making. Taxes affect all citizens; they touch all parts of the economy. Insofar as they redistribute income they can become the subject of major clashes over the principles of free enterprise, over the proper role of the government in relation to the poor.

And indeed there are organized groups whose aim is to push general views of federal taxing policy—in particular, groups who want to limit that policy as much as possible. More important, the mass public is involved in taxes in a way in which it is not involved in the regulation of business. The public cares about taxes. In any election, national or local, tax rates are likely to be an issue. In public-opinion polls citizens are always against tax increases. And government officials—particularly when an election is coming up—are very wary about raising taxes.

Even in this area one finds a tendency to disaggregate policy to a series of narrow decisions. One reason for this is suggested by the complexity of the tax system in the United States. Federal income taxes are the largest single item on the citizen's tax bill, but he pays many other kinds of taxes as well. And these tax burdens are decided in the states, in localities, by special districts, by school districts. This disaggregated decision making has the usual results: Decisions are made for one narrow constituency without considering their impact on other groups. The tax decisions of one school district in a metropolitan area affect all other parts of that area in that they may stimulate population movement in or out of the district, thereby affecting the policies of its neighbors. Indeed, as we have shown, one of the causes of the metropolitan crisis is differences among the school systems within metropolitan areas. Yet each school district makes its own tax decisions. (This system is being challenged in the courts because of the inequalities it produces.)

Even federal income-tax policy is subject to disaggregation into a series of particular decisions for small constituencies. We can see this by looking more closely at how federal tax policy is made. The public is involved in tax policy because of its concern about high taxes and because of government officials' concern with how public attitudes will affect the next election. And the President is concerned as well, particularly when higher taxes are needed to support foreign or domestic programs he favors or when he wants to use tax policy to slow down or speed up the economy. But in both cases the pressure is a rather general one—for higher or lower tax revenue. It doesn't involve a specific division of the tax burden among groups.

Congress' Role in Tax Policy   When it comes to specific tax policy, Congress plays a major role. It supervises tax policy more than most other policies. In effect, though, it is not Congress as a whole that acts on tax matters but two specialized committees: the House Ways and Means Committee and the Senate Finance Committee.

The procedure is not very different from that used in the regulation of business, although the formal structure is quite different. Congress does not assign tax policy to a body formally independent of it, as it does with much business regulation. The independent regulatory commissions are separate agencies; the House Ways and Means Committee and the Senate Finance Committee are parts of Congress. But a similar pattern may be seen. Congress starts with a vague general principle—a progressive income tax. The committee fills in the blanks. And it does so in a way very similar to the regulation of business, in which decisions are made with a single constituency in mind (the business or industry to be regulated) but with little concern for overall public policy.

How Tax Laws Are Written   Numerous studies have been made of the process by which tax laws are written. They agree that tax laws are a series of specific decisions about specific types of income. Various industries, businesses, and other types of economic interests make requests for tax relief: exemptions, lower rates, special treatment for depreciation. In this they are often represented by a congressman or senator with a strong interest in that area, usually because it is heavily represented in his state or district. In these matters most members of Congress tend to think of themselves as defending the interests of their constituents, and since all other members of Congress are doing so, a congressman who does not play this role would be in danger of losing support.

The procedures for making tax law make it easy to respond to such requests. For one thing, the law is complicated and contains a great range of alternatives. Thus income can be taxed as regular income or as capital gains, the latter at a much lower level. It would be a major concession by Congress, which would lead to criticism in the press and by the public, if a certain kind of income were completely exempt from taxes or even given an arbitrarily lower rate. But to move one kind of income from regular salary to capital gains appears to be a much more technical decision, to which others are less likely to object. And indeed most special tax advantages come not from changing the basic tax rate but from more subtle adjustments.

Second, the decisions are taken on an "interest-by-interest" basis; that is, they are disaggregated decisions. When the question of tax relief for a particular kind of farmer comes up, Congress tends to deal with it in terms of what is equitable in that case. It often seems easy, and not harmful to others, to offer a particular group relief from a tax burden it considers too high. There are more general principles involved: Who will have to pay higher taxes to compensate for the lower taxes paid by this group? What social programs will be hurt by the reduced revenues that result from the tax

Table 17.2
Capital Gains
Benefit the Rich

Adjusted Gross Income	Average Amount Saved Through Capital Gains Tax Exemption
Under $3,000	$ 1.66
$5,000–7,000	7.44
$10,000–15,000	16.31
$50,000–100,000	2,616.10
Over $100,000	38,126.29

Source: Based on data from *The Washington Monthly,* January 1973.

advantage just offered? Is the advantage given to this group equal to advantages received by others? But since each adjustment for each group is considered separately, these broader questions are not asked.

The system of adjustments for specific interests is also highly technical and does not get much public attention, despite the general concern with high taxes and despite the potentially hot issue of unfair tax advantages. The public can be aroused by high taxes or clear unfairness. But when the tax adjustments for some groups are hidden in the complexities of the tax law, little opposition can be aroused.

One result of all this is that special tax benefits go to wealthier citizens. They are more likely to pressure Congress for relief from taxes and more likely to have the kind of earnings that benefit from special exemptions. As Table 17.2 shows, benefits from capital-gains exemptions are more likely to help those with high incomes.

Nor does Congress as a whole play much of a role. Indeed over the years the House Ways and Means Committee has developed ways of pushing through the House, without hearings and with little debate, "minor" tax bills that often cost the Treasury large sums.

These bills come up as "members' bills" brought up by congressmen to deal with specific cases of alleged tax inequity rather than to change general tax law. Each year the Ways and Means Committee brings a long list of such bills before the House. They are called up under a rule that allows them to pass by unanimous consent without debate.

Only later is it discovered that some of these bills have given to a particular industry or firm a major tax break not available to others, a benefit that costs the U.S. Treasury millions of dollars. There is no better example of what we mean by a disaggregated decision.

The final result is a hodgepodge of separate benefits guided by no overall structure. This can be seen by looking at the oil-depletion allowance, which for many years gave the oil industry a 22 percent deduction against gross earnings because of the depletion of its resources. The logic of this provision was that it would stimulate exploration for new sources of oil needed for national defense, among other things.

Over time similar, though smaller, deductions have been allowed for other industries using natural resources that may disappear. Allowances are made for the gravel and sand industry, though no one has argued that we have to locate more gravel and sand for national defense. Allowances are made for the coal industry. And here the logic is opposite to that of the oil-depletion allowance. It is not that we are running out but that there is too much coal; it could not be sold because of competition from gas and oil. Indeed the depletion allowance for oil (which leads to the production of more oil) creates the problem of the coal industry — by increasing the availability of the competing product!

In short, the various allowances to the mineral industry follow no general plan. Rather, each represents an adjustment to that industry made in the light of its particular appeal.

Tax policy thus works out in ways not unlike the regulation of business. The public is somewhere in the background pushing for lower taxes. But its voice is absent when it comes to the details of the tax law and how it is applied. The President is involved when there is a need for more tax revenue, or when the Treasury Department wants to use the tax power to regulate the economy. But this involvement is rather general as well, and does not determine how the tax burden is divided among groups. Congress is involved, but only in a general sense. It sets an overall framework within which tax law is made. The most effective actors — the ones who in some real sense make the tax law — are the businesses and other interests working closely with particular congressional committees and specific congressmen. A policy that seems hard to disaggregate winds up disaggregated to the nth degree.

The result of these various tax loopholes is that many billions of dollars of income are exempt from federal taxes. In 1972 it was estimated that $166 billion of income was exempt, and the federal government lost $55 billion in tax revenue by not taxing that income. The exemptions for specific interests add up. (See Table 17.3.)

Returning Tax Policy to Public View

In the previous chapter we described the tension between disaggregated and incremental policies and more centralized and comprehensive policies. There are times when tax policies come before a wider audience; when concern for a more general "public interest" is placed against the narrow interests that ordinarily determine policy. In 1974 and 1975 a number of events took tax policy out of congressional committees and brought it to the attention of the public as well as the executive branch.

Three events combined to produce the more general concern with tax matters: (1) The energy crisis brought the oil industry and its 22 percent depletion allowance under public scrutiny; (2) the recession led the Ford administration to use tax policy to try to stimulate the economy; and (3) the revelation during the Watergate hearings of

Table 17.3
One Estimate of Income That
Escapes Federal Taxes

Tax Preference or Privilege	Estimated Income Removed From Tax Base in 1972	Estimate Loss in Tax Revenue
	(BILLIONS OF DOLLARS)	
Tax exemption for transfer payments, including social-security pensions	$ 55.1	$13.1
Special deductions, double exemptions for the aged and blind, and the retirement income credit	42.2	14.2
Special benefits for homeowners, including deductions of mortgage interest	28.7	9.6
Special tax treatment of capital gains on sales of securities, other things	26.0	13.7
Exemption of interest earned on life insurance investments	9.1	2.7
Tax exemption of interest on state and local bonds	1.9	1.2
Tax exemption of up to $100 in annual dividends per person	1.9	0.7
Excess depletion and depreciation allowances	1.1	0.6
Total	$166.0	$55.8

Source: "Individual Income Tax Erosion by Income Classes," a study by Joseph A. Pechman and Benjamin A. Okner, Brookings Institution, published by the Joint Economic Committee of Congress on May 8. Reprinted from *U.S. News and World Report*, May 22, 1972. Copyright © 1972, U.S. News and World Report, Inc.

President Nixon's attempts to avoid taxes led to public concern with tax reform. Under these circumstances the chances for more general tax reform increased. For instance, pressures mounted in 1975 to phase out or abolish the 22 percent oil-depletion allowance, though what the final result would be was uncertain.

The general concern with tax policy that grew out of the events just mentioned tells us something important about disaggregated policy making: Policy making remains successfully disaggregated when few people pay attention to it. When some area of public policy becomes a matter of general public concern, the dominant position of narrow but intensely concerned interests is challenged. We describe this situation more fully in the following section.

Inflation, Recession, Energy: Tuning the Economy

Economic crises create pressure for centralization of economic policy and comprehensive planning. We have just seen how the economic crisis of the 1970s modified the tendency for tax policy to be disaggregated. But the impact of the crisis was more general than that; it affected not only tax policy but overall economic policy.

Since the days of the New Deal, the federal government has taken some responsibility for regulating the ups and downs of the business cycle. If business appears to lag, the government intervenes with its two major weapons: monetary policy and fiscal policy. Monetary policy refers to the supply of money in the economy. By reducing interest rates the Federal Reserve Board increases the supply of money and stimulates business. Fiscal policy refers to the amount of money the government raises through taxes and the amount it spends on domestic and foreign programs. If business lags, the government decreases taxes (giving citizens more money to spend) and increases spending. Each of these actions stimulates the economy.

The combination of these powers makes the federal government a "manager" of the economy. If any aspect of government policy resembles the comprehensive planning model, it is this "fine tuning" of the economy, which takes place largely under the direction of the executive branch. The economic crisis triggered by the energy shortage and the combination of inflation and recession created pressure for even more comprehensive planning. The planning, however, was made more difficult by the fact that inflation and recession came at the same time. The traditional policy for fighting recession—increasing the supply of money by lowering interest rates, cutting taxes, increasing government spending—were exactly the policies that made inflation worse.

Powers of the Executive

The economic crisis illustrates the great power of the White House when it comes to emergencies. On August 15, 1971, President Nixon startled the nation by announcing a large-scale program of price and wage controls coupled with a surcharge on imported goods. Nixon had always been opposed to such controls. But he believed the severe balance-of-payments problems the United States faced at that time (we were buying more goods from abroad than we were selling) required such drastic action.

The President took similar action in the winter of 1973–1974. In the face of an embargo by the Middle Eastern oil-producing nations, the United States suffered a severe energy shortage. Drivers waited in long lines for gasoline; homeowners were afraid their supplies of heating oil would run out. The President created a Federal Energy Office and appointed an "energy czar" to head it. A number of policies were introduced through executive orders: Gas stations were ordered closed on Sundays, the speed limit was reduced to 55 miles per hour, heating-oil deliveries were curtailed. Such regulations had not previously been attempted by the federal government.

Here is another example. About six months after he took office, President Ford, in a move to reduce oil consumption, announced that he would raise the import fees on oil by $3 a barrel. The move would raise the price of oil and, he hoped, cut consumption.

All of these actions were taken by executive order, that is, on the initiative of the President. They did not require that a law be passed by Congress. Where does this executive power come from? In most cases it comes from powers the President has under various congressional laws. The power over oil imports comes from national-security laws. He can control the flow of imports if there is a threat to national security. Nixon imposed wage and price controls under the emergency authority given him by the Economic Stabilization Act of 1970. In addition, Congress passed a bill setting up the Federal Energy Administration, which gave the executive branch wide powers over the economy.

These executive powers reflect the fact that management of our complex economy, especially in times of crisis, requires central control and a good deal of technical expertise. To achieve these a number of White House agencies were created. The Council of Economic Advisers, made up of three top economists, has come to play a major role. And President Ford set up an Economic Advisory Board to "oversee the formulation, coordination, and implementation of all economic policy." Members of the Board include the Secretary of the Treasury, the special assistant to the President for economic matters, the chairman of the Council of Economic Advisers, the director of the Office of Management and Budget, and the Secretaries of State, Agriculture, and Labor.

Is the White House All-Powerful?

Our discussion so far seems to suggest that the White House dominates economic policy making, issuing broad executive orders with no external check. How does such centralized power square with separation of powers or with the tendency for policy making

Chairman Arthur Burns of the Federal Reserve Board testifies before the House Banking and Currency Committee.

to be disaggregated into a number of smaller decisions on specific issues? The answer is as follows: Though an economic emergency like the "stagflation" (stagnation plus inflation) that greeted President Ford when he came to office calls for more centralized control over the economy, the forces of decentralization still limit the power of the President.

The Executive Branch   The executive branch is not always unified. The economic crisis revealed many disagreements among President Ford's advisers over what policy to pursue. Secretary of the Treasury Simon and Chairman of the Council of Economic Advisers Greenspan wanted a sharp cut in government spending; Office of Management and Budget Head Ash was opposed, as were the heads of departments whose programs would be cut. Policy may appear to be centralized in the executive branch, but within that branch there are many conflicts.

In addition, the President has far from complete control over the executive agencies that make economic policy. In particular, his control over the Federal Reserve Board is limited by the fact that the governors of the Board serve fourteen-year terms and are not under the President's direct control. Congress wanted the Board to be independent of the President. Though the Board works closely with the President's economic advisers, it often takes positions opposed to Presidential policy.

Congress   The constitutional powers of Congress over the economy are great. Fiscal policy—adjusting federal spending and taxes—is one of the main ways of regulating the economy. And Congress has control over both appropriations and taxes. The President can recommend new taxes or an increase or decrease in the federal budget. But Congress has to approve. And much of the struggle over tax and spending policy under President Ford was between Ford's plans and plans proposed by Congress.

The "Affected Interests"   Much policy making has been dominated, as we have shown, by a coalition between the "affected interest" and the government agency dealing with that interest. This is the standard pattern in government regulation of business. During a crisis the attention of the press, the public, and Congress is focused on the regulatory process, and "cosy" arrangements between the regulator and the business being regulated are more difficult. Yet even in this area there were complaints that the Federal Energy Administration was too careful of the interests of the businesses being regulated. One critic claimed:

> The FEA is becoming an advocate for energy producers within the bureaucreacy. It has gone to bat for the electric utilities and won at least a temporary relaxation in air quality standards. It has worked with the Atomic Energy Commission to shorten the licensing time for

atomic plants. It has helped independent oil companies find steel tubing. It has helped sponsors of refineries and electric plants negotiate the environmental thickets that hold them back. It has shown utilities how to operate more efficiently and pass fuel costs on to consumers.[2]

And as we saw, the FEA was found to be heavily staffed by former oil company officials.

Summary   Economic and energy policy is not made by a group of economists in the White House who make comprehensive plans without any interference from the other actors in the policy process. There is more centralized and comprehensive planning in these fields than in most others. But the White House is still limited by political pressures from Congress, from business interests, and from within the executive branch itself.

Medical Care

The Medicare Program

In the early summer of 1965, President Johnson signed into law the medicare program—a program of government support for the medical expenses of citizens over 65. The program represented a major step in a long battle over the role of the government in relation to medical expenses. The issue had been on the agenda for decades. Around the time of World War I, bills to set up state health-insurance programs had been introduced in various state legislatures. In the early 1930s, the New Deal administration had considered adding health insurance to its social-security legislation. In 1948, Harry Truman had made government-supported health insurance a major part of his campaign program.

In each case the proposals came to nothing. A strong campaign was mounted by the American Medical Association, whose opposition to "socialized medicine"—as it labeled any program of government health insurance—had become a dominant feature of the public debate on the issue. The early state programs failed in the state legislatures; the New Deal program was never even submitted for fear that the addition of a controversial measure like health insurance would hurt the chances of the rest of the social-security program. And Truman's program died in committee in both houses of Congress. It never even came to a floor vote in 1949.

Policy on medical care shows how the absence of government action is nevertheless a policy. Medical costs for the American population had been rising rapidly with the improvement of medicine and the increase in specialization. Paradoxically, the success of medical care was itself one of the sources of higher medical costs: People live longer, and medical expenses are particularly high for the aged

² Eliot Marshall, "Enough Energy by 1985?" *New Republic,* September 28, 1974, 17.

Table 17.4
Health Care and People
Over 65

With One-Tenth of the Population, the Aged Account for One-Quarter of Medical Spending		
	Share of Population	Share of Health Spending
65 and over	9.9%	27.4%
Ages 19–64	54.4%	56.5%
Under 19	35.7%	16.1%

For Practically Every Type of Care, Bills Are Highest for the Aged

	Health Spending per Person in 1971		
	65 and Over	Ages 19–64	Under 19
Hospital care	$410	$158	$ 41
Nursing home	151	2	—
Physicians' services	144	69	45
Drugs	87	37	20
Dentists' services	19	27	16
Other health services	50	30	18
Total	$861	$323	$140

Source: U.S. Department of Health, Education and Welfare. Reprinted from *U.S. News and World Report,* January 22, 1973. Copyright © 1973, U.S. News and World Report, Inc.

(See Table 17.4.) By the 1940s the United States had become the only industrialized nation of the world with no program of government health insurance, and many nations, such as Germany, had had such programs since the nineteenth century.

The program passed in 1965 was hailed as a great breakthrough for government health insurance. But it did not bring the United States into line with the other nations. The medicare program was limited to medical expenses for the aged. In several major ways the program is an example of incremental policy making. Although more comprehensive medical-care plans had been prepared, the program that was able to pass Congress was one that involved incremental modifications of existing programs. For one thing, government assistance to the aged was a well-established program. This made a medical-care program for the aged more likely to pass. Furthermore, it was set up as an insurance program, in which benefits become an "earned right" based on previous payments into the social-security program. This too was in line with past practices. In this way medicare became an extension of the social-security laws. It was a major step, but it was by no means a comprehensive program for medical care.

But one thing must be noted about incremental changes. Over time a number of small steps can add up to a comprehensive change. The supporters of federal medical assistance would have preferred a broader program. They supported the narrower one because its passage was possible by 1965 and because they felt it was a basis on which further small steps could be taken toward a comprehensive

Mrs. Minna Van Ness, 102, and her daughter receive their medicare cards.

program. Each incremental step becomes a take-off point for the next. And indeed the AMA shared this perspective, though its evaluation of the situation was much more negative. For the AMA the medical-care program for the aged was a cause of concern because it was the "foot in the door" for comprehensive medical care.

The Actors in Medical-Care Legislation

Who were the major actors in this long history of medical-care legislation? In terms of impact the issue of medical costs touches everybody. Of course such expenses are a greater burden for poorer families. However, it was not just the very poor for whom medical care was a burden, for they could often get treatment in free clinics. The burden fell just as heavily on middle-income families, particularly when major illnesses hit them. And above all, medical costs were a major burden on the aged. Medical needs soar in later years, just when income is declining.

The Public at Large   For a number of years public-opinion polls had found the American people in favor—usually by two to one—of government health-insurance plans, despite the AMA's campaign against them. But this public support can be thought of as only a vague and general pressure on the government. Much more is needed to carry a new social program through Congress.

The Aged: A Noncohesive Group   Interestingly enough, even after the issue began to focus on medical care for the aged there was little direct involvement of the aged as a cohesive group. There were some organizations associated with the aged—senior citizens councils, golden age clubs—but these were small compared with the major lobbying groups such as the AMA. This illustrates a generalization presented earlier—it's hard to get organized pressure from "consumer" groups. Although the aged were major consumers of medical services and would be greatly helped by this legislation, they did not represent a self-conscious and organized group.

Interest Groups   The major public actors were organized interest groups. The proponents included the AFL-CIO, other labor unions, and charitable organizations. The opponents were led by the AMA and included the American Hospital Association, the Life Insurance Association of America, and other more general organizations like the National Association of Manufacturers (NAM) and the U.S. Chamber of Commerce. It was these organizations—because they were *organized*—who could carry on the battle, particularly in Congress.

But notice one major imbalance between the organizations that favored the medical-care program and those that opposed it. Those who favored it were well-organized and powerful groups such as the AFL-CIO. But these were organizations for whom medical care

MEDICAL CARE

was only a side issue. Labor unions, after all, have many other purposes and more direct involvement in such matters as wages and labor conditions. When it comes to such matters as wages, the unions are *producers* of services; when it comes to medical expenses, they are *consumers*. And, since citizens and groups become more active in relation to their interests as producers than as consumers, the unions are likely to be more effective and active on wage policy than on medical policy.

The contrast with the opponents of medical insurance is striking. The opponent groups were led by the organizations representing the major producers of medical treatment — the AMA and the American Hospital Association. And such an organization as the Life Insurance Association of America was also involved as a producer, since medical-insurance programs would compete with private insurance. The involvement of these groups was much more intense and steady. And they were involved in many ways. For one thing, they claimed the special status of producer groups — the status of experts. In addition, the AMA conducted a long campaign to persuade the public that medical insurance was "un-American." In this way the debate rose to a more general level.

The AMA had several advantages. It was well financed. Medical problems were its main concern. And it could mobilize much of its membership. The nature of its membership is important. Doctors are members of a highly respected profession, they are spread throughout the country, and they are likely to be important citizens in their localities — just the kind of constituency to catch the attention of members of Congress.

The Presidency If the battle had been between the interest groups alone, the stalemate might never have been broken. But there were other important actors, in the White House and in Congress. Much of the pressure for medical-care legislation came from the Presidency. Truman made medical insurance one of his major legislative goals. In this he had the support of some influential members of Congress, such as Senator Robert Wagner of New York, who introduced some of the major bills. Truman did not succeed. His program was blocked by a hostile congressional coalition of Republicans and conservative Democrats. But his support kept the prospects of medical insurance alive.

During the Eisenhower years the program had little White House support. But it came alive again under President Kennedy and culminated with the medicare bill under President Johnson. Without the strong push from the White House, no progress would have been made.

Government Specialists In this process a key role was played by the government specialists who shaped the legislation. Officials of the Federal Security Agency — men like Wilbur J. Cohen and I. S. Falk —

had worked on medical-care problems for years. Over the years they had become the leading administrative spokesmen at congressional committee hearings. They played a major role in drafting the legislation and adjusting it in ways that would make it acceptable to Congress.

Congressional Committees As with tax legislation, the crucial arena for medicare legislation was Congress, or rather the relevant congressional committees. The two powerful committees in this case, as in the tax case, were the House Ways and Means Committee and the Senate Finance Committee, with the House committee and its chairman, Wilbur Mills, playing a major role. The annual hearings before this committee were the main public battleground in the war over medical insurance. It was here that the various interest groups testified. It was here that legislation would have to be initiated if it was to be successful in the House of Representatives.

The situation points up a key paradox of Congress' representative role. Congress is the institution most capable — in principle — of representing the views of the public: Its members are elected from all parts of the country; they consider themselves representatives of their constituents; and unlike the independent regulatory commissions, they have broad constituencies. Each congressman represents many interests in his district, and all congressmen together represent a wide range of citizens and groups. Thus Congress should be able to make policy according to the public's wishes.

But the organization of Congress is such that it rarely acts as a body. Rather, the key role is played by particular congressmen on committees. In 1961 President Kennedy, who favored a medical-insurance program, had a Democratic majority in Congress. But this majority was, as was often the case, not enough to push through a legislative program. It included many conservative southern Democrats, who often joined the Republicans in opposition to the administration. It was only when Representative Mills decided to support the medicare plan that it was passed. In his change of mind the public did play a role — though indirectly. The landslide victory of Lyndon Johnson in 1964 brought with it both a larger Democratic majority and an apparent demand from the people for some new legislation. "By changing from opponent to manager [of the medicare bill], Mills assured himself control of the content . . . at a time when it might have been pushed through the Congress despite him."[3]

Conclusions on the Medicare Issue

Of course, as we have seen from other legislative areas, what may really count is not the decision to have legislation but the details of how that legislation is written and applied. And in working out these

[3] Theodore R. Marmor, "The Congress: Medicare Politics and Policy," in Allan P. Sindler, ed., *American Political Institutions and Public Policy* (Boston: Little, Brown, 1969), p. 53.

Government programs create paperwork: The forms at left were needed for a hospital case before medicare; those at right were needed under the medicare program.

details Representative Mills "called on committee members, HEW officials, and interest group representatives to lend their aid in drafting a combination bill."[4] In this way interest groups like the AMA—though they may have lost the overall battle against the legislation—did have some influence in the writing of the bill. For instance, one of the effects of the bill has been a large increase in the income of doctors, primarily because the bill did not define what it meant by "reasonable charges." The result has benefited doctors, since they define that term as they wish.

What can be said about the actors in the medicare issue? For one thing, it shows that no one is all-powerful. The AMA did not have its way; it would have preferred no legislation. The President—even when he had a majority of the same party in Congress, as Truman and Kennedy did—could not push through the legislation he wanted. The public, though it favored some program according to the polls, was unable to make Congress act.

If any institution appeared all-powerful, it was perhaps the House Ways and Means Committee and its chairman. But even he was movable when the forces changed. And he would not probably have held the position against a medical program for as long as he did if he had not had the support of the AMA.

Yet the political efficacy of an organization like the AMA cannot be denied, especially when it has powerful allies at strategic points in Congress. Such a combination can be a powerful force, especially when it is dedicated to holding the line against innovation. It is true that a bill was ultimately passed despite the objections of the AMA. But it held the line for a long time. Germany had a health-insurance program in 1883!

Furthermore, by holding the line it also played a major role in setting the agenda of the debate on medical care. The bill that was passed was still quite limited, at least compared to other, more comprehensive plans that had been proposed. And this limitation was largely due to the belief—probably correct—among the proponents of medical insurance that nothing more extensive could be passed. In this sense the anti-medical insurance forces remained strong even when they seemed to have been defeated.

Medicare represented an incremental change in the government's involvement in health insurance. And as such it becomes the basis for the next step. The next step is likely to be a more comprehensive national health-insurance program. A number of competing plans are currently under consideration. The AMA no longer opposes all such programs. Rather, the debate is on what kind of program—how comprehensive? paid for in what way? run by whom? These are not minor questions. As we have stressed, the details of a policy may be more important than its overall goals. But as one observer has put it, the issue is no longer "whether" but "what kind of" a program.

[4] Ibid., p. 52.

Desegregation of the Public Schools

The process of policy making on school desegregation differs from medical-care policy in one important way: The major consumers of medical services, who would benefit from new laws—the aged and their organizations—were not major actors in pushing for legislative action. The major "consumers" of education, who would benefit from desegregated schools—blacks and organizations representing them—were major actors. In particular, the National Association for the Advancement of Colored People (NAACP) was important in pushing for change. This difference helps us understand the conditions under which groups can take a major role in the policy process. The aged do not form a cohesive and self-aware group. They are probably more divided by other social characteristics—religion, place of residence, race, income level—than they are united by their age. Blacks, on the other hand, though they are by no means a fully cohesive and organized group, have a greater basis for cohesion and organization. They have a common history, tend to live in racial neighborhoods, and throughout American history have suffered a special deprived status.

The Role of the Supreme Court

Segregation in public schools was formally adopted as policy by about twenty states in the 1890s. State law explicitly declared that white and nonwhite pupils had to attend separate schools. Such laws—as well as many other laws requiring segregation in the use of public facilities—were coupled with legislation limiting black participation in politics. And these undercut any improvement in the status of blacks since the Civil War.

The laws requiring segregation in the schools were challenged in the Supreme Court as violating the equal-protection clause of the Fourteenth Amendment. But in 1896 in a famous 7–1 decision— *Plessy* v. *Ferguson*—the Supreme Court held that the Constitution did not bar separate schools as long as they were equal. The "separate but equal" doctrine was to be the law of the land for decades.

But as we have seen, the mere statement of a policy—even by a government body as respected and powerful as the Supreme Court— does not automatically put it into effect. To see what the policy means, one has to observe how it works in practice. In connection with the separate-but-equal doctrine, the Court's views went into effect only in part. The schools were indeed separate, but they were rarely equal. The "separate" doctrine was enforced, since that was the practice already and local officials were in favor of keeping the schools segregated. The "equal" doctrine was not enforced, because equal schools were costly, local officials were not really interested (since blacks had no political power, barred as they were from voting), and the Court had no way to check on the equality of facilities.

The Role of the NAACP The first challenge to school segregation was led by the NAACP, an organization founded by a small group of educated blacks headed by W. E. B. DuBois shortly after the turn of the century. After unsuccessful attempts to work through the legislative branch, the NAACP turned its attention to the courts. In Congress action could be stopped by a determined bloc representing the one-party, all-white politics of the southern states. The court was above such direct political pressures. Also, the wording of the Fourteenth Amendment, declaring that no state could "deny to any person within its jurisdiction the equal protection of the laws," seemed inconsistent with the practices of the southern states—though the Court had not yet ruled that way.

The NAACP's appeals through the courts followed the by now familiar incremental approach: trying to make step-by-step changes in the rules applying to segregation. At first they challenged the equality of the schools. In 1938 the Supreme Court ruled that the State of Missouri was not giving black students equal education by providing scholarships to an out-of-state law school, there being only an all-white law school in Missouri.[5] Equal education required that the state open a law school for blacks within Missouri. Note that the Court allowed for a separate school but was beginning to enforce equality.

In 1950 the Court went further, saying separate law schools—one for each of the races—were inadequate. Their very separateness made them unequal.[6] In 1954 the Supreme Court handed down its landmark Brown decision that segregation in the public schools led to unequal treatment of pupils and was unconstitutional.

The movement by the Court to the school-desegregation decision was an incremental one. It dealt first with the issue of equality, only later with separation. It ruled first on graduate schools—not as hot an issue as the public schools—and only later on the public schools. And the school-desegregation decision itself, with its call for "all deliberate speed" and allowances for delays in carrying out specific plans, certainly fits the incremental mold.[7]

The role played by the NAACP through the Supreme Court shows how a group can bypass the legislative branch of the government. The Court acted where Congress was unable or unwilling to act. But a group that wants to do this needs many resources. For one thing, it has to be able to make a constitutional case. Without the Fourteenth Amendment the NAACP would not have gotten far with this tactic. Another thing it needs is a lot of time and effort. The constitutional road is a long one; cases have to be carefully prepared and argued up from the lower courts. The NAACP's success took many decades of steady work. Finally, it needs a great deal of skill; and the NAACP had this in a competent group of lawyers led by Thurgood Marshall,

[5] Missouri ex rel. *Gaines* v. *Canada* 305 U.S. 337 (1938).
[6] *Sweatt* v. *Painter* 339 U.S. 629 (1950).
[7] *Brown* v. *Board of Education* 347 U.S. 483 (1959).

who later became the first nonwhite justice on the Supreme Court.

Our analysis of what happens to general statements of law—by Congress or by the courts—should warn the reader that the battle for equal schooling did not end with a statement by the Supreme Court that segregated schools are unconstitutional. Administration of the program was turned over to local school districts and to the states—all under the supervision of the federal courts. But, as with the regulation of business, this meant in effect that those who carried out the law were those who were to be regulated. After all, the local school districts and the states had been carrying out the segregation laws. These local districts dragged their feet, helped by the state legislatures in the South, which found various ways to block court-ordered desegregation. The result was that a decade after the Court decision less than 2 percent of black children in the South went to integrated schools.

The slowness is in part a result of the separation of powers in America. Although the Supreme Court can interpret the Constitution and such interpretations are the "supreme law of the land," the power for enforcing that law lies in the states and localities. They can effectively block federal action, especially if that action is a decision of the Supreme Court not backed up by the other branches of the federal government.

President Eisenhower had used the U.S. Army to keep Governor Orville Faubus of Arkansas from blocking the court-ordered integration of Little Rock High School, and in that way had thrown the executive power behind the Supreme Court. But Eisenhower never spoke out directly on the issue of segregation and never pressed for legislation to follow up the Supreme Court's ruling. And Congress was inactive as well.

DESEGREGATION OF THE
PUBLIC SCHOOLS

511

Chicago	85%
Baltimore	76%
Washington, D.C.	89%
Los Angeles	78%
Mobile, Alabama	85%
Nationwide	61%

Source: U.S. Department of Health, Education and Welfare.

Progress toward ending legal segregation had to wait until other parts of the federal government could take action. Kennedy put his administration behind a bill enforcing school desegregation, and so did Johnson—with more force and success. The Civil Rights Act, sponsored by the Johnson administration, was passed in 1964. This Act put the power of the executive branch behind integration. The attorney general was given the power to initiate desegregation suits if asked to do so by local residents; the Office of Education had the power to survey the extent of segregation in a district. The federal government could thus become a powerful offset to local authorities.

De Facto Desegregation—A Major Issue

With federal support more progress was made toward ending de jure segregation in the South. But this of course did not end school segregation. What was becoming clear in the 1960s was that school segregation was only partly due to state law. At the end of the 1960s, there was at least as much segregation in the North as in the South (perhaps more), because in the North segregated schools were a result of the segregated residential patterns that had evolved in northern cities over the decades. (See Table 17.5.)

De facto segregation may turn out to be harder to handle than de jure segregation. For one thing, it is deeply rooted in the social structure and geographic layout of American cities. School integration requires either a change in residential patterns—a long-term and difficult process—or large-scale busing of children. On the busing issue large groups of people, both black and white, tend to get aroused.

Unlike most of the issues we have been discussing, school desegregation has not been turned into a disaggregated issue. In America, as pointed out earlier, many policies are disaggregated; a policy is made to benefit a specific constituency—the railroads, say, or a particular type of farmer—without at the same time considering its effect on other groups in society. Such policy-making produces little opposition because the benefits given one group are not seen by others as costly to them.

Matters of school desegregation, particularly those that involve busing, often involve direct conflict between those favoring integrated schools and parents who see busing as a direct cost to them. A policy seen as beneficial to blacks is seen as costly to some whites.

Under such circumstances the number of relevant political actors increases. Disaggregated issues tend to be decided quietly; issues that involve clashes among constituencies are noisier. There are a number of actors. The press plays a major role, since open conflict becomes news.

The courts are active, sometimes closely supervising the desegregation of the schools through busing. Local and state governments are active, since both levels have a role in education. The federal government is involved. Congress has tried to limit the use of federal educational funds for busing, a position that may put it at odds with the Supreme Court. And within the local community many parents and community leaders are active on each side.

In short, it is a policy with many, many actors. Out of such a conflict may come social change, but it is unlikely to come smoothly.

Policy Making in Foreign Affairs: Vietnam

If there was a crisis in American politics in the 1960s and early 1970s, the two issues on which it centered were race and Vietnam. Race, as we have shown, is a "naturally" divisive issue, particularly if one race sees benefits given to the other as directly harmful to it. Usually a war has just the opposite effect. In most cases wars have led to national unity, as in the two world wars. And even the Korean War, which did not have as much popular support as World War I and World War II, did not lead to the kinds of stresses that grew out of Vietnam.

This is not a book about Vietnam. The histories of U.S. involvement will be written and rewritten, and we can only touch lightly on the complexities of that issue. But the history of policy making on Vietnam can tell us a lot about governmental policy making. Vietnam shows how foreign policy is made in "ordinary" times and how it is made in the unusual situation in which a foreign-policy issue has aroused major public controversy.

Vietnam policy under President Kennedy and during the first years under President Johnson was made the way foreign policy is usually made—with little public or congressional attention. Vietnam policy after 1964 or 1965 was a much more public issue. Yet even then it took quite a while for Congress to get much control over Vietnam policy.

Vietnam Under President Kennedy

Roger Hilsman, a leading student of foreign policy and Kennedy's Assistant Secretary of State for Far Eastern Affairs said, "Any discussion of the making of United States foreign policy must begin with the President."[8] Despite the power over foreign affairs that

[8] Roger Hilsman, *The Politics of Policy Making in Defense and Foreign Affairs* (New York: Harper & Row, 1971), p. 17.

would seem to belong to Congress—based on its power to declare war and to appropriate funds, as well as on the power of the Senate to ratify treaties—foreign affairs has traditionally been the province of the President. He—or rather his administration—oversees day-to-day foreign affairs; only the executive branch has the expertise and information needed for foreign policy making. Nor have the powers of Congress limited the President. President Truman sent American troops to Korea without a congressional declaration of war or even a resolution supporting the move. And the American involvement in Vietnam took place largely through a series of Presidential decisions.

It would be a mistake, though, to consider the President a free agent when it comes to foreign policy. To begin with, policies, as we have seen, have a history. At any moment a President must make decisions in the light of what has gone on in the past. Thus when Kennedy took office in 1961 he inherited commitments made under Eisenhower to support the government of South Vietnam. As early as 1961 there were several hundred American military men in Vietnam working directly with the South Vietnamese government.

A President is limited in another way. He is very dependent on the foreign-policy bureaucracy. They do not make decisions on foreign policy—at least not the major ones—but they can structure the decision for the President by the advice they give him, by the information they control. In "ordinary" foreign policy making, such as Kennedy's policy on Vietnam before it became a public issue under Johnson, the major actors are the Presidency and the agencies that give the Presidency information: the State Department, the CIA, the military.

Thus in 1962, using information from the CIA on the needs of the South Vietnamese government, President Kennedy ordered an increase in American troops in Vietnam from a few hundred men to 12,000 men. The nature of the step is important. It was considered a limited response to a particular issue, not an open-ended commitment to preserve the South Vietnamese government at any cost. At least there is no evidence that the administration foresaw the bombings and the half-million men who would be there in a few years. In this way it was an incremental policy, one that modified an earlier policy.

But Vietnam policy was also guided by an overall strategy based on a desire to keep communism from spreading. According to the "domino theory," the loss of South Vietnam would topple the other Asian nations. Thus Vietnam policy in the 1960s took the form of small incremental steps guided by an overriding concern not to "lose" South Vietnam.

The Role of Congress in Vietnam Policy The role of Congress during this era is fairly easy to summarize: It was minimal. In 1961, 1962, and 1963 Congress had little to do with Vietnam. Its attention was turned to other problems. Its first major involvement came in the summer of 1964, during President Johnson's first year in office. In response to a Presidential request on the heels of an alleged attack by North Vietnamese gunboats on two American destroyers, Congress passed almost unanimously the so-called Tonkin Gulf resolution. It expressed support for the President in Vietnam and allowed him "to take all necessary measures to repel any armed attack against the armed forces of the United States and to prevent further aggression."

The event illustrates the relative roles of the President and Congress in foreign affairs. That the President asked for such a resolution shows that there is some sharing of power over foreign affairs. Otherwise such support would not be needed. Yet the resolution shows how little sharing there was. The President, as well as many members of Congress, felt that the resolution was not necessary; the President already had the powers it gave him. In other words, congressional support was not a necessity but, rather, a way to strengthen the President's position.

Nor did Congress, in this first stage of Vietnam policy, use its power over appropriations to limit Presidential action in Vietnam. The consultative role of the Senate was summed up by Senator Fulbright in describing the Presidential decision to bomb North Vietnam in February 1965:

> The President called the congressional leadership to the White House and had the Director of the CIA, the Secretary of Defense, etc., all demonstrate to us the reasons why the only course of action open to us was to bomb. This was the "consultation" of the President with Congress on that important decision. Mike Mansfield and I were the only ones at that meeting to demur on the bombing . . . the President just did not give a damn.[9]

In short, then, the actors on Vietnam policy until late 1964 or early 1965 were fairly limited. Policy was made in the White House; the major actors were the President and his close foreign-policy advisers in the State Department, the Department of Defense, on the White House staff, and on the National Security Council, and all based their decisions on information from the CIA and the military. It is not clear when the decision to make a long-term commitment in Vietnam was made. But many believe such a decision was made fairly early in 1964, before the Tonkin Gulf incident. If this is the case, it was made largely in the White House. If there was opposition—and there is some evidence that there was—it came from within the administration itself, not from outside.

Vietnam Under President Johnson

The "second stage" of the Vietnam war dates from sometime in 1965. There were two changes from the earlier stage. For one thing, the American involvement grew steadily, culminating in 1968 with

[9] Quoted in Eugene Eidenberg, "The Presidency: Americanizing the War in Vietnam," in Sindler, p. 122.

over a half-million American troops in Vietnam, large-scale bombings, and what is generally agreed to have been domination of the war effort by American troops. At the same time, Vietnam came to public attention. In 1964, when the American people were asked in a survey to name the most important problem facing the nation, 8 percent mentioned Vietnam. By 1966, that figure had risen to 46 percent, and during the late 1960s Vietnam was consistently mentioned as the most important problem facing the nation. And public expression was not limited to public-opinion polls. Rather, some groups showed their concern in a growing number of protest marches and demonstrations.

Protest against the war also moved to the floor of the Senate, where senators like Fulbright, McGovern, Kennedy, and McCarthy came out against Vietnam policy. And in 1968 first McCarthy and then Kennedy entered the Presidential primary races against President Johnson. The result was the President's withdrawal from the campaign.

Public involvement continued after a new administration under President Nixon entered office. Student protest reached a new high after the President sent troops into Cambodia, and congressional critics spoke out.

But in some ways things didn't change much. Vietnam exploded as an issue in America. Congress was aroused, and many members were critical; the public was concerned, and large groups became active in opposition. Yet the major way Vietnam policy was shaped — by the President on the basis of advice of his staff — did not change much. They operated in a new environment where policy was under close scrutiny and constant attack, an environment quite different from that of the early 1960s. The President, however, remained what Hilsman has called the "ultimate decider."

Consider how the roles of the various actors changed in the years after 1965. The Tonkin Gulf resolution represented the high point of Senate backing of the President in Vietnam. From then on the Senate — or, rather, certain senators — became more critical. A series of public hearings in 1968 brought out information showing that the administration had not been candid and had used the Tonkin Gulf incident to take advantage of the Senate. Various resolutions were introduced in the Senate expressing disapproval of Presidential policy, calling for withdrawal of troops, and the like. But in all of these attempts the Senate acted as a critic of Presidential activity. It did not intervene directly in the process of decision making on Vietnam. It could embarrass the administration — and indeed the pressure may have been a major factor in Johnson's decision not to seek reelection. But it did not shape policy. Nor did Congress use its power over appropriations to limit the administration. Vietnam appropriations were criticized but usually passed.

There are many reasons for the relatively weak position of Congress when it comes to foreign policy. For one thing, the constitu-

U.S. troops leaving Vietnam.

Homecoming.

tional balance of power lies in the direction of the President. The President's role as Commander-in-Chief of the armed forces was the main basis for sending troops to Korea and Vietnam. Once such commitments are made, Congress is reluctant to deny appropriations necessary to support the troops.

More important than constitutional power is the administration's greater ability to coordinate policy, to get information on foreign affairs, to present its position to the American people. The President controls the bureaucracy in the State Department, the Defense Department, and the Central Intelligence Agency (CIA), as well as a large White House staff. Congress has few such resources.

Foreign affairs is only one of the many subjects congressmen must deal with, and for all but a few it is not the most important. Senators and representatives, as we pointed out, are first and foremost representatives of their states and districts; they know local needs and problems. But such knowledge is not very helpful in foreign affairs. They are specialists in local needs. Foreign affairs take time and win few local votes.

Pressure from Congress   This is not to argue that the growing congressional opposition to the war did not have an effect on the policy makers in the White House. They were aware of pressure to end U.S. involvement in the war. They also felt great pressure from the public, seen in negative ratings in public-opinion polls as well as in large anti-war demonstrations like those that followed the invasion of Cambodia in 1970. But despite these pressures the major decisions on Vietnam, right up to the "Christmas bombing" decision of the Nixon administration on the eve of the ceasefire agreement, were made by the White House.

Vietnam: Its Impact on Foreign Policy

During the period when the United States was directly involved in the Vietnam war, Congress complained but did little to change the course of U.S. policy. After direct American military involvement ended with the ceasefire at the beginning of 1973, Congress took a more active role. It explicitly limited the use of American military forces in Vietnam and Cambodia. In 1973 it passed, over the President's veto, a law setting a limit of sixty days on the ability of the President to commit U.S. forces abroad without the consent of Congress. (In the Korean and Vietnam wars, the President had committed troops without the consent of Congress.) Furthermore, Congress' previous habit of complaining about but going along with administration requests for aid to Vietnam ended in 1975 when it refused a large request for emergency aid. Shortly thereafter the Saigon regime collapsed.

Congress was able to take a more active foreign-policy role because of the weakness of the Presidency during the Watergate investigations and by the revelations that the administration had

POLICY MAKING IN FOREIGN
AFFAIRS: VIETNAM

South Vietnamese refugees arrive.

misled Congress and the public about the bombing of Cambodia four years earlier. Nor did Congress limit its foreign-policy activity to Southeast Asia. It limited the aid that the President could give Turkey after the Cyprus conflict; it limited U.S. aid to such countries as South Korea and Chile. And it set limits on the trade agreement the Ford administration was negotiating with the Soviet Union.

This all led Secretary of State Kissinger to complain: "The growing tendency for Congress to legislate in detail the day-to-day or week-to-week conduct of our foreign affairs raises grave issues." He wondered if the United States could carry out an effective foreign policy if it could not speak with a unified voice. He argued that Congress should limit its involvement in foreign policy making so as to give the administration the flexibility and consistency it needed for foreign policy.[10]

Many in Congress were sympathetic to this position. Congress is not organized to supervise the day-to-day operation of foreign policy, nor is it effective in making more general policy. The information and skills are more often located in the executive branch. But Congress was so dissatisfied with the administration that it seemed unlikely to return the powers it had taken away.

Controversy

The American political agenda—the issues before the public and the government—does change. From year to year new issues arise and old ones fade. One has only to follow the headlines for a few months to see this happen. But does this mean the American political system is flexible and responsive to new issues?

One Side

Yes, it does. Any important social issue can make it onto the political agenda. Just consider the past couple of decades. All sorts of issues have come before us: equal opportunities for blacks and other minorities, as well as the rights of women. The consumer movement has grown from small beginnings to a major force. Or consider the increasing importance of pollution as an issue. One cannot say issues have been "suppressed."

The mass media help get issues before the public and the government. They are quick to pick up new trends. In fact one can

[10] *New York Times,* January 25, 1975.

argue that they are more likely to exaggerate the importance of minor issues than to suppress major ones.

Can those who claim issues are suppressed name one such issue?

The Other Side

It may be true that all kinds of issues come onto the political scene. But this does not mean the political system is open and flexible. For one thing, when important new issues have come to the attention of the public and the government, they have almost always done so very late in the game, after many years of being ignored. Furthermore, they are usually put on the agenda by groups who have to go outside the ordinary political channels to do so. Sometimes it takes violence or other direct action to catch the attention of political decision makers. And just because an issue gets into the newspapers does not mean the government responds to it.

Besides, not all issues make it to the front of the political stage. Some important ones are never raised. Just ask the people who are fundamentally critical of American society. A right-wing critic might mention the welfare state as something taken for granted. No one suggests ending the many welfare programs in America. A left-wing critic might mention the capitalistic basis of our economy. No one raises the issue of fundamental economic change.

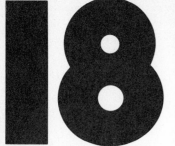

18

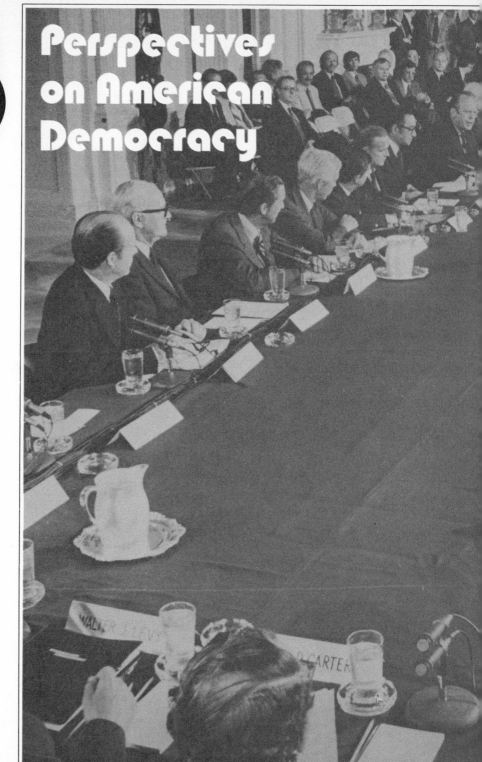

Perspectives on American Democracy

Is America a democracy? This is perhaps the most controversial question to ask about American politics. It certainly is the hardest to answer. How you answer it depends on what you think the word *democracy* stands for. It also depends on how you look at different facts. We do not attempt an answer here, but we will review two contrasting views of democracy in America. The facts stressed in one view lead to the conclusion that "yes, on balance, America is a democracy," while the contrasting view stresses other facts and concludes that "no, America is not really a democracy."

The first view is often summarized under the label *pluralistic democracy,* and it has two major themes:

1. Power is widely shared in American society.
2. As voters and as members of interest groups, the citizens have meaningful control over public policy.

The second perspective has been called the *power elite thesis* and takes the opposite position on these themes:

1. Power is in the hands of a small group of people.
2. The average citizen is ineffective when it comes to the making of public policy.

Pluralist Democracy

In the pluralist view power is fragmented. It is scattered among numerous competing interests. No single interest has total control, and no part of the population is totally excluded. The competition among different interests—management vs. labor, rural vs. urban, southerners vs. northerners, isolationists vs. interventionists—expresses itself as the struggle between organized groups. Each group gets part of what it wants, but no group ever gets all it wants. Compromise prevails. The group struggle takes place in the public arena, with the government acting as umpire so a workable balance is achieved and the entire society benefits. In the pluralist view what begins as conflict between selfish and local interests ends up benefiting society as a whole.

Three conditions in American society support a pluralistic politics. There is, first, social pluralism or the variety of groups in the population. Many different types of people migrated to the United States during its first two centuries, resulting in a society that has correctly been called a "community of communities." Religious, ethnic, and racial differences prevail. The lifestyles of rural America continue side by side with the lifestyles brought about by urbanization. It is the American creed to tolerate different lifestyles, and though this tolerance has sometimes been strained, the famous "melting pot society" has not in fact produced a homogeneous society.

There is, second, the tendency of Americans to form groups to satisfy a wide range of public and private needs. This was seen in Chapter 7, where we saw that not all American citizens belong to organizations. This is important, and we discuss it later. Still, there are a large number of formal and informal associations. The right to form groups is protected in the First Amendment freedom of association, and the habit of forming groups is as old as the Republic, as de Tocqueville pointed out:

> In no country in the world has the principle of association been more successfully used, or applied to a greater multitude of objects, than in America. In the United States, associations are established to promote the public safety, commerce, industry, morality, and religion. There is no end which the human will despairs of attaining through the combined power of individuals united in a society.[1]

Perhaps the number of those involved in group activity has been exaggerated, but there is a complex network of private associations linking the individual citizen and his government.

A third important condition of pluralistic politics is the structure of American government. The formal powers of government were purposely fragmented, primarily through the separation-of-powers system, in which different duties are assigned to the judiciary, executive, and legislature, and through the federal principle, in which different duties are assigned to national, state, and local governments. This fragmentation of power gives citizens many points of access to government. Numerous agencies and officials make decisions that affect different interests, with the result that there is a large number of groups.

What is striking about the pluralist theory is, of course, its view of power. Power is viewed as fragmented or dispersed. Partly this is because different groups are active in different areas of public life. Thus the groups that compete in the arena of public education are not the same as those that compete in the arena of veterans' benefits. If the National Federation of Teachers is powerful when it comes to federal aid to education, it has little influence over health plans for returning servicemen. The opposite is true of the Veterans of Foreign Wars. The fact that different groups compete in different policy areas goes far toward explaining why no single interest ever gets a monopoly of political power. Moreover, any given group varies in its political success. It wins one battle but loses the next. The American Medical Association has certainly won its share of battles in the struggle to prevent establishment of public medicine and national health-insurance programs, but it has not won all the battles.

What emerges is a system not only of fragmented but also of balanced powers, according to the pluralists. The great economic interests of society—business, labor, agriculture, consumers—share

---

[1] Alexis de Tocqueville, *Democracy in America*, trans. Phillips Bradley (New York: Knopf, 1944), I, p. 198.

power. The same can be said of the interests of geographic areas: Some policies benefit the South, others the Midwest or the Northeast. No single region can monopolize public policy.

The portrait of American society painted by the pluralist has the various groups struggling for access and advantage: trade unions trying to improve wages and working conditions while management organizations try to protect corporate profits and investment capital; concerned parents agitating for a bond issue to raise teacher salaries but opposed by the homeowner association that wants to keep property taxes low; doves marching to end the war even as hawks are holding rallies to demand an increase in the military effort. These group conflicts are the basis of American politics.

The conflict is never too disruptive, however, because the various interests presumably agree about the basic rules by which the political game is played. Despite sharp and divisive differences over policy, there is agreement about how differences are to be resolved — elections, due process, peaceful assembly and petitioning, legislative debate, court decisions, majority will, and so forth. This underlying agreement reduces the social harm of group conflict. As the conflict proceeds within the proper channels, the opposing groups reach a compromise.

Resolution of conflicts is greatly aided by the government. In the pluralist view the state has no particular interest in the outcome of group conflict. It serves all interests — and thus all of society — by setting the framework within which differences are peacefully resolved. The government also watches that no single interest monopolizes the power of society. If one interest group — say, business and commerce — appears to be growing too strong, then the government supports the claims of the farmers or those of the workers. This process ensures that no part of society is subordinated to another.

The public plays an active role at two critical points. First, it supplies the mass membership that makes interest groups important actors in the policy process. Labor can stand up to business because 19 million American workers belong to trade unions. The antipollution policies of the last decade are at least partly in response to public pressure by the many environmental-protection groups in society.

In pluralistic democracy the public is in control in another and even more important way. The public chooses its own representatives to umpire the struggle among competing groups. These elected representatives pay close attention to what they believe the public wants in the way of public policy. That is, their powers are not free from public control. Because staying in office depends on satisfying the voting public, representatives choose policies they think are in the public interest.

According to this view America is a pluralistic-representative democracy. Power is widely shared and public policy is largely under the control of citizens as they express their preferences through their group memberships and through the vote. This outlook can be diagramed as shown in Figure 18.1.

Figure 18.1
A Pluralistic-Representative
Democracy

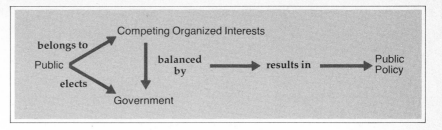

Some Doubts About Pluralist Democracy

The pluralist view has received sharp criticism. The critics say it misrepresents the power structure in the United States and that the elements of pluralism that do operate have unfortunate results.

One big problem with the pluralist view is the assumption that no groups in American society are excluded from the group process. The critics stress the fact that many individuals remain unorganized and some interests are never expressed through the group process. A good example is consumer interests. The unorganized consumer is hurt by the inflationary policies shaped jointly by big labor and big business. Even federal agencies that try to regulate advertisements or ensure fair competition find themselves largely captured by the industrial interests they are supposed to regulate. The individual consumer is a small voice in a world dominated by giant corporations, huge labor unions, and the mass media. The popularity of Ralph Nader suggests how eager the consumer is to have his interests protected. The difficulties Nader faces suggest how much the balance is in favor of organized rather than unorganized interests.

The problem of the unorganized interest is made worse by the fact that the membership in groups is far from universal. Trade unions have big budgets and effective lobbying staffs. It is understandable that in congressional committees or the Department of Labor trade unions are viewed as the voice of the working class. But only one out of four American workers belongs to a union. Migrant workers, farm laborers, domestic help, small-business employees, and many industrial workers, especially in the South and West, are not unionized. Some unions limit membership, as when members of minority races are unable to join apprentice programs; thus the construction trades have been all white for many years. If organized labor is the voice of the working class, very many workers have no voice.

A similar bias can be seen in the professions. The AMA has long been viewed as the official spokesman for the medical profession, but fewer than half of the practicing doctors today belong to the AMA. The doctor who refuses to join or who finds it hard to become a member is typically in public health or in a university-based hospital. He is often unhappy with the conservative views of the AMA leadership, and even more unhappy with the AMA's influence in medical policy making. As long as health policy is dominated by the "organized viewpoint," the liberal view is not represented. Liberal doctors trying to form their own organization, like nonunionized workers, find that the political system puts all the resources in the hands of those who are already organized.

Many more examples could be given, but the point is clear. When social policies are promoted or blocked in the name of organized interests, many citizens are left out. The critics of pluralism also point out that the bias in pluralistic politics favors the more conservative interests of society and the more privileged groups.

The reason for the conservative bias is simple. Established organizations are more powerful than organizations in the process of being born. The former have their budgets, their professional lobbying staff, their contacts in Washington and the state capitals, and a long record of public involvement. The upstarts lack all these things. But it is usually the upstart organizations that are dissatisfied with the status quo and want to bring about reform. They are met, and often beaten back, by the "conservatives" who shaped the status quo and, understandably, want to protect it.

The pressure-group system has also an upper-class bias. If one looks closely at the interests regularly and effectively represented in the group process, it is clear that business and commercial organizations dominate. American politics serves their needs, as might be expected in a society committed to capitalism. Of the organizations that have access to Congress and executive agencies, 60–75 percent represent the business community. In addition to the two giants— the National Association of Manufacturers and the U.S. Chamber of Commerce—there are hundreds of trade associations and independent corporations that maintain lobbies. Business associations have a decided advantage in the group struggle because of the society's commitment to capitalism and because the commercial interests benefit from the high social status of their leaders. Perhaps most important, it is business groups and businessmen who provide most of the cash for political campaigns and party activities.

The class bias of the pressure-group system is evident when we look at organizations that are supposed to represent the lower classes. The most active members of any group are its middle-class members, and its leaders are nearly always better educated than its average members. Thus such well-established minority-group organizations as the NAACP or the Urban League are directed by blacks whose social background and education make them very different from the ghetto resident or southern sharecropper. The same is true even of labor unions. In case after case the executives who shape the political program of the labor movement are not themselves workers but, instead, people with college educations and often law degrees. Because large organizations—even those with a mass base—lack internal democracy, the critics conclude that power rests in the hands of an upper-class leadership.

Besides, say the critics, competition among organized interests has been exaggerated in the pluralist view. It is true that there is a plurality of groups. It is *not* true that they compete with one another. And government doesn't act in a way that produces the best outcome for the entire society. A more accurate view of power sees that interest groups dominate the area of public life that directly concerns them. In this view *capture* is a better word than *competition* to describe group politics.

In an extended criticism of pluralism, it is argued that the all-important distinction between private power and public authority has been nearly eliminated in American society. "This has been accomplished not by public expropriation of private domain—as would be true of the nationalization that Americans fear—but by private expropriation of public authority."[2] In this criticism pluralism is nothing but a façade behind which powerful private interests rule with the blessing of public authority and public funds.

Dissatisfaction with pluralism as a description of power in American society has led to a view stressing a power elite. It is easy to see why. Because only the wealthiest interests in society are effectively organized and because they have used the government for their own benefit, a reasonable view of power holds that a very small group of men are able to direct society according to their preferences.

Elitist Rule

Neither the mass public nor elected representatives nor interest groups have power. American society is ruled by a power elite. These are the men and women who "are in command of the major hierarchies and organizations of modern society. They rule the big corporations. They run the machinery of the state and claim its prerogatives. They direct the military establishment. They occupy the strategic command posts of the social structure, in which are now centered the effective means of the power and wealth and the celebrity which they enjoy."[3] In his influential book *The Power Elite*, C. Wright Mills swept aside previous interpretations of American politics and proposed instead a view that was deeply pessimistic about the fate of democracy.

There are three sources of power in American society today, Mills suggested: the large corporations, the military establishment, and the political leaders. The economy is no longer a series of small productive units competing in the marketplace but "has become dominated by two or three hundred giant corporations, administratively and politically interrelated, which together hold the keys to economic decisions." The political order is no longer a decentralized arrangement with state and local autonomy, but "has become a centralized, executive establishment which has taken up into itself many powers previously scattered, and now enters into each and every cranny of the social structure." The military is no longer a weak

[2] Theodore J. Lowi, *The End of Liberalism* (New York: Norton, 1969), p. 102.
[3] C. Wright Mills, *The Power Elite* (New York: Oxford University Press, 1956), p. 4.

Former White House aide General Alexander Haig takes command of NATO forces.

institution limited by the traditional American distrust of standing armies, but "has become the largest and most expensive feature of government, and, although well versed in smiling public relations, now has all the grim and clumsy efficiency of a sprawling bureaucratic domain."[4]

The powerful, Mills wrote, are people who can get their way even if others oppose them. It is clear to Mills that the powerful are those who head the corporate economy, the political system, and the military. Men and women in charge of these dominant institutions are truly a power elite. They make the life-and-death decisions for the society. They not only do their duty, they define what their duty is. History is made by this elite, as may be seen in such dramatic events as the Cuban missile crisis, the escalation of the war in Vietnam, the wage-price freeze, taking the dollar off the gold standard, and supporting China's entry into the United States.

These decisions are not made by an actively involved public, by the huge number of elected representatives holding office in American politics, or by the leaders of interest groups. They are made by those who control the three dominant institutions. Other people control the middle levels of power; in this category belong most legislators, party bureaucrats, small-scale businessmen, interest-group leaders, city mayors, and even state governors. Below this middle level of power is the public, a powerless mass having political interests but no political information that is manipulated without being consulted and that is acted upon rather than responded to.

The hold of the power elite on society is aided by the interlocking nature of the three dominant institutions. According to Mills, it is

[4] Ibid., p. 7.

naïve to think there are separate economic, military, and political elites, and it is wrong to view the economic, military, and political areas as independent of one another. Power in American society results from the interlocking of the three sectors. Economic elites cooperate with political elites, and military elites are involved in political and corporate decisions. Indeed the different elites know one another; they went to the same private schools, the same well-known universities and law schools, and they now vacation in the same resorts and appear at the same social gatherings. Their children marry each other. More important, the elites are often interchangeable. A retired general is invited to join the board of directors of a major defense industry; the president of Ford Motor leaves the corporate world to become Secretary of Defense; the defeated Presidential candidate joins a major New York law firm that handles the affairs of giant corporations. These are not three separate elites competing with one another, but a single elite that shares responsibility for three different sectors of society.

Private wealth is a big advantage in getting into elite circles, though the elite is not limited to the wealthy. Elite status can be obtained by people from various social backgrounds. But this does not mean entry into the top positions is entirely open. On the contrary, it is impossible or very difficult unless you share the general view of the dominant elite. The elite do not of course agree on many matters of specific policy, but they agree that private property is preferable to public ownership, that military force should be used to protect American interests abroad, that the public treasury must be used to support a faltering economy, and that the mass public requires and expects strong, wise leadership.

This observation is particularly important to the power-elite thesis. Even though America has the trappings of a democracy, effective democratic control is missing because citizens have become part of a mass either unable or unwilling to deal with the complexities of public policy.

In the first place, the mass public doesn't want to be bothered. The average citizen cares more for his family, his job, and how he spends his time than for the complicated problems of society. Perhaps because he is largely indifferent to public issues, the average citizen is also ill informed about broad questions as well as specific issues.

Thus the elite thesis does not find in the public a source of effective democratic control. It also dismisses most of the elected representatives, and even organized interest groups. It finds, instead, that power is concentrated in the hands of an elite that controls corporations, the military establishment, and the executive center of government. Competition may take place at the middle levels of power, but the higher levels are in general agreement about the direction American society should take. This viewpoint might be diagramed as shown in Figure 18.2.

Vice-President Rockefeller meets with Egyptian representatives.

529

Figure 18.2
The Power Elite

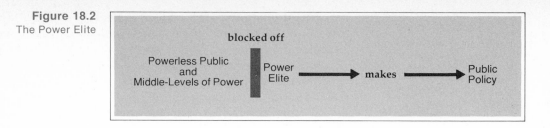

Some Doubts About the Power-Elite Thesis

The elite thesis has not escaped criticism. We cannot review all the criticisms, many of which come from the pluralist viewpoint. We concentrate on one important observation.[5]

It may be true that a small group of people make many of the major decisions for society, and it is likely that these are the people directing the large corporations, the military, and the executive branch of government. It is not true that this small group is a *power* elite. In fact, it is powerless against active, popular opposition. A policy that loses widespread support will be pushed aside. And any policy that gets such support will eventually become the law of the land, no matter how much it might hurt the interests of the elite. Examples might be pollution control and consumer protection. Finally, it is not only the corporate, military, and political elites who have veto power; the public does too. There is evidence to suggest that the elites were willing and even eager to move much faster on civil rights during the 1950s and 1960s than the general public. Social harmony and general stability work to the advantage of the elites, and integrating middle-class neighborhoods (where they do not live), providing more blue-collar jobs (which they do not compete for), or improving ghetto schools (which their children do not attend) are not social policies that challenge elite control or privileges. But the elite did not have the power to move the American public faster than it was willing to move. The elite, in short, is not a *power* elite.

Critics hold that the elite theorists overlook the importance of what might be called "constitutional opposition." Effective opposition to current leadership can be hampered but not ignored. This doesn't usually happen. For the most part the elite do govern more or less as they see fit. But the threat of opposition is never absent. Especially potent is the opposition that can express itself through the vote. And consumer revolts, wildcat strikes, draft resistance, mass rallies, and similar demonstrations can supplement the voting process.

Of course the elite in the United States has used tactics of questionable legality to suppress political opposition outside acceptable channels. And the elite is not afraid to manipulate political symbols,

---

[5] The point made below is developed more fully in Robert Paul Wolfe, *The Poverty of Liberalism* (Boston: Beacon, 1968), chap. 3.

keep secret what should be public information, and attempt to control or intimidate the mass media when threatened by an opposition movement; hence the practice during the 1960s of calling anti-war spokesmen unpatriotic and suppressing negative reports from Vietnam while exaggerating the optimistic ones. Such tactics, however, are not the same as disbanding Congress, refusing to hold elections, banning newspapers, forcefully retaining office despite an electoral defeat, or calling out troops to intimidate voters. These are common practices in nations where the elite is in fact a *power* elite.

What remains is the idea that for the most part elites do rule. What is denied is that they rule despite widespread popular opposition to their decisions. If enough citizens are angry or dissatisfied with current policies, sooner or later this opposition will lead to action, and the ruling group will either change its tune or lose its position. That this seldom happens only proves that the elite manages to mix propaganda, persuasion, manipulation, and acceptable policies in a way that minimizes opposition. The American public is ruled largely by default.

A Glimpse of the Future

These contrasting views — pluralism and elitism — take different facts and give them very different political interpretations. The contrasts are important because they help us understand the ways in which power might be organized and exercised in the society. But there is a common theme in both the pluralist and elitist views. This theme gives us a glimpse of the future.

An Expanding Government　The point of agreement between elitists and pluralists is straightforward. The responsibilities and powers of government are expanding. It is true, of course, that this observation could have been made at practically any time in the last 200 years of American history. But the observation has taken on special meaning in the past few decades. There is an expanding *rate* of growth. Less and less is it the case that the government is one of many institutions in society, sharing power with the business sector, the religious sector, the education sector. More and more it is the case that government is *the* dominant institution in America.

What accounts for the continually expanding powers of government? What does it mean that government is today the central force in our society? Throughout the text partial answers to these questions have been given. In these final pages we conclude with a few things to watch for in the future.

The Demand for Equality
Americans are proud that the nation was founded on the principles of equality. But Americans have taken care to insist that equality refers not to condition but to opportunity and treatment.

Every citizen does not deserve the same rewards. Every citizen should have a fair shot at the unequal rewards.

If this is the principle, we know that the practice has sometimes been flawed. The list is long of groups denied equal treatment and equal opportunity: Irish, Italian, Eastern European immigrants; American Indians and Spanish-speaking Americans; blacks and women; the poor and the physically disabled.

Where do disadvantaged groups press their claims when they are treated unfairly? Increasingly in recent years the claims have been pressed on government. Not the church, not private business, not charity, but the government is looked upon as the effective agency for bringing about equal opportunities. Government has responded with programs and policies and laws. Government grows accordingly. Thus the more claims for equality pressed upon government, the larger a government budget and bureaucracy needed to satisfy these claims.

American society is passing through a period of considerable concern about equality. We have had other such periods: The Jacksonian era was one; so was the progressive era at the turn of the century. That the present is such a period increases the pressures on government. It also increases the potential for political disagreements and disputes.

Equality and Conflict Enlarging the scope of government enlarges the scope of political conflict. It is not that Americans disagree with the principle of equal opportunity. But in two ways they do disagree about how far the principle should be extended.

First, there are citizens bothered by the sheer growth of government. These citizens feel that government, however well-intentioned, is an awkward and costly instrument of social reform. Government tries to help disadvantaged groups but perhaps does as much damage as it does good. For instance, a government medical program seems like a good idea, especially if it ensures decent health care for groups too poor to pay the rising costs of hospitals and doctors. But then there is a new and costly government bureaucracy to contend with. And it is possible that the quality of medical service will decline if doctors and hospital administrators feel cramped by government regulations and paperwork.

The second source of disagreement with government action in the field of equality sees a tension between two principles: equality and freedom. Protecting the equality of one group can easily hamper the freedom of another. Busing children to schools might increase equality of educational opportunity; it might also decrease the freedom of parents to choose the kind of school they want for their children. Programs designed to provide equal rights for women are viewed by some persons as destroying the traditional freedom of institutions to run their own affairs, such as when a business firm is told that it should hire more women.

Poor People's march on Washington.

As government takes on more and more responsibilities for equality of opportunity and treatment, it also becomes the arena within which battles are fought over the principles and programs of equality. Some of the battles will be over the substance of the programs; others will be over the merits of greater government power.

Here we see a pattern that will repeat itself in many other areas of American social and political life in the coming decades. Problems are identified: inequality of opportunity, industrial pollution, unemployment, fragile international monetary system, slippage in security arrangements. The government is looked upon as the source of programs and policies to deal with the problems. The government grows. It grows in the number of people it employs, in the share of the national income it needs, and in the volume of regulations and laws it passes. Because government becomes the central agency dealing with America's problems, it becomes the arena within which legitimate differences of viewpoint about those problems become expressed. Thus there is an increase in political conflict.

Collective Goods

In the earliest pages of this text we learned that certain social benefits are not likely to be produced if left to the voluntary action of individuals or to the working of the free marketplace. Such social benefits are called collective goods. The example used earlier was the clean air produced if cars are equipped with antipollution devices. Clean air is a social benefit. Moreover, it is a benefit from which it is nearly impossible to exclude any particular person. Every person gets to breathe the clean air, even the person who does not install the antipollution device. In fact, the rational person would use his money elsewhere, not install the device, and still have the benefit of clean air produced by others purchasing the antipollution device.

A GLIMPSE OF THE FUTURE

If everyone acted rationally, however, no one would install the device. There would be no social benefit to enjoy. A collective good, then, is one from which you cannot exclude people who do not contribute. Because noncontributors cannot be excluded, some system of coercion is necessary to make sure that everyone does contribute.

The system of coercion is of course the government. Government provides collective goods. It does so through regulations and taxes. It does not depend on the voluntary compliance or contribution of individual citizens.

We first introduced the idea of collective goods in order to answer one question: Why government? We reintroduce the idea in order to answer another question: Why does government grow? The more benefits in society that become defined as collective goods, the greater become the powers and responsibilities of government.

As we enter the last part of the twentieth century, there is a marked tendency to define various social goals or benefits as collective goods. National defense, of course, has always been thought of as a collective good. (It is difficult to exclude a citizen from the protection of a military security system; you can hardly let an enemy bomber fly across the country and bomb only those houses of noncontributors.) Added to national defense are a number of things not considered collective goods only a few decades ago. One example is a clean environment, which only in very recent years has been considered a collective good and therefore a government responsibility. Another example is medical research. If cures for infectious diseases are found, every citizen will benefit, because every citizen will be inoculated in order to prevent an infectious disease from getting started. A public highway system is considered a collective good. So are public parks. So is a stable economy.

The tendency to define certain benefits as collective goods cannot but expand the powers of government. It is the justification for government intervention in the economic sector, in social and family life, in research and education. To bring about a collective good such as national defense requires laws, programs, and agencies. Government powers expand, and government grows.

Collective Goods and Conflict It might seem that there would be no conflict over whether government should provide collective goods. Who could oppose national security or clean air and water or a highway system? But there *is* conflict. There is, in the first place, serious conflict over priorities. Should taxpayers' money be spent on building a faster fighter plane, cleaning polluted rivers, or improving the highway system? Mathematicians and economists have demonstrated that there are no rules for determining the socially preferred ordering for a series of collective goods. There is no way of knowing which collective good is better than another. To call things collective goods does not eliminate conflict. It increases it. For now there becomes a struggle over the priorities.

There is a second source of conflict. It turns out that there are reasonable differences of opinion about what actually constitutes a collective good. Some economists believe that too many social benefits are being defined as collective goods, incorrectly so. They argue that the present trend toward collective goods is really the result of a government bureaucracy trying to expand its powers. And this trend is not producing the kind of society Americans want. The free-market system is more likely to produce such a society. For instance, when enough citizens prefer clean air to fast cars (or jobs in the factories that produce those cars), they will use their purchasing power to punish the polluters. The market will respond; cars that pollute will no longer be manufactured. The preferences of society will have been realized.

For government to try to take over the task of the marketplace only messes things up. It creates a bureaucracy that then justifies itself by spending taxpayers' money and regulating the lives of individual citizens.

The persons who stick to this view strongly oppose the trend toward defining various social goals as collective goods. They oppose the growth of government. They oppose an arrangement in which government and not the individual decides how best to spend the money an individual earns by his own labor.

Our glimpse of the future sees the continual growth of government powers and responsibilities, but it also sees greater conflict in society about how these powers are used and even about whether government should be taking on greater responsibilities.

Planning for Scarcity

Yet another trend in American society is contributing to the growth of government. This is the trend toward increased planning—the attempt to anticipate and prepare for the future. Will there be enough doctors in the year 2000? If not, start spending more money on medical education now. Will there be enough wood pulp to satisfy our needs for paper in the year 2000? If not, support research that might discover alternative methods of making paper. Will there be too few open spaces for wildlife in the year 2000? If so, now is the time to stop the developments that destroy wilderness areas.

Whose task is it to anticipate and plan for the future? The simple answer is that it is everyone's task. But this won't work. So we turn the task over to an institution large enough, rich enough, and powerful enough to think about the future and to try to control events now that are thought to affect the future. That institution is the government. Planning means a growth of government powers.

The planning task of government has taken on increased urgency in recent years. This is because of a shift from abundance to scarcity.

The period from the end of the Second World War (1945) until the early 1970s convinced many Americans that ours was a society of abundance. There was an enormous increase in educational opportunities, and literally hundreds of new colleges and universities were started. There was a substantial increase in the purchasing power of many Americans. And there were nice things to buy. American technology mass-produced such important labor-saving devices as automatic washing machines and dishwashers. It also produced entertainment through television and movies. Even work seemed to be easier. Shorter working hours and longer (paid) vacations became the custom. And there was an increase in the number of "high-status" jobs as professional and technical positions became available in government, in education, and in some of the newer industries. The result of all this was a growing and largely satisfied middle class.

Few Americans noticed that this abundance was based upon fragile conditions. The "American way of life" was based in part on cheap labor, some provided in this country by the rural poor and the underpaid blacks; the remainder was provided by cheap labor abroad. The minerals needed by American industry were in part mined by cheap labor in South America and parts of Africa; the fresh fruit enjoyed by Americans was picked by migrant workers in California or local workers in Honduras.

Even less noticed by Americans was the importance of a constant supply of cheap energy, energy that filtered swimming pools and lit theater marquees, that heated university libraries in the winter and air-conditioned them in the summer, that drove motor boats and campers, that brought big-time sports into everyone's living room. The source of this cheap energy was cheap oil.

It is no longer as cheap. Neither is the labor that provided many of the services and products enjoyed by middle-class America in the 1950s and 1960s. It turns out that the world does not have an unending supply of resources and labor available to support the way of life many Americans have become used to.

Thus we enter a period in which abundance has become scarcity, or at least a period in which we can no longer assume a constantly increasing standard of living. For the past generation there was no doubt that their lives would be better than those of their parents. For the present generation, this is very much in doubt.

There is now a concern about how best to hold on to what we have. One result has been to place more emphasis on planning, on individual planning at the family level and on social planning at the governmental level. The energy crisis best illustrates this emphasis, but it is not the only illustration. The sharp increase in the cost of imported oil has led government into long-range planning about future energy needs and energy sources. There is momentum for a growing government.

Planning, Scarcity, and Conflict As the government extends its planning function, it does so in a way that contributes to deep social conflicts. A time of scarcity is a time when those already advantaged battle to hold on to what they have, battle to expand their wealth and security if possible, and battle to pass it along to their children. The less advantaged groups in society shout "foul." In a time of limited growth, fewer jobs, and sacrifices for the future, it does not seem to them fair that those already well off should continue to be so.

Government is in the middle of this conflict. It tries to distribute national wealth and yet plan for the future in the midst of conflicting, competing, and irreconcilable claims. Once again we find conditions that appear to lead to both greater government powers and greater political conflict.

Bibliography

Chapter 1 The American Economy and Political Life

A classic work on capitalism and democracy is Joseph A. Schumpeter's *Capitalism, Socialism, and Democracy,* 3d ed. (New York: Harper & Row, 1950). For a less favorable view of similar issues, written from a Marxist point of view, see Paul A. Baran and Paul M. Sweezy, *Monopoly Capital: An Essay on the American Economic and Social Order* (London: Pelican, 1968) and Ralph Miliband, *The State in Capitalist Society* (New York: Basic Books, 1969).

Two works by John Kenneth Galbraith provide useful perspectives on American economic society. These are *The Affluent Society* (Boston: Houghton Mifflin, 1958) and *The New Industrial State* (Boston: Houghton Mifflin, 1967).

A textbook by Paul A. Samuelson provides not only basic facts about the American economy but also lucid interpretation; see his *Economics,* 9th ed. (New York: McGraw-Hill, 1973).

Current statistics on government programs and expenditures can be found in various publications by the Office of Management and Budget and in publications of the Congressional Quarterly Service. See, for instance, the latter's *Federal Income Policy,* a background report on economic developments and legislation.

Chapter 2 The Constitutional Framework

The Federalist, originally written as newspaper essays urging the adoption of the new Constitution, under the authorship of Alexander Hamilton, James Madison, and John Jay, remains the most lucid interpretation of various constitutional principles. See also Max Farrand, *The Framing of the Constitution* (New Haven, Conn.: Yale University Press, 1926). Charles A. Beard, in his famous *Economic Interpretation of the Constitution of the United States* (New York: Macmillan, 1913), attempts to show that economic interests of influential delegates to the Constitutional Convention explain many of the Constitution's provisions. For refutations of Beard's thesis, see Forest McDonald, *We the People: The Economic Origins of the Constitution* (Chicago: University of Chicago Press, 1958) and Robert E. Brown, *Charles Beard and the Constitution* (Princeton, N.J.: Princeton University Press, 1956).

Two useful works on American political ideas are Louis Hartz, *The Liberal Tradition in America* (New York: Harcourt Brace Jovanovich, 1955) and Richard Hofstadter, *The American Political Tradition* (New York: Knopf, 1951). Robert A. Dahl, *A Preface to Democratic Theory* (Chicago: University of Chicago Press, 1956) deals in a more formalistic way with certain key ideas in democratic thought, including the Madisonian formulations that so substantially influenced the Constitution.

A readable and informative account of the Constitutional Convention and of the battles over ratification is Catherine Drinker Bowen, *Miracle at Philadelphia* (New York: Bantam, 1968). This book would make excellent light reading as background to our discussion.

Chapter 3 Political Equality, Social Inequality

The classic treatment of American egalitarian values is Alexis de Tocqueville, *Democracy in America,* ed. Phillips Bradley, 2 vols. (New York: Knopf, 1945), a report on this perceptive Frenchman's visit to the United States in the 1830s. Similar historical comments, though written from a contemporary perspective, can be found in Seymour Lipset, *The First New Nation* (London: Heineman, 1963). Perhaps the most convincing essay ever written on citizenship is that of T. H. Marshall, "Citizenship and Social Class," as reproduced in his *Class, Citizenship, and Social Development* (Garden City, N.Y.: Doubleday, 1964). The distinction between legal, political, and social-rights citizenship used in our chapter is drawn from this essay.

The literature on equality in America is very large indeed. Useful data can be found in Christopher Jencks et al., *Inequality: A Reassessment of the Effect of Family and Schooling in America* (New York: Basic Books, 1972). A collection of critical essays is in Maurice Zeitlin, ed., *American Society, Inc.* (Chicago: Markham, 1970). Michael Harrington's *The Other America* (Baltimore: Penguin, 1963) is credited with helping to bring poverty forcefully to the attention of the government, and thus helping to prepare the way for the antipoverty programs. For facts and figures about the wealthier classes, see Ferdinand Lundberg, *The Rich and the Super-Rich* (New York: Bantam Books, 1968).

Chapter 4 Political Participation in America

For a comprehensive study of participation in America, see Sidney Verba and Norman H. Nie, *Participation in America: Political Democracy and Social Equality* (New York: Harper & Row, 1972). The classic study of voting in America is Angus Campbell, Philip E. Converse, Warren E. Miller, and Donald E. Stokes, *The American Voter* (New York: Wiley, 1960). A recent updating is found in Norman H. Nie, Sidney Verba and John Petrocik, *The Changing American Voter* (Cambridge: Harvard University Press, 1976).

For a study of the participation of American blacks, see Donald R. Matthews and James W. Prothro, *Negroes and the New Southern Politics* (New York: Harcourt Brace Jovanovich, 1966) and Alan A. Altshuler, *Community Control: The Black Demand for Participation in Large American Cities* (New York: Pegasus, 1970).

For a consideration of participation in America in comparative perspective, see Gabriel A. Almond and Sidney Verba, *The Civic Culture: Political Attitudes and Democracy in Five Countries* (Boston: Little, Brown, 1965).

For a discussion of violence in American politics, see Jerome H. Skolnick, *The Politics of Protest,* Staff Report to the National Commission on the Causes and Prevention of Violence (New York: Ballantine, 1969).

Chapter 5 Recruitment of Political Leaders

Material on the careers and social backgrounds of political leaders can be found in Donald R. Matthews, *The Social Background of Political Decision-Makers* (Garden City, N.Y.: Doubleday, 1954) and in Suzanne Keller, *Beyond the Ruling Class* (New York: Random House, 1963). A report by W. Lloyd Warner et al., *The American Federal Executive* (New Haven: Yale University Press, 1963) has detailed information on the social and personal characteristics of civilian and military leaders in the federal government.

Important theoretical commentary on the process of political recruitment into top positions appears throughout C. Wright Mills, *The Power Elite*

(New York: Oxford University Press, 1956). Elaboration of certain themes appearing in this chapter can be found in Kenneth Prewitt, *The Recruitment of Political Leaders* (Indianapolis: Bobbs-Merrill, 1970) and in Kenneth Prewitt and Alan Stone, *The Ruling Elites* (New York: Harper & Row, 1973). The idea of "skill revolutions" is developed by Harold Lasswell in *Politics: Who Gets What, When, and How* (New York: McGraw-Hill, 1936).

Chapter 6 Political Beliefs in America

Two classics about American political belief systems are Alexis de Tocqueville, *Democracy in America,* ed. Phillips Bradley, 2 vols. (New York: Knopf, 1945) and James Bryce, *The American Commonwealth,* 3d ed., 2 vols. (New York: Macmillan, 1899).

Gabriel A. Almond and Sidney Verba, *The Civic Culture: Political Attitudes and Democracy in Five Countries* (Boston: Little, Brown, 1965) views the political beliefs in America compared to other democracies. It is the source for the comparative information in this chapter and for the data on education and attitudes. An in-depth study of citizen attitudes on politics is in Robert E. Lane, *Political Ideology: Why the American Common Man Believes What He Does* (New York: Free Press, 1962).

Two other major works on the American public are V. O. Key, Jr., *Public Opinion and American Democracy* (New York: Knopf, 1961) and Angus Campbell, Philip E. Converse, Warren E. Miller, and Donald E. Stokes, *The American Voter* (New York: Wiley, 1960). Both are sources for many specific items in this chapter. Good coverage of the beliefs of Americans is also found in Kenneth M. Dolbeare and Patricia Dolbeare, *American Ideologies* (Chicago: Markham, 1971).

For an analysis of the structure of political opinion, see Philip E. Converse's essay "The Nature of Belief Systems in Mass Politics," in David E. Apter, ed., *Ideology and Discontent* (New York: Free Press, 1964), pp. 206–261; and Norman H. Nie, "Mass Belief Systems Revisited," *Journal of Politics*, 36 (August 1974), 590–591. For the sources of political beliefs in the process of socialization, see Richard Dawson and Kenneth Prewitt, *Political Socialization* (Boston: Little, Brown, 1969) and Kent Jennings and Richard Niemi, *The Political Character of Adolescents* (Princeton, N.J.: Princeton University Press, 1974).

Chapter 7 Social Origins of Conflict

Two of the best books on the group bases of American politics are V. O. Key, Jr., *Public Opinion and American Democracy* (New York: Knopf, 1961) and Angus Campbell, Philip E. Converse, Warren E. Miller, and Donald E. Stokes, *The American Voter* (New York: Wiley, 1960).

For material on ethnicity in America, see Nathan Glazer and Daniel P. Moynihan, *Beyond the Melting Pot* (Cambridge, Mass.: Harvard University Press, 1963) and Andrew M. Greeley, *Why Can't They Be Like Us?* (New York: Institute of Human Relations Press, 1969). Michael Novak's *The Rise of the Unmeltable Ethnics: Politics and Culture in the Seventies* (New York: Macmillan, 1971) deals with white ethnics.

On American blacks, see the classic by Gunnar Myrdal, *An American Dilemma: The Negro Problem and Modern Democracy,* 20th Anniversary Edition (New York: Harper & Row, 1962); Donald R. Matthews and James W. Prothro, *Negroes and the New Southern Politics* (New York: Harcourt Brace Jovanovich, 1966); and Talcott Parsons and Kenneth B. Clark, eds., *The Negro American* (Boston: Beacon, 1967).

Chapter 8 Interest Groups in America

The classic statement of the benefits of interest-group representation is David B. Truman, *The Governmental Process* (New York: Knopf, 1951). The counter position is well expressed in Grant McConnell, *Private Power and American Democracy* (New York: Knopf, 1966) and in Theodore J. Lowi, *The End of Liberalism* (New York: Norton, 1969). E. E. Schattschneider's *The Semi-Sovereign People* (New York: Holt, Rinehart & Winston, 1960) is a critical analysis of the pressure system in the U.S.

A subtle theoretical statement relevant to the dynamics of organization is found in Mancur Olson, Jr., *The Logic of Collective Action: Public Goods and the Theory of Groups* (Cambridge, Mass.: Harvard University Press, 1965). Murray Edelman's *The Symbolic Uses of Politics* (Urbana: University of Illinois Press, 1964) is relevant for the kinds of interests that can be served by group activity.

Lester W. Milbrath's *The Washington Lobbyists* (Chicago: Rand McNally, 1963) covers the activity of lobbyists. James Q. Wilson's *Political Organizations* (New York: Basic Books, 1973) is a sophisticated analysis of how organizations motivate their members to contribute and what makes some successful.

Chapter 9 Political Parties and Elections

The standard reference work on American political parties is V. O. Key, Jr., *Politics, Parties, and Pressure Groups,* 5th ed. (New York: T. Y. Crowell, 1964). This work includes a detailed treatment of party organization, the nominating process, campaign techniques, party finance, and related topics. It also includes some historical discussion. For additional historical treatment as well as analytic interpretation, see the collection of studies in William Chambers and Walter Burnham, eds., *The American Party Systems: Stages of Political Development* (New York: Oxford University Press, 1967).

For the argument that our political parties are not sufficiently programmatic and responsible, see the thesis developed in E. E. Schattschneider, *Party Government* (New York: Holt, Rinehart & Winston, 1942). For further analysis on the same topic the treatment of Austin Ranney, *The Doctrine of Responsible Party Government* (Urbana: University of Illinois Press, 1956) is very helpful.

The thesis that American political parties will converge toward a "centrist" position is well developed in Anthony Downs, *An Economic Theory of Democracy* (New York: Harper & Row, 1957). Finally, the analysis of American voting behavior is best illustrated in two publications of the Survey Research Center at the University of Michigan: Angus Campbell, Philip E. Converse, Warren E. Miller, and Donald E. Stokes, *The American Voter* (New York: Wiley, 1960) and, by the same authors, *Elections and the Political Order* (New York: Wiley, 1966).

Chapter 10 Congress: Representation and Legislation

A provocative book on Congress, very much in the muckraking tradition, is the Ralph Nader Congress Project report, *Who Runs Congress?* (New York: Bantam, 1972). A more balanced though still critical review appears in the collection of essays edited by Senator Joseph S. Clark, *Congressional Reform: Problems and Prospects* (New York: T. Y. Crowell, 1965). This book ends with Clark's own recommendations for "making Congress work." Published in the same year are the solid, informative essays in David B. Truman, ed., *The Congress and America's Future* (Englewood Cliffs, N.J.: Prentice-Hall, 1965).

The flavor of the House of Representatives is evoked in the late Clem Miller's *Member of the House* (New York: Scribner, 1962), a collection of newsletters written by this very gifted congressman. The book-length treatment of the Senate by Donald R. Matthews, *U.S. Senators and Their World* (New York: Vintage, 1960) includes readable discussion as well as useful data on a series of topics.

Much of the scholarly literature on Congress, of which there is a great deal, appears in journal articles. These are often collected in readers. For a representative selection of articles, see Robert L. Peabody and Nelson Polsby, eds., *New Perspectives on the House of Representatives* (Chicago: Rand McNally, 1963) and Leroy N. Riselbach, ed., *The Congressional System* (Belmont, Calif: Wadsworth, 1970). Recent monograph studies of importance include Richard F. Fenno, Jr., *Congressmen in Committees* (Boston: Little, Brown, 1973) and David R. Mayhew, *Congress: The Electoral Connection* (New Haven, Conn.: Yale University Press, 1971).

Chapter 11 The Presidency

A useful general book is Clinton Rossiter's *The American Presidency* (New York: Harcourt Brace Jovanovich, 1956). Two books written in the 1960s that make a case for stronger Presidential leadership are James M. Burns, *Deadlock of Democracy: Four-Party Politics in America* (Englewood Cliffs, N.J.: Prentice-Hall, 1963) and Richard E. Neustadt, *Presidential Power* (New York: Wiley, 1960). It is said that both of these works were closely read by John Kennedy and may well have been the inspiration for his ambitions for the Presidency, as illustrated in the quotation that begins this chapter. A very telling critique of the Burns and Neustadt proposals can be found in Garry Wills, *Nixon Agonistes: The Crisis of the Self-Made Man* (Boston: Houghton Mifflin, 1969), which includes as well some fascinating interpretive discussions of what the election of Richard Nixon to the Presidency tells American society about itself.

Presidents and the Presidency have, of course, long fascinated observers. Many journalistic accounts have been written, and some of them contain rich descriptive material as well as sound analysis. Often, however, the reader will find that the preferences of the author color his perspective. The weaknesses as well as the strengths of such accounts appear in two highly readable books written about the Kennedy years: Theodore C. Sorensen, *Decision-Making in the White House* (New York: Columbia University Press, 1963) and Arthur M. Schlesinger, Jr., *A Thousand Days* (Boston: Houghton Mifflin, 1965). On the Johnson Presidency, see Robert D. Novack and Rowland Evans, *Lyndon B. Johnson: The Exercise of Power* (New York: New American Library, 1966), which includes a useful account of his first years in office, when he managed to put through Congress much domestic legislation, but stops short of the years when Vietnam dominated his administration. For Johnson's own account of his Presidency, see his *The Vantage Point* (New York: Popular Library, 1971).

Nixon's Presidency, especially the final segment concerning the Watergate affair, will be the topic of many books, both popular and scholarly. For an account of how two *Washington Post* reporters helped uncover Watergate, see Carl Bernstein and Bob Woodward, *All the President's Men* (New York: Simon & Schuster, 1974). Arthur Schlesinger's *The Imperial Presidency* (New York: Popular Library, 1973) deals with the growth of Presidential powers and their potential for abuse. Finally, for spontaneous, unrehearsed commentary on the workings of the Nixon Presidency, directly from the oval office of the White House, see *The Presidential Transcripts* (various editions, 1974), the transcript of the White House tapes that led to Nixon's resignation.

Chapter 12 The Supreme Court in American Politics

A standard work is Robert G. McCloskey's *The American Supreme Court* (Chicago: University of Chicago Press, 1960), as is Alexander Bickel's *The Least Dangerous Branch* (Indianapolis: Bobbs-Merrill, 1962). There are numerous casebooks on constitutional law; a useful one is Alpheus T. Mason and William B. Beaney, eds., *American Constitutional Law* (Englewood Cliffs, N.J.: Prentice-Hall, 1965).

Herbert Jacob, *Justice in America* (Boston: Little, Brown, 1965) covers many relevant topics not reviewed in this chapter, especially material on the organization of American courts and appellate proceedings. For a broad and provocative view of the role of law in American society, see the collection of essays edited by Robert Paul Wolff, *The Rule of Law* (New York: Simon & Schuster, 1971).

Richard Richardson and Kenneth Vines, *The Politics of Federal Courts* (Boston: Little, Brown, 1970) reviews the lower federal courts in the United States, and Henry Abraham, *The Judicial Process* (New York: Oxford University Press, 1968) includes in a discussion of the Supreme Court and judicial review useful comparative material about court systems in European countries.

Chapter 13 The Separation of Powers

The works for the preceding three chapters—on Congress, the President, and the courts—are all relevant for the separation of powers. On the bureaucracy, see Alan A. Altshuler, ed., *The Politics of the Federal Bureaucracy* (New York: Dodd, Mead, 1968) and Francis E. Rourke, *Bureaucracy, Politics and Public Policy* (Boston: Little, Brown, 1969).

On the relationship between Congress and the executive, see Nelson W. Polsby, *Congress and the Presidency* (Englewood Cliffs, N.J.: Prentice-Hall, 1971).

Chapter 14 The Individual and the State

On the general problems of majority rule and minority rights, see the important analysis by Alexis de Tocqueville, *Democracy in America* (New York: Oxford University Press, 1947) and the illuminating treatment by Robert A. Dahl, *Preface to Democratic Theory* (Chicago: University of Chicago Press, 1965). John Stuart Mill's *On Liberty* (New York: Appleton, 1947), originally published in 1851, is the classic philosophical statement of the libertarian defense of freedom of speech. Bertrand Russell's *Authority and the Individual* (New York: Simon & Schuster, 1949) deals with the tension between political authority and individual freedom, and Henry David Thoreau's 1849 essay *On the Duty of Civil Disobedience* (New Haven, Conn.: Yale University Press, 1928) is a remarkable plea for the individual to resist unjust governmental authority. A widely read history on American civil liberties is Zechariah Chafee, Jr., *Free Speech in the United States* (Cambridge, Mass.: Harvard University Press, 1941). A more recent work on the Bill of Rights and the court's interpretation of it is Henry J. Abraham, *Freedom and the Court: Civil Rights and Civil Liberties in the United States* (New York: Oxford University Press, 1972). On freedom of religion, see Leo Pfeffer, *Church, State and Freedom* (Boston: Beacon, 1953). The report of the Commission on Obscenity and Pornography (Washington, D.C.: Government

Printing Office) covers this topic thoroughly. Anthony Lewis' *Gideon's Trumpet* (New York: Random House, 1964) covers a classic case involving the rights of accused criminals.

Chapter 15 White House, State House, City Hall: Federalism in America

On federalism in America, see Morton Grodzins, *The American System* (Chicago: Rand McNally, 1966); Richard Leach, *American Federalism* (New York: Norton, 1970); James L. Sundquist, *Making Federalism Work* (Washington, D.C.: The Brookings Institution, 1969); and Michael D. Reagan, *The New Federalism* (New York: Oxford University Press, 1972). William H. Riker's *Federalism: Origin, Operation, Significance* (Boston: Little, Brown, 1964) is a more systematic analysis than most.

For a discussion of the urban problem, see James Q. Wilson and Edward C. Banfield, *City Politics* (Cambridge, Mass.: Harvard University Press, 1963); Robert C. Wood, *1400 Governments: The Political Economy of the New York Metropolitan Region* (Garden City, N.Y.: Doubleday, 1964); and Michael Danielson, ed., *Metropolitan Politics* (Boston: Little, Brown, 1971). For a general discussion of community government, see Alan A. Altshuler, *Community Control: The Black Demand for Participation in Large American Cities* (New York: Pegasus, 1970).

Chapter 16 The Policy Process

A good account of how policy is made in the all-important area of budgeting is Aaron Wildavsky, *The Politics of the Budgetary Process* (Boston: Little, Brown, 1964). An explication and defense of incremental policy making are found in Charles E. Lindblom, *The Policy-Making Process* (Englewood Cliffs, N.J.: Prentice-Hall, 1968), p. 68. A critique of this mode of policy making is in Theodore J. Lowi, *The End of Liberalism* (New York: Norton, 1969).

On the ways in which policies can have symbolic rather than substantive meaning, see Murray Edelman, *The Symbolic Uses of Politics* (Urbana: University of Illinois Press, 1964), and Murray Edelman, *Politics as Symbolic Action* (Chicago: Markham, 1971).

On the problem of policy implementation, see Jeffrey L. Pressman and Aaron D. Wildavsky, *Implementation* (Berkeley and Los Angeles: University of California Press, 1973). Theodore L. Beeker and Malcolm M. Feeley's *The Impact of Supreme Court Decisions* (New York: Oxford University Press, 1973) deals with the actual effects of Supreme Court decisions.

Chapter 17 Public Policies: Domestic and Foreign

The literature on the policies discussed in Chapter 17 is vast. James L. Sundquist's *Politics and Policy: The Eisenhower, Kennedy and Johnson Years* (Washington, D.C.: The Brookings Institution, 1968) deals with the passage of social legislation under three Presidents.

A few works on each issue area: Regulation of business: Marver Bernstein's *Regulating Business by Independent Commissions* (Princeton, N.J.: Princeton University Press, 1965) is the standard work. Tax policy: Joseph A. Peckman and Benjamin A. Okner, *Who Bears the Tax Burden?* (Washington, D.C.: The Brookings Institution, 1974) analyzes the impact of taxes on income distribution in the United States. Inflation, recession, energy: Any good economics textbook will deal with this. On the alternatives faced in making the federal budget, see Edward R. Fried et al., *Setting National Priorities: The 1974 Budget* (Washington, D.C.: The Brookings Institution, 1973).

Medical care: A comprehensive account of medicare legislation is Theodore R. Marmon, *The Politics of Medicare* (Chicago: Aldine, 1973). Desegregation of the schools: A good collection of essays on race relations is *The Negro American,* ed. Talcott Parsons and Kenneth B. Clark (Boston: Beacon, 1967). See also Milton D. Morris, *The Politics of Black America* (New York: Harper & Row, 1975). Vietnam: David Halberstam's *The Best and the Brightest* (New York: Random House, 1972) is a detailed account of the making of Vietnam policy in the White House. Roger Hilsman's *The Politics of Policy Making in Defence and Foreign Policy* (New York: Harper & Row, 1971) covers Vietnam policy making and the policy-making process more generally.

Chapter 18 Perspectives on American Democracy

The literature on pluralism and elitism and the debate between the two perspectives is large. The standard book-length treatments of pluralism include David Truman, *The Governmental Process,* 2d ed. (New York: Knopf, 1971) and Robert Dahl, *Who Governs?* (New Haven, Conn.: Yale University Press, 1961). Critiques of pluralism, though not necessarily from the elitist perspective, can be found in Grant McConnell, *Private Power and American Democracy* (New York: Vintage, 1970) and Theodore Lowi, *The End of Liberalism* (New York: Norton, 1969); both of these books describe how American government responds to narrow private interests. For treatment of American society from the elitist perspective, see C. Wright Mills, *The Power Elite* (New York: Oxford University Press, 1956); William Domhoff, *Who Rules America?* (Englewood Cliffs, N.J.: Prentice-Hall, 1967); and Ralph Miliband, *The State in Capitalist Society* (New York: Basic Books, 1969). A review of both pluralist and elitist perspectives can be found in Kenneth Prewitt and Alan Stone, *The Ruling Elites* (New York: Harper & Row, 1973).

The Constitution of the United States

[*Preamble*]
We the people of the United States, in Order to form a more perfect Union, establish Justice, insure domestic Tranquility, provide for the common defence, promote the general Welfare, and secure the Blessings of Liberty to ourselves and our Posterity, do ordain and establish this Constitution for the United States of America.

ARTICLE 1

Section 1
[*Legislative Powers*]
All legislative Powers herein granted shall be vested in a Congress of the United States, which shall consist of a Senate and a House of Representatives.

Section 2
[*House of Representatives, How Considered, Power of Impeachment*]
The House of Representatives shall be composed of Members chosen every second Year by the People of the several States, and the Electors in each State shall have [the] Qualifications requisite for Electors of the most numerous Branch of the State Legislature.

No Person shall be a Representative who shall not have attained to the Age of twenty five Years, and been Seven Years a Citizen of the United States, and who shall not when elected, be an Inhabitant of that State in which he shall be chosen.

Representatives and direct Taxes shall be apportioned among the several States which may be included within this Union, according to their respective Numbers, which shall be determined by adding to the whole Number of free Persons, including those bound to Service for a Term of Years, and excluding Indians not taxed, three fifths of all other Persons. The actual Enumeration shall be made within three years after the first Meeting of the Congress of the United States, and within every subsequent Term of ten Years, in such Manner as they shall by Law direct. The Number of Representatives shall not exceed one for every thirty Thousand, but each State shall have at Least one Representative; and until such enumeration shall be made, the State of New Hampshire shall be entitled to chuse three, Massachusetts eight, Rhode-Island and Providence Plantations one, Connecticut five, New York six, New Jersey four, Pennsylvania eight, Delaware one, Maryland six, Virginia ten, North Carolina five, South Carolina five, and Georgia three.

When vacancies happen in the Representation from any State, the Executive Authority thereof shall issue Writs of Election to fill such Vacancies.

The House of Representatives shall chuse their Speaker and other Officers; and shall have the sole Power of Impeachment.

Section 3

[The Senate, How Constituted, Impeachment Trials]

The Senate of the United States shall be composed of Two Senators from each State, chosen by the Legislature thereof, for six Years; and each Senator shall have one Vote.

Immediately after they shall be assembled in Consequence of the first Election, they shall be divided as equally as may be into three Classes. The Seats of the Senators of the first Class shall be vacated at the Expiration of the second Year, of the second Class at the Expiration of the fourth Year, and of the third Class at the Expiration of the sixth Year, so that one third may be chosen every second Year; and if Vacancies happen by Resignation, or otherwise, during the Recess of the Legislature of any State, the Executive thereof may make temporary Appointments until the next Meeting of the Legislature, which shall then fill such Vacancies.

No Person shall be a Senator who shall not have attained to the Age of thirty Years, and been nine Years a Citizen of the United States, and who shall not, when elected, be an Inhabitant of that State for which he shall be chosen.

The Vice-President of the United States shall be President of the Senate, but shall have no Vote, unless they be equally divided.

The Senate shall chuse their other Officers, and also a President pro tempore, in the Absence of the Vice-President, or when he shall exercise the Office of President of the United States.

The Senate shall have the sole power to try all impeachments. When sitting for that Purpose, they shall be on Oath or Affirmation. When the President of the United States [is tried] the Chief Justice shall preside: And no Person shall be convicted without the Concurrence of two thirds of the Members present.

Judgment in Cases of Impeachment shall not extend further than to removal from Office, and disqualification to hold and enjoy any Office of honor, Trust or Profit under the United States: but the Party convicted shall nevertheless be liable and subject to Indictment, Trial, Judgment and Punishment, according to Law.

Section 4

[Election of Senators and Representatives]

The Times, Places and Manner of holding Elections for Senators and Representatives, shall be prescribed in each State by the Legislature thereof; but the Congress may at any time by Law make or alter such Regulations, except as to the Places of chusing Senators.

The Congress shall assemble at least once in every Year, and such Meeting shall be on the first Monday in December, unless they shall by Law appoint a different Day.

Section 5

[Quorum, Journals, Meetings, Adjournments]

Each House shall be the Judge of the Elections, Returns and Qualifications of its own Members, and a Majority of each shall constitute a Quorum to do Business; but a smaller Number may adjourn from day to day, and may be authorized to compel the Attendance of absent Members, in such Manner, and under such Penalties as each House may provide.

Each House may determine the Rules of its Proceedings, punish its Members for disorderly Behaviour, and, with the Concurrence of two thirds, expel a Member.

Each House shall keep a Journal of its Proceedings, and from time to time publish the same, excepting such Parts as may in their Judgment require Secrecy; and the Yeas and Nays of the Members of either House on any question shall, at the Desire of one fifth of those Present, be entered on the Journal.

Neither House, during the Session of Congress, shall, without the Consent of the other, adjourn for more than three days, nor to any other Place than that in which the two Houses shall be sitting.

Section 6
[Compensation, Privileges, Disabilities]
The Senators and Representatives shall receive a Compensation for their Services, to be ascertained by Law, and paid out of the Treasury of the United States. They shall in all Cases, except Treason, Felony and Breach of the Peace, be privileged from Arrest during their Attendance at the Session of their respective Houses, and in going to and returning from the same; and for any Speech or Debate in either House, they shall not be questioned in any other Place.

No Senator or Representative shall, during the Time for which he was elected, be appointed to any civil Office under the Authority of the United States, which shall have been created, or the Emoluments whereof shall have been encreased during such time; and no Person holding any Office under the United States, shall be a Member of either House during his Continuance in Office.

Section 7
[Procedure in Passing Bills and Resolutions]
All Bills for raising Revenue shall originate in the House of Representatives; but the Senate may propose or concur with Amendments as on other Bills.

Every Bill which shall have passed the House of Representatives and the Senate, shall, before it becomes a Law, be presented to the President of the United States; if he approves he shall sign it, but if not he shall return it, with his Objections to that House in which it shall have originated, who shall enter the Objections at large on their Journal, and proceed to reconsider it. If after such Reconsideration two thirds of that House shall agree to pass the Bill, it shall be sent, together with the Objections, to the other House, by which it shall likewise be reconsidered, and if approved by two thirds of that House, it shall become a Law. But in all such Cases the Votes of both Houses shall be determined by Yeas and Nays, and the Names of the Persons voting for and against the Bill shall be entered on the Journal of each House respectively. If any Bill shall not be returned by the President within ten Days (Sundays excepted) after it shall have been presented to him, the Same shall be a Law, in like Manner as if he had signed it, unless the Congress by their Adjournment prevent its Return, in which Case it shall not be a Law.

Every Order, Resolution, or Vote to which the Concurrence of the Senate and House of Representatives may be necessary (except on a question of Adjournment) shall be presented to the President of the United States; and before the Same shall take Effect, shall be approved by him, or being disapproved by him, shall be repassed by two thirds of the Senate and House of Representatives, according to the Rules and Limitations prescribed in the Case of a Bill.

Section 8
[Powers of Congress]

The Congress shall have the Power To lay and collect Taxes, Duties, Imposts and Excises, to pay the Debts and provide for the common Defence and general Welfare of the United States; but all Duties, Imposts and Excises shall be uniform throughout the United States.

To borrow Money on the credit of the United States;

To regulate Commerce with foreign Nations and among the several States, and with the Indian Tribes;

To establish an uniform Rule of Naturalization, and uniform Laws on the subject of Bankruptcies throughout the United States;

To Coin Money, regulate the Value thereof, and of foreign Coin, and fix the Standards of Weights and Measures;

To provide for the Punishment of counterfeiting the Securities and current Coin of the United States;

To establish Post Offices and post Roads;

To promote the Progress of Science and useful Arts, by securing for limited Times to Authors and Inventors the exclusive Right to their respective Writings and Discoveries;

To constitute Tribunals inferior to the supreme Court;

To define and punish Piracies and Felonies committed on the high Seas, and Offences against the Law of Nations;

To declare War, grant Letters of Marque and Reprisal, and make Rules concerning Captures on Land and Water;

To raise and support Armies, but no Appropriation of Money to that Use shall be for a longer Term than two Years;

To provide and maintain a Navy;

To make Rules for Government and Regulation of the land and naval Forces;

To provide for calling forth the Militia to execute the Laws of the Union, suppress Insurrections and repel Invasions;

To provide for organizing, arming, and disciplining the Militia, and for governing such Part of them as may be employed in the Service of the United States, reserving to the States respectively, the Appointment of the Officers, and the Authority of training the Militia according to the discipline prescribed by Congress;

To exercise exclusive Legislation in all Cases whatsoever, over such District (not exceeding ten Miles square) as may, by Cession of particular States, and the Acceptance of Congress, become the Seat of the Government of the United States, and to exercise like Authority over all Places purchased by the Consent of the Legislature of the States in which the Same shall be, for the Erection of Forts, Magazines, Arsenals, dock-Yards, and other needful Buildings — And

To make all Laws which shall be necessary and proper for carrying into Execution the foregoing Powers, and all other Powers vested by this Constitution in the Government of the United States, or in any Department or Officer thereof.

Section 9
[Limitation upon Powers of Congress]

The Migration or Importation of such Persons as any of the States now existing shall think proper to admit, shall not be prohibited by the Congress prior to the Year one thousand eight hundred and eight, but a Tax or duty may be imposed on such Importation, not exceeding ten dollars for each Person.

The Privilege of the Writ of Habeas Corpus shall not be suspended, unless when in Cases of Rebellion or Invasion the public Safety may require it.

No Bill of Attainder or ex post facto Law shall be passed.

No Capitation, or other direct, Tax shall be laid, unless in Proportion to the Census or Enumeration herein before directed to be taken.

No Tax or Duty shall be laid on Articles, exported from any State.

No Preference shall be given by any Regulation of Commerce or Revenue to the Ports of one State over those of another; nor shall Vessels bound to, or from, one State, be obliged to enter, clear, or pay Duties in another.

No Money shall be drawn from the Treasury, but in Consequence of Appropriations made by Law; and a regular Statement and Account of the Receipts and Expenditures of all public Money shall be published from time to time.

No title of Nobility shall be granted by the United States: And no Person holding any Office of Profit or Trust under them, shall, without the Consent of the Congress, accept of any present, Emolument, Office, or Title, of any kind whatever, from any King, Prince, or foreign State.

Section 10

[Restrictions upon Powers of States]
No State shall enter into any Treaty, Alliance, or Confederation; grant Letters of Marque and Reprisal; coin Money; emit Bills of Credit; make any Thing but gold and silver Coin a Tender in payment of Debts; pass any Bill of Attainder, ex post facto Law, or Law impairing the Obligation of Contracts, or grant any Title of Nobility.

No State shall, without the Consent of the Congress, lay any Imposts or Duties on Imports or Exports, except what may be absolutely necessary for executing its inspection Laws: and the net Produce of all Duties and Imposts, laid by any State on Imports or Exports, shall be for the Use of the Treasury of the United States; and all such Laws shall be subject to the Revision and Control of [the] Congress.

No State shall, without the Consent of Congress, lay any Duty of Tonnage, keep Troops, or Ships of War in time of Peace, enter into any Agreement or Compact with another State, or with a foreign Power, or engage in War, unless actually invaded, or in such imminent Danger as will not admit of delay.

ARTICLE 2

Section 1

[Executive Power, Election, Qualifications of the President]
The executive Power shall be vested in a President of the United States of America. He shall hold his Office during the Term of four Years, and, together with the Vice-President, chosen for the same Term, be elected as follows:

Each State shall appoint, in such Manner as the Legislature thereof may direct, a Number of Electors, equal to the whole Number of Senators and Representatives to which the State may be entitled in the Congress: but no

Senator or Representative, or Person holding an Office of Trust or Profit under the United States, shall be appointed an Elector.

The Electors shall meet in their respective States, and vote by Ballot for two Persons of whom one at least shall not be an Inhabitant of the same State with themselves. And they shall make a List of all the Persons voted for, and of the Number of Votes for each; which List they shall sign and certify, and transmit sealed to the Seat of the Government of the United States, directed to the President of the Senate. The President of the Senate shall, in the Presence of the Senate and House of Representatives, open all the Certificates, and the Votes shall then be counted. The Person having the greatest Number of Votes shall be the President, if such Number be a Majority of the whole Number of Electors appointed; and if there be more than one who have such Majority, and have an equal Number of Votes, then the House of Representatives shall immediately chuse by Ballot one of them for President; and is no Person have a Majority, then from the five highest in the List the said House in like Manner chuse the President. But in chusing the President, the Votes shall be taken by States, the Representation from each State having one Vote; A quorum for this purpose shall consist of a Member or Members from two thirds of the States, and a Majority of all the States shall be necessary to a Choice. In every Case, after the choice of the President, the Person having the greatest Number of Votes of the Electors shall be the Vice-President. But if there should remain two or more who have equal Votes, the Senate shall chuse from them by Ballot the Vice-President.

The Congress may determine the Time of chusing the Electors, and the Day on which they shall give their Votes; which Day shall be the same throughout the United States.

No person except a natural born Citizen, or a Citizen of the United States, at the time of the Adoption of this Constitution, shall be eligible to the Office of President; neither shall any Person be eligible to that Office who shall not have attained to the Age of thirty five Years, and been fourteen Years a Resident within the United States.

In Case of the Removal of the President from Office, or of his Death, Resignation, or Inability to discharge the Powers and Duties of the said Office, the Same shall devolve on the Vice-President, and the Congress may by Law provide for the Case of Removal, Death, Resignation or Inability, both of the President and Vice-President, declaring what Officer shall then act as President, and such Officer shall act accordingly, until the Disability be removed, or a President shall be elected.

The President shall, at stated Times, receive for his Services, a Compensation, which shall neither be encreased nor diminished during the Period for which he shall have been elected, and he shall not receive within that Period any other Emolument from the United States, or any of them.

Before he entered on the Execution of his Office, he shall take the following Oath of Affirmation:—"I do solemnly swear (or affirm) that I will faithfully execute the Office of the President of the United States, and will to the best of my Ability, preserve, protect and defend the Constitution of the United States."

Section 2

[Powers of the President]

The President shall be Commander in Chief of the Army and Navy of the United States, and the Militia of the several States, when called into the actual Service of the United States; he may require the Opinion, in writing, of the principal Officer in each of the executive Departments, upon any subject relating to the Duties of their respective Offices, and he shall have Power to grant Reprieves and Pardons for Offences against the United States, except in Cases of Impeachment.

He shall have Power, by and with the Advice and Consent of the Senate, to make Treaties, provided two thirds of the Senators present concur; and he shall nominate, and by and with the Advice and Consent of the Senate, shall appoint Ambassadors, other public Ministers and Consuls, Judges of the supreme Court, and all other Officers of the United States, whose Appointments are not herein otherwise provided for, and which shall be established by Law: but the Congress may by Law vest the Appointment of such inferior Officers, as they think proper in the President alone, in the Courts of Law, or in the Heads of Departments.

The President shall have Power to fill up all Vacancies that may happen during the Recess of the Senate, by granting Commissions which shall expire at the End of their next Session.

Section 3
[Powers and Duties of the President]
He shall from time to time give to the Congress Information of the State of the Union, and recommend to their Consideration such Measures as he shall judge necessary and expedient; he may, on extraordinary Occasions, convene both Houses, or either of them, and in Case of Disagreement between them, with Respect to the Time of Adjournment, he may adjourn them to such Time as he shall think proper; he shall receive Ambassadors and other public Ministers; he shall take Care that the Laws be faithfully executed, and shall commission all the Officers of the United States.

Section 4
[Impeachment]
The President, Vice-President and all civil Officers of the United States, shall be removed from Office on Impeachment for, and Conviction of, Treason, Bribery, or other high Crimes and Misdemeanors.

ARTICLE 3

Section 1
[Judicial Power, Tenure of Office]
The judicial Power of the United States, shall be vested in one supreme Court, and in such inferior Courts as the Congress may from time to time ordain and establish. The judges, both of the supreme and inferior Courts, shall hold their Offices during good Behavior, and shall, at stated Times, receive for their Services, a Compensation, which shall not be diminished during their Continuance in Office.

Section 2
[Jurisdiction]
The judicial Power shall extend to all Cases, in Law and Equity, arising under this Constitution, the Laws of the United States, and Treaties made, or which shall be made, under their Authority;—to all Cases affecting Ambassadors, other public Ministers and Consuls;—to all Cases of admiralty and maritime Jurisdiction;—to Controversies to which the United States shall be a Party;—to Controversies between two or more States;—

between a State and Citizens of another State;—between Citizens of different States;—between Citizens of the same State claiming Lands under Grants of different States, and between a State, or the Citizens thereof, and foreign States, Citizens or Subjects.

In all Cases affecting Ambassadors, other public Ministers and Consuls, and those in which a State shall be Party, the supreme Court shall have original Jurisdiction. In all the other Cases before mentioned, the supreme Court shall have appellate Jurisdiction, both as to Law and Fact, with such Exceptions, and under such Regulations as the Congress shall make.

The Trial of all Crimes, except in Cases of Impeachment, shall be by Jury; and such Trial shall be held in the State where the said Crimes shall have been committed; but when not committed within any State, the Trial shall be at such Place or Places as the Congress may by Law have directed.

Section 3
[Treason, Proof and Punishment]

Treason against the United States, shall consist only in levying War against them, or in adhering to their Enemies; giving them Aid and Comfort. No Person shall be convicted of Treason unless on the Testimony of two Witnesses to the same overt Act, or on Confession in open Court.

The Congress shall have Power to declare the Punishment of Treason, but no Attainder of Treason shall work Corruption of Blood, or Forfeiture except during the Life of the Person attainted.

ARTICLE 4

Section 1
[Faith and Credit Among States]

Full Faith and Credit shall be given in each State to the public Acts, Records, and judicial Proceedings of every other State. And the Congress may by general Laws prescribe the Manner in which such Acts, Records and Proceedings shall be proved, and the Effect thereof.

Section 2
[Privileges and Immunities, Fugitives]

The citizens of each State shall be entitled to all Privileges and Immunities of Citizens in the several States.

A Person charged in any State with Treason, Felony, or other Crime, who shall flee from Justice, and be found in another State, shall on Demand of the executive Authority of the State from which he fled, be delivered up, to be removed to the State having Jurisdiction of the Crime.

No person held to Service or Labour in one State, under the Laws thereof, escaping into another, shall, in Consequence of any Law or Regulation therein, be discharged from such Service or Labour, but shall be delivered up on Claim of the Party to whom such Service or Labour may be due.

Section 3
[Admission of New States]

New States may be admitted by the Congress into this Union; but no new State shall be formed or erected within the Jurisdiction of any other State; nor any State be formed by the Junction of two or more States, or Parts of States, without the Consent of the Legislatures of the States concerned as well as of the Congress.

The Congress shall have Power to dispose of and make all needful Rules and Regulations respecting the Territory or other Property belonging to the United States; and nothing in this Constitution shall be so construed as to Prejudice any Claims of the United States, or of any particular State.

Section 4
[Guarantee of Republican Government]
The United States shall guarantee to every State in this Union a Republican Form of Government, and shall protect each of them against Invasion; and on Application of the Legislature, or of the Executive (when the Legislature cannot be convened) against domestic Violence.

ARTICLE 5

[Amendment of the Constitution]
The Congress, whenever two thirds of both Houses shall deem it necessary, shall propose Amendments to this Constitution, or, on the Application of the Legislatures of two thirds of the several States, shall call a Convention for proposing Amendments, which, in either Case, shall be valid to all Intents and Purposes, as Part of this Constitution, when ratified by the Legislatures of three fourths of the several States, or by Conventions in three fourths thereof, as the one or the other Mode of Ratification may be proposed by the Congress; Provided that no Amendment which may be made prior to the Year One Thousand eight hundred and eight shall in any Manner affect the first and fourth Clauses in the Ninth Section of the first Article, and that no State, without its Consent, shall be deprived of its equal Suffrage in the Senate.

ARTICLE 6

[Debts, Supremacy, Oath]
All Debts contracted and Engagements entered into, before the Adoption of this Constitution, shall be as valid against the United States under this Constitution, as under the Confederation.

This Constitution, and the Laws of the United States which shall be made in Pursuance thereof; and all Treaties made, or which shall be made, under the Authority of the United States, shall be the supreme Law of the Land; and the Judges in every State be bound thereby, any Thing in the Constitution or Laws of any State to the Contrary notwithstanding.

The Senators and Representatives before mentioned, and the Members of the several State Legislatures, and all executive and judicial Officers, both of the United States and of the several States, shall be bound by Oath or Affirmation, to support this Constitution, but no religious Test shall ever be required as a Qualification to any Office or public Trust under the United States.

ARTICLE 7

[Ratification and Establishment]
The Ratification of the Conventions of nine States, shall be sufficient for the Establishment of this Constitution between the States so ratifying the Same.

Done in Convention by the Unanimous Consent of the States present the

Seventeenth Day of September in the Year of our Lord one thousand seven hundred and Eighty seven and of the Independence of the United States of America the Twelfth In witness whereof We have hereunto subscribed our Names.

Go. Washington
Presidt and deputy from Virginia

New Hampshire	John Langdon Nicholas Gilman
Massachusetts	Nathaniel Gorham Rufus King
Connecticut	Wm Saml Johnson Roger Sherman
New York	Alexander Hamilton
New Jersey	Wil: Livingston David Brearley Wm Paterson Jona: Dayton
Pennsylvania	B. Franklin Thomas Mifflin Robt. Morris Geo. Clymer Thos. FitzSimons Jared Ingersoll James Wilson Gouv Morris
Delaware	Geo. Read Gunning Bedford jun John Dickinson Richard Bassett Jaco: Broom
Maryland	James McHenry Dan of St Thos. Jenifer Danl Carroll
Virginia	John Blair James Madison Jr.
North Carolina	Wm Blount Richd Dobbs Spaight Hu Williamson
South Carolina	J. Rutledge Charles Cotesworth Pinckney Charles Pinckney Pierce Butler
Georgia	William Few Abr Baldwin

Amendments to the Constitution

[The first ten amendments, known as the Bill of Rights, were proposed by Congress on September 25, 1789; ratified and adoption certified on December 15, 1791.]

AMENDMENT I

[Freedom of Religion, of Speech, of the Press, and Right of Petition]
Congress shall make no law respecting an establishment of religion, or prohibiting the free exercise thereof; or abridging the freedom of speech, or of the press; or the right of the people peaceably to assemble, and to petition the Government for a redress of grievances.

AMENDMENT II

[Right to Keep and Bear Arms]
A well regulated Militia being necessary to the security of a free State, the right of the people to keep and bear Arms, shall not be infringed.

AMENDMENT III

[Quartering of Soldiers]
No Soldier shall, in time of peace be quartered in any house, without the consent of the Owner, nor in time of war, but in a manner to be prescribed by law.

AMENDMENT IV

[Security from Unwarrantable Search and Seizure]
The right of the people to be secure in their persons, houses, papers, and effects, against unreasonable searches and seizures, shall not be violated, and no Warrants shall issue, but upon probable cause, supported by Oath of affirmation, and particularly describing the place to be searched, and the persons or things to be seized.

AMENDMENT V

[Rights of Accused in Criminal Proceedings]
No person shall be held to answer for a capital, or otherwise infamous crime, unless on a presentment or indictment of a Grand Jury, except in cases arising in the land or naval forces, or in the Militia, when in actual service in time of War or public danger; nor shall any person be subjected for the same offense to be twice put in jeopardy of life or limb; nor shall be compelled in any criminal case to be a witness against himself, nor be deprived of life, liberty, or property, without due process of law; nor shall private property be taken for public use, without just compensation.

AMENDMENT VI

[Right to Speedy Trial, Witnesses, etc.]
In all criminal prosecutions, the accused shall enjoy the right to a speedy and public trial, by an impartial jury of the State and district wherein the

crime shall have been committed, which district shall have been previously ascertained by law, and to be informed of the nature and cause of the accusation; to be confronted with the witnesses against him; to have compulsory process for obtaining witnesses in his favor, and to have the Assistance of Counsel for his defence.

AMENDMENT VII

[Trial by Jury in Civil Cases]
In Suits at common law, where the value in controversy shall exceed twenty dollars, the right of trial by jury shall be preserved, and no fact tried by a jury, shall be otherwise reexamined in any Court of the United States, than according to the rules of the common law.

AMENDMENT VIII

[Bails, Fines, Punishments]
Excessive bail shall not be required, nor excessive fines imposed, nor cruel and unusual punishments inflicted.

AMENDMENT IX

[Reservation of Rights of the People]
The enumeration in the Constitution, of certain rights, shall not be construed to deny or disparage others retained by the people.

AMENDMENT X

[Powers Reserved to States or People]
The powers not delegated to the United States by the Constitution, nor prohibited by it to the States, are reserved to the States respectively, or to the people.

AMENDMENT XI

[Proposed by Congress on March 4, 1793; declared ratified on January 8, 1798.]
[Restriction of Judicial Power]
The Judicial power of the United States shall not be construed to extend to any suit in law or equity, commenced or prosecuted againse one of the United States by Citizens of another State, or by Citizens or Subjects of any Foreign State.

AMENDMENT XII

[Proposed by Congress on December 9, 1803; declared ratified on September 25, 1804.]
[Election of President and Vice-President]
The Electors shall meet in their respective states, and vote by ballot for President and Vice-President, one of whom, at least, shall not be an inhabitant of the same state with themselves; they shall name in their ballots the person voted for as President, and in distinct ballots the person voted for as Vice-President and they shall make distinct lists of all persons voted for as President, and of all persons voted for as Vice-President, and of the number of

votes for each, which lists they shall sign and certify, and transmit sealed to the seat of the government of the United States, directed to the President of the Senate;—The President of the Senate shall, in the presence of the Senate and House of Representatives, open all the certificates and the votes shall then be counted;—The person having the greatest number of votes for President, shall be the President, if such number be a majority of the whole number of Electors appointed; and if no person have such majority, then from the persons having the highest numbers not exceeding three on the list of those voted for as President, the House of Representatives shall choose immediately, by ballot, the President. But in choosing the President, the votes shall be taken by states, the representation from each state having one vote; a quorum for this purpose shall consist of a member or members from two-thirds of the states, and a majority of all the states shall be necessary to a choice. And if the House of Representatives shall not choose a President whenever the right of choice shall devolve upon them, before the fourth day of March next following, then the Vice-President shall act as President, as in the case of the death or other constitutional disability of the President.—The person having the greatest number of votes as Vice-President, shall be the Vice-President, if such number be a majority of the whole number of Electors appointed, and if no person have a majority, then from the two highest numbers on the list, the Senate shall choose the Vice-President; a quorum for the purpose shall consist of two-thirds of the whole number of Senators, and a majority of the whole number shall be necessary to a choice. But no person constitutionally ineligible to the office of President shall be eligible to that of Vice-President of the United States.

AMENDMENT XIII

[*Proposed by Congress on January 31, 1865; declared ratified on December 18, 1865.*]

Section 1
[*Abolition of Slavery*]
Neither slavery nor involuntary servitude, except as a punishment for a crime whereof the party shall have been duly convicted, shall exist within the United States, or any place subject to their jurisdiction.

Section 2
[*Power to Enforce This Article*]
Congress shall have the power to enforce this article by appropriate legislation.

AMENDMENT XIV

[*Proposed by Congress on June 16, 1866; declared ratified on July 28, 1868.*]

Section 1
[*Citizenship Rights Not to Be Abridged by States*]
All persons born or naturalized in the United States, and subject to the jurisdiction thereof, are citizens of the United States and of the State wherein they reside. No State shall make or enforce any law which shall abridge the privileges or immunities of citizens of the United States; nor shall any State deprive any person of life, liberty, or property, without due process of law;

nor deny to any person within its jurisdiction the equal protection of the laws.

Section 2
[Apportionment of Representatives in Congress]
Representatives shall be apportioned among the several States according to their respective numbers, counting the whole number of persons in each State, excluding Indians not taxed. But when the right to vote at any election for the choice of electors for President and Vice-President of the United States, Representatives in Congress, the Executive and Judicial officers of a State, or the members of the Legislature thereof, is denied to any of the male inhabitants of such State, being twenty-one years of age, and citizens of the United States, or in any way abridged, except for participation in rebellion or other crime, the basis of representation therein shall be reduced in the proportion which the number of such male citizens shall bear to the whole number of male citizens twenty-one years of age in such State.

Section 3
[Persons Disqualified from Holding Office]
No person shall be a Senator or Representative in Congress, or elector of President and Vice-President, or hold any office, civil or military, under the United States, or under any State, who, having previously taken an oath, as a member of Congress, or as an officer of the United States, or as a member of any State legislature, or as an executive or judicial officer of any State, to support the Constitution of the United States, shall have engaged in insurrection or rebellion against the same, or given aid or comfort to the enemies thereof. But Congress may by a vote of two-thirds of each House, remove such disability.

Section 4
[What Public Debts Are Valid]
The validity of the public debt of the United States, authorized by law, including debts incurred for payment of pensions and bounties for services in suppressing insurrection or rebellion, shall not be questioned. But neither the United States nor any State shall assume or pay any debt or obligation incurred in aid of insurrection or rebellion against the United States, or any claim for the loss or emancipation of any slave; but all such debts, obligations and claims shall be held illegal and void.

Section 5
[Power to Enforce This Article]
The Congress shall have power to enforce, by appropriate legislation, the provisions of this article.

AMENDMENT XV

[Proposed by Congress on February 26, 1869; declared ratified on March 30, 1870.]

Section 1
[Negro Suffrage]
The right of citizens of the United States to vote shall not be denied or abridged by the United States or by any State on account of race, color, or previous condition of servitude.

Section 2
[*Power to Enforce This Article*]

The Congress shall have power to enforce this article by appropriate legislation.

AMENDMENT XVI

[*Proposed by Congress on July 12, 1909; declared ratified on February 25, 1913.*]
[*Authorizing Income Taxes*]

The Congress shall have power to lay and collect taxes on incomes, from whatever source derived, without apportionment among the several States, and without regard to any census or enumeration.

AMENDMENT XVII

[*Proposed by Congress on May 13, 1912; declared ratified on May 31, 1913.*]
[*Popular Election of Senators*]

The Senate of the United States shall be composed of two Senators from each State, elected by the people thereof, for six years; and each Senator shall have one vote. The electors in each State shall have the qualifications requisite for electors of the most numerous branch of the State legislatures.

When vacancies happen in the representation of any State in the Senate, the executive authority of such State shall issue writs of election to fill such vacancies: *Provided*, That the legislature of any State may empower the executive thereof to make temporary appointments until the people fill the vacancies by election as the legislature may direct.

This amendment shall not be so construed as to affect the election or term of any Senator chosen before it becomes valid as part of the Constitution.

AMENDMENT XVIII

[*Proposed by Congress on December 18, 1917; declared ratified on January 16, 1919.*]

Section 1
[*National Liquor Prohibition*]

After one year from the ratification of this article the manufacture, sale, or transportation of intoxicating liquors within, the importation thereof into, or the exportation thereof from the United States and all territory subject to the jurisdiction thereof for beverage purposes is hereby prohibited.

Section 2
[*Power to Enforce This Article*]

The Congress and the several States shall have concurrent power to enforce this article by appropriate legislation.

Section 3
[*Ratification Within Seven Years*]

This article shall be inoperative unless it shall have been ratified as an amendment to the Constitution by the legislatures of the several States, as provided in the Constitution, within seven years from the date of the submission hereof to the States by the Congress.

AMENDMENT XIX

[Proposed by Congress on June 4, 1919; declared ratified on August 26, 1920.]
[Woman Suffrage]
The right of citizens of the United States to vote shall not be denied or abridged by the United States or by any State on account of sex.

Congress shall have power to enforce this article by appropriate legislation.

AMENDMENT XX

[Proposed by Congress on March 2, 1932; declared ratified on February 6, 1933.]

Section 1
[Terms of Office]
The terms of the President and Vice-President shall end at noon on the 20th day of January, and the terms of Senators and Representatives at noon on the 3rd day of January, of the years in which such terms would have ended if this article had not been ratified; and the terms of their successors shall then begin.

Section 2
[Time of Convening Congress]
The Congress shall assemble at least once in every year, and such meeting shall begin at noon on the 3rd day of January, unless they shall by law appoint a different day.

Section 3
[Death of President Elect]
If, at the time fixed for the beginning of the term of the President, the President elect shall have died, the Vice-President elect shall become President. If a President shall not have been chosen before the time fixed for the beginning of his term, or if the President elect shall have failed to qualify, then the Vice-President elect shall act as President until a President shall have qualified; and the Congress may by law provide for the case wherein neither a President elect nor a Vice-President elect shall have qualified, declaring who shall then act as President, or the manner in which one who is to act shall be selected, and such person shall act accordingly until a President or Vice-President shall have qualified.

Section 4
[Election of the President]
The Congress may by law provide for the case of the death of any of the persons from whom the House of Representatives may choose a President whenever the right of choice shall have devolved upon them, and for the case of the death of any of the persons from whom the Senate may choose a Vice-President whenever the right of choice shall have devolved upon them.

Section 5
Sections 1 and 2 shall take effect on the 15th day of October following the ratification of this article.

Section 6

This article shall be inoperative unless it shall have been ratified as an amendment to the Constitution by the legislatures of three-fourths of the several States within seven years from the date of its submission.

AMENDMENT XXI

[Proposed by Congress on February 20, 1933; declared ratified on December 5, 1933.]

Section 1

[National Liquor Prohibition Repealed]
The eighteenth article of amendment to the Constitution of the United States is hereby repealed.

Section 2

[Transportation of Liquor into "Dry" States]
The transportation or importation into any States, Territory, or possession of the United States for delivery or use therein of intoxicating liquors, in violation of the laws thereof, is hereby prohibited.

Section 3

This article shall be inoperative unless it shall have been ratified as an amendment to the Constitution by conventions in the several States, as provided in the Constitution, within seven years from the date of the submission hereof to the States by the Congress.

AMENDMENT XXII

[Proposed by Congress on March 21, 1947; declared ratified on February 26, 1951.]

Section 1

[Tenure of President Limited]
No person shall be elected to the office of the President more than twice, and no person who has held the office of President, or acted as President, for more than two years of a term to which some other person was elected President shall be elected to the office of the President more than once. But this Article shall not apply to any person holding the office of President when this Article was proposed by the Congress, and shall not prevent any person who may be holding the office of President, or acting as President, during the term within which this Article becomes operative from holding the office of President, or acting as President during the remainder of such term.

Section 2

This Article shall be inoperative unless it shall have been ratified as an amendment to the Constitution by the legislatures of three-fourths of the several States within seven years from the date of its submission to the States by the Congress.

AMENDMENT XXIII

[Proposed by Congress on June 17, 1960; declared ratified on May 29, 1961.]

Section 1
[District of Columbia Suffrage in Presidential Elections]
The District constituting the seat of Government of the United States shall appoint in such manner as the Congress may direct:

A number of electors of President and Vice-President equal to the whole number of Senators and Representatives in Congress to which the District would be entitled if it were a State, but in no event more than the least populous State; they shall be in addition to those appointed by the States, but they shall be considered, for the purposes of the election of President and Vice-President, to be electors appointed by a State; and they shall meet in the District and perform such duties as provided by the twelfth article of amendment.

Section 2
The Congress shall have power to enforce this article by appropriate legislation.

AMENDMENT XXIV

[Proposed by Congress on August 27, 1962; declared ratified on January 23, 1964.]

Section 1
[Bars Poll Tax in Federal Elections]
The right of citizens of the United States to vote in any primary or other election for President or Vice-President, for electors for President or Vice-President, or for Senator or Representative in Congress, shall not be denied or abridged by the United States or any State by reason of failure to pay any poll tax or other tax.

Section 2
The Congress shall have power to enforce this article by appropriate legislation.

AMENDMENT XXV

[Proposed by Congress on July 6, 1965; declared ratified on February 10, 1967.]

Section 1
[Succession of Vice-President to Presidency]
In case of the removal of the President from office or of his death or resignation, the Vice-President shall become President.

Section 2
[Vacancy in Office of Vice-President]
Whenever there is a vacancy in the office of the Vice-President, the President shall nominate a Vice-President who shall take office upon confirmation by a majority vote of both Houses of Congress.

Section 3
[Vice-President as Acting President]
Whenever the President transmits to the President pro tempore of the Senate and the Speaker of the House of Representatives his written declaration that he is unable to discharge the powers and duties of his office, and until

he transmits to them a written declaration to the contrary, such powers and duties shall be discharged by the Vice-President as Acting President.

Section 4
[Vice-President as Acting President]
Whenever the Vice-President and a majority of either the principal officers of the executive departments or of such other body as Congress may by law provide, transmit to the President pro tempore of the Senate and the Speaker of the House of Representatives their written declaration that the President is unable to discharge the powers and duties of his office, the Vice-President shall immediately assume the powers and duties of the office as Acting President.

Thereafter, when the President transmits to the President pro tempore of the Senate and the Speaker of the House of Representatives his written declaration that no inability exists, he shall resume the powers and duties of his office unless the Vice-President and a majority of either the principal officers of the executive department or of such other body as Congress may by law provide, transmit within four days to the President pro tempore of the Senate and the Speaker of the House of Representatives their written declaration that the President is unable to discharge the powers and duties of his office. Thereupon Congress shall decide the issue, assembling within forty-eight hours for that purpose if not in session. If the Congress, within twenty-one days after receipt of the latter written declaration, or, if Congress is not in session, within twenty-one days after Congress is required to assemble, determines by two-thirds vote of both Houses that the President is unable to discharge the powers and duties of his office, the Vice-President shall continue to discharge the same as Acting President; otherwise, the President shall resume the powers and duties of his office.

AMENDMENT XXVI

[Proposed by Congress on March 23, 1971; declared ratified on July 5, 1971.]

Section 1
[Lowers Voting Age to 18 Years]
The right of citizens of the United States, who are eighteen years of age or older, to vote shall not be denied or abridged by the United States or by any State on account of age.

Section 2
The Congress shall have power to enforce this article by appropriate legislation.

Presidential Elections 1789-1972

Year	Candidates	Party	Popular Vote	Electoral Vote
1789	**George Washington**			69
	John Adams			34
	Others			35
1792	**George Washington**			132
	John Adams			77
	George Clinton			50
	Others			5
1796	**John Adams**	Federalist		71
	Thomas Jefferson	Democratic-Republican		68
	Thomas Pinckney	Federalist		59
	Aaron Burr	Democratic-Republican		30
	Others			48
1800	**Thomas Jefferson**	Democratic-Republican		73
	Aaron Burr	Democratic-Republican		73
	John Adams	Federalist		65
	Charles C. Pinckney	Federalist		64
1804	**Thomas Jefferson**	Democratic-Republican		162
	Charles C. Pinckney	Federalist		14
1808	**James Madison**	Democratic-Republican		122
	Charles C. Pinckney	Federalist		47
	George Clinton	Independent-Republican		6
1812	**James Madison**	Democratic-Republican		128
	DeWitt Clinton	Federalist		89
1816	**James Monroe**	Democratic-Republican		183
	Rufus King	Federalist		34
1820	**James Monroe**	Democratic-Republican		231
	John Quincy Adams	Independent-Republican		1
1824	**John Quincy Adams**	Democratic-Republican	108,740 (30.5%)	84
	Andrew Jackson	Democratic-Republican	153,544 (43.1%)	99
	Henry Clay	Democratic-Republican	47,136 (13.2%)	37
	William H. Crawford	Democratic-Republican	46,618 (13.1%)	41
1828	**Andrew Jackson**	Democratic	647,231 (56.0%)	178
	John Quincy Adams	National Republican	509,097 (44.0%)	83
1832	**Andrew Jackson**	Democratic	687,502 (55.0%)	219
	Henry Clay	National Republican	530,189 (42.4%)	49
	William Wirt	Anti-Masonic ⎫		7
	John Floyd	National Republican ⎭	33,108 (2.6%)	11

Year	Candidates	Party	Popular Vote	Electoral Vote
1836	**Martin Van Buren**	Democratic	761,549 (50.9%)	170
	William H. Harrison	Whig	549,567 (36.7%)	73
	Hugh L. White	Whig	145,396 (9.7%)	26
	Daniel Webster	Whig	41,287 (2.7%)	14
1840	**William H. Harrison**	Whig	1,275,017 (53.1%)	234
	(John Tyler, 1841)			
	Martin Van Buren	Democratic	1,128,702 (46.9%)	60
1844	**James K. Polk**	Democratic	1,337,243 (49.6%)	170
	Henry Clay	Whig	1,299,068 (48.1%)	105
	James G. Birney	Liberty	62,300 (2.3%)	
1848	**Zachary Taylor**	Whig	1,360,101 (47.4%)	163
	(Millard Fillmore, 1850)			
	Lewis Cass	Democratic	1,220,544 (42.5%)	127
	Martin Van Buren	Free Soil	291,263 (10.1%)	
1852	**Franklin Pierce**	Democratic	1,601,474 (50.9%)	254
	Winfield Scott	Whig	1,386,578 (44.1%)	42
1856	**James Buchanan**	Democratic	1,838,169 (45.4%)	174
	John C. Frémont	Republican	1,335,264 (33.0%)	114
	Millard Fillmore	American	874,534 (21.6%)	8
1860	**Abraham Lincoln**	Republican	1,865,593 (39.8%)	180
	Stephen A. Douglas	Democratic	1,382,713 (29.5%)	12
	John C. Breckinridge	Democratic	848,356 (18.1%)	72
	John Bell	Constitutional Union	592,906 (12.6%)	39
1864	**Abraham Lincoln**	Republican	2,206,938 (55.0%)	212
	(Andrew Johnson, 1865)			
	George B. McClellan	Democratic	1,803,787 (45.0%)	21
1868	**Ulysses S. Grant**	Republican	3,013,421 (52.7%)	214
	Horatio Seymour	Democratic	2,706,829 (47.3%)	80
1872	**Ulysses S. Grant**	Republican	3,596,745 (55.6%)	286
	Horace Greeley	Democratic	2,843,446 (43.9%)	66
1876	**Rutherford B. Hayes**	Republican	4,036,572 (48.0%)	185
	Samuel J. Tilden	Democratic	4,284,020 (51.0%)	184
1880	**James A. Garfield**	Republican	4,449,053 (48.3%)	214
	(Chester A. Arthur, 1881)			
	Winfield S. Hancock	Democratic	4,442,035 (48.2%)	155
	James B. Weaver	Greenback-Labor	308,578 (3.4%)	
1884	**Grover Cleveland**	Democratic	4,874,986 (48.5%)	219
	James G. Blaine	Republican	4,851,981 (48.2%)	182
	Benjamin F. Butler	Greenback-Labor	175,370 (1.8%)	
1888	**Benjamin Harrison**	Republican	5,444,337 (47.8%)	233
	Grover Cleveland	Democratic	5,540,050 (48.6%)	168
1892	**Grover Cleveland**	Democratic	5,554,414 (46.0%)	277
	Benjamin Harrison	Republican	5,190,802 (43.0%)	145
	James B. Weaver	People's	1,027,329 (8.5%)	22
1896	**William McKinley**	Republican	7,035,638 (50.8%)	271
	William J. Bryan	Democratic; Populist	6,467,946 (46.7%)	176

Year	Candidates	Party	Popular Vote	Electoral Vote
1900	**William McKinley** (**Theodore Roosevelt**, 1901)	Republican	7,219,530 (51.7%)	292
	William J. Bryan	Democratic; Populist	6,356,734 (45.5%)	155
1904	**Theodore Roosevelt**	Republican	7,628,834 (56.4%)	336
	Alton B. Parker	Democratic	5,084,401 (37.6%)	140
	Eugene V. Debs	Socialist	402,460 (3.0%)	
1908	**William H. Taft**	Republican	7,679,006 (51.6%)	321
	William J. Bryan	Democratic	6,409,106 (43.1%)	162
	Eugene V. Debs	Socialist	420,820 (2.8%)	
1912	**Woodrow Wilson**	Democratic	6,286,820 (41.8%)	435
	Theodore Roosevelt	Progressive	4,126,020 (27.4%)	88
	William H. Taft	Republican	3,483,922 (23.2%)	8
	Eugene V. Debs	Socialist	897,011 (6.0%)	
1916	**Woodrow Wilson**	Democratic	9,129,606 (49.3%)	277
	Charles E. Hughes	Republican	8,538,221 (46.1%)	254
1920	**Warren G. Harding** (**Calvin Coolidge**, 1923)	Republican	16,152,200 (61.0%)	404
	James M. Cox	Democratic	9,147,353 (34.6%)	127
	Eugene V. Debs	Socialist	919,799 (3.5%)	
1924	**Calvin Coolidge**	Republican	15,725,016 (54.1%)	382
	John W. Davis	Democratic	8,385,586 (28.8%)	136
	Robert M. La Follette	Progressive	4,822,856 (16.6%)	13
1928	**Herbert C. Hoover**	Republican	21,392,190 (58.2%)	444
	Alfred E. Smith	Democratic	15,016,443 (40.8%)	87
1932	**Franklin D. Roosevelt**	Democratic	22,809,638 (57.3%)	472
	Herbert C. Hoover	Republican	15,758,901 (39.6%)	59
	Norman Thomas	Socialist	881,951 (2.2%)	
1936	**Franklin D. Roosevelt**	Democratic	27,751,612 (60.7%)	523
	Alfred M. Landon	Republican	16,681,913 (36.4%)	8
	William Lemke	Union	891,858 (1.9%)	
1940	**Franklin D. Roosevelt**	Democratic	27,243,466 (54.7%)	449
	Wendell L. Willkie	Republican	22,304,755 (44.8%)	82
1944	**Franklin D. Roosevelt** (**Harry S Truman**, 1945)	Democratic	25,602,505 (52.8%)	432
	Thomas E. Dewey	Republican	22,006,278 (44.5%)	99
1948	**Harry S Truman**	Democratic	24,105,812 (49.5%)	303
	Thomas E. Dewey	Republican	21,970,065 (45.1%)	189
	J. Strom Thurmond	States' Rights	1,169,063 (2.4%)	39
	Henry A. Wallace	Progressive	1,157,172 (2.4%)	
1952	**Dwight D. Eisenhower**	Republican	33,936,234 (55.2%)	442
	Adlai E. Stevenson	Democratic	27,314,992 (44.5%)	89
1956	**Dwight D. Eisenhower**	Republican	35,590,472 (57.4%)	457
	Adlai E. Stevenson	Democratic	26,022,752 (42.0%)	73
1960	**John F. Kennedy** (**Lyndon B. Johnson**, 1963)	Democratic	34,227,096 (49.9%)	303
	Richard M. Nixon	Republican	34,108,546 (49.6%)	219

Year	Candidates	Party	Popular Vote	Electoral Vote
1964	**Lyndon B. Johnson**	Democratic	43,126,233 (61.1%)	486
	Barry M. Goldwater	Republican	27,174,989 (38.5%)	52
1968	**Richard M. Nixon**	Republican	31,783,783 (43.4%)	301
	Hubert H. Humphrey	Democratic	31,271,839 (42.7%)	191
	George C. Wallace	American Independent	9,899,557 (13.5%)	46
1972	**Richard M. Nixon** **(Gerald Ford,** 1974)	Republican	46,631,189 (61.3%)	521
	George McGovern	Democratic	28,422,015 (37.3%)	17

Note: Because only the leading candidates are listed, popular-vote percentages do not always total 100. The elections of 1800 and 1824, in which no candidate received an electoral-vote majority, were decided in the House of Representatives.

Glossary

accountability The principle according to which officials in a democracy are held responsible for their actions by those who elected or appointed them.

advice and consent Senatorial power, granted in Article II, Section 2 of the Constitution, to approve Presidential treaties and certain Presidential appointments such as ambassadors and justices of the Supreme Court. Treaties require a two-thirds vote of the Senate for ratification.

agenda The list of items to be considered at a meeting or legislative session; more generally, the list of politically relevant issues.

amendment An alteration or addition to a bill, motion, or constitution. Congressional bills may be amended at virtually any point before they are passed. As specified in Article V of the U.S. Constitution, constitutional amendments may be proposed by a two-thirds vote of both houses of Congress or by a convention assembled by Congress at the request of the legislatures of two-thirds of the states. To be ratified, a constitutional amendment must be approved by the legislatures of three-fourths of the states or by conventions called for that purpose in three-fourths of the states.

amicus curiae brief Literally, a brief filed by a "friend of the court"; thus a brief filed by one who is not a party to a lawsuit—but who may very well be affected by its outcome—stating a legal principle for the consideration of the court.

appeal A legal proceeding in which a case is carried from a lower court to a higher court for review or reexamination.

aristocracy Rule or government by a small group of privileged notables, usually selected by birth or wealth.

assimilation The process of absorption and amalgamation of a minority into the dominant social group. When a group is assimilated, its members lose their distinctiveness.

Bill of Rights The first ten amendments to the U.S. Constitution.

bourgeois Middle class; may refer to those who own private property.

budget A statement of estimated income and expenses. The President is responsible for preparing the annual budget for the federal government.

capitalism An economic system based on the private ownership of land and natural wealth and of the means of production, distribution, and exchange, in which there is a minimum of government interference in the economy.

centralization The gravitation of political power and decision-making responsibility from units or agencies that are geographically small or functionally specific to ones that are larger or more general (cf. decentralization).

checks and balances The principle according to which various government institutions exercise certain checks on the activities of other government institutions. Examples of this system include the President's power to veto acts of Congress and the courts' power to declare legislative acts unconstitutional.

Chicano A citizen of Mexican-American descent.

citizen A member of a state, either native-born or naturalized, who owes allegiance to its government and enjoys the protection of its laws.

closed primary An election in which a party's candidates are selected, whose participants include only those who have declared themselves to be party members or supporters (cf. direct primary).

coalition A political union containing disparate political elements. American political parties, for example, are coalitions including members of many different ideological and social groups.

collective good A benefit available to everyone in society regardless of whether any particular individual worked toward the attainment of that benefit.

Commander-in-Chief The President's role, specified in Article II, Section 2 of the Constitution, as supreme commander of the armed forces and of the state militias when they are called into federal service. Acting in his role as Commander-in-Chief, the President can deploy troops abroad without a congressional declaration of war.

communal activity Political activity in which citizens join together and act as a group to pressure the government. Communal activity may involve either ad hoc or formally constituted organizations.

conference committee A joint Senate–House committee convened to reconcile the differences between the versions of a bill passed in the Senate and the House of Representatives.

confirmation The Senate's power to approve nominations made by the President for certain posts such as ambassadors or Supreme Court justices.

congressional caucus A meeting by the members of one party in either the House or the Senate in which various partisan decisions are made. Congressional party leaders—whips, floor leaders, candidates for presiding officer—are chosen in such meetings.

Connecticut compromise The agreement reached at the Constitutional Convention that Congress would consist of two chambers: the House of Representatives, in which the size of state delegations would be fixed according to population; and the Senate, in which each state, regardless of population, would be represented equally.

conscientious objector One who refuses to serve in the military because his religion or his conscience instructs him not to.

consensus Underlying agreement in opinion.

conservatism Political philosophy stressing the importance of maintaining social stability and the need for strong political and social institutions to restrain the natural passions of men; often, political philosophy urging maintenance of the status quo (cf. liberalism).

conspiracy An agreement among individuals to commit an illegal act. Many laws, designed to discover criminal acts in their planning stages, define conspiracy as a crime.

constituency The district represented by a legislator; in broader terms, the set of interests represented by a governmental unit such as a congressional committee or an executive agency.

constituent A resident of a legislative district.

constitution The fundamental law—written or unwritten—that sets up the government of a nation, state, or any other organized body of men; specifies the duties and powers of the various government agencies; and elaborates the relationship between the citizens and their government.

decentralization The process of passing political power and decision-making responsibility from larger political units or agencies to ones that serve smaller geographical or narrower functional constituencies (cf. centralization).

depletion allowance A tax deduction that may be taken by owners of oil and gas wells and other minerals, supposedly to encourage costly exploration for such natural resources (cf. tax deduction).

differential impact of government decisions The degree to which government decisions and policies affect different citizens differently—benefiting some citizens, leaving some unaffected, perhaps even harming others.

direct primary An intraparty election in which the voters choose the candidates who will run on a party's ticket in the forthcoming general election (cf. closed primary).

disfranchise (or disenfranchise) To deny the privileges and rights of citizenship, especially voting.

due process of law The protection, guaranteed in the Fifth and Fourteenth Amendments to the Constitution, that acts of government that would deprive the individual of life, liberty, or property cannot be merely arbitrary but must be in accordance with established judicial procedures.

Electoral College The body of electors from each state who, after a Presidential election, actually choose the new President and Vice-President. Each state selects a slate of electors in the November election. Normally they vote as a unit for the candidates who received a plurality of votes in that state in the general election. The candidates who receive the majority of electoral votes, who may or may not be the same men who received the nationwide plurality of popular votes, become the President- and Vice-President-elect.

ethnic group A group whose members share such traits as common national background, religion, customs, culture, language, or historical experience. Catholic Americans of eastern or southern European origin are sometimes referred to as "ethnics."

executive agreement An international agreement concluded by the President that needs no senatorial approval to be operative.

extradition Transference of a person to the nation or state in which he has been accused of committing a crime by the government of another nation or state.

federalism A system of government in which power is shared between a central government and state or regional governments.

Federalist Papers A series of essays written by Alexander Hamilton, James Madison, and John Jay in defense of the newly drafted U.S. Constitution.

filibuster Obstruction of Senate action on a bill by the use of dilatory tactics. A common filibuster technique is to take advantage of the Senate's provision for unlimited debate in order to "talk a bill to death."

fiscal policy Use of economic tools—adjusting taxes, increasing or decreasing government spending on public projects, balancing the federal budget, or engaging in deficit spending—to stabilize the national economy or to spur economic growth.

floor leaders Party leaders, one from each party in each house of Congress, who are responsible for marshaling the party's forces in legislative battles.

gerrymandering Drawing the boundaries of legislative districts in an unnatural way in order to gain partisan advantage.

grandfather clause A provision, used in southern states to enfranchise whites who had been disqualified from voting by literacy tests or property qualifications, that held that disenfranchised people could vote if they, or a lineal ancestor, had been able to vote on January 1, 1867.

grant-in-aid A subsidy given by the federal government to a state or local government (or by a state government to a local government) to be used for some specified purpose according to prescribed standards.

habeas corpus A writ ordering an official who has a person in custody to bring that person to court and demonstrate why he is being held. The necessity of producing such a writ constitutes an important guarantee against arbitrary arrest.

impeachment A formal accusation of a public official for misconduct in office made by the lower house of a legislature (a necessary step before the accused can be tried by the upper house of the legislature).

impoundment Literally, seizing and holding in legal custody; in the political context, Presidential refusal to spend funds appropriated by Congress.

independent agency An agency of the executive branch of the federal government, such as the Veteran's Administration, that is not contained within one of the executive departments.

independent regulatory commission An agency, such as the Securities and Exchange Commission, set up outside the major executive departments and responsible for regulating a given sector of the economy. An independent regulatory commission is generally shielded from partisan politics and from Presidential control.

independent voter A voter who identifies with neither major political party and casts his ballot on a case-by-case basis according to the specific candidates or issues involved in a given race.

individualism A doctrine holding that the liberty and well-being of the individual are to be placed above those of society; also, a belief that the lot of the individual is a function of his own character and abilities rather than of social forces.

inflation An economic situation in which an increase in prices is accompanied by a loss of purchasing power.

Jim Crow law Any of a great variety of laws passed by southern states requiring segregation of blacks and whites (cf. segregation).

land-grant college A college established under the terms of the Morrill Act of 1862, which provided that land owned by the national government would be given to the states so that they could establish agricultural and technical colleges.

libel and slander Statements, either written (libel) or oral (slander), that defame the character of a person without justification.

liberalism Political philosophy emphasizing political, social, and economic changes in order to promote the well-being of the individual (cf. conservatism).

lobbyist An individual, often representing a special-interest group, who seeks to influence the contents of pending legislation, the outcome of legislative votes, or the decisions of executive agencies.

loyalty oath An oath requiring an individual to repudiate certain beliefs. In recent years loyalty oaths have required that a person swear that he does not advocate, or belong to an organization that advocates, overthrow of the government by violence.

majority rule The principle underlying democracy that the will of the greater number, a number over 50 percent, shall prevail in making political decisions and in choosing public officials (cf. plurality).

National Association for the Advancement of Colored People (NAACP) A national interest group that seeks to promote the well-being of racial minorities, particularly blacks.

open-occupancy law A law making it illegal to discriminate on the basis of race in the sale or rental of dwelling units.

patronage The power to make partisan appointments or to distribute, on a partisan basis, various jobs, franchises, contracts, or favors.

plebiscite A vote by the people on some measure that has been submitted to them for their approval by political authorities.

plurality The largest number of votes. When more than two strong candidates run for a given office, the winner will usually secure a plurality rather than a majority (cf. majority rule).

pocket veto A Presidential power giving him an effective veto over legislation passed at the end of a legislative session. If a President holds a piece of legislation without signing or vetoing it for ten days—during which time Congress adjourns—then the bill does not become law.

political efficacy A citizen's belief that he can influence the affairs of government by his own actions.

politicization The process of becoming politically aware and politically relevant.

popular sovereignty The concept that the locus of political authority ultimately rests with the people.

president pro tempore The presiding officer of the Senate in the absence of the Vice-President. The President *pro tem* is always from the party holding a majority in the Senate, regardless of the party of the Vice-President.

private sector The part of the economy that is privately owned and in general run for profit.

professional official An officer of an organized trade or professional group whose full-time occupation is to lead the group rather than to practice the profession represented by the group.

proportional representation (PR) An electoral system in which legislative seats are apportioned to parties or factions according to their approximate electoral strength.

public domain Lands such as national forests or grazing lands that are owned by the government.

radical One who advocates immediate and sweeping political, social, or economic changes.

ranking member The member of the majority party with the longest continuous service on a given committee and usually its chairman (cf. seniority rule).

refer to committee Sending a bill that has been introduced into one of the houses of Congress to a standing committee.

roll-call vote A vote in Congress in which the legislators' votes of "yea" or "nay" are recorded.

rule of law The principle underlying American democracy that stresses supremacy of law over the actions of elected officials.

Rules Committee The standing committee of the House of Representatives that controls the flow of legislation from the other standing committees to the floor of the House.

segregation The separation of blacks and whites in public and private facilities—schools, buses, theaters, restaurants, and so on. De jure segregation is grounded in law; de facto segregation has no legal basis but exists in reality.

seniority rule The traditional congressional practice of awarding a committee chairmanship to the member of the majority party with the longest uninterrupted service on that committee (cf. ranking member). A few successful challenges to this practice have occurred in recent years.

separation of powers The principle according to which governmental power is shared by the three branches of government—legislative, executive, and judicial.

Speaker of the House The presiding officer and in general the most powerful member of the House of Representatives. The Speaker is elected by the entire House but has in fact been previously selected by a caucus of the representatives from the majority party.

special district A local governmental unit that is created to provide a single service such as maintenance of parks or mosquito abatement.

split ticket A ballot on which the voter has selected candidates of different parties for different offices (cf. straight ticket).

State of the Union address An annual address to Congress in which the President assesses the problems that face the nation and presents a legislative program to deal with them.

state sovereignty The principle, espoused by many before the Civil War, that ultimate authority rests with the separate states rather than with the national government.

straight ticket A ballot on which the voter has selected candidates of a single party for different offices (cf. split ticket).

tariff A tax on imports that protects domestic products from foreign competition by raising the prices of foreign products.

tax deduction A subtraction—for example, for medical expenses or interest payments on a mortgage—that reduces the amount of income that can be taxed. When a deduction is taken, taxable income is reduced, and therefore the amount paid in taxes is reduced.

tax exemption Income not subject to taxation, such as income from municipal bonds.

three-fifths compromise Agreement at the Constitutional Convention that slaves would be counted as three-fifths of one person in apportioning seats in the House of Representatives.

welfare state A state that assumes responsibility for the well-being and security of its citizens by providing such economic and social services as unemployment insurance, subsidized housing, and health care.

whip Assistant floor leader, selected in party caucus in either house of Congress, who is responsible for acting as a liaison between party leaders and party members and for making sure party members are present for crucial votes.

wiretapping Use of electronic devices to intercept private conversations, especially telephone conversations.

writ of mandamus An order commanding an individual, corporation, or public official to perform some duty.

Index

differential impact and, 7
economic issues and, 27
elections and, 114
ethnic, 170
forces of localism in, 478
group conflicts and, 524
importance of, 12–13
judicial appointments and, 356
need for, 5–9
policies and, 458
political agenda and, 466–471
public opinion and, 152–154, 156–159
radical, 150–151
state capitalism and, 35
Supreme Court and, 330–361
understanding of, 12
Population, United States, 9–10
Populist Party, 234
Power
pluralistic view of, 523
transfer of, 224–225
Power elite, 485. *See also* Elitist rule
Presidency, 296–325
Constitution and, 296
diplomacy and, 299–300
executive agreements and, 300–301
foreign policy and, 390–391
foreign policy powers, 300–301
growth of powers, 296–308, 379
legislative programs and, 301–302
President as commander-in-chief and the, 297–298
proposal origination and, 303–305
remoteness of, 258
road to the, 310–322
staffing and managing, 302–303
war powers of the, 298–299
Watergate affair and the, 379–389
See also Executive branch
President
advisers, 376–377
agency compliance and, 374–375
cabinet, 377–378
challenges within party, 312
Congress and the, 369–372
congressional struggles with, 369–372
control of executive branch, 375
economic crisis and, 500–502
federal bureaucracy and, 372–375
foreign policy and, 514
health insurance programs and, 506
personality of, 322–325
political attitudes and, 144
removal from office, 381
as symbol, 308–310

term limits, 311
See also Presidency
Presidential advisers, 376–377
Presidential campaigns
costs, 320–321
electoral college and, 319
strategy and, 318–319
Presidential candidates
campaigns, 318–322
in-party and, 311
nominating, 313
out-party and, 312
primary elections and, 313–314
public financing, 312
Presidential Election Campaign Fund, 321–322
Presidential elections, 222
Presidential hopefuls, 310–311
Presidential nominating conventions, 315–316
choosing nominee, 317–318
delegate selection, 316
Presidential power, R. M. Nixon and, 379–380
Presidential primaries, 314–315
Presidential programs
restraints on, 306–308
tactics for enactment, 305–306
Presidential removal
Congress and, 381–383
Constitution and, 381–385
Pressure groups
class bias of, 526
congressional committees, 214
court system and, 214–215
election campaigns and, 215
executive branch and, 214
federal power growth and, 443–444
organizations as, 206–210
political agenda and, 469, 470–471
power of, 206
as quasi-government, 215–216
resources of, 206–210
tariff legislation and, 211–213
tax legislation and, 210–211
See also Groups, Interest groups
Price and wage controls, 500–501
Primary elections, 313–314
Prior restraint, 405
Private enterprise, subsidies to, 18–19
Private property, due process and, 343
Progressive income tax, 31
Progressive Party, 234
Property rights
protection of, 410
public interest and, 411

Protestant vote, 173
Protest movements. *See* Political protest movements
Protest politics
effectiveness of, 102–103
motivation and, 100–102
violence and, 99–100
Public, diversity in the, 155
Public Finance Bill (1974), 94–95
Public funds, organizations controlling, 216
Public hearings, congressional committees and, 280–281
Public interest
property rights and the, 411–412
tax policy and the, 498–499
Public opinion
democracy and, 398
effect of, 152–154
voting and, 156–159
Public schools, desegregation of, 509–513
Public tolerance, limits to, 154–155

Race. *See* Ethnicity and race
Racial discrimination
Brown v. *Board of Education of Topeka*, 347–348
NAACP's fight against, 346
Supreme Court and, 344–348
Sweatt v. *Pointer*, 346–347
Racial hostility, 147–150
Radical politics, 150–151
Railroads, ownership of, 29
Rayburn, Sam, 272
Realigning elections, 236
Recession, 499–501
Regional groups, 179–180
Regulated economy, 21–24
Regulatory commissions, independent, 488–491
Religion. *See* Freedom of religion
Religious groups, 180–181
Representation
compromise and, 257
Congress and, 257–259
Representative assemblies, 257
Representative government, 49–50
Connecticut Compromise and, 46
Republican congressmen, legislation supported by, 244–245
Republican Party
differs from Democratic Party, 237–247
ethnic politics and, 171
image of, 239–240
organizational fragmentation within, 226–227